PROBLEMS WITH PRAYERS

STUDIES IN THE TEXTUAL HISTORY OF EARLY RABBINIC LITURGY

BY

STEFAN C. REIF

WALTER DE GRUYTER · BERLIN · NEW YORK

∞ Printed on acid-free paper which falls within the guidelines of the ANSI
to ensure permanence and durability.

ISBN-13: 978-3-11-019091-5
ISBN-10: 3-11-019091-5

ISSN 0585-5306

Bibliographic information published by the Deutsche Nationalbibliothek

Die Deutsche Nationalbibliothek lists this publication in the Deutsche Nationalbibliografie;
detailed bibliographic data are available in the Internet at http://dnb.d-nb.de.

STEFAN C. REIF

PROBLEMS WITH PRAYERS

STUDIA JUDAICA

FORSCHUNGEN ZUR WISSENSCHAFT
DES JUDENTUMS

HERAUSGEGEBEN VON
E. L. EHRLICH UND G. STEMBERGER

BAND XXXVII

WALTER DE GRUYTER · BERLIN · NEW YORK

For 'other women' in my life ~

In memory of my mother Annie (1916–2002),
who worked so hard to fund my primary education
and lovingly inspired my earliest ambitions ~

To honour my sisters, Cynthia and Sharron,
whose love, loyalty and devotion are an example of what is best is
sibling relationships ~

And for my grand-daughter, Naama,
who was not yet born when an earlier book was dedicated to my other
grandchildren, and to encourage her always to be as articulate as now

Preface

Background to the volume

When I took early retirement a few months ago, I was asked on numerous occasions about my main motivation and I had no hesitation in replying that I was anxious to devote any remaining, energetic years to the interests that had first led me to choose an academic career, namely, research, publication and lecturing. What greatly appealed to me was the possibility of declining those tasks about which I am less than enthusiastic (and often have to do with apparently pointless bureaucratic procedures) and concentrating on a range of projects that I had commenced during my years of academic tenure but not yet succeeded in completing. Such projects include volumes on liturgical topics, the lives of Genizah researchers, and medieval Jewish Bible commentary, and the current collection of essays represents the first of these to reach fruition.

In choosing a particular selection of essays out of a larger number that have previously appeared in conference proceedings, *Festschriften* and other collective volumes, and adding to those some new chapters, I have been guided by the need to adhere to a reasonably consistent theme. That theme is simply summarized as the pursuit of the historical within the liturgical and further explanations and clarifications of my methodology are to be found in the first chapter. I have tried to weld together the essays so that they can be understood as part of an overall scholarly thesis but they may also be read totally independently by those interested in their respective topics. With this in mind, I have sometimes repeated myself in text and in footnotes, thereby relieving the reader of the need to jump from one chapter to another in order to clarify or amplify a point. I have also done my best to adopt a fairly consistent bibliographical style within the references but, again, only so far as dictated by the needs of respective chapters. Since full bibliographical details of all publications have been given in each chapter, I have thought it redundant to repeat these in a bibliography at the end of the volume.

For many of my previous books and articles, my wife, Shulie, did most of the complicated computer work, as well as carefully sub-editing the text and the footnotes. She did basic work on many of the chapters of this volume but her serious illness in recent months has prevented her from completing the tasks. She has advised whenever she could, but, with the exception of some help from my son, Aryeh, and from colleagues in the Genizah Research Unit at Cambridge University Library, I have been left to my own devices. The result will inevitably not reach the high standard that she has devotedly maintained for me over the years. I am most grateful to the publishers of this volume, Walter de Gruyter, for their confidence and support; to the editors of the series, Professor Ernst L. Ehrlich and Professor Günter Stemberger, for accepting the volume; and to Dr Albrecht Döhnert, de Gruyter's editor-in-chief of theology, Jewish studies and religious studies, for much kindness and helpful guidance.

Original provenance of some chapters

The second chapter is based on 'Jewish Liturgy in the Second Temple Period: Some Methodological Considerations', in: *Proceedings of the Eleventh World Congress of Jewish Studies 1993* (Jerusalem: World Union of Jewish Studies, 1994), 1–8, and the third chapter on 'The Second Temple Period, Qumran Research and Rabbinic Liturgy: Some Contextual and Linguistic Comparisons' in: E. Chazon and A. Pinnick (eds), *Liturgical Perspectives: Prayer and Poetry in Light of the Dead Sea Scrolls*, Leiden; Brill, 2003, 133–149. The fourth chapter is essentially what I published in 'Prayer in Ben Sira, Qumran and Second Temple Judaism' in: R. Egger-Wenzel (ed.), *Proceedings of the International Ben Sira Conference, Durham, Ushaw College, 2001*, Berlin and New York: de Gruyter, 2002, 321–41, and an earlier version of chapter 5 appeared as 'The Bible in Jewish Liturgy' in: A. Berlin and M. Z. Brettler (eds), *The Jewish Study Bible*, Oxford and New York: Oxford University Press, 2004, 1937–48. The studies of the priesthood and of the shema' are making their first appearance in print. Chapter 8 first appeared as 'Jerusalem in Jewish Liturgy' in: L. I. Levine (ed.), *Jerusalem: Its Sanctity and Centrality in Judaism, Christianity and Islam*, New York: Continuum, 1998, 424–37; chapter 9 was originally included as 'Some Notions of Restoration in Early Rabbinic Prayer' in: J. M. Scott (ed.), *Restoration: Old Testament, Jewish and Christian Perspectives*, Leiden: Brill, 2001, 281–304; and chapter 10 was recently published as 'Approaches to Sacrifice in Early Jewish Prayer' in: R. Hayward and B. Embry (eds), *Studies in Jewish Prayer*, Oxford: Oxford University Press for University of Manchester, 2005, 135–50.

Various parts of the study of the physical transmission of the liturgical medium originate in three publications: 'Codicological

Aspects of Jewish Liturgical History', *Bulletin of the John Rylands University Library of Manchester* 75/3 (1993), 117–31; 'Written Prayers from the Genizah; Their Physical Aspect and its Relationship to their Content' (Hebrew) in: J. Tabory (ed.), *From Qumran to Cairo: Studies in the History of Prayer*, Jerusalem: Orhot Press, 1999, 121–130; and 'From Manuscript Codex to Printed Volume: a Jewish Liturgical Transition?' in: R. Langer and S. Fine (eds), *Liturgy in the Life of the Synagogue*, Winona Lake, Indiana; Eisenbrauns, 2005, 95–108. The piece on Maimonides is being published for the first time while chapter 13 is based on different parts of the same three publications used in chapter 11, as well as on 'The Importance of the Cairo Genizah for the Study of the History of Prayer' (Hebrew) in: *Kenishta*, ed. J. Tabory, Ramat Gan: Bar Ilan University Press, 2001, 43–52, and on 'Some Recent Developments in the Study of Medieval Jewish Liturgy' in: N. de Lange (ed.), *Hebrew Scholarship and the Medieval World*, Cambridge: Cambridge University Press, 2001, 60–73.

The next three chapters were written for *Festschriften*, as follows: 'Some Observations on Solomon Luria's Prayer-Book', in: *Tradition and Transition: Essays Presented to Chief Rabbi Sir Immanuel Jakobovits to celebrate twenty years in office*, ed. J. Sacks, London: Jews' College Publications, 1986, 245–57; 'Liturgical Difficulties and Genizah Manuscripts' in: S. Morag, I. Ben-Ami and N. A. Stillman (eds), *Studies in Judaism and Islam Presented to Shelomo Dov Goitein*, Jerusalem: Magnes, 1981, 99–122; and '"Al-Ha-Nissim' in a forthcoming volume in honour of Colette Sirat being edited by Judith Olszowy-Schlanger and Nicholas de Lange. The seventeenth chapter is an updated translation into English of what appeared in Hebrew as 'We-'ilu Finu. A Poetic Aramaic Version' in: S. Elizur, M. D. Herr, G. Shaked, A. Shinan (eds), *Knesset `Ezra: Literature and Life in the Synagogue: Studies Presented to Ezra Fleischer*, Jerusalem: Ben-Zvi, 1994, 269–83, while the final chapter appeared in German as 'Ein Genisa-Fragment des Tischdank' in: W. Homolka (ed.), *Liturgie als Theologie: Das Gebet als Zentrum im judischen Denken*, Berlin: Frank & Timme, 2005, 11–29. A Hebrew version is scheduled to appear in a *Festschrift* for Aron Dotan. I am deeply grateful to all the relevant publishers for kindly granting permission to use some of my material from their publications and to the Syndics of Cambridge University Library for permitting the reproduction of their Genizah fragments in the plates at the end of the volume.

Cambridge, U. K.; Bet Shemesh, Israel   August 2006

Contents

1

Introduction

The collection of Jewish liturgical studies that constitutes the present volume is intended to complement the study that I published more than a dozen years ago under the title of *Judaism and Hebrew Prayer: New Perspectives on Jewish Liturgical History* (Cambridge, 1993). In that earlier monograph, I presented an overview of the development of Jewish liturgy from biblical until modern times, attempting as I did so to offer some fresh perspectives on the topic in its entirety. I traced the emergence and evolution of the major rites and practices, adopting a broad approach that took account not only of the requirements of Jewish religious law but also of theological, political and social factors and the impact of Christianity and Islam. By its very definition, such an approach was bound to relate to general trends rather than to detailed examples and I was conscious at that time that I ought at some future date to offer the reader some closer analyses of how these and other factors left their marks on the precise formulation of prayer texts. There are some aspects of the studies included at the beginning of the current volume that still opt, to at least a limited degree, for the broad sweep, but they are appropriate because their topics had yet to be seriously treated when I penned the previous work and because they do contain detailed as well as general assessments. By and large, however, most of the chapters contain substantial data derived from primary sources and the evidence of manuscripts.

The seventeen chapters that follow this introduction are essentially a summary of most of my liturgical research over the course of the past twelve years. Eleven of the studies have appeared (or will shortly appear) in collective volumes and in conference proceedings while three are fresh treatments and the remaining three have been adapted from earlier publications. Details of their origins will be provided at the end of this introductory chapter. Much of the research I have done relates directly to Genizah manuscripts, a source that has been close to my heart for some thirty-three years and one that often provides testimony to liturgical (as well, of course, as non-liturgical) developments that greatly predate what we know from other manuscript material and from printed works. But even when my research is concerned with pre-Genizah history such as, say, the late Second Temple period or the early geonic era, the Genizah evidence stands quietly at the rear waiting to be summoned. This is because it knows that the researcher must ultimately decide how to date,

characterize and conceptualize its contents and how to explain where
they vary significantly from what became, or is regarded (rightly or
wrongly) as having become, the standard rabbinic liturgy sanctioned
by the Iraqi Jewish authorities from the ninth to the eleventh centuries.

The aim of these introductory remarks it to set the scene for the
studies themselves by noting what I had to say in my earlier volume
and summarizing some of my more recent findings. I shall sound a few
warning notes, cite the evidence from Qumran and Ben Sira in order to
contextualize the developments of the first two Christian centuries, and
then turn to liturgical themes and specific prayers, most of which are
highly illuminated by the precious fragments from the Cairo Genizah. I
shall then draw some broad conclusions. Readers will then be able to
pursue in more detail, and with reference to source material, the
particular topics that interest them in any order, or in none, since my
summary and conclusions will already be behind them and since I
have, in any case, tried to ensure that each study may read
independently.

Earlier findings

Since this volume sets out from where my earlier one left off, let me
briefly recall what I had to say about the Genizah evidence in that
earlier publication. I made the point that just as it is now beyond doubt
that standard and authoritative versions of midrashic and targumic
material are a product only of the later geonic period, so it is possible to
argue convincingly a similar case in the matter of liturgy. Pluralism,
multiformity, and variation were characteristic of the late talmudic and
early geonic periods, although it is not yet clear whether they represent
a continuation of, or a reaction against, the notions of the earlier
rabbinic teachers. That very much depends on whether one subscribes
to the view that such notions and such teachers were or were not
already themselves wholly authoritative. Be that as it may, I listed the
types of liturgical non-conformity to be found among the Genizah texts,
including novel benedictions, some of them disapproved by some
talmudic and post-talmudic teachers, and alternative versions of such
central prayer-texts as the 'amidah, the qaddish and the grace after meals.

I also drew attention to the uses made of biblical texts that are
unfamiliar or unacceptable in the dominant versions, or had been
thought to have disappeared at an earlier stage, such as the liturgical
recitation of the Decalogue. What had also emerged from the Genizah
source were messianic, pietistic and mystical renderings of central parts
of the liturgy, otherwise lost or eliminated, and clear indications not
only of what appeared to be hybrid rites but also of a lack of liturgical

unanimity even in specific areas and communities. Aramaic and Arabic were sometimes used where the later standard had opted exclusively for Hebrew and the vast numbers of liturgical poems newly discovered testified to the fact that such a literary genre had almost ousted the regular and simpler forms of prayer from their central place. Indeed, according to Ezra Fleischer's interpretation of the liturgical history of the geonic period, the Genizah variants do not reflect an earlier lack of unanimity among the talmudic authorities but a revolutionary displacement of their versions with those of the later liturgical poets.

Scholarly controversy

Since Fleischer's interpretation was an important part of the scholarly discussion of the early 1990s, it is important to make further reference to it in the present context and to the reactions it spawned. Fleischer was adamant that there was no obligatory Jewish prayer in any communal contexts during the Second Temple Period; that the apocryphal, hellenistic and early Christian sources said nothing of such prayer; and that the customs adopted and practised at Qumran were those of sectarians. Only at Yavneh was the novel idea introduced of praying thrice daily and Rabban Gamliel laid down a clear formulation of the prayers. This was closely followed in the Babylonian centres and the liturgical traditions of those communities are consequently closer to the original than those of Eretz Israel which are the product of later poetic tendencies.

Although agreeing with the overall argument that the communal prayers of the tannaitic rabbis, *as they came to be formulated and legislated in the second century*, were not recited in earlier synagogues, I was troubled by what appeared to me to be the anachronisms, generalizations and dogmatic conclusions in some of Fleischer's informed but controversial presentation. I did not wish to rule out completely the possibility that when Jews came together in communal contexts they might have prayed, as well as studying and providing communal facilities, and I felt that the definition of the Qumranic material as sectarian, and therefore somehow irrelevant to the early development of rabbinic liturgical practice, was misleading. Other sources did hint at communal Jewish prayer and Palestinian texts were, in my view, just as likely, if not more likely than Babylonian ones, to be original and authentic. Similar patterns of liturgical development, however differently expressed, could be detected for each generation and were a more impressive interpretation of historical change than a theory of unrelated revolutions led by bombastic individuals. A synchronic approach to the talmudic sources was still dictated by the lack of definitive criteria for establishing a reliable diachronic analysis.

What then has to be added on the basis of the work of the last fifteen years to this argument about the late Second Temple and early rabbinic and Christian periods? Firstly, given the increased evidence of the dynamic religious variety of that time, and the attendant stresses and strains, one must be wary, in the matter of methodology, of assuming that sects, philosophies and religious practices can be clearly and categorically defined or that credit can be given to a few outstanding individuals for major developments. The critical historian should, rather, be on the lookout for the degree to which religious traditions were mutually influential, overlapping and multifarious and for the manner in which individuals might be championing notions that have evolved in their own, or in other environments. As Moshe Greenberg (*Biblical Prose Prayer as a Window to the Popular Religion of Ancient Israel* Berkeley, 1983) and Lee Levine (*The Ancient Synagogue: The First Thousand Years*, New Haven, 1999) have forcefully and convincingly argued, the growing importance and formality of what had started out life as individual prayer, as well as the evolution of the synagogue as a centre of worship, may represent tendencies towards the democratic, egalitarian and popular, as against the oligarchic, elitist and exclusivist values of the Temple and the priesthood.

Qumran and Ben Sira

The evidence from the Dead Sea manuscripts points to the regular recitation at stipulated times or occasions of communal prayers, although there is no overall consistency of formulation or context. Some parts of such prayers are reminiscent of what was formulated by the tannaitic rabbis but, as in other cases of similarity between their religious traditions, it is not clear if there was a direct line of transmission or whether the medium was an oral or written one. While the material familiar from Qumran makes a re-appearance in rabbinic liturgy, the format, the vocabulary and the usage have all taken on a distinctive character that reflects the ideology of early talmudic Judaism. There was clearly more than one provenance for the development of hymns and prayers during the Second Temple period. Among the sources from which the early rabbis apparently drew their liturgical inspiration (perhaps in some cases indirectly) were the Temple and its priesthood, contemporary circles of pietists and mystics, proto-synagogal gatherings such as the *ma'amadot*, and local custom. There is ample evidence in the talmudic and geonic eras that this process of liturgical innovation, adaptation and adjustment did not come to an end in the second-century so that it hardly seems valid to extrapolate backwards from the late geonic period to the early talmudic one in an effort to reconstruct precisely what constituted the earliest rabbinic formulations.

If we now offer a three-way comparison between Ben Sira, Qumran and the Rabbis, it has to be acknowledged that the apocryphal book has less in common with other two sources than the latter two have with each other. To cite some examples, Ben Sira has no mention of regular prayers at specific times, of poetic formulations for special occasions, or of a special liturgical role for sabbaths and festivals and there is little stress in his book on angels, apocalyptic notions and the end of time. On the other hand, like the Rabbis after him, Ben Sira clearly sees the possibility of worshipping God in a variety of ways and contexts, including the educational and the intellectual, and has the greatest respect for the Jerusalem Temple – he perhaps more practically and the Rabbis more theoretically.

The use of hymns, prayers and benedictions, as well as of biblical words and phrases to which fresh meanings have been given, is common to all three sources. They also all include as central themes in their entreaties the election of Israel, the status of Zion, the holiness of Jerusalem, the return of the Davidic dynasty, and the manifestation of God's great power now and in the future. Ben Sira undoubtedly takes the matter of worship beyond that of most of the Hebrew Bible but does not reflect the same liturgical intensity as that found at Qumran. He thus sets the tone for some rabbinic developments but is apparently not the source for various others.

Priesthood

A brief sketch of the *kohen* (or, priest) in Jewish history testifies to some interesting religious tendencies, especially in the areas of worship. Priesthood was undoubtedly one of the central religious functions of the world of the Hebrew Bible. In the periods leading up to the Babylonian Exile and immediately thereafter, priests were probably at their most powerful and influential but this situation changed in the Hellenistic era. In response to the ambitions of some priestly families to extend even further their religious and political power, especially in Jerusalem, other groups offered alternative understandings of their role in both the present and the eschatological future and approved of the participation of non-priests in religious ritual.

The early forms of rabbinic Judaism and Christianity were concerned about the status and function of priests within their religious practices and how they related to the wider body of their coreligionists. The earliest talmudic-midrashic sources are ambivalent in their assessment of priestly characteristics but the trend was ultimately towards replacing priests with rabbis in the academy and prayer-leaders in the synagogue. The first generations of liturgical poets, on the other hand, made efforts to glorify the priesthood, the Temple and the associated activities and it is tempting to see in this something of a response to the arrangements in the Byzantine Church.

The halakhic authorities of the early Middle Ages presupposed the validity of the biblical restrictions on some of the priest's activities as well as of his right to pronounce the priestly blessing in the synagogue and to take precedence in other liturgical spheres. As the centuries passed, however, some doubts were raised about his genealogical and spiritual status and this led the priests to mount counter-attacks in order to maintain their privileges. Even before the rise of progressive interpretations of Judaism in the modern world, the priesthood had lost virtually all but its ceremonial role, and those interceptions tended to abolish what remained. In more recent decades, however, there has been something of a tendency towards the restoration of some religious functions that had gradually lapsed.

Shema'

At the axial age, one encounters the broader use of one paragraph, and maybe even two paragraphs, of the *shema'* , or at least parts of these two passages, as well as of the Decalogue. There is a particular awareness of, and affection for, such passages and they are regarded as bearing a special theological message. They are consequently used as amulets, phylacteries or simply as sacred texts. What emerges from New Testament texts is that there also existed a tendency (perhaps inspired by hellenistic, philosophical notions) to see the whole religious message summarized in one brief biblical text, as interpreted by tradition, be it from the Decalogue, the *shema'* , or what current scholarship knows as the Holiness Code.

The *shema'* developed among the early rabbis as a declaration of their acceptance of the kingdom of God, rather than any other kingdom (such as that of Rome), and of all the commandments of the Torah. The devotion required in the light of such a declaration was interpreted as relating to all aspects of human nature, as demanding martyrdom when necessary, and as requiring a total acceptance of God's ultimate justice and the use of all one's assets. According to some halakhic midrashim, the messages carried by the *shema'* are that Israel has a special role and that its special devotion to God may be traced back to the Patriarchs. Israel's constant loyalty is a form of martyrdom and the first paragraph of the *shema'* is liturgically superior to the Decalogue and to the other two passages, given its special message of God's kingship and the yoke of its acceptance by Israel. What has therefore happened is that a biblical source, or set of sources, has been hijacked and used as a banner to proclaim some central but broad religious messages and then gradually employed more particularistically as the liturgical expression of Israel's special role as understood in rabbinic theology.

Biblical texts

By the time that the talmudic rabbis of the early Christian centuries were debating the matter of the inclusion of biblical verses and chapters in their standard prayers for daily, sabbath and festival use, there were a number of these that were well established by popular tradition within the liturgical context. Minor examples are the sets of verses, included in the *musaf* ('additional') *'amidah* for New Year and illustrating the three themes of kingship, remembrance and *shofar* (ram's horn) that stand at the centre of that prayer, as well as the verses used on special fast-days proclaimed in times of drought. More common and more major examples are the *shema'* , the Decalogue, the *hallel* ('praise'), the Passover *Haggadah*, the Song at the Sea (Ex. 15), the priestly benediction (Num. 6:24–26) and the trisagion (Isa. 6:3). The role of biblical material in the liturgy was a lively and controversial one.

Rabbinic formulations were regarded as preferable to biblical precedents, and biblical verses were to be differentiated from rabbinic prayers. Could, for instance, the verses from Isa. 12:6 and Ps. 22:4 be employed at any point in the *qedushah* benediction of the *'amidah* without valid halakhic objections being raised? The early rabbinic teachers sometimes even made changes in liturgical formulations out of polemical considerations. A good example concerns the use of the Biblical Hebrew word ''*olam*' (meaning 'world' as well as 'eternity' in post-biblical Hebrew) in such a way as to ensure that the notion of a future world was not excluded. Nevertheless, the liturgical pre-existence of such specific items as the *shema'* , and others mentioned above, provides positive proof that earlier attitudes had been different.

Perhaps what the talmudic rabbis feared was the potential influence of some groups who were regarded by them as sectarian and who had opted for the inclusion of biblical texts among their prayers. The Jews whose literary remains were found at Qumran, by the Dead Sea, were of such an ilk, and medieval Karaites, whose prayers were exclusively composed of biblical texts, pursued a similar liturgical philosophy. The situation among the Rabbanite Jews changed from the beginning of the Islamic period when, instead of merely a few favourite verses (such as Ps. 51:17, 84:5 and 144:15) and complete Psalms (such as Ps. 145), substantial blocks of biblical verses, groups of chapters and individual verses, especially from the book of Psalms, came to be incorporated in the traditional daily prayers, and then in the first prayer-books. Either the popular urge to include biblical items was so powerful that the halakhic authorities had to submit to it or it was determined that the most attractive religious practices should not be left exclusively to the theological opposition.

Jerusalem

Moving further into this more theological use of liturgy, a comparison of the manner in which Jerusalem is handled in various rabbinic prayers, with careful attention being given to the variants to be found in Genizah fragments, is also instructive. While the Temple was still standing, a realistic picture emerges of that institution and its service, with the priests at their centre and the people of Israel at their edge, all of them the beneficiaries of the special favour expressed by God for Zion, a term that alludes to the whole religious arrangement. During the talmudic period, there is the keen anticipation of a recovery from the disasters that befell these institutions and the expectation of an almost imminent restoration of the city of Jerusalem, the Temple and its service, and the special relationship with God that they represent. God's compassion and mercy will bless Israel with security, and the people's prayers, as well as their offerings, will attract divine favour.

As the passing centuries eliminate even the vaguest folk memories of actual Jerusalem institutions, so the prayers chosen most commonly to relate to them become less embedded in reality and convey a more futuristic and messianic message. God's infinite power will bring unexpected joy and recompense to those suffering the pain of exile and persecution. A detailed picture is painted of an idealized future, with Jerusalem functioning with more than its former glory. The Temple and the Davidic kingdom are presupposed and each group of Jews is seen to be playing a part in the scene. Economy of expression and simplicity of language, particularly as championed by Babylonian formulations, give way to the kind of generous augmentation and colourful vocabulary that are more characteristic of Palestinian prayer texts.

Restoration

If one examines the theme of restoration in the rabbinic liturgy in a similar manner, one encounters three themes: 1) that God will rectify the situation; 2) the restoration to Israel of Divine favour and warm relations to Israel; and 3) prophetic and messianic visions. Here it is more difficult to separate the themes chronologically and thematically but possible to reach some important broader conclusions. There are undoubtedly instances in which the same words have been interpreted in significantly different ways by various generations. References to Davidic rule, to the holy city and to divine worship did not necessarily convey the same concepts to the Jews of every centre and in each century. Nevertheless, it may confidently be concluded that the standard rabbinic prayers in their totality include all three themes and that the widespread textual, linguistic and theological variations testify to a dynamic process of development, though not one that displays one consistent tendency. It seems likely that this process was affected by the history of the Jewish people as it evolved from epoch to epoch and from centre to centre. Social, political and religious ideas undoubtedly left their mark on the texts of the prayers and, while the nature of such marks are identifiable, the details of their arrival and departure remain obscure in the early centuries of the first Christian millennium. What may be suggested for at least some periods is that, as the idea of restoration became less confidently and expeditiously expected, so it tended to be expressed progressively more in the language of the utopian visionary.

Sacrifices

If we now move on to the subject of the cultic service, there was clearly substantial talmudic discussion about the future of and/or the replacement of sacrifice and its relative theological importance in rabbinic Judaism. Although there was from the outset a strong body of opinion contending that there was no connection or continuation, there was also a tendency to seek ways of incorporating details of sacrifices into the prayers, and not simply opting for the view that prayers had wholly replaced sacrifices. This tendency subsequently strengthened in the post-talmudic period and is evidenced in the earliest prayer-books. There was also a major move on the part of the liturgical poets to restore the cult to a central role, especially by way of poetic versions of the *avodah* ritual for Yom Kippur, while a belief in the mystical, even magical use of language encouraged the recitation of the relevant passages concerning the cult.

The tenth century saw an enthusiastic interest on the parts of both Karaites and Rabbanites in special circumambulations of Jerusalem and in the recitation of connected prayers but, it must be admitted, without any central concern for details of the sacrificial cult. The Jewish liturgy ultimately incorporated, in conflated format, and not always in a fully logical presentation, two independent trends towards either Torah study or cultic restoration. The kabbalists of the late medieval and early modern periods, for their part, saw a prophylactic value in the recitation of passages concerning the sacrifices and this gave such texts an increased status in the regular prayers. To propose, therefore, that sacrifice was replaced by prayer is undoubtedly a gross over-simplification of a long and complicated liturgical process.

Physical medium

Studies of the physical medium used for the transmission of the liturgical texts, as reflected in the Genizah material, also reveal an interesting course of development. It would appear that some fragments represent early attempts on the part of individuals rather than communities to commit oral traditions to writing. As with other areas of rabbinic literature, the adoption of the codex gave the texts a greater degree of canonicity, leading to a growing concern for precise formulation. The single leaf evolved into the more lengthy codex, the private individual became the professional scribe, and the texts that had once been brief and provisional notes gradually turned into formal prayer-books. This ultimately led later generations to append to such prayer-books their own notes, instructions, commentaries and decorations, thus enhancing both their religious status and their physical attractiveness.

Maimonides and son

Maimonides's liturgical work reveals a number of tensions about theological priorities and preferences, especially as they relate to religious idealism versus social reality. He was capable of innovation where the circumstances demanded it, particularly where the public reputation of Judaism was at stake. He was, however, broadly committed to the continued application of talmudic principles on the one side, and to the promotion of the religiosity of prayer on the other, while remaining aware of the distinction between legal requirement and customary practice. What is uncovered in his comments is a contentment with basic Hebrew liturgy and a desire never to lose sight of the main theme of a prayer or set of prayers. He demonstrates a preference for intense preparation over unnecessary expansion, especially of the mystical or superstitious variety. His preferred liturgy appears to be Egyptian/North African and to stand between the centralized Babylonian rite emanating from the geonic authorities and the variegated traditions that flowed from it. On the other hand, there is evidence that in some respects he adhered to a Sefardi (Andalusian) liturgical tradition at home. His preferred liturgy made a major impact only on the Yemenite (*baladi* not *shami*) rite and appears to have lost much of its influence in the increasingly powerful centres of Europe. The substantial inroads later made by the mystics into the liturgical field were at least to some degree initiated by his son, Abraham, and do not reflect his overall approach, while the father's discomfort with the Palestinian liturgical rites led to a powerful and ultimately successful campaign by the son for their elimination.

As Mordechai Friedman has meticulously demonstrated, Genizah documents reveal that the war of words between Abraham Maimuni, the new communal leader, and his opponents continued from the time of his father's demise in 1204 virtually until his own death in 1237. Initially, the practice of referring to the leader of the Jewish community in parts of the synagogal liturgy (*reshut*), as well as in official documents, as an expression of allegiance, had to be abandoned by the leadership because of objections to Abraham's authority and ideology and it took almost a decade before he was able to re-assert this right for himself. Only by taking such action could the leadership forestall the creation of additional synagogues that would regard themselves as independent of the communal leadership. His opponents saw Abraham's pietistic campaign not as a defence of tradition but as a radically novel religiosity bent on mimicking Sufi practice and his rejection of Palestinian practice as an attempt to destroy well-established and authentic rituals. So incensed and desperate were they that on more than one occasion they appealed to the Muslim authorities to rule that his modes of worship were unconscionably innovative. He, for his part, was so convinced of the rectitude of his arguments that he found support for them in tannaitic sources. According to his interpretation, there was already then an established custom uniformly to kneel in rows facing the ark where the scrolls were kept and to conduct all the prayers in the direction of Jerusalem.

Luria's liturgy

Solomon Luria, in sixteenth-century Poland, stood in a long line of rabbinic authorities who saw a need to 'correct' the Hebrew of their liturgy from its rabbinic form to that of the Masoretic Bible. He cited numerous predecessors of a similar mind and made use of an extensive number of liturgical manuscripts and editions. For him, the language of the prayers had to reflect a certain logic and he was prepared to amend what he had inherited in order to achieve this. If, for instance, there was a danger of misunderstanding or of inadvertently expressing what amounted to a heretical thought, he would propose an alternative text. Such a text would often, but not always, have a precedent in an authoritative source. On the other hand, change for the sake of uniformity with another, perhaps more dominant rite, was not to his liking. If he could find a biblical verse that supported the retention of a traditional liturgical text, this would be sufficient reason to reject any change. His preference was also generally for language that was communal rather than individual, for a limitation on unnecessary liturgical expansions, and for what he regarded as more grammatically accurate forms.

In truth

The Genizah texts also shed light on the original sense of the first sentence of the post-*shema'* paragraph in the evening prayers: אמת ואמונה כל זאת קים עלינו. Taking the Yemenite vocalization קִים in the *pi'el* perfect and the absence of the words כי הוא in many Genizah texts as the starting points, there are various possible interpretations. A convincing sense could be 'has fulfilled all this for us', i.e. God has kept his promise just recited in the third paragraph of the *shema'*, to be our God, 'and we are Israel His people'. The first two words could also be made to yield a better sense if it is recalled that the first of them is often used in the liturgy in the sense of באמת and both are given this sense here. Additional support for such a meaning is available in the variant reading באמת ובאמונה instead of אמת ואמונה which occurs in the morning *ge'ulah* benediction. The translation would then be 'In truth and faith, God has fulfilled all this for us'. Alternatively, אמת is only the introductory 'Truly' and not part of the remainder of the sentence, and just as in the third part of the sentence a claim is made about the fulfilment of God's promise so in the second part is the trustworthiness of what has been recited acknowledged in the words אֱמוּנָה כל זאת. Such a sense and vocalization would admirably fit Ginzberg's theory about the origins of the prayer as an אמן to what has gone before. it would also be linguistically significant. The translation would then be 'Truly, all this is acknowledged'.

This novel treatment of the passage does not, however, provide any reference to the future redemption, apparently presupposed by Rashi and the *Tosafot* in their commentaries on BT, Ber 12a. It may, of course, be the case that they are reading the idea into קים עלינו but, if not, the possibility that קים was here originally קָיָּם as it appears in so many other cases, or יְקַיֵּם, should be considered. Perhaps mention should also be made of the possibility that there is here a remnant of some form of קים אמונה, 'keeping a promise'. Changes in other such petitions for the future redemption are well-known and the last phrase ואנחנו ישראל עמו, which would not fit well as the concluding portion of such a petition, would therefore have to be a later addition.

There is the remote possibility that there is here some long-forgotten allusion to a popular text or its interpretation, a text such as Neh. 10:1 in which the expression כל זאת occurs in the context of 'making a covenant'. It may be added that the words ברית and אמנה are governed by none other a verb than קום in the *pi'el* in one of the Zadokite Documents (ed. C. Rabin, p. 39).

Genizah texts of *'Al Ha-Nissim*

Neither the recitation nor the definitive wording of this prayer were talmudically ordained. The prayer was introduced by the geonic authorities and given expression in historical, poetic and supplicatory styles, perhaps each of them originally separate, but ultimately combined. Although the general structure of the text is agreed in all the versions, there are interesting textual variants. On the linguistic side, one can detect in a number of fragments tendencies towards the replacement of mishnaic philology, vocabulary and orthography with their biblical Hebrew counterparts, sometimes because the transmitters were ill-at-ease with the meanings they attached to mishnaic forms, and towards the use of biblical verses as prototypes. There was a clear tension between those who stressed the historical miracle and those who wished not only to offer thanks for the past but also to make entreaty for the future. Also controversial was the degree to which strong elements of eschatology, the supernatural and lyricism should be included in standard *'amidah* benedictions. There are also political considerations (such as in the use of the term מלכות הרשעה), theological concerns about associating Israel with destruction and God with *lèse majesté*, and ambivalence about whether phrases are to be understood politically, theologically or intellectually (as with זדים ביד עוסקי תורתך).

Aramaic poem

A close examination of an Aramaic poem in T-S NS 160.11 (ואלו פומנה) raises broader issues that are worthy of further discussion. Its style parallels and echoes those of Targum Onqelos and the fixed prayers of the early medieval period. Its vocabulary, grammatical forms and modes of expression closely match the language of the halakhic authorities who held spiritual and cultural sway over much of the Mediterranean area at the end of the geonic period. At the same time, it has to be acknowledged that, although there are no clear indications of the kind of Galilean Aramaic that is characteristic of so many targumic versions to be found in the Genizah collections, there are some linguistic elements that appear to have originated among the communities of the land of Israel. Given the incontrovertible existence of trilingualism on the part of the Jews in the post-geonic period, it hardly seems surprising to encounter texts in which there are switches between languages. It is not unlikely that one of the aspects of this linguistic and literary process was the development whereby Aramaic dialects came to be used that did not represent particular geographical areas. The scholarly authors of the later period chose to write Aramaic in order to expand the range of their literature and made use of a variety of earlier styles and characteristics that were borrowed from a number of different sources.

The manner in which our author re-works the material before him is basically similar to that employed by the Aramaic targumists when they added to the scriptural source but remained thoroughly loyal to its basic content. Recently published research work on such targumim have demonstrated the existence of many types of translation and supplement. In addition to the well-known Targum Onqelos, Pseudo-Jonathan and Yerushalmi renderings, there were also targumic collections that followed the sabbath and festival lectionaries or treated particular chapters or verses of scripture, as well as more general types of *tosefta* (additamenta) versions. In a number of respects, our Aramaic poem, though connected to the fixed liturgy rather than to the biblical text, is similar to such targumim and makes use of words and expressions that are linguistically typical of targumic Aramaic.

What we may therefore have here is a composition that is similar in aim and usage to those Aramaic liturgical poems of post-talmudic Byzantium and later Franco-Germany but certainly does not employ a language and style that is wholly comparable with theirs. It seems reasonable to suppose that it is an example of a literary genre that belongs to the history of Hebrew poetry at the end of the geonic period and that is linked to the emergence of the new centres of Jewish life that replaced those of Babylon and the Palestinian Jewish homeland. As long, however, as no similar such poems have been found and identified, it will not be possible to be more precise about its historical and literary milieu.

A few sentences should now deal with the context in which our previously unknown Aramaic poem was recited. Such a recitation was obviously attached to the *nishmat* prayer. Since the ritual practices of

Babylon and Palestine differed as to when that prayer was recited, there are two possibilities that immediately come to mind. Our poem was recited either in the sabbath morning service or as part of the weekday prayers. But there is also a third historical option. Perhaps our author's intention was to include his composition among the special prayers recited on Passover. In that case, it could have been attached to the morning service of the festival, or of its intermediate sabbath, like the other poems that appear on the remaining folios of the fragment, or it might have been recited as part of the *hallel* section of the Passover Haggadah of the first evening. Since the Genizah has revealed fragments that contain novel Aramaic versions of parts of the Haggadah that are generally familiar to us in Hebrew, such a phenomenon need not be regarded as rare or exceptional. The references in lines 5 and 12 to 'youngest speakers' and a gathering of 'young and old' (Aramaic originals: זעטוטין ודעדקין and במיכנש סבין ודרדקין) may certainly allude to the Jewish communal gathering in the synagogue but one cannot rule out the important possibility that the author has in mind the domestic Passover seder. If so, what emerges is that the community in which he operated apparently had the custom of extending the range of the *hallel* beyond what is to be found in the prayer-book of R. Sa'adya Gaon and in many Genizah fragments.

Genizah grace

A number of more general conclusions, that are important for an accurate understanding of Jewish liturgical history, may also be derived from the data provided by a Genizah fragment of the grace after meals and from its relationship with other versions. The twelfth-century rabbinic liturgies clearly still displayed a considerable variety of textual detail that remained in flux even if the major factors had become more solidified. The crystallization of the definitively recognizable rites of Europe and the orient was only in its early stages. There were still tensions between traditional transmission and novelty, between inconsistency and standardization, and between the biblical and rabbinic varieties of Hebrew language. The image of God, the nature of his relationship with the worshipper, and the notion of the messianic era were all concepts that were, in their smaller detail if not in their major configuration, open to liturgical adjustment. Historians should be ready to find among the manuscript sources numerous examples of texts that are not purely Babylonian or Palestinian and should place *Seder Rav Amram*, as it has come down to us, among the *formae mixtae* of the post-geonic period and not within the purer Babylonian versions of the ninth century. Our manuscript appears to

belong to a genre that is in or close to North Africa and still retains
mixed Babylonian and Palestinian elements as well as similarities to the
modified version of *Seder Rav Amram* and the prayer-book of
Maimonides. The prayer-book of Solomon ben Nathan is simply
another example of the variety of 'western' and 'oriental' liturgical
elements that still existed in North Africa in the twelfth century.

Conclusions

Ben Sira, Qumran and the Rabbis share some of the liturgical genres
and a number of the dominant themes. Ben Sira moves beyond the
biblical definition of worship but does not testify to the regular
recitation of prayers at stipulated times or on specific occasions such as
is found at Qumran. The Rabbis are inspired by various such earlier
traditions but create their own formulation and usage. Although they
grant the priesthood some privileges, its role in the synagogue
gradually becomes little more than vestigial and symbolic.

Beginning its Jewish liturgical life as some form of amulet, the
shema' comes to be seen as the summary of a central religious message
and then as a declaration of faith in the divine kingdom and in the
importance of the religious commandments (מצות). Once established in
such a role, it is then regarded as the banner of other major aspects of
rabbinic theology.

Some biblical verses and passages are used as tannaitic liturgical
compositions but there is some apprehension among the talmudic
rabbis about opting for biblical rather than rabbinic formulations. After
the rise of Islam, and the success of early medieval Karaism, more
substantial liturgical use is made by the rabbinic tradition of biblical
texts, albeit never with the authoritative liturgical status of the *'amidah*.

In the period immediately following the destruction of the Judean
state, there is a confidence that Jerusalem, the Temple and the cult,
which had been of critical significance to many of the Jewish people,
will be restored and God's favour again attracted. As the memory of
the reality fades, so the nature of the prayers about these institutions
becomes more idealistic and includes more colourful, futuristic and
messianic elements.

The topic of restoration includes three themes in rabbinic liturgy:
physical improvement, divine favour and messianic ideology. The
specific manifestations of such themes are viewed differently by
changing generations and in varied locations, often as a result of
historical developments.

Although some of the early talmudic rabbis were of the opinion
that there was little or no connection or continuation between the

sacrificial system and the daily prayers, others felt not only that the latter were the direct replacement of the former but also that ways should be sought of incorporating details of the sacrifices into the prayers. This view found further expression among the liturgical poets of the post-talmudic period and among those who saw such an incorporation either as part of Torah-study or an entreaty for the future.

It seems likely that most prayers were originally transmitted in an oral form and that the commitment to the written folio increased as the codex was more widely adopted by the Jews. Once that form became more standard, and indeed more lengthy, so did it attract to itself more content and a greater degree of authority. This process also laid the foundations for the addition of notes, commentaries and decorations by subsequent generations.

The liturgical preferences of Maimonides in the twelfth century are for talmudic principles, mishnaic Hebrew, personal religiosity and intense preparation but he is capable of innovation when public circumstances demand it and aware of the distinction between legal requirement and customary practice. In a liturgical situation that was obviously still somewhat fluid, his preferred public liturgy seems to have been Egyptian/North African but he sometimes adhered to Sefardi (Andalusian) tradition in his personal behaviour. His reservations about following the rites of Eretz Israel and about the place of mysticism were not shared by his son, Abraham, who was willing to involve himself in considerable communal controversy in order to eliminate the Palestinian customs and to implement Sufi-like changes in the local prayer customs.

What is especially intriguing about Solomon Luria is the fact that he straddled the medieval and modern worlds. He supported his views by reference to authoritative predecessors but at the same time cited evidence from manuscripts and early editions. He was anxious that the correct religious message should be imparted but also wished to maintain high standards of Hebrew language and grammar. He was prepared to opt for textual adjustment if logic demanded but only if he could not find some justification for retaining the standard version without betraying his rational values.

In the first of four detailed textual studies, it becomes clear that in the opening paragraph of the *ge'ulah* benediction following the *shema'* in the evening office, and beginning אמת ואמונה, the semantic range, the syntax and the vocalization of the first five words are all controversial. We may here be dealing with an original meaning that has been lost, some objection to one sense that has lead to the substitution of another, or a misunderstanding that has crept into the text as a result of a false

analogy with another phrase. The impetus for change may be
theological, linguistic or grammatical.

Our second case concerns the recitation and formulation of the 'al
ha-nissim prayer in the 'amidah during the festival of Hanukkah which
were products of the post-talmudic period. Although much of the text
is fairly standard, the variations documented in the Genizah
manuscripts offer some interesting testimony. In addition to some
intriguing political, theological and intellectual considerations, there
were clearly tensions about whether the prayers should be in biblical or
mishnaic Hebrew, whether the stress should be on past events or future
hopes, and whether the atmosphere of the prayer should be poetic or
prosaic.

The third text is that of an Aramaic poem that appears to be part of
the Passover liturgy, either synagogal or domestic, and that treats the
biblical source much as the Targumim did. Although it is similar in aim
and usage to the poetry of post-talmudic Byzantium and later Franco-
Germany, its language and style are different from theirs. It
consequently testifies to the insertion into the standard prayers of
poetic Aramaic expansions that have links with earlier and later genres
but are by no means identical with them.

A Genizah manuscript containing the whole text of the grace after
meals constitutes our fourth example. Although this version is unlikely
to be earlier than the twelfth century, and few of its elements are totally
innovative, it is impossible to identify it in its totality (only in specific
parts of its content) with any one liturgical rite known from that period
or the centuries immediately before or after it, or indeed to see its
source in any purely Babylonian or Palestinian form. It is perhaps
closest to a North African rite that still has both 'western' and 'oriental'
aspects to it.

What therefore emerges from all these studies and the associated
conclusions? There were undoubtedly forms of communal Jewish
prayer before Rabban Gamliel and most Qumran scholars currently
subscribe to the view that this was not a practice limited to only one
small sect. It is possible to detect a process of liturgical evolution from
the Second Temple period to the tannaitic, amoraic and geonic eras.
Attitudes to the use of biblical verses and to the status of the priest is
not uniform through these periods but appears to be dependent on
external factors, revealing both negative and positive responses to the
customs of other groups. Rabbinic liturgy is affected by changing
political circumstances and by adjustments in theology. Liturgical poets
do not necessarily have a revolutionary impact on the prayers but
sometimes continue and expand earlier talmudic traditions. The
physical medium left a major mark on the liturgical content, style and

status. Although there are efforts to establish the basic Babylonian forms, there remains even as late as the twelfth century a considerable degree of fluidity and the clearly definable rites do not emerge wholly and successfully until the thirteenth and fourteenth centuries. Close textual analysis testifies to alterations, misunderstandings and controversies, behind which lie theological, political, intellectual and linguistic considerations.

2

Liturgy in the Second Temple Period: Methodology

Introduction

In any relatively narrow field of research it is undoubtedly a useful exercise to give oneself pause at regular intervals, to relate one's efforts to what is transpiring in the wider context, and to take stock of what has and can be achieved in one's own topic of interest. In performing such an exercise one is driven to think again about the general philosophy and methodology of a subject, the intricate and detailed examination of which may have evolved into something of a obsession, and to look afresh at problems and solutions in the light of ideas that have been fostered elsewhere. When invited to lecture on the present topic at an international symposium,[1] it occurred to me that the subject being considered was basically an historical one, however closely linked to theology, archaeology, language and literature, and that it might benefit from a few broad remarks about how general historians have recently come to view their scholarly endeavours. There will of course be those for whom this may constitute well-trodden ground and I can only excuse myself by claiming that there are few presentation, however familiar in part, that do not by their overall treatment of a theme inspire new thoughts and ideas on the part of those to whom they are offered and for whom open-mindedness is not a characteristic of academic indecision and weakness.

What is history?

Students of history have in recent decades conducted a lively debate about what does and does not constitute history and about the extent to which historical research may be related as much, if not more, to the present and the future as it is to the past. Such discussions touch on

---

1   I am grateful to Professor Lee Levine for having arranged a symposium on this general topic at the 1993 World Congress of Jewish Studies, and for having laid down for the participants some clear parameters for their contributions. His invitation to me to participate and the exchange between Professor Ezra Fleischer and myself in *Tarbiz* 60 (1991), pp. 677–88 provided the impetus for the present treatment of the theme.

philosophy, politics and morality and assuredly move greatly beyond the study of one specific element of a particular people's *religions-geschichte* such as concerns us here.[2] Indeed, such historians often express impatience and a lack of confidence in the scholarly abilities of those who occupy themselves with such specifics precisely because they cannot be trusted to see the interpretative wood for the factual trees. Let us then attempt to respond to such criticism by drawing from the reservoir of historiographical theory some notions that have come to be widely held and that may be of assistance to us in approaching any aspect of Second Temple period history.

There are numerous differences of approach and of emphasis that distinguish twentieth-century historical research from its nineteenth-century predecessor but the one that perhaps overshadows all the others concerns the status of facts in any attempt to improve our understanding of the past. Until well into the twentieth century it was believed that the true student of the past could stand outside his own chronology and locality and could, by an enthusiastic and judicious marshalling of progressively more intricate data from chosen sources, replace the folktales of tradition with the scientific analysis of the present, producing a picture of the past *wie es eigentlich gewesen ist*. In the amusing and perceptive words of E. H. Carr, 'three generations of German, British and even French historians marched into battle intoning the magic words *"wie es eigentlich gewesen [ist]"* like an incantation – designed like most incantations, to save them from the tiresome obligation to think for themselves.'[3] Not quite subscribing to the view that 'history is a pack of lies',[4] more recent historians are no less committed to the pursuit of reliable information and fresh sources; it is just that they recognize that neither the historian nor his source can ever be regarded as dispassionate and that academic history is a matter of placing everyone and everything in its context and interpreting their significance accordingly and with as little subjectivity as one can manage. In framing a number of important questions that the researcher should ask about his sources, G. Kitson Clark cautions the

---

2   Some of the relevant issues are touched on in the entry 'History' in *The New Encyclopaedia Britannica*, vol. 20 (Chicago, 1991), pp. 572–74 and much of the debate was fired by the controversial study of the subject by E. H. Carr, *What is History? The George Macaulay Trevelyan Lectures delivered in the University of Cambridge January–March 1961* (Basingstoke and London, 1961; second edition, ed. R. W. Davies, 1986).

3   Carr, *What is History?* (see n. 2 above), p. 3, and the whole chapter entitled 'The historian and his facts' in that volume, pp. 1–24.

4   In a reference to the views of Charles Kingsley, Professor of Modern History at the University of Cambridge from 1860 to 1869, William Stubbs, Bishop of Oxford, wrote the lines 'The Reverend Canon Kingsley cries / History is a pack of lies'; see *Letters of William Stubbs, Bishop of Oxford, 1825–1901*, ed. W. H. Hutton (London, 1904), p. 162 (letter of December 1871 to J. R. Green).

potential historian about the danger of being 'habitually cynical about the statements made by one class of person or about one type of event, while trusting the statements made by other classes of person or about other types of event'.[5] If one fails to take account of the relevant sources, one's views are no more than speculative; if one pays exclusive attention to what they have themselves to say without offering an overall interpretation, one is compiling footnotes and not writing history.

If doubts may justifiably be expressed about the possibility of objectivity on the part of those who have what they consider to be a clinical view of the past, how much more must such scepticism be applied to earlier sources that had no such pretensions but for whom religion and history were virtually indistinguishable. Sources are not all equally valid, relevant or informative, and to question their value and uncover their motivation are not acts of scholarly anarchism but a *sine qua non* of a balanced and critical analysis. J. H. Hexter has expressed it very well: 'the historian. . . must formulate rough hypotheses, often very rough, about what happened and how it happened, and then examine the available record to verify or correct his hypotheses. But at the outset, from an almost limitless range of conceivable hypotheses he must select for investigation the very few that lie somewhere in the target area; he must select only those for which the surviving records hold forth some hope of verification; and he must have a sense of what records among a multitude are likely to provide the evidence he needs'.[6] The definition of periods and movements and the creation of terminology to describe them should be seen as aids to understanding history and not as a straitjacket employed to restrain the struggles of those who are bent on reaching out for alternative descriptions and expositions.

And what of interpretations of history that ascribe major developments to individual personalities and single causes? Of course particular men and women have left more of a mark than others on the story of humanity's progress or its opposite, and some causes may be evaluated as more central than others but an awkward social, economic and religious complexity is more convincing to the sophisticated historian than a convenient political simplicity. To quote E. H. Carr again, 'the desire to postulate individual genius as the creative force in history is characteristic of the primitive stages of historical consciousness', and Alexis de Tocqueville already postulated in 1840 that 'historians who write in aristocratic ages are wont to refer all

5   G. Kitson Clark, *Guide for Research Students Working on Historical Subjects* (Cambridge, 1960), pp. 28–29.
6   J. H. Hexter, *Doing History* (London, 1971), p. 24.

occurrences to the particular will or temper of certain individuals...'
while those 'who live in democratic ages exhibit precisely opposite
characteristics.'[7] Similar judgements might be made of the search for
the fact that launched a thousand relationships. The modest caution of
contemporary historians, once contrasted with the confident
conclusions of the natural scientists, seems lately to be spreading from
libraries to laboratories and no scholar who wishes to be taken
seriously any longer believes that if an idea is repeated often enough
and stridently enough, it becomes worthy of canonicity.

Second Temple period

If we may now particularize the discussion and move to a
consideration of what is known as the Second Temple period, it must
immediately be acknowledged that here too recent years have seen a
considerable divergence of views about both the evidence and its
interpretation. While in the nineteenth and early twentieth centuries
Jewish and Christian scriptures and their authoritative religious
literature were regarded as the major sources for understanding the
period, more recent decades have seen the explosion of further data
relating to Palestinian archaeology, Hellenistic Jewry and the Qumran
scrolls, as well as a greater application of information derived from the
non-Jewish world to an understanding of its Jewish equivalent.[8] It was
once thought easier to write ancient and medieval history than to
analyse the events of the modern period because the very paucity of
source material inhibited its interpreters from offering many alternative
viewpoints. It is therefore perfectly fair to expect the explosion of data
to have been accompanied by a matching expansion of critical
theorizing about its significance, and to an extent that has indeed
occurred.

Some have continued to see the period as a preparatory one that
leads from the 'Old Testament' world to its 'New Testament' or
rabbinic successor while others have laid emphasis on the unique
religious developments of the time.[9] The remarkable influence

---

7   Carr, *What is History?* (see n. 2 above), p. 39; Tocqueville, *Democracy in America*, vol. 2
     (E.T. Henry Reeve, London, 1862), p. 102.

8   This is clearly exemplified by a comparison of the theories, sources and bibliography
     contained in the original E. Schürer, *Geschichte des jüdischen Volkes im Zeitalter Jesu
     Christi* (Leipzig, 1886–1890) with the revised English edition, *The History of the Jewish
     People in the Age of Jesus Christ 175BC–AD135*, eds G. Vermes, F. Millar and M.
     Goodman (3 vols; Edinburgh, 1973–87).

9   E.g. J. Jeremias, *Jerusalem zur Zeit Jesu: kulturgeschichtliche Untersuchung zur
     neutestamentlichen Zeitgeschichte* (Göttingen[3], 1962) translated as *Jerusalem in the Time
     of Jesus: an Investigation into Economic and Social Conditions during the New Testament*

exercised by the culture of Greece and Rome has intrigued one group of scholars while it has been the polemical response to such a challenge that has occupied the minds of some of their colleagues.[10] There have been studies that read as if mysticism dominated religious ideology in the two or three centuries leading up to the destruction of the Temple and alternative theses that create the impression that law and ritual observance were central at all times.[11] The whole field of research has been richly fertilized by the notions that there were multiple Judaisms or at least that Judaism was multifarious; by new archaeological discoveries about the Temple, Jerusalem and other important structures; and by the growing number and variety of texts from the Dead Sea area.[12] There has even been an awareness on the part of some scholars that we may be dealing with wider social, political and economic factors rather than simply with theological history, and a few have ventured to suggest that in addition to piling batches of undigested information on to stacks of raw material, as some representatives of the *Wissenschaft des Judentums* and their successors

---

Period (London, 1969); S. Safrai, *The Jewish People in the Days of the Second Temple* (Hebrew; Tel Aviv, 1970); and J. Neusner, *Judaism in the Beginning of Christianity* (Philadelphia, 1982) and *Reading and Believing: Ancient Judaism and Contemporary Gullibility* (Atlanta, 1986).

10 E.g. S. Lieberman, *Greek in Jewish Palestine: Studies in the Life and Manners of Jewish Palestine in the II–IV Centuries C.E.* (New York², 1962) and *Hellenism in Jewish Palestine: Studies in the Literary Transmission, Beliefs and Manners of Palestine in the I Century B. C. E. – IV Century C. E.* (New York², 1962); V. Tcherikover, *Hellenistic Civilization and the Jews* (E. T. from the German, Philadelphia, 1959); E. Bickerman, *From Ezra to the Last of the Maccabees: Foundations of Post-biblical Judaism* (New York, 1970) and *The Jews in the Greek Age* (London, 1988); M. Hengel, *Judaism and Hellenism: Studies in their Encounter in Palestine during the Early Hellenistic Period* (from the German edition of Tübingen, 1973; 2 vols; London, 1974); M. Stern, *Greek and Latin Authors on Jews and Judaism* (3 vols; Jerusalem, 1974–84).

11 There is a growing awareness that, for all his pioneering efforts and brilliance, Scholem over-emphasised the role of mysticism and Albeck, for his part, took it for granted that later halakhic concepts applied in earlier times; see G. Scholem *Jewish Gnosticism, Merkabah Mysticism and Talmudic Tradition* (New York², 1965) and H. Albeck, *Introduction to the Mishna* (Hebrew; Tel Aviv², 1960); translated into German as *Einführung in die Mischna* (Berlin and New York, 1971), and my review of the latter in *JJS* 19 (1974), pp. 112–18.

12 J. Neusner, W. S. Green and E. Frerichs (eds), *Judaisms and their Messiahs at the Turn of the Christian Era* (Cambridge, 1987); Y. Yadin (ed.), *Jerusalem Revealed: Archaeology in the Holy City 1968–74* (Jerusalem, 1976); L. I. Levine (ed.), *Ancient Synagogues Revealed* (Jerusalem, 1981), especially the articles by Levine, E. M. Myers and G. Foerster; E. M. Meyers and J. F. Strange, *Archaeology, the Rabbis and Early Christianity* (London, 1981); G. Vermes, *The Dead Sea Scrolls in English* (London³, 1987); E. Tov, 'The unpublished Qumran texts from Caves 4 and 11', *JJS* 43 (1992), pp. 101–36 (including bibliography); and B. Z. Wacholder, 'A note on E. Tov's list of preliminary editions of the unpublished Dead Sea Scrolls', *JJS* 44 (1993), pp. 129–31.

were inclined to do, we should be asking searching questions about sources, methodology and definitions.[13]

Along which lines then should such questions be asked and what are the shortcomings that remain to be made good in this major area of Jewish history? One inadequacy that should perhaps immediately be noted is the tendency to overstress one aspect of the overall picture at the expense of all the others. No scholar can be a specialist in 'Old Testament', 'New Testament', Septuagint, Hellenism, Apocrypha and Pseudepigrapha, Talmud, Midrash, Targum and Qumran, nor can one researcher master archaeology, law, mysticism, socio-economic and political development and religious thought, but what all those writing about the period can surely appreciate is that no impressive description of any one of these topics can be achieved if it fails to take account of the existence of all or most of the others. In the words of H. Butterfield, 'for the historian the only absolute is change'[14] and, given such an assessment of all events, it is impossible to understand any period without attempting to discover how its various constituents relate to each other. Since few or multiple factors may trigger developments, one is unlikely to identify the most major catalysts of a reaction unless one recognizes the various possibilities and their probable interconnection. No groups or individuals stand outside the time and place in which they operate[15] and to claim that they may be understood without reference to such chronological and local factors is to demonstrate a naive faith in the kind of absolute terms or pure elements that can lay little claim to existence in human history.

That being the case, caution must be exercised in identifying the precise and unique characteristics and achievements of any Second

---

13   Among other important publications representing a variety of approaches are to be numbered *The Jewish People in the First Century: Historical Geography, Political History, Social, Cultural and Religious Life and Institutions,* eds S. Safrai and M. Stern (2 vols; Assen and Philadelphia, 1974–76); *Cambridge History of Judaism,* eds W. D. Davies, L. Finkelstein and J. Sturdy (3 vols published; Cambridge, 1984–99; fourth volume scheduled for publication in 2006); H. Maccoby, *Early Rabbinic Writings* (Cambridge, 1988); *Jewish Writings of the Second Temple Period: Apocrypha, Pseudepigrapha, Qumran Sectarian Writings, Philo, Josephus,* ed. M. E. Stone (Assen and Philadelphia, 1984); S. J. D. Cohen, *From the Maccabees to the Mishnah* (Philadelphia, 1987); *Mikra: Text, Translation, Reading and Interpretation of the Hebrew Bible in Ancient Judaism and Early Christianity,* ed. M. J. Mulder (Assen and Philadelphia, 1988); E. P. Sanders, *Judaism: Practice and Belief 63BCE–66CE* (London and Philadelphia, 1992); and L. L. Grabbe, *Judaic Religion in the Second Temple Period: Belief and Practice from the Exile to Yavneh* (London and New York, 2000), pp. 129–49.

14   H. Butterfield, *The Whig Interpretation of History* (London, 1931), p. 58, cited by Carr (see n. 2 above), p. 115.

15   *Pace* the view of E. Fleischer as expressed in his article 'On the beginnings of obligatory Jewish prayer', *Tarbiz* 59 (1990), p. 401 and his response to my criticism in the next volume of the same journal (see n. 1 above).

Temple group no less than those of any individuals of the period. In the first place, the sources, both primary and secondary, that provide the basic information about such groups and individuals may rarely be taken at face value (which sources can?) and without reference to the contexts from which they sprang into being. Instead of happily and naively welcoming all the data that they provide, one must ask oneself who compiled these traditions, how they were disseminated and with what readership or audience in mind. It is equally important to understand the motivations and ideologies that lay behind their creation and to uncover the inevitable layers of later rewriting that cover the earlier strata of records.

At the same time, one should take into careful consideration the fact that reasons given in the literature for the development of a particular tradition, especially of a religious nature, may bear little resemblance to the original impetus for its emergence and that the interpreter must exercise not only scepticism about the available data but also an imagination lively enough to attempt a reconstruction of the circumstances in which they were created. Just because the writers of the period may not have seen the events of their day in terms of social, political and economic history or religious phenomenology, does not mean that we are precluded from doing so in our own. Consequently, the definition of particular groups with sharply delineated characteristics, the description of central institutions with clear-cut roles to play, the employment of specific terminology with overtones that belong to a different age, and the attribution of revolutionary creativity to a few individuals are all highly dubious methods for the historian to pursue.[16] One need only mention the terms 'Pharisees', 'Synagogue', 'Halakhah' and 'Men of the Great Synagogue' for an immediate appreciation of the message that I am trying to convey.

Liturgical forms

And so, finally, to the Second Temple period liturgy and to the factors and considerations that are to be taken into account in any putative notions about the nature of that phenomenon. If we can justifiably ask

---

16 Examples of such methods are to be found in the simple acceptance of the definitions offered by Josephus for the various Jewish philosophies of his age; in the views of Safrai in his articles on 'The Temple', 'The Synagogue' and 'Education and the Study of Torah' in *The Jewish People* (see n. 13 above), pp. 865–970 and in 'The Temple and the Divine Service' in *The World History of the Jewish People. First Series: Ancient Times. Volume Seven: The Herodian Period*, eds M. Avi-Yonah and Z. Baras (New Brunswick, 1975), pp. 284–337; and in the evaluation by Fleischer of Rabban Gamliel's role in the article 'On the beginnings' cited in n. 15 above.

ourselves what history is, we may most certainly inquire after the meaning of both the 'Second Temple period' and 'liturgy'.[17] By defining a period of time in relation to the dates of existence of one of its institutions one is in danger of overestimating, or at least wrongly estimating, that institution's importance for the period under discussion and of presupposing that its creation and destruction were necessarily the dominant factors in all aspects of its history. All such periodization is flawed (think of the 'pre-Christian', 'proto-Rabbinic' or 'inter-testamental' periods for instance) but one may continue to utilize it if one makes genuine efforts to avoid the kind of circular arguments that explain Second Temple period phenomena by way of their existence in Second Temple period times. The period is simply a convenience and must not prevent us from looking behind or ahead of it for aspects of its content.

By a similar token, liturgy is by linguistic definition the formal service of deities in the Classical world and equivalent to the Temple ritual in the Jewish religious system and the Eucharist for Christianity.[18] What is, however, surely intended when the word is used more loosely by historians is the whole gamut of worship that is to be identified in and around the period in question. If this is indeed the case, earnest researchers must ask themselves whether service might not take forms that would go further than standard concepts of worship. Are the reading of sacred texts, their study and exegesis not also acts of service according to some understandings of their function? Similarly, it would be perfectly appropriate to include the acts of eating and fasting and any rituals associated with them in the general area of liturgy. At the more obvious ends of the scales, of course, are to be reckoned benedictions, prayers and amulets in the various forms that they apparently took. There is no doubt that as far as the Qumran material is concerned, formal liturgical texts were in extensive use although it is not yet totally clear whether such texts reflect a standard preoccupation of the wider contemporary society or a special feature of the sect nor in which way later Jewish and Christian prayers are to be linked with them.[19] It also remains unclear whether the activities of priests, levites

---

17   This is precisely what I have attempted to do in the third chapter of my *Judaism and Hebrew Prayer* (Cambridge, 1993), especially pp. 53–75 and in an essay contributed to the third volume of the *Cambridge History of Judaism* (Cambridge, 1999), pp. 326–57.

18   See the definition of the Greek word *leitourgia* given in *A Greek-English Lexicon*, eds H. G. Liddell and R. Scott (Oxford[9], 1983), p. 1036.

19   The literature and the problem regarding Qumran and Rabbinism are clearly cited by E. and H. Eshel and A. Yarden in their Hebrew article 'A scroll from Qumran which includes part of Psalm 154 and a prayer for King Jonathan and his kingdom' *Tarbiz* 60 (1991), pp. 295–324. With regard to Qumran and Christianity, contrast the views of P. F. Bradshaw, *Daily Prayer in the Early Church* (London, 1982), pp. 20–22

and Israelites at the Temple included some prayers as well as the psalms and formulae associated with some of their rituals. What emerges from all the evidence and its interpretation is the distinct impression that liturgy was expressed in many ways and that these ways will have been inter-related in Jewish society as a whole.

The same impression holds good for the various institutions associated with worship in its wide definition. The Temple was undoubtedly a centre of elitism and formality but a variety of sources testify to a growing involvement on the part of the populace and the increasing presence of alternative manifestations of liturgy. The expansion of its buildings for wider use, the more common occurrence of prayer in its environs, the notion of the *ma'amad*, and the possible importation of such popular items as the *hallel* (the archetypal collection of psalms) and the *shema'* are among examples worthy of consideration in this connection.[20] As far as the synagogue is concerned, its existence as a building in the land of Israel does not predate the first century BCE and even at that time its function was as much to do with scripture, ritual practice and hospitality as anything more strictly concerned with prayers and benedictions.[21] It is even possible that its basic characteristics were imported into the homeland from diaspora communities where such a function was doubly useful in protecting religious identity as well as centralizing its practical expression.[22] If liturgical formulations such as those found as Qumran were more widely in use and popular benedictions and the spontaneous prayers of the specially pious were looking for a centre in which they could coalesce, it is difficult to see how the synagogue can be ruled out as a possible location for such a development.[23]

---

and J. T. Burtchaell, *From Synagogue to Church. Public Services and Offices in the Earliest Christian Communities* (Cambridge, 1992), pp. 255–57 and 267–71. See also chapters 3–4 below.

20 Reif, *Judaism and Hebrew Prayer* (see n. 17 above), pp. 57–59, 65–76 and 82–87.

21 See L. I. Levine, 'Ancient synagogues: a historical introduction' in *Ancient Synagogues Revealed* (see n. 12 above), pp. 1–10; 'The Second Temple synagogue: the formative years' in *The Synagogue in Late Antiquity*, ed. L. I. Levine (Philadelphia, 1987), pp. 7–31; and 'The sages and the synagogue in late antiquity' in *The Galilee in Late Antiquity*, ed. L. I. Levine (New York and Jerusalem, 1992), pp. 201–22, all of which work is encapsulated in his most useful volume *The Ancient Synagogue: The First Thousand Years* (New Haven and London, 2000).

22 See the articles by J. G. Griffiths, 'Egypt and the rise of the synagogue', *JTS*, NS 38 (1987), pp. 1–15 and L. L. Grabbe, 'Synagogues in pre-70 Palestine: a re-assessment', *JTS*, NS 39 (1988), pp. 401–10.

23 Most of the evidence (as presented in the articles cited in nn. 21–22 above) points to a variety of functions for the synagogue including those noted in the famous Theodotos inscription but not necessarily restricted to them; see L. Roth-Gerson, *The Greek Inscriptions from the Synagogues in Eretz-Israel* (Hebrew; Jerusalem, 1987), pp. 76–86.

It is no less likely that the ultimate mutation of the synagogal assembly (if I may be guilty of such a tautology) into the formal house of worship in some later times and places owes its origins to the first attempts to centralize existing customs, including perhaps some that had been associated with the Temple and the Temple Mount. What should not be forgotten is that the home too had long functioned as a Jewish liturgical *locus*, as more than adequately documented in the Hebrew Bible with regard to such matters as personal supplication and pedagogical rituals. It seems reasonable to assume that during the period under discussion the rites of *qiddush* and *havdalah* became established although it is unclear whether these were an evolution of earlier practices or a reaction by which ceremonial moved from the Temple to the home or, indeed, from the larger group to the smaller domestic setting.[24] Where it is likely that such a reaction did take place is in the matter of the development of the Passover *seder*, where a biblical ritual tied to the Temple sacrifice found its alternative and ultimately central setting in the home.[25]

If, then, it is true that in dealing with the liturgy of the period we must be wary of identifying clear-cut practices, easily defined groups, superlative individuals and absolute notions, the corollary is that our academic objective must be the pursuit of the mutual influences exercised by religious customs, the overlapping traditions that might be characteristic of a number of different philosophies, the individuals who express the essence of their particular environment, and the patchwork of concepts that make up the chequered history of ideas. The stresses and tensions that may be located in any area of human activity and at any time or place were most certainly present among the Jews of our period as they strove to express their desire for communication with the divine. Perhaps the growing importance and formality of what had begun as individual prayer were a genuine expression of what Moshe Greenberg perceived as the 'democratic and egalitarian nature' of Jewish worship[26] and the development of the synagogal centre was, as Levine has suggested, a means whereby the local populace were offered a system that could compete with what was on offer for their more elitist and intellectual brothers and sisters.[27]

And, mentioning sisters, was the woman's role complementary, challenging or identical to that of the man in various liturgical

---

24   Reif, *Judaism and Hebrew Prayer* (see n. 17 above), pp. 69–70 and 87.

25   B. M. Bokser, *The Origins of the Seder: The Passover Rite and Early Rabbinic Judaism* (Berkeley, 1984).

26   M. Greenberg, *Biblical Prose Prayer as a Window to the Popular Religion of Ancient Israel* (Berkeley, 1983), pp. 45–57.

27   See Levine's work cited in n. 21 above.

respects?[28] Did the *shema'* and the *'amidah*, and the liturgical use of the Decalogue, originate in economically, socially and intellectually distinguishable contexts and was there a composite rather than a single response to what constituted a religious requirement in matters liturgical?[29] Other areas in which there was obviously considerable competition between alternatives are those of language, geography and spirituality. Was the ideal a Hebrew formulation of a mystical bent in a Palestinian context or a Greek philosophical structure developed in Egypt, to identify the possibilities only at their extremes? And what effect did the Ancient Near Eastern or Classical traditions have on the Jewish liturgy? The chapters that follow this one may at least partly indicate where and how we are to seek the answers to such questions.

I fear that my excursion into theory, methodology and historiography has raised many questions and offered few solutions about the direction in which the topic should ideally be moving. But, to paraphrase Aqavya ben Mahalel,[30] unless we know how we set out, where we are going, and by what means we are to be judged, there is the distinct possibility of our journey being futile. *Hereux qui comme Ulysse a fait un beau voyage.*[31]

---

28 Useful summaries of the liturgical role of women in the period under discussion are offered by Susan Grossman and Hannah Safrai in *Daughters of the King: Women and the Synagogue*, eds S. Grossman and R. Haut (Philadelphia, New York and Jerusalem, 1992), pp. 15–49.

29 T. Zahavy, 'Three stages in the development of early rabbinic prayer' in *From Ancient Israel to Modern Judaism; Intellect in Quest of Understanding: Essays in Honor of Marvin Fox*, eds J. Neusner, E. S. Frerichs and N. M. Sarna, vol. 1 (Atlanta, 1989), pp. 233–65; and 'The politics of piety, social conflict and the emergence of rabbinic liturgy' in *The Making of Jewish and Christian Worship*, eds P. F. Bradshaw and L. A. Hoffman (Notre Dame and London, 1991), pp. 42–68; R. Kimelman, 'The shema' and its rhetoric: the case for the shema' being more than creation, revelation and redemption', *Journal of Jewish Thought and Philosophy* 2 (1992), pp. 111–56; and 'The shema' liturgy: from covenant ceremony to coronation', in *Kenishta: Studies of the Synagogue World*, ed. J. Tabory (Ramat Gan, 2001), pp. 9–105. See also chapter 7 below.

30 Mishnah, *'Avot* 3.1.

31 Joachim Du Bellay (1522–60), *Les Regrets et Autres Oeuvres Poëtiques*, eds J. Jollife and M. A. Screech (Geneva, 1966), no. 31, p. 98.

3

Qumran Research and Rabbinic Liturgy

Introduction

It is widely recognized that most proponents of *Wissenschaft des Judentums*, at least in the first century of its existence, were at one time or another engaged in research on the history of Jewish liturgy. Although their interests in this connection ranged widely within the rabbinic tradition from texts to theology, from prose to poetry, and from the mystical to the mundane, there was always also a preoccupation on the part of some scholars with the precise relationship between the earliest manifestations of rabbinic liturgy and the broader history and literature of the Jews during the Second Temple period. Tending as they did to see the religious histories of Christianity and Rabbinic Judaism in diachronic terms, they combed the late books of the Hebrew Bible, the Apocrypha and Pseudepigrapha, and the literary sources of Hellenistic Judaism, to identify the material that could most closely be related to the earliest talmudic-midrashic traditions. While the Christian scholars tended to see the New Testament and the early Church as the faithful transmitters of major Second Temple ideas and practice, their Jewish counterparts preferred to locate such a continuation in the extensive literature of the talmudic-midrashic sources.[1]

---

1   For bibliographical guidance, see J. Tabory, *Jewish Prayer and the Yearly Cycle: A List of Articles*, supplement to *Kiryat Sefer* 64 (Jerusalem, 1992–93), and a substantial collection of addenda to that publication that appeared together with his facsimile edition of the Hanau prayer-book of 1628, eds J. Tabory and M. Rapeld (Ramat Gan, 1994). Tabory has also surveyed the field in a Hebrew article entitled *'Tefillah'* in supplementary volume 3 of the *Encyclopaedia Hebraica* (Jerusalem and Tel-Aviv, 1995), cols 1061–68, and in his English article 'The prayer book (siddur) as an anthology of Judaism', *Prooftexts* 17/2 (1997), pp. 115–32. See also R. Sarason's three articles: 'On the use of method in the modern study of Jewish liturgy' in *Approaches to Ancient Judaism: Theory and Practice*, ed. W. S. Green (Missoula, Montana, 1978), pp. 97–172; 'Recent developments in the study of Jewish liturgy' in *The Study of Ancient Judaism. 1. Mishnah, Midrash, Siddur*, ed. J. Neusner (New York, 1982), pp. 180–87; 'Religion and worship: the case of Judaism' in *Take Judaism for Example: Studies Toward the Comparison of Religions*, ed. J. Neusner (Chicago, 1983), pp. 49–65. See also S. C. Reif, *Judaism and Hebrew Prayer: New Perspectives on Jewish Liturgical History* (Cambridge, 1993), pp. 1–21; chapter 13 below; and 'The importance of the Cairo Genizah for the study of the history of prayer' in *Kenishta: Studies of the Synagogue World*, ed. J. Tabory (Ramat Gan, 2001), pp. 43–52 (Hebrew section).

Earlier views

This Jewish scholastic tendency in the field of liturgical research may be
traced in the work of many scholars from Reform circles in mid-
nineteenth-century Germany to modern Orthodox stalwarts in mid-
twentieth-century Israel but is perhaps best exemplified in the work of
an American liturgical specialist who ultimately headed the rabbinical
school of the Conservative movement. Louis Finkelstein devoted much
of his early research to the history of the traditional Hebrew prayers
and it is now some eighty years since he produced detailed studies of
the *'amidah* and the *birkat ha-mazon*, later supplemented by articles on
the *shema'* and the *hallel*. These studies, which appeared in the form of
lengthy articles in scholarly periodicals, contained a mass of evidence
from talmudic, geonic and midrashic literature, from Genizah and
other manuscript folios (some of them containing unique material),
from medieval halakhic compositions and liturgical commentaries, and
from early printed editions.[2] Finkelstein's analysis, though containing
important theological, literary and historical elements, and making
comparisons with Christian and Karaite traditions, was primarily
textual and he reached very precise conclusions about the origin and
development of these central Jewish prayers. Having compared all the
rites, versions and citations, and laying particular stress on what he had
drawn from the Genizah sources, he felt able to eliminate what he
regarded as later accretions and to present, in tabulated format, a text
that could be defined as a pristine version originating in Judea in the
Second Temple period, probably as early as pre-Maccabean times. In
his view, the role of Rabban Gamliel in the second century of the
current era had been to establish the authentic and authoritative nature
of such a version and through his powerful leadership to transmit its
purity to future generations. In the wake of Finkelstein's definitions, it
became fairly common for general studies of Second Temple Judaism to

---

2   L. Finkelstein, 'The development of the amidah', *JQR*, NS 16 (1925), pp. 1–43 and
     127–70; 'The birkat ha-mazon', *JQR*, NS 19 (1928–29), pp. 211–62; "La kedouscha et
     les benedictions du schema', *REJ* 93 (1932), pp. 1–26; and 'The origin of the hallel',
     HUCA 23/2 (1950–51), pp. 319–37. For recent assessments of Finkelstein as scholar
     and educator, see M. B. Greenbaum, 'The Finkelstein era', H. E. Goldberg, 'Becoming
     history: perspectives on the Seminary faculty at mid-century' and B. R. Shargel, 'The
     texture of Seminary life during the Finkelstein era', in *Tradition Renewed: A History of
     the Jewish Theological Seminary*, ed. J. Wertheimer (2 vols; New York, 1997), 1.161–232,
     353–437 and 515–64.

cite his work among the most important studies of Jewish liturgy in
that period.[3]

The notion that there were single and standard manifestations of
Jewish thought, religious practice, sacred literature, popular language
and liturgical rite that existed in the Second Temple, and that may be
traced in direct lines of evolution into the early Christian centuries, has
been seriously challenged by numerous scholarly developments since
the time of Finkelstein. The discovery, exploitation and publication of
the Qumran corpus has undoubtedly made the most major impact and
will shortly engage our closer attention. There have, however, also been
other changes of outlook on the part of specialists in the period that
have made their mark on the scientific understanding of its Jewish
liturgical history. In the previous chapter I have argued the need for a
change in the methodology required to reach such a scientific
understanding. It seems to me that the broader Near Eastern
background and the more specific Hellenistic culture have to be taken
into account; that social, economic and political factors are now to be
given more recognition than they once were; that the role of
archeological and inscriptional evidence is continuing to grow in
significance; and that, above all, the definition of what constitutes
history must be permitted to add a powerful voice to the discussion.
[4]More specifically, the views of Joseph Heinemann and Ezra Fleischer,
diametrically opposed and mutually contradictory in so many ways as
they are, nevertheless have in common that they both force the
liturgical historian to think again about what preceded the tannaitic
traditions in general and the achievements of Rabban Gamliel in
particular. As far as Heinemann was concerned, there never was one
original version and the Genizah texts, far from being distillable to one
pure essence, should rather be analysed as testifying to a variety and
complexity of content that characterized Jewish liturgy from its
foundations during the Second Temple period. Such an inherent lack of
textual consistency was more consonant with a proposed orality of
transmission than with the notion of a standard formulation committed
to writing. What the scholar could and should do was to employ the
form-critical method to uncover the varied ritual, educational and
individual contexts in which the different sets of prayers had their
origins and to identify the common themes and factors that run

---

3   See, for example, the revised English edition of E. Schürer, *The History of the Jewish
     People in the Age of Jesus Christ (175 B.C. – A.D. 135)*, vol. 2, eds G. Vermes, F. Millar
     and M. Black (Edinburgh, 1979), p. 456.
4   See chapter 2 above.

through the varied formulations.[5] For his part, Fleischer saw the variegated nature of liturgical texts from the Genizah as testimony to the revolutionary impact of the liturgical poets on the central Jewish prayers in the geonic period, an impact that he regarded as having its origin in the mishnaic authorization for textual innovation in the 'amidah. The recitations and compositions of such poets spawned a host of novel versions for what had previously been the standard liturgy. That liturgy had been created virtually *de novo* by Rabban Gamliel in the second century, had existed in written form, and had throughout the talmudic period enjoyed a more authoritative status than any of the varied formulations that are cited from time to time by the other rabbis.[6] What appears to be a central pillar in both historical reconstructions is the conviction that it is impossible to identify a standard 'amidah-type or similar liturgical text that was broadly used in Jewish religious communities to meet a religious obligation in the final two or three centuries of the Second Temple period.

In the course of the last decade or two, the liturgical texts available from Qumran have increased considerably in number and variety and consequently represent the latest phase of the challenge to which reference was earlier made. The question that needs to be answered is whether this new evidence and its close study and careful publication have reinforced the conviction that is common to the Heinemann and Fleischer views or have, even in a limited fashion, moved more in the direction of justifying that aspect of Finkelstein's approach that presupposed that scholars could uncover standard liturgical texts dating from the pre-Christian period that were the undisputed ancestors of later Jewish and Christian worship. When I was, some fifteen years ago, writing my general history of normative Hebrew prayer in the Jewish religious community, I decided not to give any more than brief attention to the Qumran evidence because I was unsure of the degree to which it could justifiably be regarded as directly mundane to the topic.[7] Having looked at liturgical items such as the

---

5   The original Hebrew edition, with the English title *Prayer in the Period of the Tanna'im and Amora'im: Its Nature and Its Patterns* (Jerusalem, 1964) was updated by the author and translated into English by R. Sarason. It was published as *Prayer in the Talmud: Forms and Patterns* (Berlin, 1977), with an introduction that offers a summary and justification of his novel approach.

6   E. Fleischer, 'On the beginnings of obligatory Jewish prayer', *Tarbiz* 59 (1990), pp. 397–441; 'Rejoinder to Dr Reif's remarks', *Tarbiz* 60 (1991), pp. 683–88. Compare also his *Eretz-Israel Prayer and Prayer Rituals as Portrayed in the Geniza Documents* (Hebrew; Jerusalem, 1988); 'Annual and triennial reading of the Bible in the Old Synagogue', *Tarbiz* 61 (1992), pp. 25–43; 'The *Shemone Esre* – its character, internal order, contents and goals', *Tarbiz* 62 (1993), pp. 179–223; and 'Le-sidrey ha-tefillah be-vet ha-kenesset', *Asufot* 7 (1993), pp. 217–60.

7   Reif, *Judaism and Hebrew Prayer* (see n. 1 above), pp. 48–52, 55, 60, 66–69, 77–78, 82.

Hodayot, Benedictions, Songs of the Sabbath Sacrifice and *Words of the Luminaries*, and the literature then available on these, I noted that they went beyond what was known from biblical, apocryphal and pseudepigraphical literature and hinted that this might lend some credence to the connection originally made by Kaufmann Kohler a century ago between the liturgy of the Essenes and that of the early rabbis.[8] Such themes as the choice of Israel, the centrality of Zion, the elimination of evil and the survival of the saints occurred at Qumran and in the relevant rabbinic texts and there were possible parallels with the later *'amidah, vidduy* and *taḥanun*. At the same time, there were no clear indications about matters of recitation, participation and context and I therefore offered the following tentative conclusions:

> Certainly, the Qumran scrolls provide the earliest testimony to liturgical formulations of a communal nature designated for particular occasions and conducted in a centre totally independent of Jerusalem and the Temple, making use of terminology and theological concepts that were later to become dominant in Jewish and, in some cases, Christian prayer...
> The question that has yet to be asked, let alone answered, is whether that process is to be understood as a unique feature of the way of life represented at Qumran, which was later adopted and adapted by the rabbinic inheritors of Jewish religious practice, or as an example of popular liturgical piety that was common to various Pharisaic and Essene groups and subsequently survived in the tannaitic traditions.[9]

Given that additional texts and more extensive studies of the subject are now available, the time has come to discuss the matter afresh and to offer a re-assessment of its current state.

Weinfeld's theory

The scholar who has been most prolific in comparing the liturgical texts from Qumran with those of rabbinic literature is undoubtedly Moshe Weinfeld and his articles therefore represent a good starting point for this fresh analysis. Indeed, a mere glance at the titles of these scholarly papers and at their summaries and conclusions, some published before I completed the research for my volume on Hebrew prayer, and others

---

8   K. Kohler, 'Ueber die Ursprünge und Grundformen der synagogalen Liturgie: Eine Studie', *MGWJ* 37 (1893), pp. 441–51 and 489–97. Compare also his further comments in his articles on 'Didascalia', 'Essenes' and 'Liturgy' in *Jewish Encyclopaedia* (New York, 1906) and on 'The origin and composition of the eighteen benedictions', *HUCA* 1 (1924), pp. 387–425, reprinted in *Contributions to the Scientific Study of Jewish Liturgy*, ed. J. J. Petuchowski (New York, 1970), pp. 52–90.

9   Reif, *Judaism and Hebrew Prayer* (see n. 1 above), pp. 49–50 and 66.

at a later date, would seem to justify a conclusion that goes significantly beyond what I was then prepared to venture and therefore to call for a more definitive acknowledgement of the Qumran corpus as the obvious source and precedent for rabbinic liturgy. Weinfeld devotes considerable attention to such liturgical topics as the *qedushah*, *'amidah*, *birkat ha-mazon* and morning benedictions, closely examining the relevant texts in both Qumranic and rabbinic literature and dealing with terminology, content and overall context. He identifies many individual words, in both verbal and nominal forms, and numerous short phrases that the two literatures have in common. He also finds similar theological themes such as creation and calendar, the closeness of the supplicant to God, and the removal of satanic power. Parallel uses of verses and of sections of the Psalms are located and he points to a number of instances in which links are made between the same two or three topics. For example, *qedushah*, morning light and angels are found in close proximity in both sets of sources, as are repentance, knowledge of God and forgiveness, and there is a possible parallel between sets of texts both of which link the joy of a wedding and the comforting of a mourner.[10]

From the point of view of subject matter, there can be no denying that there are similar theological themes, that one can point to parallel tendencies to deal with groups of topics in contexts that are not dissimilar, and that the language used has its common factors. There are, however, a number of criteria that combine to call into question whether these basic similarities are sufficient to indicate that rabbinic liturgy is directly borrowed from Qumran. The precise word-order, the complete phraseology, and the structure of the syntax are by no means parallel and the liturgical use made of the language differs in the two corpora. The topics covered and the links made are among those that constituted the stuff of contemporary religious thinking and may therefore be theologically rather than liturgically meaningful. Many of the parallels have common precedents in the books of the Hebrew Bible

---

10   M. Weinfeld, 'Traces of *qedushat yozer* and *pesukey de-zimra* in the Qumran literature and in Ben-Sira', *Tarbiz* 45 (1975–76), pp. 15–26; 'The prayers for knowledge, repentance and forgiveness in the eighteen benedictions — Qumran parallels, biblical antecedents and basic characteristics', *Tarbiz* 48 (1979), pp. 186–200; 'On the question of morning benedictions at Qumran', *Tarbiz* 51 (1982), pp. 495–96; 'Grace after meals at the mourner's house in a text from Qumran', *Tarbiz* 61 (1992), pp. 15–23; 'Grace after meals in Qumran', *JBL* 111 (1992), pp. 427–40; 'Prayer and liturgical practice in the Qumran sect', in *The Dead Sea Scrolls: Forty Years of Research*, eds D. Dimant and U. Rappaport (Leiden, New York, Köln and Jerusalem, 1992), pp. 241–58; 'The angelic song over the luminaries in the Qumran texts' in *Time to Prepare the Way in the Wilderness: Papers on the Qumran Scrolls by Fellows of the Institute for Advanced Studies of the Hebrew University, Jerusalem, 1989–90*, eds D. Dimant and L. H. Schiffman (Leiden and New York, 1995), pp. 131–57.

and this is not always clarified. In addition, Weinfeld permits himself
to use rabbinic material in a chronologically indiscriminate manner,
citing sources that range over many centuries and numerous
communities, rather than limiting himself to items that may with some
confidence be dated to the early Christian centuries.[11] It is true that, in
the case of a fair number of liturgical texts, limited linguistic and
thematic similarities will be acceptable even to those who are more
sceptical about their overall significance for making direct links
between Qumran and the rabbinic synagogue and academy. The
instance of the claimed parallel between 4Q434[a] and the post-prandial
grace recited at the home of the mourner in the rabbinic tradition is,
however, to all intents and purposes somewhat speculative and far
from convincing.[12]

Weinfeld's arguments in connection with that Qumran fragment,
and indeed with regard to 4Q37 (4QDeut[j]) and 4Q41 (4QDeut[n]), led me
to consider whether the use of current computer-based searches might
not establish linguistic similarities that could conceivably strengthen
his position. I therefore began to make use of the software available
from Oxford University Press and Brill in Leiden in their second
CDRom in the series entitled *The Dead Sea Scrolls Electronic Reference
Library*, edited by Timothy Lim, to comb the available Qumran sources
for direct parallels to rabbinic texts, paying particular attention to the
grace after meals.[13] To date, I have searched only for the major
vocabulary and content that are characteristic of limited sections of the
birkat ha-mazon in its various textual witnesses but the results
nevertheless seem worthy of consideration. Given the limited context
here, I have in any case been able to include only a few illustrations. In
4Q504, for example, we encounter notions such as the divine love of
Israel, the choice of Jerusalem, the special status of Zion, the
uniqueness of the Davidic kingdom, God's great name, and the

---

11 In his article 'Traces' (see n. 10 above), for instance, he cites halakhic, liturgical, poetic and midrashic sources, all of which are many centuries later than Qumran in their literary form, without demonstrating why he regards them as incorporating earlier material; see nn. 7, 10, 22, 25, 55, 62 and 67 in that article.

12 In his articles on the grace after meals (see n. 10 above), for instance, he has again correctly pointed to a number of similar themes but has neither taken sufficient account of the influence of biblical precedents nor justified the presupposition of so precise a liturgical context for these Qumranic fragments; see also n. 32 below for a reference to Falk's assessment of these similarities.

13 *The Dead Sea Scrolls Electronic Reference Library*, ed. Timothy Lim, the second CD-Rom published in 1999 by Oxford University Press in Oxford and Brill in Leiden. This was available to me at the library of Tyndale House in Cambridge and I welcome this opportunity of recording my gratitude to the President, Dr Bruce Winter, and to the library staff there for their many kindnesses.

removal of satanic and evil power.[14] The roots אכל , שבע and ברך coincide in 4Q370, references to the exodus from Egypt and the feeding (כלכל) of the Jewish people in 4Q393, and the notion of a shortage of food, by way of the use of the verb חסר and the noun לחם is to be found in 4Q416–7.[15] The writer in 4Q504 takes pride in the fact that his group are 'called by God's name' and that same divine name is described as 'the great name' in a number of Qumranic contexts.[16] If we move beyond the vocabulary and content of the grace, we may note another interesting example. The Davidic occupation of the royal throne is described as eternal in 4Q252, echoing Deuteronomy 17:18, 1 Kings 2:45, as well as Daniel 2:44 and 7:14, and finding a parallel in the third post-*haftarah* benediction dealing with the messianic age.[17]

The manner in which these and similar citations are reminiscent of rabbinic texts is undoubtedly intriguing but we must be careful not to draw conclusions that go beyond the evidence before us. There are here concepts and linguistic usages that are similar but there is very little that is actually identical and the order of the phraseology and the syntactical structure are by no means parallel. The standardized formats and contexts of the rabbinic formulations appear to have no clear-cut precedents at Qumran. Both sets of texts have biblical precedents but they utilize them in different ways, each opting for the kind of adjustments that take account of its own predilections. With regard to Israel, Jerusalem and the Temple, the religious groups that lie

---

14   For 4Q504 (4QDib.Hamᵃ), see M. Baillet, *DJD* VII (Oxford, 1982), pp. 137–68 and F. García Martínez and E. J. C. Tigchelaar, *The Dead Sea Scrolls Study Edition*, vol. 2 (Leiden, Boston and Köln, 1998), pp. 1009–19. See also M. R. Lehmann, 'The writings of Ben Sira, the Dead Sea Scrolls and temple worship in the liturgy of Yom Kippur' in *Piyyut in Tradition*, vol. 2, eds B. Bar-Tikva and E. Hazan (Hebrew; Ramat Gan, 2000), pp. 13–18.

15   For 4Q370 (4QAdmonition Based on the Flood), I.1–2, see C. Newsom in *DJD* XIX (1995), pp. 85–97 and García Martínez, *Study Edition* (see n. 14 above), p. 733; for 4Q393 (4QCommunal Confession, *olim* Liturgical Work), see *A Preliminary Edition of the Unpublished Dead Sea Scrolls: The Hebrew and Aramaic Texts from Cave Four*, fascicle 3, eds B. Z. Wacholder and M. G. Abegg (Washington, 1993), p. 267 and D. Falk in *DJD* XXIX (1999), pp. 45–61; for 4Q416–7 (4QInstructionᵇ⁻ᶜ), fragment 1, II.23–24, see the same *Preliminary Edition*, fascicle 2 (Washington, 1992), pp. 54–76, García Martínez, *Study Edition* (see n. 14 above), pp. 847–61 and J. Strugnell and D. J. Harrington in *DJD* XXXIV (1999), pp. 73–210.

16   See n. 14 above and 1QM (1QWar Scroll), XI.2; see E. L. Sukenik, *The Dead Sea Scrolls of the Hebrew University* (Jerusalem, 1955), pp. 1–19 and García Martínez, *Study Edition* (see n. 14 above), vol. 1 (Leiden, Boston and Köln, 1997), pp. 113–45, esp. p. 131.

17   For 4Q252(4QcommGenA), V.1–4, see G. Brooke, *DJD* XXII (1996), pp. 185–207 and García Martínez, *Study Edition*, vol. 1 (see n. 15 above), pp. 501–5; see also the *haftarah* references in S. Baer, *Seder 'Avodat Yisra'el* (Rödelheim, 1868), p. 227 and *Oṣar Ha-Tefillot*, ed. A. L. Gordon (corrected and expanded edition, Vilna, 1923, Hebrew pagination), p. 351.

behind the various textual constructions have a variety of theological motivations for their preferences. One may even tentatively suggest that divine attributes such as טוב, חסד and רחמים are regarded at Qumran as the models for human piety and idealistic behaviour while the stress in the rabbinic texts is more on the blessings they convey on Israel.[18]

Linguistic analysis

At this point it is necessary to make reference to a comparative linguistic analysis of the texts from Qumran and from rabbinic sources that was made by Chaim Rabin and to assess the degree to which it is relevant to the current discussion. Although the original English article appeared in 1965 and its Hebrew translation in 1972, Rabin's reputation was such that it is still often cited and it has without question exercised a formative influence on subsequent approaches to the subject.[19] Rabin argued for the existence in Palestine in the middle of the Second Temple period of 'a literary language in which BH (=Biblical Hebrew) and MH (=Mishnaic Hebrew) elements coexisted upon a mainly MH grammatical foundation'. He suggested reasons why the authors of the texts found at Qumran consciously chose to move in the direction of a BH style while their later rabbinic counterparts reacted to this and related developments by committing themselves even more enthusiastically to the MH flavour of their own linguistic usage. For our purposes here, it is important to deal not so much with his overall linguistic theory but what he has to say about the liturgical field. Adopting the view, particularly as earlier expressed by Talmon,[20] that

---

18 See the examples of such usage in 4Q266 (4QD^a), fragment 2, I.12 and 22, with text in García Martínez, *Study Edition*, vol. 1 (see n. 15 above), p. 582; 4Q418 (4QInstruction^d), fragment 81.19, with text in García Martínez, vol. 2 (see n. 14 above), p. 872; 4Q504 (4QDibHam^a), fragment 4.5, with text in García Martínez, 2.1010; 4Q506 (4QpapDibHam^c), fragments 131–32.11, with text in García Martínez, 2.1020; 4Q521 (4QMessianic Apocalypse), fragment 2, II.11, with text in García Martínez, 2.1044; 1QRule (1QS) IV.3, with text in García Martínez, 1.77; 1QHymns^a (1QHodayot^a), XVIII (=X+30).16, with text in García Martínez, 1.186. For the corresponding rabbinic texts that I have compared, see L. Finkelstein, 'The birkat ha-mazon', *JQR*, NS 19 (1928–29), pp. 211–62.

19 C. Rabin, 'The historical background of Qumran Hebrew' in *Scripta Hierosolymitana* 4 (Jerusalem, 1965), pp. 144–61, with a later Hebrew version published in *Qoveṣ Ma'amarim Bilshon Ḥz"l*, vol. 1, ed. M. Bar-Asher (2 vols; Jerusalem, 1972), pp. 355–82.

20 S. Talmon, 'The order of prayers of the sect from the Judaean desert', *Tarbiz* 29 (1959), pp. 1–20; 'The <<Manual of Benedictions>> of the sect of the Judaean desert', *RQ* 2 (1960), pp. 475–500. Talmon's work on this topic is summarized in 'The emergence of institutionalized prayer in Israel in the light of the Qumran literature' in his *The World of Qumran from Within: Collected Studies* (Leiden and Jerusalem, 1989), pp. 200–243.

the Qumran sect was familiar with the benedictions of the *shema'* and the *'amidah* 'in a sequence not unlike that of the rabbinic version', Rabin concluded that 'anything characteristic of the prayers is therefore common inheritance of the Qumran Sect and of Pharisaism'.[21]

At first glance, this appears to be at odds with our findings as described above and to require either a reconsideration of these or a challenge to the kind of view espoused by Rabin. A closer examination of his article does, however, reveal that he makes a number of additional points that indicate clearly that he was proposing a more refined assessment of the situation. He alludes to the fact that the 'common inheritance' appears to have included a store of expressions and some similar vocabulary but is at the same time cautious enough to disclaim any possibility of recovering the original linguistic form of such prayers. The Qumran texts adapted whatever they inherited with a view to matching it to their own style and the rabbis remained loyal to an idiom of MH that was exclusively used for their prayers but fixed the precise textual formulation of the latter only in the post-talmudic period.[22] It is therefore clear that Rabin, even from the limited texts available to him forty years ago, is tending to the view that commonality of subjects and vocabulary is not to be confused with identity of liturgical context, order and formulation.

The findings of another, later article of his are also worthy of summary in the current context. There he argues that a better understanding of Jewish liturgical history is to be achieved by adopting aspects of the structuralist approach, by stressing the synchronic as well as the diachronic analysis, and by pointing to the legal and theological elements in the language of the prayers. What he presupposes is a long and complicated development from a format that may well have been originally oral, through a process of literary improvement and linguistic selection, towards the establishment of independent parameters, and a status that could even ultimately exercise a formative influence on the emergence of contemporary, spoken Hebrew.[23] Such views are by no means at odds with the notion that what had been liturgically expressed in varieties of language, structure and context in Second Temple times came to be formulated

---

21   The two quotations from Rabin are to be found on pp. 156 and 153 of his English article cited in n. 19 above.

22   Rabin, 'The historical background' (see n. 19 above), pp. 153–56.

23   C. Rabin, 'The linguistic investigation of the language of Jewish prayer' in *Studies in Aggadah, Targum and Jewish Liturgy in Memory of Joseph Heinemann*, eds J. J. Petuchowski and E. Fleischer (Jerusalem and Cincinnati, 1981), Hebrew section, pp. 163–71.

and utilized in a generally more standardized fashion in what became the authorized rabbinic traditions of subsequent periods.

No less relevant to this discussion are the views of another, more contemporary specialist in the history of the Hebrew language in the Second Temple period, Avi Hurvitz. In a helpful overview of developments, he has defined the language of the Qumran scrolls as a form of late Biblical Hebrew and has drawn attention to the biblical elements in the Hebrew of rabbinic prayer. He has also contrasted the spontaneous and classical nature of the language used for prayer in the First Temple period with its later equivalent, as for instance, recorded in the book of Ezra, and has noted linguistic movements in the direction of rabbinic compositions, as well as similarities between the rabbinic and Qumranic usages. At the same time, however, he has pointed to the possibility that the commitment to Biblical Hebrew may have been the result of a conscious mimicry and, even more significantly for the topic here being considered, has stressed that it is the roots of rabbinic liturgy that one can find in the Second Temple period and not the precise formulation of its actual prayers.[24]

Qumran specialists

Recognizing the fact that my own perspective is one that is firmly fixed in the historical study of rabbinic sources rather than in the literary analysis of the Judean scrolls, I am aware of the need to turn now to the work of a sample selection of current Qumran specialists and to bring into the equation how they have recently come to view the overall liturgical history of the Second Temple period from their own particular outlook. Fortunately for the purposes of this study, there are a number of important monographs and articles that have appeared in recent years and that provide fresh evidence, clear analyses and convincing conclusions. What is perhaps even more to the point is that they do not represent one school of thought but range across the field, incorporating views and interpretations that originate in European, North American and Israeli institutions. They are therefore of

---

24   A. Hurvitz, *The Transition Period: A Study in Post-Exilic Hebrew and its Implications for the Dating of Psalms* (Hebrew; Jerusalem, 1972), especially pp. 36–63. See also E. Qimron, *The Hebrew of the Dead Sea Scrolls* (Atlanta, 1986). The late Shelomo Morag identified prominent grammatical traits in the language of the Dead Sea scrolls that he regarded as representative of an old dialectal variation that was preserved in a spoken (*not* literary) Hebrew of the Qumran period and was not directly related to Biblical Hebrew. He did not, however, make any reference to the relationship between Qumran Hebrew and the language of rabbinic prayer. See his article 'Qumran Hebrew: some typological observations', *VT* 38 (1988), pp. 148–64.

considerable assistance to the project to relate, in a scientifically sound manner, what happened among the rabbis to what was recorded at Qumran.[25]

Bilhah Nitzan's study *Qumran Prayer and Religious Poetry* appeared in English translation in 1994 and was based on the Hebrew original that appeared in Tel Aviv in 1989.[26] In that important and extensive treatment of the subject, Nitzan devoted some of the discussion to the relationship between Qumranic and rabbinic prayer. Although both are dependent on the same biblical sources, they each demonstrate unique characteristics. Blessings and prayers occur in both sets of texts but in each case with its own formulas. Although they do share some ideas, it would be exaggerated to claim close and precise parallels of pattern. The priestly benediction has a much more central role in the arrangement of poetic and ceremonial compositions at Qumran while the structure and use of the *qedushah* is considerably less crystallized there than among the rabbis.

Other specific features of the Judean scrolls are, according to Nitzan, that they supplement biblical content with apocalyptic material and reformulate apocalyptic myths in the biblical style, as well as expressing the sanctity of the sabbath by the use of ritual poetry specifically suited to that day and of a more elevated style than the weekday prose. What emerges from all this data is that both groups may be said to have fixed liturgy but only the rabbinic variety is of a fully uniform nature and that the Qumranic use of benedictions is not to be seen as a precedent for the later rabbinic employment of this genre. More accurately, the liturgical developments at Qumran should be plotted at a point, between the biblical beginning and the rabbinic progression, that is close to the position occupied by the Apocryphal

---

25 Among the earlier studies that laid the foundations for the later research discussed in more detail below were D. Flusser, 'Psalms, hymns and prayers' in *Jewish Writings of the Second Temple Period*, ed. M. E. Stone (Assen and Philadelphia, 1984), pp. 551–77; J. Charlesworth, 'Jewish hymns, odes and prayers (c. 167 BCE–135 CE)' in *Early Judaism and its Modern Interpreters*, eds R. A. Kraft and G. W. E. Nickelsburg (Philadelphia, 1986), pp. 411–36; C. A. Newsom, *Songs of the Sabbath Sacrifice: A Critical Edition* (Atlanta, 1985) and '"Sectually Explicit" literature from Qumran' in *The Hebrew Bible and its Interpreters*, eds W. H. Propp, B. Halpern and D. N. Freedman (Winona Lake, 1990), pp. 167–87; L. H. Schiffman, 'The Dead Sea Scrolls and the early history of Jewish liturgy' in *The Synagogue in Late Antiquity*, ed. L. I. Levine (Philadelphia, 1987), pp. 33–48; J. Maier, 'Zu Kult und Liturgie der Qumrangemeinde', *RQ* 14 (1989–90), pp. 543–86.

26 B. Nitzan, *Qumran Prayer and Religious Poetry* (Leiden, New York and Köln, 1994), translated by Jonathan Chipman from the Hebrew original *Tefillat Qumran Ve-Shiratah Be-Ziqatan La-Miqra* (Jerusalem, 1989).

and Pseudepigraphical literature. This conclusion is obviously not merely of chronological significance.[27]

Some attention must also be given to the conclusions reached in studies recently penned by Eileen Schuller and Esther Chazon on the place of the Qumranic liturgical texts in the search for the origins of rabbinic prayer. Schuller has made it clear that the non-canonical psalms enjoyed a provenance that was both earlier and broader than that of Qumran and that they were employed for liturgical purposes. She has demonstrated that although they make use of the more common biblical precedents in the formulation of the terms with which they describe themselves, they also contribute innovative developments to this whole process.

Schuller's analysis of the *Hodayot* has revealed that they, more specifically, reflect the experiences and teachings of the Qumranic sect and that they exist in a variety of collections. She has pointed to elements of Aramaic influence and to words and expressions in the non-canonical psalms that have their equivalents in other Hebrew texts of the late Second Temple period and in the early years of the post-Destruction era. She has also provided clear evidence that formulations and concepts known in tannaitic Judaism and early Christianity are already adumbrated in such psalms as that found in 4Q372 1 and has stressed the importance of the Qumranic scrolls for plotting the development of the use and formulation of the Jewish liturgical benediction.[28]

Perhaps the most important of Esther Chazon's many findings and conclusions is her overall assessment that although there are some sectarian liturgical elements at Qumran, there is now a wealth of evidence to indicate that many of the hymns and prayers found there

---

27 Nitzan, *Qumran Prayer* (see n. 26 above), especially pp. 13, 20–22, 31, 75–80, 111–16, 170–71, 200, 225–26, 272, 317–18, 358 and 368; see also the review of Nitzan's volume by E. Glickler Chazon in *Dead Sea Discoveries* 2 (1995), pp. 361–65.

28 E. Schuller, *Non-Canonical Psalms from Qumran: A Pseudepigraphic Collection* (Atlanta, 1986); 'Some observations on blessings of God' in *Of Scribes and Scrolls: Studies on the Hebrew Bible, Intertestamental Judaism and Christian Origins presented to John Strugnell on the Occasion of his Sixtieth Birthday*, eds H. W. Attridge, J. J. Collins and T. H. Tobin (Lanham, New York and London, 1990), pp. 133–43; 'The Psalm of 4Q372 1 within the context of Second Temple prayer', *CBQ* 54 (1992), pp. 67–79; 'Prayer, hymnic and liturgical texts from Qumran' in *The Community of the Renewed Covenant*, eds E. Ulrich and J. VanderKam (Notre Dame, 1994), pp. 153–71; 'The Cave Four hodayot manuscripts: a preliminary description', *JQR* 85 (1994), pp. 137–50; 'The use of biblical terms as designations for non-biblical hymnic and prayer compositions' in *Biblical Perspectives: Early Use and Interpretation of the Bible in Light of the Dead Sea Scrolls*, eds M. Stone and E. G. Chazon (Leiden, Boston and Köln, 1998), pp. 207–22; and 'Prayer at Qumran' in *Prayer from Tobit to Qumran: Deuterocanonical and Cognate literature, Yearbook 2004*, eds R. Egger-Wenzel and J. Corley (Berlin and New York, 2004), pp. 411–28.

represent the religious activities of the 'common Judaism' of the Second
Temple period. Although more work has to be done on explaining such
phenomena as the occurrence of different prayers for the same
occasion, it can no longer be doubted (even if she and others had some
earlier hesitations) that communal prayer at fixed times predated the
rabbis of the Mishnah and that the content, language, form and
function of rabbinic prayer cannot justifiably be regarded as totally
innovative.[29] As Chazon herself clearly expresses it, 'although we
cannot know to what extent the texts of 4Q503 and Q408 were used by
the Qumran community or by its contemporaries, we can be reasonably
sure that daily prayers of this type were said by different Jewish groups
in the late Second Temple period and were considered important
enough to be incorporated into the liturgy that was institutionalized by
the rabbis in the aftermath of the destruction of the Second Temple in
70 CE.'[30]

In his contribution to the third volume of the *Cambridge History of
Judaism*, Daniel Falk has covered the topic of 'Prayer in the Qumran
Texts' and expressed some cautious views concerning its historical link
with rabbinic liturgy. He places the origins of Qumranic prayer texts in
a variety of provenances, including the Temple, the priesthood, the
levitical groups and the *ma'amadot* and describes how some are linked
to the calendar, some to special events, and some to penitential themes.
He accepts that there are parallels of subject and language with
rabbinic texts and identifies some particularly striking similarities
between the *Festival Prayers* and the later synagogal liturgy. He is,
however, convinced that we are dealing with independent
exploitations of the biblical models and not a direct link between
Qumran and the talmudic traditions.[31] He consequently rejects
Weinfeld's view that the major rabbinic prayers have their prototypes
among the Judean scrolls. He acknowledges that 'thematic resonances
with the later synagogue liturgy cane be heard frequently in the

---

29   E. G. Chazon, 'Prayers from Qumran and their historical implications', *Dead Sea
     Discoveries* 1 (1994), pp. 265–84; 'New liturgical manuscripts from Qumran',
     Proceedings of the Eleventh World Congress of Jewish Studies, Jerusalem, 1993, Division A
     (Jerusalem, 1994), pp. 207–14; (with M. J. Bernstein), 'An introduction to prayer at
     Qumran' in *Prayer from Alexander to Constantine: A Critical Anthology*, ed. M. Kiley *et
     al.* (London and New York, 1997), pp. 9–13; 'Hymns and prayers in the Dead Sea
     Scrolls' in *The Dead Sea Scrolls after Fifty Years: A Comprehensive Assessment*, eds P. W.
     Flint and J. C. VanderKam, vol. 1 (Leiden, Boston and Köln, 1998), pp. 244–70; 'The
     qedushah liturgy and its history in light of the Dead Sea Scrolls' in *From Qumran to
     Cairo: Studies in the History of Prayer*, ed. J. Tabory (Jerusalem, 1999), pp. 7–17.
30   Chazon, 'Hymns' (see n. 29 above), p. 257.
31   D. K. Falk, 'Prayer in the Qumran texts' in *The Cambridge History of Judaism*, vol. 3,
     The Early Roman Period, eds W. Horbury, W. D. Davies and J. Sturdy (Cambridge,
     1999), pp. 852–76.

Qumran prayers' but argues that it 'does not necessarily follow from this that we have incipient forms of the synagogue liturgy in the Dead Sea Scrolls.' His preferred conclusion is that 'the prayers found at Qumran belong to a broad stream of prayer tradition in which the rabbis also stood'.[32]

Being in the happy position of having more texts and interpretations now available to him, Falk has been able to devote a monograph to a close study of many daily, sabbath, and festival prayers in the Dead Sea scrolls.[33] He sets out to identify where lines of continuity may be established in the history of Jewish prayer and whether the traditions represented at Qumran are sectarian or of broader significance. The points made in his *CHJ* article are here discussed and exemplified at length and he stresses the importance of recognizing that prayer in the Dead Sea Scrolls is not a uniform phenomenon but has a variety of forms, functions and socio-liturgical settings that are perhaps being welded together at Qumran.

What is most important for him is that the Temple appears to have stood at the centre of many of these liturgical traditions which is why they appear in many, variant types of Jewish literature emanating from the axial age. 'In the Temple,' writes Falk, 'the prayers of the priests, the songs of the Temple singers, and the popular prayers of the people remained disparate, brought into proximity only by their somewhat loose connection with the Temple service.' Jewish, and indeed Christian, institutionalized prayer had its origins not directly in the Qumranic context but in the 'attraction of prayer to the Temple cult, rather than the need to provide a replacement for the sacrificial system'. The notion that Qumranic prayer had a variety of functions is further supported in a recent article in which it is cogently argued that prayer at Qumran was motivated by a desire 'to ensure righteousness, holiness and atonement for the community and for the rest of the land'.[34]

Conclusions

It remains only to offer a few brief conclusions for those students of rabbinic liturgy who are anxious to know what relevant lessons may be learned from recent Qumran studies for their own historical reconstructions:

---

32 Falk, 'Prayer' (see n. 31 above), p. 871.
33 D. K. Falk, *Daily, Sabbath and Festival Prayers in the Dead Sea Scrolls* (Leiden, Boston and Köln, 1998).
34 Falk, *Daily* (see n. 33 above), p. 254; R. C. D. Arnold, 'Qumran prayer as an act of righteousness', *JQR* 95 (2005), pp. 509–29.

1. There is, in the broad context of Second Temple Judaism, clear evidence for the existence, at least among some groups, of a practice to recite regular prayers at specific times but the relevant literature in its totality does not reveal any obvious consistency of text and context for these.

2. There are written texts from Qumran that record such prayers and they have elements in common with the rabbinic liturgy of the second Christian century. This by no means rules out the possibility that there were also oral liturgical traditions during that period, nor does it imply that early rabbinic prayer moved totally from orality to wholly fixed texts.

3. In various religious spheres, the Jews at Qumran and the rabbis sometimes express themselves uniquely while at others they follow well-established precedents. As far as liturgy is concerned, rabbinic prayer incorporates material broadly known from Qumran but imposes upon it a fresh order, style and distinctive formulation. This innovative aspect reflects the traditions of tannaitic Judaism and its own approach to the Hebrew language and to the Biblical canon. The later development of rabbinic prayer, in both oral and written forms, has its own range of dynamic characteristics and caution must be exercised in using post-talmudic and geonic texts for the reconstruction of earlier trends.

4. Given the breadth of the liturgical material found at Qumran, there was clearly more than one provenance for the development of hymns and prayers during the Second Temple period. Among the sources from which the early rabbis drew their liturgical inspiration (perhaps in some cases indirectly) were the Temple and its priesthood, contemporary circles of pietists and mystics, proto-synagogal gatherings such as the *ma'amadot*, and local custom.[35] If we are then to answer the question raised earlier in the context of the Finkelstein-Heinemann-Fleischer debate about the existence of standard liturgy,

---

35   See P. Schäfer, *Geniza-fragmente zur Hekhalot Literatur* (Tübingen, 1984); M. Bar-Ilan. *The Mysteries of Jewish Prayer and Hekhalot* (Hebrew; Ramat Gan, 1987); M. D. Swartz, *Mystical Prayer in Ancient Judaism: An Analysis of Ma'aseh Merkavah* (Tübingen, 1992); and Rachel Elior, 'From earthly temple to heavenly shrines: prayer and sacred liturgy in the Hekhalot literature and its relation to temple traditions', *Tarbiz* 64 (1995), pp. 341–80. Since the original penning of this essay, additional studies have appeared; see, for instance, J. R. Davila, *Liturgical Works* (Grand Rapids, Michigan and Cambridge, UK, 2000) and *Liturgical Perspectives: Prayer and Poetry in Light of the Dead Sea Scrolls*, eds E. G. Chazon, R. A. Clements and A. Pinnick (Leiden and Boston, 2003). They are of considerable value for the details they add to the whole picture but they do not appear to call into question the summaries and conclusions being offered here.

we may conclude that there was no standard set of liturgy widely employed by Jewry but, at the same time, there were undoubtedly texts that were used in certain Jewish circles as standard liturgy for specific occasions.

4

Prayer in Ben Sira, Qumran and Second Temple Judaism

Treatment to date

On first applying myself to the actual preparation (as distinct from the broad consideration) of the contents of this chapter, it occurred to me that the challenge was not a daunting one. The topic was such an obviously important one, with broad ramifications, that there would be no shortage of earlier studies that could easily serve as guides and precedents and my task would merely be to copy the overall picture that had previously been painted, with an additional flourish here and an occasional highlight there. I therefore confidently undertook the necessary bibliographical search for comprehensive and systematic presentations of the whole topic represented in my title and was soon faced with an interesting result. Not only was there no close study of the liturgical content of Ben Sira in the broader context of the Jewish worship of his day but neither was there any concise summary of how Ben Sira relates to matters of prayer, worship and liturgy throughout his book. Although this state of affairs meant that I was obliged to research, think and write for myself to a degree that I had not expected, it was at the same time personally encouraging since it justified my choice of topic and provided the opportunity of making at least some first moves towards the provision of what was undoubtedly a *desideratum*. While no scholarly predecessor had wholly covered the ground I had proposed to examine, there were undoubtedly studies that had addressed, or touched on, certain aspects of the topic and it was clear that my initial responsibility would therefore be to summarize some such work, to assess aspects of its character and to illustrate my remarks with a few examples.[1]

It should be stated at the outset that, given the limited space available here for this particular treatment, my approach in meeting this first obligation will have to be highly eclectic and the treatment will

---

1   I am grateful to Dr Jeremy Corley, of Ushaw College, Durham, and to Professor Renate Egger-Wenzel, of the Institut für Alt- und Neutestamentliche Wissenschaft at the University of Salzburg, for their kind initiative in inviting me to deliver a paper on this topic at the Durham conference of July, 2001, which led to the publication of the volume *Ben Sira's God*, ed. R. Egger-Wenzel (Berlin and New York, 2002).

need to be broadly thematic rather than tightly chronological, permitting me to give the flavour of some of what has been written without engaging in anything like a thorough bibliographical analysis. Given that Ben Sira's period is dominated by the Second Temple, it is not inappropriate to commence with a note to the effect that almost all the commentators on his book place stress on the Jerusalem cult and the author's devotion to this central element of Jewish life in the Judean state of his day. As will shortly become clear, not all of them succeed in doing so without betraying what are to my mind some specific and gratuitous elements of tendentiousness. For his part, Coggins, while stressing how highly Ben Sira regards the role of the priest both historically and contemporarily, justifiably and judiciously raises the issue, as so many others do, of whether he may even himself have been a priest, citing the main evidence for this contention but remaining unconvinced that it is persuasive.[2] More remarkably and questionably, Oesterley, having traced overall reverence, delight and zeal in Ben Sira's attitudes to Temple rituals and priestly functions, also somehow manages to detect in them a weakening of the commitment to the Jerusalem cult. Basing himself on verses that say no more than that sacrifice, to be efficacious, has to be sincere and pious, rather than mechanical and hypocritical, he argues, in a leap of scholarly as well as theological faith, that Ben Sira 'is, in effect, offering a plea for the abandonment of material sacrifice' and concludes that 'he never directly affirms the atoning effect of sacrifices.'[3] To his credit, Lange, in a weighty article, focuses more cautiously on alleged polemics regarding the cult and on the relative dates of Ecclesiastes and Ben Sira.[4]

For other scholars, it is Ben Sira's relationship with later rabbinic liturgy that is of the greatest relevance and importance. At the beginning of the twentieth century, Elbogen was anxiously searching for parallels between Ben Sira and the rabbinic 'amidah and listed various phrases that seemed to him to qualify, and a similar line was later pursued by Idelsohn.[5] For Gevaryahu, Ben Sira was to be seen as a

2   R. J. Coggins, *Sirach* (Sheffield, 1998), p. 49.

3   W. O. E. Oesterley, *The Wisdom of Jesus the Son of Sirach or Ecclesiasticus in the Revised Version with Introduction and Notes* (Cambridge, 1912), pp. lxxi–lxxii.

4   A. Lange, 'In Diskussion mit dem Tempel: zur Auseinandersetzung zwischen Kohelet und weisheitlichen Kreisen am jerusalemer Tempel' in *Qohelet in the Context of Wisdom*, ed. A. Schoors (Leuven, 1998), pp. 113–59.

5   I. Elbogen, *Der jüdische Gottesdienst in seiner geschichtlichen Entwicklung* (Frankfurt am Main, 1931; reprint, Hildesheim, 1962), pp. 29–31, 43, 48, 50, 53–54, 68, 73, 244 and 278; Hebrew edition התפילה בישראל בהתפתחותה ההיסטורית, eds J. Heinemann, I. Adler, A Negev, J. J. Petuchowski and H. Schirmann (Tel Aviv, 1972), pp. 22–23, 31, 34, 37, 39, 41–42, 54, 58, 185 and 208; English edition, *Jewish Liturgy: A Comprehensive History* (English translation and edition by Raymond P. Scheindlin; Philadelphia, Jerusalem

typical formulator of prayers in his day and this activity was to be linked with the presupposed existence of the synagogue. He also identified liturgical themes such as threats from the non-Jewish world, exile and redemption.[6] Rivkin, on the other hand, will have none of this supposition about the existence of the synagogue and uses Ben Sira to argue powerfully that there was no such institution in the middle of the Second Temple period.[7] In his introduction to the books of the Apocrypha, Brockington does cover the hymns and praises of Ben Sira fairly well but here too he most certainly has other theological fish to fry, indulging himself in a statement of his own spiritual preferences rather than a fair assessment of Ben Sira's religious values, or indeed those of his contemporary co-religionists. 'One might think', he writes, 'that such an attitude would have lifted Ben Sira above the level of nationalism and led him to think in terms of universalism as did some of the prophets before him. That was evidently far more than the ordinary Jew could reach.'[8]

A most useful treatment is provided by Johnson in a short but important monograph on apocryphal and pseudepigraphical prayer in which many of the relevant sources are listed throughout the study.[9] The book of Ben Sira does not, however, receive individual attention in that work but is cited only within the larger context, a policy I myself followed in an earlier volume on the history of Hebrew prayer.[10] Integral links between different aspects of religious expression is another topic that is found by some scholars in their examinations of liturgical developments in the period under discussion. Newman, for example, sees the role of exegesis in the penitential prayers of the Second Temple period and points out the literary models used in prayers, including some by Ben Sira.[11] She does not, however, pay any attention to the rabbinic liturgy or to the evidence from Qumran. In his

---

and New York, 1993), pp. 26–27, 35, 38, 43, 45, 47, 49, 62, 66, 194 and 217; A. Z. Idelsohn, *Jewish Liturgy and its Development* (New York, 1932), pp. 20–22 and 110.

6   H. Gevaryahu, 'Shimon Ben-Sira: the image of a Jerusalem scholar' in *David Gross Anniversary Volume*, ed. S. Kodesh (Hebrew; Jerusalem, 1983), pp. 256–74.

7   E. Rivkin, 'Ben Sira and the nonexistence of the synagogue: a study in historical method' in *In the Time of Harvest: Essays in Honor of Abba Hillel Silver on the Occasion of his 70th birthday*, ed. D. J. Silver (New York and London, 1963), pp. 320–54.

8   L. H. Brockington, *A Critical Introduction to the Apocrypha* (London, 1961), pp. 71–84, with the cited piece on p. 83.

9   N. B. Johnson, *Prayer in the Apocrypha and Pseudepigrapha: A Study in the Jewish Concept of God* (Philadelphia, 1948), pp. 7, 11, 16, 20, 25–26, 28–29, 36, 38, 40–43, 46, 48–50, 54–59, 61–62 and 66.

10 S. C. Reif, *Judaism and Hebrew Prayer: New Perspectives on Jewish Liturgical History* (Cambridge, 1993), pp. 45–46 and 346.

11 J. H. Newman, *Praying by the Book: The Scripturalization of Prayer in Second Temple Judaism* (Atlanta, 1999), pp. 73, 114, 133, 137, 153, 160–63, 177, 179, 182, 194, 213, and 238.

careful and useful review of recent research, Reiterer has little to cite in
the area of liturgy but does stress the connection between the different
theological areas as portrayed in the work of Jolley. As the latter
scholar puts it, 'Torah is to be used in study and worship as the guide
to how one should live... Torah and wisdom are inseparably linked
together in Sirach in a synergistic relationship.'[12] As will become
apparent as this chapter unfolds, I am greatly dependent here on
Segal's *Sefer Ben Sira Ha-Shalem* and on Skehan/Di Lella's *Wisdom of Ben
Sira* and it will therefore perhaps be appropriate to cite both these
works before I conclude this short summary of work done.[13] In his
introduction, Segal barely refers to prayer at all but does deal with
sacrifices. He points out that Ben Sira values these highly and honours
the priesthood but that, at the same time, he views both these
institutions within the total Jewish religious context.[14] Di Lella also
notes the centrality of cult and prayer for Ben Sira and their place in his
total religious outlook. He argues not just that social justice is part of
this outlook for Ben Sira but that it is 'more important and central',
perhaps going a little further in this connection than I, or some others,
might wish to do.[15]

Current approach

Given the summaries just offered of what has, or has not, been
accomplished to date, it should be clear that it would now be useful for
students of Ben Sira if such literature could be supplemented by the
provision of a critical overview of the total liturgical picture capable of
being drawn on the basis of the relevant Ben Sira texts. There are also
additional reasons why such an analysis would be timely. Until some
twenty years ago, the study of Jewish liturgical history had been
something of a 'Cinderella' in the broader field of Hebrew and Jewish
studies, a state of affairs that lead numerous scholars, myself included,

---

12   F. V. Reiterer, 'Review of recent research on the book of Ben Sira' in *The Book of Ben
     Sira in Modern Research*, ed. P. C. Beentjes (Berlin and New York, 1997), pp. 23–60,
     citing M. A. Jolley, The function of Torah in Sirach' (Southern Baptist Theological
     Seminary dissertation, 1993), on p. 50.

13   M. H. Segal, *Sefer Ben Sira Ha-Shalem* (2nd revised edition, Jerusalem, 1958); P. W.
     Skehan and A. A. di Lella, *The Wisdom of Ben Sira: A New Translation with Notes,
     Introduction and Commentary* (New York, 1987). The Hebrew and English texts used
     in this article have been cited from these two volumes respectively for purposes of
     comment. I am grateful to the publishers, Bialik Institute in Jerusalem and
     Doubleday/Random House in New York for kindly permitting this use. The
     alternative verse citations are those given in Arabic rather than in Hebrew numerals
     in Segal's volume.

14   Segal, *Ben Sira Ha-Shalem* (see n. 13 above), introduction, pp. 33–34.

15   Skehan/Di Lella, *Ben Sira* (see n. 13 above), introduction, pp. 87–88.

to call, at about that time, for the subject to receive the attention it truly deserved.[16] Whether as a result of such a call, or for other reasons, just such a development has taken place and a much larger number of books and articles, containing more extensive and more varied treatments of the field, have made their appearance and stimulated considerably more debate.[17] Among the periods that have received particular attention have been the Second Temple period and the early Christian centuries and the time has now surely come to set Ben Sira in such context. Furthermore, the new availability of many Qumran texts has provided insights into areas previously known only to a limited degree and liturgy has been a particular beneficiary of the publication, translation and study of such texts. As has already been noted in an earlier chapter, a number of recently published volumes have greatly illuminated the liturgical activities recorded at Qumran.[18] This has meant that instead of guessing at the nature of Jewish prayer and worship during and immediately after the Second Temple period, we now have some definite and relevant data on which to base our speculations. What I therefore propose to do in the next part of this chapter is to summarize the central liturgical content and ideology of Ben Sira by way of some major textual examples, before moving on to the consideration of other elements to be found in remaining texts, and a comparison of these findings with the broader liturgical situation.

Major texts

1. Simeon the High Priest and Public Worship (50:23–36 or 50:16–24)

Hebrew text

23. ויריעו וישמיעו קול אדיר	להזכיר לפני עליון:
24. כל בשר יחדיו נמהרו	ויפלו על פניהם ארצה:
25. להשתחות לפני עליון	לפני קדוש ישראל:
26. ויתן השיר קולו	ועל המון העריכו נרו:
27. וירנו כל עם הארץ	בתפלה לפני רחום:
28. עד כלותו לשרת מזבח	ומשפטיו הגיע אליו:
29. אז ירד ונשא ידיו	על כל קהל ישראל:

---

16 My own contribution to this appeal was an article entitled 'Jewish liturgical research: past, present and future', *JJS* 34 (1983), pp. 161–70.

17 For excellent bibliographical guidance to these, see J. Tabory, *Jewish Prayer and the Yearly Cycle: A List of Articles*, supplement to *Kiryat Sefer* 64 (Jerusalem, 1992–93); a substantial collection of addenda to that publication that appeared together with his facsimile edition of the Hanau prayer-book of 1628, eds J. Tabory and M. Rapeld (Ramat Gan, 1994); and 'A list of articles about synagogues' in *Kenishta: Studies of the Synagogue World*, ed. J. Tabory (Ramat Gan, 2001), pp. 63–147.

18 See chapter 3 above, 'Qumran specialists'.

.30 וברכת יייי בשפתיו	ובשם יייי יתפאר:
.31 וישנו לנפול שנית	ל..... מפניו:
.32 עתה ברכו נא את יייי אלהי ישראל	המפליא לעשות בארץ:
.33 המגדל אדם מרחם	ויעשהו כרצונו:
.34 יתן לכם חכמת לבב	ויהי בשלום ביניכם:
.35 יאמן עם שמעון חסדו	ויקם לו ברית פינחס:
.36 אשר לא יכרת לו ולזרעו	כימי שמים:

English text

16. The sons of Aaron would sound a blast, the priests on their trumpets of beaten metal;
    A blast to resound mightily as a reminder before the Most High.
17. Then all the people with one accord would quickly fall prostrate to the ground
    In adoration before the Most High, before the Holy one of Israel.
18. Then hymns would reecho, and over the throng sweet strains of praise resound.
19. All the people of the land would shout for joy, praying to the Merciful One,
    As the high priest completed the service at the altar by presenting to God the sacrifice due;
20. Then coming down he would raise his hands over all the congregation of Israel;
    The blessing of the Lord would be upon his lips, the name of the Lord would be his glory.
21. Then again the people would lie prostrate, receiving the blessing from the Most High.
22. And now, bless the God of all, who has done stupendous things on earth;
    Who makes humans grow from their mother's womb, and does with them according to his will!
23. May he grant you wisdom of heart, and may he abide among you as peace;
24. May his kindness towards Simeon be lasting; may he fulfil for him the covenant with Phinehas
    So that it may not be abrogated for him or for his descendants, while the heavens last.
23. May he grant us joy of heart and may there be peace in our days in Israel, as in the days of old.
24. May his kindness remain constantly with us and may he save us in our days!

Summary

After the wine libation has been offered, the priests ceremonially sound the trumpets and all the people[19] involve themselves in the act of divine worship by prostrating themselves before God. Prayer and song (led by

---

19   Given the parallel with v. 24, the Hebrew עם הארץ (v. 27) does not here convey the sense of a privileged group, as it does in the Hebrew Bible (e.g. Genesis 23:7 and 2 Kings 11:14), but is more akin to its later rabbinic meaning of 'the general public'.

the levites?) accompany the latter part of the cultic ritual and when the high priest has concluded his ministrations at the altar he blesses the people, apparently still at that stage with the literal use of the tetragrammaton,[20] and they then once more prostrate themselves.[21] Ben Sira invites the priests (or, less likely, the people?) to praise God for the wonders of creation and prays for wisdom (or, according to the Greek, for joy and kindness) and peace for them, as well as for an eternal priesthood, to which he shows himself, throughout the passage, closely attached.[22]

2. Parents, Cult, Priesthood, Tithes and Charity (7:28–38 or 7:27–36)

Hebrew text

ואם תחוללך אל תשכח:	28. [בכל לבך כבד אביך
ומה תגמל להם כגמולם לך:]	29. זכר כי מהם היית
ואת כהניו הקדיש:	30. בכל לבך פחד אל
ואת משרתיו לא תעזב:	31. בכל מאודך אהב עושך
ות[ן חל]קם כאשר צוותה:	32. כבד אל והדר כהן
זבחי] צדק ותרומת קדש:	33. לחם אברים ותרומת [יד
למען תשלם ברכתך:	34. וגם לאביון [הושי]ט יד
וגם ממת אל תמנע חסד:	35. תן מתן לפני כל חי
ועם אבלים התאבל:	36. אל תתאחר מבוכים
כי ממנו תאהב:	37. אל תשא לב מאוהב
ולעולם לא תשחת:	38. בכל מעשיך זכור אחרית

English text

27. With your whole heart honor your father; your mother's birth pangs forget not.
28. Remember, of these parents you were born; what can you give them for all they gave you?
29. With all your soul fear God, revere his priests.
30. With all your strength love your Maker, neglect not his ministers.
31. Honor God and respect the priest; give him his portion as you have been commanded:
    The flesh of sacrifices, contributions, his portion of victims, a levy on holy offerings.
32. To the poor also extend your hand, that your blessing may be complete;
33. Give your gift to anyone alive, and withhold not your kindness from the dead;
34. Avoid not those who weep, but mourn with those who mourn;

---

20 Contrast PT, *Yoma* 3.7 (40d), where a change in practice is presupposed.
21 For variations in the order and content of the ritual, compare 2 Chronicles 29:27–29 and Mishnah, *Tamid* 6.3–7.3.
22 See also, e.g., 45:9–40 or 6–22 and 50:6–31 or 5–21. For a broader exegetical study of Simon the High Priest and chapter 50, see O. Mulder, *Simon the High Priest in Sirach 50. An Exegetical Study of the Significance of Simon the High Priest as Climax to the Praise of the Fathers in Ben Sira's Concept of the History of Israel* (Leiden and Boston, 2003).

35. Neglect not to care for the sick – for these things you will be loved.
36. In whatever you do, remember your last days, and you will never sin.

Summary

Respect for God and one's parents is set alongside honour for the priest and meeting one's obligations to him in the matters of tithes and his share of the sacrifices.[23] This is immediately followed by instructions to assist the poor, the unfortunate and those in mourning,[24] all of this in order to ensure that one's life is blessed and one is loved.[25] The reference to the מת (v. 35) may be to the dying,[26] or to the dead, who need burial,[27] or to the leper,[28] but amounts in all cases to an act of kindness.

3. Correct Nature and Wider Context of Worship (7:8–15)

Hebrew text

8. אל תקשור לשנות חטא	כי באחת לא תנקה:
9. [אל תאמר לרב מנחתי יביט	ובהקריבי לאל עליון יקח:]
10. אל תאיץ בצבא מלאכת עבודה	הי כאל נחלקה:
11. אל תקצר בתפלה	ובצדקה אל תתעבר:
12. אל תבז לאנוש במר רוח	זכר כי יש מרים ומשפיל:
13. אל תחרוש חמס על אח	וכן על רע וחבר יחדו:
14. אל תחפץ לכחש על כחש	כי תקותו לא תנעם:
15. אל תסוד בעדת שרים	ואל תישן דבר בתפלה:

English text

8. Do not plot to repeat a sin; not even for one will you go unpunished.
9. Say not, 'He will appreciate my many gifts; the Most High will accept my offerings.'
10. Be not brusque in your prayers; neither put off doing a kindness.
11. Laugh not at an embittered person; there is One who exalts and humbles.

---

23 Whether one points אֲבָרִים or אֵבָרִים (under the influence of Psalms 78:25), the reference is still to some aspect of what is due to the priests; see also Ben Sira 45:9–50 or 6–26. The pointing אֲבָרִים is in itself controversial; see S. C. Reif, *Shabbethai Sofer and his Prayer-book* (Cambridge, 1979), pp. 149 and 259–60. On the matter of respecting parents, see also Ben Sira 3:1–15 or 16. M. Kister has important comments on this passage, particularly as it relates to Deuteronomy 6:5, in his article 'Some notes of biblical expressions and allusions and the lexicography of Ben Sira' in *Sirach, Scrolls and Sages*, eds T. Muraoka and J. F. Elwolde (Leiden, Boston and Köln, 1999), pp. 183–86.
24 The concern with playing a part in mourning practices is also reflected in other texts; see n. 45 below.
25 For another passage in which the major Torah precepts are holistically regarded as worship, see Ben Sira 34:19–36:17 or 34(31):21–36(33):22.
26 As in 2 Kings 20:1: כי מת אתה ולא תחיה.
27 As in Genesis 47:29: ועשית עמדי חסד ואמת אל נא תקברני במצרים.
28 As in BT, *Nedarim* 64b on Numbers 12:12: מצורע דומה למת.

12. Contrive no mischief against your brother, nor against your friend and companion.
13. Take no pleasure in telling lie after lie; it never results in good.
14. Do not hold forth in the assembly of the elders, nor repeat yourself when you pray.
15. Hate not laborious work; work was assigned by God.

Summary

Persistent sinners are advised that offerings in the Temple may not bring forgiveness of sin. People are instructed not to show contempt for their less fortunate fellows or to plan violence or deceit against them. Nor should they chatter indiscreetly[29] in important company. Within the context of these ethical prescriptions, there are also warnings about giving the appropriate attention to prayer[30] and charity and, possibly also (if the phrase מלאכת עבודה (v. 10) is so explained), to manual labour.

4. David's Role in Composing Hymns and Music at Specific Times (47:11–17 or 47:8–11)

Hebrew text

לאל עליון [בדבר כ]בוד:	11. בכל מעשהו נתן הודות
ובכל [יום הללו תמי]ד:	12. בכל לבו אוהב עושהו
ו[ק]ו[ל] [מזמור בנבל]ים תיקן:	13. נגינות שיר ל[פני מזבח
ויתקן מועדים שנה בש]נה:	14. [נתן] ל[חגים הדר
לפני בק[ר] ירון משפט:	15. בה[ללו] את שם קדשו
וירם לעולם קרנו:	16. [גם] ייי העביר פשעו
וכסאו הכין על ירושלם	17. [וי]תן ל[ו] חק ממלכת

English text

8.   With his every deed he offered thanks; of God Most High he proclaimed the glory.
    With his whole heart he loved his Maker
9c.   and daily had his praises sung;
10a.   He added beauty to the feasts
10b.   and solemnised the seasons of each year
9a.   With string instruments before the altar,

---

29   Deriving the verb in 15a/14a from the root סוד in the sense of 'conversing intimately', as in Ben Sira 9:21, Jeremiah 23:18–22 and Job 15:8.
30   It is possible that 15b/14b alludes to the gratuitous repetition of prayer which Ben Sira is condemning as much as its exaggerated abbreviation but there is no indication that fixed formulae are here presupposed. Kister may be right in seeking a sense that is a better parallel to the first half of the verse and opting for a meaning of שנה דבר similar to Proverbs 17:9 and pointing תְּפִלָּה and not תְּפִלָּה; see M. Kister, 'Genizah manuscripts of Ben Sira' in *The Cambridge Genizah Collections: Their Contents and Significance*, ed. S. C. Reif (Cambridge, 2002), pp. 40–41. For a thorough treatment of the cultic content of Ben Sira 7, see F. V. Reiterer, 'Gott und Opfer' in *Ben Sira's God* (see n. 1 above), pp. 136–79 and 371–74.

9b.   providing sweet melody for the psalms
10c.   So that when the Holy Name was praised,
10d.   before daybreak the sanctuary would respond.
11.   The Lord forgave him his sins and exalted his strength forever. He conferred on him the rights of royalty and established his throne in Israel.

Summary

David loved and praised God and composed songs and music for special occasions. He composed hymns for recitation in the sanctuary, expressing himself liturgically every morning.[31] Because of this, his sin was forgiven, he was granted success, and his dynasty was permanently established in Jerusalem.[32]

5. The Scribe has Liturgical as well as Intellectual Duties
(39:7–12 or 39:5–8)

Hebrew text

ולפני עליון יתחנן:	.7 לב ישית לשחר עושהו
ועל עונותיו יעתיר:	.8 ויפתח פיו בתפלה
רוח בינה ימלא:	.9 אם אל עליון ירצה
ויודה ליי בתפלה:	.10 הוא יביע דברי חכמה
ובמסתריו יתבונן:	.11 הוא יכין עצה ודעת
ובתורת יי יתפאר:	.12 הוא יביע מוסר ושכל

English text

5.   His care is to rise early to seek the Lord, his Maker, to petition the Most High,
     To open his lips in prayer, to ask pardon for his sins.
6.   Then if it pleases the Lord Almighty, he will be filled with the spirit of understanding;
     He will pour forth his words of wisdom and in prayer give praise to the Lord.
7.   He will direct his counsel and knowledge aright, as he meditates upon God's mysteries.
8.   He will show the wisdom of what he has learned and glory in the Law of the Lord's covenant.

---

31   The Hebrew text has משפט, with the possible meaning of 'custom' or 'form', while a gloss, and the Greek, read מקדש. David is to such an extent idealized as the most outstanding example of one who conducts the praise of God that his role here is clearly identified (or confused?) with that of the high priest.
32   Less central attention is given to Jerusalem in the Greek and Syriac, which refer more generally to Israel.

Summary

The scribe is expected to develop intellectually, to understand God's mysteries, and to express himself intelligently and ethically. He should at the same time, however, appreciate that all this is intended as a religious exercise. He should also therefore humbly and enthusiastically seek and praise God,[33] pray for the forgiveness of his sins, and take pride in mastering (and teaching?) the Torah.

6. Prayer and Fasting Require Repentance (34:26–28 or 34:30–31)

Hebrew text

מה יועיל ברחיצתו:	26. טובל ממת ושב ונוגע בו
ושב והולך ועושה אלה:	27. כן אדם צם על חטאיו
ומה יועיל בתעניתו:	28. תפלתו מי ישמע

English text

30. If a person again touches a corpse after he has bathed, what did he gain by the purification?

31. So with a person who fasts for his sins, but then goes and commits them again:
    Who will hear his prayer, and what has he gained by his mortification?

Summary

Just as there is no point in undergoing purification through ritual immersion and then immediately attracting impurity, so fasting and praying for forgiveness[34] cannot be efficacious if one sets about sinning again. The subsequent three verses parallel ethical behaviour and the offering of sacrifices and appear to equate their religious value.

7. Successful Prayer at Sennacherib's Invasion (48:26–29 or 48:19–21)

Hebrew text

ויחילו כיולדה:	26. [אז נ]מוגו בגאון לבם
ויפרשו אליו כפים:	27. [ויקראו] אל אל עליון
ויושיעם ביד ישעיהו:	28. [וישמע] בקול תפלתם
ויהמם במגפה:	29. [ויך במ]חנה אשור

---

33 *Pace* Segal, *Ben Sira Ha-Shalem* (see n. 13 above), p. 259 and Di Lella, *Ben Sira* (see n. 13 above), p. 452, there is no clear indication in this text that the reference is necessarily to the composition of formal prayers (such as are found in the later rabbinic tradition, according to Segal); the author may just as well have spontaneous prayer in mind.

34 Note the close association here of the acts of fasting and praying and their joint contribution to the forgiveness of sin; see also Ben Sira 18:18–22 or 14–23.

English text

19. The people's hearts melted within them; they were in anguish like that of childbirth.
20. But they called upon the Most High God and lifted up their hands to him; He heard the prayer they uttered and saved them through Isaiah.
21. God struck the camp of the Assyrians and routed them with a plague.

Summary

When they were terrified by Sennacherib's hosts, not only Hezekiah but 'they' (Isaiah? all the people?) prayed to God and raised their hands in worship. God heard their prayer and rescued them, through Isaiah, by striking the Assyrians with a plague that sent them on their way in confusion.[35]

8. Prayer for the Rescue of God's People Israel (36:1–17 or 36:1–22)

Hebrew text

.1	הושיענו אלהי הכל · ו[שים] פחדך על כל הגוים:
.2	הניף על עם נכר · ויראו את גבורותיך:
.3	כאשר נקדשת לעיניהם בנו · כן לעינינו הכבד בנו:
.4	וידעו כאשר ידענו · כי אין אלהים זולתך:
.5	חדש אות ושנה מופת · האדר יד ואמץ זרוע וימין:
.6	העיר אף ושפוך חמה · והכניע [צר] והדוף אויב:
.7	החיש קץ ופקוד מועד · כי מי יאמר לך מה תעשה:
.8	[באף אש יאכל שריד · ומרעי עמך ימצאו שחת:]
.9	השבת ראש פאתי מואב · האומר אין זולתי:
.10	אסוף כל שבטי יעקב · ויתנחלו כימי קדם:
.11	רחם על עם נקרא בשמך · ישראל בכור כניתה:
.12	רחם על קרית קדשך · ירושלים מכון שבתיך:
.13	מלא ציון את הודך · ומכבודך את היכלך:
.14	תן עדות למראש מעשיך · והקם חזון דבר בשמך:
.15	תן את פעלת קווך · ונביאיך יאמינו:
.16	תשמע את תפלת עבדיך · כרצונך על עמך:
.17	וידעו כל אפסי ארץ · כי אתה אל עולם:

English text

1. Come to our aid, God of the universe,
2. And put all the nations in dread of you!
3. Raise your hand against the foreign folk, that they might see your mighty deeds.
4. As you have used us to show them your holiness, so now use them to show us your glory.
5. Thus they will know, as we know, that there is no God but you.
6. Give new signs and work new wonders;

---

35 The textual variants presupposed in the texts before the Greek and the Syriac translators modify the description of the prayer and the response to it but without significant alteration of the liturgical significance of the passage.

7. Show forth the splendor of your right arm;
8. Rouse your anger, pour out wrath,
9. Humble the enemy, scatter the foe.
10. Hasten the ending, appoint the time when your mighty deeds are to be proclaimed:
11. Let raging fire consume the fugitive, and your people's oppressors meet destruction;
12. Smash the heads of the hostile rulers, who say, 'There is no one besides me!'
13. Gather all the tribes of Jacob,
16. That they may inherit the land as in days of old.
17. Show mercy to the people called by your name: Israel whom you named your firstborn.
18. Take pity on your holy city, Jerusalem, the foundation for your throne.
19. Fill Zion with your majesty, your temple with your glory.
20. Give evidence of your deeds of old; fulfil the prophecies spoken in your name,
21. Reward those who have hoped in you, and let your prophets be proved true.
22. Hear the prayers of your servants, for you are ever gracious to your people; Thus it will be known to all the ends of the earth that you are the eternal God.

Summary

Ben Sira prays for God to demonstrate his power and reputation in a miraculous way, as he did in the past, and to save his people Israel by swiftly destroying their most arrogant enemies. In this way, the other peoples of the world will recognize his uniqueness. With his special affection, God should ingather the exiles of his people, Israel, and show his glory in Zion and Jerusalem. By answering such prayers, God will testify to the reliability of the prophetic message and the world will recognize his universal divinity.[36]

---

36 Of particular significance for Jewish liturgical history is the occurrence here of theological themes, as well as elements of phraseology and vocabulary, that are broadly reminiscent of later rabbinic liturgy. This is especially true of vv. 1–4, 7, 10–13 and 16–17 and Segal, *Ben Sira Ha-Shalem* (see n. 13 above), pp. 226–29 notes the similarities, perhaps without drawing sufficient attention to the fact that there are also important variations of detail; see also Kister, 'Some notes' (see n. 23 above), pp. 164–66. The Greek refers to 'Aaron's blessing' at the end of the passage but there is insufficient reliability about the authenticity of this text as a reflection of the original to permit any liturgical conclusions. For further historical and literary comment on this chapter, see M. Gilbert, 'Prayer in the book of Ben Sira: function and relevance' in *Prayer from Tobit to Qumran: Deuterocanonical and Cognate literature, Yearbook 2004*, eds R. Egger-Wenzel and J. Corley (Berlin and New York, 2004), pp. 118–22.

9. Hallel in the style of Psalms 136 from the time of the Zadokite high priesthood (51:21–35 or 51:12 .i–xvi)

Hebrew text

כי לעולם חסדו:	הודו לייי כי טוב .21
כי לעולם חסדו:	הודו לאל התשבחות .22
כי לעולם חסדו:	הודו לשומר ישראל .23
כי לעולם חסדו:	הודו ליוצר הכל .24
כי לעולם חסדו:	[הוד]ו לגואל ישראל .25
כי לעולם חסדו:	[הו]דו למקבץ נדחי ישראל .26
כי לעולם חסדו:	הודו לבונה עירו ומקדשו .27
כי לעולם חסדו:	הודו למצמיח קרן לבית דוד .28
כי לעולם חסדו:	הודו לבוחר בבני צדוק לכהן .29
כי לעולם חסדו:	הודו למגן אברהם .30
כי לעולם חסדו:	הודו לצור יצחק .31
כי לעולם חסדו:	הודו לאביר יעקב .32
כי לעולם חסדו:	הודו לבוחר בציון .33
כי לעולם חסדו:	הודו למלך מלכי מלכים .34
תהלה לכל חסידיו	וירם קרן לעמו .35
הללויה:	לבני ישראל עם קרובו

English text

i. Give thanks to the Lord for he is good, for his mercy endures forever;
    Give thanks to the God of [our] praises, for his mercy endures forever;
    Give thanks to the Guardian of Israel, for his mercy endures forever;
    Give thanks to him who formed all things, for his mercy endures forever;

v. Give thanks to the Redeemer of Israel, for his mercy endures forever;
    Give thanks to him who has gathered Israel's dispersed, for his mercy endures forever;
    Give thanks to him who rebuilt his city and his sanctuary, for his mercy endures forever;
    Give thanks to him who makes a horn to sprout for the house of David, for his mercy endures forever;
    Give thanks to him who has chosen the sons of Zadok as his priests, for his mercy endures forever;

x. Give thanks to the Shield of Abraham, for his mercy endures forever;
    Give thanks to the Rock of Isaac, for his mercy endures forever;
    Give thanks to the Mighty One of Jacob, for his mercy endures forever;
    Give thanks to him who has chosen Zion, for his mercy endures forever;
    Give thanks to the King of the kings of kings, for his mercy endures forever;

xv. He has raised up a horn for his people, be this his praise from all his dutiful ones,
    For the children of Israel, the people close to him, Praise the Lord!

Summary

According to the recent research of O. Mulder, this hymn of praise is an authentic part of the original Hebrew composition, omitted by the author's grandson for social and political reasons. But, even if, as many scholars have suggested, this hymn of praise may not have been composed by Ben Sira himself, it must still date to a period no later than

152 BCE since it mentions the Zadokite dynasty of priests that came to an end at that date. It is not the verses borrowed from the book of Psalms, and the similarity to Psalm 136, that are particularly noteworthy in this context,[37] but the liturgical phraseology. With the exception of the reference to the Zadokites, all the expressions have precise parallels or at least equivalents in the rabbinic liturgy, especially the 'amidah.[38]

10. Praise God for his Bounty (32:17–18 or 32:11–13)

Hebrew text

17. פטר לביתך ושלם רצון   ביראת אל ולא בחסר כל:
18. ועל כל אלה ברך עושך   המרוך מטובתו:

English text
11. When it is time to leave, tarry not; be off for home without delay,
12. And there enjoy doing as you wish, but without sin or words of pride.
13. Above all, give praise to your Maker, who showers his favors upon you.

Summary
Ben Sira advises his readers to maintain the appropriate courtesies when paying visits. He appears to counsel the recitation of a blessing acknowledging God's bounty and the wording has minor similarities to the rabbinic grace after meals.[39]

11. Blessing God on Seeing a Rainbow (43:13 or 43:11)

Hebrew text

13. ראה קשת וברך עושיה,   כי מאד נאדרה [בכב]וד:

English text
11. Behold the rainbow! Then bless its Maker, for majestic indeed is its splendor.

---

37   These are discussed at length by Di Lella, *Ben Sira* (see n. 13 above), pp. 569–71. Mulder's treatment is included in his article 'Three Psalms or two prayers in Sirach 51' in *Prayer from Tobit to Qumran* (see n. 36 above), pp. 182–87.

38   See Segal, *Ben Sira Ha-Shalem* (see n. 13 above), pp. 356–57 and Di Lella, *Ben Sira* (see n. 13 above) p. 571. Segal argues that this psalm was composed by Ben Sira himself, used for public worship in his day, and then omitted from the text when no longer liturgically relevant. To be more cautious, the evidence permits us to say no more than that the psalm had a liturgical function in the middle of the second pre-Christian century.

39   It seems fairly clear from the text that the author has in mind the recitation of a blessing thanking God for the food one has just eaten but there is no indication here that the reference is necessarily to a formal, authoritative or communal benediction.

Summary

The manifestation of God's power in the natural world is the theme of 42:21–43:38 (or 42:15–43:33) and the specific reference to the glories of the rainbow includes an exhortation to praise God for having created it.[40]

Other texts

Other, generally shorter, texts deal with more specific items in the liturgical field. Ben Sira takes the idea of the hymn further than its prototype in Psalms which is probably why some have sought to identify Greek elements, such as the *encomium* in its structure.[41] He treats the genre more consistently and systematically and devotes specific sections to the praise of God, creation, wisdom, and the historical heroes of the Jewish people.[42] In addition to such hymns, there are also prayers to God that request encouragement, that are of the supplicatory variety, and that make specific appeals.[43] Among such appeals are requests for strength in avoiding sin in general and slanderous talk in particular.[44] Mourning customs are presupposed but caution is advised with regard to their possible exaggeration[45] and there is no indication of formal or standardized prayer-texts for such *rites de passage*. In order to improve the degree of efficacy of one's prayers, one should genuinely repent and make efforts to be wholly sincere, as well as forgiving others and avoiding anger.[46] The clear impression is given that the wise and the poor have better prospects in this connection.[47] Links are regularly made between prayer and other religious duties such as Torah, cult and respect for others.[48] It is also suggested that good health is dependent on prayer as well as on doctors.[49] In the context of relating the activities of Jewish historical heroes, it is

---

40   Rabbinic custom includes blessings in appreciation of natural phenomena and this practice is clearly adumbrated here; but the caution expressed in the previous footnote is again relevant.

41   See, e.g., T. R. Lee, *Studies in the Form of Sirach 40–50* (Atlanta, 1986).

42   Ben Sira 39:20–47 or 15–35 and 16:28–18:13 or 16:24–18:14; 42:21–43:13 or 42:15–43:11; 24:1–30 or 1–29 and 14:23–15:10 or 14:20–15:10; 44:1–45:50 or 45:26.

43   Ben Sira 37:21 or 15; 17:19–27 or 24–32; see also text 6 above.

44   Ben Sira 22:32–23:35 or 22:27–23:21. See Gilbert, 'Prayer in the book of Ben Sira' (see n. 36 above), pp. 117–18.

45   Ben Sira 7:36 or 34 (in text 2 above); 22:6–11or 6–12; 38:16–25 or 16–23.

46   Ben Sira 17:24 or 29; 21:1–4 or 1–3; 28:2–5; see text 6 above.

47   Ben Sira 15:9–10; 21:6 or 21:5; see text 5 above. See Gilbert, 'Prayer in the book of Ben Sira' (see n. 36 above), pp. 126–28.

48   Ben Sira 3:1–15 or 1–16; 45:5–8 or 4–5; see also texts 2–3 above.

49   Ben Sira 38:9–15.

regularly noted that they prayed when circumstances demanded and the expression that occurs and recurs is קרא אל אל עליון.[50]

Summary of liturgical content

Ben Sira had a high opinion of the Temple and the priesthood and a strong conviction about their central role in Jewish religious practice. He incorporates many of the liturgical elements recorded in the Hebrew Bible but with the addition of a greater public involvement in and around the Temple Mount and perhaps of a development of the musical aspect of liturgy. He prefers a holistic approach to Jewish liturgy that makes a close association between Torah, ritual, social precepts, wisdom, prayer and charity, all of them by necessity requiring high degrees of conviction and sincerity. He makes extensive use of the hymn of praise as a way of expressing his commitment to the central elements of the Jewish religious tradition and also appears to employ the benediction to acknowledge welcome developments. He formulates personal supplications and appeals to God with a common use of language and vocabulary that mimics and borrows those of the Hebrew Bible but undoubtedly goes beyond it. He provides no evidence of any fixed set of texts that represents formal prayer regularly recited on particular occasions, that is to say, he does not testify to a fixed liturgy outside the Temple.

Evidence from Qumran

What emerged from the analysis offered in the previous chapter now requires to be summarized briefly in this context in order to make it clear how it relates to Ben Sira and to the rabbis. I shall offer only the conclusions, without annotation, and leave the reader to seek the sources in the footnotes of that chapter.

There is now a wealth of evidence to indicate that many of the hymns and prayers found there represent the religious activities of the 'common Judaism' of the Second Temple period. Although more work has to be done on explaining such phenomena as the occurrence of different prayers for the same occasion, it can no longer be doubted that communal prayer at fixed times predated tannaitic Judaism and that the content, language, form and function of rabbinic prayer cannot justifiably be regarded as totally innovative. The *hodayot* reflect the

---

50 Ben Sira 46:7 or 5; 47:6 or 5; 48:27 or 20 (in text 7 above); see also similar expressions in 50:23–25 or 16–17 (in text 1 above), 7:9 (in text 3 above), 47:11 or 8 (in text 4 above), 39:7–9 or 5–6 (in text 5 above), and 46:27 or 16.

experiences and teachings of the qumranic sect and they exist in a variety of collections. Words and expressions in the non-canonical psalms have their equivalents in other Hebrew texts of the late Second Temple and early post-destruction periods and there are elements of Aramaic influence. The close relationship with aspects of the rabbinic liturgical evidence is also noteworthy. We encounter familiar, national notions such as the divine love of Israel, the choice of Jerusalem, the special status of Zion, and the uniqueness of the davidic kingdom. There are also broader theological themes that the two groups have in common such as God's great name, creation and calendar, the closeness of the supplicant to God, and the removal of satanic and evil power. There are many individual words, in both verbal and nominal forms, and numerous short phrases, that the literatures of Qumran and the Rabbis share. There are also parallel uses of verses and of sections of the psalms. Other specific features of the Judean scrolls are that they supplement biblical content with apocalyptic material and reformulate apocalyptic myths in the biblical style, as well as expressing the sanctity of the sabbath by the use of ritual poetry.[51]

Conclusions

It should by now have become apparent that the Qumran approach and that of the Rabbis have a little more in common with each other than either or both of them have with Ben Sira. They both presuppose a practice to recite regular prayers at specific times while there is no mention of such a custom in Ben Sira. Sabbaths and festivals feature strongly in both of them and there are poetic formulations for special occasions while these characteristics do not appear in Ben Sira. Apocalyptic elements, angelology and eschatology appear to play a more significant role at Qumran and with the Rabbis than in Ben Sira's composition. On the other hand, Ben Sira's holistic liturgical approach is more reminiscent of that of the rabbis than that of Qumran and his devotion to the Temple cult is followed at least in theory by rabbinic Judaism. Similarly, Ben Sira links Torah and wisdom with prayer in a manner that calls to mind the later views of the Rabbis. All three sources have in common the use of hymns of praise, supplicatory prayers and benedictions, as well as the occurrence of words and phrases that are in essence biblical but subsequently take on special forms and meanings. They also share as central themes in their entreaties the notions of the election of Israel, the status of Zion, the holiness of Jerusalem, the return of the davidic dynasty, and the

---

51   See nn. 15, 25–34 of chapter 3 above.

manifestation of God's great power now and in the future. What therefore seems likely is that the Rabbis ultimately borrowed extensively from the kinds of circles which produced Ben Sira and the Dead Sea Scrolls, and from some others, but, in the matter of detailed liturgical expression, they championed a fresh order, style and distinctive formulation. Ben Sira undoubtedly takes the matter of worship beyond that of most of the Hebrew Bible but does not reflect the same liturgical intensity as that found at Qumran. He thus sets the tone for some rabbinic developments but is apparently not the source for various others.[52]

---

52 I prepared this chapter for its original publication during a period as a Fellow of the Center for Advanced Judaic Studies at the University of Pennsylvania in Philadelphia, September–December 2001. I am most grateful to the Center, its Director Professor David Ruderman, and his dedicated staff, for their kind invitation and their generous assistance.

5

Use of the Bible

Introduction

The Hebrew Bible has, from Israel's earliest period until modern times, always provided a powerful inspiration for Jewish religious thought and practice. At the same time, for most of Judaism's history, one of the Jewish people's central means of liturgical expression has undoubtedly been the traditional rabbinic prayer-book or *siddur*, or its earlier oral equivalent. The relationship between these two pieces of literature therefore deserves close consideration in any set of essays that is attempting to explain aspects of the historical and religious background to Jewish liturgical development. In this context the *siddur* will be understood in its broadest chronological and geographical sense, and not exclusively as it was constructed by one particular community at any specific date.

The prayers being described and assessed here for their biblical content and connection are those recited in the morning, afternoon and evening on a daily basis. They consist primarily of the *shema'* (morning and evening), with its introductory and concluding benedictions;[1] the *'amidah* ('standing prayer') with its nineteen benedictions of praise, entreaty and thanksgiving;[2] and a set of varied items that are prefixed and appended to these two central pieces. Brief reference is also made to the sabbath and festival prayers which abbreviate some of the central weekday prayer texts and expand others to take account of the special nature of these days, and to communal, domestic and personal rituals that have gradually been incorporated into the pre-medieval, medieval and modern liturgies. The chapter includes an explanation of how the rabbinic tradition opts to relate to the Hebrew Bible and how the prayer-books of the various periods tackled the problem of this relationship. There are sections on the language and theology of the prayers vis-à-vis their biblical connections, and on some of the best known biblical passages included in the liturgy. The importance of the mystical element and the special needs of contemporary prayer also feature briefly.

---

1   See chapter 7 below.
2   See chapter 9 below.

Is Jewish liturgy biblical?

The appearance of biblical texts is so singularly prominent in many
parts of the *siddur* that the immediate impression given to the reader is
that the Jewish liturgy is borrowed directly from Jewish authoritative
scripture. Such a conclusion might understandably be drawn not only
by those with little close acquaintance with this classical Jewish work
but also by those who are familiar with its contents from a devotional
rather than an historical perspective.[3] A mere glance at the traditional
prayers confirms that the language is Hebrew, that the theology rings
biblical bells, and that the relationship presupposed is that between
God and Israel. Following biblical models, gratitude is expressed,
praise offered and supplication made and there is no lack of special
requests for divine assistance in matters mundane, as well as spiritual.
The names of biblical heroes frequently occur and topics such as
sacrifice, Temple, priest and levite are also to be found.

If one examines the index to the use of the Psalms appended to the
'Singer's prayer-book', first published for Anglo-Jewry in 1890, one
finds that no less than seventy-four out of a total of 150 Biblical Psalms
occur in the context of the standard prayers.[4] Are we not then entitled
to suppose that the *siddur* is the direct continuation of trends
represented by Abraham's entreaty for Sodom, Jacob's bargaining with
God, Moses's request for the healing of Miriam, Samson's appeal for
vengeance through his death, Hannah's prayer for a child,[5] the Temple
ritual and the composition of psalms? Some of the roots of the Jewish
prayers are indeed to be found in the biblical soil, but historical
accuracy forces us to draw a distinction between the notions of 'liturgy
in the Hebrew Bible' and 'the Hebrew Bible in Jewish liturgy.' Both
historically and thematically, the story is a more complicated one. The
use of the Bible in liturgy, though extensive, is in fact selective. Some

3   The late British Chief Rabbi, J. H. Hertz, was perhaps promoting an ecumenical
     agenda when he stressed that the 'climax of the Hebrew genius for prayer is the
     Book of Psalms', arguing that it was 'still the inspiration both of Jew and Christian'
     and that 'the post-Biblical singers in Israel continued the work of the Prophets and
     Psalmists'; see his revised and annotated edition of the 'Singer's' or 'authorised
     prayer-book' that appeared in one volume in 1946 but had been issued in parts
     beginning in 1941.
4   *The Authorised Daily Prayer Book of the United Hebrew Congregations of the British
     Empire, with a New Translation by the Rev. S. Singer* (London, 1890), to which the index
     to the Psalms was added in the fifth edition of 1897–98. I am grateful to Bernard
     Jackson, Esra Kahn, Joseph Schischa, Jeremy Schonfield and Dalia Tracz for their
     kind assistance in checking early editions.
5   Genesis 18:23–25; Genesis 28:16–22; Numbers 12:13; Judges 16:30; 1 Samuel 1:10–16.

texts are omitted because of their central significance to Christianity while others are theologically unpopular.[6] There is also a tendency to favour those biblical texts that are both chronologically and conceptually closer to rabbinic notions.

Pre-Rabbinic traditions

The biblical passages just cited, and many similar to them, indicate that the earliest biblical sources provide later Jewish practice with the inspiration for personal, improvised prayer, in prose format, with patterns in common speech forms. This type of prayer constituted a democratic and egalitarian way of approaching God, not at all similar to the formal, sacrificial cult of the Jerusalem Temple.[7] During the Second Temple period, the tendency developed to link the personal prayer and the formal liturgy. From the Apocryphal and Pseudepigraphical sources, it is apparent that there was an increasing number of benedictions, hymns and praises, mystical formulations of considerable variety, a concern for the absorption of Torah knowledge, and a growing use of the Temple precincts on special liturgical occasions.[8]

The Hellenistic Jewish authors, Philo and Josephus, make it clear that Jews prayed and studied in various contexts, at times with priestly guidance and involvement, especially on the sabbath, and that biblical texts played a part in such rituals. Their reports of Jewish prayer are often motivated not so much by an interest in reporting the wording of contemporary prayer forms but by a desire to expand on the biblical narrative and thus to present Jewish scripture in a favourable light to the Hellenistic world. [9] Though unquestionably devoted to the Temple cult in the second pre-Christian century, Joshua Ben Sira linked Torah and wisdom with prayer. He also used words and phrases that are essentially biblical but take on special forms and meanings.[10] The Qumran scrolls provide clear evidence of a practice, at least among

---

6   An example of the former is Psalms 51:7 and of the latter, the book of Job.

7   M. Greenberg, *Biblical Prose Prayer as a Window to the Popular Religion of Ancient Israel* (Berkeley, 1983).

8   J. Charlesworth, 'Jewish hymns, odes and prayers (*c.* 167 BCE–135 CE)' in *Early Judaism and its Modern Interpreters*, eds R. A. Kraft and G. W. E. Nickelsburg (Philadelphia, 1986), pp. 411–36; and *Prayer from Tobit to Qumran: Deuterocanonical and Cognate Literature, Yearbook 2004*, eds R. Egger-Wenzel and J. Corley (Berlin and New York, 2004).

9   J. Leonhardt, *Jewish Worship in Philo of Alexandria* (Tübingen, 2001); T. M. Jonquière, *Prayer in Josephus* (doctoral dissertation at the University of Utrecht, under the supervision of P. W. van der Horst, 2005).

10   See chapter 4 above.

some groups, to recite regular prayers at specific times. Some of these
were linked to the calendar, some to special events, and some to
penitential themes, but there is no obvious consistency of text and
context.[11]

Rabbinic innovation and development

Rabbinic prayer incorporated material from a broad set of prayer
traditions known at Qumran, as well as from various other contexts of
the Second Temple period, among them the Temple, the priesthood,
communal gatherings for biblical readings (ma'amadot), pietistic and
mystical circles with eschatological and angelological interests, and
popular practice. Among the themes that they shared with earlier
Jewish groups were the election of Israel, the status of Zion, the
holiness of Jerusalem, the return of the Davidic dynasty, and the
manifestation of God's great power now and in the future. What the
Rabbis did was to impose upon such inherited traditions a fresh order,
style and distinctive formulation, and they transmitted them in oral
form until the compilation of the first written texts of the *siddur* in the
ninth century. They absorbed the earlier elements but effectively
created a new structure that represented a *formal* liturgy. In essence,
this constituted a collection of personal prayers and benedictions,
which had been given a communal flavour and dimension, and a
preferred synagogal context.[12]

There was never total agreement about the precise place of prayer
in the theological hierarchy of Judaism but there certainly existed a
universal consensus about the need for it to be practised by the
observant Jew.[13] As medieval rabbinic Judaism progressively
committed its liturgical traditions to short and simple codices, to larger
and more elegant manuscripts, to printed volumes, and ultimately to
the contemporary formats of photocopies and digitized images, so the
siddur grew in its independence, authority and centrality for the
practitioners of the faith. A use of the Hebrew Bible was always part of

---

11 *Liturgical Perspectives: Prayer and Poetry in Light of the Dead Sea Scrolls*, eds E. Chazon
    and A. Pinnick (Leiden, Boston and Köln, 2003); see also E. Chazon (ed.), *Qumran
    Cave 4. 20, Poetical and Liturgical Texts. Pt.2*; in consultation with James VanderKam
    and Monica Brady; based in part on earlier transcriptions and comments by John
    Strugnell (Oxford, 1999).
12 See chapter 3 above.
13 Compare the views of Maimonides and Nahmanides, the former arguing that the
    requirement to pray is a precept deriving from the Written Torah (*Mishneh Torah,
    Tefillah* 1.1) while the latter contends that it is only rabbinically ordained (see his
    commentary on the *Sefer Ha-Miṣvot* of Maimonides, positive commandment 5).

these developments but found its expression in the traditional Jewish liturgy in a number of interesting and novel ways.[14]

By the time that the talmudic rabbis of the early Christian centuries were debating the matter of the inclusion of biblical verses and chapters in their standard prayers for daily, sabbath and festival use, there were a number of these that were well established by popular tradition within the liturgical context. Minor examples are the sets of verses, purposefully borrowed from each of the three parts of the Hebrew Bible, that were included in the *musaf* ('additional') *'amidah* for New Year and illustrated the three themes of kingship, remembrance and *shofar* (ram's horn) that stand at the centre of that prayer, as well as the verses used on special fast-days called in times of drought.[15] More common and more major examples are the *shema'*, the Ten Commandments, the *hallel* ('praise'), the Passover *Haggadah*, the Song at the Sea, the priestly benediction and the *qedushah*, and these will shortly be examined in more detail. What will be revealed by such an examination is that the issue of the role of biblical material in the liturgy was a lively and controversial one.

There is evidence that rabbinic formulations were regarded as preferable to biblical ones, and that Bible verses were differentiated from rabbinic prayers. Could, for instance, the verses from Isaiah 12:6 and Psalms 22:4 be employed at any point in the *qedushah* benediction of the *'amidah* without valid halakhic objections being raised?[16] The early rabbis sometimes even made changes in liturgical formulations out of polemical considerations. A good example concerns the use of the Biblical Hebrew word *'olam'* (meaning 'world' as well as 'eternity' in post-biblical Hebrew) in such a way as to ensure that the notion of a

---

14 See M. Schmelzer, 'Hebrew manuscripts and printed books among the Sephardim before and after the Expulsion' in *Crisis and Creativity in the Sephardic World, 1391–1648*, ed. B. R. Gampel (New York, 1997), pp. 257–66; see also chapter 11 below.

15 Examples, some of which are first recorded in BT, *Rosh Hashanah* 31b and PT, *Rosh Hashanah* 4.7 (59c), are, according to the Ashkenazi rite: Exodus 15:18, Numbers 23:21, Deuteronomy 33:5, Psalms 22:29, 93:1 and 24:7–10, Isaiah 44:6, Obadiah 1:21, Zechariah 14:9, Deuteronomy 6:4 for 'kingship'; Genesis 8:1, Exodus 2:24, Leviticus 26:42, Psalms 111:4–5, 106:45, Jeremiah 2:2, Ezekiel 16:60, Jeremiah 31:19, Leviticus 26:45 for 'remembrance'; Exodus 19:16 and 19 and 20:15, Psalms 47:6, 98:6, 81:4–5 and 150:1–6, Isaiah 18:3 and 27:13, Zechariah 9:14–15; Numbers 10:10 for 'shofar'. For one of the Sefardi selections of texts, see M. Gaster, *The Book of Prayer and Order of Service according to the Custom of the Spanish and Portuguese Jews* (London, 1901–6), vol. 2 (1903), pp. 117–22. On the fast-days, see Mishnah, *Ta'anit* 2.2–3.

16 PT, *Berakhot* 1:8 (3d), and the interpretations offered by N. Wieder, *The Formation of Jewish Liturgy in the East and the West: A Collection of Essays* (Hebrew; 2 vols; Jerusalem, 1998), 1.285–91 (originally published in *Tarbiz* 43 (1974), pp. 46–52) and I. Ta-Shema, *'Eyn omrim berakhah pasuq'* in the memorial volume for Yitzchak Raphael, *Sefer Raphael*, ed. J. E. Movshovitz (Hebrew; Jerusalem, 2000), pp. 643–51.

future world was not excluded.[17] Nevertheless, the liturgical pre-
existence of such specific items as the *shema'*, and others mentioned
above, provides positive proof that earlier attitudes had been different.
Perhaps what the talmudic rabbis feared was the potential influence of
some groups who were regarded by them as sectarian and who had
opted for the inclusion of biblical texts among their prayers. The Jews
whose literary remains were found at Qumran, by the Dead Sea, were
of such an ilk, and medieval Karaites, whose prayers were exclusively
composed of biblical texts, pursued a similar liturgical philosophy.[18]
The situation among the Rabbanite Jews changed from the beginning of
the Islamic period when, instead of merely a few favourite verses (such
as Psalms 51:17, 84:5 and 144:15) and Psalms (such as Psalms 145),
substantial blocks of biblical verses, groups of chapters and individual
verses came to be incorporated in the traditional daily prayers, and
then in the first prayer-books.[19] Either the popular urge to include
biblical items was so powerful that the halakhic authorities had to
submit to it or it was determined that the most attractive religious
practices should not be left exclusively to the theological opposition.

Early prayer-books

In the early prayer-books, therefore, the introduction of the morning
prayers by the recitation of Psalms 145–50 (called the *pesuqey de-zimra*,

---

17   Mishnah, *Berakhot* 9.5; see J. G. Weiss, 'On the formula *melekh ha-'olam* as anti-Gnostic
     protest', *JJS* 10 (1959), pp. 169–71, E. J. Wiesenberg, 'The liturgical term *melekh ha-
     'olam*', *JJS* 15 (1964), pp. 1–56 and J. Heinemann, 'Once again *melekh ha-'olam*', *JJS* 15
     (1964), pp. 149–54.
18   C. Rabin, 'The historical background of Qumran Hebrew' in *Scripta Hierosolymitana* 4
     (Jerusalem, 1965), pp. 144–61, with a later Hebrew version published in *Qoveṣ
     Ma'amarim Bilshon Ḥz"l*, vol. 1, ed. M. Bar-Asher (Jerusalem, 1972), pp. 355–82, and
     'The linguistic investigation of the language of Jewish prayer' in *Studies in Aggadah,
     Targum and Jewish Liturgy in Memory of Joseph Heinemann*, eds J. J. Petuchowski and E.
     Fleischer (Jerusalem and Cincinnati, 1981), Hebrew section, pp. 163–71; A. Hurvitz,
     *The Transition Period: A Study in Post-Exilic Hebrew and its Implications for the Dating of
     Psalms* (Hebrew; Jerusalem, 1972), especially pp. 36–63; E. Qimron, *The Hebrew of the
     Dead Sea Scrolls* (Atlanta, 1986); L. Nemoy, *Karaite Anthology: Excerpts from the Early
     Literature* (New Haven and London, 1952); P. S. Goldberg, *Karaite Liturgy and its
     Relation to Synagogue Worship* (Manchester, 1957); P. Birnbaum (ed.), *Karaite Studies*
     (New York, 1971); Wieder, *The Formation of Jewish Liturgy* (see n. 16 above), 1.242–52
     (originally published in *Sinai* 98 (1986), pp. 39–48).
19   E.g. the verses used in the Ashkenazi rite for supplicatory purposes from Psalms 6,
     25, 130:8, 2 Samuel 24:14, 2 Chronicles 20:12, Psalms 25:6, 33:22, 79:8, 123:3,
     Habakkuk 3:2, Psalms 103:14, 78:38, 40:12, 106:47, 130:3–4, 103:10, Jeremiah 14:7,
     Psalms 25:6, 20:2,10, Daniel 9:15-17, 9:18–19, Isaiah 64:7, Joel 2:17, Deuteronomy 6:4
     at the daily morning service, and Psalms 119:142, 71:19 and 36:37 at the Sabbath
     afternoon service.

or 'Biblical verses of praise'), a custom known in earlier times, was not the only use of that book of the Bible.[20] Sets of Psalms made up of such chapters as Psalms 19, 33–34, 90–93, 98, 100, 103, 121–24 and 135–36, came to be added, in different groupings according to the various rites, for use on sabbaths and festivals.[21] Catenae of verses were similarly used to preface the central liturgy and grew in range and extent as the medieval centuries passed. They included passages from 1 Chronicles 16 and 29 and from Nehemiah 9, as well as from a variety of pentateuchal, prophetic and hagiographical books.[22] They were often strung together by a common theme such as God's salvation and protection or his gifts, including the revelation of the Torah. One of the most popular concatenations, originally associated with sessions of Torah study and entitled *qedushah de-sidra*, was the one beginning with the verses from Isaiah 59:20–21.[23] As the prayer-book and the synagogal ritual became progressively more formalized in the high and later Middle Ages, so other opportunities were taken of introducing biblical texts. An examination of the earliest known versions of the grace after meals, for instance, reveals that some rites were anxious to conclude the body of each benediction with a biblical verse while others preferred to restrict the content to rabbinic formulations. In later texts of the same

---

20 *Massekhet Soferim*, ed. M. Higger (New York, 1937), 18.1, p. 309 (E.T., ed. I. W. Slotki, London, 1965, 17.11, p. 298), where it is assumed that the reference in BT, *Shabbat* 118b is to such a set of Psalms.

21 See *Soferim*, ed. Higger (n. 20 above), 18.2–4, pp. 310–14 and ed. Slotki (n. 20 above), 18.1–3, pp. 299–301; S. Baer, *Seder 'Avodat Yisra'el* (Rödelheim, 1868), p. 62; *Siddur Oṣar Ha-Tefillot*, ed. A. L. Gordon (corrected and expanded edition, Vilna, 1923, Hebrew pagination), pp. 94b–95a; I. Elbogen, German edition = G, *Der jüdische Gottesdienst in seiner geschichtlichen Entwicklung* (Frankfurt am Main, 1931; reprint, Hildesheim, 1962), pp. 112–13; Hebrew edition = H, התפילה בישראל בהתפתחותה ההיסטורית (eds J. Heinemann, I. Adler, A. Negev, J. Petuchowski and H. Schirmann, Tel Aviv, 1972), p. 86; English edition = E, *Jewish Liturgy: A Comprehensive History* (English translation and edition by R. P. Scheindlin, Philadelphia, Jerusalem and New York,1993), p. 95; Gaster, *Prayer* (see n. 15 above), vol. 1 (London, 1901), pp. 16–18 and 92–99; and B. S. Jacobson, *Netiv Binah* (Hebrew; 5 vols; Tel Aviv, 1968–83), 2.135–39.

22 Baer, *Seder*, p. 72; *Oṣar Ha-Tefillot*, p. 115b; Elbogen, *Gottesdienst*, G, pp. 85–86, H, p. 67, E, pp. 75–76; Gaster, *Prayer*, 1.14–16 and 22–23; Jacobson, *Netiv* 1.218–20. For the above references, see n. 21.

23 The other verses included Psalms 22:4, Isaiah 6:3, Ezekiel 3:12, Exodus 15:18, 1 Chronicles 29:18, Psalms 73:33, 86:5, 119:142, Micah 7:20, Psalms 86:20, 46:8, 84:13, 20:10, 30:13, Jeremiah 17:7, Isaiah 26:4, Psalms 9:11, Isaiah 42:21, Psalms 8:10, 31:25, Numbers 14:17, Psalms 25:6 and Isaiah 9:11. See Baer, *Seder*, pp. 127–29; *Oṣar Ha-Tefillot*, pp. 212a–214b; Elbogen, *Gottesdienst*, G, p. 79, H, p. 62, E, pp. 70–71; Gaster, *Prayer*, 1.49–50; Jacobson, *Netiv*, 1.360–65. For the above references, see n. 21. See also below, the section on the *qedushah*.

prayer, the passages appended to the final benediction include a significant number of biblical verses, especially at the conclusion.[24]

Conscious as they were of these tendencies and of the need to stress that rabbinic Judaism was not in any sense rejecting the Hebrew Bible in favour of the Talmud, leading scholars such as Sa'adya ben Joseph, the rabbinic leader in the tenth-century Babylonian centre of Sura, and Maimonides, his counterpart in twelfth-century Cairo, had statements to make on the matter. The former attempted to demonstrate that the rabbinic prayers were not unprecedented and innovative but formulations of liturgical genres that already appeared in the Hebrew Bible. This apparently allowed him to opt for the inclusion of biblical psalms without subscribing to Karaite notions about those compositions' exclusive right to represent Jewish liturgy.[25] The latter, for his part, argued that it was only because the Jewish people's knowledge of Hebrew had deteriorated severely after the Babylonian exile that they could no longer be left to their own liturgical devices, but had to be guided by being provided with rabbinic structures.[26] Thus, these two leading authorities set about merging the two major sources of Judaism, the Bible and the Talmud, in theological terms, just as this had been achieved by practical religious custom in the ritual context.

Medieval additions

It was laid down that when the worshippers made their entry into the synagogue they should recite verses from such sources as Numbers 24:5 and Psalms 5:8, 26:8, 55:15, 69:14 and 95:6.[27] Similarly, the removal and return of the Torah scroll in connection with the lectionary, attracted a growing number of biblical verses, some of which did not even appear in the text of the prayer-book until well after the invention of printing. The most common of these on a weekday were Numbers 10:35 and Isaiah 2:3 before the biblical reading, and Psalms 148:13–14

---

24 The verses used to conclude the first, second and third benedictions were, respectively, Psalms 145:16, Deuteronomy 8:10 and Psalms 147:2; see L. Finkelstein, 'The Birkat Ha-Mazon', *JQR*, NS 19 (1928–29), pp. 243–58.

25 In his introduction to the prayer-book, *Siddur R. Saadja Gaon*, eds I. Davidson, S. Assaf and B. I. Joel, (Jerusalem, 1941, Jerusalem², 1963), pp. 1–13. See also N. Ilan, 'Saadiah Gaon's translation of *mikhtam*', *JJS* 56 (2005), pp. 298–305, especially pp. 304–5.

26 *Mishneh Torah, Tefillah*, 1.4; ed. M. Hyamson, *The Book of Adoration* (Jerusalem, 1965), f. 98b.

27 Baer, *Seder*, p. 122; *Oṣar Ha-Tefillot*, p. 206a; Elbogen, *Gottesdienst*, G, pp. 198–205, H, pp. 147–52, E, pp. 158–63; Gaster, *Prayer*, 1.1; Jacobson, *Netiv*, 2.212–17. For the above references, see n. 21.

and Numbers 10:36 after it. Among other verses introduced in connection with the synagogal use of the Torah scroll were Psalms 86:8 and 132:8–10, Proverbs 4:2 and 3:16–18, Lamentations 5:21, 2 Samuel 22:31 and Deuteronomy 4:35. Many of these make no direct reference to the Torah (e.g. Proverbs 4:2) but were understood in this way by post-biblical Judaism and one is a 'doctored' version of Deuteronomy 4:44 and Numbers 4:37.[28] Later (more voluntary) additions to the conclusion of the formal service were the Binding of Isaac (Genesis 22) and the Manna (Exodus 16), as well as some other, less commonly recited passages.[29] One of the contributions of the early modern mystics was to champion the recitation of the Song of Songs as an introduction to Friday evening prayers and to follow that by the recitation of Psalms 95–99 and 29, and then of Proverbs 31:10–31 before the sabbath meal.[30] Liturgists in the early Reform movement was generally more attached to biblical passages than to rabbinic texts and some consequently removed the rabbinic benedictions that talmudic tradition had attached to the reading of the lectionaries and to the recitation of such items as *hallel*.[31]

Language of the liturgy

The Hebrew of the *siddur* is very reminiscent of its biblical counterpart but by no means identical with it. The basic vocabulary and phraseology of praise and supplication is borrowed from the Psalms and there are occasionally linguistic usages that are characteristic of

28 Baer, *Seder*, p. 125; *Oṣar Ha-Tefillot*, p. 209ab; Elbogen, *Gottesdienst*, G, pp. 198–205, H, pp. 147–52, E, pp. 158–63; Gaster, *Prayer*, 1.47; Jacobson, *Netiv*, 2.240–44. For the above five references, see n. 21. See also J. M. Cohen, 'Ve-zot ha-Torah – a liturgical reassurance', *Judaism* 40.4 (1991), pp. 407–18; and R. Langer, 'Early medieval celebrations of Torah', *Kenishta* 2 (2003), pp. 99–118 (Hebrew), especially 116–18. Another 'doctored' text is Isaiah 45:7 which is cited at the beginning of the morning pre-*shema*' benedictions with the word *ha-kol* ('everything') substituting for *ha-ra*' ('evil'); see Baer, *Seder*, p. 76; *Oṣar Ha-Tefillot*, p. 127a; Elbogen, *Gottesdienst*, G, p. 17, H, p. 13, E, p. 17; Gaster, *Prayer*, 1.26; Jacobson, *Netiv*, 1.231. For the above five references, see n. 21.
29 Baer, *Seder*, pp. 155–60; *Oṣar Ha-Tefillot*, pp. 223a–227b; but compare Elbogen, *Gottesdienst*, G, p. 81, H, p. 64, E, p. 72, who makes no reference to these additions at the end of the morning service. For the above references, see n. 21.
30 Elbogen, *Gottesdienst* (see n. 21 above), G, pp. 389–93, H, pp. 288–91, E, pp. 291–95; A. Idelsohn, *Jewish Liturgy and its Development* (New York, 1932), pp. 47–55; Jacobson, *Netiv* (see n. 21 above), 2.29–68. R. Goetschel (ed.), *Prière, mystique et Judaïsme* (Paris, 1987), especially the contributions of M. Hallamisch and B. Sack on pp. 121–31 and 179–86.
31 Full details of such trends are to be found in J. J. Petuchowski, *Prayerbook Reform in Europe. The Liturgy of Liberal and Reform Judaism* (New York, 1968); see especially pp. 265–76.

Biblical rather than Rabbinic Hebrew. The overall style, syntax and linguistic flow are, however, very much dependent on those that are familiar from other rabbinic literature and there is no doubt that the early talmudic leaders were anxious not to confuse the two forms of the language. Perhaps one of the ways in which Rabbinic Judaism created its own identity was by rejecting a preference for the Biblical Hebrew style in the formulation of its traditions and committing itself to its own linguistic usage.[32]

Through its history of almost two millennia, the language of rabbinic prayer underwent a long and complicated development from a format that may well have been oral in origin, through a process of literary improvement and linguistic selection, towards the establishment of independent parameters. It achieved a status that could even ultimately exercise a formative influence on the re-emergence of contemporary, spoken Hebrew in the modern period. Be that as it may, the process was always accompanied by a tension between those who were anxious to re-forge the link with the Hebrew Bible and those who saw the need for the language of rabbinic prayer to grow independently, whatever its deepest roots. The 'biblicisors' of each generation made their stand. They fought off the challenges of Greek, Aramaic and later vernaculars and expressed preference for wording the prayers in a style that followed more closely the biblical precedent. When the Ben Asher text of the Hebrew Bible became the standard in the second Christian millennium, it was their circles that fought valiantly to apply its principles to the language of the liturgy. They were not averse to the employment of strange strategies to achieve their aims.[33]

In the case of the sixteenth-century Polish rabbinic scholar, Solomon Luria, he argued that the sabbath day should be termed 'shabbat', and not 'manoaḥ' in Hebrew, because Manoaḥ in the Hebrew Bible is not used for 'rest' but as the name of Samson's father, about whom the Talmud makes derogatory remarks. Similarly, the verse in Numbers 24:5 should not be used in the synagogue because it originates not in scripture itself but in the words of the Gentile pseudo-

32 See L. I. Rabinowitz, 'The Psalms in Jewish liturgy', *Historia Judaica* 6 (1944), pp. 109–22; J. Heinemann, '*Sefer Tehillim kemikor lenusaḥ ha-tefillah*' in *Studies in Jewish Liturgy*, ed. A. Shinan (Hebrew; Jerusalem, 1981), pp. 176–79; and M. P. Weitzman, 'Biblical elements in Jewish prayer' in *Israel Yeivin Festschrift* (=*Language Studies* 5–6; Hebrew; Jerusalem, 1992), pp. 25–39, as well as the references to the work of Rabin and Hurvitz cited in n. 18 above.
33 For further discussion and details of the sources, see S. C. Reif, *Judaism and Hebrew Prayer: New Perspectives on Jewish Liturgical History* (Cambridge 1993), pp. 61–64, 113–15, 176–78, 210–11, 230–32, 248–50, 262–66.

prophet, Balaam.[34] Although these 'biblicisors' made an impact, particularly at times and places that had a need for a stronger identification with the Hebrew Bible (as, for instance, in central and western Europe immediately after the Reformation or during Jewish emancipation), their efforts were neither intended nor destined to remove parts of the rabbinic liturgy from their place in traditional Jewish literature. Such a result was achieved only by the non-traditional movements beginning in the late eighteenth and early nineteenth centuries.

Theology of the siddur

A similar situation pertains to the theology of the *siddur*. The common prayers undoubtedly reflect the religious ideology of Rabbinic Judaism. The divine authority of Oral Torah is presupposed in many contexts and the obligation to perform the 613 religious precepts, as formulated by rabbinic interpretation, underlies various texts. There is a conviction that goodness will be rewarded and evil punished and that repentance brings forgiveness. The study of Torah makes its appearance both as one of the observant Jew's duties and in the form of texts that are cited from rabbinic literature. These are so successfully welded into the body of the prayer-book that they are effectively treated as liturgy rather than education. The ideology underlying their inclusion is that the absence of the Temple ritual prescribed in the Pentateuch can be compensated for by the recitation of the biblical and talmudic passages that describe its detailed requirements.[35]

Having first been formulated in the period following the destruction of the Temple, the expulsion from the holy city of Jerusalem, and the loss of the independent Jewish homeland, the rabbinic prayers lay powerful stress on Israel's appeal to God for the restoration of these religious and national symbols. Much is made of God's choice of Israel for a special religious role and there are polemical undertones in some prayers that appear to be aimed at Christianity or Islam. At the same time, there is an enthusiasm for the

---

34 Luria's responsa first appeared in print in Lublin, 1574, and no. 6, dealing with the prayer-book was translated by B. Berliner, 'Rabbi Solomon Luria on the prayer-book' in *Jews' College Jubilee Volume*, ed. I . Harris (London, 1906), pp. 123–39; the reference to Balaam appears on p. 134 of that translation. For some typical comments by Luria, see chapter 14 below, especially section C about Manoaḥ.

35 There appear to be two aspects to this ideology, one that regards the mere recitation itself as achieving what once resulted from the offering of sacrifices while the other stresses the need for an understanding of the passages though serious study; see BT, *Ta'anit* 27b, *Menaḥot* 110a and *Shabbat* 30a. I have discussed this in detail in chapter 10 below.

'righteous proselyte' and a fervent hope (following biblical eschatological models) that the whole world will ultimately come to recognize God's sovereignty. The ultimate redemption, like that of Israel from Egypt, will be an impressive manifestation of God's power and will include the arrival of the Messiah and the resurrection of the dead. The assumption is frequently made that the worshipper can enjoy a close relationship with God and that practical matters in human life require God's blessing for them to flourish.[36] Formal catechisms are not a feature of rabbinic prayer although there are certainly texts such as the *shema'* that include the relevant theological principles. A poetic summary of Maimonides's 'Thirteen Principles of Faith', known from its opening word as the *yigdal* hymn, is included for recitation before formal prayer in the morning and for singing after the Friday evening service but this is late, optional, controversial, and an exception rather the rule. In some communities, the thirteen principles were also recited in their prose form at the conclusion of the morning prayers.[37]

It will be obvious to anyone with a modicum of biblical knowledge that most of the religious ideology just charted is either represented in an earlier form in the Hebrew Bible or has a basis in some of its texts. Sometimes, the only change in a phrase is the adjustment of the singular to the plural to take account of the change from individual request to communal petition. The notions of a special relationship between God and Israel, of direct access to his favour, and of revelation and redemption from the divine source, are all familiar features of the biblical books. By the same token, the nature of rabbinic theodicy, eschatology and religious law is largely shaped by ideas to be found in the Written Torah.

Shema' and Ten Commandments

What is widely regarded as Rabbinic Judaism's most famous prayer, the *shema'*, is in fact a section borrowed from Deuteronomy 6:4–9, with a second paragraph from Deuteronomy 11:13–21 and a third from Numbers 15:37–41. In the Hebrew Bible, these passages are not specifically marked as prayers. In a Hebrew papyrus inscription from the second century BCE, named after W. L. Nash who purchased it in

---

36 For summaries of the religious ideology of the *siddur*, see A. Millgram, *Jewish Worship* (Philadelphia, 1971), pp. 391–434; and Alan Mintz, 'Prayer and the prayerbook' in *Back to the Sources: Reading the Classic Jewish Texts*, ed. B. W. Holtz (New York, 1984), pp. 403–29.

37 Baer, *Seder*, p. 160; *Oṣar Ha-Tefillot*, p. 52a and 224b; Elbogen, *Gottesdienst*, G, pp. 87–88, H, pp, 68–69, E, p. 77; Jacobson, *Netiv*, 1.148–52. For all the above references, see n. 21.

Egypt in 1903, the text of the first two verses appears together with that of the Ten Commandments, in a formulation that corresponds closely to the Greek translation of the Exodus version.[38] Whether that papyrus is to be identified as an amulet or as a piece of liturgy, it testifies to a Jewish use of these two biblical texts as something other than a direct quotation, since they do not occur together in the Pentateuch. Such a use was therefore being made before the earliest manifestation of either Christianity or Rabbinic Judaism and further evidence is provided by the Hellenistic Jewish writers, as well as from the mishnaic traditions of the second century CE.[39] They indicate that both the *shema'* and the Ten Commandments already then had a special and well-established liturgical significance, apparently because they gave expression to the most central religious ideas of the Jews. Attempts were indeed made to draw parallels between the occurrences of such ideas in the two passages.[40]

In the case of the *shema'*, there appears to have been a gradual development from the use of one paragraph to the acceptance of three, and to its recitation, in some (as yet unclear) form of special chant, in both the morning and evening prayers. On the other hand, the independent status of the Ten Commandments led to controversy and a diminution of its liturgical function. It was once so central to liturgical use that it was included among the biblical texts inserted in the *tefillin* ('phylacteries') boxes by such sects as those who lived by the Dead Sea. Later, it came to be regarded with suspicion when it was polemically cited by groups regarded by Rabbinic Judaism as heretical. Their argument was that such a central liturgical use permitted the conclusion that only such parts of the Pentateuch were authoritative. Such a challenge encouraged the Rabbis to rule against the liturgical recitation of the passage in spite of its impressive pedigree, a ruling that was widely followed at least in Babylonian Jewry.[41] Interestingly, the finds from the Cairo Genizah document a continuing use of the Ten Commandments among the Palestinian Jews, in a place of honour in the prayer-book just before the commencement of the *shema'* benedictions. Having apparently brought the practice with them from

---

38   For a bibliography of research on the Nash Papyrus, see *Encyclopaedia Judaica* 12, col. 833; see also M. H. Segal, 'The Nash Papyrus', *Leshonenu* 15 (1947), pp. 27–36, reprinted in his *Masoret U-Viqoret* (Tel Aviv, 1957), pp. 227–36, and S. C. Reif, 'The Nash Papyrus', *Cambridge* 15 (1984), pp. 41–45.
39   Josephus, *Antiquities* 4.viii.13, 212–13 (ed. Loeb, pp. 577–78); Leonhardt, *Jewish Worship* (see n. 9 above), pp. 98 and 140; Mishnah, *Berakhot*; Elbogen, *Gottesdienst* (see n. 21 above), G, p. 554, H, p. 443, E, p. 434. See also chapter 7 below.
40   See, e.g., Sifrey, *Va-Ethanan*, §34, ed. Finkelstein, pp. 60–61, and PT, *Berakhot* 1.8 (3c).
41   BT, *Berakhot* 13a–17b; Y. Yadin, *Tefillin from Qumran (X Q Phyl 1–4)* (Jerusalem, 1969); PT, *Berakhot* 1.3 (3c) and BT, *Berakhot* 12a.

the Holy Land when they fled the Crusades, they were loath to abandon it in favour of the dominant Babylonian custom but their rite ultimately all but disappeared. Some authorities in Spain proposed its inclusion but it was not until the early modern period that the passage was again included in the *siddur* on a regular basis, and then not as an integral part of the prayers but as an appendix to the morning service for those few Jews who might wish to add voluntarily to their daily recitation of biblical passages.[42]

For its part, the *shema'* was, by the end of the talmudic period, already surrounded by rabbinic benedictions and liturgical poems, and inextricably bound together with the *'amidah* both evening and morning. Given that its recitation in the communal context might not therefore take place immediately after rising in the morning, or just before settling down to sleep at night, which had been part of the original intent, a secondary use of the prayer for those purposes was adopted. Its two manifestations were referred to respectively as the '*Shema'* of Rabbi Judah the Patriarch' and the '*Shema'* by the Bedside' and they were inserted into the prayer-book.[43] The custom of remaining seated for the *shema'*, which was initially that of the Babylonian communities, in contradistinction to the requirement to stand for the *'amidah*, was perhaps a way of expressing the conviction that rabbinic prayers still had a higher liturgical status than the recitation of scripture. Moreover, the thirteenth-century controversy in Spain about whether to recite the *shema'* declaratively or silently might again have had to do with approaches to its communal liturgical significance.[44] Many of the earliest Reform prayer-books retained the *shema'* in Hebrew but there were some more radical versions in which it was severely truncated. In the more recent versions produced by the progressive movements, various options are offered. Since its recitation does not require a *minyan* (quorum of ten men), Orthodox women's prayer groups include it in their recently constructed services without major controversy.[45]

---

42 E. E. Urbach, 'The place of the Ten Commandments in ritual and prayer' in *The Ten Commandments as Reflected in Tradition and Literature throughout the Ages*, ed. B.-Z. Segal (Hebrew; Jerusalem, 1985), pp. 127–45 (E. T., ed G. Levi, Jerusalem, 1990, pp. 161–89); E. Fleischer, *Eretz-Israel Prayer and Prayer Rituals as Portrayed in the Genizah Documents* (Hebrew; Jerusalem, 1988), pp. 259–74; Solomon ben Abraham Adret, *Responsa (She'elot U-Teshuvot Rashba)*, parts 1–3 (Bnei Braq, 1958–59), part 3, no. 289; see also above n. 29.

43 Baer, *Seder*, pp. 46 and 573; *Oṣar Ha-Tefillot*, pp. 70b and 278b; Elbogen, *Gottesdienst*, G, p. 91, H, p. 71, E, p. 79; Gaster, *Prayer*, 1.8, 76; Jacobson, *Netiv*, 1.176 and 3.245–64. For the above references, see n. 21.

44 M. Margulies (Margaliot), *The Differences between Babylonian and Palestinian Jews* (Hebrew; Jerusalem, 1937), pp. 75 and 91–94; *Rashba* (see n. 42 above), part 1, no. 452.

45 Petuchowski, *Prayerbook Reform* (see n. 31 above), pp. 47, 59–60 and 72; A. Weiss,

Hallel

Tracing in the rabbinic prayer-book the fate of other pieces of Hebrew scripture that have a Jewish liturgical history going back for at least two millennia may also be profitable for the overall picture being painted. Although the word *hallel* does occur with reference to other biblical passages, its oldest liturgical definition relates to the recitation of Psalms 113–18. Such a collection of scriptural passages is reported by the Mishnah to have been part of the Temple ritual during the offering of the paschal lamb.[46] Whether or not the custom is, from a critical, historical perspective, as ancient as Temple times, it was incorporated into the domestic ritual on the first night of Passover in post-Temple times and the nature of its recitation is the subject of early rabbinic discussion. Three teachers from the tannaitic period compared its declamation with that of the Song at the Sea (Exodus 15), namely, antiphonally by prayer-leader and community, but each had a different concept of the precise form taken by such an exchange.[47] Such a fluidity of view about the precise nature of the recitation of *hallel* had its equivalent in the later rules about its use in the standard prayers. In spite of its more than respectable origins, it was limited to certain festivals, and even then with an abbreviated format for the New Moon. Even with regard to the first night (or, according to some rites, first two nights) of Passover, some communities incorporated it into the synagogal services while others restricted it to domestic use in the *Haggadah* (Exodus story and exposition). It was, however, important enough for a benediction to be formulated (perhaps not in early talmudic times) to precede it and, consequently, for some of the nineteenth-century Reform prayer-books to allow its retention as a biblical passage but without such a benediction.[48]

Passover Haggadah

The earliest rabbinic sources take it for granted that there is a domestic liturgy on the first Passover night but its earliest format was not

---

Women at Prayer (Hoboken, N.J., 1990), pp. 22–24 and 43–56.

46   Mishnah, *Pesaḥim* 10.6–7.

47   Mekhilta of R. Ishmael on Exodus 15:1; ed. J. Z. Lauterbach (Philadelphia, 1933), 2, pp. 7–8.

48   Baer, *Seder*, p. 328; *Oṣar Ha-Tefillot*, p. 442a; Elbogen, *Gottesdienst*, G, p. 496, H, p. 371, E, p. 377; Jacobson, *Netiv*, 3.264–312 (for the above references, see n. 21); Petuchowski, *Prayerbook Reform* (see n. 31 above), pp. 265–76.

lengthy. It constituted the usual festival benedictions relating to the wine and the meal, some references to the unleavened bread, the paschal lamb and the bitter vegetables of Exodus 12:8, the exposition of the passage from Deuteronomy 26:5–8 summarizing the Egyptian bondage and the Exodus and ending with a special redemption blessing, and the *hallel*. This domestic celebration generated a large number of additional liturgical and pedagogical offshoots, many of them with biblical content. Already in talmudic times, the early rabbinic interpretations of the Exodus story and of the requirement to relate it (Exodus 12:26, 13:8 and 14, and Deuteronomy 6:20) were incorporated and expanded, as were the references to the meal and the special foods which cited Exodus 12:27, 12:39 and 1:14. In the Middle Ages, the persecution of the Jews elicited a liturgical response in the form of the recitation of biblical verses calling for Divine retribution, as in Psalms 79:6–7, Psalms 69:25 (and other verses in that chapter), and Lamentations 3:64–66.[49] The secular Zionists of the twentieth century created novel texts that stressed the themes of springtime and of national freedom, already recorded in the Exodus story, but with a contemporary application.[50]

Song at the Sea

Talmudic discussion of the antiphonal recitation of the Song at the Sea revolved around what the rabbis presupposed to have been its original format in the mouths of Moses and the Children of Israel. The reader of such comments is, however, led to wonder whether there was also a liturgical use in their own day that they had in mind. If there was, it was evidently a ritual originally reserved for the sabbath afternoon service and only in post-talmudic times made its way into the sabbath morning and even the daily prayers. It then took a place of honour – in the Palestinian ritual even as a virtually independent ceremony – at the conclusion of the block of Psalms known as the *pesuqey de-zimra* (Psalms 145–50; see above), that linked the morning benedictions and readings with the *shema'* and its benedictions.[51]

---

49   E. D. Goldschmidt, *The Passover Haggadah: Its Sources and History* (Hebrew; Jerusalem, 1969), pp. 26–29, 51–58 and 62–64.

50   E.g. Y. H. Yerushalmi, *Haggadah and History: A Panorama in Facsimile of Five Centuries of the Printed Haggadah from the Collections of Harvard University and the Jewish Theological Seminary of America* (Philadelphia, 1975), plates 166, 170, 174–75, 178, 182–85 and 190.

51   BT, *Soṭah* 30b; Judah ben Barzilai al-Bargeloni, *Sefer Ha-'Ittim*, ed. J. Schor (Berlin and Cracow, 1903; New York, 1959), p. 249; BT, *Rosh Ha-Shanah* 31a; Fleischer, *Eretz-Israel* (see n. 42 above), pp. 215–57.

Priestly Benediction

A silver amulet dating from the seventh-century BCE contains a version of the priestly benediction closely resembling that recorded in Numbers 6:24–26 and demonstrates that even at that early period some special liturgical significance was already attached to the benediction. It certainly played a role in the worship performed in the Second Temple and there is no doubt that elements of priestly liturgy were absorbed into the proto-rabbinic prayers.[52] At the same time, the extensive talmudic sources record tensions about whether priests are to retain their privileged position or are to be succeeded by the rabbis. For the Tanna, R. Simeon, it was not priesthood but a good reputation that had maintained an attractive religious standing and a mishnaic statement seems to regard the priestly benediction as separate from the standard prayer context. Other teachers, however, preferred a compromise to such a categorical differentiation. What is clearly attested are changes in the use of the Divine Name, the custom of raising the hands in blessing, the nature of the accompanying ritual, and the Jewish constituency to whom the priestly benediction is addressed. Although biblical privileges were to a large extent retained, and the priestly genealogy and role continued to be recognized, intellectual and halakhic leadership became more democratically available.[53]

As the rabbinic liturgy acquired a more formal nature in the early medieval period, the recitation of the priestly benediction was denied to the priest except in restricted circumstances and there were some arguments for weakening even that privilege, especially among the Jewish communities in Christian lands.[54] The benediction even came to be part of the biblical readings of the daily 'morning benedictions' that were originally recited by every pious individual at home and were later absorbed into the synagogal ritual.[55] The halakhic authorities in

---

52 G. Barkay, *Ketef Hinnom. A Treasure Facing Jerusalem's Walls* (Israel Museum, catalogue no. 274, Jerusalem, 1986); Mishnah, *Tamid* 5:1.

53 Qohelet Rabbah 7.1.3; Mishnah, *Berakhot* 5.4; BT, *Soṭah* 37b–39b; see also L. A. Hoffman, *The Canonization of the Synagogue Service* (Notre Dame and London, 1979), pp. 54 and 110–13 and E. (Yitschak) Zimmer, 'Mo'adey Nesi'at Kappayim', *Sinai* 100 (1987), pp. 452–70. See chapter 6 for further details.

54 See e.g. the rulings (in Hebrew) of Isaac ben Sheshet, *Responsa* (*She'elot U-Teshuvot Rivash*) (Jerusalem, 1993), no. 94; Samuel ben Moses de Medina, *Responsa* (*She'elot U-Teshuvot Maharashdam*) (Lemberg, 1862), *Even Ha-'Ezer*, no. 235; Solomon Luria, *Yam Shel Shelomo* (Bnei Braq, 1960), *Bava Qamma* 5, section 35; and Joseph ben Moses Trani, *Responsa* (*She'elot U-Teshuvot Mahariṭ*) (Lemberg, 1861), section 1, no. 149.

55 Baer, *Seder*, p. 38; *Oṣar Ha-Tefillot*, p. 59b; Elbogen, *Gottesdienst*, G, p. 91, H, pp. 70–71, E, p. 79; Gaster, *Prayer*, 1.4; Jacobson, *Netiv*, 1.159–60. For all the above bibliographical references, see n. 21.

the Middle Ages generally maintained the biblical restrictions and some of the special honour that applied to the priests, but they were content to leave the matter of the restoration of their total power to the messianic age and did not therefore legislate specifically for priests. The priests did at times mount counter-attacks in attempts to restore their earlier authority but generally with only limited success.[56] The use of the priestly benediction in the domestic service preceding the Friday evening meal by the father (not the priest or the prayer-leader) to bless his children was apparently promoted in the sixteenth-century (by the mystics?) and amounted to a further process of democratization.[57] With the rise of the modern progressive movements, even those last few ceremonial roles and restrictions left to the priests were abolished in all but the traditional communities. In the latter, there were doubts about the priestly role in the nineteenth and early twentieth centuries but these seem to have been widely overcome in more recent decades, as reflected in current editions of the Orthodox prayer-book.[58]

Qedushah

Although the recitation of the *qedushah*, or trishagion, from Isaiah 6:3 is accorded importance in the Talmud, it is not clear precisely what piece of liturgy is intended by the Hebrew term and on which occasions it was at that time employed in the prayers. In the post-talmudic period, however, it was certainly used regularly in a number of different contexts in the prayers, especially together with such verses as Ezekiel 3:12, Psalms 146:10 and Isaiah 5:16. It was employed in connection with the study of Torah, as well as in the prayer-leader's repetition of the *'amidah* and in the first benediction preceding the morning *shema'*, as a

---

56 As in the case of the liturgical poets when they were describing the *'Avodah* service of Yom Kippur; see E. Fleischer, *Hebrew Liturgical Poetry in the Middle Ages* (Hebrew; Jerusalem, 1975), p. 175 and J. Yahalom, *Az Be'eyn Kol: Priestly Palestinian Poetry: A Narrative Liturgy for the Day of Atonement* (Hebrew; Jerusalem, 1996), p. 56; see also chapter 10 below.

57 Baer, *Seder*, p. 195; *Oṣar Ha-Tefillot*, p. 307b; Gaster, *Prayer*, 1, p. 91; Jacobson, *Netiv*, 2, pp. 109–14 (for the above references, see n. 21). It is interesting that Elbogen makes no specific reference to this custom and that there is conisiderable lack of enthusiasm for it in *Oṣar Ha-Tefillot*.

58 Elbogen, *Gottesdienst* (see n. 21 above), G, p. 72, H, p. 57, E, p. 66; J. A. Romain, *Faith and Practice: A Guide to Reform Judaism Today* (London, 1991), pp. 191–93. Compare the treatment of the priestly benediction in the first edition of the 'Singer's prayer-book' (see n. 4 above) with the attitude displayed in later Orthodox prayer-books such as *Siddur Qol Ya'aqov. The Complete ArtScroll Siddur. A New Translation and Anthological Commentary*, ed. N. Scherman (Brooklyn, 1984); see also Reif, *Hebrew Prayer* (see n. 33 above), p. 305.

description and emulation of the angelic choir praising God.[59] Since there are precedents for such a daily liturgy in the Qumran literature, the custom might well have been transmitted by pietistic groups, at that time and later, and thus incorporated into the rabbinic liturgy. They found the adoption of what they regarded as the heavenly liturgy as a mystical activity that extended their religious experience and sharpened their spiritual sensitivity.[60] Whether or not the successors of such groups initiated in Palestine, Pirqoi ben Baboi reports in the ninth century that its communities did not recite the pre-*shema' qedushah* on a daily basis until the Babylonian Jews living in Jerusalem and elsewhere created a degree of contention about its omission. In the tenth century, Sa'adya Gaon included the *qedushah* only in the communal, and not the individual context, but gradually it became the widespread custom to allow its recitation even by the individual in at least the non-*'amidah* contexts. It need hardly be pointed out that many of the nineteenth-century rationalists were no happier with the expanded and angelological versions of this mystical item than they were with other such material and retained little more than the biblical sources.[61]

Mystical input

Later mystics also played a part in the expansion of the biblical dimension in the rabbinic *siddur*. The major impact was made by those of the city of Safed in the sixteenth century but they had predecessors in North Africa, Spain and Germany two and three centuries earlier, as well as successors in Eastern Europe a similar amount of time later. The achievement of blissful communion with God required special levels of devotion and these could be reached by the recitation of special prayers

---

59   Baer, *Seder*, pp. 77–79; *Oṣar Ha-Tefillot*, pp. 129a–131b; Elbogen, *Gottesdienst*, G, pp. 61–67, H, pp. 47–54, E, pp. 54–62; Jacobson, *Netiv*, 1, pp. 233–35. For the above references, see n. 21. See also the reference to the *qedushah de-sidra* in an earlier section of this chapter on 'The Early Prayer-books'.
60   E. G. Chazon, 'The *qedushah* liturgy and its history in light of the Dead Sea scrolls' and M. Idel, 'The *qedushah* and the observation of the heavenly chariot' in *From Qumran to Cairo: Studies in the History of Prayer*, ed. J. Tabory (Jerusalem, 1999), pp. 7–17 (English section) and pp. 7–15 (Hebrew section).
61   L. Ginzberg, *Geonica* (2 vols; New York, 1909), 2.48–53 and *Genizah Studies in Memory of Doctor Solomon Schechter* 2 (New York, 1929), pp. 544–73; J. Mann, 'Les "Chapitres" de Ben Bâboi et les relations de R. Yehoudaï Gaon avec la Palestine', *REJ* 70 (1920), pp. 113–48; S. Spiegel, '*Lefarashat ha-pulmus shel Pirqoy ben Baboy*' in the Hebrew section of the *Harry Austryn Wolfson Jubilee Volume* (Jerusalem, 1965), pp. 243–74; E. Fleischer, 'The diffusion of the *qedushshot* of the *'amidah* and the *yozer* in the Palestinian Jewish ritual', *Tarbiz* 38 (1969), pp. 255–84; *Siddur R. Saadja Gaon* (see n. 25 above), pp. 36–37; Petuchowski, *Prayerbook Reform* (see n. 31 above), pp. 59, 69, 81, 85, 88, 92, 196–97 and 209.

and biblical verses. These latter were often borrowed from the Psalms
but it was not always the actual content and simple sense that was
being used. The number, the enunciation and the special combination
of certain letters was held to have a mystical effect and the belief was
that the first letter of each verse recited could contribute to this effect.
Verses were added to prayers in order to strengthen their potency and
were incorporated into amulets to protect the living and to entreat for
the souls of the dead.[62] If, for example, verses from Lamentations 3:56,
Psalms 119:106, 122, 162, 66 and 108 were recited before the sounding
of the *shofar*, the relevant letters made up a Hebrew phrase that invited
a diminution of Satan's powers.[63]

Psalms for special days

The *siddur* also contains biblical chapters and verses which, though not
as central as those noted earlier, were placed there for more contextual
reasons. On the sabbath, obvious choices were Psalms 92 and Exodus
31:16–17, on *Hanukkah* it was logical to opt for Psalms 30, the sounding
of the *shofar* could be introduced by Psalms 47, and the themes of
Psalms 24, Psalms 27 and Psalms 130 matched the mood of the days
before and after New Year and the Day of Atonement. Since there was
a rabbinic tradition that claimed that certain Psalms (Psalms 24, 48, 82,
94–95, 81 and 93) had been recited in the Temple on particular days of
the week, it was natural to follow such an alleged precedent, although
it is not clear that such a ritual had been adopted in the daily version of
the earliest talmudic liturgy (Mishnah, *Tamid* 7.4).[64] Authorities, such as
the early medieval *Seder Rav Amram*, noted objections to the tendency
to extend the use of these Psalms beyond the morning services, on the
grounds that although the incense – details of which are also included
at the end of the service – was offered in the Temple morning and
evening, the relevant Psalm was recited only in the morning.[65]

---

62 For further discussion, see Reif, *Hebrew Prayer* (see n. 33 above), pp. 173–75 and 240–
   47, and M. Idel, *Kabbala: New Perspectives* (New Haven and London, 1988), pp. 156–99
   and *Messianic Mystics* (New Haven and London, 1998), pp. 104–6, 141, 174, 229–33;
   and see n. 30 above.
63 *Oṣar Ha-Tefillot*, p. 523b; see also Jacobson, *Netiv*, 5.114–16. Baer, *Seder* (see n. 21
   above, p. 394) makes no mention of this custom while Elbogen (G, p. 391, H, p. 289,
   E, p. 294) regards it as a mockery of true prayer ('einen Hohn auf jeden echten
   Gottesdienst'). For the above references, see n. 21. For a different set of verses, see
   Gaster, *Prayer* (see n. 15 above) 2, p. 110.
64 *Soferim* (see n. 20 above), ed. Higger, 18.2–4, 11 (ed. Slotki, 18.1–3 and 19.2). I am not
   wholly convinced by P. L Trudinger's acceptance of such a custom as reliably dating
   from the Second Temple period (*The Psalms of the Tamid Service*, Leiden, 2004).
65 Mishnah, *Tamid* 7.4; *Seder Rav Amram*, ed. N. Coronel (Warsaw, 1865), p. 14b; ed. A.

Miscellaneous addition of verses

The study (subsequently no more than the recitation) of passages from talmudic literature, to which was appended a special doxology entitled *Qaddish*, inevitably provided an opportunity of citing verses that stressed the importance of Torah and the eternal bliss its study was said to guarantee. Among such texts were Deuteronomy 33:4, Isaiah 42:21 and 60:21, Psalms 29:11, Proverbs 3:17–18, 18:10 and 9:11. [66] When the custom arose of inserting supplicatory prayers after the recitation of the morning *'amidah*, there were many verses, especially from Psalms, that were regarded as suitable for such a context and both Psalms 6 (or Psalms 25) and the Thirteen Divine Attributes (Exodus 34:6–7) were pressed into service.[67] At nightfall, God's protection was invoked by the recitation of such verses as Psalms 20:10, 46:8, 78:38, 84:13, and 134:1–3. Verses from Exodus 15 (e.g. 11 and 18) were obviously appropriate for the theme of the redemption from Egypt.[68] The domestic rituals that preceded the sabbath meals and marked its conclusion (*qiddush* and *havdalah*), though they began as purely popular rabbinic customs, fairly distinct from anything in the Hebrew Bible, eventually attracted to themselves the addition of verses regarded as relevant to the topic or to the atmosphere.[69]

New prayers

One of the trends that was typical of the Palestinian Jewish communities of the pre-Crusader period was to follow up references to past events in the Jewish religious experience with hopes for similar developments in the future. Although such a liturgical expansion met

---

L. Frumkin (Jerusalem, 1912), p. 164b; ed. D. Hedegård (Lund, 1951), p. 57 (Hebrew), pp. 134–35 (English); ed. E. D. Goldschmidt (Jerusalem, 1971), p. 40.

66 *Oṣar Ha-Tefillot*, p. 368b; Gaster, *Prayer*, 1, p. 58; Jacobson, *Netiv*, 2, pp. 259–60. For the above references, see n. 21.
67 Baer, *Seder*, pp. 223 and 590; *Oṣar Ha-Tefillot*, pp. 203a and 192a; Elbogen, *Gottesdienst*, G, pp. 76–77, 128, 200 and 222, H, pp. 60–61, 97, 149 and 166, E, pp. 68–69, 107, 160 and 177–78.; Gaster, *Prayer*, 1.39 and 44; Jacobson, *Netiv*, 1.351 and 3.466. For the above references, see n. 21.
68 Baer, *Seder*, pp. 86, 163 and 167–69; *Oṣar Ha-Tefillot*, pp. 146b–47b, 266b–267b and 271b; Elbogen, *Gottesdienst*, G, pp. 22–26 and 99–106, H, pp. 17–20 and 76–81, E, pp. 21–24 and 85–90; Gaster, *Prayer*, 1.67 and 69; Jacobson, *Netiv*, 1.257–60, 402–3 and 409. For the above references, see n. 21.
69 Baer, *Seder*, pp. 197–98 and 311–12; *Oṣar Ha-Tefillot*, pp. 318b and 430ab; Elbogen, *Gottesdienst*, G, pp. 107–112 and 120–22, H, pp. 82–86 and 91–93, E, pp. 91–95 and 101–3; Jacobson, *Netiv*, 2.127 and 388. For the above references, see n. 21.

with the opposition of those authorities who preferred the prayers to deal with one discrete theme at a time, it was broadly adopted in a number of instances and in those cases the hope for the ideal future was tied to the citation of a biblical verse that might be interpreted as having predicted it.[70] Where novel prayers were introduced into the liturgy in the late medieval and early modern period, biblical verses were added to them in order to give them a more authentic flavour and an additional degree of authority. In the case of the prayer for the secular ruler, use was made of Psalms 144:10, Psalms 145:13, Isaiah 43:16, and Jeremiah 23:6, but a glance at the total original contexts of each of these verses reveals an emphasis on God's supreme power and the ultimate kingdom of David rather than on their temporal equivalents.[71]

The English Chief Rabbinate's prayer-book of 1890 included a number of new prayers for such *rites de passage* as childbirth, charity collection, the house of mourning, and taking up residence in a new house, as well as some for young children to recite. All of these were richer in Psalms and other scriptural quotations than they were in traditional liturgical phraseology.[72] The same philosophy was adopted by those in the progressive movements when they formulated new pieces of liturgy for events and circumstances that had previously lacked them.[73] Twentieth-century prayers introduced in communities of various religious hues for the State of Israel and its Defense Forces, though less biblically dominated, also incorporate such verses as Deuteronomy 20:4 and 30:3–5, and the last part of Isaiah 2:3. Here too, the earlier tension between subservience to biblical quotations and the use of newer liturgical language and forms is evident.[74] The clear indication is that the biblical quotation, though by no means ubiquitous, continues to be indispensable.

---

70   A good example is the *ge'ulah* benediction immediately before the *'amidah* in the morning service; see Baer, *Seder*, p. 86; *Oṣar Ha-Tefillot*, p. 147b; Elbogen, *Gottesdienst*, G, pp. 22–26 , H, pp. 17–20, E, pp. 21–24; Jacobson, *Netiv*, 1.259–60. For the above references, see n. 21.

71   B. Schwartz, '*Hanoten Teshua*. The origin of the traditional Jewish prayer for the government', *HUCA* 57 (1986), pp. 113–20.

72   *The Authorised Daily Prayer Book* (see n. 4 above), pp. 300–303, 311–13 and 322–26.

73   E.g. *Siddur Lev Chadash: Services and Prayers for Weekdays and Sabbaths, Festivals and Various Occasions*, eds J. D. Rayner and C. Stern (London, 1995), pp. 533–611.

74   See *Siddur Rinat Yisrael*, ed. Shelomo Tal (Jerusalem, 1970), pp. 274 and 278, and *Siddur Tefillah* published by Koren (Jerusalem, 1982), pp. 185 and 188.

6

Priesthood in Early Sources

Introduction

The definition of 'early Jewish' is admittedly something of a hot theological potato, arguments for its chronological parameters ranging from as late as the early Christian centuries to as early as the second pre-Christian millennium. Whichever view is taken, it is impossible to understand early Jewish and rabbinic notions without making brief reference to the canonical Hebrew Bible that is the source of all such later ideas. This is not, of course, to say that there is no ideological and practical evolution in the religious ideas and practice, merely to stress that the course of that evolution cannot be safely traced without seeking at least a part of its origins in the Hebrew Bible. This is particularly true in the case of priesthood since it undoubtedly had a high profile in the Hebrew Bible. The object here will therefore be to begin by describing that profile both for its own sake and in order to understand what occurred in Jewish religious history in subsequent periods, before moving on to consider some later aspects of the priesthood's religious and historical development in various Jewish contexts.[1]

Background in the Hebrew Bible

It is widely presupposed in the Hebrew Bible that the priest enjoys a central role in matters relating to the cult. Although this function may perhaps have been allocated in earlier times to heads of families, first-born sons, royalty and a number of shrines, this was not the situation in the biblical documents that reflect what might be called the more

---

1   The inspiration for this broad survey arose out of a kind invitation by Dr Margaret Barker and Dr George Bebawi to lecture at a seminar on 'Concepts of the Priesthood in Early Jewish and Christian Sources' arranged by them for the Centre for Advanced Religious and Theological Studies at the Faculty of Divinity in the University of Cambridge and held on 24 September, 2001. The first draft was prepared while I was a Fellow of the Center for Advanced Judaic Studies at the University of Pennsylvania in Philadelphia, September–December 2001. I am most grateful to the Center, its Director Professor David Ruderman, and his dedicated staff, for this welcome appointment and for their generous assistance.

standard legislation and what ultimately proved to be the successful
theology. In such sources the function is reserved for a particular
dynasty, with eponymous ancestors such as Aaron, Zadok and
Melchizedek, and relates to the Temple in Jerusalem. The priest is
formally appointed and mediates for Israel by way of the sacrificial
ceremonies and other liturgical functions. He enjoys distinct privileges,
including a holy status, access to the sacred site, sacramental clothing,
the gift of parts of the offerings, the receipt of special tithes, and the
right to dispense oracles and to pronounce the divine blessing on the
people (Numbers 6:22–27). At the same time, he is required to maintain
a ritual purity and to avoid contact with impurity such as that
represented by dead bodies, and suffers other significant restrictions,
among them marital limitations, and the prohibition of alcohol while
functioning ritually. These advantages and disadvantages are
especially enhanced in the case of the כהן גדול or 'high priest'.[2]

The priest also has functions that are performed outside the
Jerusalem Temple, although it may be argued that some of them have
their origins in the cultic setting. He operates, for instance, in various
contexts as a physician, judge, teacher and charity worker. Whenever
any allusion is made to the religious hierarchy of ancient Israel, the
assumption is that the priest has a major role. There are times when
there is undoubtedly tension and competition between him on the one
side and the king, the prophet and/or the sage on the other.[3] He does
not always come out of this successfully but the continuity of the
theological system cannot be maintained without his significant
participation. As a result of this dominant role, the literature and the
ideology of the Hebrew Bible are permeated with practices and ideas
that have their origins in priestly circles and are strongly promoted by
their members. The notion of turning Israel into what is called 'a
priestly kingdom and a sacred nation' is one of the best and most
succinct examples.[4] Scholars do not always agree about which precisely
are to be counted among such priestly practices and ideas, and about

---

2   For useful treatments of the priesthood and its significance in the biblical period, see
    the entries under כהן by J. Bergman, H. Ringgren and W. Dommerhausen in the
    Theological Dictionary of the Old Testament, eds H. Ringgren, G. J. Botterweck and H.-J.
    Fabry, vol. 7 (E. T., D. E. Green, Grand Rapids, 1995), pp. 60–75, and Richard D.
    Nelson, *Raising Up a Faithful Priest: Community and Priesthood in Biblical Theology*
    (Louisville, Ky, 1993).
3   Examples of verses are: Judges 17:10: והיה לי לאב ולכהן; Jeremiah 32:32: אשר עשו להכעסני
    מלכיהם שריהם כהניהם ונביאיהם; Lamentations 2:6: וינאץ בזעם אפו מלך וכהן ; see also Jeremiah
    6:13 and 23:34. For a number of important essays on such tensions, see *The Priests in
    the Prophets: The Portrayal of Priests, Prophets and other Religious Specialists in the Latter
    Prophets*, eds L. L. Grabbe and A. O. Bellis (Edinburgh, 2005).
4   ממלכת כוהנים וגוי קדוש (Exodus 19:6).

the range of their influence in the many centuries during which the Hebrew Bible was being composed and transmitted, but none would seriously propose that they are anything but centrally important.

Second Temple period

Though mostly still part of the period covered by the Hebrew Bible, the age that ranged from the fifth century BCE to the first century CE saw some significant developments in the matter of the priesthood that need to be noted, however briefly, in this overview. In such areas as music and song, a more organized and specified role evolved for the levites as the priests' assistants in the Temple. The liturgical role of the priests appears to have expanded from the sacrifice itself, which had, if any, a very limited connection with prayer recitation, to broader Temple activities, including some interchange with the people in attendance. This also seems to have evolved into a leading activity within the proto-synagogal context that included Torah education and the performance of other biblical precepts. The increased political activity of the priests led to the emergence of what may justifiably (even if a trifle anachronistically) be called a sect or a party. One of the consequences was the possibility of combining, at times, the priestly and royal functions, even when this met with strong opposition in some quarters. The priesthood also acquired a social, economic and cultural status that was highly conservative about the retention of biblical status and privileges but did not necessarily have a negative view about participation in aspects of life that had been imported into Judea from the Greek and Roman worlds.[5] This led to various responses on the part of other groups and the present discussion will limit itself to the two that are the most widely familiar and best documented, namely, those of Qumran and the Rabbis. Early Jewish-Christianity had its own response too but this is for description and evaluation in another context.[6]

5　For religio-historical background, as understood through different approaches, see L. L. Grabbe, *Judaic Religion in the Second Temple Period: Belief and Practice from the Exile to Yavneh* (London and New York, 2000), pp. 129–49; S. Safrai and M. Stern (eds), *The Jewish People in the First Century: Historical Geography, Political History, Social, Cultural and Religious Life and Institutions* (2 vols; Assen and Philadelphia, 1974–76), 2.561–630 (M. Stern); E. P. Sanders, *Judaism: Practice and Belief 63 BCE – 66CE* (London and Philadelphia, 1992), pp. 77–102 and 170–89.

6　See Margaret Barker, *The Great High Priest: The Temple Roots of Christian Liturgy* (London and New York, 2003).

Qumran

What is meant here by Qumran is the literature that has been discovered in and around that area in the course of the past half-century and more. The intention here is not to enter into the argument about whether that group represented one definable and identifiable form of Judaism. It is rather to refer to the ideas found in the texts that were regarded by the group as religiously important enough to use and preserve.[7] Just as in the Hebrew Bible, the priest occurs in these texts as instructor, judge and supervisor but there are important expansions. First of all, there are clear indications of a breakaway from the Jerusalem priesthood and a rejection of the Temple as then constituted and administered. Qumran's own priesthood is legitimized and that of Jerusalem execrated and regarded as expelled. The notion of sacrifice has therefore to be spiritualized and the role of the priest channelled into other areas of activity in the present time and into a heavenly function in the future.

At Qumran, the priest takes a leading part in the sect's renewal of the covenant and its reception of new members, in the Torah education of the sect, and in the sacral features of the communal meal. His ritual responsibility for pronouncing blessings on Israel is expanded but, interestingly, he has to share a judicial role with the levites and the Israelites. The continuing ideological (or, perhaps, theoretical) importance of the priesthood for Qumran is demonstrated by the existence of an angelic priesthood in some of its liturgical texts and a priestly messiah in its eschatology. Significantly, that messiah takes precedence over his royal counterpart. In sum, then, the broadening of the notion of priesthood is accompanied by its greater spiritualization and perhaps, as a consequence, by a diminution of its practical power. Schiffman does indeed identify a gradual weakening of priestly power as the sect develops over the three centuries of its existence.[8]

Talmudic comments on the past

Bearing in mind the chronological, geographical, linguistic and thematic range of talmudic-midrashic comment and the difficulty of

---

7   See the entry 'Priests' by Robert A. Kugler in *Encyclopedia of the Dead Sea Scrolls*, eds
     L. H. Schiffman and J. C. VanderKam (Oxford and New York, 2000), pp. 688–93, and
     'High Priests' by D. K. Falk, pp. 361–64.
8   L. H. Schiffman, *Reclaiming the Dead Sea Scrolls: the History of Judaism, the Background
     of Christianity, the Lost Library of Qumran* (Philadelphia, 1994), index, p. 523.

identifying the origins of each statement, what researchers therefore have to do in cases such as this is to try to give an overview of the relevant sources without always committing themselves to the establishment of precise historical attributions. Given that important qualification, the first point to be made is that there are some apparently old statements that reflect an early rabbinic or proto-rabbinic dissatisfaction with the ethical, political and cultic activities of the priesthood during the Second Temple Period. There are passages that attribute violence, corruption and greed to the priesthood and that are severely critical of the Hasmoneans for taking over the high priesthood to which their family was not entitled ('Be satisfied with the royal crown and leave the high priesthood to the appropriate descendants of Aaron').[9]

Other talmudic statements appear to decry priestly tendencies to be over zealous in the application of Torah legislation, a characteristic (it is claimed) that will not be found in Elijah the Prophet when he heralds the arrival of the messianic age. The early tannaitic sources (say, from about the second century) report that the Tetragrammaton was originally pronounced in its authentic and original way by the high priests (there is some doubt as to whether this refers to the Holy of Holies on Yom Kippur or, more simply, the priestly blessing) but that this was changed when the standard of behaviour became too low, presumably on the part of the priests in the Temple.[10]

Continuing in the area of liturgy, seven of the original eight benedictions reported to have been recited by the high priest in the Temple have their equivalents, or even direct parallels, in the later rabbinic prayers while one of them, which is said to have concluded הבוחר בכהנים ('You are praised, Lord...for choosing the priests'), has disappeared in its own right and been absorbed into a benediction on the theme of peace, which constitutes the final blessing of the 'amidah, despite the fact that it continues to include the full text of the priestly benediction. Indeed, the Palestinian Talmud states categorically that one can have an 'amidah without the priestly benediction but no such a benediction without an 'amidah.[11] Richard A. Henshaw's claim that 'with the capture of the Temple in 70 CE the cultic function of the priesthood ceased, although priestly families continued to bless the people in synagogue service' cannot be described as anything but a considerable over-simplification.[12]

---

9   Tosefta, Yoma 1.12 and Menaḥot 13.21; BT, Pesaḥim 57b, Yoma 71b and Qiddushin 66a.

10   Mishnah, 'Eduyot 8.3 and 8.7; PT, Yoma 3.7 (40d); BT, Qiddushin 71a.

11   Mishnah, Soṭah 7.7 and Yoma 7.1; PT, Yoma 7.1 (44b) and Ta'anit 4.1 (67b).

12   In Eerdman's Dictionary of the Bible ed. D. N. Freedman (Grand Rapids, Michigan and Cambridge, UK, 2000), p. 1083.

Talmudic comments on the present

The combination in rabbinic Judaism's central rabbinic prayer, the
'amidah, of these two elements – one concerning the priestly benediction
and the other more broadly relating to the rabbinic theology of shalom –
may reflect a tension about the status of the priesthood in the amoraic
period. The question that faced the talmudic scholars was whether the
rights and privileges of the priest should continue or were in one way
or another to be taken over by the rabbis.[13] The theological expression
of this conundrum occurs in the notion that Israel is blessed with three
crowns, the crown of Torah, the crown of priesthood and the crown of
kingship ('but the crown of a good name is greater than all of them').[14]
On the more practical, halakhic side, it should be borne in mind that
the earliest rabbis or proto-rabbis emulated the example of the priests
with regard to the adoption of special strictness regarding ritual purity
and the maintenance of separate religious identity, as set out in Exodus
19:6. Although there appears to have been wide agreement that direct
Torah legislation regarding ritual contamination by the dead and the
prohibition about marriage with a divorcee remained in their place,
there are interesting references to the temporary suspension of the
former in special circumstances.[15] About other matters there was also
some serious discussion. Priests are declared to be 'the representatives
of the Merciful One', are credited with being enthusiastic about
everything they do, and are accorded the honours of being called first
to read the Torah, of leading the recitation of the grace after meals, and
of having first choice of whatever good things are being offered.[16] Some
of the teachers appear to take a special delight in priestly lineage,
perhaps in response to the Exilarch's claims about his own descent
from the davidic dynasty, and value highly marriage into a priestly
family. Further indications that the Babylonian teachers had a more
favourable view of priesthood, or a greater interest in it, may be found
in their compilation of a talmudic tractate on qodashim and their
familiarity with the Sifra midrash on Leviticus.[17]

---

13   On the struggle, see C. Hezser, The Social Structure of the Rabbinic Movement in Roman
     Palestine (Tübingen, 1997), pp. 480–89 and M. S. Jaffee, Torah in the Mouth: Writing
     and Oral Tradition in Palestinian Judaism 200 BCE to 400 CE (Oxford, 2001), pp. 65–67.
14   Mishnah, Avot 4.2.
15   PT, Berakhot 3.1 (6a) and BT, Berakhot 19b.
16   BT, Yoma 19a, Shabbat 20a, Giṭṭin 59b.
17   See I. Sonne, 'The paintings of the Dura Synagogue', HUCA 20 (1947), pp. 268–72
     and G. Herman, Ha-Kohanim Be-Bavel Bi-Tequfat Ha-Talmud: Zekhuyot Yeter U-
     Ma'amad Ḥevrati (M.A. dissertation; Hebrew University of Jerusalem, 1998), as cited

On the other hand, there are statements about priests being congenitally stubborn and about the entitlement of the rabbinic teachers to claim at least the same rights as those traditionally granted to the priests.[18] Two mishnaic passages (from at least as early as the second century) warrant particular attention. The first is a piece of advice in the name of the contemporary of Jesus, Hillel, that calls upon Jews to be disciples of Aaron by loving and pursuing peace; here there may be a hidden polemic that implies 'you do not need to be of the *seed of Aaron* to have high standards, only to follow his best qualities.'[19] The other passage lists priorities in matters of Jewish status beginning with the priest and working downwards via the levite, the ordinary Jew, the *mamzer* or illegitimate Jew, the Temple servant, the proselyte and the freed slave. Having made that prioritization, it then has second thoughts, probably reflecting an alternative view, and argues that all this is dependent on equal knowledge of Torah. If that is not to be presupposed, the situation is different and, for instance, an illegitimate scholar takes precedence over an ignorant high priest![20] There are two interesting midrashic comments that would seem to constitute polemics against those claiming a wider availability of priesthood than that previously approved by Judaism. One of them rejects the notion that priesthood comes from Melchizedek and restricts it to the progeny of Abraham, thus taking issue with early Christian exegesis. A second explains that the rebellion of Korah against Moses was based on his desire for the priesthood to be available to everyone and not exclusively to the family of Moses and Aaron, i.e. the tribe of Levi.[21]

With regard to the status of the priest among the early liturgical poets of the late Byzantine period in the land of Israel (some of whom are known to have been priests themselves), recent research has pointed out that they demonstrate a distinct tendency to restore the central significance of both the Temple ritual and those who had carried it out. The Yom Kippur *'avodah* was re-enacted in the synagogue by way of special compositions and their dramatic recitation not only by cantor-poets but also specifically by those of them who were priests. This undoubtedly amounted to an expression of greater interest in Temple matters and an attempt to restore the priest's liturgical role and consequently brought about something of a rehabilitation of the

in J. L. Rubenstein, *The Culture of the Babylonian Talmud* (Baltimore and London, 2002), pp. 88–90.

18   BT, *Qiddushin* 70b and *Nedarim* 62ab.
19   Mishnah, *Avot* 1.12.
20   Mishnah, *Horayot* 3.8.
21   BT, *Nedarim* 32b and *Bereshit Rabbah* 55.7, ed. Theodor-Albeck, 2.592, on which see E. Kessler, *Bound by the Bible: Jews, Christians and the Sacrifice of Isaac* (Cambridge, 2004), pp. 52–55; BT, *Sanhedrin* 110a.

priesthood in at least some rabbinic circles. Also of relevance to the late talmudic and immediately post-talmudic period is the fact that archaeological discoveries have testified to a considerable interest in Temple and priesthood on the part of Jewish builders and artists. Motifs relating to both these topics, and representing various activities associated with each of them, are to be found among the pieces of physical evidence uncovered in recent years.[22]

Medieval priestly benediction

As is well known, the post-talmudic or geonic period – that is, the period between the seventh and eleventh centuries – saw a serious attempt to transform the variety, the elasticity and the trend towards the dialectic rather than the dogmatic that had become characteristic of the late talmudic period. The preference was now for centralization, authority and clear guidance and this affected the liturgical area as much as any other area of religious activity. One of the questions that arose was the role of the priest in the daily worship. Was he always to recite the priestly blessing that is included within the final benediction of the 'amidah, or was the prayer-leader to substitute for him at times, and, if so, on which precise occasions? It would seem that in the land of Israel the tendency was to allow him a continued privilege on such occasions as fast-days and completely to omit the recitation of the benediction on weekdays. In Iraq, on the other hand, there were moves towards restricting the privilege at some services on fast-days and allowing the prayer-leader to recite it at the daily service, perhaps thereby moving towards a liturgy more centrally controlled by the prayer-leader.[23]

The argument continued into the later medieval period and indeed into more modern times. Those arguing for the priests' special right to recite the benediction could point simply to the biblical origins, the Temple background, and the associated rabbinic benediction. The

22   L. I. Levine, *The Ancient Synagogue: The First Thousand Years* (New Haven and London, 2000), pp. 491–500; J. Yahalom, *Az Be'eyn Kol: Priestly Palestinian Poetry: A Narrative Liturgy for the Day of Atonement* (Hebrew; Jerusalem, 1996), p. 56; E. Fleischer, *Hebrew Liturgical Poetry in the Middle Ages* (Hebrew; Jerusalem, 1975), p. 175; M. Swartz, 'Ritual about myth about ritual', *Journal of Jewish Thought and Philosophy* 6 (1997), pp. 135–55, and 'Sage, priest and poet: typologies of religious leadership in the ancient synagogue' in *Jews, Christians, and Polytheists in the Ancient Synagogue: Cultural Interaction during the Greco-Roman Period*, ed. Steven Fine (London and New York, 1999), pp. 101–17; and S. Fine, 'Between liturgy and social history: priestly power in late antique synagogues?', *JJS* 56 (2005), pp. 1–9.
23   L. A. Hoffman, *The Canonization of the Synagogue Service* (Notre Dame and London, 1979), pp. 54 and 110–13.

opposition, for its part, did not express itself as rejecting these elements as such since they were unassailably authoritative. What it did was to find reasons that might disqualify the priests. They were no longer ritually pure; they did not enjoy the correct frame of mind (שמחה); the ceremony lengthened the service and this constituted a kind of public nuisance (טרחא דציבורא), or a waste of time (ביטול תורה) needed for Torah study; there were services that were more suitable than others for a recitation specifically by the priests rather than by the prayer-leader, e.g. those with a public reading of scripture, or with an additional (מוסף) service, or the major festivals.[24] Interestingly, the tendency to limit the priestly recitation of the benediction in the synagogue was more pronounced in the Jewish communities of Christian countries than in those that existed under Islam and one could speculate about underlying reasons for this. The trend may have been polemically motivated and have originated in the sphere of the institutional and organizational. That is to say, giving the priest a central role was too much like Christianity or there was a preference for the prayer-leader to be given virtually exclusive control of the synagogue service. In the modern period of Jewish history, following emancipation and enlightenment, progressive movements made changes that were motivated by considerations other than the strict application of Jewish religious law. The synagogal ritual was altered to bring greater decorum, more vernacular, less elitism, a more ceremonial clergy, and an atmosphere that could be favourably compared with major Christian worship. In that context, the priests were deprived of their role in almost all areas and even some modern Orthodox communities of the nineteenth and early twentieth centuries accepted certain such limitations, eliminating the priests' recitation of the blessing from Numbers in the synagogal liturgy. In a number of British synagogues under the authority of the Chief Rabbi, such a recitation was re-introduced in the second half of the twentieth century.[25]

Medieval halakhic position

It will be recalled that the Talmud records three primary privileges accorded by the rabbinic halakhah to the priests, namely, to read the Torah first, to lead the grace after meals, and to have first choice when

---

24   Eric (Yitschak) Zimmer, 'Mo'adey nesi'at kappayim', Sinai 100 (1987), pp. 452–70.
25   On aspects of the ambivalence in the modern orthodox prayer-book towards the recitation of the priestly benediction by the priests themselves, rather than by the prayer-leader, see S. C. Reif, Judaism and Hebrew Prayer: New Perspectives on Jewish Liturgical History (Cambridge, 1993), pp. 286 and 305.

good things are being offered. Unsurprisingly, therefore, the medieval halakhic authorities include this ruling in their codes, but they do not generally appear to treat the subject of the priests as an independent topic, including it when it is relevant to other areas such as liturgy. They do, of course, take it for granted that biblical legislation about contact with corpses and non-marriage with a divorcee (and the matter of the redemption of the first born) still applies. What we are seeing here is, on the one hand, a halakhic acceptance of the fact that the fuller role of the priest can be re-activated only in the messianic age when the Temple is restored and, on the other, a preference not to legislate for such speculative matters.[26]

The exception to this is Maimonides who, for various reasons, included in his code everything relating to Judaism, including cultic and messianic matters. He therefore devoted part of his *Mishneh Torah* to the sacred utensils of the Temple and to the status of those who use them. He distinguishes between priests and levites and counts it as a positive precept to grant the priests their special status both inside and outside the Temple. Jews are obliged to offer them special honour, to offer them priority in all sacred matters, including those three rights mentioned in the Talmud. What is rather fascinating is that, in connection with the priests, he includes in his code the kind of medical matter originating in the Talmud that he often omits if he, as a contemporary physician, disapproves of it.[27] Basing himself on a passage in the Talmud Yerushalmi, he notes that because the priests in the Temple stood on the cold floor, ate a great deal of meat, and had scanty clothing, they suffered stomach problems.[28] A special medical officer had therefore to be appointed to attend to their physical needs and this is duly codified by him. Even more interestingly, the item about scanty clothing is inserted by Maimonides himself while he omits the next section which explains that some wines can cure the medical problem while others cannot.

Some halakhic authorities tended to make a distinction between the priests as they were in biblical times and as they will again be in messianic times on the one hand, and priests of their own day on the other. If it was a fact that their direct genealogical descent could no

---

26 See the useful and concise summary of the halakhic position and sources by G. J. Blidstein in the *Encyclopaedia Judaica*, vol. 13, cols 1088–89 and in J. D. Eisenstein's *Ozar Yisrael* (Hebrew: third edition; ed. Shapiro, Vallentine, London, 1935), p. 259. See also S. Emanuel, 'The responsa of R. Meir of Rothenburg – Prague edition', *Tarbiz* 57 (1988), p. 561.

27 Maimonides, *Mishneh Torah, Kley Ha-Miqdash* 4.1–2 and 7.14; E. T., *The Code of Maimonides. Book Eight. The Book of Temple Service*, trans. M. Lewittes (New Haven and London, 1957), pp. 53 and 68.

28 PT, *Sheqalim* 5.2 (48d).

longer be guaranteed, then their entitlements could at best be no more than customary usage rather than legal requirement and at worst might even be denied to them in some circumstances. The matter did, however, remain controversial and other halakhists were unhappy about such an interpretation.[29] What we are again here witnessing is a stance against the maintenance of priestly privileges that seeks to hide behind arguments other than the rational and radical, and to seek halakhic justification for changes in priestly status. Once more, the modern movements were more direct about their revolutionary proposals. Remarkably, recent genetic research has established that a high percentage of those Jews claiming priestly descent have common genetic factors and that these may be traced back to the seventh or eight century BCE.[30]

Medieval reality

There are some interesting facts about the priests, how they were treated, and how they conducted themselves, in the various medieval sources, especially the fragments from the 'high middle ages' emanating from the Cairo Genizah and mainly to be found at Cambridge University Library.[31] As far as marriage is concerned, there are no records of priests marrying freedwomen (who had the same forbidden status as divorcees) but there is a notorious case of one who, when refused marriage to a divorcee, went off to the Muslim courts and contracted marriage with her there, and was excommunicated by Maimonides for his effrontery.[32] Another case concerns a priest who declared that his wife had not been a virgin when they married and whose children were disqualified as priests by one judge, only to be re-

---

29 See e.g. the rulings (in Hebrew) of Isaac ben Sheshet, *Responsa (She'elot U-Teshuvot Rivash)* (Jerusalem, 1993), no. 94; Samuel ben Moses de Medina, *Responsa (She'elot U-Teshuvot Maharashdam)* (Lemberg, 1862), *Even Ha-'Ezer*, no. 235; Solomon Luria, *Yam Shel Shelomo* (Bnei Braq, 1960), *Bava Qamma* 5, section 35; and Joseph ben Moses Trani, *Responsa (She'elot U-Teshuvot Maharit)* (Lemberg, 1861), section 1, no. 149.

30 See 'Y chromosomes of Jewish priests', *Nature* 385 (2 January, 1997); P. Hirshberg and J. Logan, 'Decoding the priesthood', *Jerusalem Report* (10 May, 1999). Interestingly, the earliest extra-biblical evidence for the priestly benediction is to be found in a silver amulet from the seventh century BCE; see G. Barkay, *Ketef Hinnom. A Treasure Facing Jerusalem's Walls* (Israel Museum, catalogue no. 274, Jerusalem, 1986) and 'The priestly benediction on the Ketef Hinnom plaques' (Hebrew), *Cathedra* 52 (1989), pp. 37–76.

31 For details of the collection, see S. C. Reif, *A Jewish Archive from Old Cairo: The History of Cambridge University's Genizah Collection* (Richmond, Surrey, 2000).

32 S. D. Goitein, *A Mediterranean Society: The Jewish Communities of the Arab World as Portrayed in the Documents of the Cairo Geniza*, 5 vols and index volume (Berkeley, Los Angeles and London, 1967–93), 1.436; vol. 2 (1971), p. 399; vol. 3 (1978), pp. 82–83.

instated later by another. The issue was whether his claim was justified or made in spiteful anger and, if the former, whether this meant that his wife should be defined as immoral i.e. a זונה in the technical sense according to the legal source in Leviticus.[33] Among the recognized ways of honouring the priest, in addition to the talmudic requirements, were wishing him the merit of serving in the restored Temple, asking him to sign documents first, and referring in the liturgy of the relevant sabbath to the priestly watches that once served in the Temple. There was also the custom of making a special cloak for the priest to use when he recited the priestly benediction in the synagogue.[34]

On the other hand, there were times when the power of the priests threatened to get out of hand and applications were made to halakhic authorities for responses to this. In one such instance, the approach was to Hai ben Sherira Gaon (939–1038) in the Iraqi (Babylonian) rabbinic centre of Pumbedita and concerned the behaviour of the Jewish priests of Tunisia, either in that geographical location or in the Holy Land where some of them had settled. The accusation was that organized groups of priests were demanding consumables as priestly dues, assigning to themselves leadership roles, and fomenting controversy in the community. The Gaon's response constituted a strongly worded criticism of their practices. He argued that gifts to the priests could be consumed only in a state of ritual purity (attainable only while the Temple stood) and dictated to them how they should properly behave. His view was that those who failed to behave in an acceptable and modest fashion were providing *prima facie* evidence that their priestly lineage was suspect.[35]

Conclusions

1. The priest was undoubtedly one of the central figures in the political, religious and socio-economic establishment in the period of the Hebrew Bible. The caste appears to have reached the acme of its power at the end of the First Temple period and early in the Second Temple period, i.e. between the seventh and fourth centuries BCE.

---

33   Goitein, *Mediterranean Society* (see n. 32 above), 3.101, where he appears to have mistakenly understood the court's decision to have been made on the basis of the need for virginity (Leviticus 21:13, applicable only to a high priest) when it may in fact have been based on the assumption that if she had been a non-virgin on marriage she must have behaved immorally (Leviticus 21:7, applicable to any priest).

34   Goitein, *Mediterranean Society* (see n. 32 above), 3.426; vol. 4 (1983), p. 196 and vol. 5 (1988), pp. 402 and 620.

35   M. Ben-Sasson, *The Emergence of the Local Jewish Community in the Muslim World: Qayrawan, 800–1057* (Hebrew; Jerusalem, 1997), pp. 169–71.

2. As members of the group tried to wrest exclusive power and influence for themselves during the early Hellenistic period, they created a negative response on the part of some sections of society and alternative families of priests began to re-interpret and spiritualize their role in the present and in the eschatological future, and to broaden the participation of non-priestly Israelites in religious ritual – but the aristocratic families remained dominant at least in Jerusalem.

3. The rise of Christianity and early rabbinic Judaism led to discussions in the earliest rabbinic sources about the status and role of the priest, the rabbi and the ordinary Jew. Although there were both favourable and unfavourable assessments of the priests (perhaps indicating lively differences of opinion), there are discernible tendencies towards the replacement of the priest with the rabbi in educational matters and with the prayer-leader or *hazzan* in the synagogue. At the same time, some of the liturgical poets strove to restore priesthood and Temple matters to the centre of their religious agenda.

4. In the early medieval period, the biblical restrictions were taken for granted and the priest maintained his right to pronounce the priestly benediction in the synagogue and to take precedence in a few limited spheres. In the latter part of the middle ages, however, questions were raised, albeit of a theoretical nature, about the reliability of his genealogical status and his spiritual worthiness. In some communities the priests attempted to restore their power and influence and this led to clashes with halakhic authorities from which the latter emerged victorious.

5. Before the revolutionary religious developments of the modern period, the priest had already, within the traditional halakhic system, been deprived of all but a few ceremonial roles and restrictions. With the rise of the modern progressive movements, even these were abolished in all but orthodox communities. Even in the latter, there were doubts about the priestly role in the nineteenth and early twentieth centuries but these seem to have been widely overcome in more recent decades and a symbolic status restored, especially with a rehabilitation of the priestly benediction.

7

The Theological Significance of the *Shema'*

Introduction

If one tunes into Israeli Radio's popular and secular 'Station 2' at 05.59 on a weekday morning, one is greeted by the mellifluous sound of a confident and reverential voice punctiliously enunciating, in an oriental accent, the Hebrew text of Deuteronomy 6:4–9. Checking the manuscript collections at Cambridge University for the oldest Hebrew papyrus in the world leads one to a brown and barely legible text some 2,200 years old that includes Deuteronomy 6:4.[1] In the course of the twenty-two centuries that separate these two manifestations of interest, Jews have written these and related texts in the forms of inscriptions and amulets, have transcribed them on to parchment for insertion into the *tefillin* (phylacteries) worn during daily worship and into *mezuzot* attached to doorposts, and have recited them in their standard morning and evening prayers. It seems reasonable therefore to conclude that the *shema'*, which acquired its name from the first words of the passage ('hearken, Israel'), has long enjoyed a high reputation as a religiously valuable and versatile piece of Hebrew literature, and that the origins of its popularity are to be sought not only in the axial era that saw the rise of Christianity and rabbinic Judaism but also in the Second Temple period that immediately preceded it. In 1909, Solomon Schechter, who should be credited with major insights into rabbinic thought and religiosity, as well as an eye for precious manuscripts, made a simple but far-reaching statement about this ancient item of Jewish liturgy.[2] His definition was that the *shema'* 'not only contains a metaphysical statement (about the unity of God), but expresses a hope and belief – *for everything connected with this verse has a certain dogmatic value* [my italics – SCR] – in the ultimate universal kingdom of God.'[3] When carefully assessed, Schechter's comment may be seen to be ascribing to the *shema'* theological, liturgical, eschatological and dogmatic importance, covering as it does such weighty topics as the nature of the Divine,

---

1   See below, the section headed 'Extra-biblical evidence'.
2   On Solomon Schechter, see the entry and bibliography in the *Oxford Dictionary of National Biography*, formerly known as the *New Dictionary of National Biography* (Oxford, 2004), 49.207–10.
3   S. Schechter, *Some Aspects of Rabbinic Theology* (London, 1909), p. 64.

optimistic expectations, valuable beliefs and eschatological confidence.
The purpose of this chapter is, having first outlined the function of the
shema' in the traditional Jewish liturgy, to examine the basic sense of
the biblical texts used in the *shema'*, and to trace how they, together
with the Decalogue, came to be utilized by the Jews in the late biblical
and post-biblical periods. Sources will then be cited from early rabbinic
and closely-related contemporary literature that illuminate the
evolving role of the *shema'*. Such an analysis and survey should help to
clarify the degree to which the *shema'* was theologically significant, and
the nature of such significance, in the context of early rabbinic thought.

In order to establish the broader liturgical framework for such
theological developments, a few remarks will first be devoted to the
role of the Hebrew Bible in the history of Jewish prayer traditions and
to the overall development of Jewish liturgical practice in the Second
Temple period. It is undoubtedly the case in rabbinic liturgy that
biblical texts have consistently enjoyed a prominent place, that the
biblical precedent has often been followed in matters of language and
theology, and that personalities and topics familiar from the Hebrew
Bible occur in many of the compositions. As in the biblical model, God
is thanked, praised and entreated, and requests for divine assistance
range widely from the spiritual to the mundane. At the same time, it
should be acknowledged that this extensive use of the Hebrew Bible is
also selective and that, when style and content are being emulated,
preference has tended to be given to later rather than earlier biblical
texts.[4] As far as pre-rabbinic liturgy is concerned, what late biblical
books, the apocryphal and pseudepigraphical works, and the literature
revealed at Qumran have in common is the use of hymns of praise,
supplicatory prayers and benedictions, as well as the occurrence of
words and phrases that are in essence part of the earlier biblical stock
but subsequently take on special forms and meanings. They also share
as central themes in their entreaties the notions of the election of Israel,
the status of Zion, the holiness of Jerusalem, the return of the davidic
dynasty, and the manifestation of God's great power in the present and
in the future. The early rabbinic liturgy adopts these characteristics but,
in the matter of detailed liturgical expression, it champions a fresh
order, style and distinctive formulation.[5]

For the present purpose, what is being defined as the traditional
Jewish liturgy is the collection of standard prayers that were

---

4   See 'The Bible and the synagogue' by Avigdor Shinan, *The Jewish Study Bible*, eds
     Adele Berlin and Marc Zvi Brettler (Oxford and New York, 2004), pp. 1929–37 and
     chapter 5 above.
5   See the collected essays in *Liturgical Perspectives: Prayer and Poetry in Light of the Dead
     Sea Scrolls*, ed. Esther G. Chazon (Leiden and Boston, 2003).

universally adopted and approved by rabbinic communities in talmudic, post-talmudic (= geonic), medieval and early modern times. The basic content of such a liturgy for the daily usage consists of the *shema'* and the *'amidah* for morning and evening services and of the *'amidah* alone for the afternoon services. The sources and development of that state of affairs are in themselves complicated and worthy of attention but need not concern us in the present context. For its part, the *'amidah* is made up of a selection of rabbinic benedictions praising and thanking God and making various basic requests relating to daily life. The *shema'*, on the other hand, is at its core three pentateuchal passages so that it might justifiably be argued that it is not prayer at all but a lectionary. It is, however, introduced and concluded with rabbinic benedictions that provide the liturgical context and flavour for the whole section, and there are two additional phrases, immediately before and after Deuteronomy 6:4, that are not part of the original biblical texts.

The three pentateuchal passages that came to constitute the *shema'* of the early rabbinic liturgy are Deuteronomy 6:4–9, Deuteronomy 11:13–21 and Numbers 15:37–41.[6] Of the two benedictions that precede these three passages, the first concerns the natural world, namely, the change from night to day in the morning prayer and from day to night in the evening prayer, while the second concentrates on the election of Israel and its duty to study and perform the precepts of the Torah. In the morning service, the three passages are followed, before the *'amidah*, by one benediction relating to the redemption of Israel, historically in the Exodus from Egypt, and again in the future in the eschatological context. The evening service adds a second post-*shema'* benediction appealing for God's protection and, according to some rites, there is also a third benediction which, for its part, expands on the themes of redemption and protection and adds to them the subject of God's kingship.[7] In the talmudic and post-talmudic periods, it became

6   See Reuven Kimelman, 'The shema' liturgy: from covenant ceremony to coronation' in *Kenishta: Studies of the Synagogue World*, ed. J. Tabory (Ramat Gan, 2001), pp. 9–105. This lengthy article, which supersedes two earlier published versions, cites many important texts and has some thoughtful insights, a number of which have been particularly useful to me in the preparation of this much briefer and more narrowly focused piece.

7   I. Elbogen, German edition = G, *Der jüdische Gottesdienst in seiner geschichtlichen Entwicklung* (Frankfurt am Main, 1931; reprint, Hildesheim, 1962), pp. 16–26; Hebrew edition = H, התפילה בישראל בהתפתחותה ההיסטורית (eds J. Heinemann, I. Adler, A. Negev, J. J. Petuchowski and H. Schirmann, Tel Aviv, 1972), pp. 12–20; English edition = E, *Jewish Liturgy: A Comprehensive History* (trans. and ed. Raymond P. Scheindlin, Philadelphia, Jerusalem and New York, 1993), pp. 16–24; B. S. Jacobson, *Netiv Binah*, (Hebrew; 5 volumes; Tel Aviv, 1968–73), 1.54–56 and 228–60; J. J.

customary to insert between Deuteronomy 6:4 and 6:5 a eulogy
stressing God's eternal kingship in the form ברוך שם כבוד מלכותו לעולם ועד
(= 'may the name of his glorious kingship be blessed forever and ever'),
and for the individual to precede the first verse with the three words אל
מלך נאמן (= 'God, faithful king') – two customs that will be briefly
discussed later in this article.[8]

Analysis of biblical passages

What, then, of these three passages in their original contexts? What was
the basic sense of the verses? Which phrases are particularly
problematic and which are central? Are there any dominant themes in
each of the passages and how do the latter relate to each other? The
lyrical beginning of the first passage (Deuteronomy 6:4–9) indicates
that a special text is about to be transmitted and the statement about
God is unequivocal about his 'oneness'. Although the remainder of the
passage is addressed to the second person singular, the description of
the Lord in the second phrase is as 'our God' and it is not clear how
that phrase relates to the third phrase. Recent consensus would appear
to prefer to understand the latter as 'the Lord our God is unique'. The
listener is instructed, in a style that has moved away from the direct
imperative of the previous verse, to love God with all possible thought,
passion and 'muchness', that is, of intensity so that all God's words are
constantly on one's mind. Precisely which of God's words are intended
is unclear although the phrase 'which I am commanding you today'
could indicate that the reference is to more than the Decalogue heard at
Sinai, and perhaps even to all the deuteronomic laws and teachings. On
the other hand, we could here be dealing with a later insertion that
deliberately sets out to encourage such a broader understanding. The
transmission of the traditions is to be guaranteed by constant repetition
and by the oral education of children. The divine message is to be
treated as a physical ornament on one's body and is to be publicly
displayed. The interpretations of the original text here range from those
that see such phrases as totally metaphorical to those that presuppose
from an early date the use of amulets or similar media. The overall
message is that Israel, as part of its covenant with God, must subscribe
to the notion of a unique divinity and to a pure form of monotheism.
What perhaps underlies this instruction is a polemic against alternative

---

Petuchowski, 'The liturgy of the synagogue' in *Approaches to Ancient Judaism* 4, ed.
W. S. Green (Chico, 1983), pp. 18–24.
8   See below, the section headed 'Appended rabbinic phrases'.

understandings of divinity. The total devotion to God here demanded of Israel is reminiscent of what was expected in the Ancient Near East of vassals by those who exercised control over them. The context of Deuteronomy 6 is one that revolves around moral exhortation and the lessons of history, and the style is didactic and homiletical. Although the passage is theologically intense, it is not, either in its original essence or in its complete form, greatly different from many other parts of Deuteronomy, nor does it appear to be especially central to that book.[9]

The second passage (Deuteronomy 11:13–21) occurs in a context that deals with the lessons of the historical experience in Egypt and Sinai, the special gift of the land and its successful inheritance, and the expectation of reward and punishment. It repeats the themes of the total devotion of the individual and the people to God, the transmission of God's words by way of intense education, and the instruction to treat them like personal ornaments and public banners. The minor variations from the first passage consist of the inclusion of the notion of serving God as well as loving him, a change in a number of instances from the second person singular to the second person plural, and the replacement of the root שנן, indicating oral repetition, with the root למד in the *pi'el*, constituting a broader term for teaching. So much for verses 13 and 18–19. The remaining verses promise, in addition, that love, obedience and attention to God's commands (not just his words) will lead to agricultural success while the absence of these will bring failure and death. The final verse promises length of days of superhuman (eternal?) quality in the promised land. The overall message here, then, belongs in the field of theodicy and, given the broader context, may fairly be explained as promising reward for correct behaviour and punishment for the opposite, not only on the farm but in the totality of life. It may therefore be regarded as theologically more wide-ranging than that of the first passage.[10] The Talmud Yerushalmi records a most interesting dispute in this connection between two Palestinian rabbis who flourished at the end of the third and the beginning of the fourth centuries.[11] The Babylonian-born Ḥanina could see no essential distinction between the contents of the first two paragraphs and opted for the recitation of only the first,

---

9   See, for example, *The Oxford Bible Commentary*, eds J. Barton and J. Muddiman (Oxford, 2001), 'Deuteronomy' by C. Bultmann, p. 142; *JPS Torah Commentary: Deuteronomy*, compiled by J. H. Tigay (Philadelphia and Jerusalem, 1996), pp. 76–79.

10 Bultmann, 'Deuteronomy' (see n. 9 above), p. 144; Tigay, *Deuteronomy* (see n. 9 above), pp. 113–15.

11 PT, *Berakhot* 2.1 (4a).

while his colleague Ilai saw a subtle distinction between the two and apparently therefore justified the recitation of both:

מה בין פרק ראשון ומה בין פרק שני? הראשון ליחיד והשני לציבור, והראשון לתלמוד והשני למעשה

'What then distinguishes these passages from each other? While the first passage deals with the individual and with Torah study, the second deals with the community and with the performance of the Torah's precepts.'

The third passage (Numbers 15:37–41) is concerned with the permanent precept concerning the attachment of fringes, with blue threads, to every four-cornered garment, which is intended to draw the attention of the wearer to all God's commands and their observance and to cultivate a high degree of sanctity among the Israelites. Strong objection is expressed to any departure from such commands in the direction of more hedonistic pursuits. God identifies himself as the one who brought Israel out of Egypt in order to become their God, adding that He is the Lord, their God. The overall message here not only concerns a physical medium and its religious function, the need for total obedience to God's message, and God's relationship with Israel, all of which have their parallels in the first two passages, but also moves on to the matter of holiness and the avoidance of religious pollution, giving a central role to the rescue of God's people from Egypt.[12]

Comparison with Decalogue

If Rabbinic Judaism's *shema'* is, as Schechter indicated, of theological, liturgical, eschatological and dogmatic importance, with the implication that it is being used in a kind of catechismal fashion, the next question to be addressed is how such a passage, or combination of passages, compares to the more obvious candidate for such a catechismal use, namely, the Decalogue (Deuteronomy 5:6–18). There are certainly some obvious similarities. Both passages occur in the early part of Deuteronomy, refer specifically to themselves as the direct instructions of God, and contain references to the uniqueness of God. They share material that constitutes a warning against idolatry, that stresses the special religious relationship between parents and children, that promises longevity as a reward, and that mentions the Exodus. They may both therefore be regarded as tantamount to summaries of the theological essentials. At the same time, there are significant differences. The passage containing the Decalogue has an obvious integrity as a literary and theological unit, probably from pre-

---

12 *Oxford Bible Commentary* (see n. 9 above), 'Numbers' by T. E. Freitheim, p. 121; *JPS Torah Commentary: Numbers*, compiled by J. Milgrom (Philadelphia and Jerusalem, 1990), pp. 127–28.

pentateuchal times, the style of the Decalogue is apodictic, and the negative precept is dominant even among the more positively expressed commandments. The flavour of the Decalogue is of moral and religious instruction of a general kind rather than detailed practical and ritual law, the exception being the laws relating to the sabbath which may have been expanded from a simpler form. There is no mention of personal relationship with God or of the requirement for total loyalty and devotion, the means of transmission and education are absent, and there are no specific references that tie the contents to social, environmental or chronological circumstances.[13]

What, then, is the evidence for the use of the *shema'* and the Decalogue in the late biblical era and the subsequent Second Temple period? The first point to establish is that there was a familiarity with the texts, or with the same notions as are included in the texts, so that we can exploit such data in assessing the degree to which these passages were more central or more specially significant during those centuries. Regarding the Decalogue, we can point to a number of biblical texts, four of which will be sufficient for our present purposes:[14]

1. Hosea 4:2: אלה וכחש ורצח וגנב ונאף = 'swearing, lying [or breaking one's oaths, or swearing falsely], murdering, stealing and committing adultery';

2. Jeremiah 7:9: הגנב רצח ונאף והשבע לשקר וקטר לבעל והלך אחרי אלהים אחרים = 'stealing, murdering, committing adultery, swearing falsely, offering incense to Baal and following other gods';

3. Psalms 50:7: שמעה עמי ואדברה ישראל ואעידה בך אלהים אלהיך אנכי = 'Listen, my people, and I shall speak, Israel, and I shall testify against you, I am God, your God', with references to stealing, adultery and lying in vv.18–19;

4. Psalms 81:10–11, perhaps the clearest example: לא יהיה בך אל זר ולא תשתחוה לאל נכר. אנכי ה' אלהיך המעלך מארץ מצרים = 'You shall have no other god nor worship any foreign god; I am the Lord, your God, the one raising you out of the land of Egypt.'

Recent research has also argued that there are allusions to the first paragraph of the *shema'* in other biblical texts. According to R. W. L. Moberley, the parallelism between the language in 2 Kings 23:25 and that of Deuteronomy 6:5 indicates that 'Josiah is portrayed as a prime

---

13 *JPS Torah Commentary: Exodus*, compiled by Nahum M. Sarna (Philadelphia and Jerusalem, 1991), pp. 107–15; Tigay, *Deuteronomy* (see n. 9 above), pp. 62–72; M. Weinfeld, *The Decalogue and the Recitation of "Shema": the Development of the Confessions* (Hebrew; Tel Aviv, 2001), pp. 41–98. Weinfeld's volume is rich in source material and full of thought-provoking suggestions and has been most useful for the preparation of this brief study. See also Ephraim E. Urbach, 'The place of the Ten Commandments in ritual and prayer' in *The Ten Commandments as Reflected in Tradition and Literature throughout the Ages*, ed. B.-Z. Segal (Hebrew; Jerusalem, 1985), pp. 127–45 (E. T., ed G. Levi, Jerusalem, 1990, pp. 161–89).

14 Weinfeld, *Decalogue* (see n. 13 above), p. 99.

example of what it means to fulfil the Shema'. Particularly indicative in this connection is the Hebrew phrase in the Kings verse: אשר שב אל ה' בכל לבבו ובכל נפשו ובכל מאדו ככל תורת משה.[15] Paul Overland has pointed to the allusions to Deuteronomy 6:4–9 to be found in Proverbs 3:1–12 and has suggested that the latter text represents a sage's intensification and clarification of the former, in accordance with his own intellectual and religious preferences.[16] According to J. Gerald Janzen's discussion of the word 'eḥad, Deutero-Isaiah 'was preceded and perhaps influenced...by the theological reflection that produced the Shema in Deuteronomy 6:4–5.' He also finds allusions to the shema''s language and theological notions in Jeremiah 32:39–41 and possibly also in Job 23:13 and 31:15, and Daniel 2:9. Perhaps most convincing is Zechariah 14:9, which reads like a theological development of the first verse of the shema': והיה ה' למלך על כל הארץ ביום ההוא יהיה ה' אחד ושמו אחד = 'On the day on which the Lord is [regarded as] king over the whole earth, the Lord will be one and his name one'.[17] An important, general point to be made here is that all these references, or alleged references, to the shema' are to the first paragraph, i.e. Deuteronomy 6:4–9.

Extra-biblical evidence

Some broader background for various aspects of our discussion is also available from the ancient Near East and is noteworthy, although it cannot be recounted in detail in the present limited context.[18] The statement about the Lord who is God that introduces the shema' and the mention of his characteristics amount to a phenomenon known from other ancient Semitic declarations about a god's uniqueness. The requirement for full devotion is familiar from numerous vassal treaties, as is the confirmation that constitutes the first post-shema' liturgical section. The possibility that the tying and the writing referred to in vv. 8–9 are not metaphorical but physical also receives support from the broader Semitic field. One Canaanite text from Ugarit describes how 'on his head tefillin were hanging between his eyes' (and, transcribed

---

15　R. W. L. Moberly, 'Toward an interpretation of the shema' in Theological Exegesis: Essays in Honor of Brevard S. Childs, eds C. Seitz and K. Greene-McCreight (Grand Rapids, Michigan and Cambridge, U.K., 1999), pp. 124–44.

16　P. Overland, 'Did the sage draw from the shema: a study of Proverbs 3:1–12', CBQ 62 (2000), pp. 424–40.

17　J. G. Janzen, 'An echo of the shema in Isaiah 51:1–3', JSOT 43 (1989), pp. 69–82, following up on his earlier study 'On the most important word in the shema (Deuteronomy vi 4–5)', VT 37 (1987), pp. 280–300.

18　The evidence is conveniently brought together by Weinfeld, Decalogue (see n. 13 above), pp. 126–43.

into Hebrew letters, it would read ‏(ראשה תפלי תלי בן עני‏).[19] There is a reference among the Elephantine Papyri to a ‏תפלה די כסף‏[20] and there are ancient Egyptian and Samaritan customs according to which sacred texts were attached to parts of doors.[21] Less convincing but worthy of note is the possibility that the root ‏טטף‏ may be related to the roots ‏טפף‏ and ‏נטף‏ that are used in connection with hanging female jewellery and amulets.[22] More important is the silver amulet found in Ketef Hinnom and dated to the seventh century BCE which contains a version of the priestly benediction to be found in Numbers 6:22–27.[23]

Most significant of all is the famous Nash Papyrus which is housed at Cambridge University Library.[24] Discovered in Egypt early in the twentieth century by the London surgeon, Walter Llewellyn Nash, it was entrusted to two Cambridge scholars to decipher, analyse and publish. Stanley A. Cook, later Regius Professor of Hebrew at the University of Cambridge, and Francis C. Burkitt, subsequently Norrisian Professor of Divinity there, both wrote on the subject and were not wholly in agreement. The Nash Papyrus contains twenty-four lines of square Hebrew containing a text of the Decalogue that is sometimes in agreement with Exodus and sometimes with Deuteronomy and occasionally supports the text presupposed by the Septuagint. Appended to the Decalogue is the first verse of the *shema'*, prefaced by a verse, not found in the Masoretic Text of the Hebrew Bible but similar to that which occurs in the Septuagint:

‏[אלה החקים] והמשפטים אשר צוה משה את [בני] [ישראל] במדבר בצאתם מארץ מצרים‏
'[These are the statutes] and judgements that Moses commanded [the children of Israel] in the desert when they came out of the land of Egypt.'

Cook argued that this is a pre-Masoretic form of the text rather than a lectionary, phylactery, charm or liturgy, and therefore important for the

---

19   RŠ24.245 (=*Ugaritica* V, III, 3) discussed by M. H. Pope and J. H. Tigay, 'A description of Baal', *Ugarit-Forschungen* 3 (1971), p. 118.

20   Bezalel Porten and Ada Yardeni (eds), *Textbook of Aramaic Documents from Ancient Egypt*, vol. 3 (Jerusalem, 1993), p. 260, text C3.28 (Cowley 81), line 106.

21   Graham Davies, 'A Samaritan inscription with an expanded text of the shema'', *PEQ* 131 (1999), pp. 3–19.

22   Weinfeld, *Decalogue* (see n. 13 above), p. 139.

23   G. Barkay, *Ketef Hinnom: A Treasure Facing Jerusalem's Walls* (Catalogue 274; Jerusalem: Israel Museum, 1986) and 'The priestly benediction on the Ketef Hinnom plaques' (Hebrew), *Cathedra* 52 (1989), pp. 37–76.

24   Or. 233, about 14 x 6 cms; for details see S. C. Reif, *Hebrew Manuscripts at Cambridge University Library: A Description and Introduction* (Cambridge, 1997), p. 65 and plate 4. For a bibliography of research on the Nash Papyrus, see *Encyclopaedia Judaica* 12, col. 833; see also M. H. Segal, 'The Nash Papyrus', *Leshonenu* 15 (1947), pp. 27–36, reprinted in his *Masoret U-Viqoret* (Jerusalem, 1957), pp. 227–36, and Reif, 'The Nash Papyrus', *Cambridge* 15 (1984), pp. 41–45. See also Ezra Fleischer, *Eretz-Israel Prayer and Prayer Rituals as Portrayed in the Genizah Documents* (Hebrew; Jerusalem, 1988), pp. 259–74.

textual history of the Hebrew Bible. Burkitt for his part – and I believe his view to be the more sound and better supported by other evidence – opted for a popular pre-rabbinic version used for liturgical purposes and relevant to the history of Jewish religiosity and worship.[25]

Our understanding of the Nash Papyrus was, of course, considerably influenced by the discovery of the Dead Sea Scrolls, and the resultant advances in Hebrew palaeography led to its redating to some two or three centuries earlier. Items found among the scrolls at Qumran included *tefillin* (phylacteries) and *mezuzot* containing texts that both varied from, and corresponded to, what became traditional in rabbinic practice. Of most relevance to this discussion is that both the Decalogue and the first two paragraphs of the *shema'* have their place in such items. In the case of the *tefillin*, they occur together with Exodus 13:1–10 (קדש לי כל בכור, covering first-born, Passover feast and the source-verse for *tefillin*) and Exodus 13:11–16 (והיה כי יבאך, also covering these three themes), in a slightly different order from that of the rabbinic tradition; that is to say, the *shema'* passages are separated as second and fourth, and not together as third and fourth, as later became the norm.[26] It has also been suggested that the texts in 1QS X:10–14 that refer to special communication with God, and the blessing of his name, at the beginning and end of each day, may be an allusion to the recital of the *shema'* and the Decalogue, possibly even accompanied by some kind of formal benediction.[27]

Josephus also has a passage which helps to build the overall picture of the situation in the late Second Temple period. It reads:

> Twice each day, at the dawn thereof and when the hour comes for turning to repose, let all acknowledge before God the bounties which He has bestowed on them through their deliverance from the land of Egypt: thanksgiving is a natural duty, and is rendered alike in gratitude for past mercies and to incline the giver to others yet to come. They shall inscribe also on their doors the greatest of the benefits which they have received from God and each shall display them on his arms; and all that can show forth the power of God and His goodwill towards them, let them bear a

---

25 Stanley A. Cook, 'A pre-masoretic biblical papyrus', *Proceedings of the Society of Biblical Archaeology* 25 (1903), pp. 34–56; F. C. Burkitt, 'The Hebrew papyrus of the Ten Commandments', *JQR* 15 (1903), pp. 392–408.

26 Yigael Yadin, *Tefillin from Qumran: XQ Phyl 1-4* (Jerusalem, 1969).

27 Daniel K. Falk, 'Qumran prayer texts and the Temple' in *Sapiential, Liturgical and Poetical Texts from Qumran: Proceedings of the Third Meeting of the International Organization for Qumran Studies, Oslo, 1998*, eds D. K. Falk, F. García Martínez and E. M. Schuller (Leiden, Boston, Köln, 2000), pp. 115–17, and his forthcoming article 'Qumran and the synagogue liturgy' which he was kind enough to share with me.

record thereof written on the head and on the arm, so that men may see on every side the loving care with which God surrounds them.[28]

As far as Philo is concerned, the references are less clear but it may confidently be stated that he saw biblical readings as central to synagogal activity, that he knew about the daily recitation of the *shema'*, and that he may even have alluded to the inclusion of the *shema'* and the Decalogue in the *tefillin* of his day.[29]

At the axial period, then, we have encountered the broader use of one paragraph, and maybe even two paragraphs, of the *shema'*, or at least parts of these two passages, as well as of the Decalogue. There is a particular awareness of, and affection for, such passages and they are regarded as bearing a special theological message. They are consequently used as amulets, phylacteries or simply as sacred texts.

New Testament

What did leading Jewish groups of the first two centuries have to say about the religious significance of the *shema'* and similar texts? The sources that will make it possible to formulate a response to this question are undoubtedly to be found in the New Testament traditions that emanated from early Christian or Judaeo-Christian circles and in the codified views and midrashic comments that represent the ideas of the tannaitic teachers. A theological discussion between Jesus and the Scribes is recorded in Mark 12:28–34 and deals with the matter of which is the foremost of the biblical commandments. Jesus opts for two passages, namely, the first two verses of the *shema'* in Deuteronomy 6:4–5 and the instruction to love one's neighbour in Leviticus 19:18. A similar dialogue is reported between Jesus and an unidentified questioner in Mark 10:17–19 about which of the precepts in the Hebrew Bible promise eternal life to those who adhere to them. Jesus points to those in the Decalogue that prohibit murder, adultery, theft and dishonesty and that require respect for one's parents (Exodus 20:12). According to Matthew 22:34–40, the Pharisees and Sadducees challenged Jesus by demanding to know which is the greatest commandment in the Torah. Jesus gives essentially the same reply as in Mark 12 but adds that everything else in the Torah and the Prophets is dependent on these two. What emerges from these texts is that there existed in that age a tendency (perhaps inspired by hellenistic,

---

28 *Antiquities* 4.viii.13, 212–13 (Cambridge, Mass., and London, 1930, 1967²), pp. 577–78. T. M. Jonquière, *Prayer in Josephus* (doctoral dissertation at the University of Utrecht, under the supervision of P. W. van der Horst, 2005).

29 J. Leonhardt, *Jewish Worship in Philo of Alexandria* (Tübingen, 2001), pp. 98 and 140.

philosophical notions) to see the whole religious message summarized
in one brief biblical text, as interpreted by tradition, be it from the Ten
Commandments, the *shema'*, or what current scholarship knows as the
Holiness Code.[30]

Selected tannaitic comments

If attention is first paid to the mishnaic traditions, which may fairly be
stated to originate in the first two centuries CE and may possibly, in
some cases, reflect earlier practices, there are a number of key texts that
are of distinct importance to our discussion. An anonymous (and
therefore old?) report in *Tamid* 5.1 appears to presuppose the existence
during the Second Temple period, and on the Temple Mount, of a
prototype of rabbinic prayer.[31] Mention is made of benedictions and
biblical readings and the list includes items that ultimately became part
of the *'amidah* and of the *shema'* benedictions, as well as the *shema'* itself
and the Decalogue. Given that a list of items is always susceptible to
amendments by editors and redactors to take account of their own
contemporary practice, we should not automatically assume the
reliability of every benediction and reading noted here; but the fact that
the transmitted text does not include other fairly prominent items from
the later rabbinic liturgy allows us to conclude that we are dealing with
a *prima facie* piece of evidence for the liturgical use of the *shema'* in late
Second Temple times. What may perhaps represent an addendum is
the mention of the second and third paragraphs of the *shema'*.

A tradition recorded in *Berakhot* 2.5 cites the objection of Rabban
Gamliel II's students to the fact that he was inconsistent on the matter
of a bridegroom's recitation of the evening *shema'* on the first night of
his marriage, choosing not to follow his own ruling that such a man is
exempt from this liturgical obligation on that occasion. His argument
was that he could not, even in such circumstances, contemplate freeing

---

30 A recent discussion of the passage in Matthew is the well documented and closely
    argued article by Paul Foster, 'Why did Matthew get the *shema* wrong? A study of
    Matthew 22:37', *JBL* 122 (2003), pp. 309–33. Foster rightly questions the liturgical
    form and use of the *shema'* passages in the Second Temple period but seems to me
    too sceptical about the evidence, especially in the New Testament, for the existence
    of at least a shorter form in the pre-Christian and early Christian periods. See also
    David Flusser, 'The Ten Commandments and the New Testament' in *The Ten
    Commandments* (see n. 13 above), pp. 219–46. On the matter of regarding one passage
    as the summary of a broader religious message, see also Serge Ruzer, 'The double
    love precept in the New Testament and in the Rule of the Congregation' (Hebrew),
    Tarbiz 71 (2002), pp. 353–70.
31 אמר להם הממונה ברכו ברכה אחת והן ברכו. קראו עשרת הדברים, שמע, [+והיה שמוע, ויאמר?] ברכו את העם
    שלש ברכות: אמת ויציב, ועבודה, וברכת כהנים. ובשבת מוסיפין ברכה אחת למשמר היוצא.

himself from what he defined, without further qualification or explanation, as 'the yoke of the kingdom of heaven'.[32] Such a definition is also applied to the *shema'* , but specifically only to its first paragraph, by R. Joshua b. Qorḥa (mid-second century) when he explains the order of the three *shema'* passages, as reported in *Berakhot* 2.2. The yoke of the kingdom of heaven precedes the yoke of the commandments and they precede the Numbers 15 passage because the last-mentioned was recited only in the morning and not in the evening.[33] This latter assumption is also made by R. Eleazar b. Azariah, who explains (*Berakhot* 1.5) that he was seventy before he found a convincing explanation for the inclusion of that passage in the evening.[34] Another anonymous ruling in *Berakhot* 9.5 declares that God must be thanked for whatever he does, whether the effect on the Jew appears good or bad. This is supported by the citation of Deuteronomy 6:5 in which the double occurrence of the letter *bet* in the word לבבך is seen to refer to both these effects. The word נפש is interpreted as an allusion to the loss of one's life, i.e. martyrdom, and the word מאד as a reference to all one's possessions or to what God metes out (= 'measures out', from the root מדד) to us.[35] What may be concluded from the mishnaic sources just cited is that the *shema'* appears to have been a major liturgical item inherited by the rabbis from a ritual attached to the Temple but with no clearly defined content or length. It developed among the early rabbis as a declaration of their acceptance of the kingdom of God, rather than any other kingdom, and of all the commandments of the Torah. The devotion required in the light of such a declaration was interpreted as relating to all aspects of human nature, as demanding martyrdom when necessary, and as requiring a total acceptance of God's ultimate justice and the use of all one's assets.

Various halakhic midrashim include comments that clarify the status and understanding of the *shema'* on the part of the early rabbis.

---

32 מעשה ברבן גמליאל שקרא בלילה הראשון שנשא. אמרו לו תלמידיו: לא לימדתנו רבנו שחתן פטור מקריאת שמע בלילה הראשון. אמר להם: איני שומע לכם לבטל ממני מלכות שמים אפילו שעה אחת.

33 אמר רבי יהושע בן קרחה: למה קדמה שמע לוהיה אם שמע? אלא כדי שיקבל עליו עול מלכות שמים תחלה, ואחר כך יקבל עליו עול המצות. והיה אם שמע לויאמר? שוהיה אם שמע נוהג ביום ובלילה, ויאמר אינו נוהג אלא ביום.
Could it be that we have here a new stress on the passage dealing with the fringes (ציצית) and their blue thread, as part of a polemical response to the alleged superiority of Roman life and culture? As a reaction to the Roman use of blue dye for royalty, the Jews indicated that they were no less regal, as indicated by the wearing of the fringes. For bibliography on the use of purple dyes in the ancient Mediterranean world, see the website http://www.tekhelet.com/old_pub.htm.

34 מזכירין יציאת מצרים בלילות. אמר רבי אלעזר בן עזריה: הרי אני כבן שבעים שנה ולא זכיתי שתאמר יציאת מצרים בלילות עד שדרשה בן זומא.

35 חייב אדם לברך על הרעה כשם שמברך על הטובה, שנאמר ואהבת את ה' אלהיך בכל לבבך ובכל נפשך ובכל מאדך. בכל לבבך בשני יצריך, ביצר הטוב וביצר הרע; ובכל נפשך אפילו הוא נוטל את נפשך; ובכל מאדך בכל ממונך. ד"א בכל מאדך בכל מדה ומדה שהוא מודד לך הוה מודה לו במאד מאד.

Four appear in the commentary of Sifrey on Deuteronomy 6:4–9. The first (§31) interprets the first person plural pronominal suffix on the word אֱלֹהֵינוּ as indicating that God has especially attached his name to Israel,[36] while the second (§32), by an exegesis of Psalms 44:23, has God regarding Israel's righteousness as a constant act of martyrdom.[37] R. Meir on Deuteronomy 6:5 (§32) relates the 'heart' to Abraham's love of God, the 'soul' to Isaac's willingness to be martyred, and the word מאד to the gratitude (מודה) expressed by Jacob to God.[38] In the fourth passage (§34), linguistic and thematic associations are made between the passages included in the rabbinic *tefillin* (as mentioned above) and, on the basis of these, it is argued that the Decalogue does not share such characteristics, no doubt with the intention of polemicizing against its inclusion in the *tefillin*.[39]

The reference in the third paragraph of the *shema'* (Numbers 15:39) to the mention (=recitation) of God's precepts in association with the fringes is stated in Sifrey's comment there (§115) to be an allusion to the first and not the second paragraph since it is argued that the first paragraph, unlike its counterpart, includes an acceptance of the yoke of the kingdom of heaven without mention of idolatry.[40] According to these midrashim, the *shema'* indicates that Israel has a special role and that its devotion to God begins with the Patriarchs. Israel's constant loyalty is a form of martyrdom and the *shema*"s first paragraph is liturgically superior to the Decalogue and to its other two passages, given its special, dual message of God's kingship and Israel's submission to its yoke.

---

36 ה' אלהינו: למה נאמר והלא כבר נאמר ה' אחד, מה תלמוד לומר אלהינו עלינו החל שמו ביותר

37 ובכל נפשך: אפילו הוא נוטל את נפשך וכן הוא אומר כי עליך הורגנו כל היום נחשבנו כצאן טבחה, רבי שמעון בן מנסיה אומר וכי היאך איפשר לו לאדם ליהרג בכל יום אלא מעלה הקדוש ברוך הוא על הצדיקים כאילו הם נהרגים בכל יום.

38 רבי מאיר אומר הרי הוא אומר ואהבת את ה' אלהיך בכל לבבך, כאברהם אביך כענין שנאמר ואתה ישראל עבדי יעקב אשר בחרתיך זרע אברהם אהבי. ובכל נפשך, כיצחק שעקד עצמו על גבי המזבח כענין שנאמר וישלח אברהם את ידו ויקח את המאכלת. בכל מאדך, הוי מודה לו כיעקב אביך שנאמר קטנתי מכל החסדים ומכל האמת אשר עשית את עבדך כי במקלי עברתי את הירדן הזה ועתה הייתי לשני מחנות.

39 וקשרתם, אלו בקשירה ואין ויאמר בקשירה, שהיה בדין אם יביא קדש לי והיה כי יביאך שאינם בשנון הרי הם בקשירה, ויאמר, שהוא בשנון אינו דין שיהא בקשירה, תלמוד לומר וקשרתם אלו בקשירה ואין ויאמר בקשירה. עדיין אני אומר אם קדש לי, והיה כי יביאך, שקדמום מצות אחרות הרי הם בקשירה, עשר הדברות שלא קדמום מצות אחרות, אינו דין שיהו בקשירה, אמרת קל וחומר הוא, אם ויאמר שהוא בשנון אינו בקשירה, עשר הדברות שאינם בשנון, אינו דין שלא יהו בקשירה, הרי קדש לי, והיה כי יביאך יוכיחו, שאינם בשנון והרי הם בקשירה והם יוכיחו לעשר דברות, שאף על פי שאינם בשנון שיהו בקשירה תלמוד לומר וקשרתם, אלו בקשירה ואין עשר דברות בקשירה.

40 וראיתם אותו וזכרתם את כל מצות ה' ועשיתם אתם, זו פרשת שמע אתה אומר זו פרשת שמע או אינו אלא פרשת והיה אם שמוע אמרת צא וראה איזהי פרשה שיש בה קיבול מלכות שמים ומיעט בה עבודה זרה אין אתה מוצא אלא פרשת שמע.

Other rabbinic traditions

There are some other early rabbinic traditions that are of interest here. In Tosefta, *Berakhot* 2.13, R. Meir argues that it is not necessary to recite the words of the *shema'* audibly and cites (without winning the halakhic argument) the example of the pupils of R. Akiva, including himself, whose recitation of the *shema'* was not audible to a Roman official standing nearby.[41] There is also a disagreement between R. Yose and R. Judah, noted in Tosefta, *Rosh Ha-shanah* 2, about whether Deuteronomy 6:4 and 4:39 should be included in the catena of verses that make up the 'kingship' section of the additional *'amidah* for New Year.[42] A lengthy exposition in the name of R. Levi appears in the Talmud Yerushalmi, *Berakhot* 1:8, according to which the two passages of the *shema'* are recited each day because they include allusions to each of the commandments in the Decalogue.[43] In this connection it should be recalled that there are talmudic reports, both Palestinian[44] and Babylonian,[45] that the Decalogue ought, by virtue of its theological centrality, to be recited every day but that the practice was discontinued in the context of disputes with groups defined by the rabbis as heretical.

What emerges from these traditions is that in the second century there was clearly discussion about identifying the *shema'* as primarily meaning the acceptance of the kingdom of God and about the degree to which the Jew should pursue this notion, given its capability of being construed by Romans or Romanophiles as antipathy towards their rule

---

41 Ed. Zuckermandel, 2.14, p. 4: פעם אחת היינו יושבין לפני רבי עקיבא והיינו קורין את שמע ולא היינו משמיעים לאזנינו מפני קסדור אחד שהיה עומד על הפתח אמרו לו אין שעת סכנה ראייה.

42 Ed. Zuckermandel, 4.7, p. 213: שמע ישראל וכו' וידעת היום והשבת וכו' ר' יוסי אומר אומרן עם המלכיות ר' יהודה אומר לא היה אומרן עמהן.

43 Ed. Krotoschin, 3c: מפני מה קורין שתי הפרשיות הללו בכל יום. ר' לוי ור' סימון. ר' סימון אמר מפני שכתוב בהן שכיבה וקימה. ר' לוי אמר מפני שעשרת הדברות כלולין בהן.

44 PT, *Berakhot* 1.8 (3c): א"ר בא אין מן הדא לית ש"מ כלום שעשרת הדברות הן הן גופה של שמע, דרב מתנה ור' שמואל בר נחמן אמר תרויהון אמרין בדין הוה שיהו קורין עשרת הדברות בכל יום ומפני מה אין קורין אותן, מפני טענת [טינת] המינין שלא יהו אומ' אלו לבד' ניתנו למשה בסיני.

45 BT, *Berakhot* 12a: א"ר יהודה אמר שמואל אף בגבולין בקשו לקרות כן אלא שכבר בטלום מפני תרעומת המינין תניא נמי הכי ר' נתן אומר בגבולין בקשו לקרות כן אלא שכבר בטלום מפני תרעומת המינין רבה בב"ח סבר למקבעינהו בסורא א"ל רב חסדא כבר בטלום מפני תרעומת המינין אמימר סבר למקבעינהו בנהרדעא א"ל רב אשי כבר בטלום מפני תרעומת המינין. But, around 400 CE, the Church Father, Jerome, in his commentary on Ezekiel 24:15, reports a continuing use of the Decalogue in Babylon, perhaps in *tefillin*; see A. Habermann, 'The phylacteries in Antiquity' (Hebrew), *Eretz Israel* 3 (1954), p. 177. There are also Genizah texts in which it appears between the morning psalms and the beginning of the *shema'* benedictions; see J. Mann, 'Genizah fragments of the Palestinian order of service,' *HUCA* 2 (1925), pp. 283–84, reprinted in *Contributions to the Scientific Study of Jewish Liturgy* (ed. J. J. Petuchowski, New York, 1970) and Fleischer, *Eretz Israel* (see n. 24 above), pp. 259–74.

and that of the Emperor. There were also moves towards regarding the *shema'* as at least equivalent to the Decalogue, and ultimately as capable of usurping its theological centrality in the liturgy.[46] The second chapter of *Berakhot* in the Babylonian Talmud deals at length with the *shema'* and the evidence shows that there was a wide range of views about what constituted the *shema'* for the purposes of its daily liturgical recitation: the first verse only; the first three verses; the first paragraph; the first two paragraphs; the first two paragraphs plus the opening and closing sections of the third paragraph; all three paragraphs. From a number of sources, it is clear that as the *shema"*s importance grew its recitation in the synagogal liturgy became a more formal affair. There are technical terms for this formal recitation involving the use of the roots פרס and כרך but there is no unanimous view as to precisely what this entailed. The prayer leader led with the beginning of a verse, or a whole verse, or a whole passage, and the congregation followed by repeating what he had intoned or, perhaps, by repeating his recitation and continuing themselves with the next part of the text.[47]

There are also theological comparisons between the *shema'* and the *'amidah* and contrasting views about whether the recitation of the former is required not only according to rabbinic law but also according to its biblical precedent, and is therefore a requirement of considerable importance.[48] Among a host of homiletical statements made in other rabbinic sources about the *shema'*, the claim is made that it is equivalent to offering sacrifices in the Temple, or to the study of Torah, that it leads to prayers being answered and to eternal bliss, that it brings God's special protection, and that a variety of evils arise out of its neglect.[49] Indeed, the angelic choir on high does not begin its praise of God until Israel has recited the *shema'* here below, and its formulation of the trisagion includes the *shema'*. While the heavenly praises are recited only once a day, Israel's recitation of the *shema'* takes place twice.[50]

---

46 See Kimelman, 'Shema' liturgy' (see n. 6 above), pp. 68–80.

47 Mekhilta of R. Ishmael on Exdus 15:1 (ed. J. Z. Lauterbach, 2.7): ר' נחמיה אומר רוח הקודש
    שרת על ישראל והיו אמרים שירה כבני אדם שהן קורין את שמע ויאמרו לאמר [שמות טו:א]; BT, *Soṭah* 30b:
    Tosefta Pesaḥim רבי נחמיה אומר כסופר הפורס על שמע בבית הכנסת שהוא פותח תחילה והן עונין אחריו
    3.15 (ed. Zuckermandel 2:19, p. 160): כיצד כורכין את שמע שמע אומרין שמע ישראל ה' אלהינו ה' אחד ולא
    היו מפסיקין ר' יהודה אומ' מפסיקין היו אלא שאין אומ' ברוך שם כבוד מלכותו לעולם ועד. For a full
    discussion, as well as details of primary and secondary sources, see Kimelman,
    'Shema' liturgy' (see n. 6 above), pp. 92–97.

48 See especially BT, *Berakhot* 21a.

49 See the texts cited in the introductory section to M. M. Kasher, *Sefer Shema' Yisra'el*
    (Hebrew; Jerusalem, 1980), pp. 9–16.

50 Sifrey, *Ha'azinu*, §306; *Batei Midrashot*, compiled by S. A. Wertheimer, ed. A. J.
    Wertheimer (Jerusalem, 1954), 1.116 and 2.471 (from *Hekhalot Rabbati* and *Midrash R.
    'Aqiva*); BT, *Ḥullin* 91b.

Appended rabbinic phrases

Before concluding, it remains to say a few words about the theological significance of the insertion of the sentence ברוך שם כבוד מלכותו לעולם ועד (= בשכמל"ו)[51] after the first verse of the *shema'*, and of the phrase אל מלך נאמן to introduce it. There appears to be a tannaitic tradition (or claim?) that בשכמל"ו was the formula used in the Second Temple instead of 'amen' and on hearing the pronouncement of the Divine Name on Yom Kippur.[52] There are a number of reasons for questioning whether that precise wording was indeed of Temple origin. The biblical, apocryphal and qumranic texts that are most closely parallel to the rabbinic version do not include together all four elements of 'blessing' (ברוך), God's 'honoured name' (שם כבודו), the divine 'kingship' (מלכותו) and 'forever' (לעולם).[53] There is considerable ambivalence in the talmudic and midrashic sources about the origins of the phrase בשכמל"ו, it being variously attributed to Jacob, Moses and the angels.[54] One talmudic tradition also indicates some hesitation about the justification for reciting a rabbinic text immediately after the first verse of such an authoritative biblical one, thereby explaining why it is normally recited in a whisper.[55] Furthermore, the central rabbinic significance of the Aramaic response יהא שמיה רבא מברך לעלם ('May his great name be blessed forever') and the existence in the targumic tradition of the blessing בריך שום יקריה לעלמא ('May his honoured name be blessed forever') point in the direction of an original blessing that seems likely

---

51 For a full discussion, see Kimelman, 'Shema' liturgy' (see n. 6 above), pp. 97–103.

52 Mishnah, *Yoma* 3.8 and 6.2; BT, *Ta'anit* 16b.

53 See, for example, Psalms 72:9, Psalms 145:11 and Nehemiah 9:5; Tobit 11:14 and 13:1; 4Q511, frgms. 63-64, col. IV and 4Q286 [Berakhot[a]], frgm. 7, col. I. line 7.

54 *Devarim Rabbah* 2.35: מהיכן זכו ישראל לקריאת שמע, משעה שנטה יעקב למיתה קרא לכל השבטים ואמר להם שמא משאני נפטר מן העולם אתם משתחוים לאלוה אחר, מנין שכך, כתיב [בראשית מח:ב] הקבצו ושמעו בני יעקב וגו' מהו ושמעו אל ישראל אביהם, אל ישראל אביכם הוא, אמרו לו, שמע ישראל ה' אלהינו ה' אחד, והוא אומר בלחישה ברוך שם כבוד מלכותו לעולם ועד. אמר ר' לוי ומה ישראל אומרים עכשיו שמע אבינו ומהיכן זכו ישראל לקרות. *Devarim Rabba* 2.31: ישראל אותו הדבר שצויתנו נוהג בנו, ה' אלהינו ה' אחד שמע, אמר ר' פנחס בר חמא ממתן תורה זכו ישראל לקרות שמע, כיצד את מוצא לא פתח הקב"ה בסיני תחלה אלא בדבר זה, אמר להן שמע ישראל אנכי ה' אלהיך, נענו כולן ואמרו ה' אלהינו ה' אחד, ומשה אמר ברוך שם כבוד בשעה שישראל אומרין מלכותו לעולם ועד. *Bereshit Rabbah* 65.21 (ed. Theodor-Albeck, p. 739): שמע ישראל המלאכים שותקין ואחר כך[בעמדם] תרפינה כנפיהן ומה הן אומרין ברוך כבוד ה' ממקומו וברוך שם כבור מלכותו [לעולם ועד].

55 BT, *Pesaḥim* 52a: באותה שעה פתח יעקב אבינו ואמר בשכמל"ו אמרי רבנן היכי נעביד נאמרוהו לא אמר משה רבינו לא נאמרוהו אמר יעקב התקינו שיהו אומרים אותו בחשאי וכו' אמר ר' אבהו התקינו שיהו אומרים אותו בקול רם מפני תרעומת המינין ובנהרדעא דליכא מינין עד השתא אמרי לה בחשאי.

to have been along the lines of ברוך שם כבודו לעולם ('May his honoured
name be blessed forever').[56]

The addition of the word מלכות and the insertion of the benediction
after the first verse of the *shema'* therefore constituted a categorical
affirmation by the rabbis that the theological significance of the verse
was that it represented Israel's 'acceptance of the yoke of the kingdom
of God'. It marked a recognition that the biblical texts were now being
treated as adjustable rabbinic liturgy rather than pure Scripture. To add
authoritative weight to the recitation of the phrase in this form, it was
linked with the Temple, Jacob, Moses and the angelic choir, and any
anxiety was assuaged by the compromise decision to distinguish
between the body of the biblical text and the inserted rabbinic blessing
by declaiming the former and whispering the latter, unless there were
major polemical reasons for equating the two texts. The alternative
Aramaic version of the blessing, which was employed in a different
liturgical context,[57] was allowed to remain in its simpler form. The later
insertion of the other phrase that here concerns us, namely אל מלך נאמן,
also represented a typical rabbinic compromise but appears to have less
theological significance. There was doubt about whether the
benediction immediately before the *shema'* should or should not have
the word 'amen' appended to it, and a way of following both views
was to propose the use of the phrase אל מלך נאמן. Its three letters
represented 'amen', it was a description of God which did not interrupt
the theme of God and his relationship with Israel, and it provided the
three passages of the *shema'* with 248 words, a number which was
among the favourites of the rabbis.[58] That development was, however, a
post-talmudic one. In that later period, a number of additional
liturgical roles were assigned to the *shema'* and it was customary
among the Jewish communities of the Holy Land to introduce it with a
specific benediction praising God for having instructed us to affirm
wholeheartedly his kingship and unity.[59] To discuss these matters
would, however, take us beyond the confines of our present study and
involve us in wider-ranging matters of history, theology, dogma and
liturgy.

56 Sifrey, *Ha'azinu*, §306; Pseudo-Jonathan on Deuteronomy 6:4; Targum Jonathan on
    Psalms 72:19. See also J. Heineman, *Prayer in the Talmud: Forms and Patterns* (revised
    English edition; Berlin and New York, 1977), pp. 136 and 256–57.
57 See Andreas Lehnardt, *Qaddish: Untersuchungen zur Entstehung und Rezeption eines
    rabbinischen Gebetes* (Tübingen, 2002), pp. 81–86.
58 BT, *Shabbat* 119b: מאי אמן אמר ר' חנינא אל מלך נאמן. Elbogen (see n. 7 above), G, pp. 21–22;
    H, p. 16; E, p. 20; Mann, 'Genizah fragments' (see n. 45 above), pp. 288–89.
59 Mann, 'Genizah fragments' (see n. 45 above), pp. 286–88.

Conclusion

In spite of his brilliant contribution to a historical understanding of rabbinic prayer, Ismar Elbogen was more than occasionally inclined to indulge in theologically motivated polemics about certain developments in Jewish liturgy. In one of his summaries of the evolution of synagogal worship, he expresses himself thus (in Scheindlin's English translation from the German original):

As a result of its dissemination, synagogue worship took on a different character and instruction was displaced as its main purpose by prayer and reverence. The profession of faith, the *Shema'*, was recited as before, but the original significance of these scriptural readings was progressively lost, and they were given a scholastic interpretation, according to which the commandment of twice-daily prayer and the memorial commandments of phylacteries, fringes and mezuza were derived from them.[60]

Apart from its polemical tone, such a statement is something of a simplification. The trends were undoubtedly more complicated and the relationship between the Hebrew Bible and rabbinic customs ever remained complex. There was indeed ultimately a tendency to stress the halakhic element but, as has emerged from the above analysis, this was not the only trend. The drive to centralize such Torah precepts was one impetus for changes in the use and interpretation of the *shema'*. There were, however, other factors that related to the role of the Torah precepts, the status of Israel, the kingdom of God, martyrdom and suffering, the importance of daily prayer that contained both the *shema'* and the *'amidah*, divine protection and ultimate reward. If Elbogen was not quite accurate in his estimate, Schechter was by no means mistaken in his.

---

60 Elbogen (see n. 7 above), G, pp. 246–47; H, p. 187; E, p. 196. I am grateful to my dear friend and colleague, Professor Robert Gordon for inviting me to lecture on this topic at the Old Testament Seminar in the University of Cambridge, for helpful comments on the text, and for kindly agreeing to allow me to publish the study here rather than in the volume that he is currently editing, containing some papers given at the Seminar.

8

Jerusalem

Introduction

There can be little doubt that Jerusalem occupies an honoured place in the medley of religious ideas formulated and transmitted by Jewish circles through countless generations. Equally incontrovertible is the notion that liturgy has, during those many centuries, functioned as a central medium for the expression of Judaism's most cherished principles of faith and practice. In the words of the late A. M. Habermann, 'the mention of Jerusalem was obligatory in all the statutory prayers.'[1] It therefore follows that any characteristic selection of Hebrew literature should include significant examples of the occurrence of Jerusalem in liturgical texts. The fact is, however, that an examination of Reuven Hammer's recently published volume, *The Jerusalem Anthology: A Literary Guide*, fails to support such a presupposition. In what is a useful and extensive volume, all manner of works, of diverse content, and from numerous periods are cited for their remarks about the City of David but there is only one minor reference to the standard rabbinic prayer-book.[2] It seems to me that this by no means represents an oversight on the part of the learned author but is, rather, a reflection of a basic problem in the study of Jewish liturgy which is singularly relevant to any treatment of the subject in hand. As such, it deserves some attention at the beginning of this chapter in the context of a limited methodological discussion that will attempt to explain and justify the approach being taken here.

Methodology

Although there is also a liturgical role for Jerusalem in biblical, apocryphal, qumranic, Christian and Muslim texts, what will be examined here is the theme as it occurs in rabbinic prayer-texts. If one was of a mind to do so, one could simply take the traditional siddur of

---

1   *Encyclopaedia Judaica* 9 (Jerusalem, 1971), cols 1560–63, which has a useful summary of Jerusalem's appearances in statutory prayer and in liturgical poetry.

2   R. Hammer, *The Jerusalem Anthology: A Literary Guide* (Philadelphia and Jerusalem, 1995). The sole reference is to the burial *qaddish* and is included in the 'Fourth Gate' of the volume, p. 150, dealing with the geonic period.

any of the major rites, before the substantial revisions of the modern period, and summarize the cases in which Jerusalem makes an appearance. One would then have a comprehensive catalogue of texts that had been fairly standard for the best part of a whole millennium but had also, by virtue of their very canonicity and ritualization, lost the link with their original incorporation. Since I feel committed to provide more than a literary index, I have set myself the task of tackling the subject of Jerusalem in the first millennium of rabbinic, liturgical history. It is there that one is likely to find the evidence that will prove so central to any understanding of what Jews, Christians and Muslims had in common and how they differed in their approaches to the Holy City. That is the period during which only two major rites appear to have existed, in Babylon and the Land of Israel, and it predates both the widespread standardization based on the former rite and the subsequent renewal of ritual fractionization in both Europe and the Orient.[3] And here, in the formative era of rabbinic liturgy, one is confronted by precisely the problem that apparently faced Hammer and faces anyone else who wishes to place liturgical texts that clearly had their origin in that wide span of time in a particular geographical, chronological or theological context.

That problem relates to the scientific use of liturgical texts from the talmudic-midrashic literature, from the geonic corpora, and from the earliest sources preserved in the Cairo Genizah. There are of course general difficulties in dealing with any material from such origins. There are undoubtedly oral and written stages; clear indications of provenance are rare; and traditions often appear isolated. The matter of dating, contextualizing and expounding the texts is consequently a challenging task. As far as liturgy is concerned, that task is made even more complicated by further considerations. To what extent may we assume that the text preserved in one generation precisely matches its format in an earlier one? Is there not a tendency to adjust versions to accommodate them to current thought? When a scribe cites a prayer, might he not absent-mindedly record what is familiar to him rather than what he is supposed to be transmitting? What is more, it is all too facile a solution to subscribe to the general principle that all short, simple Babylonian texts (from the Talmud, for example) represent the pristine form while all longer, more complex Palestinian versions (from the Genizah, for example) may universally be judged to be later accretions. These and other difficulties have led scholars from the period of the *Wissenschaft des Judentums* until our own day to eschew

---

3   For an historical overview of liturgical developments in this period, see S. C. Reif,
     Judaism and Hebrew Prayer: New Perspectives on Jewish Liturgical History (Cambridge,
     1993), pp. 122–52.

the kind of detailed historical reconstruction of liturgical history that would explain what dictated many textual choices in favour of a less speculative approach that concentrates on an account of what these choices simply were.[4] As Dov Rappel has, however, strongly contended, the theological history of rabbinic liturgy deserves no less attention than its text-critical analysis since every variant carries with it a meaningful religious message of some sort.[5] How then shall we best proceed in attempting to meet both these needs in this brief and necessarily modest examination of the place of Jerusalem in the first few centuries of rabbinic liturgy?

What I propose to do is to examine a few of the major prayers (but not liturgical poems) that were incontrovertibly central to the rabbinic tradition as they are documented in the talmudic and geonic sources, which are in many cases representative of authoritative viewpoints, and as they are found in the Genizah fragments, which are often more indicative of less conformist trends. Each such examination will include a survey of the role that Jerusalem and closely associated subjects play in the texts and a report on the nature of significant textual variations that relate directly to that role. I shall deliberately refrain from defining texts as specifically Babylonian or Palestinian in order not to confuse textual evidence with its assumed provenance nor unjustifiably to restrict the interpretative possibilities. Some additional information of a similar nature will then be adduced about less prominent prayers. At that point, an effort will be made to summarize the various notions relating to Jerusalem that have been identified and to estimate their individual and overall significance in the realm of religious ideas. In the concluding section of the chapter, I propose to offer some options that are available to historians in their analysis of the development and absorption of such ideas among the rabbinic Jews of the period. I am, however, aware that no more than the groundwork will by then have been completed and that the matter of historical reconstruction, speculative as it must remain at this stage of our knowledge, will await attention in another context.

Temple service

A start may be made with a liturgical tradition that lays strong claim to be one of the earliest to be documented in the talmudic-midrashic

---

4   For discussion of some of the methodological problems in the scientific study of Jewish liturgy, see Reif (see n. 3 above), pp. 1–21 and chapter 2 above.
5   His views and studies are collected in *Pithey She'arim: Gates to the Jewish Liturgy*, eds Y. and N. Rappel (Hebrew; Jerusalem and Tel Aviv, 2001).

literature. It describes a ritual that took place in the Temple on Yom Kippur and, given that it has no real parallels or equivalents in the post-Temple period to contaminate its textual purity, it may be regarded a reliable testimony to an important list of theological priorities inherited by the rabbis. The beginning of the seventh chapter in the mishnaic tractate Yoma records that after the high priest had read out some relevant pentateuchal passages he pronounced eight benedictions for the Torah, Temple-service ('avodah), Thanksgiving, Forgiveness of Sin, Temple (miqdash), Israel, Priests and other (more general) matters.[6] The Tosefta identifies the first benediction as that familiar to us from synagogal (or, perhaps, academic) use; the next three as those included in the 'amidah; the fifth, sixth and seventh as individual (unique perhaps?) benedictions; and the last as a special plea for the security of the Jewish people.[7] Further comment is provided in the talmudic tractates. The Palestinian Talmud cites the doxological conclusions for all the benedictions and the ones that are of special interest to us in the present context are those for the Temple-service, Temple and Priesthood. The latter two allude to God's special choice of these two institutions by the use of the phrases ha-boḥer bamiqdash and ha-boḥer ba-kohanim, and to the awesome worship of God in the imperfect tense by the use of the phrase she'otekha nira' we-na'avod. What is of special significance here is an alternative phraseology offered for the Temple. Instead of noting its divine selection, the third-century Palestinian 'amora Rabbi Idi opts for a phrase about the Temple that refers to the divine presence in Zion (hashokhen beṣiyyon).[8]

---

6   Mishnah, *Yoma* 7.1; see E. E. Urbach, *The Sages: Their Concepts and Beliefs* (E. T., 2 vols; Jerusalem, 1975), 1.655–67: ומברך עליה שמונה ברכות על התורה ועל העבודה ועל ההודאה ועל מחילת העון ועל המקדש ועל הכהנים ועל שאר תפלה.

7   Tosefta, *Yoma* 3.13, ed. Zuckermandel, p. 189; S. Lieberman, *Tosefta Ki-Fshuṭah*, Part 4 (Hebrew; New York, 1962), pp. 800–803: שמונה ברכות היה מברך באותו היום על התורה כדרך שמברך בבית הכנסת על העבודה (ועל ההודאה) ועל מחילת העון כסידרן ועל המקדש ברכה בפני עצמה ועל ישראל ברכה בפני עצמה ושאר תפלה בקשה תחינה שעמך ישראל צריכין להיושע מלפניך וחותם בשומע תפלה כל העם קורין בשלהן כדי להראות חזיית לציבור. Although the first benediction is given a synagogal milieu, it seems strange that this should be differentiated from that of the next three, namely, the prayers. Perhaps an earlier version of the text had a reference to the *bet ha-midrash* where the Torah benediction no doubt originated, later amended to reflect new realities. See also I. Elbogen, German edition = G, *Der jüdische Gottesdienst in seiner geschichtlichen Entwicklung* (Frankfurt am Main, 1931; reprint, Hildesheim, 1962), pp. 170–72; Hebrew edition = H, התפילה בישראל בהתפתחותה ההיסטורית (eds J. Heinemann, I. Adler, A. Negev, J. Petuchowski and H. Schirmann, Tel Aviv, 1972) , pp. 128–30; English edition = E, *Jewish Liturgy: A Comprehensive History* (English translation and edition by R. P. Scheindlin, Philadelphia, Jerusalem and New York,1993), pp. 140–41.

8   PT, *Yoma* 7.1, ed. Krotoschin, f. 44b: ומברך עליה שמונה ברכות על התורה הבוחר בתורה על העבודה שאותך נירא ונעבוד על הודיה הטוב לך להודות

Little is added to the discussion by the Babylonian Talmud which merely cites (but not in the Munich manuscript) a tannaitic tradition virtually at one with that of the Tosefta.[9] What then of Jerusalem the city? Its only mention in this context is in variant texts of the Mishnah which cite it between Israel and the priests and therefore create a textual problem by referring to nine, rather than eight items.[10]

Grace and 'amidah

Another liturgical phenomenon that is widely recognized as having had its origins in the pre-rabbinic period is the grace after meals. What remain more open questions are the degree to which its four benedictions are a revolutionary innovation of the tannaitic rabbis and whether each was appended to a basic text-form at a different point of development.[11] In this case, however, there is little difficulty in locating the context in which Jerusalem occurs since the third benediction is devoted to that subject and its doxological conclusion is exclusively concerned with that city. The problem here is that on approaching the sources emanating from the first Christian millennium, one is confronted with a wide variety of content. The closing benediction itself, if we include both the sabbath and weekday versions, may refer simply to the building of Jerusalem, to the consolation of Zion through the building of Jerusalem, or to David's God and the building of Jerusalem. Such complexity appears positively straightforward when compared with the situation as regards the subjects covered in the body of the benediction, according to a variety of textual and literary

---

על מחילת העון מוחל עונות עמו ישראל ברחמים על המקדש הבוחר במקדש ואמר רבי אידי השוכן בציון על ישראל הבוחר בישראל על הכהנים הבוחר בכהנים על שאר תפלה ותחינה ובקשה שעמך ישראל צריכין להיושע לפניך בא"י שומע תפילה.

There is some doubt about the precise identification of the Idi cited here since he is entitled 'Rabbi' and not 'Rav' and is apparently therefore not the Palestinian teacher with the strong Babylonian background.

9 BT, *Yoma* 70a; see R. N. Rabbinovicz, *Variae Lectiones* (*Diqduqey Soferim*) (Munich and Przemysl, 1867–97), IV (Munich, 1871), pp. 203–4: ומברך עליה שמונה ברכות ת"ר על התורה

כדרך שמברכים בבית הכנסת על העבודה ועל ההודאה ועל מחילת העון כתקנה ועל המקדש בפני עצמו ועל הכהנים בפני עצמן ועל ישראל בפני עצמן ועל שאר תפלה ת"ר ושאר התפלה רנה תחינה בקשה מלפניך על עמך ישראל שצריכין להיושע וחותם בשומע תפילה ואחר כך כל אחד ואחד מביא ספר תורה מביתו וקורא בו כדי להראות חזותו לרבים.

10 For the variant texts in the Mishnah, see J. Meinhold (ed.), *Joma (Der Versöhnungstag). Text, Übersetzung und Erklärung* (Giessen, 1913), p. 79.

11 S. Baer, *Seder 'Avodat Yisra'el* (Rödelheim, 1868), pp. 554–62; B. S. Jacobson, *Netiv Binah* (Hebrew; 5 vols; Tel Aviv, 1968–83) 3.33–97; J. Heinemann, *Prayer in the Talmud: Forms and Patterns* (revised English edition, Berlin and New York, 1977), pp. 115–22.

traditions.[12] It is obviously not possible in the present context to record all the variants but if the briefest and most extensive lists are set side by side, the purpose of indicating the range of content will have been well served. The simplest formulation would appear to have included a request for God's mercy to be shown to his people Israel, his city Jerusalem, his Temple (מעון, היכל) , and, perhaps as early additions to such a formulation, to his glorious habitation Zion and to the Davidic dynasty. Some versions place an emphasis on the secure provision of food while others make a link between that subject and the main theme of the benediction by stressing that the worshipper's consumption of food and drink by no means indicates that he has forgotten the plight of Jerusalem and its need for restoration. In a number of texts, that theme of restoration is spelt out, in some cases after the benediction, with pleas for some or all of the developments that are presupposed by references to the consolation of Zion, to the building of Jerusalem, and to the return there of God's presence and rule, of the Davidic (=messianic) kingdom, of the sacrificial system, and of the Jewish population.

Given that the fourteenth benediction of the daily 'amidah shares with the third benediction of the birkat ha-mazon just discussed the central theme of Jerusalem, it is by no means surprising to find that they have in common many of the related topics that are to be found in the body of the text.[13] The major difference between them is that in the

---

12   J. Mann, 'Genizah fragments of the Palestinian order of service,' *HUCA* 2 (1925), pp. 332–38, reprinted in *Contributions to the Scientific Study of Jewish Liturgy* (ed. J. J. Petuchowski, New York, 1970); L. Finkelstein, 'The birkat ha-mazon', *JQR, NS* 19 (1928–29), pp. 211–62; A. Scheiber, '*Qiṭ'ey birkat ha-mazon*', *SRIHP* 7 (Jerusalem and Tel Aviv, 1958), pp. 147–53; Y. Ratzaby, '*Birkot mazon mefuyyaṭot*', *Sinai* 113 (1994), pp. 110–33. Three basic forms are:

a. רחם י' א' על ישראל עמך ועל ירושלים עירך ועל היכלך ועל מעונך (ועל ציון משכן כבודך ועל מלכות בית דוד) בא"י בונה ירושלים

b. נחמינו י' א' בציון עירך ברנה ובשכלול בית מקדשך ורחם י' א' עלינו ועל ישראל עמך ועל ירושלים עירך ועל ציון משכן כבודך ועל הבית הגדול שנקרא שמך עליו ועל מלכות בית דוד משיחך במהרה תחזירנה למקומה כי לך י' מיחלות עינינו ותבנה ותבנה ציון עיר קדשך ותמלוך עלינו אתה לבדך ותושיענו למען שמך ואע"פ שאכלנו ושתינו חרבן ביתך הגדול והקדוש לא שכחנו ואל תשכיחנו לעד כי חסיד וקדוש וברוך ונאמן אתה ונאמר בונה ירושלים י' נדחי ישראל יכנס בא"י הבונה ברחמיו את ירושלים אמן בחיינו אמן במהרה בימינו תבנה ציון ברנה ותכון עבודה בירושלים וארמון על משפטו ורומי הרשעה תפול

c. רחם י' א'...רועינו זננו מפרנסנו מכלכלנו הרוח לנו מהרה מצרותינו ועל תצריכנו לידי מתנת בשר ודם שמתנתם מעוטה וחרפתם מרובה בשם קדשך הגדול והנורא בטחנו ויבא אליהו ומשיח בן דוד בחיינו

See also chapter 18 below. Avi Schmidman is currently completing a doctoral dissertation at Bar-Ilan University on the poetic forms of the grace after meals which may take the study of the Jerusalem theme a little further.

13   Baer, *Seder 'Avodat Yisra'el* (see n. 11 above), pp. 96–97; Jacobson, *Netiv Binah* (see n. 11 above), 1.285–86; Elbogen (see n. 7 above), G, pp. 52–54; E, pp. 47–48; H, pp. 41–42; Heinemann, *Prayer in the Talmud* (see n. 11 above), pp. 48–50, 70–76, and 288–91, and *Studies in Jewish Liturgy*, ed. A. Shinan (Hebrew; Jerusalem, 1981), pp. 3–11

case of the *'amidah* benediction there are two options, of sound talmudic pedigree, for the treatment of the restored kingdom of David. According to one, it appears as part of the Jerusalem benediction while, according to the other, it is treated in an independent benediction. Inevitably, there are indications of conflated versions and of contamination by the text of the grace after meals but three archetypal formulations stand at the centre of most textual witnesses, as has recently been pointed out by Yechezkel Luger.[14] The first of these, which is perhaps the closest to the simpler format recorded for the grace, invokes God's mercy first on Israel his people, on Jerusalem his city, and on his Temple (היכל, מקדש, מעון), and then on his glorious habitation Zion; pleads for the building of an eternal Jerusalem; and concludes with a doxology that refers to God as the builder of Jerusalem. In the second formulation, the messianic kingdom of David is added to the subjects of God's projected mercy which are again Israel, Jerusalem and Zion, the last-mentioned appearing on its own, without any specific word for the Temple itself. That institution receives attention after the addendum referring to the Davidic kingdom, when a plea is made for the reconstruction of God's house and palace. Since the option to include the Davidic kingdom in the Jerusalem benediction is here being exercised, the doxology understandably describes the recipient of the prayer as the God of David and the builder of Jerusalem. The third archetypal formulation again has the simpler doxology on the one theme, as well as a plea for the building of an eternal Jerusalem but any similarity with either of the other two formulations ends there. God is in simple terms requested kindly to return to his city of Jerusalem (or, according to a textual variant, make it his habitation) and there is no mention whatsoever of any of its other institutions.

Three benedictions

In the context of his study of the talmudic origins of rabbinic liturgy, Joseph Heinemann helpfully points out that there are three other

---

(originally published in *Hayyim (Jefim) Schirmann Jubilee Volume*, eds S. Abramson and A. Mirsky, Jerusalem, 1970, pp. 93–101).

14   Y. Luger, *The Weekday Amidah in the Cairo Genizah* (Hebrew; Jerusalem, 2001), pp. 150–58. The two options are perhaps already presupposed in Tosefta, *Berakhot* 3.25, ed. Zuckermandel, p. 9. The three archetypal formulations are:

a. רחם י' א' עלינו ועל ישראל עמך ועל ירושלים עירך ועל היכלך ועל מקדשך ועל מעונך ועל ציון משכן כבודך ובנה את ירושלים בנין עולם בא"י בונה ירושלים

b. רחם עלינו י' א' ברחמיך הרבים על ישראל עמך על ירושלים עירך על ציון משכן כבודך ועל מלכות בן דויד משיחך בנה ביתך ושכלל היכלך בא"י אלקי דוד בונה ירושלים

c. לירושלים עירך ברחמים תשוב ותבנה אותה בנין עולם בא"י בונה ירושלים

benedictions which use similar formulations in dealing with the topic
of Jerusalem and which occur, respectively, in the service for the fast-
day of the Ninth of Av, in the benedictions that follow the *haftarah*
reading, and in the benedictions that are recited at a wedding feast.
Although Heinemann's agenda is somewhat different from ours, and
his comparative list of readings makes no distinction between the
talmudic and geonic evidence on the one hand and the early mediaeval
sources on the other, a careful and eclectic use of the information he
compiled about these three liturgical items will be of considerable
assistance to us in the present context.[15] The special prayer formulated
in talmudic times for the Ninth of Av and inserted at some point in the
'*amidah* during one or all of the services to be held on that day is
designed to make specific mention of the fate of Jerusalem. In its
simplest form, it first reads very much like the fourteenth benediction
itself, craving God's mercy (not his compassion)[16] on Israel his people,
Jerusalem his city, and Zion his glorious habitation, while then adding
to the list the ruined city, whose plight and divinely promised ultimate
restoration are duly noted. As far as the doxology is concerned, God is
again cited as the builder of Jerusalem, or in more complex manner as
either the God of David and the builder of Jerusalem or the consoler of
Zion and the builder of Jerusalem. The initial word of the second
blessing after the prophetic reading also occurs as either רחם or נחם and
the doxological variants once more contain references to either the
consolation of Zion, this time with her children, or to the building of
Jerusalem. Since the benediction directly concerns Jerusalem, the
remainder of the content is also of importance for our discussion. The
titles of Jerusalem are here given as 'Zion your city' and 'our house of
life'[17] and there is also a call for swift vengeance on behalf of those who
have been saddened, presumably by its loss.

If Jerusalem stands as a theme in its own right in both of these
benedictions, its relevance to the wedding feast is somewhat more
problematic. One must assume that the philosophy behind its inclusion
is that even at times of self-indulgence and joy one should remember
the tragic loss of the historic and spiritual centre. Be that as it may,
there is still ambiguity about whether to place the stress on the joyous
occasion or on the loss and this makes itself particularly felt in two of

---

15   Heinemann, *Prayer in the Talmud* (see n. 11 above), pp. 70–76. See also PT, *Berakhot*
     4.3, ed. Krotoschin, f. 8a, and Tractate *Soferim* 13.11, ed. M. Higger, p. 247.
16   The Hebrew root רחם is common in the early versions but the alternative נחם was
     ultimately preferred for the Ninth of Av, perhaps because it is more closely
     associated with tragic loss.
17   It is unclear whether the Hebrew בית חיינו refers to the Temple's eternal significance,
     its close association with God as the source of all life, or its function as the guarantor
     of Israel's survival. This is reflected in the medieval liturgical commentaries.

the benedictions. In the fourth, the joy of the barren woman, joyfully gathering her children to her, clearly serves as a metaphor alluding to the return of the Jews to Jerusalem since the doxology praises God as the one who will gladden Zion through (the return of) her children. The subject of the fifth benediction is the joy of the participants, requested of God, as he produced it in Adam by creating a wife for him, but the doxology varies in different traditions. One placed the emphasis exclusively on God's gift of joy to the bride and groom; another on such a gift to his people (or Zion) and on the building of Jerusalem; and a third on the creation of his people's joy in Jerusalem.[18]

'Avodah

Since this analysis has perforce alluded to such Jerusalem institutions (if they may, for want of a better term, be categorized as such), it will not be appropriate to leave the 'amidah without devoting some attention to the seventeenth benediction, that entitled 'avodah and dealing with the Temple service, at least in so far as the textual data are relevant to the matter of Jerusalem. This benediction is particularly important since it is highly likely that elements of it have their origin in Temple times.[19] Here, the textual options are basically two, even if there is the usual phenomenon of examples that are not wholly consistent with either option but incorporate elements of both. In the first of these, the text remains true to the title given to the benediction in various talmudic passages, namely ברכת העבודה, by making use of the root עבד twice in the body of the text and once in the doxology. God is asked to express his favour by dwelling in Zion and a future is described in which his servants will serve him there and the reciters of the prayer will worship him in Jerusalem. The final phrase of the text is that God will then find favour in them and the doxological conclusion that the reciters of the benediction will serve him. The second formulation has a somewhat different style, order and content. It entreats God to favour his people and their prayer, to restore the service to his Temple (דביר ביתך), and to accept favourably their service (עבודה), including an

---

18   In addition to Heinemann, *Prayer in the Talmud* (see n. 11 above), see BT, *Ketubbot* 7b–8a, and N. Wieder, 'Fourteen new Genizah-fragments of Saadya's Siddur together with a reproduction of a missing part' in *Saadya Studies*, ed. E. I. J. Rosenthal (Manchester, 1943), pp. 270–72, republished with additional notes in his *The Formation of Jewish Liturgy in the East and the West: A Collection of Essays* (2 vols; Hebrew; Jerusalem, 1998), 2.648–58.

19   *Wa-yiqra Rabbah* 7.2, ed. M. Margaliot, 1.151; *Pesiqta de-Rabbi Kahana* 24.5, ed. B. Mandelbaum, 2.353; and Rashi's commentary on BT, *Berakhot* 11b, where he interestingly offers a reconstruction of the text in Temple times.

ambiguous reference to 'fire-offerings' that could allude to either the restoration or the acceptance. There then follows a final appeal for sight of God's merciful return to Zion, followed by a doxology that describes him as the one who restores his presence to Zion.[20]

It will perhaps be useful to spell out more precisely the differences between the two archetypes. The first formulation has a text that centres on what will happen liturgically in a future Zion followed by a doxology that stresses (and presupposes?) divine service there, while the second has a form of words that centres on God's acceptance of Jewish liturgy, followed by a doxology that stresses (and presupposes?) his return to Zion. The mention of Jerusalem is unique to the first version and that of prayer (as distinct from service) unique to the second, while the concern with finding God's favour is common to them both. Whether or not the prayer entitled *ya'aleh we-yavo* was originally more closely associated with another liturgical context, by the geonic period it is certainly part of the *'avodah* benediction and consequently deserves some attention at this point in the discussion.[21] The prayer is inserted on festive occasions and expresses the hope that on this special day God will remember his special Jewish connections. What these connections are is a matter of textual controversy although it may safely be said that certain circles tended to expand the list into a kind of litany. Perhaps there was a simple form which referred to no

---

20 Mann, 'Genizah fragments' (see n. 12 above), pp. 419–20; Elbogen (see n. 7 above), G, pp. 55–57; E, pp. 50–51; H, pp. 43–44; E. Fleischer, 'On the text of the 'avodah benediction', *Sinai* 60 (1967), pp. 269–75; Luger, *The Weekday Amidah* (see n. 14 above), pp. 173–83. Elbogen (E, p. 212) is correct about variant liturgical texts reflecting changing religious views but his claims about the theological differences between Babylon and Palestine in the case of the *'avodah* benediction are not justified by the additional textual evidence now available. The alternatives are:

a. רצה י' א' ושכון לציון [בציון] יעבדוך עבדיך בירושלים נשתחוה לך ואתה ברחמיך תחפץ בנו ותרצנו בא"י שאותך [ביראה] נעבוד

b. רצה י' א' בעמך [ישראל] ובתפלתם והשב [ה]עבודה לדביר ביתך [ואשי] ישראל ותפלתם תקביל ברצון ותהא לרצון תמיד עבודת ישראל [עמך] ותחזינה עינינו בשובך לציון ברחמיך [ותרצה בנו כמו אז] בא"י המחזיר שכינתו לציון

The later midrashic text is found in Midrash Psalms (ed. S. Buber, Vilna, 1891) 17, p. 64b, and Midrash Samuel (ed. S. Buber, Vilna², 1925), 31, p. 47b: השב שכינתך לציון וסדר עבודתך לירושלים עירך. See also U. Ehrlich, 'The earliest version of the *amidah* – the blessing about the temple worship' in *From Qumran to Cairo: Studies in the History of Prayer*, ed. J. Tabory (Jerusalem, 1999), pp. 17–38, and his edition of some Genizah fragments of the Palestinian rite in *Kobez Al Yad* 19 [29] (2006), pp. 1–22.

21 Tractate *Soferim* 19.5, ed. Higger, 327; L. J. Liebreich, 'Aspects of the New Year liturgy', *HUCA* 34 (1963), pp. 125–31; Luger, *The Weekday Amidah* (see n. 14 above), pp. 173–76; L. A. Hoffman, *The Canonization of the Synagogue Service* (Notre Dame and London, 1979), pp. 93–100. There is no scholarly consensus about the earliest context(s) of the *ya'aleh we-yavo* prayer. The textual alternatives are:

a. וזכרון עמך עירך מקדשך היכלך מעונך נאוך

b. וזכרון אבותינו וזכרון ירושלים עירך וזכרון כל עמך בית ישראל

more than the divine remembrance of the worshippers, God's people Israel. Be that as it may, one dominant formulation in the post-talmudic period also opted for a number of references associated with Jerusalem, not only mentioning God's city, without specific name, but also using a number of poetic terms for the Temple. The other specified Jerusalem by name, also cited 'our fathers', and in some versions included the Davidic messiah, but made no mention of the Temple.

Other contexts

Before an attempt is made to summarize and analyse the textual evidence, attention must be drawn to some additional data relating to Jerusalem's treatment in five other contexts, where it is of less central significance than in the cases noted above. In the *musaf* prayer for the pilgrim festivals, the basic theme is the future offering, on the respective occasions, of the requisite sacrifices ordained in the Pentateuch. Again there are two basic styles. In the first (thoroughly documented by Fleischer), biblical verses play an important part, the formulation is not greatly at odds with those used for the other *'amidot* of the day, and there are simple references to the return to Zion and Jerusalem, to the joyous sighting of the Temple, and to the festal offerings. The second version is more complex, differs from the other *'amidot*, and expands on the theme of the return to Jerusalem and the future offerings in the Temple. It decries the current inability to make the pilgrimage to the Temple site and looks forward not only to the return of the people and the sacrifices but also to the restoration of God's presence and of the specific duties of the priests, levites and Jewish population.[22] In the second post-*shema'* benediction of the evening service, God is entreated to protect the worshippers from catastrophes and to ensure their peace and security. While one version of the doxology remains with the general theme of God's protection of Israel, the other extends this to include God's 'stretching the canopy of

22   Mann, 'Genizah fragments' (see n. 12 above), pp. 325–32; Elbogen (see n. 7 above), G, pp. 132-40; E, pp. 111–17; H, pp. 100-105; E. Fleischer, *Eretz-Israel Prayer and Prayer Rituals as portrayed in the Geniza Documents* (Hebrew; Jerusalem, 1988), pp. 93–159. The alternatives are:

a. והביאנו י' א' לציון עירך ברנה ולירושלים בית מקדשך בשמחת עולם... ועינינו תאיר בבית מאווינו ושם נראה לפניך... ונעשה לפניך את חובתנו

b. נקרא שמך אתה אשר והקדוש הגדול בבית בחירתך לפניך ולהשתחוות ולראות לעלות יכולים אנו איו עליו... שתשוב ותרחם עליו ועלינו... ותבניהו... והביאנו לציון ברנה ולירושלים עירך בשמחת עולם... בנה ביתך כבתחלה כונן מקדשך על מכונו והראנו בבנינו ושמחנו בתקונו החזיר שכינה לתוכו יעלו כהנים לעבודתם ולוים לשירה ולזמרה השב ישראל אל נוהו ושבטי ישורון אל נחלתם וארמון על משפטו ישב שם נעלה ונראה לפניך...

peace' over his people Israel, consoling Zion and building Jerusalem.[23] The matter of peace is itself the subject of the final *'amidah* benediction and in some versions the blessing is invoked not only on God's people Israel but also on his city, or, more specifically, on Jerusalem.[24] As far as the *qaddish* is concerned, the version that came to be used at the burial service and at a *siyyum* ceremony goes beyond the simple praise of God and contains a passage of messianic character. This is regarded by Heinemann as a genuine *bet ha-midrash* element rather than a later addition, as was suggested by Elbogen. The theme there is that God will establish his kingdom, revive the dead, build Jerusalem, reconstruct the Temple and replace heathen ritual with authentic worship.[25] Finally, it is interesting to note that the text of the *ge'ulah* benediction included in the Passover Haggadah also includes a messianic section, in various formulations, which looks forward to the restoration of the Temple and the sacrifices and to the joy to be engendered by that development and by the 'the building of your city'. Another version, however, refers more simply to next year's joyous celebration of the Temple service in 'Zion your city'.[26]

Conclusions

What then emerges if we now attempt to capture an image of the thematic wood rather than the textual trees, first bringing into view the overall treatment of the city and its special institutions, and then

---

23 Mann, 'Genizah fragments' (see n. 12 above), pp. 302–25, especially p. 304; Elbogen (see n. 7 above), G, pp. 101–2; E, pp. 87; H, p. 78; Hoffman, *The Canonization* (see n. 21 above), p. 77. See also PT, *Berakhot* 4.5 (8c):

בא"י הפורש סוכת שלום עלינו ועל עמו ישראל מנחם ציון ובונה ירושלים אמן בא"י שומר עמו ישראל

24 Mann, 'Genizah fragments' (see n. 12 above), pp. 307 and 310–11; Elbogen (see n. 7 above), G, p. 59; E, pp. 53; H, p. 46; Heinemann, *Prayer in the Talmud* (see n. 11 above), p. 57; Luger, *The Weekday Amidah* (see n. 14 above), pp. 196–99: שים שלום על ישראל עמך ועל עירך ועל נחלתך וברכנו כולנו כאחד.

25 D. de Sola Pool, *The Kaddish* (Leipzig, 1909), pp. 79–89; Elbogen (see n. 7 above), G, pp. 92–98; E, pp. 80–84, especially 83; H, pp. 72–75; Heinemann, *Prayer in the Talmud* (see n. 11 above), pp. 266–69. There are also some useful insights and an interesting anthology in D. Telsner, *The Kaddish: Its History and Significance*, ed. G. A. Sivan (Jerusalem, 1995): יתגדל ויתקדש שמה רבא דעתיד לחדתא עלמא ולאחאה מיתיא ולמפרק חייא ולמבני קרתא דירושלם ולשכללא היכלא קדישא ולמעקר פלחנא נכראה מן ארעא ולאתבא פלחנא דשמיא לאתרה.

26 Mishnah, *Pesaḥim* 10.6, ed. E. Baneth (Berlin, 1927), p. 254, and the footnotes provided there; E. D. Goldschmidt, *The Passover Haggadah: Its Sources and History* (Hebrew; Jerusalem, 1969), pp. 56–57: הגיענו למועדים ולרגלים אחרם הבאים לקראתנו לשלום שמחים בבנין [נ"א בציון] עירך וששים בעבודתך ונאכל שם מן הזבחים ומן הפסחים...On the matter of the phrase *'or ḥadash'* inserted into the first pre-*shema'* benediction of the morning prayers, according to some rites, see N. Wieder, '*Peraqim be-toledot ha-tefillah*', *Sinai* 77 (1975), pp. 116–18, reprinted with additional notes in his *Formation of Jewish Liturgy* (see n. 18 above), 1.155–80.

moving on to the activities of God and of Israel, as they are all described in the sources examined earlier? The city is referred to as Zion, as the city of God, and simply as Jerusalem. The Temple enjoys a larger number of epithets, the basic forms alluding to it as a holy place (מקדש), glorious habitation (משכן כבוד) or house of God, while the more lyrical terms include היכל, מעון, דביר and בית חיים, all of which, while clearly conveying the general sense, present problems for the precise translator. The act of liturgy, or divine service, attracts the term עבודה but there are also more specific references to sacrifices, as well as instances in which prostration and prayer are included in the formulations. The Jewish people involved one way or another with Jerusalem are priests, levites, Israel and Zion's children and there are mentions of the royal Davidic dynasty. Apart from the references to its worship of God, reports of Israel's activities are fairly limited, with notes about her exile, her renewed sight of the holy place, and her return. As is only to be expected in praises of God and his power, on the other hand, the divine activities vis-à-vis Israel and her institutions receive considerable attention. They include (as well as his divine status) his presence and his potentially favourable treatment of Israel;[27] his mercy, compassion and building programme; his vengeance and his blessing of happiness; and his eternal restoration of Israel's lost glories.

The data collected and the themes identified are also capable of being interpreted in the context of the variety of religious ideas to be found in Jewish liturgical material in the period under discussion. There is some ambivalence about whether it is the Temple or the city that is spiritually predominant. While the Temple is sometimes seen as God's place, it also functions in a special way to the benefit of Israel. The service of God may be expressed and his favour obtained not only through the Temple rituals, past and future, but also through other acts of worship. The separate functions of Israel, the priesthood and the levites are blurred in contexts in which more general reference is made to Zion and her children. The theological and political significance of Davidic rule and the building of Jerusalem are stressed in some prayers while in others the dominant theme may be the cultic shortcomings of exile and how these will be made good by the restoration, or Israel's tragedy and how its pain may be assuaged by God's mercy or the exercise of his power as purveyor of joy or recompense. Descriptions of

---

27 Fleischer has indeed identified the central element of the עבודה benediction as the attempt to obtain God's favour (רצון) and suggested that the original doxology was הרוצה בעבודה. It may just as well have been הבוחר בעבודה but his basic point remains valid; see his article in *Sinai* cited in n. 20 above. See also the relevant Ben Sira texts in 51:27 and 51:33, ed. M. H. Segal, *Sefer Ben Sira Ha-Shalem* (2nd revised edition, Jerusalem, 1958), p. 355.

the future may be oriented towards security, the recovery of what was lost, or the messianic aeon. It may be presupposed either that it is primarily God's presence that requires to be restored to Zion or that his special favour will be obtained when Jerusalem again becomes the centre of his cultic service.[28]

As already indicated at an earlier point in this chapter, a chronological approach to the ideas and formulations to be found in early Jewish liturgy is one that is fraught with methodological danger. It is nevertheless an important interpretative option and must as such be offered, albeit with the necessary caution. If it is assumed that the scholar may with some degree of confidence identify early tannaitic material, distinguish it from later talmudic and geonic sources, and date the contents of the Genizah texts to the end of the first Christian millennium, a reconstruction of the development of liturgical ideas becomes possible. In the period before 70 CE, a realistic picture emerges of the Temple and its service, with the priests at their centre and the people of Israel at their edge, all of them the beneficiaries of the special favour expressed by God for Zion, a term that alludes to the whole religious arrangement. During the talmudic period, there is the keen anticipation of a recovery from the disasters that befell these institutions and the expectation of an almost imminent restoration of the city of Jerusalem, the Temple and its service, and the special relationship with God that they represent. God's compassion and mercy will bless Israel with security, and the people's prayers, as well as their offerings, will attract divine favour. As the passing of the centuries puts paid to even the vaguest folk memories of actual Jerusalem institutions, so the prayers chosen most commonly to relate to them become less embedded in reality and convey a more futuristic and messianic message.[29] God's infinite power will bring unexpected joy and recompense to those suffering the pain of exile and persecution. A detailed picture is painted of an idealized future, with Jerusalem functioning with more than its former glory. The Temple and the Davidic kingdom are presupposed and each group of Jews is seen to be playing a part in the scene. Economy of expression and simplicity of language, particularly as championed by the Babylonian formulations,

---

28   Many of these notions are of course mutually compatible and even those that appear to stress opposing concepts may be doing so because they are operating in different contexts. One's interpretation of the evidence ultimately depends on the degree to which one expects to find total consistency in a set of prayer texts from a given time or provenance.

29   It is hardly necessary to point out that the predominance of a particular kind of theological message in one historical or religious context does not mean that it was not previously in existence in an earlier or alternative one.

give way to the kind of generous augmentation and colourful vocabulary that are more characteristic of Palestinian prayer texts.

What if, however, the dating of tannaitic material is more problematic and the talmudic traditions as they have come down to us are less than reliable witnesses to the precise prayer forms of the talmudic period? Perhaps geonic testimonies are not disinterested records of liturgical developments but contain more than their share of propaganda on behalf of their own notions and ambitions. Is there always such a clear-cut distinction between what is authoritative and Babylonian on the one hand and what is deviant and Palestinian on the other? Conceivably, Genizah texts of the ninth and tenth centuries are authentic bearers of liturgical traditions that predate the geonic tendency to standardization but became popular only afterwards.[30] It must be allowed that such doubts would call into question some of the chronological reconstruction just attempted. At the same time, however, it would still be possible to maintain that the religious ideas identified in the liturgical texts examined, in all their variety and difference of emphasis, stand testimony to changing conceptions of Jerusalem and its institutions on the part of Jews in the first Christian millennium. The changes may be due as much to the different milieux from which various forms of liturgy emerged as to chronological developments over a period of centuries. But a synchronic rather than a diachronic analysis would still detect the same rich variety of theological notions appertaining to Jerusalem as that described above. The problem is that any attempt to set their emergence and development in particular historical contexts suffers seriously from a lack of matching historical data. Whatever the methodological preference, there can be no avoiding the conclusion that Jerusalem stood close to the hearts and minds of Jewish worshippers whenever and wherever they formulated prayers that were central to their reflections on the present and their aspirations for the future.

---

30 What is being touched on here is the wider methodological debate about Jewish liturgical history which is reflected, for instance, in the differences between my views and those of E. Fleischer; see Reif, *Judaism and Hebrew Prayer* (see n. 3 above), pp. 5, 54, 77, 90, 105–6, 119 and 136; Fleischer, 'On the beginnings of obligatory Jewish prayer', *Tarbiz* 59 (1990), pp. 397–441 and his rejoinder to me in *Tarbiz* 60 (1991), pp. 683–88; Reif, 'On the earliest development of Jewish prayer', *Tarbiz* 60 (1991), pp. 677–81; and chapter 2 above.

9

Notions of Restoration

Topic

Scholars invited to explore the expanses of rabbinic prayer in search of the finest samples of a theological product widely defined as 'restoration' might be forgiven for making the *'amidah* their first port of call. Given that the 'standing prayer' is generally regarded as the most ancient, central and characteristic of the liturgical formulations promoted by talmudic Judaism, they would rightly expect to find there the most authentic creations of the particular spiritual territory being scoured. Having been safely garnered and packaged, such goods could then be displayed among the variety of wares made available to the consumer in the market for religious notions of such a genre. And the *'amidah* would not disappoint such expectations; for there, at the centre of this famous anthology of benedictions, in the eleventh example, one encounters a text that apparently promises precisely what one is seeking and that advertises its potential relevance by the use of the introductory word השיבה, namely, 'Restore'.

Sample text

Any researcher worth an academic tenure would, of course, be aware that one cannot simply pluck a version from any rabbinic prayer-book and discuss its relevance to the history of Jewish religious ideas in the first Christian millennium. One should rather take as one's starting-point the earliest *siddurim*, or formal collections of liturgy, acknowledging that these date from the last centuries of that millennium but hoping to find there at least some reflections of the kind of ideology that had established itself among the rabbinic teachers and worshippers of the earlier talmudic period. The prayer-book with the soundest textual witnesses from among these pioneering archetypes is undoubtedly that of Sa'adya Gaon who flourished as the head of the rabbinical school of Sura at the beginning of the tenth century.[1] His version of the eleventh benediction would surely then

---

1   The standard edition is *Siddur R. Saadja Gaon*, eds I. Davidson, S. Assaf and B. I. Joel, (Jerusalem, 1941, Jerusalem², 1963). For more recent work, see N. Wieder, *The*

provide at least an initial guide to what early rabbinic liturgy had to say about the topic of restoration.

The text, to which we shall shortly return in more detail, is simple enough. It appeals to God to restore the people's judges and mentors to their former state and praises the Divine King for loving what is right and just. The matter becomes more complicated when one compares other evidence relating to the benediction, or attesting to its formulation, and dating from that same geonic period or its earlier talmudic counterpart. All at once, we are confronted with phrases that seem to deal with alternative subjects such as the quality of human life and the extent and nature of Divine power. What is more, the talmudic rabbis unusually had no formal title for this benediction and there is no unanimity about the words to be used in the concluding doxology, which often carries the key to understanding the broader context. Indeed, it emerges that there is no consensus about what precisely the whole benediction wishes to see restored. Is it a fair system of theodicy or the elementary punishment of the wicked? Are we looking forward to messianic judgement or the integrity of law-courts? Could there be here a polemic against non-Jewish courts, or against the alleged misjudgements of apostates from Judaism, or sectarians? [2]

This lack of textual and contextual clarity certainly makes one thing clear. Such liturgical material may not accurately supply the required theological information here being sought quite as readily as we might have supposed. The difficulties about reliably exploiting one small paragraph counsel caution and pause and are symptomatic of a number of methodological problems that have to be noted before any progress can be made in drawing on the rabbinic prayer-book for the history of Jewish religious ideas. That classic source does, of course, provide rich seams of spirituality, philosophy and history but so many movements and disturbances have taken place in their overall structure over the generations that it is no longer an easy matter to identify which was laid down when and how the deposits relate to each other. In order successfully to take on and meet the challenge issued by the topic of this chapter, it will therefore be necessary to offer some comments about where rabbinic liturgy originated and how it was transmitted and modified. Also required will be a tentative explanation

---

Formation of Jewish Liturgy in the East and the West: A Collection of Essays (Hebrew; 2 vols; Jerusalem, 1998), pp. 561–658; R. Brody, 'Saadya Gaon on the limits of liturgical flexibility' in *Genizah Research after Ninety Years*, eds J. Blau and S. C. Reif (Cambridge, 1992), pp. 40–46; and R. Brody, 'The conclusion of Se'adya Gaon's prayerbook', *Tarbiz* 63 (1994), pp. 393–401 and 'Note on the conclusion of Se'adya Gaon's prayerbook', *Tarbiz* 68 (1999), pp. 279–81.
2   See text and translation of no. 3 below. See also, more generally, chapter 16 below.

of the ideological background against which liturgical subject matter
was played out and a brief assessment of the degree to which it is
feasible firmly to attach particular ideas to specific periods in a clearly
definable, diachronic development. Such methodological considerations are intended to lay the foundations for a justification of the
manner in which the topic is subsequently treated and the conclusions
thereby reached.

Early rabbinic transmission

One of the over-riding paradoxes about talmudic literature is that,
while it provides an extensive and authentic expression of the rabbinic
Judaism that became so powerful in the first few Christian centuries, its
very success in that respect has contributed to obscuring the manner in
which it was achieved. In earlier and later periods of Jewish religious
development, we are able to identify layers of development, competing
interpretations and a broader context in which they operated, largely
because the literature sub-divides itself for us and there is much
external material with which to compare it. As far as the talmudic
period is concerned, the numerous clusters of traditions, variegated
though they are in respect of attribution, style, subject and intent, have
been fused into one mass. Through a long process of transmission and
redaction, the generations of the learned and the loyal have ensured
that the body of texts that has become for them almost canonical in its
status and importance has also acquired a style and flavour of its own.
Inbuilt into the system has been a tendency to harmonize its
constituents and to present its contents as uniform and authoritative,
the sole representative of the Jewish religious tradition in the Classical
and Byzantine eras.[3]

This presents particular difficulties in the field of liturgy. Although
there is still evidence in the talmudic sources that the Babylonian and
Palestinian communities followed different liturgical customs, it is

---

3   Some discussion of the major problems may be found in *The Formation of the
    Babylonian Talmud*, ed. J. Neusner (Leiden, 1970); *The Jewish People in the First Century:
    Historical Geography, Political History, Social, Cultural and Religious Life and Institutions*,
    eds S. Safrai and M. Stern (2 vols; Assen and Philadelphia, 1974–76); *The Literature of
    the Sages. First Part: Oral Tora, Halakha, Mishna, Tosefta, Talmud, External Tractates*, ed.
    S. Safrai (Assen, Maastricht and Philadelphia, 1987); H. Maccoby, *Early Rabbinic
    Writings* (Cambridge, 1988); *Mikra: Text, Translation, Reading and Interpretation of the
    Hebrew Bible in Ancient Judaism and Early Christianity*, ed. M. J. Mulder (Assen and
    Philadelphia, 1988); J. Sussmann and D. Rosenthal, מחקרי תלמוד: קובץ מחקרים בתלמוד
    ותחומים גובלים (Jerusalem, 1990–93); G. Stemberger, *Introduction to the Talmud and
    Midrash* (E. T., Edinburgh, 1996); *Cambridge History of Judaism*, vol. 3, eds W. D.
    Davies, J. Sturdy and W. Horbury (Cambridge, 1999).

often difficult to identify the precise differences because of the manner
in which the later, usually Babylonian, customs have come to dominate
the relevant texts. Since there is no longer any doubt that the diaspora
synagogues in the broader Graeco-Roman world followed their own
traditions in such areas as language, iconography and administration, it
is highly unlikely that their prayer-texts fully matched those of their
Babylonian counterparts.[4] Sadly, however, there is little evidence to
indicate the precise nature of their devotions. Furthermore, the very
nature of liturgy conspires with these historical and theological
considerations to add to the problem. The recitation of prayers is no
mere theory of religion; it is an active and dynamic element in rabbinic
practice, familiar to a large proportion of the adherents to the faith, for
many of them on a daily, or at least a weekly basis. Traditions that
incorporate liturgical formulas of earlier or distant communities are
therefore inevitably prone to alteration and standardization in the light
of the experience and commitments of those who inherit and transmit
them.

There is another factor that further complicates matters and was
even perhaps integral to the emergence, expansion and success of the
rabbinic tradition. The medium for that tradition's message was
primarily an oral one. While other Jews had opted for the written form,
the rabbinic communities preferred to pass on their talmudic and
related traditions by word of mouth, perhaps in an effort to distinguish
the Oral Torah from the Written Torah, perhaps to retain a unique and
powerful educational experience. This is not to say that there was no
process of editing. Textual interpretations and legal discussions had for
centuries been acquiring an increasingly formal structure but there is
no reason to suppose that such a structure could not be adopted and
developed without recourse to writing. Oral transmission was seen as a
special feature of the revelation to Israel and there was a serious
suspicion that a commitment to writing was a betrayal of the authentic
historical experience. It therefore follows that, in spite of the care taken
to pass on the traditions in a sound form, there was still a considerable
degree of fluidity in all the texts being orally transmitted.[5]

4   For recent treatments of these and related topics, see L. A. Hoffman, *The Canonization
     of the Synagogue Service* (Notre Dame and London, 1979); P. F. Bradshaw and L. A.
     Hoffman (eds), *The Making of Jewish and Christian Worship* (Notre Dame and London,
     1991) and *The Changing Face of Jewish and Christian Worship* (Notre Dame and
     London, 1991); S. C. Reif, *Judaism and Hebrew Prayer: New Perspectives on Jewish
     Liturgical History* (Cambridge, 1993); L. I. Levine, *The Ancient Synagogue: The First
     Thousand Years* (New Haven and London, 2000).
5   For aspects of the history of Jewish books and scribes and the importance of orality,
     see *The Hebrew Book: An Historical Survey*, eds R. Posner and I. Ta-Shma (Jerusalem,
     1975); M. Beit-Arié, *Hebrew Codicology: Tentative Typology of Technical Practices*

Given that there is an almost total absence of Hebrew manuscripts between the second and the ninth centuries – a phenomenon that may not be accidental but may relate to the strength of the oral tradition just noted – we can only speculate about the nature of written liturgy in the late talmudic and early geonic periods. We do, however, have some talmudic traditions that permit us to derive some technical information. Until the eighth century, the individual folio, made of papyrus, leather, or possibly cloth, was the main writing material for any rabbinic liturgical text that did achieve such formal recognition. Alternatively, a less strictly controlled version of the scroll than that in use for the Hebrew Bible might have been employed. When, in, say, the ninth and tenth centuries, the codex became the fashionable medium for talmudic Jews, at first with the use of papyrus or vellum but later exclusively with vellum, it contained a few gatherings simply stitched together, tended to be of a small, manageable size, and perhaps, like a scroll, was written only on one side. While individual folios, whether or not joined, continued to be classified as *diphthera*, the scroll form was known as *gewil*, and the later Arabic term for the bound volume, namely, *mushaf*, was eventually adopted by the Jews of the Orient to describe what is more generally familiar to western scholarship as the codex.[6]

Employed in Hebrew Dated Medieval Manuscripts (Jerusalem[2], 1981); S. D. Goitein, *A Mediterranean Society: The Jewish Communities of the Arab World as Portrayed in the Documents of the Cairo Geniza*, 5 vols and index volume (Berkeley, Los Angeles and London, 1967–93), vol. 2 (1971), pp. 228–40; S. C. Reif, 'Aspects of mediaeval Jewish literacy' in *The Uses of Literacy in Early Mediaeval Europe*, ed. R. McKitterick (Cambridge, 1989), pp. 134–55; B. Gerhardsson, *Memory and Manuscript* (Lund and Copenhagen, 1961; republished with a new preface by the author and a foreword by J. Neusner, together with *Tradition and Transmission in Early Christianity*, Grand Rapids and Livonia, Michigan, 1998); M. J. Carruthers, *The Book of Memory: A Study in Medieval Culture* (Cambridge, 1990); and W. A. Graham, *Beyond the Written Word: Oral Aspects of Scripture in the History of Religion* (Cambridge, 1987; paperback edition, 1993).

6   Information about the Jewish adoption and use of the codex may be found in S. Lieberman, *Hellenism in Jewish Palestine: Studies in the Literary Transmission, Beliefs and Manners of Palestine in the I Century B. C. E. – IV Century C. E.* (New York[2], 1962), pp. 203–9; E. G. Turner, *The Typology of the Early Codex* (Philadelphia, 1977); C. M. Roberts and T. C. Skeat, *The Birth of the Codex* (London[2], 1983); R. H. Rouse and M. A. Rouse, 'Codicology, Western European' in *Dictionary of the Middle Ages* (New York, 1982-89), vol. 3 (1983), pp. 475–78; M. Beit-Arié, 'How Hebrew manuscripts are made' in *A Sign and a Witness: 2,000 years of Hebrew Books and Illustrated Manuscripts*, ed. L. S. Gold (New York and Oxford, 1988), pp. 35–46; I. M. Resnick, 'The codex in early Jewish and Christian communities', *JRH* 17 (1992), pp. 1–17. Papyrus is still used for some of the older Genizah material (e.g. Cambridge MS T-S 6H9–21) and there are also examples of cloth being used for the recording of texts (e.g. T-S 16.31). See also C. Sirat, *Les Papyrus en Caractères Hébraïques trouvés en Egypte* (Paris, 1985) and her brief note on T-S 6H9–21 in *Genizah Fragments* 5 (April, 1983), pp. 3–4. The

Although the use of the codex was ultimately destined to have a revolutionary effect on many aspects of the rabbinic liturgy, including its size, content and status, the primary purpose of the prayer-text at that early stage was to provide the basic wording, some rubrics for its use, and also possibly some sort of justification for its being chosen out of the many alternatives still circulating. Perhaps the small, primitive and rather fully covered sheets of vellum precluded any additional attention, or perhaps there was still doubt about the use of a written format. Certainly, there are responsa that appear to testify that the issue of orality versus textuality was still a live one in the eighth and ninth centuries. What is particularly important and noteworthy for us in our present discussion is that such physical developments encouraged a number of literary and liturgical ones. As it became more common to write down the rabbinic traditions, including the prayers, in a respectful and systematic manner, so the tendency grew to regard such texts as having something of a canonical nature. The single leaf evolved into the codex, the private individual became the professional scribe, and brief and provisional notes evolved into formal prayer-books.[7]

Methodological aspects

How do such considerations affect this examination of the topic of restoration? What I propose to do is to examine a few of the major benedictions that are of relevance to the subject and to compare their textual formats, as derived from the authoritative talmudic and geonic sources, with those found in the less conformist Genizah fragments. I shall refrain from presupposing that all short, simple Babylonian texts represent the pristine form while all longer, more complex Palestinian versions (from the Genizah, for example) may universally be judged to be later accretions. Rather than confidently (but unjustifiably) associating specific formulations with particular places and periods, I shall adopt a less speculative approach that simply gives an account of the textual options that existed. Since I subscribe to the view that most liturgical variants convey a meaningful religious message of some sort,

pentateuchal codex was known to the oriental Jews as *mashaf torah*, as in e.g. T-S 12.791, or *mashaf de-'orayta*, as in e.g. T-S A41.41.

7   S. C. Reif, 'Codicological aspects of Jewish liturgical history', *BJRULM* 75/3 (1993), pp. 117–31, and 'The Genizah and Jewish liturgy: past achievements and a current project', *Medieval Encounters* 5.1 (1999), pp. 29–45. For a fuller Hebrew version of the relevant part of the latter, see Reif, 'Written prayers from the Genizah: their physical aspect and its relationship to their content' in *From Qumran to Cairo: Studies in the History of Prayer*, ed. J. Tabory (Jerusalem, 1999), pp. 121–30. For an updated treatment of the broader topic, see chapter 11 below.

I shall also attempt to summarize the theological import of each version. Once the data have been analysed in this way, it should be possible to draw some general conclusions of assistance to the historian of religious ideas.[8]

But none of these ideas came into existence or continued to operate in a liturgical or theological vacuum. With regard to liturgy, it is not only important to take account of the developments in the geonic and medieval periods as they are well reflected in the prayer-books during the period that they crystallized, expanded and became authoritative. Attention has also to be paid to the earlier sources from which the rabbinic prototypes seem to have been drawn or by which their content was apparently inspired during the Second Temple period. The evidence from Qumran makes it clear that there were groups who recited regular prayers at specific times but there is no obvious consistency of text and context for these. There are written texts from Qumran that record such prayers and they have elements in common with the rabbinic liturgy of the second Christian century, even if the latter ultimately chose to transmit them in oral form. Given the breadth of the liturgical material found at Qumran, there was clearly more than one provenance for the development of hymns and prayers during the Second Temple period. Rabbinic prayer, borrowing from such contexts, incorporates earlier material but imposes upon it a fresh order, style and distinctive formulation. This innovative aspect reflects the traditions of early talmudic Judaism and its own approach to the Hebrew language and to the biblical canon.[9]

On the theological side, the notion of restoration belongs to the broader notion of visions of the future and talmudic literature has its share of these, even if it cannot fairly be argued that they enjoyed a central role or were consistently and systematically conceived and expressed. Some of the ideas concerned individuals and how they were to be rescued from life's various vicissitudes, to see justice done, and to be blessed with a good quality of life. That was at the mundane and more immediate level while in the more idealized and utopian future, they could look forward to a time when their souls, perhaps more collectively than individually, would experience the ultimate reward of the good and punishment of the wicked, as well as eternal bliss and the resurrection of the dead. Other concepts were even more nationally oriented and concerned the re-establishment of the royal, cultic and political institutions and the return of the Jews from the countries of their diaspora to their holy land. Such hopes could constitute realistic

---

8   See chapter 7 above.
9   See chapter 4 above.

expectations of developments not to be long delayed or could be of a more eschatological nature. In that case, the messianic figure became more spiritualized, the atmosphere took on a more apocalyptic hue, and the events included war and catastrophe before leading to a satisfactory theological denouement.[10]

'Amidah texts

If we may now return to the *'amidah*, the first point to be made is that this anthology of benedictions contains entreaties for the return of supposedly ideal situations at the personal as well as the national level. The famous rabbinic scholar of eleventh-century France, Rashi (= Rabbi Solomon ben Isaac) demonstrates an awareness of this in his comments on a talmudic passage dealing with these benedictions. In response to Rava's claim that redemption is the subject of the seventh benediction because the ultimate redemption will occur in the sabbatical year, Rashi stresses that such an interpretation is justified only because the Hebrew root גאל is used in both cases but not because it refers to the same kind of redemption or rescue in each case. In the seventh benediction, the prayer is for God to rescue us from our constant and mundane tribulations while the ultimate redemption will gather us in from our exile, rebuild Jerusalem and re-establish the royal house of David. These three subjects are treated in a different section of the *'amidah* and are each accorded an independent benediction.[11] Taking our lead from Rashi, it will, in this presentation, be more appropriate for us to deal with those benedictions in which the restoration touches on very specific developments rather than alluding more broadly to better times and conditions. Each benediction will be identified, cited in Hebrew from the tenth-century text of R. Sa'adya Gaon, given my own English rendering, compared with other versions, and analysed for the relevant theological content.

1. Daily *'amidah*, second benediction, known as גבורות :

Hebrew text

אתה גבור לעולם ייי רב להושיע מכלכל חיים בחסד מחיה מתים ברחמים רבים רופא חולים ומתיר אסורים ומשען לאביונים ומקיים אמונתו לישני עפר מי כמוך בעל גבורות ומי דומה לך ממית ומחיה ב א ייי מחיה המתים

---

10   For a most useful and informative treatment of the relevant theology to be found in early rabbinic sources, see E. E. Urbach, *The Sages: Their Concepts and Beliefs* (E. T., 2 vols; Jerusalem, 1975), 1.649–92, and 2.990–1009.

11   See BT, *Megillah* 17b, where the *'amidah* benedictions are discussed, and Rashi's comments on that passage.

English translation
Your miraculous powers are eternal, Lord, and are exercised in many ways. [In winter: You make the wind blow and the rain fall.] You generously sustain the living and most mercifully restore the dead to life. You cure the sick, release the captive and support the poor. He keeps his promise to those who sleep in the dust. Who is like you, Master of such powers, and who may be compared to you, bringer of death and restorer of life? You are praised, Lord, as the restorer of the dead to life.[12]

The theme of this benediction is that God alone has the special power of bringing about changes in those aspects of life that are often considered uncontrollable and that can bring, at the very least, considerable discomfort, and at the worst, various degrees of tragedy. The simplest forms of the benediction refer to God's exercise of his power through his provision of rain and food and his restoration of life to the dead. The most extensive forms of the benediction include repetitions of the themes of power and restoration, and include among the examples the thwarting of tyranny and oppression and (unless phrases such as סומך נופלים and זוקף כפופים are metaphorical) the restoration of physical normality.[13] If due account is taken of the title of the benediction, the order of the contents and the nature of the themes mentioned, it seems more likely that the ability to restore the dead to life was added to a benediction dealing with God's overall powers than *vice versa*. If that is a valid conclusion, it would be reasonable to

---

12 *Siddur R. Saadja* (see n. 1 above), p. 18; S. Baer, *Seder 'Avodat Yisra'el* (Rödelheim, 1868), p. 89; *Siddur Oṣar Ha-Tefillot*, ed. A. L. Gordon (corrected and expanded edition, Vilna, 1923, Hebrew pagination), pp. 156b–159a.
13 S. Schechter, 'Genizah specimens: liturgy', *JQR* 10 (1898), p. 656; I. Elbogen, German edition = G, *Der jüdische Gottesdienst in seiner geschichtlichen Entwicklung* (Frankfurt am Main, 1931; reprint, Hildesheim, 1962), pp. 27–41 and 44–45; Hebrew edition = H, התפילה בישראל בהתפתחותה ההיסטורית (eds J. Heinemann, I. Adler, A. Negev, J. Petuchowski and H. Schirmann, Tel Aviv, 1972), pp. 20–32 and 34–35; English edition = E, *Jewish Liturgy: A Comprehensive History* (English translation and edition by R. P. Scheindlin, Philadelphia, Jerusalem and New York,1993), pp. 24–37 and 39; J. Mann, 'Genizah fragments of the Palestinian order of service,' *HUCA* 2 (1925), pp. 306, 309–10, reprinted in *Contributions to the Scientific Study of Jewish Liturgy* (ed. J. J. Petuchowski, New York, 1970), pp. 416, 419–20; L. Finkelstein, 'The development of the amidah', *JQR*, NS 16 (1925), pp. 142–45; L. Ginzberg, *A Commentary on the Palestinian Talmud* (4 vols; New York, 1941 and 1961), vol. 4, ed. D. Weiss-Halivni, pp. 164–68, 184–91; S. Assaf, 'Mi-seder ha-tefillah be-Ereṣ Yisra'el' in *Sefer Dinaburg*, eds Y. Baer, J. Guttmann and M. Shova (Jerusalem, 1949), p. 117; J. Heinemann, *Prayer in the Period of the Tanna'im and Amora'im: Its Nature and Its Patterns* (Hebrew; Jerusalem², 1966), pp. 31, 40–41; revised English edition, *Prayer in the Talmud: Forms and Patterns* (Berlin and New York, 1977), pp. 26–29, 58; B. S. Jacobson, *Netiv Binah* (Hebrew; 5 vols; Tel Aviv, 1968–83), 1.273–74; E. Fleischer, *Eretz-Israel Prayer and Prayer Rituals as Portrayed in the Geniza Documents* (Hebrew; Jerusalem, 1988), pp. 35–36, n. 52; Y. Luger, *The Weekday Amidah in the Cairo Genizah* (Hebrew; Jerusalem, 2001), pp. 53–62.

postulate that the concluding doxology did not originally refer to the restoration theme but to God's miraculous powers. Whatever the chronology of the themes, they are all included here as examples of what are to be regarded here and now as the divine characteristics. When and how they are or will be demonstrated is another matter.

2. Daily *'amidah*, tenth benediction, known as קבוץ גלויות:

Hebrew text

תקע שופר גדול לחירותנו ושא נס מהרה לקבצנו ברוך אתה ייי מקבץ נדחי עמו ישראל

English translation
Sound a powerful horn for our freedom and raise a speedy banner for our ingathering. You are praised, Lord, as the one who gathers in the exiles of his people Israel.[14]

This benediction constitutes an entreaty to God to bring about the end of the Jewish people's captivity and exile and the restoration of their unity. The briefer versions simply record these two pleas, sometimes omitting the mention of the people of Israel in the concluding doxology while those that have a more extensive text refer to the current dispersion over the four corners of the earth and pray for a joyous, swift and liberated journey of return. The longer forms also use an imperative verb (קבצנו) and refer specifically, not just metaphorically, to a restoration to Israel's own land and to God's holy habitation.[15] There are strong grounds for presupposing that the simple liturgical formulation of a request for the re-strengthening of the population of the homeland as against its dissipation into a growing diaspora could have been made at any time during the Second Temple period. The inclusion of certain additional factors in the benediction does, however, indicate other considerations. The use of more powerful words such as נדחים and חירות point in the direction of a political restoration. The special status given to the land and the cultic centre conveys a spiritual message. The metaphorical language used to describe the beginning of the restoration is more reminiscent of a prophetic vision than of a request for an imminent change of situation.

---

14 *Siddur R. Saadja* (see n. 1 above), p. 18; Baer, *'Avodat Yisra'el* (see n. 12 above), p. 92; *Oṣar Ha-Tefillot* (see n. 12 above), pp. 333–35.

15 Schechter, 'Genizah specimens', p. 657; Elbogen, G, p. 50; H, p. 39; E, pp. 44–45; Mann, 'Palestinian order of service', pp. 296, 306, 309–10; Finkelstein, 'The development of the amidah', pp. 12–15, 154–55; Ginzberg, *Palestinian Talmud*, vol. 3, pp. 324–25; Assaf, '*Mi-seder ha-tefillah*', p. 118; Jacobson, *Netiv Binah*, 1.281–82; Luger, *Weekday 'Amidah*, pp. 114–18. For fuller sources see n. 13 above.

3. Daily *'amidah*, eleventh benediction, with no talmudic title:

Hebrew text

השיבה שופטינו כבראשונה ויועצנו כבתחלה ברוך אתה ייי מלך אוהב צדקה ומשפט

English translation

Restore our judges as they first were and our mentors as they were at the outset. You are praised as the King who is devoted to what is right and just.[16]

What is here being requested is the restoration of some sort of pristine state in which correct judgements are made by those of the Jewish people with special responsibilities for such activities. Such correct judgements are given the stamp of divine approval by being linked in the doxological conclusion with the kind of qualities to which God is himself partial. The body of the benediction as recorded by Sa'adya Gaon is as short as it occurs anywhere but the epithets used to describe God at its end may well have been simpler in origin, referring to him as no more than a devotee (אוהב) or a king of משפט. The longer versions of the benediction include references to the removal of sorrow, to the eternal reign of God, and to just rulership.[17] It will be recalled that we had reason to note the contents of this benediction at an earlier point in the discussion and to draw attention to the fact that there was no consensus at any stage among the commentators as to their general import. It is not and was not clear which judges and judgements (or misjudgements) the worshipper has in mind; whether the ideology being promoted is theological or juridical; and at what point in time the expected improvement is to be expected. In that case, each phrase that is not found in the most skeletal format of the benediction may represent an attempt at interpreting at least part of its basic sense vis-à-vis what the future should hold. The fact that later developments tended to include all or most of these by no means proves that they originally stood together as a unified testimony to one particular notion of restoration.

4. Daily *'amidah*, fourteenth benediction, known as בונה ירושלים:

Hebrew text

רחם ייי אלהינו עלינו על ישראל עמך ועל ירושלים עירך ועל היכלך ועל מעונך ועל ציון משכן כבודך ובנה
ברחמיך את ירושלים ברוך אתה ייי בונה ירושלים

---

16 *Siddur R. Saadja* (see n. 1 above), p. 18; Baer, *'Avodat Yisra'el* (see n. 12 above), pp. 92–93, *Oṣar Ha-Tefillot* (see n. 12 above), pp. 335–36. See Isaiah 1:26 for the biblical source of the phraseology.

17 Schechter, 'Genizah specimens', p. 657; Elbogen, G, pp. 50–55; H, pp. 39–40; E, p. 45; Mann, 'Palestinian order of service', pp. 306, 309–310; Finkelstein, 'The development of the amidah', pp. 14–15, 154–55; Ginzberg, *Palestinian Talmud*, vol. 3, pp. 325–29; Assaf, 'Mi-seder ha-tefillah', p. 118; Heinemann, *Prayer* (see n. 13 above), Hebrew edition, p. 141; English edition, pp. 223–24; Jacobson, *Netiv Binah*, 1.282–83; Luger, *Weekday Amidah*, pp. 119–32. For fuller sources see n. 13 above.

English translation
Show mercy, Lord, our God, to us, to your people Israel, to your city Jerusalem, to your temple, to your habitation, and to Zion, your esteemed residence, and mercifully build Jerusalem. You are praised, Lord, as the builder of Jerusalem.[18]

What is here being requested is a change of divine sentiment towards the Jews and their special centre in Jerusalem that will lead to its being rebuilt. The simplest form of the benediction prays for God's return to Jerusalem and links this with its physical restoration. In the more complex varieties of the entreaty, reference is made to some or all of a number of associated bodies, such as the worshippers, the Jewish people, the city and the Temple, the last two being described by a variety of poetic epithets. Some texts look forward to a speedy restoration while others are more concerned with its permanency, and there are some references to the people returning joyfully to the holy city. As is well known, the benediction for the Davidic dynasty (next to be discussed below) is not always included in texts of the *'amidah*. In some witnesses it is replaced by a brief reference to that subject in this benediction for Jerusalem, with or without a specific mention of the messianic element, and in others it appears both here and independently. Where it does appear here, the concluding doxology may also refer to God as the God of David as well as the builder of Jerusalem.[19] Given the variety of its textual format, there is no clarity in the overall benediction as to the precise geography, chronology and theology of what is to be restored. Is the stress on the rebuilt, physical city of the near future and its repopulation by the Jews, or on the reconstructed Temple of the idealized messianic age and the bliss this will bring to those who participate in the restored cult?

---

18 *Siddur R. Saadja* (see n. 1 above), p. 18; Baer, *'Avodat Yisra'el* (see n. 12 above), p. 96; *Oṣar Ha-Tefillot* (see n. 12 above), pp. 339–40.

19 Schechter, 'Genizah specimens', pp. 657, 659; Elbogen, G, pp. 52–54; H, pp. 41–42; E, pp. 47–48; Mann, 'Palestinian order of service', pp. 306, 309–310; Finkelstein, 'The development of the amidah', pp. 33–38, 158–59; Ginzberg, *Palestinian Talmud*, vol. 3, pp. 329–30; Assaf, *'Mi-seder ha-tefillah'*, p. 118; Heinemann, *Prayer* (see n. 13 above), Hebrew edition, pp. 35–40, 48–51, English edition, pp. 48–56, 70–76, 288–91 and *Studies in Jewish Liturgy*, ed. A. Shinan (Hebrew; Jerusalem, 1981; originally published in *Hayyim (Jefim) Schirmann Jubilee Volume*, eds S. Abramson and A. Mirsky, Jerusalem, 1970, pp. 93–101), pp. 3–11; Luger, *Weekday Amidah*, pp. 150–58; Jacobson, *Netiv Binah*, 1.285–86. For fuller sources see n. 13 above, and chapter 7 above. See U. Ehrlich, 'On the ancient version of the benediction 'Builder of Jerusalem' and the benediction of David' (Hebrew), *Pe'amim* 78 (1999), pp. 16–43 and his edition of some Genizah fragments of the Palestinian rite in *Kobez Al Yad* 19 [29] (2006), pp. 1–22; see also Tosefta *Berakhot* 3.25, ed. Zuckermandel, p. 9.

5. Daily *'amidah*, fifteenth benediction, with no talmudic title:

Hebrew text

את צמח דויד עתה תצמיח וקרנו תרים בישועתך ברוך אתה ייי מצמיח קרן ישועה

English translation

Now make the offspring of David flourish and raise his head high by granting your succour. You are praised, Lord, as the one who generates pride by granting succour.[20]

In those cases in which manuscripts testify to an independent benediction – and they are by no means a small proportion – the message is brief and direct, even if the precise meaning and immediate relevance is not obvious. As expressed, the benediction calls for a proud and successful Davidic dynasty and the textual variations are generally minor. The pronoun אתה replaces the adverb עתה; there are disagreements about the inclusion of a conjunctive *waw*; there is doubt whether a *qal* or *hiph'il* form is to be used with the verb רום; and some texts hope that the request may be met swiftly. Perhaps more significantly, one version includes, immediately before the doxological conclusion, an expression of the people's continuous longing for divine succour. Interestingly, that concluding formula unexpectedly makes no mention whatsoever of David but appears to concentrate on the broader notion of succour.[21] It is not our present task to argue whether the one benediction has here become two, or *vice versa*, but rather to identify what the issues might have been that could conceivably have led to a move in one direction or the other. If the entreaty here is for the successful continuation of what is seen as Davidic leadership, it is a request for the here and now and an expression of support for, say, the Patriarch in Palestine or the Exilarch in Babylon. If this were regarded as central, it might warrant its own benediction. If a restoration of national institutions is the theme, it would fit well with that version of the previous benediction that listed a number of these and looked forward to the (perhaps distant?) future in which they would recur in what might be a form more splendid than ever. If the benediction were to remain independent, it might opt for a more general and less Davidic or messianic theme, as appears to have occurred in the case of the concluding doxology.

---

20   *Siddur R. Saadja* (see n. 1 above), p. 18; Baer, *'Avodat Yisra'el* (see n. 12 above), p. 97; *Oṣar Ha-Tefillot* (see n. 12 above), p. 341.

21   Elbogen, G p. 54; H, p. 42; E, pp. 48–49; Mann, 'Palestinian order of service', pp. 300, 310; Finkelstein, 'The development of the amidah', p. 160; Ginzberg, *Palestinian Talmud*, vol. 3, pp. 277–79; Heinemann, *Prayer* (see n. 13 above), Hebrew edition, pp. 37, 140; English edition, pp. 52–53, 222; Jacobson, *Netiv Binah*, 1.287; Y. Liebes, '*Mazmiaḥ qeren yeshu'ah*', *Jerusalem Studies in Jewish Thought* 3 (1983–84), pp. 313–48 and the subsequent discussion in 4 (1984–85), pp. 181–217 and 341–54; Fleischer, *Eretz-Israel Prayer*, p. 19, n. 3, p. 181; Luger, *Weekday Amidah*, pp. 159–65. For fuller sources see n. 13 above.

6. Daily 'amidah, seventeenth benediction, known as עבודה:

Hebrew text

רצה ייי אלהינו בעמך ובתפלתם והשב עבודה לדביר ביתך ואשי ישראל ותפלתם תקבל ברצון ותהא לרצון
תמיד עבודת ישראל ותחזינה עינינו בשובך לציון ברחמים ותרצה בנו כמו אז ברוך אתה ייי המחזיר שכינתו
לציון

English translation

Find favour, Lord, our God, in your people and in their prayer, and restore the ritual to the centre of your shrine. Accept as favourable the offerings and prayers of Israel and may Israel's ritual always be favourable. May we witness your merciful return to Zion and may you favour us as you did in the past. You are praised, Lord, as (the one) who restores his divine presence to Zion.[22]

This first of the last three benedictions that are standard in all 'amidah prayers deals with Israel's worship of God and the special relationship it enjoys with him. The plea is that the worship should be unflawed and efficacious and that God should assist this process by restoring his presence to Zion. In the shorter version, God is asked to dwell in Zion and the plea made that his servants should serve him there and that the reciters of the prayer should worship him in Jerusalem. The final request is that God should mercifully take delight in them and favour them and the doxological conclusion praises God as the one to whom the worshippers will direct their ritual. The longer version, for its part, requests divine favour for his people Israel and the restoration of the Temple ritual. This request is then expanded to include their prayers as well as their offerings, the body of the benediction concluding with a vision of the return of God to Zion, this theme being repeated in the doxological conclusion. There are, in addition, colourful, poetic expansions that refer to the restoration of a pristine Jerusalem and the details of the sacrificial process to be conducted there.[23] What emerges is that there is a group of texts that place the stress on what appears to be the current or immediate continuation of the Temple cult

---

22 *Siddur R. Saadja* (see n. 1 above), p. 19; Baer, *'Avodat Yisra'el* (see n. 12 above), p. 98; *Oṣar Ha-Tefillot* (see n. 12 above), pp. 345–46.

23 Schechter, 'Genizah specimens', p. 657; Elbogen, G, pp. 55–57; H, pp. 43–44; E, pp. 50–51; Mann, 'Palestinian order of service', pp. 306–307, 309–10; Finkelstein, 'The development of the amidah', pp. 162–64; Ginzberg, *Geonica* (2 vols; New York, 1909), 1.107, 119; Heinemann, *Prayer* (see n. 13 above), Hebrew edition, pp. 52, 57–58, 63–64, English edition, pp. 77, 87, 98–100; Jacobson, *Netiv Binah*, 1.289–91; Fleischer, *Eretz-Israel Prayer*, pp. 34–43, 63, 72–73, 76, 309, n. 71 and 'Le-nusaḥ birkat ha-avodah', *Sinai* 60 (1966), pp. 269–75; Luger, *Weekday Amidah*, pp. 173–83. For fuller sources see n. 13 above. See also U. Ehrlich, 'The earliest version of the *amidah* – The blessing about the temple worship' in *From Qumran to Cairo* (see n. 7 above), pp. 17–38, and his edition of some Genizah fragments of the Palestinian rite in *Kobez Al Yad* 19 [29] (2006), pp. 1–22.

accompanied by God's presence in the holy city and his approval and that are predicated upon the concluding principle that he alone should be worshipped. An alternative set of versions is more centrally concerned with the extension of the concept of worship to the area of communal prayer but also refers to the restoration of God's presence to Zion at its conclusion. There is therefore something of a paradox here in that the final theme fails to match the central concern of the previous text.

7. Festival *'amidah* for *musaf* service, fourth (central) benediction:

Hebrew text

אלהינו ואלהי אבו' מפני חטאינו גלינו מארצנו ונתרחק מעל אדמתנו ואין אנו יכולין לעלות לראות
להשתחות לפניך בבית בחירתך בבית הגדול והקדוש אשר אתה שמך נקרא עליו מפני היד שנשתלחה
במקדשך יהי רצון מלפניך ייי אלהינו אב הרחמן מלך יעקב שתשוב ותרחם עליו ועלינו ברחמיך הרבים
ותבנהו מהרה ותגדל כבודו אבינו מלכנו אלהינו גלה מלכותך עלינו מהרה הופע והנשא לעיני כל חי קרב
פזורנו מבין הגוים ונפוצותינו כנס מירכתי ארץ והביאנו לציון ברנה ולירושלם עירך בשמחת עולם ונעשה
לפניך קרבן חובתנו... מלך רחמן רחם עלינו מלך בראשית העתר לנו טוב ומטיב הדרש לנו שוב עלינו
בהמון רחמיך בגלל אבותינו שעשו את רצונך בנה ביתך כבתחלה כונן את מקדשך על מכונו הראנו בבנינו
שמחנו בתקונו החזיר שכינה לתוכו יעלו כהנים לעבודתם ולויים לשירה ולזמרה השב ישראל אל נוהו
ושבטי ישורון אל נחלתם וארמון על משפטו ישב שם נעלה ונראה לפניך שלוש פעמים בשנה...

English translation

Our God, and the God of our fathers, for our sins we have been exiled from our land and removed far from our territory so that we are unable to come up and appear before you at worship in your chosen abode, in the great and holy house to which your own name is attached, because of the power that has occupied your sanctuary. May it be your will, Lord, our God, merciful father, king of Jacob, that you once again show great mercy to it and to us and that you rebuild it speedily with increased esteem. Our divine and royal father, quickly restore your rulership over us and appear exalted in the eyes of all the living. Bring back as a symbolic act from the ends of the earth those of us who are scattered and dispersed among the nations. Bring us to Zion with rejoicing and to your city Jerusalem with eternal happiness so that we can bring you the required offering... Merciful king, show mercy to us; king of the universe, respond to our plea; model of all that is good, meet our request and return to us in your abundant mercy for the sake of our fathers who acted as you wished. Build your house as it was at first, reconstruct your sanctuary in its true form, grant us the sight of its restoration. Gladden us through its restoration and bring back the divine presence within it. Let the priests ascend to their worship and the levites to their song and their music. Repatriate Israel to where it belongs and the tribes of Yeshurun to their inheritance and let the divine abode be occupied in the rightful manner. We shall then go up and appear there before you three times a year... [24]

---

24   *Siddur R. Saadja* (see n. 1 above), pp. 151–52: Baer, *'Avodat Yisra'el* (see n. 12 above), pp. 347–56; *Oṣar Ha-Tefillot* (see n. 12 above), pp. 913–28.

The basic themes common to the various versions of this benediction are the restoration of God's exclusive rulership over his people Israel and the demonstration of his power to the world at large; the joyous return of the Jewish exiles from various parts of the world to Jerusalem and to the Temple; and the people's appearance and cultic participation at the Temple in accordance with the ancient pilgrim rite. The shorter version, such as that generally to be found in texts demonstrating allegiance to the Palestinian rite, adds to the future vision a universal acknowledgement of God's sovereignty supported by the use of part of a verse from Psalms 103:19 ('God's royal authority will be established throughout the world'), as well as poetic embellishments of the manner in which the restoration will be experienced. There are also some textual variants in which more specific reference is made to the joyous rebuilding of an eternal Zion and the glorious appearance of God in Jerusalem.[25]

The prayer entitled *ya'aleh we-yavo* also appears in this version and, although it seems more concerned with immediate deliverance than long-term restoration, and with God remembering his special Jewish connections, it includes a number of references to Jerusalem, not only mentioning God's city, without specific name, but also using a number of poetic terms for the Temple.[26] The additional material contained in the longer version, such as appears in the Sa'adyanic text, does broaden the theological treatment of the subject. The introductory section firmly blames the Jewish exile on the people's sins while bewailing the occupation of the Temple area by other powers and predicates the restoration on the renewal of God's special relations with Israel.[27] Later in the prayer, the appeal for a successful hearing is justified by reference to the religious loyalty of the Patriarchs and the vision of the future includes the specific functions of the priests, levites and ordinary Israelites and a summary of the situation by the citation of the last part of Jeremiah 30:18 (understood as 'the Temple will occupy its proper place').

---

25 Elbogen, G, pp. 132–40; H, pp. 100–105; E, pp. 111–17; Mann, 'Palestinian order of service', pp. 325–32; Jacobson, *Netiv Binah*, vol. 4.14–27; Fleischer, *Eretz-Israel Prayer*, pp. 93–159. For fuller sources see n. 13 above.

26 *Soferim* 19.5 (ed. Higger, p. 327); L. J. Liebreich, 'Aspects of the New Year liturgy', *HUCA* 34 (1963), pp. 125–31; Hoffman, *Canonization* (see n. 4 above), pp. 93–100; see also chapter 8 above, on the *'avodah* benediction.

27 The alternative formulation, in which stress is not placed on Israel's sins, may reflect the kind of view found in BT, *Berakhot* 3a which, if the variant readings are carefully examined, appears to imply that God regretted that he had destroyed his Temple and exiled the Jews; see R. Rabbinovicz, *Variae Lectiones* (*Diqduqey Soferim*) (Munich and Przemysl, 1867–97), I (Munich, 1867), pp. 4–5.

Other prayers

Although the intention here is to concentrate on what may be gleaned from the 'amidah, it should be noted that the theme of restoration also occurs in a number of other ancient rabbinic prayers. It may therefore be helpful to the discussion to make at least brief reference to the contents of some of these before attempting to analyse the data collected and to offer some tentative conclusions. As far as the birkat ha-mazon (grace after meals) is concerned, the simplest formulation would appear to have included a request for God's mercy to be shown to his people Israel, his city Jerusalem, and his Temple. Some texts refer to the cultic centre rather poetically as היכל and מעון, while others prefer the more prosaic phrase הבית הגדול והקדוש. What appear to be among early additions to the simplest formulation are references to Zion as the glorious habitation and to the Davidic dynasty. Some versions place an emphasis on the secure provision of food while others make a link between that subject and the main theme of the benediction by stressing that the worshippers' consumption of food and drink by no means indicates that they have forgotten the plight of Jerusalem and its need for restoration. In a number of texts, that theme of restoration is spelt out, in some cases after the benediction, with pleas for some or all of the developments that are presupposed by references to the consolation of Zion, to the building of Jerusalem, and to the return there of God's presence and rule, of the Davidic (sometimes specifically described as the messianic) kingdom, of the sacrificial system, and of the joyous Jewish population.[28]

Account should also be taken of the contents of the nahem (or rahem) prayer, one of the haftarah benedictions, the qaddish and the Passover Haggadah. The first-mentioned, a special prayer formulated in talmudic times for the Ninth of Av and inserted at some point in the 'amidah during one or all of the services to be held on that day, is designed to make specific mention of the fate of Jerusalem. In its simplest form, it first reads very much like the fourteenth benediction

---

28   Baer, 'Avodat Yisra'el (see n. 12 above), p. 554; Oṣar Ha-Tefillot (see n. 12 above), pp. 482–85; Heinemann, Prayer (see n. 13 above), Hebrew edition, pp. 73–77, English edition, pp. 113–22; Jacobson, Netiv Binah (see n. 13 above), 3.59–64; Mann, 'Palestinian order of service' (see n. 13 above), pp. 332–38; L. Finkelstein, 'The birkat ha-mazon', JQR, NS 19 (1928–29), pp. 211–62; A. Scheiber, 'Qiṭ'ey birkat ha-mazon', SRIHP 7 (Jerusalem and Tel Aviv, 1958), pp. 147–53; Y. Ratzaby, 'Birkot mazon mefuyyaṭot, Sinai 113 (1994), pp. 110–33; see chapter 8 above, the section dealing with the grace and the 'amidah. See also Tosefta, Berakhot 3.25, ed. Zuckermandel, p. 9 and n. 19 above; and chapter 18 below.

itself, craving God's mercy (rather than his compassion) on Israel his people, Jerusalem his city, and Zion his glorious habitation. An additional reference is then made to the ruined city, whose plight is recorded and whose ultimate restoration, as divinely promised, is confidently predicted. As far as the concluding formula is concerned, God is again cited as the builder of Jerusalem, or in more complex manner as either the God of David and the builder of Jerusalem, or the consoler of Zion and the builder of Jerusalem.

The initial word of the second blessing after the prophetic reading also occurs as either רחם or נחם and the variant concluding formulas once more contain references to either the consolation of Zion, this time with her children, or to the building of Jerusalem. The city's titles of Jerusalem are here given as ציון עירך and בית חיינו and there is also a call for swift vengeance on behalf of those who have been saddened, presumably by its loss.[29] As far as the *qaddish* is concerned, the version that came to be used at the burial service and at a *siyyum* ceremony (for concluding the study of a talmudic tractate) goes beyond the simple praise of God and contains a passage of messianic character, probably originating in the early rabbinic academy. Its theme is that God will establish his kingdom, revive the dead, build Jerusalem, reconstruct the Temple and replace heathen ritual with authentic worship.[30] Finally, it is interesting to note that the text of the *ge'ulah* benediction included in the Passover Haggadah (Mishnah, *Pesaḥim*, 10.6) also includes a messianic section, in various formulations, which looks forward to the restoration of the Temple and the sacrifices and to the joy to be engendered by that development and by 'the building of your city' (בנין עירך). Another version, however, refers more simply to next year's joyous celebration of the Temple service in 'Zion your city' (ציון עירך).[31]

A linguistic analysis of the prayer texts dealt with above reveals factors that are fairly common to most aspects of early rabbinic liturgy as well as a few characteristics that are more specifically relevant to

29 Heinemann, *Prayer* (see n. 13 above), Hebrew edition, pp. 48–51, English edition, pp. 70–76; see also PT, *Berakhot*, 4.3 (ed. Krotoschin, f. 8a) and *Soferim* 13.11 (ed. Higger, p. 247).

30 D. de Sola Pool, *The Kaddish* (Leipzig, 1909), pp. 79–89; Elbogen, (see n. 13 above), G, pp. 92–98; H, pp. 72–75; E, pp. 80–84; Heinemann, *Prayer* (see n. 13 above), Hebrew edition, pp. 23, 170–72, English edition, pp. 24–25, 266–68. There is also an interesting anthology in D. Telsner, *The Kaddish: Its History and Significance*, ed. G. A. Sivan (Jerusalem, 1995) and some useful insights in L. Wieseltier, *Kaddish* (New York, 1998).

31 Mishnah, *Pesaḥim* 10:6, ed. E. Baneth (Berlin, 1927), p. 254, and the footnotes provided there; E. D. Goldschmidt, *The Passover Haggadah: Its Sources and History* (Hebrew; Jerusalem, 1969), pp. 56–57.

particular pieces.[32] The vocabulary, grammar and spelling are those regularly found in the standard rabbinic liturgy originating in the talmudic period and are distinct from their equivalents in Biblical Hebrew. Some wording is borrowed from the Hebrew Bible but this is done by way of direct quotation in only a limited proportion of cases.[33] More usually, the material derived from the biblical books or parallel to texts to be found there has its own rabbinic flavour and is well integrated into the overall liturgical style and format.[34] There are instances in which a substantial part of a biblical verse is included within a particular prayer without being identified through the use of an introductory phrase such as ככתוב or כאמור.[35] Some formulations tend to be poetic, others resemble the style of a litany, while there are also cases in which simple prose predominates.[36] There are variations among the versions in the tenses and conjugations of verbs, the choice of roots, and the use of epithets, and these have not traditionally been regarded as of major significance to the exegesis of the prayers.

Three concepts

It will now be appropriate to identify three central concepts of restoration as they occur in the material just analysed. According to the first, the process is one by which God is expected to correct the inadequacies, inequalities, injustices, abnormalities and discomforts of life through his miraculous powers, including תחית המתים, but without reference to precisely when or in which epoch this will occur. The restoration of the dead to life is at an early stage of rabbinic prayer considered central enough for it to be given a place, even a primary place, among the divine corrections being requested. Belonging to this kind of notion, which may be defined as more immediate and mundane, are those prayers that see the future of the diaspora, the Temple, Jerusalem, the holy land, and the Jewish people with its major

---

32 C. Rabin, 'The historical background of Qumran Hebrew' in *Scripta Hierosolymitana* 4 (Jerusalem, 1965), pp. 144–61, with a later Hebrew version published in *Qoveṣ Ma'amarim Bilshon Ḥz"l*, vol. 1, ed. M. Bar-Asher (2 vols; Jerusalem, 1972), pp. 355–82, and 'The linguistic investigation of the language of Jewish prayer' in *Studies in Aggadah, Targum and Jewish Liturgy in Memory of Joseph Heinemann*, eds J. J. Petuchowski and E. Fleischer (Jerusalem and Cincinnati, 1981), Hebrew section, pp. 163–71; A. Hurvitz, *The Transition Period: A Study in Post-Exilic Hebrew and its Implications for the Dating of Psalms* (Hebrew; Jerusalem, 1972), especially pp. 36–63.
33 See e.g. the phrases ממית ומחיה in text no. 1 above and השיבה שופטינו כבראשונה in text no. 3 above.
34 Compare e.g. the formulation of text no. 2 above with Isaiah 11:12.
35 A good example is the phrase וארמון על משפטו ישב at the end of text no. 7 above, which is borrowed from Jeremiah 30:18.
36 Contrast the varying styles of texts nos. 2–3, 4 and 6 above.

institutions and leadership, in terms of improvements on their current state and restorations of what is regarded as the authentic norm. Also to be included in this genre are prayers that request the removal of suffering and sorrow, whether of the personal or the national variety.

A second understanding of the idea of restoration that can be identified among the standard rabbinic prayers concerns the relationship between God and Israel. The idea is that God should re-establish the warm relations he once enjoyed with Israel, should remove the subjugation which they are currently experiencing, and should re-impose on them the direct, divine rule to which they were subject in earlier times. A kind of *imitatio dei* works here in reverse, God providing the quality leadership and authority that is acutely required by Israel. Emphasis is placed on the efficacy of Israel's worship and the restoration of God's presence to Zion. In spite of their past sins, divine favour is restored to Israel, perhaps as an acknowledgement of the merits of the eponymous ancestors, and stress is laid on the principle of God's exclusive right to worship.

It is a prophetic, messianic and poetic message that pervades the third notion of restoration found in the liturgical texts examined above. God's power will be gloriously made manifest to the whole world and his eternal rule will be universally established and acknowledged. Heathen control and worship will be eradicated and Israel's suffering at their hands will be avenged. The Jews will be gathered from the four corners of the earth and ceremoniously restored to Zion where the Temple and its detailed ritual will be reinstated in their pristine form. The festal pilgrimages, with all their joy, will be restored to the rebuilt city of Jerusalem and the priests, levites and common people will fully perform their religious obligations there.

In connection with this third approach, which may justifiably be described as having a predominantly ascetic character, it is perhaps relevant to note the existence in the latter part of the geonic age of special prayers and biblical verses recited by pilgrims on their visits to Jerusalem. Recent research, especially by Reiner, Fleischer and Ben-Shammai, has added significantly to our knowledge of the ceremony and the recitations that accompanied each part of the approach to the holy city, the circumambulation of its walls, and the final arrival at the Temple Mount. The ritual may be traced in both Rabbanite and Karaite circles, and it would appear that it was the 'Mourners of Zion' who instituted the practice. Locals and pilgrims participated in ceremonies in the course of which they recited the book of Lamentations and other poems that bemoaned the loss of Jerusalem and the Temple and expressed sorrow about their current state. The biblical verses recited at each gate were chosen to match its name and the special prayers and supplications were added to these verses only at the first and last 'stations'. Some of these were known from other liturgical contexts and took the form of benedictions, and poetic items were also used, in one case borrowed from the mystical *hekhalot* texts.[37] Whether such data permit us to conclude, maximally, that such texts in their turn had an influence on the choice of the wording of the regular prayers, or, minimally, that they do no more than reflect another aspect of the ascetic tendency just noted, remains a moot point. What is beyond doubt is that they occupy an important place in Jewish liturgical responses to the possible restoration of the Holy City.

It would considerably ease the task of the historian of religious ideas if it could confidently be stated that each of the three themes just described appears in a particular benediction, or originates at a specific date in an identifiable place, or is championed by a special individual or group. Not only does the oral and literary history of the early rabbinic liturgy, as previously discussed, rule this out. Even the division into three such themes is in itself something of a subjective and speculative exercise. One has to admit that the notions overlap, that there is a lack of clarity about the process of addition and omission, and that those responsible for the developments remain largely anonymous. Particularly in the liturgical field, matters must be viewed synchronically as well as diachronically, since the moves may not be consistently in one direction but may at times take one step forward before taking two steps back. In addition, there are instances in which the same words have been interpreted in significantly different ways by various generations. References to Davidic rule, to the holy city and to divine worship did not necessarily convey the same concepts to the Jews of every centre and in each century. Nevertheless, it may confidently be concluded that the standard rabbinic prayers in their totality include all three themes and that the widespread textual, linguistic and theological variations testify to a dynamic process of development, though not one that displays one consistent tendency. It seems likely that this process was affected by the history of the Jewish people as it evolved from epoch to epoch and from centre to centre. Social, political and religious ideas undoubtedly left their mark on the texts of the prayers and, while the nature of such marks are identifiable, the details of their arrival and departure remain obscure in the early

---

37   E. Reiner, 'Concerning the Priest Gate and its location', *Tarbiz* 56 (1987), pp. 279–90; E. Fleischer, 'Pilgrims' prayer and the gates of Jerusalem', in *Mas'at Moshe: Studies in Jewish and Islamic Culture Presented to Moshe Gil*, eds E. Fleischer, M. A. Friedman and J. A. Kraemer (Hebrew; Jerusalem and Tel Aviv, 1998), pp. 298–327; and H. Ben-Shammai, 'A unique lamentation on Jerusalem by the Karaite author Yeshu'a ben Judah' in the same Gil *Festschrift*, pp. 93–102; and see chapter 13 below.

centuries of the first Christian millennium. What may be suggested for at least some periods is that, as the idea of restoration became less confidently and expeditiously expected, so it tended to be expressed progressively more in the language of the utopian visionary.

10

Approaches to Sacrifices

Introduction

In the various interpretations of Judaism that are now current, practical liturgical responses of various types are offered to the matter of the Temple rituals that were of such central significance to the Jewish people before the destruction of its cultic centre in 70 ce. Prayers for their full, ultimate restoration, together with passages recording all their details, such as are found in Orthodox siddurim, stand at one end of the spectrum, while at the other, represented by the radical Reform practice, there is a reluctance to make any reference to it at all. Not uncommonly in matters liturgical, the American Conservative prayer-books opt for a compromise and find ways of making mention of the rites that were once followed in the Temple by simply reciting their details.[1] It should not, however, be supposed that all the traditionalists of the modern period have been content with the role ascribed to the sacrifices in their standard liturgies. Abraham Berliner (1851–1929), who was lecturer and librarian at the Orthodox Rabbinical Seminary in Berlin, founded by Azriel Hildesheimer, was a major supporter of the Adass Jisroel secessionist congregation and had little truck with the Reform movement.[2] Nevertheless, in his scholarly notes on the prayer-book, he railed against those who rattled off the details of the sacrifices in a ritualistic fashion without knowledge of their origins and content.[3]

Where there does, however, appear to be some degree of unanimity among Jewish religious groups of various hues is in the interpretation of the historical relationship between Temple ritual and synagogue liturgy. In this matter, one encounters the well-established and oft-repeated notion that sacrifice was replaced by prayer, and the notion is by no means the exclusive mantra of either the more traditional or the more progressive movements. For the leader of separatist German

---

1 A summary of the overall attitudes to this and similar liturgical customs on the parts of various current interpretations of Judaism, together with details of the relevant prayer-books, are to be found in my volume *Judaism and Hebrew Prayer: New Perspectives on Jewish Liturgical History* (Cambridge, 1993), pp. 294–331.

2 I. Wolfsberg, 'Professor Abraham Berliner' in *Ḥokhmat Yisra'el Be-Ma'arav Eyropa*, ed. S. Federbusch (Hebrew; Jerusalem, 1958), pp. 101–8.

3 A. Berliner, *Randbemerkungen zum täglichen Gebetbuche* (Berlin, 1909), p. 17.

orthodoxy in the nineteenth century, Samson Raphael Hirsch, the
'present Divine service' is 'only a faint echo of that originally ordained
by God in the Sanctuary in Jerusalem' but by that very definition is
nevertheless its replacement.[4] The subject of animal sacrifices offered in
the Temple was of such central liturgical concern to the late Chief Rabbi
of the United Hebrew Congregations of the Commonwealth, Lord
Jakobovits, that he included an essay on the topic in his edition of the
Orthodox prayer-book.[5] As well as arguing for their theological
significance and value, and contending that they 'are absolutely central
to the very structures of our principal daily prayers', he states
categorically that 'prayer ... replaced them'.[6] The same idea, though
originating and occurring in a different ideology, is given expression in
the non-Orthodox camps through their conviction that the synagogue
service has replaced the Temple ritual. In the words of Benjamin Szold
of Baltimore, 'Therefore we do not unduly lament over the Temple that
is destroyed ... We mourn not despairingly over the downfall of
Jerusalem ... Thou hast given us another home in place of that which
we lost in the land of our fathers.'[7]

Whatever the theological views of the liturgical practitioners, the
question facing the historian of ideas relating to Jewish worship is
whether the substitution of the sacrificial system with the recitation of
prayers was always seen by the rabbis as a simple and uncontroversial
matter. This brief study will attempt to describe and assess the relevant
responses on the part of major talmudic and post-talmudic sources
during the first millennium of rabbinic Judaism. The material discussed
will range from the halakhic to the liturgical, the poetic, the mystical

---

4   *The Hirsch Siddur: The Order of Prayers for the Whole Year* (E.T.; Jerusalem and New
     York, 1969), p. 41.
5   On his life and work, see Chaim Bermant, *Lord Jakobovits: the Authorised Biography of
     the Chief Rabbi* (London, 1990) and M. Persoff, *Immanuel Jakobovits: A Prophet in Israel*
     (London, 2002).
6   'Animal sacrifices in Judaism: probings into a psycho-religious drama' in *The
     Authorised Daily Prayer Book of the United Hebrew Congregations of the Commonwealth.
     Based on the original translation of the Rev. S. Singer. Published for the Centenary of the
     first edition,* ed. I. Jakobovits, E.T. by E. Cashdan (London, 1990), pp. 897–902.
7   '*Avodat Yisra'el: Israelitish Prayer-book for all the Public Services of the Year,* originally
     arranged by B. Szold, second edition revised by M. Jastrow and H. Hochheimer
     (Philadelphia, 1873), p. 589. The original German edition was *Israelitisches Gebetbuch
     für dem öffentlichen Gottesdienst im ganzen Jahre* (Baltimore, 1873) and read more
     stridently: 'Wir klagen nicht, o Gott, um den gefallenen Tempel...Wir klagen nicht
     über den Sturz Jerusalems, deiner heiligen Stadt...[du] hast uns hier auf dem Boden
     einer neuen Heimath das Vaterland wiedergegeben, das wir im Lande der Väter für
     immer verloren hatten.' Part of the passage by Szold is cited by Leon A. Jick, 'The
     Reform Synagogue' in *The American Synagogue: A Sanctuary Transformed,* ed. Jack
     Wertheimer (Cambridge and New York, 1987), p. 90, but without accurate details of
     the two editions or their interesting variations.

and the pietistic, in order to reach a broad understanding of how the topic of the apparently defunct sacrificial system was handled by each generation of rabbinic Jews.

Talmudic-midrashic sources

It should be stated at the outset that the documentary evidence for the notion that the Temple rituals were replaced by rabbinic prayer is not found in the Mishnah itself but in the Tosefta and the Talmudim, at times cited within traditions that are identified as tannaitic by amoraim of the third and fourth centuries. When a source is sought for the timing of the 'amidah prayers of morning and afternoon, it is the daily offering in the Temple that is cited as the precedent. The performance of divine worship that has lost its location on the Temple Mount finds an alternative place in the Jewish heart at prayer. The biblical and Second Temple notion of עבודה ('service') is re-interpreted as עבודה שבלב ('service of the heart') and cultic acts have thus become metamorphosized into spiritualized liturgy.[8]

But a number of other passages indicate that such a view was by no means unanimous. It is alternatively suggested that the daily 'amidah owes its origin to the biblical Patriarchs, Abraham, Isaac and Jacob, and verses are imaginatively interpreted to support the idea that each of them instituted one of the three daily 'amidot. It is also proposed that the inspiration comes from the changing phases of the day. Is it not natural for people to thank God in the morning for having survived the night, to entreat Him at noon to see out safely the remainder of the day, and to express the wish at night that the light of dawn should once more be witnessed?[9] It is perhaps the more ascetically minded of the talmudic teachers who opt for the view that the liturgical act of fasting, leading as it does to a physical contraction of the body fats and fluids, is the equivalent of the burning up on the altar of the corresponding animal products, or the even more radical concept that rabbinically formulated prayer is in fact superior to the sacrificial system once practised in the Temple. On the opposite, conservative side, some rabbis held tenaciously to the view that nothing could ever win divine favour more successfully than that system and they promoted the

---

8   Tosefta, Berakhot 3.1 (ed. Zuckermandel, p. 5); PT, Berakhot 4.1 (7a); BT, Berakhot 26b. See also Jubilees 22:6–9.
9   BT, Berakhot 26b; PT, Berakhot 4.1 (7a).

custom of attaching to the mention of the Temple a prayer that it
should be speedily restored.[10]

Those seeking a successor that could function no less centrally in
rabbinic theology than the Temple had done in the earlier religious
infrastructure of the Jews were not restricted to the field of prayer. One
of the dominant views is that the study of Torah, especially at night, is
the equivalent of every form of sacrifice and incense offered in the
Temple and some teachers take this further and argue that it totally
removes the requirement for such offerings, that it develops a close
relationship between the Torah student and God, and that God actually
prefers study to the cult. There is indeed a piece of exegesis relating to 1
Samuel 2:3 and Exodus 15:16 that appears to argue that a reasonable
degree of intellectual development is tantamount to the rebuilding of
the Temple because in the first of these texts the word דעות
('knowledge') occurs between two divine epithets while in the latter the
word מקדש ('sanctuary') does the same.[11]

The talmudic sources indicate that there was some confusion as to
whether ritual acts once performed in the Temple were continued,
either in their totality or to only a limited degree, in the synagogue, or
whether they had become effectively obsolete until its future
restoration. One interesting view, based on an interpretation of Psalms
118:27, is not only that the species of plants used on the feast of Sukkot
can still be brought together ritually by a Jewish individual but that
such a person has performed an act that is equivalent to building an
altar and offering a sacrifice. Similarly, while the verse in Deuteronomy
27:7 makes a close association between the offering of sacrifices with its
attendant consumption of meat and the joy of the festivals, there is
another verse that advises the Jew how to achieve such a level of joy
without the Temple. The advice is based on Psalms 104:15 and
promotes the idea that the drinking of wine can bring about happiness
on a festival even in the absence of sacrifices. In some talmudic circles
the equivalent religious value of the cult was located among various
examples of ethical behaviour rather than within any liturgical activity.
Humility was regarded as of the same value as offering the whole
gamut of sacrifices while charitable deeds were seen as having the
same power to effect atonement for Israel's sins as the Temple had once
had. Kindness to impoverished scholars was particularly lauded, the

---

10   BT, *Berakhot* 17a and 32b; *Avot de-Rabbi Nathan*, Recension A, chapter 4, ed. S.
     Schechter, p. 20, now republished with additional annotation by M. Kister, *Avoth de-
     Rabbi Nathan: Solomon Schechter Edition* (New York and Jerusalem, 1997); BT, *Rosh
     Ha-Shanah* 30a.
11   BT, *Menaḥot* 110a; *Avot de-Rabbi Nathan* (see n. 10 above), Recension A, chapter 4, p.
     18; BT, *Shabbat* 30a; BT, *Sanhedrin* 92a.

act of granting them hospitality being equated with offering the daily sacrifice and the charity of filling their wine glasses being seen as parallel to pouring a wine libation in the Temple.[12] A rather different, and somewhat more mystical view, was destined to have a major impact on the later development of various aspects of rabbinic liturgy. A statement ascribed to God in the course of a conversation with Abraham declared that the passages recording the order of the Temple sacrifices had been divinely ordained so that when God heard them being formally recited He would regard it as if the offerings themselves had been made and would forgive the sins of those who had recited them.[13]

It is not our task in the present context to evaluate the attributions of these above statements, precisely to date their origins and literary evolution, or to assess the degree to which they had an immediate halakhic application. For our purposes, the fact that such views were given expression in the early rabbinic period, and were not suppressed from within the corpora of traditions, is sufficient to indicate that a complex religious debate was taking place that is relevant to our topic. There was a serious interchange of ideas among the talmudic teachers about the future and/or the replacement of sacrifice and its relative theological importance in evolving Judaism. At first, a strong body of opinion contended that there was little or no connection or continuation. Gradually, space appears to have been found for alternative notions that gave sacrifices a continuing liturgical role but, as the following discussion will demonstrate, the transition was not a simple one.[14]

Tractate Soferim

One of the most important sources concerning rabbinic liturgical practice in the centuries immediately after the talmudic period is *Massekhet Soferim*. The date and provenance of this 'minor tractate' have by no means been definitively established but we may say with confidence that it reflects customs from the middle of the geonic period

---

12 BT, *Sukkah* 48a; BT, *Pesaḥim* 109a; BT, *Sanhedrin* 43b; *Avot de-Rabbi Nathan* (see n. 10 above), Recension A, chapter 4, p. 21; BT, *Berakhot* 10b; BT, *Yoma* 71a.
13 BT, *Ta'anit* 27b.
14 These various talmudic notions have been explained as intellectual, mystical and eschatological responses by J. Neusner, 'Emergent Rabbinic Judaism in a time of crisis: four responses to the destruction of the Second Temple', *Judaism* 21 (1972), pp. 313–27.

and records a substantial degree of Palestinian custom.[15] It will be recalled from earlier remarks that the Talmud itself already laid emphasis on the formal recitation of texts relating to the Temple sacrifices and to the theological value of such a practice. In this connection there are a number of traditions that are documented in *Soferim* and that may therefore be regarded as important developments in the period during which it was compiled. It is laid down that during each festival the biblical verses relating to that festival and, in some instances, to the sacrifices that were originally brought in the Temple on that festival, are to be recited.[16] Another custom mentioned in the tractate is the recitation of specific psalms on particular days on the basis of the tannaitic tradition that this is what was done in the Temple and the conclusion that this is equivalent to building a new altar and making a sacrifice on it.[17]

Reference is also made in *Soferim* to the 175 sabbath readings from the Pentateuch which represented the Palestinian Jewish lectionary (according to its triennial cycle) and, in a somewhat opaque comment, they are equated with the daily burnt-offering in the Temple.[18] That daily burnt-offering is also mentioned in a ruling that requires the recitation of the *qedushah* on Ḥanukkah, New Moon and the intermediate days of Pesah and Sukkot because that offering is specified in the pentateuchal legislation for sacrifices on those days.[19] While these attempts were being made to give a more active role to such cultic matters, it has to be acknowledged that the prayer that is, according to *Soferim*, to be recited on the New Moon and that makes detailed reference to the messianic age, looks forward to rejoicing, glad tidings, Torah study, Jewish independence and the traditional fixing of the New Moon in considerable detail but makes only brief allusion to the rebuilding of the Temple and none to the sacrifices.[20] What we then have in the halakhah-oriented guidance provided by *Soferim* is a tendency to give some increased liturgical attention to the Temple ritual but by no means any trend towards restoring it to any central place in Jewish liturgy.

---

15 M. B. Lerner, 'Massekhet Sofrim' in *The Literature of the Sages. First Part: Mishna, Tosefta, Talmud, External Tractates*, eds S. Safrai and P. J. Tomson (Assen/Maastricht and Philadelphia, 1987), pp. 397–400.
16 *Massekhet Soferim*, ed. M. Higger (New York, 1937), 17.5, pp. 302–3 and 20.8–9, pp. 349–52 (E.T., ed. I. W. Slotki, London, 1965, 17.11, pp. 296–98 and 20.10–12, pp. 315–16).
17 *Soferim* (see n. 16 above), ed. Higger, 18.2, pp. 310–13; ed. Slotki, 18.1, pp. 299–300.
18 *Soferim* (see n. 16 above), ed. Higger, 16.8, pp. 291–92; ed. Slotki, 16.10, p. 292.
19 *Soferim* (see n. 16 above), ed. Higger, 20.5, p. 345; ed. Slotki, 20.7, p. 313.
20 *Soferim* (see n. 16 above), ed. Higger, 19.7, pp. 331–33; ed. Slotki, 19.9, p. 307.

Poetic Yom Kippur ritual

For their part, however, those who were more intensely involved in the development and expansion of Jewish liturgical poetry saw the synagogal references to ceremonials ('*Avodah*) that had been conducted by the high priest on Yom Kippur in Temple times as fertile ground for cultivating a much richer crop of cultic allusions and for promoting a more staple diet of emotive responses to its loss. Such references had gradually been included in the liturgy in talmudic times but had limited themselves to the unadorned reports originating in the Pentateuch and the Mishnah.[21] The liturgical poets embellished these reports to a considerable extent, as has been succinctly summarized by Ezra Fleischer in his classic introduction to the Hebrew liturgical poetry of the medieval period (in my own translation):

The details of the Yom Kippur ritual in the Temple follow the traditional pre-classical piyyutic style and are presented in a realistic manner, being treated in a restrained and accurate fashion. The liturgical poems that accompany them, on the other hand, are more emotive and give intense and enthusiastic expression to the feelings that the traditional liturgical poetry attaches to the detailed ceremonial. Here the poets use colourful and exaggerated figures to describe the glorious and beautiful appearance of the high priest when he performed the ritual, the outstanding joy of the generations who viewed it, and the miserable state of those who did not live at that time but only after the destruction of the Temple.[22]

It may even be the case, as has been argued by Joseph Yahalom, that some of the ideas and descriptions relating to the sacrificial cult and used in these poems have their origins in earlier Jewish traditions that were once valued and transmitted by groups of priests. When the latter's role diminished in significance in the talmudic age, their traditions were relegated to a lower level of use and importance but the situation was reversed during the post-talmudic period. At that stage, the liturgical poets took central stage and, with so many of them belonging to the priesthood, were able to re-instate the Temple

---

21 I. Elbogen, German edition = G, *Der jüdische Gottesdienst in seiner geschichtlichen Entwicklung* (Frankfurt am Main, 1931; reprint, Hildesheim, 1962), p. 217; Hebrew edition = H, התפילה בישראל בהתפתחותה ההיסטורית (eds J. Heinemann, I. Adler, A. Negev, J. Petuchowski and H. Schirmann, Tel Aviv, 1972), p. 162; English edition = E, *Jewish Liturgy: A Comprehensive History* (English translation and edition by R. P. Scheindlin, Philadelphia, Jerusalem and New York,1993), p. 174.

22 E. Fleischer, *Hebrew Liturgical Poetry in the Middle Ages* (Hebrew; Jerusalem, 1975), p. 175.

traditions, including detailed accounts of the sacrifices, to an honoured position in Jewish liturgy.[23]

A closer examination of the ideas of these poets will permit a better understanding of how they were attempting to re-absorb the notion of sacrifices into the mainstream of liturgical thought and practice. Particularly through their lyrical embellishments of the 'Avodah, they stressed that the world's creation had been undertaken by God precisely for the sake of the cult and attempted a rehabilitation of the biblical concept of purification through Temple rituals that had gradually been replaced in rabbinic thought by the idea of individual atonement. While the talmudic rabbis had been at best equivocal about the functions of the priest after the Temple's destruction, the composers of the *piyyuṭim* concerning the 'Avodah idealized and glorified his role. For them, he was the people's direct contact with the divine presence and able to assure their participation in the ritual drama. Unlike Christianity, they did not lay emphasis on the victim in the sacrificial act but they did make much of the actual details surrounding its offering. What was in effect happening was that the composers and reciters of this liturgy about the cult were using the synagogal setting as a backdrop against which to act out an epic drama of contact between the human and the divine through the sacrificial ritual. In this way they were offering an alternative response, at once both more traditional and more radical, to the various explanations that had been proposed by the talmudic rabbis for the loss of the religious achievements that had been experienced on the Temple Mount in Jerusalem. Perhaps even more significantly for later liturgical developments in the rabbinic prayer-book, this alternative response was characterized by the process of recitation.[24] The poets were picking up and expanding on the talmudic statement, noted earlier, that recitation of the sacrificial details would be counted by God as the equivalent of making the offerings themselves and would thereby bring the forgiveness that those rituals had once promised.[25] By adopting such a position, they were to an extent struggling to wrest back from the rabbinic scholar the religious power that had been

---

23   J. Yahalom, *Az Be'eyn Kol: Priestly Palestinian Poetry: A Narrative Liturgy for the Day of Atonement* (Hebrew; Jerusalem, 1996), p. 56.

24   All this is very well presented and summarized by Michael Swartz, particularly in his two articles 'Ritual about myth about ritual', *Journal of Jewish Thought and Philosophy* 6 (1997), pp. 135–55, and 'Sage, priest and poet: typologies of religious leadership in the ancient synagogue' in *Jews, Christians, and Polytheists in the Ancient Synagogue: Cultural Interaction during the Greco-Roman Period*, ed. Steven Fine (London and New York, 1999), pp. 101–17.

25   See n. 13 above.

granted to him by the talmudic sources primarily because of his halakhic expertise and devotion to study.

Yeṣirah

However early it may be dated, the *Sefer Yeṣirah* was also of undoubted importance to the Hebrew literary tradition and to Jewish thought in the post-talmudic period and reflects the approaches adopted by those who were particularly attracted to mysticism, speculative thought and wisdom literature. These areas, no less than the legal and poetic traditions, exercised an influence on the content of the developing liturgy that was destined to grow in the course of the medieval centuries. What *Yeṣirah* has to say about the Temple cult is therefore of relevance to this discussion of the various understandings of its role in synagogal prayer. Here again, recitation and verbalization are of central significance but in this instance the emphasis is on the intrinsic spiritual value of the language in which they take place rather than on the matter of cultic forgiveness. The letters of the Hebrew alphabet are understood to represent the constituents of the Temple and to have taken over its cosmic function and the power once to be found in the sacrificial system is now located in the Hebrew language. It is that medium that brings together God and the Jewish people, as once did the sacrificial rituals. It is not difficult to see how such a notion would encourage and strengthen the tendency to include in the liturgy the recitation of those passages that detail the rituals once performed in the Temple. Peter Hayman's analysis of paragraph 38 of *Yeṣirah* provides a clear and helpful précis of what that work was trying to say:

> ... the author wishes to transfer from the Temple to the Hebrew language that total symbolic structure which we have found in so many earlier versions of Judaism. Instead of the three Temple courts, symbolizing maybe three heavens, we have 'three matrices *Alef, Mem, Shin'*; instead of the *Menorah* and the seven cubit measurements we have 'seven double letters'; instead of the twelve gates of the outer courts we have the 'twelve simple letters'. Instead of the universe being sustained by the Temple cultus, it is now sustained by the power of the Hebrew language on the lips of God and, maybe also, on the lips of men. Once the Temple was the yesod (the foundation) now it is the 'twenty-two fundamental letters' (*'esrim ushtayim 'otiyot yesod*).[26]

---

26 P. Hayman, 'Some observations on *Sefer Yeṣira*: (2) the temple at the centre of the universe', *JJS* 37 (1986), pp. 176–82. See also his article 'Was God a magician: *Sefer Yeṣira* and Jewish magic', *JJS* 40 (1989), pp. 225–37. See also his edition *Sefer Yeṣira: Edition, Translation and Text-critical Commentary* (Tübingen, 2004).

Early musaf prayer

It is true that the *musaf* prayer – essentially of course the *'amidah* – differs from the other prayers in that it has a direct precedent among the Temple sacrifices, while they are linked with such sacrifices only by means of rather convoluted exegesis. In addition, it began its life as an exclusively communal act of worship and was only later added to the liturgical obligations of the individual. Nevertheless, the earliest form of the *musaf* appears not to have differed greatly from its *shaharit* equivalent in simply making reference to the hope for a renewal of revelation, and possibly also for a universal knowledge of God, and to God's blessing of Israel through the particular festival on which it is being recited.[27] It was the liturgical innovator and promoter of the early third century, Rav, who appears to have expressed a preference for an additional reference to be inserted into the *musaf* that consisted of details of the sacrifice once made in the Temple on that festival and it was his view that came to dominate the form of the prayer in the middle ages.[28] But the process was not a simple or consistent one as is demonstrated by the evidence of early Genizah texts. One of these still records what seems to have been a simple form of the passage that precedes the concluding doxology of the central benediction:[29]

והשיאנו יי אלהינו את ברכת מועדיך לשלום כאשר אמרת ורצית כן תברכנו סלה כי בישראל עמך
בחרת ואותנו קדשת ונעשה ונעשה לפניך את חובתינו תמידי יום וקרבן מוסף ב א יי מקדש ישראל ויום צום
הכפורים מוחל וסולח לעונותינו ולעונות עמך בית ישראל ברחמים בעבור שמו הגדול:

It will be noted that, in addition to the theme of God's blessing and sanctification of Israel through the observance of the festival, the final sentence before the doxological conclusion requests that the Jewish people might in the future again be able to perform their obligatory daily sacrifices as well as to make their additional (*musaf*) offering but does not yet specify the details of these sacrifices or cite the biblical verses that record them. This text would then represent a period before

---

27   Elbogen (see n. 21 above), G, p. 264; H, p. 198; E, p. 207.

28   PT, *Berakhot* 4.6 (8c): רב אמר צריך לחד' בה דבר. ושמואל אמר א"צ לחד' בה דבר. ר' זעירא בעי קומי רבי
יוסי מה לחדש בה דבר. א"ל אפי' אמר ונעש' לפניך את חובותינו תמידי יום וקרבן מוסף יצא:

29   Cambridge University Library (henceforth = CUL), T-S 8H23.8. On this fragment, see N. Wieder, 'Genizah studies in the Babylonian liturgy', *Tarbiz* 37 (1968), pp. 153–54, reprinted in *The Formation of Jewish Liturgy in the East and the West* (Hebrew; 2 vols; Jerusalem, 1998), 1.31–32; E. Fleischer, *Eretz-Israel Prayer and Prayer Rituals as Portrayed in the Geniza Documents* (Hebrew; Jerusalem, 1988), pp. 133, 136–37 and 140 and 'Fragments of Palestinian prayer collections from the Genizah' (Hebrew), *Kobez Al Yad*, NS 13 (1996), p. 134; and S. C. Reif, 'Festive titles in liturgical terminology' (Hebrew) in *Proceedings of the Ninth World Congress of Jewish Studies 1985/1*, Division C (Jerusalem, 1986), p. 70.

which such additions were made and a context in which there was still doubt about the degree to which the sacrificial cult was again to be given central significance. That the move towards granting it such a significance in this part of the liturgy remained controversial becomes apparent from the close examination of the variant versions of this sentence, as they have been cited by Naphtali Wieder, who has convincingly argued that textual adjustments became necessary because of the new content of the *musaf* prayer:[30]

> The early Palestinian poet, Yannai, has: כי בו תישעה מיד עמוסיך תמידי יום
> וקרבן מוסף
> Genizah text, Westminster College, Cambridge Arabic I 12 reads: ותירצה
> לפניך תפילת עמוסיך כתמידי יום וקרבן מוסף
> The Persian rite opts for: ותירצה לפניך תפלת בניך כתפילת עמוסיך כתמידי יום
> [ו]קרבן מוסף

To my mind, what is being reflected in these various versions is the argument about the place of sacrifices in rabbinic prayer. Firstly, in the talmudic period, Rav suggests that a reference to the future pilgrimage to Jerusalem at festival periods should note the restoration of the relevant sacrifices. The details of these are then expanded, making it necessary to re-justify the original sentence by linking it with prayer. Yannai reflects the views of the poets of Eretz Israel at the end of the talmudic period who, as has earlier been argued, were devoted to the idea of the restored sacrificial cult *per se* and to the lyrical expansion of its details. According to him, the request is for God to favour the daily and *musaf* offerings being made by his chosen people, the word עמוסיך referring to the Jewish people and their resumed sacrifices, when the cult is again a real event. But according to the Westminster Genizah text, which is also represented in the remnants of Palestinian versions that survived in the Italian, French and English versions of the middle ages, God should find favour in the prayer of the chosen people, just as he once did, historically, in the Temple cult. In the Persian rite (also linked with that of Eretz Israel), the simile is used again and the subject is prayer and not sacrifice. But in this case, the word עמוסים has been understood as referring to the Patriarchs and the plea is that God should find favour in the prayers of today's Jews just as he did with those offices created by the Patriarchs, the equivalent of the sacrifices once offered in the Temple. This is a neat way of including both ideas about the origins of the *'amidah* that are recorded in the Talmud, at the same time as giving the central role to prayer.[31]

---

30   Wieder, *Jewish Liturgy* (see previous note), 2.616–18.
31   See the sources cited in nn. 8 and 9 above.

Torah as study or as cult

If the textual variants just cited testify to a counter-attack on the part of
those who were adamant that synagogal prayer had replaced Temple
ritual as the central experience of Jewish liturgy, there are also
indications from the late geonic period that tensions continued in the
matter of how precisely sacrifices were to be classified and
incorporated within the developing rabbinic liturgy. In Natronai ben
Hilai Ha-Gaon's nuclear prayer-book of the ninth century, he lays out
instructions for the recitation of various passages in the introductory
section of the morning prayers.[32] These include the accounts of the daily
offering in the Temple recorded at the beginning of Numbers 28 and
the fifth chapter of the mishnaic tractate *Zevaḥim*, beginning איזהו מקומן.
Lest it be thought that this is in some sense an idealization of the
sacrificial ritual, he makes it clear that at least part of the justification
lies elsewhere. He cites the talmudic passage[33] that includes a number
of views about the kind of text before which one is to recite the
benediction for Torah study and concludes that the reading of these
two cultic instructions is mandated in order to fulfil the all-inclusive
view that selections from the Pentateuch and the Mishnah are to be
among those that are to be studied for this purpose.[34] For Natronai's
successor as the head of the Sura academy, Sa'adya ben Joseph Ha-
Gaon, the emphasis is undoubtedly on Torah study through
pentateuchal and mishnaic passages, as 'a tradition', but not on the
sacrificial ritual as such.[35]

For their part, the Genizah fragments, mostly dating from the late
geonic period, testify to a continuing fluidity about the degree to which
passages dealing with the sacrificial system are to be given liturgical
importance. One set of fragments appears to prefer the priestly
benediction, either Numbers 6:22–26 or 6:24–26, immediately after the
three Torah benedictions[36] and before the mishnaic passage from Pe'ah
1:1 recording those kindly deeds that are without legal stipulation as to
amounts, and those that bring reward in the after-life as well as in this

---

32   L. Ginzberg, *Geonica* (2 vols; New York, 1909), 2.109–10 and 114–17.
33   BT, *Berakhot* 11b.
34   Natronai also includes R. Ishmael's *baraita* at the beginning of *Sifra* among the
     passages to be recited since that is a midrashic text and he has therefore met all the
     possible obligations listed among the views expressed in the talmudic passage.
35   *Siddur R. Saadya Gaon*, eds I. Davidson, S. Assaf and B. I. Joel (Jerusalem, 1963²), p.
     358; Wieder, *Jewish Liturgy* (see n. 29 above), 2.562.
36   See n. 33 above.

world.[37] Another set include both the priestly benediction and the daily
offering, usually Numbers 28:1–8, but usually with the latter being
recited first.[38] There are also those that have the passage about the daily
offering immediately after the Torah benedictions but break off at that
point, leaving us in the dark as to whether the priestly benediction may
immediately have followed.[39] At this juncture in the prayers, it is
unusual among the fragments to find the fifth chapter of *Zevaḥim* or R.
Ishmael's *baraita*.[40]

On the other hand, another Cambridge Genizah fragment places
the matter of the restoration of the Temple cult squarely among those
items for which special supplication is made immediately after the
recitation of the morning benedictions and which obviously therefore
loomed large in the writer's theological wish-list. In an unusual
combination of entreaties and benedictions, the text includes a wish for
Torah knowledge and adherence to the divine will, a benediction of
thanks for the creation of mankind in God's image, and a request for
the avoidance of dishonesty.[41] It then continues with a prayer for the
rebuilding of Jerusalem and the restoration of the Temple that actually
concludes with the benediction used in this connection in the daily
'amidah, the *hafṭarah*, wedding benedictions and the grace after meals.[42]
The text reads: כן יהי רצון ורחמים מלפניך י"י אלהינו ואלהי אבותינו שתבנה [עי]רך
בימינו ותכונן היכלך בחיינו ותשמחינו בבנין עירך ותעורר ישיני עמך ותחיש קץ הפלאות ותחדש
ימינו כקדם ותנחמינו מהרה בבנין בית מקדשך כאשר אמרת והבטחת ברוך אתה י"י בונה ברחמיו
את ירושלים:

Later medieval developments

If one examines the later medieval rites, and indeed some of their
modern counterparts, one encounters two groups of readings, each of
which appear to be offering the worshipper the opportunity of reciting
biblical and rabbinic texts, including those centred on the sacrificial
cult. They are separated by longer or shorter sets of other material and
this separation may have permitted the inclusion of both groups in
spite of their similar liturgical aim of meeting the requirement to study

37   E.g. CUL, T-S NS 157.15, NS 160.27 and NS 230.90; T-S AS 105.151 and AS 120.95.
38   E.g. CUL, T-S NS 154.80 and NS 158.2.
39   E.g. CUL, T-S 8H9.15, NS 121.7 and AS 103.63; on the first of these, see Wieder,
     Jewish Liturgy (see n. 29 above), 1.204.
40   But see CUL, T-S NS 123.11 and NS 123.12.
41   CUL, Add.3160.1; see J. Mann, 'Genizah fragments of the Palestinian order of
     service,' *HUCA* 2 (1925), pp. 269–338, reprinted in *Contributions to the Scientific Study
     of Jewish Liturgy* (ed. J. J. Petuchowski, New York, 1970), which requires some minor
     corrections, as incorporated in the text here transcribed.
42   For sources and discussion of this Jerusalem benediction, see chapter 8 above.

a broad selection of Torah. Elbogen identifies the first as consisting of the priestly benediction, the daily offering and the mishnaic passage from the tractate *Pe'ah*, as already detailed above, and the second as the daily offering, the fifth chapter of *Zevaḥim* and R. Ishmael's *baraita*.[43] He offers the tentative suggestion that the former group may have been Palestinian in origin but the Genizah witnesses cited above and the earlier evidence from the talmudic and post-talmudic period may indicate that there was also another consideration in the gradual formulation of such passages. Perhaps there were some circles that wished to lay stress on the practical details of the Temple service, as a way of enacting a form of restoration, while others opted for passages that were less centred on the cult, as a way of encouraging the intellectual aspect of Torah study.

There are two additional pieces of research that would appear to indicate the existence of such a tension at the end of the geonic age and the beginning of the medieval period. Recent manuscript study by Fleischer and Ben-Shammai have added substantially to our knowledge of the special ceremonies, prayers and biblical verses recited by pilgrims on their visits to Jerusalem. The walls of Jerusalem were circumambulated before the Temple Mount was finally reached and specific sets of verses and prayers were recited at each of the gates of the city. Those who inspired and instituted this ritual were the 'Mourners of Zion' who were intensely moved by the references to the Temple and deeply lamented the loss of that institution. What is of particular interest is that these liturgical ceremonials, with their practical manifestations of love for the lost centre, were conducted by both Rabbanites and Karaites, perhaps another indication that the division of custom was not controlled by geographical or sectarian preference but by liturgico-theological concerns.[44]

My own close examination of those benedictions in the *'amidah* that are concerned with the restoration of lost Jewish institutions also appears to be of relevance to the present discussion. Some texts stress the rebuilt city of Jerusalem, the return of the Jews from the exile, the presence of God in Zion and the re-establishment of his rulership over Israel and, indeed, over the whole world. Others seem to be more directly concerned with the reconstructed Temple of the idealized messianic age, the people's appearance at the pilgrim festivals and the

---

43 Elbogen (see n. 21 above), G, pp. 90–91; H, pp. 70–71; E, pp. 78–79.

44 E. Fleischer, 'Pilgrims' prayer at the gates of Jerusalem', in *Mas'at Moshe: Studies in Jewish and Islamic Culture Presented to Moshe Gil*, eds E. Fleischer, M. A. Friedman and J. A. Kraemer (Hebrew; Jerusalem and Tel Aviv, 1998), pp. 298–327; H. Ben-Shammai, 'A unique lamentation on Jerusalem by the Karaite author Yeshu'a ben Judah' in *Mas'at Moshe*, pp. 93–102.

related festive rites, and the details of the sacrificial cult. It should be acknowledged that the texts do not always represent one tendency or the other but often constitute a combination of various themes. At the same time, there does at times seem to be a trend in one direction or the other and such a trend may cease to be easily identifiable as the texts evolve through the ages and borrow elements from each other.[45]

Since mention has briefly been made of the practice to recite the fifth chapter of the mishnaic tractate *Zevaḥim*, a few points should be made about this custom. The earliest codifications of the practice occur in the liturgies of Natronai, Amram and Maimonides, that is to say, in Babylon of the eighth and ninth centuries and followed in Egypt in the twelfth century.[46] Since the manuscripts of the liturgical work of Amram ben Sheshna Gaon often reflect the customs of the European rites of the high middle ages rather than any purer Babylonian tradition, one should generally be cautious about dating its contents to ninth-century Sura.[47] In this case, however, the other two sources appear to indicate that the reading is an authentic one. At this early stage, as is clear from what has been previously stated, the passage may have been either an exercise in re-enacting the Temple ritual or the replacement of the latter with an intellectual equivalent by way of textual study.

There is no doubt, however, that later developments were more influenced by kabbalistic notions which encouraged an increase in the liturgical importance attached to sacrificial matters and a consequent expansion of the passages detailing them. Reference was still made to the talmudic passages in *Menaḥot* and *Ta'anit*[48] but the recitation was additionally thought to be of prophylactic value against such disasters as the plague, and the mishnaic chapter was seen as special because it recorded no disagreement between the tannaitic teachers anywhere in its text.[49] The developments of the late medieval and early modern period are, however, beyond the scope of this study. Suffice it to say, in order to bring the argument full circle and to return to the remarks of

---

45 See chapter 8 above.
46 For Natronai, see n. 32 above; *Seder Raw Amrom Gaan* [sic] (Warsaw, 1865), p. 2; *Seder Rav 'Amram Ha-Shalem*, ed. A. L. Frumkin (Jerusalem, 1912), p. 55a (=109); *Seder R. Amram*, part 1, ed. D. Hedegård (Lund, 1951), Hebrew text, p. 10, English text, p. 24; *Seder Rav Amram*, ed. E. D. Goldschmidt (Jerusalem, 1971), p. 7.
47 Wieder, *Jewish Liturgy* (see n. 29 above), 1.53 and 1.163; Reif, *Hebrew Prayer* (see n. 1 above), pp. 185–87; and R. Brody, 'The enigma of *Seder Rav 'Amram'* (Hebrew) in *Knesset Ezra: Literature and Life in the Synagogue: Studies Presented to Ezra Fleischer*, eds S. Elizur, M. D. Herr, G. Shaked and A. Shinan (Jerusalem, 1994), pp. 21–34.
48 See nn. 11 and 13 above.
49 A. Berliner, *Randbemerkungen* (see n. 3 above), p. 28; *Bet Yosef* (commentary of R. Joseph Karo) on *Ṭur, Oraḥ Ḥayyim*, section 50.

Berliner which were cited at the beginning of the discussion, that Seligmann Baer is concerned to include in his commentary on the prayers an instruction to read the chapter from *Zevahim* with proper understanding of its content. To this end, he even attaches to it the fifteenth-century commentary of R. Obadiah of Bertinoro.[50] Again, the intellectual may be seen to be counter-attacking the mystic.

Summary

There was clearly substantial talmudic discussion about the future and/or replacement of sacrifice and its relative theological importance in rabbinic Judaism. Although there was from the outset a strong body of opinion that there was no connection or continuation, there was also a tendency to seek ways of incorporating details of sacrifices into the prayers, and not simply opting for the view that prayers had wholly replaced sacrifices. This tendency subsequently strengthened in the post-talmudic period, as documented in the earliest prayer-books. The liturgical poets also moved to restore the cult's central role, especially by way of poetic versions of the 'Avodah ritual for Yom Kippur, while a belief in the mystical, even magical, use of language encouraged the recitation of the relevant passages concerning the cult. The tenth century saw an enthusiastic interest on the parts of both Karaites and Rabbanites in special circumambulations of Jerusalem and in the recitation of connected prayers but, it must be admitted, without any central concern for details of the sacrificial cult. On the other hand, the textual variations in the prayers concerning Jewish restoration from about the same era reflect a tension between different notions of the future of Jerusalem. The Jewish liturgy ultimately incorporated, in conflated format, and not always in a fully logical presentation, two independent trends towards either Torah study or cultic restoration. The kabbalists of the late medieval and early modern periods, for their part, saw a prophylactic value in the recitation of passages concerning the sacrifices and this gave such texts an increased status in the regular prayers. To propose, therefore, that sacrifice was replaced by prayer is undoubtedly a gross over-simplification of a long and complicated liturgical process.[51]

50   S. Baer, *Seder 'Avodat Yisra'el* (Rödelheim, 1868), p. 50.

51   What I have written here is therefore a more nuanced interpretation of the subject than the briefer and less precise comments I offered in *Hebrew Prayer* (see n. 1 above), p. 138.

11

From Codex to LaTeX:
The Physical Transmission

Previous research

Since I have, in an earlier Hebrew study published elsewhere, discussed the literary and cultural background of rabbinic Judaism's liturgical developments in the Byzantine period , it will be useful in the context of this chapter to begin by noting a number of the conclusions that I reached in connection with that age.[1] As far as the general history of the Jewish communities of that time is concerned, the centres that existed in the homeland, in Iraq and in Egypt varied from one another with regard to the dominant cultures, religions and languages that surrounded them, and experienced different sets of circumstances, both favourable and otherwise, that made major impacts on their daily lives. Although it is true that there were times when they enjoyed close relations and mutual influences, as well as similar degrees of autonomy and toleration, the situation by and large was that the culture of each of these Jewish centres was by no means identical to those of its counterparts.[2] In the matter of the transmission of rabbinic traditions in the talmudic and post-talmudic periods, we have no evidence of complete codices being used for that purpose from the time of Bar Kokhba until the ninth century. It was not until the geonic period that a significant change took place and that rabbinic prayer-texts began to be committed to writing, albeit in a somewhat haphazard fashion and on to primitive codices of no more than a few folios.[3] It is clear from the archaeological and literary evidence that the synagogues of Palestine and the Diaspora in the first Christian centuries had no consistency of

---

1   Reif, 'Jewish prayers in their literary and cultural contexts during the Roman-Byzantine period' (Hebrew) in *Continuity and Renewal: Jews and Judaism in Byzantine-Christian Palestine*, ed. L. Levine (Jerusalem, 2004), pp. 389–401.

2   See, for example, *The Jewish People in the First Century. Historical Geography, Political History, Social, Cultural and Religious Life and Institutions*, eds S. Safrai and M. Stern (2 vols; Assen and Philadelphia, 1974–76); *Eretz Israel from the Destruction of the Second Temple to the Muslim Conquest*, eds Z. Baras, S. Safrai, Y. Tsafrir and M. Stern (Hebrew; Jerusalem, 1982 and 1988); and *Jerusalem, Its Sanctity and Centrality to Judaism, Christianity and Islam*, ed. L. I. Levine (New York, 1999).

3   Further details and documentation for this development are provided below in the section entitled 'Adopting the codex'.

structure, style or function. The Jewish teachers of the first two
Christian centuries (*Tanna'im*) expressed variant views concerning the
physical location of communal worship and the degree of holiness to
be ascribed to the relevant building. Rabbinic attitudes in these
connections altered from place to place and from time to time and only
gradually did the talmudic leadership come to accept the notion that
the synagogue had inherited the spiritual status of the Jerusalem
Temple.[4]

I also argued that the length, division and calendar of the
synagogal lectionaries of the Jewish communities of the Holy Land
were by no means monolithic in the period under discussion. On the
other hand, the situation in Babylon was apparently more consistent,
although it has to be acknowledged that the difference between that
consistency and its absence in Palestine may also have a chronological
element to it. At any rate, the eastern diaspora was long known for
completing the pentateuchal readings in one year while many in the
western homeland preferred to prolong the process for about three and
a half years.[5] The *Tanna'im* regarded the recitation of their prayers and
the practice of their synagogal customs as integral parts of a spiritual
life controlled by the requirements of halakhah and committed their
traditions to all manner of collections, the vast majority of them orally
transmitted. The Babylonian and Palestinian Talmuds are often at odds
and the object of the rabbinic dialectic that they record was essentially
to clarify the nature of a halakhic topic rather than to offer a conclusive
view of its application.[6]

The religious context in which the Aramaic targumim emerged was
that of the scriptural readings in the synagogue accompanied by their
public translation. Such targumim were originally a spontaneous
phenomenon, orally transmitted and spawning various versions. In the
course of the talmudic period, the Targum Onqelos became the most
authoritative and widespread Aramaic translation but there were other
versions that retained their importance for a number of subsequent
centuries.[7] With regard to the targum's sister genre of midrash, it is still

---

4   See, for example, Steven Fine, *This Holy Place. On the Sanctity of the Synagogue during
     the Greco-Roman Period* (Notre Dame, 1997).

5   A fairly recent discussion of the issues is by S. Naeh, 'The Torah reading cycle in
     Palestine: a re-examination', *Tarbiz* 67 (1998), pp. 167–87.

6   Some interesting points are made by Ruth Langer in her volume *To Worship God
     Properly: Tensions between Liturgical Custom and Halakhah in Judaism* (Cincinnati, 1998)
     and in her critique of the liturgical theories of E. Fleischer in *Prooftexts* 19 (1999), pp.
     179–204.

7   See, for example, the relevant articles in *The Aramaic Bible: The Targums in their
     Historical Context*, eds D. R. G. Beattie and M. McNamara (Sheffield, 1994) and the
     extensive literature cited there.

difficult to ascertain whether its original provenance was in the synagogue or the academy, or in both of them. What is clear is that there existed various types of midrash, that a variety of preachers delivered their homilies in different contexts, and that aggadot of a multifarious nature are to be found in different collections. Detailed comparative analysis of the variant texts of such pieces of midrash provide ample testimony to a long and complicated process that began with oral traditions and ultimately encompassed numerous and varied stages of redaction and editorial modification through the ages.[8] As far as the creation of liturgical poetry (*piyyut*) is concerned, there are certainly some common factors with the contemporaneous development of lectionaries, midrashim and targumim. What does not, however, exist among the earlier forms of Jewish poetic expression is a literary type that may confidently be identified as the prototype for the later emergence of *piyyut*. The origins of such liturgical poetry may be traced to the second half of the talmudic period and its characteristics at that time were simplicity and clarity. Only later did it adopt the use of the rhyme, the allusive epithet, and a more formal and complex structure.[9]

By way of summary, the dominant and decisive characteristic of Jewish culture and literature in the period leading up to the Byzantine era was that of novel and dynamic development. To a great extent, geographical and chronological considerations were at the heart of what transpired in the socio-political, theological and cultural fields and it is clear that external influences were no less significant than internal ones. The commitment of rabbinic traditions to formal, written structure was, at best, a limited procedure, and creative improvisation played a central role in the emergence of a variety of literary genres. My central proposition was that interpretations that argued for a more conservative and monolithic tendency on the part of Jewish liturgical composition would have to explain why liturgy stood in such stark contrast to parallel types of rabbinic literature.

If, then, a formal written structure for Jewish liturgy was the product of the post-talmudic and early medieval periods, it will now be necessary to explain how that transformation came about and how different systems of transmission characterized the various ages. The

---

8   Two important treatments are R. Kasher, 'The interpretation of scriptures in rabbinic literature' in *Mikra. Text, Translation, Reading and Interpretation of the Hebrew Bible in Ancient Judaism and Early Christianity*, ed. M. J. Mulder (Assen, Maastricht and Philadelphia, 1988), pp. 547–94, and G. Stemberger, *Introduction to the Talmud and Midrash* (E. T., Edinburgh, 1996), pp. 254–393.

9   A recent monograph, which incorporates much of the scholarship of such specialists as E. Fleischer and J. Yahalom, is that of L. J. Weinberger, *Jewish Hymnography: a Literary History* (London and Portland, 1998).

manner in which I shall attempt to do this will be to offer brief responses to the same basic questions in each of five periods of Jewish liturgical history. How and by whom was Jewish liturgy recorded in the Second Temple, talmudic, geonic, medieval and modern periods? Through which cause and with what effect did changes occur in the means employed to transmit such traditions?

Pre-rabbinic developments

That the means existed for recording both sacred and non-sacred texts in the late biblical epoch is of course self-evident to anyone with even the most elementary knowledge of the Jewish literature, epigraphy and archaeology of that period. Texts were recorded on stone, pottery, papyrus, leather and metal and it is through the remnants of artefacts made of such materials that a picture has been built up of a wide range of religious, political and social behaviour on the part of Second Temple Jewry.[10] Of particular relevance is the fact that its disparate communities flourished not only in the Jerusalem area but also in the more culturally symbiotic centres of Judah and the diaspora, such as those of Egypt and by the shores of the Dead Sea.[11] While it appears to have been the general practice to copy and transmit texts of the Hebrew Bible on leather and papyrus and to use other materials for more mundane purposes, it is not possible to point to any one medium by which liturgy was recorded or recited among the various groups claiming to belong to the house of Israel. A variety of practices in a number of contexts require to be noted. Formally structured psalms, as included in the canonical book and in addition to these, were not only recorded as sacred writ but were also chanted at holy sites and ceremonies, the best known example being the levitical activity on the Temple Mount in Jerusalem.[12] Other biblical passages, or close

10   See the relevant sections of D. W. Thomas (ed.), *Documents from Old Testament Times* (Edinburgh and London, 1958) and G. I. Davies, *Ancient Hebrew Inscriptions: Corpus and Concordance* (2 vols; Cambridge, 1991 and 2004).
11   B. Porten, *Archives from Elephantine: the Life of an Ancient Jewish Military Colony* (Berkeley and Los Angeles, 1968); R. de Vaux, *The Archaeology of the Dead Sea Scrolls*, revised English edition (London, 1973); G. Vermes, *The Dead Sea Scrolls, Qumran in Perspective* (London, 1977), and 'Qumran publications', *JJS* 43 (1992), pp. 99–100; E. Tov, 'The unpublished Qumran texts from Caves 4 and 11', *JJS* 43 (1992), pp. 101–36.
12   J. H. Charlesworth, 'A prolegomenon to a study of the Jewish background of the hymns and prayers in the New Testament', in G. Vermes and J. Neusner (eds), *Essays in Honour of Yigael Yadin* (= *JJS* 33, 1982), pp. 265–85; D. Flusser, 'Psalms, hymns and prayers', in *Jewish Writings of the Second Temple Period*, ed. M. E. Stone (Assen and Philadelphia, 1984), pp. 551–77; Reif, *Judaism and Hebrew Prayer: New Perspectives on Jewish Liturgical History* (Cambridge, 1993), chapters 2 and 3. See also chapter 4 above.

approximations to the canonical versions of them, including the *shema'*, the priestly benediction and the Ten Commandments, were also committed to writing not only on scrolls but also as discrete items in the form of amulets of one sort or another.[13]

As far as individual and communal prayers linked to special needs and occasions are concerned, a distinction requires to be drawn between, on the one hand, the Qumran evidence, which points to written formulae, and, on the other, what may perhaps be justifiably referred to as the proto-rabbinic circles, where the earliest forms of the *'amidah*, the grace after meals and other common benedictions were taking similar shape but apparently without commitment to writing.[14] Prototypes existed in the equivalent prayers recorded in the Hebrew Bible and were used by the pious and the populace to meet needs as they occurred but one fails to encounter any formal prayers of novel relevance and structure outside the Qumran community in the pre-rabbinic period.[15] Taken together with the use of the earliest synagogues for all manner of social and religious activities, perhaps including personal prayer as a minor element, and the centrality of Torah study on the sabbath for any popular (rather than pietist) notion of liturgy as such, such phenomena may indicate a reticence on the part of a significant section of the Jewish community to accept the expansion into liturgy of the concept of authorized textuality and of a commitment to writing that was becoming characteristic of some of their peers.[16] As the availability of leather and papyrus increased,[17] the

---

13   S. C. Reif, 'The Nash Papyrus', *Cambridge* 15 (1984), pp. 41–45; G. Barkay, *Ketef Hinnom. A Treasure Facing Jerusalem's Walls* (Israel Museum, catalogue no. 274, Jerusalem, 1986); Y. Yadin, *Tefillin from Qumran (X Q Phyl 1–4)* (Jerusalem, 1969); E. E. Urbach, 'The place of the Ten Commandments in ritual and prayer' in *The Ten Commandments as Reflected in Tradition and Literature throughout the Ages*, ed. B.-Z. Segal (Hebrew; Jerusalem, 1985), pp. 127–45 (E. T., ed. G. Levi, Jerusalem, 1990, pp. 161–89); R. Hammer, 'What did they bless? A study of Mishnah Tamid 5.1', *JQR*, NS 81 (1991), pp. 305–24. See also chapter 7 above.

14   M. Baillet, *DJD VII* (Oxford, 1982); E. Qimron, 'Times for praising God: a fragment of a scroll from Qumran 4Q409', *JQR*, NS 80 (1990), pp. 341–47; J. Heinemann, *Prayer in the Talmud: Forms and Patterns*, revised English edition (Berlin and New York, 1976). See also Flusser (see n. 12 above), the exchange between M. Weinfeld and R. Brody in *Tarbiz* 51 (1981–82), pp. 493–96, the liturgical texts edited in *DJD* XIX, XXIX and XXXIV, as cited above in chapter 4, n. 15, J. R. Davila, *Liturgical Works* (Grand Rapids, Michigan and Cambridge, UK, 2000) and *Liturgical Perspectives: Prayer and Poetry in Light of the Dead Sea Scrolls*, eds E. G. Chazon, R. A. Clements and A. Pinnick (Leiden and Boston, 2003).

15   E. Fleischer, 'On the beginnings of obligatory Jewish prayer', *Tarbiz* 59 (1990), pp. 397–441; S. C. Reif, 'On the earliest development of Jewish prayer', *Tarbiz* 60 (1991), pp. 677–81.

16   On the earliest use of the synagogue, see the Theodotos inscription conveniently available in L. Roth-Gerson, *The Greek Inscriptions from the Synagogues in Eretz-Israel* (Hebrew; Jerusalem, 1987), p. 76. For more general background see E. P. Sanders,

question arose about the nature of the text for which such a means of transmission was most ideally suited. Were benedictions and prayers, as well as codes of religious law and guides to religious belief, to be recorded much in the same way as biblical texts? Alternatively, was there a special power in the written word that could make it particularly apt for the revealed word of God and functional in the form of an amulet, but unsuitable or even dangerous for such popular expressions as oaths, vows and personal devotions, unless, of course, such devotions were to be accorded the status of magical communion with the divine? Such a question touches on the essential nature of the Jewish and Christian liturgies as they developed in the next period to be reviewed.[18]

Memorization and note-taking

That period, covering as it does the centuries that witnessed the development of tannaitic and amoraic Judaism, presents special problems of source interpretation because of the difficulty in dating and attributing the traditions recorded in the talmudic-midrashic literature and in assessing the degree to which the views to be found there reflect reality rather than a process of dialectics. The view here being espoused is that the varying opinions expressed by the rabbis in matters liturgical are a reflection of the tensions between, for example, individual and community, Hebrew and vernacular, male and female roles, precepts and liturgy, pietism and legalism, and spontaneity and formality.[19] Towering above all was the controversy, continuing from the earlier period, about whether the prayers were to be written and formally sanctioned or oral and unofficial. In that connection it is clearly of major importance to note what materials were available on which the rabbis could, if they so desired, record texts. In addition, of course, to biblical scrolls, references are made to the *pinax*, *diphthera* and

---

Jewish Law from Jesus to the Mishnah (London and Philadelphia, 1990), pp. 67–81 and *Judaism: Practice and Belief 63 BCE – 66CE* (London and Philadelphia, 1992), pp. 190–212.

17   Such a development is chronicled by R. Reed, *Ancient Skins, Parchments and Leathers* (London and New York, 1972) pp. 86–117.

18   The nature of such liturgies is discussed in the various essays in *The Making of Jewish and Christian Worship*, eds P. F. Bradshaw and L. A Hoffman (Notre Dame and London, 1991) and in a number of the subsequent volumes edited by the same two scholars and bearing the series title 'Two Liturgical Traditions'.

19   Heinemann (see n. 14 above); S. C. Reif, 'Some liturgical issues in the talmudic sources', *Studia Liturgica* 15 (1982–83), pp. 188–206 and chapter 4 of *Hebrew Prayer* (see n. 12 above).

tomos, all of them borrowed from the Classical world.[20] The first connotes a hard or soft writing-tablet, the second a primitively prepared leather folio, and the third a roll of sheets joined together in a scroll. The *pinax* could comprise not only one tablet but also a number of these attached at their ends and folding over to produce an effect similar to that associated with the codex. Some scholars have identified such a *pinax* as identical with the codex while others have argued convincingly that the system of binding was different in each case.[21] While the *diphthera* may have been used for individual biblical texts (not in the more controlled scroll form approved for synagogal use), the other two artefacts were primarily for recording commercial, legal and educational matters. The businessman and the lawyer attracted no criticism for doing so but there were doubts among the rabbis about the propriety of recording the *oral* Torah in such a fashion and serious objections to the consignment of prayers and bendictions to any written form.[22]

That such objections exist in talmudic literature cannot be gainsaid; their interpretation, however, depends on one's preconception of the degree to which talmudic Judaism was a standardized and formal set of beliefs and practices for a substantial section of Jewry during the period that its traditions were first being discussed and recorded. If the form of rabbinic prayer was fixed as early as the time of Rabban Gamliel, references to alternative structures and objections to written versions must refer to sectarian practice. If, as appears more convincing to me, talmudic Judaism was internally pluralistic at least as far as liturgy was concerned, such references are a reflection of contentious debates about the content and authority of prayer formulations.[23] Those who used the principle of note-taking to advantage in their own

20   S. Lieberman, *Hellenism in Jewish Palestine: Studies in the Literary Transmission, Beliefs and Manners of Palestine in the I Century B.C.E. – IV Century C. E.*, (New York[2], 1962), pp. 203–9; E. G. Turner, *The Typology of the Early Codex* (Philadelphia, 1977); C. M. Roberts and T. C. Skeat, *The Birth of the Codex* (London[2], 1983); R. H. Rouse and M. A. Rouse, 'Codicology, Western European' in *Dictionary of the Middle Ages* (New York, 1982–89), vol. 3 (1983), pp. 475–78. The relevant talmudic sources include Mishnah, *Shabbat* 12.4–5, *Avot* 3.17 (16), *Kelim* 24.7, *Bava Batra* 10.1 and *Soṭah* 2.4; PT, *Giṭṭin* 8 (49d) and *Bava Batra* 10 (17c); BT, *Bava Batra* 160ab and *Megillah* 19a.
21   M. Haran, 'The codex, the *pinax* and the wooden slats', *Tarbiz* 57 (1988), pp. 151–64, with an additional note in *Tarbiz* 58 (1989), pp. 523–24; S. Z. Havlin, 'From scroll to codex' *Alei Sefer* 16 (1989–90), pp. 151–52 and 160–61.
22   Tosefta, *Shabbat* 14.4 (13.4) and BT, *Shabbat* 115b.
23   Divergent interpretations of the evidence are offered by E. Fleischer and S. C. Reif in the articles cited in note 15 above. Parallel Christian development may be compared in D. A. Fiensy, *Prayers alleged to be Jewish: an Examination of the Constitutiones Apostolorum* (Chico, Ca., 1985). See also P. W. van der Horst's important treatment of related liturgical topics in his *Japheth in the Tents of Shem: Studies on Jewish Hellenism in Antiquity* (Leuven, 2002).

activities perhaps wished to import it into the field of liturgy, while those who doubted its legitimacy for the recall of oral Torah had even greater doubts about its use in matters pertaining to such a mystical phenomenon as prayer. This is not to say that where orality was preferred, simple alternatives were encouraged and more complex literary forms precluded. The nature of oral recording and transmission at that period is most assuredly to be distinguished from its equivalent in the modern period and orality survived well into the middle ages as a valid and even the preferred medium.[24] Variant texts inevitably flourished but they were by no means restricted to the brief and simple form, and the role of the *ḥazzan* in recalling, reciting and modifying them began to take on significance. It is true that the codex of the Classical world was adopted by Christianity when it became the dominant faith in that milieu but this should not lead historians of Hebrew literature to the uncritical assumption that the device of the bound volume was also in use by the Jews before the geonic period.[25] When, then, did note-taking develop into book-compiling and how did it affect the next stage of development in the history of Jewish liturgy?

Adopting the codex

As in the case of European history, the period of five hundred years leading up to the eleventh century has tended to be underestimated by historians. Far from being 'dark ages', these centuries in both orient and occident, but especially in the former, turn out to have been highly innovative and productive. With regard to written material pre-dating the ninth century, the remarkable fact is that we lack any Hebrew manuscripts from the time of Bar Kokhba to the earliest Genizah fragments. Inscriptional evidence testifies to the fact that material relating to the building and endowment of synagogues, the functioning of academies, and the application of halakhah was recorded on stone[26]

---

24   This is well illustrated by M. Carruthers, *The Book of Memory: a Study in Medieval Culture* (Cambridge, 1990).

25   M. Beit-Arié, 'How Hebrew manuscripts are made' in *A Sign and a Witness: 2,000 Years of Hebrew Books and Illustrated Manuscripts*, ed. L. S. Gold (New York and Oxford, 1988), pp. 35–46, and *Hebrew Codicology: Tentative Typology of Technical Practices Employed in Hebrew Dated Medieval Manuscripts* (Jerusalem², 1981), is careful to point to the absence of evidence that might support such an assumption. On the Christian usage, see I. M. Resnick, 'The codex in early Jewish and Christian communities', *JRH* 17 (1992), pp. 1–17.

26   Examples are to be found in D. Urman, 'Jewish inscriptions from Dabbura', *IEJ* 22 (1972), pp. 16–23; Y. Sussmann, 'A halakhic inscription from the Beth-Shean valley', *Tarbiz* 43 (1973–74), pp. 88–158; and J. Naveh, *On Stone and Mosaic: the Aramaic and Hebrew Inscriptions from Ancient Synagogues* (Hebrew; Jerusalem, 1978).

but actual texts of rabbinic literature have simply not survived from that period. The only hint of liturgy, if one may define it as such, are the brief blessings invoked on synagogal benefactors.[27] It is not impossible that this absence of manuscripts is historically fortuitous and that evidence will at some future date become available. On the other hand, it is more tempting to suggest that it reflects the predominantly oral nature of the halakhic, rabbinic tradition, of which liturgy was certainly a part.[28] As earlier argued, midrashim, targumim and *piyyuṭim* appear to have been transmitted orally at the early stages of their existence and it seems to me that the possibility of at least such biblical and liturgical commentaries having originally existed in such a form has received insufficient attention and consideration. Whether the same question should be asked in connection with mystical texts is open to discussion, given that the written word carries special significance for such material. While it is perhaps explicable that individual sheets of papyrus and leather should all have disappeared, it hardly seems reasonable to presuppose that complete codices would have sunk without trace during a lengthy epoch of Jewish history. Furthermore, the early adoption of the codex by the fast-growing empire of Islam could well have provided an impetus for the Jewish community to match the cultural and religious encroachments from that powerful source by making use of the same artefact.[29]

With such developments in mind, it seems sensible to view the history of written liturgy in the geonic period as one of two parts. Until the eighth century, the individual folio, made of papyrus, leather, or possibly, cloth, was the main writing material for any liturgical text that did achieve such formal recognition.[30] It is also conceivable that a less structured version of the scroll than that used for biblical texts was

---

27   E.g. many of the inscriptions listed by Naveh (see n. 26 above) in which the donors and builders are 'blessed' or 'remembered for good'; see also J. Yahalom, 'Prayers for the community in synagogue inscriptions', *Cathedra* 19 (1981), pp. 44–46.

28   This interpretation is supported by the views of R. Brody, 'The testimony of geonic literature to the text of the Babylonian Talmud', in *Meḥqerey Talmud*, eds J. Sussmann and D. Rosenthal (Hebrew; Jerusalem, 1990), pp. 237–303; B. Gerhardsson, *Memory and Manuscript* (Lund and Copenhagen, 1961; republished with a new preface by the author and a foreword by J. Neusner, together with *Tradition and Transmission in Early Christianity*, Grand Rapids and Livonia, Michigan, 1998); and G. Khan, 'On the question of script in medieval Karaite manuscripts: new evidence from the Genizah' in *Artefact and Text: the Re-creation of Jewish Literature in Medieval Hebrew Manuscripts*, *BJRULM* 75.3 (1993), pp. 133–41. See also the introductory remarks to this chapter.

29   For the papyrus evidence, see C. Sirat, *Les Papyrus en Caractères Hébraïques trouvés en Egypte* (Paris, 1985); see also her brief article on T-S 6H9–21 at Cambridge University Library in *Genizah Fragments* 5 (April, 1983), pp. 3–4.

30   Papyrus is still used for some of the older Genizah material (e.g. T-S 6H9–21) and there are also examples of cloth being used for the recording of texts (e.g. T-S 16.31).

used. When the codex, at first in papyrus and later in vellum, subsequently became the preferred medium, it was limited to no more than a few quires.[31] It is possible that just as the scroll was written only on one side, so early forms of the codex followed the same practice and that double-sided copying was a later sophistication.[32] While individual folios, or bifolia, continued to be classified as *diphthera*, the scroll form was known as *gewil*, and the later Arabic term for the bound volume, namely, *mushaf*, was eventually adopted by the Jews of the orient.[33] It would be strange if the adoption and development of the codex from the eighth century onwards had nothing to do with the emergence of the first *siddurim*. While an individual folio could be used for a brief responsum about a liturgical problem, for an abbreviated list of texts, readings or poems, or for a novel prayer-form, the codex device was infinitely more suitable for the halakhic authority who wished to provide a total written guide to all the prayers of the Jewish calendar.[34]

Not that the expanded form yet took on the characteristics of a text open to limitless glossing and commentary, a development that took place only later. At that early stage, say, in the ninth, tenth and eleventh centuries, the primary purpose of the prayer-text was to provide the basic wording, rubrics for its use, and a justification for its being chosen out of the many alternative versions that were still circulating.[35] Perhaps the small, primitive and rather fully covered

31 See the references to the work of Turner and Sirat in nn. 20 and 29 above; see also M. Bar-Ilan, '*Ha-ma'avar mi-megillah le-qodeqs*', *Sinai* 107 (1991), pp. 242–54.

32 That such a practice was also used for rabbinic texts is documented by an early Genizah manuscript, T-S AS 74.324, published by M. Bregman, 'An early fragment of Avot de-Rabbi Natan from a scroll', *Tarbiz* 52 (1983), pp. 201–22. Whether that fragment is to be dated to the fourth to fifth century as suggested by Bregman, or some centuries later, remains an open question, but it is certainly among the earliest Genizah fragments.

33 *Massekhet Soferim* 3.6 and *Sefer Halakhot Gedolot*, ed. E. Hildesheimer (3 vols; Jerusalem, 1971, 1980, 1988), 1.404. The pentateuchal codex was known to the oriental Jews as *mashaf torah*, as in e.g. T-S 12.791, or *mashafa de-'orayta*, as in e.g. T-S A41.41. For details of the scribal profession in the Genizah period see S. D. Goitein, *A Mediterranean Society: The Jewish Communities of the Arab World as Portrayed in the Documents of the Cairo Geniza*, 5 vols and index volume (Berkeley, Los Angeles and London, 1967–93), 2.228–40.

34 S. C. Reif, 'Aspects of mediaeval Jewish literacy' in *The Uses of Literacy in Early Mediaeval Europe*, ed. R. McKitterick (Cambridge, 1990), pp. 134–55. See also B. Gerhardsson, *Memory and Manuscript* (Uppsala, 1961), Carruthers, *Memory* (see n. 24 above) and W. A. Graham, *Beyond the Written Word: Oral Aspects of Scripture in the History of Religion* (Cambridge, 1987; paperback edition, 1993).

35 L. A. Hoffman, *The Canonization of the Synagogue Service* (Notre Dame and London, 1979); E. Fleischer, *Eretz-Israel Prayer and Prayer Rituals as Portrayed in the Genizah Documents* (Hebrew; Jerusalem, 1988); S. C. Reif, 'The early history of Jewish

sheets of vellum precluded any additional attention, or perhaps there was still doubt about the use of a written format. Certainly, there are responsa that appear to testify that the issue was still a live one in the eighth and ninth centuries. Yehudai rules in favour of the established practice of the academies according to which the cantor avoids errors when reciting liturgical poems on Yom Kippur and communal fasts by using a written text but trusts to memory on all other occasions. In Natronai's day written texts were apparently more common since the question was asked whether a blind person could lead the prayers, given that he could not read them. The reply was to distinguish Torah reading, for which actual sight of the text was required, and acting as representative of the worshipping community, for which memorized formulation was perfectly adequate.[36] Two further pieces of evidence indicate that by the end of the period under discussion the written version of the prayers in the codex did not yet fully dominate the scene. On the one hand, the *Seder Rav 'Amram* had been so widely disseminated and regarded as authoritative that it ensured the adoption of the basic structure of the prayers according to the Babylonian rite throughout the Jewish world, even if later recensions of the work took on local characteristics.[37] On the other hand, versions of the same prayer in different styles and languages could still exist side-by-side, no one text yet having succeeded in ousting the others from a place in the written prayer-book.[38]

Early forms of codex

It is important to compare these theories, derived as they are from a general analysis of the development of Jewish literacy and its written expression in the early Middle Ages, with the results of a recent survey that I have made of the physical characteristics of some eighty fragments of regular liturgical content in the Cambridge Genizah

---

worship' in *The making of Jewish and Christian Worship* (see n. 18 above), pp. 109–36, updated and expanded in *Hebrew Prayer* (see n. 12 above), chapter 5.

36 L. Ginzberg, *Geonica*, (2 vols; New York, 1909), 1.119–23.

37 For details, see the editor's introductory essay in *Seder Rav Amram*, ed. E. D. Goldschmidt (Jerusalem, 1971).

38 See e.g. the *qaddish* version in T-S 6H6.6 quoted by Fleischer, *Eretz-Israel Prayer* (see n. 35 above), p. 245; the study of *we-'ilu finu* in chapter 17 of this volume; and A. Samely's contribution to *Artefact and Text* (see n. 28 above), pp. 175–264. On the matter of Jewish trilingualism in the early Middle Ages, see R. Drory, 'Words beautifully put: Hebrew versus Arabic in tenth-century Jewish literature' in *Genizah Research after Ninety Years: The Case of Judaeo-Arabic*, eds J. Blau and S. C. Reif (Cambridge, 1992), pp. 53–66; S. C. Reif, 'Aspects' (see n. 34 above), pp. 134–55, especially 148–49; and Khan, 'Question of Script' (see n. 28 above).

collections.[39] The dates of these fragments range from the ninth or tenth to the twelfth or thirteenth centuries, but the majority of them appear to belong to the eleventh century. Their choice for inclusion was based entirely on the fact that physical descriptions had already been prepared in other contexts and there is no obvious, pre-existent connection between that availability and the fragments' characteristics that would invalidate their use as a random sample.[40] There appears to be no valid reason for calling into question the assumption that they are typical of many other Genizah items of similar content and chronology. The survey covers the material used and the style of handwriting; the size of the fragments and the number of folios and lines; the nature of any pointing and annotation to be found; and any identifiable, scribal techniques.

It turns out interestingly that, out of eighty fragments, forty are written on vellum and forty on paper. A majority of the texts that use the square script (thirty-four out of forty-four) are written on vellum (all but five of them of oriental provenance), while most of the texts that use a cursive or semi-cursive style of hand (thirty-one out of thirty-six) are written on paper. The maximum dimensions for the vellum fragments are 23 cm long by 24 cm broad and for the paper fragments 35 cm long by 26 cm broad. The minimum dimensions for the vellum fragments are 9 cm long by 9 cm broad and for the paper fragments 9 cm long by 8 cm broad. What emerges from all the dimensional statistics is that the average size of a vellum fragment is 15.82 cm by 14.47 cm and that of a paper fragment 16.70 cm by 12.62 cm. Although there are exceptional examples in which the number of folios reaches sixty-one in the case of the vellum or sixteen in the case of paper, the average number of folios is 2.7 for vellum and 4.8 for paper, that is, an

---

39   The classmarks of the fragments are: Add.3158, Add.3159.1–9, Add.3159.11–15, Add.3160.1–16, Add.3161–2, Add.3356, Add.3361, Add.3366, Add.3369; Or.2116.12a.3, Or.2116.19.8–11; T-S 6H2.1, T-S 6H3.7, T-S 8H9.5, T-S 8H10.6, 11, 15, T-S 8H11.4, T-S 8H16.22, T-S 8H23.10, T-S 8H24.5, T-S 10H1.4, 7, T-S 10H8.7, T-S 13H4.3; T-S A29.51, 93, T-S A40.34, T-S A41.50, T-S H2.4, 20, 49, 76, 95–96, 106, 136, 146, T-S H18.43; T-S Misc.24.137.4a, 12a, T-S Misc.28.77, 247; T-S NS 121.3, T-S NS 123.119, T-S NS 125.149, T-S NS 150.36, 59, 184.

40   Details concerning some of these fragments may be found in my volumes *Published Material from the Cambridge Genizah Collections: A Bibliography 1896–1980* (Cambridge, 1988), pp. 26, 39–40, 72–74, 91, 108, 112–14, 131, 150, 329, 411–12 and *Hebrew Manuscripts at Cambridge University Library: A Description and Introduction* (Cambridge, 1997), pp. 247–61 and 268. On the general problem of dating such fragments, see M. Beit-Arié, 'The paleography of the Geniza literary fragments', *Te'uda* 1, ed. M. A. Friedman (Tel Aviv, 1980), pp. 193–99 and 'The codicological data-base of the Hebrew palaeography project: a tool for localizing and dating Hebrew medieval manuscripts' in *Hebrew Studies*, eds D. R. Smith and P. S. Salinger (London, 1991), pp. 165–97.

overall average of 3.76.[41] As far as the lines are concerned, their number ranges from nine to thirty-two, with an average of 15.6 lines for vellum and 18.2 lines for paper, yielding an overall average of 16.86. Known systems of vocalization occur, if sometimes somewhat minimally, in thirty-seven out of eighty fragments but in this connection there appears to be no significant difference between what is to be found in the vellum as distinct from the paper, or in the cursively written texts vis-à-vis those where the square style is employed.

In the matter of the identification of the scribal techniques being employed, it should of course be stated at the outset that we are dealing here with fragments and not complete codices. In spite of that consideration, what is still nevertheless significant is the complete absence of any consistent methods. Only in rare instances is it possible to find the ruling of lines, the employment of an enlarged script (as, for instance, in headings), or remnants of an original colophon.[42] No more than occasionally does the researcher come across cases of marginal decoration or annotation, and there is only one apparent example of a list of numbers.[43] What is common is the use of abbreviations, as, for example, at the beginnings of the most familiar prayers and benedictions.[44] If account may also be taken here of content, it should be noted that the subjects covered in the texts are in the main limited to the *shema'* and its associated benedictions; the *'amidah* for weekdays, sabbaths and festivals; the Passover Haggadah and the grace after meals. Liturgical poetry and other such addenda do not generally make any appearance. Instructions and notes in Judeo-Arabic are to be found in sixteen of the vellum and twenty of the paper fragments but the use of Judeo-Arabic is proportionately smaller in material of Palestinian origin than in items of alternative provenance.

The central findings of an important piece of research recently conducted by Ezra Fleischer are also relevant to this discussion. In an extensive and informative study, Fleischer has carefully described and analysed twenty-seven Genizah fragments containing a wide variety of regular prayers of the Palestinian rite. Fleischer deduces from his investigation that the texts are all the work of a single scribe, that they were individually composed and never part of one codex, and that only occasionally are their contents consecutive. He contends that the scribe produced the texts for the use of individuals in the Palestinian

---

41 See, for example, Cambridge Genizah fragments Add.3158 and Add.3356.
42 See, for example, Cambridge Genizah fragments T-S 6H3.7, T-S 10H1.4, T-S H2.76 and T-S H2.96.
43 See, for example, Cambridge Genizah fragments Add.3159.11–12, Or.2116.19.9, 11, T-S 6H2.1, T-S Misc.24.137.4a and T-S NS 150.59.
44 See, for example, Cambridge Genizah fragment T-S 10H1.7.

communities of Egypt at the end of the eleventh or the beginning of the twelfth century.[45]

I believe that we may, on the basis of the physical data just presented, draw a number of general conclusions. The material studied provides concrete evidence of a change of allegiance from vellum to paper and of a development away from a square towards a more cursive script. The shape of the folio moves from square towards rectangular with the result that an increase in the length of the leaf is accompanied by a narrowing of the text written on it. It is of course difficult to establish the precise number of folios, given that some may be lost and others may have been ascribed to other fragmentary manuscripts and described a such, either in the Cambridge collections or in other Genizah resources. Nevertheless, one can discern an increase in the number of folios and lines as the change is made from vellum to paper. Although there is some employment of scribal techniques, there can be no doubt whatsoever that there is a lack of consistency and professionalism in this area. In addition, there is a definite tendency to insert halakhic notes, composed in Judeo-Arabic, into the text, apparently under the influence of Sa'adya and other Babylonian geonim, especially in centres where their halakhic authority reigned supreme. It seems likely that a large number of the fragments, perhaps even the vast majority of them, constitute early examples of the creation and use of the Hebrew codex. It is therefore important for specialists in paleography and literary history to distinguish carefully between what occurred during the earliest stage that the codex was in use among the Jews and what developed in the wake of such use. Another matter that requires careful consideration is the question of the means used to record the regular prayers on the one hand and the liturgical poems on the other. Were they identical in each case and, if not, in which respects did they differ?

In sum, then, what do all the above discussion and data tell us about Jewish liturgical history between the ninth and twelfth centuries and about developments in the forms taken by prayer texts during those years? It seems reasonable to propose that not long before the beginning of that period all or most of such material had been transmitted orally, and to regard some of the fragments as early attempts, probably on the part of individuals rather than communities, to commit those traditions to writing. The expansion of Jewish use of the codex encouraged this process and led to the development of fresh approaches to the nature of rabbinic literature as a whole, that is, of the oral Torah. As it became more common to write down the rabbinic

---

45   E. Fleischer, 'Qeṭa'im mi-qovṣey tefillah', Kobez al Yad, 13 [23] (1996), pp. 91–189.

traditions in a respectful and systematic manner, so the tendency grew to regard such texts as having something of a canonical nature. The single leaf evolved into the codex, the private individual became the professional scribe, and the texts that had once been brief and provisional notes gradually turned into formal prayer-books. Later generations appended to such prayer-books their own notes, instructions, commentaries and decorations, thus enhancing both their importance and their physical attractiveness. In sum, not only did the physical nature of the material influence its religious status, but that status in its turn played a part in increasing the desire to pay due honor to the concrete medium of transmission.

Changes in middle ages

The situation changed in the high middle ages. The twelfth to the sixteenth centuries were the years in which the bound codex reached the apogée of its elegance, usefulness and influence. The simple, even primitive folios and codices that are characteristic of the material found in the Cairo Genizah gradually gave way to the altogether more elaborate and systematically produced volumes that are now located in all the major collections of Hebraica around the world but are particularly well represented in this country in the southern triangle of Oxford, London and Cambridge, as well as further north in the John Rylands University Library of Manchester and the Brotherton Library of the University of Leeds. A whole range of scribal techniques evolved, qualities of vellum began to be differentiated, and paper began to challenge the place of vellum as the primary material for the transcription of texts. Quires were composed with greater care and consistency, catchwords were included, sections numerated, lines justified in a variety of ways, folios pricked and ruled, and the *masṭara* (ruling-board) was employed to facilitate the planning of the lines.[46] Although there are few Hebrew codices that can match the beauty of illuminated western manuscripts of the period, some did eventually achieve superb standards of illustration and illumination, making use not only of the more oriental style of micrography but also of art forms

---

46 Maimonides, *Mishneh Torah, Malweh we-loweh* 15.2 and *Tefillin u-mezuzah we-sefer torah* 1.6–11; *The Hebrew Book; An Historical Survey*, eds R. Posner and I. Ta-Shma (Jerusalem, 1975); C. Sirat and M. Beit-Arié, *Manuscrits Médiévaux en Caractères Hébraïques portant des Indications de Date jusqu'à 1540* (Jerusalem, 1972–86). and M. Beit-Arié, *Hebrew Codicology* (see n. 25 above) and in his collected articles entitled *The Making of the Medieval Hebrew Book: Studies in Palaeography and Codicology* (Jerusalem, 1993).

that were more typical of the west.[47] Private and public libraries had
begun to spring up in North Africa, including Egypt, as early as the
ninth and tenth centuries and the expansion of this facility ensured not
only the spread of learning but also an intense development within
each area of Jewish culture.[48]

One such area that became a major beneficiary of these new
bibliographical tendencies was that of Jewish liturgy.[49] The evidence is
not entirely balanced with regard to the geography and history of
manuscript production since the Genizah source is predominantly
early and oriental while the Spanish, Italian and Ashkenazi codices are
generally a few centuries later and reflect a more western environment.
The Fatimid and Ayyubid periods pulsate with Jewish life while the
occidental centres are still fairly silent; conversely, material remains
reduce drastically in the Mamluk period while Europe begins to
flourish.[50] Nevertheless a picture does emerge of how liturgy was
treated in the Hebrew codex as it made its increasing impact on the
structure and content of Jewish literature. The geonic tendency to
justify the text and to offer simple halakhic guidance was continued but
gradually expanded into the production of complete liturgical
compendia covering the whole liturgical calendar, not only with text
and rubrics as well as *halakhot* but also with commentaries on the text.[51]

47   C. Sirat and L. Avrin, *La Lettre Hébraïque et sa Signification: Micography as Art*
     (Jerusalem and Paris, 1981). See also the article by G. Sed-Rajna, 'The image in the
     text: methodological aspects of the analysis of illustrations and the relation to the
     text' in *Artefact and Text* (see n. 28 above), pp. 25–31.
48   Numerous Genizah fragments testify to such a development, e.g. T-S 20.44 and
     20.47, as published by E. J. Worman, 'Two book-lists from the Cambridge Genizah
     fragments', *JQR* 20 (1908), pp. 450–63, and T-S Ar.5.1 and T-S NS J271 as published
     by S. D. Goitein, 'Books: migrant and stationary: a Geniza study' in *Occident and
     Orient: a Tribute to the Memory of Alexander Scheiber*, ed. R. Dan (Budapest and Leiden,
     1988), pp. 179–98. M. Ben-Sasson delivered a paper on 'Maghreb libraries in the
     Genizah' at the third congress of the Society for Judaeo-Arabic Studies held in
     Cambridge in 1978 but it has yet to appear in print.
49   Examples maybe found in *Hebrew Manuscripts from the Palatine Library of Parma*
     (Jerusalem, 1985); *Selected Manuscripts and Prints... from the Treasures of the Jewish
     National and University Library*, eds M. Nadav and R. Weiser (Jerusalem, 1985); *A
     Visual Testimony: Judaica from the Vatican Library*, ed. P. Hiat (Florida and New York,
     1987); *A Sign and a Witness* (see n. 25 above); and Reif, *Hebrew Manuscripts* (see n. 40
     above), covering the daily and festival liturgies for various rites in entries 358–448
     on pp. 215-65.
50   Contrast the periods that attract major attention in the work of S. D. Goitein on the
     oriental communities and H. H. Ben-Sasson on their western equivalents, as in *A
     Mediterranean Society* (see n. 33 above) and *A History of the Jewish People* (Hebrew; Tel
     Aviv, 1969; English edition, London, 1976).
51   Examples are Simḥah b. Samuel of Vitry, *Maḥzor Vitry*, ed. S. Hurwitz (2 vols;
     Nuremberg², 1923) and Jacob b. Judah Ḥazzan, *The Etz Hayyim*, ed. I. Brodie (3 vols;
     Jerusalem, 1962–67); see also Cambridge University Library MS Add. 667.1, of a
     similar genre.

Such commentaries moved on from the halakhic to the exegetical and the mystical in the first instance, and then on to the philosophical, the linguistic and the literary, as all the catalogues of medieval Hebrew liturgical manuscripts make clear. While such detailed texts and commentaries were compiled by scholars for scholars and therefore reflected intellectual development at a high level, there also emerged the prayer-book in large format that contained mainly the liturgical text and was intended for use by the *ḥazzan* leading the congregation in prayer, or, following the biblical precedent, as an exemplar for members of the community wishing to check the validity of particular texts. Such a volume had invitingly large margins and inevitably attracted the enthusiastic attention of glossators, as well, of course, as 'correctors' and censors, internal and external.[52] As with all such codices, whatever their content, only a few wealthy congregants could ever actually hope to acquire their own copies but their existence in many communities meant that liturgical commentators no longer needed to provide a complete text of what they were annotating. If this distinction between the scholarly and devotional types of prayer-book is a valid one, it would also explain why *maḥzor* and *siddur* were not at an early medieval stage the mutually exclusive terms that they came to be later, when the former was applied to festival prayers and the latter to daily ones. It was only when large copies were made for cantorial use that it became practical and utilitarian to provide different volumes for specific sets of liturgical occasions.

But the prayer-books also offer space to biblical readings, sometimes with targumic renderings, to calendars and lectionary lists, to mishnaic and midrashic texts (especially the tractate *Avot*), and to collections of halakhic rulings. The nature of the poetic content, the degree to which halakhic compendia, philosophical interpretation and kabbalistic comment are included, the use of the vernacular and the extent to which the text is ornamented or, indeed, censored – all these vary from rite to rite and from centre to centre[53] but the presence of such broad elements of Jewish literary and religious expression indicate that the *siddur* has changed from being an improvised *aide-*

---

52 Among Hebrew codices at Cambridge University Library, two fine examples are Add.662 and Or.785, Ashkenazi prayer-books dating from no later than the fourteenth century; see Reif, *Hebrew Manuscripts* (see n. 40 above), entries 365 and 369, pp. 224–25 and 227–28. See also T. and M. Metzger, *Jewish Life in the Middle Ages: Illuminated Hebrew Manuscripts of the Thirteenth to the Sixteenth Centuries* (London and New York, 1985).

53 Compare, for example, the varying content of the Ashkenazi (pp. 215–29), Italian (pp. 230–40), and Sefardi (pp. 240–43) prayer-books preserved in such manuscripts as those referred to in Reif, *Hebrew Manuscripts* (see n. 49 above).

memoire for the individual to functioning as an extensive liturgical *vade mecum* for the congregation.

Menahem Schmelzer has pointed out that this process went even further. Although the majority of codices were the work of individual scribes, there were also some workshops that specialized in producing particularly impressive manuscripts and some academic centres that met the particular needs of scholars. Centres such as Spain had the reputation for producing a high quality result, often with illuminated sections, so that demand was increased and impressive private collections were gradually built up around the Jewish world.[54] In the fourteenth and fifteenth centuries, a whole range of supplementary annotations (*haggahot*) attached themselves to the basic liturgical text. Although some of these were concerned with the elucidation of the text, most were devoted to summarizing various liturgical practices. They amounted to compilations of halakhic rules and regulations that cited the views of leading authorities and the customs of particular localities. Perhaps even more interestingly, the need to incorporate such marginal notes into the manuscripts had a physical effect on the appearance of the manuscript folio. Schmelzer has himself described the process as follows:

> The intrinsic nature of the *haggahot* literature led to the intricately and deliberately shaped layouts of the Hebrew manuscript page. The challenge of copying many disjointed, individual, self-contained supplementary statements, all relating to a central text, in an esthetically pleasing manner, gave rise to scribal practice in which these supplements became arranged in ornamental patterns of a pre-planned design, frequently in the form of calligrams. In other words, the character of the literature itself was instrumental in shaping the esthetic appearance of the manuscripts in which they were copied. In addition, copyists also needed to plan the allocation of space in manuscripts which were to contain multiple works, on the margin and/or consecutively.[55]

The task was a complicated one that more often ended in failure than in success and it may even be the case that one of the results of such concentration on the physical aspect of the annotations was that their

---

54 M. Schmelzer, 'Hebrew manuscripts and printed books among the Sephardim before and after the Expulsion' in *Crisis and Creativity in the Sephardic World, 1391–1648*, ed. B. R. Gampel (New York, 1997), pp. 257–66.

55 These remarks were offered by Schmelzer at a conference held at the University of Manchester in April, 1992, on 'Artefact and Text: The Re-Creation of Jewish Literature in Medieval Hebrew Manuscripts'. The proceedings, edited by Philip S. Alexander and Alexander Samely, were published in the *Bulletin of the John Rylands University Library of Manchester* (see n. 28 above). Unfortunately, Schmelzer was unable to provide a written version of his paper for inclusion in that volume.

content tended to receive less attention and ultimately came to be neglected. There was also controversy among rabbinic authorities as to the halakhic acceptability of enriching the liturgical text with illuminations, sometimes of a brightly coloured variety. R. Meir of Rothenburg was asked in the 12th century about his failure to forbid the use in *maḥzorim* of figures of animals and birds. He ruled that this was not included in the prohibition stated in the second commandment but that it was not advisable because the presence of such illuminations would distract the attention of the worshipper using such a text.[56] On the other hand, a favourable side of codicological development for the less educated congregant was stressed by the author of the *Sefer Ḥasidim* in 12–13th century Franco-Germany. He argued that when the same phrase occurred in a number of liturgical contexts, the scribe should write it in full each time for the benefit of the non-expert worshipper who might otherwise have to search for it in the remainder of the volume and thereby cause an unwelcome interruption, or indeed an error in his devotions.[57]

Printing

The final stage in the pre-modern period would have been for the best physical elements of the most splendidly produced volumes to be gradually transferred to the smaller and more compact prayer-books that were created as much for individual as for cantorial use.[58] In many ways such volumes were the precursors of the printed edition, catering as they did as much for members of the Jewish public as for scholars or for cantors. The question is whether that transmission from the best manuscript to the best printed edition was a direct and simple one or one fraught with complications and difficulties.

It should not be forgotten that the printing-press brought about as revolutionary a change in cultural developments in its day as the computer in our own and this is particularly true in the specific instance of the printed Hebrew prayer-book. Data collection and

---

56   Meir of Rothenburg, *Responsa*, ed. I. Z. Cahana (Hebrew; 3 vols; Jerusalem, 1957–62), 2.50–52, no. 56, trans. in I. A. Agus, *Rabbi Meir of Rothenburg – His life and his Works as Sources for the Religious, Legal and Social History of the Jews of Germany in the Thirteenth Century* (New York², 1970), 1.266, no. 216.

57   *Sefer Ḥasidim*, eds J. Wistinetzki and J. Freimann (Frankfurt am Main², 1924), section 711, p. 184.

58   A good example at Cambridge University Library is Add. 438, a daily and festival prayer, according to the Sefardi rite, dating from a century before the Expulsion, consisting of the liturgical text and the rules of prayer; see Reif, *Hebrew Manuscripts* (see n. 40 above), entry no. 390, pp. 240–41.

preservation became an altogether less haphazard and difficult proposition. As long as one manuscript was available, it could be used by the printer and a rare item could be given a greater lease of life by production in numerous copies. While only a very wealthy patron could have engaged a scribe to transcribe a text for him, multiple copies made it feasible for the growing numbers of the merchant class to purchase a greater stake in learning and thereby increase their degree of involvement in decisions about its future direction.[59] The numerous incunables and sixteenth-century editions of the Ashkenazi, Sefardi and Italian prayer-books produced in the Iberian peninsula and Italy ensured that the future of such rites was no longer exclusively dependent on the employment of copyists, the memory of the *hazzan* in the synagogue or the whim of the censor or persecuter. Indeed, the mass destruction of Spanish and Portuguese Jewish communities and their cultural inheritance might have been even more disastrous for the survival of their traditions, had a small proportion of their printed editions not succeeded in escaping destruction. It should be added that the wide dissemination of printed prayer-books in Poland and the surrounding areas was matched by a similar activity in Turkey in the sixteenth century and subsequently in Germany and Holland. The amplification and reinforcement of knowledge was another feature to benefit considerably from the printed volume. Previously, a view or a piece of information was likely to be known in a limited circle and only rarely became widespread enough to win universal acceptance or to attract extensive comment, whereas now the reverse was possible. If the fate of Jewish communal worship had in earlier periods been dictated in turn by personal relevance, theological status, halakhic centralization and ritual dominance, so was it now in large measure subject to the supremacy of the printing-press and those who could or would exercise control over it.[60]

As the content of the printed *siddurim* became more sophisticated, so they came to record not only the rites themselves but rubrics about their use, reasons for their suitability, and justifications of their inclusion. The order of topics, the juxtaposition of individual items within given topics, and the relative print size of all the constituent parts said a great deal about the priorities and values of the various

---

59   This is most interestingly and impressively analysed by E. L. Eisenstein, *The Printing Press as an Agent of Change* (2 vols; Cambridge, 1979). See also J. Elbaum, *Openness and Insularity* (Hebrew; Jerusalem, 1990).

60   The specific data here concerning Jewish prayer-books is derived from Schmelzer (see nn. 54–55 above) and from the useful collection of articles from the *Encyclopaedia Judaica* reprinted in *The Hebrew Book*, eds R. Posner and I. Ta-Shma (already cited above in n. 46).

contents, as the compositor saw them, and this undoubtedly left its mark on the user of the edition. Printers of Hebrew liturgies produced a more common set of texts for daily and sabbath use in larger format for the cantor and of less imposing size for the individual, with separate volumes for festivals and booklets for special contexts and occasions such as grace after meals, Passover Haggadah and fast-days. Some of the basic characteristsics of the simpler manuscript liturgies were followed but it was apparently not yet possible to adopt their grander elements. The precise division between the volumes ultimately became a matter of distinction between Sefardi and Ashkenazi prints. Nevertheless, there was at first little to distinguish one part of the prayer-book from another, few headings, rubrics or incipits, a fairly primitive line justification, precious little commentary and text repetition as seldom as possible.[61]

But there was always a negative as well as a positive side to typographical developments. The control of text choice fell into the hands of the printers and publishers and some of their decisions were motivated more by market forces than by scholarly or halakhic considerations. Shoddy editions were therefore sometimes produced and some of the minor rites and liturgical poems were virtually consigned to oblivion for want of a popular edition. Even the new availability of a text to those ordinary congregants who had previously had to rely on the rabbi for the theory and the ḥazzan for the practice was not always a welcome circumstance. Whatever its degree of validity, a text that had been printed in hundreds of copies could soon become the norm and a community was not easily convinced that what appeared before its own eyes in printed form was not necessarily authentic.[62] And if texts were widely available to Jews, they were equally open to the critical eye of the non-Jew and the apostate. When a text was erased from a manuscript, the evidence of the erasure remained, but even if an early printer took care to leave a space where a censored text had once stood, his later contemporary took exception to the waste of space and the lack of elegance and neatly joined the passages that had survived. Alternative texts that were regarded as less 'offensive' by non-Jews were another way of dealing with the difficulty

---

61 See the rich collection of early editions at the British Library, as listed in J. Zedner, *Catalogue of the Hebrew Books in the Library of the British Museum* (London, 1867), pp. 458–86, and M. Beit-Arié, 'The affinity between early Hebrew printing and manuscripts' (Hebrew) in *Essays and Studies in Librarianship presented to C. D. Worman*, eds M. Nadav and J. Rothschild (Jerusalem, 1975), pp. 27–39 and 113.

62 Posner and Ta-Shma, *Hebrew Book* (see n. 46 above), pp. 65–203 and 209; Reif, *Shabbethai Sofer and his Prayer-book* (Cambridge, 1979), pp. 15–16 and 34–41.

so that innovations that would hardly have been tolerated for other reasons thus made their way into the unsuspecting *siddur*.[63]

A group of Polish rabbis of the sixteenth and seventeenth centuries called the printers to task for insufficient effort and liturgical standardization. In assessing the signficance of their remarks it is important to note that the 'errors' they bewailed were not simply printers' mistakes, of which there are obviously many examples, but the preservation of any linguistic traditions that did not match what they had come to regard as 'standard'. Nathan ben Samson Spira, Meshullam Faivush of Cracow, Jacob Koppel and Shabbethai Sofer of Przemysl variously censure the printers for their inadequacies.[64] Shabbethai makes numerous references to errors that he has noted in the texts of printed prayer-books.[65] In one case, he complains that the contemporary *siddurim* are wholly inconsistent in their pointing of a particular word and that what they have in common is that they are all totally at sea, erring in both theory and practice.[66] He points out that, in spite of what is wrongly printed in some *siddurim*, it is grammatically impossible for a letter to have both a *rafeh* sign and a *dagesh*.[67] He invites all those with authority to express their disapproval of the printers in the various countries of the Ashkenazi dispersion for failing to insert the necessary *rafeh* and *dagesh* in their editions of the Pentateuch and the prayer-book. This confuses the reader who is left wondering about the quality of the letters and unable to read them correctly. It is consequently no wonder that the Jewish exile is so prolonged and that their passionate prayers are ineffectual.[68] Meshullam Faivush in his reference for Shabbethai's work refers to the numerous mistakes and the unbelievable errors of all sorts that constantly occur in the prayer-books because of the printers'

---

63   W. Popper, *The Censorship of Hebrew Books* (New York, 1899; reprinted with an introduction by M. Carmilly-Weinberger, New York, 1969); Reif, *Shabbethai* (see n. 62 above), pp. 22, 35 and 293 and *Hebrew Prayer* (see n. 12 above), pp. 239–40; N. Wieder, *The Formation of Jewish Liturgy in the East and the West: A Collection of Essays* (Hebrew; 2 vols; Jerusalem, 1998), 2.453–56 and 1.368–90.

64   Reif, *Shabbethai* (see n. 62 above), pp. 15–16 and 34–39.

65   Reif, *Shabbethai* (see n. 62 above), p. 90, n. 38.

66   See Shabbethai's comments on the word כנאמך in his 'General Introduction', f. 8b, published in A. Berliner *Abhandlung über den Siddur des Schabtai ha-Sofer aus Przemysl* (Frankurt-am-Main, 1909) p. 29 and in the recent edition סדור המדקדק הגדול בקי בכל חדרי התורה מה"ר שבתי סופר ב"ר יצחק מפרעמישלא תלמיד הלבוש, יוצא לאור ע"פ כ"י בית הדין בלונדון על ידי הרב יצחק סץ והרב דוד יצחקי (5 vols., Baltimore, 1987–2002), 1.24.

67   'General Introduction', f. 10d, published in Berliner (see n. 66 above), p. 39 and Baltimore edition (see n. 66 above), 1.32.

68   'General Introduction', ff. 13bc, published in Berliner (see n. 66 above), p. 49 and Baltimore edition (see n. 66 above), 1.40.

inadequacies.[69] In his reference, Jacob Koppel describes the prayer-books as full of stupid errors in matters of pointing and textual rite and notes how difficult it is to eliminate habits that have become ingrained.[70] For its part, the Council of Three Lands complains of the inconsistency of the *siddurim* in matters of spelling and pointing and of the tendency of the Jewish public to rely on printers who publish pointed texts that are totally corrupt.[71]

As is known from my earlier research, these commitments to accurate Hebrew, to care in the choice of prayer-texts, and to the production of *siddurim* that could be regarded as educationally sound, culminated among Polish Jewry in the promotion of the idea of a model prayer-book. Meeting at the spring fair in Lublin in 1610, the Council of Three Lands (as it then was) passed a resolution calling for production of an 'authorized daily prayer-book' and the rabbis of Cracow and Przemysl persuaded Shabbethai ben Isaac Sofer (*c*.1565–*c*.1635) to undertake the task. He spent most of the decade preparing a text and commentary and, at its meeting of 9 March, 1617, the Council collectively approved his work. Among those recommending it were Joel Sirkes, Samuel Edels, Joshua Falk, Joseph Delakrut, Nathan b. Solomon Spira and Isaiah Horowitz and the text alone was published in Prague later that year.[72] Shabbethai's work demonstrates a literary, historical and critical approach, a commitment to linguistic accuracy, and a desire to educate the public. He cites manuscripts and editions in the evaluation of versions, sometimes preferring Sefardi formulae to Ashkenazi ones and is not averse to the inclusion in his prayer-book of some of the better established kabbalistic insertions.[73]

The high scholarly quality of Shabbethai's work ensured that it was not incorporated into the standard liturgical texts but there is little doubt that subsequent years did see improvements in numerous features of the Jewish prayer-books. A greater variety of fonts came to be used, pagination was added and the precise make-up of each set of prayers was made clear to the worshipper by the use of incipits, headings, helpful layouts, line justification and text repetition. Not only the format of the text but also its precise wording was of major concern to the editor of a new publication: whose version was to be followed, which linguistic conventions were to be adopted, and what were the criteria for the preferences ultimately to be expressed. Once such

---

69 Baltimore edition (see n. 66 above), 2.15.
70 Baltimore edition (see n. 66 above), 2.9.
71 I. Halperin (ed.), *Acta Congressus Generalis Judaeorum Regni Poloniae* (Jerusalem, 1945), pp. 31–36; Baltimore edition (see n. 66 above), 2.12.
72 Reif, *Shabbethai* (see n. 62 above), pp. 39–41.
73 Reif, *Shabbethai* (see n. 62 above), pp. 15–27, 33–38, 47–48 and 50–52.

decisions were made, they obviously had a major impact on the future history of any given text, so that for years, even centuries, the choice of an early printer was regarded as the standard edition. There were particular Jewish rites that fell at this first hurdle. Provençal liturgies did not receive typographical attention until the eighteenth century because of their junior status compared with the 'heavyweights' while the geographical and cultural isolation of Yemenite Jewry denied them printed prayer-books until a century later than that. No doubt a wide variety of local traditions once followed in the hundreds of synagogues of Spain and their equivalents further north in Europe simply disappeared for want of a printer's interest and a bookseller's market.[74]

The periods compared

What must now be assessed is the degree to which the evolutionary steps of the earlier periods may be said to have been duplicated in the metamorphosis of the manuscript *siddur* into the printed prayer-book. If we recall the conclusions reached above about these earlier periods, it is clear that there are a number of characteristics that they all have in common. The influence of factors that are external to the larger Jewish community is a constant theme while at the same time the differences of emphasis within the various segments of that community undoubtedly leave their mark. There is a concern for the individual as well as for the congregation and means are constantly sought for the conservation of the rabbinic tradition. Perhaps most important, and not always appreciated, is the literary effect of the physical medium used for the transmission of the prayers. The size, layout and technical details of such a medium significantly control the shape of its liturgical content and there is regularly a move from the primitive level achieved with each newly formed medium to the more impressive and sophisticated standard ultimately attained.

Nevertheless, the phenomenon of printing also had its more novel aspects. The production of numerous copies made possible an unprecedented degree of standardization and democratization and removed a significant amount of control from the rabbinic authority to the printer and publisher. The product became more user-friendly and

---

74 On the general history of Hebrew printing, including the production of prayer-books, see *Jewish Encyclopaedia* X, pp. 172–74 and XII, pp. 295–335; a collection of Hebrew articles by A. M. Habermann entitled *Studies in the History of Hebrew Printers and Books* (Hebrew; Jerusalem, 1978); reprinted articles of Joshua Bloch collected *in Hebrew Printing and Bibliography*, ed. C. Berlin (New York, 1976); Posner and Ta-Shma, *Hebrew Book* (see n. 60 above); and M. Beit-Arié, 'The affinity' (see n. 61 above).

more emphasis came to be laid on its practical use than on its potential
as a transmitter of the broader halakhic traditions. Editions were
specifically produced for particular purposes and some rare versions
were preserved by the new medium while other, more common ones,
could be assigned virtually to oblivion. The capacity of the prayer-book
to impact on Jewish education and on Hebrew knowledge was soon
appreciated and influenced some of those who produced and marketed
it. That development – as indeed the other innovations just noted –
played no small a role in the modern history of Judaism and Hebrew
literature and may still be identified in current theory and practice.[75]

What has just been written about printed Hebrew liturgies centres
on the traditional text and takes little account of the special
developments of the last two centuries, covering as they do the
emancipation, the rise of religiously progressive movements, massive
demographical adjustment, the Holocaust and the State of Israel.[76] The
present context is too limited to permit any detailed treatment but a
few brief remarks may indicate some of the trends and complete the
self-allotted task of which notice was given at the beginning of this
chapter. The alteration in the appearance of the prayer-book effected
among Ashkenazim, Sefardim and Hasidim by the liberal sprinkling of
mystical texts initially emanating from the kabbalistic school of Safed
was in many ways the most dynamic development in the history of
Hebrew liturgy since the invention of printing.[77] This desire for a new
identity was taken further by the Eastern European Hasidim when they
opted for elements of the Sefardi rite and there can be little doubt that
the result was not only a degree of liturgical iconoclasm that heralded
the move into the modern world but also something of a confusion
when printers produced editions that included characteristics of both
the traditional Ashkenazi and the innovative Hasidic rites.[78] If Eastern
European moves were iconoclastic, their equivalents in Western and
Central Europe were positively anarchistic. Under the influence of the
Jewish intellectual enlightenment of the Haskalah, linguists applied

---

75 Reif, *Shabbethai* (see n. 62 above), pp. 53–62; *Hebrew Prayer*, (see n. 12 above), pp. 256–
    331.
76 Details of modern Jewish liturgical developments may be found in Reif, *Hebrew
    Prayer* (see n. 12 above), chapters 8 and 9.
77 The transmission was by way of the eastern European qabbalist Nathan Nata
    Hannover whose collection of mystical prayers entitled *Sha'arei Siyon* was published
    many times following its early appearance in Prague, 1662 and Amsterdam, 1671. C.
    B. Friedberg in *Bet 'Eked Sefarim* (4 vols; Israel², 1951–56) lists fifty-four editions.
78 E. D. Goldschmidt, 'On the liturgy of Hassidic communities' in *On Jewish Liturgy:
    Essays on Prayer and Religious Poetry* (Jerusalem, 1978), pp. 315–21, the first part of
    which originally appeared in his edition of the Hasidic prayer-book published by
    Masada in Tel Aviv, 1965.

romantic and purist standards in forcing the Hebrew of the liturgy to match what they misguidedly saw as its biblical original and reformers opted for a vernacular not only by way of translation but also as an alternative medium.[79] The ultimate aim of such groups was to impress the non-Jewish world with a text that could be seen as equivalent to the latter's own liturgies in physical appearance and theological content and to ease feelings of embarrassment on the part of Jews who were concerned that the traditional *siddurim* failed to do so. Recent years have seen a reaction against such a trend by the readoption of some Eastern European styles across the Jewish religious spectrum but the partiality for each movement to produce its own liturgical 'flagship' has strengthened rather than weakened.[80] Since much of this volume is being written in England, it is worth noting that the latest edition of the 'Singer's Prayer-Book'[81] is produced in three styles, one to match the original 1890 format, a second to compete with Hertz's annotated version of over sixty years ago, and a third to give the appearance of an Israeli pocket edition. Typographical aspects of the right-wing 'ArtScroll Series'[82] have also been adopted. The structure of the new edition is again being adjusted to correspond with changing religious perspectives and priorities.[83]

The process of mutual influence between the medium and the message has been seen to have been a continuous one in the history of Jewish prayer and technical advances in printing, photocopying and computerization are already promising further novel developments in traditional as well as progressive circles. No doubt the achievements of the 'fax' and of 'LaTeX' will also soon provide more facts for the artful analysis of the liturgical artefact.

---

79   Reif, *Shabbethai Sofer* (see n. 62 above), pp. 51–62; J. J. Petuchowski, *Prayerbook Reform in Europe: The Liturgy of Liberal and Reform Judaism* (New York, 1968); L. A. Hoffman, *Beyond the Text: a Holistic Approach to Liturgy* (Bloomington and Indianapolis, 1987); L. A. Hoffman and N. Wiener, 'The liturgical state of the World Union for Progressive Judaism', *European Judaism* 24 (1991), pp. 10–22.

80   See, for instance, the modern Orthodox Zionist *Rinat Yisrael* published in Jerusalem in 1970 and the Koren *Siddur Tefillah* published there in 1982; the American Conservative *Sim Shalom* published in New York in 1985; the American Reconstructionist *Kol ha-Neshamah* published in Wyncole, Pa. in 1989; the American Reform *Gates of Prayer* published in New York in 1975; the British Liberal *Avodat ha-Lev* published in London in 1976; and the British Reform *Seder ha-Tefillot* published in London in 1977.

81   *Authorised Daily Prayer Book of the United Hebrew Congregations of the Commonwealth.* ed. I. Jakobovits, trans. E. Cashdan (London, 1990). The edition of Chief Rabbi J. H. Hertz was published in London in 1942–45.

82   *Siddur Qol Ya'aqov; the Complete ArtScroll Siddur: a New Translation and Anthological Commentary*, ed. Nosson Scherman (Brooklyn, 1984[1], 1986[2]).

83   S. C. Reif, 'A Singer with a new song', *L'eylah*, 32 (1991), pp. 36–39.

12

Maimonides on the Prayers

Question

The object of this brief study is to place Maimonides in the history of Jewish liturgy in general and in the development of the text of the rabbinic Hebrew prayers in particular. My interest in doing so arises out of a conviction that it will prove intriguing to establish precisely what his contribution was, on the one hand, to the broad acceptance of the Babylonian rite (or at least a form of the Babylonian rite) that preceded him, and, on the other, to the emergence of the various fixed rites – be they, for example, Yemenite, North African, Sefardi or Ashkenazi – that became characteristic of subsequent periods.

There are a number of basic questions that need to be posed. Was the great "Rambam" conservative or radical, idealistic or practical, as far as the text of the prayers is concerned? Did he opt for standardization or for variety, and did he distinguish between communal and individual responsibilities? How did he approach matters of content, length and linguistic style? Can we identify specific theological trends in his preferences, say regarding such topics as Israel and the nations? What were his attitudes to the relations between halakhah, minhag and midrash within the liturgical context? Is it possible to trace his views on the role of the Hebrew Bible within the rabbinic prayers? Above all, what were the results of his efforts in the liturgical sphere and how successful an impact did they make on later generations?

The early twentieth century's leading expert in Jewish liturgical history, Ismar Elbogen (1874–1943), did deal briefly with this subject almost a hundred years ago.[1] It is greatly to his credit that, although many of the scholarly developments concerning the Genizah texts and other manuscript evidence had yet to take place, much of what he then wrote has stood the test of time. In view of such developments, however, and the broader nature of current approaches to Jewish liturgical study, there is undoubtedly a strong case for a re-assessment of the topic.

---

1   I. Elbogen, 'Der Ritus im Mischne Thora' in *Moses ben Maimon: sein Leben, seine Werke und sein Einfluss*, eds W. Bacher, M. Brann, D. Simonsen and J. Guttmann, vol. 1 (Leipzig, 1908), pp. 319–31.

Methodology

Given his origins, migrations and lengthy scholarly and rabbinic life, it will be necessary to look at the whole of Rambam's life and establish whether there are any principles at work there that may also be relevant to the assessment of his liturgical contribution. Approaching the subject in this way will perhaps make it easier to set him and his liturgical efforts in some sorts of geographical and historical contexts. The first task is therefore to establish precisely which are the relevant sources, how reliable they are and how they are to be used. Obviously it will be necessary to undertake a close examination of what he has to say on the relevant topics in his philosophical treatise *Moreh Nevukhim*,[2] his halakhic code *Mishneh Torah*[3] and his many responsa[4] and to subject these passages and statements – particularly those that occur in his halakhic guide – to analysis, evaluation and comparison. Some examples of his preferred readings in the liturgy will be cited and they will be compared with other prayer-book texts, both those that have been published in scholarly editions and those that remain in manuscript. Lessons will be drawn from such examples and the final part of the article will list the overall conclusions that may justifiably be reached about his approach to the prayer-book on the basis of all such evidence.

Life

As is self-evident, what require to be noted here are only those factors that appear to be directly relevant to what came to represent his attitude to the Hebrew prayers, beginning with his early and formative years in Islamic Spain (*al-Andalus*) and his pride in his Sefardi heritage of the mid-12th century. Undoubtedly noteworthy are also the cultural setting of that time and place, his halakhic education within the family and young Moshe's overall plans for a novel, systematic and

---

2   I have used the English edition of S. Pines, *The Guide of the Perplexed: Moses Maimonides* (Chicago and London, 1963; second edition, 1969); see also the Judeo-Arabic and Hebrew in ed. M. Schwarz (Tel Aviv, 2002).

3   Among the translations and commentaries of *Mishneh Torah* here consulted and cited are those of S. T. Rubenstein (Jerusalem, 1959; fourth edition, 1967); N. L. Rabinovitch (Jerusalem, 1984); B. Kaplan, *Maimonides. Mishneh Torah. Hilchot Tefilah [1]. The Laws of Prayer* (Jerusalem and New York, 1988); E. Touger, *Maimonides. Mishneh Torah. Hilchot Tefilah [II] and Birkat Kohanim. The Laws of Prayer and the Priestly Blessing* (Jerusalem and New York, 1989).

4   J. Blau (ed.), *R. Moses b. Maimon: Responsa* (4 vols; Jerusalem, 1957–61 and 1986).

comprehensive coverage of Jewish law and philosophy in all their vastness. As far as his acquaintance with the "other" is concerned, the persecution of the Jews in Spain precipitated the Maimonidean family's emigration to Morocco and then subsequently to Eretz Yisrael, providing them with experiences of both the Islamic and Christian worlds and their forms of monotheism. His move at about the age of thirty to Cairo, the capital of the Fatimid empire in the eastern Mediterranean, ultimately led to communal prominence, leadership of the Jewish community, and intense medical, communal and scholarly activity. Such diverse interests inevitably brought about tensions between the purely scholarly and the religiously practical in his life and work. There were also instances of involvement in the world beyond Egypt, as exemplified in his authorship of the *Epistle to Yemen* and the special relationship thereby created with that community. A son, Abraham, was born to him in 1186 in a period of his life – he was about fifty – that was in those times undoubtedly regarded as senior citizenship and he developed a special relationship with that son domestically, communally and liturgically.[5]

Source challenge

What immediately strikes the researcher is the strength and extent of the evidence relating to his overall approach to the matter of prayer as represented in his *Mishneh Torah*, *Moreh Nevukhim* and responsa and how this situation contrasts with that pertaining to the text of his prayer-book. The version of the latter work included in the standard editions of his code is so full of omissions, abbreviations and harmonizations that it has to be ruled out as a reliable piece of evidence about his precise preferences in the matter of the liturgical text. There is in existence in the Bodleian Library at the University of Oxford a manuscript with a text of the first two books of the *Mishneh Torah* authenticated by Maimonides himself (ff.1–165) followed, after the signature of the author, by an additional nineteen folios on which the

5   S. D. Goitein, *Letters of Medieval Jewish Traders* (Princeton, 1973), pp. 207–12 and 'Moses Maimonides, man of action: a revision of the master's biography in light of the Geniza documents' in *Hommage à Georges Vajda*, eds G. Nahon and C. Touati (Louvain, 1980), pp. 155–67; B. Ben-Shammai, 'Twenty-five years of Maimonides research: a bibliography 1965–80', *Maimonidean Studies* 2 (1991), Hebrew section, pp. 17–42; M. Ben-Sasson, 'Maimonides in Egypt: the first stage', *Maimonidean Studies* 2 (1991), pp. 3–30; J. L. Kraemer, 'Six unpublished Maimonides letters from the Cairo Genizah', *Maimonidean Studies* 2 (1991), pp. 73–80 and 'Four Geniza letters concerning Maimonides' in *Mas'at Moshe: Studies in Jewish and Islamic Culture Presented to Moshe Gil*, eds E. Fleischer, M. A. Friedman and J. L. Kraemer (Hebrew; Jerusalem, 1998), pp. 381–400.

text of his prayers is offered.[6] But here too there are questions to be asked. Is this addition some sort of after-thought by the author himself, who had previously not thought it worthwhile to record the actual wording but had changed his mind? If so, this is in itself an interesting phenomenon, possibly testifying to the codifier's reluctance to become embroiled in arguments about precise detail. Or is the location of the addendum perhaps an indication that its insertion was the work of someone else and therefore to a degree suspect? The evidence in the remainder of the code does suggest that the liturgical details there match those in the text recorded in the Oxford manuscript but is one not still left with the impression that Maimonides was not *ab initio* greatly enthused by the prospect of categorically laying down the law about the detailed wording of the liturgy?[7]

Content challenge

Given that the relevant folios of the Oxford manuscript, taken together with the equivalent evidence from Maimonides's other works, provide us with some authentic notion of what he regarded as a sound text of the traditional rabbinic prayers, it remains to be established just how his text fits into the overall history of Jewish liturgy. Is it early Sefardi, North African, Eretz Yisraeli, Iraqi or Egyptian and how precisely does it relate to the texts of the Ge'onim R. Amram ben Sheshna and R. Sa'adya ben Joseph? If it does not match any one specific tradition, is it an eclectic rite built by him on the basis of his variety of preferences in numerous specific instances and therefore a personal Maimonidean rite? Also to be taken into account is the possibility that we have evidence here of his acceptance of the local Egyptian custom in spite of his own predilections for what he had himself inherited in his early days in Cordova. Part of the problem is that there is no specific mention by Rambam of the rite that he is opting for and very little about the general liturgical situation in his day. He defines the Palestinian émigrés' customs as erroneous but recognizes the strength of their communal adherence to these. An unsuccessful attempt was made by him to put a stop to the triennial cycle of biblical lectionaries but he reluctantly declined to stir up further controversy by issuing any

6   For details of this MS (Huntingdon 80), see A. Neubauer, *Catalogue of the Hebrew Manuscripts in the Bodleian Library* (Oxford, 1886), no. 577, col. 113, and M. Beit-Arié and R. A. May, *Supplement* (Oxford, 1994), cols 86–87.
7   E. D. Goldschmidt (ed.), 'The Oxford Ms. of Maimonides' book of prayer', *SRIHP* 7 (1958), pp. 183–213, reprinted in his collection of articles *On Jewish Liturgy. Essay on Prayer and Religious Poetry* (Hebrew; Jerusalem, 1978), pp. 187–216.

categorical ruling against the rites of the Jews from the Holy Land.[8] What needs, if possible, to be ascertained is whether his reluctance to come down firmly on the side of one rite or another is the reason for his initial hesitation about providing a text of the prayers. Does the evidence attest to his awareness and tolerance of the great variety of liturgical tradition still in existence in his day or to a quiet preference on his part to distinguish between personal and communal commitments and therefore, at least to some degree, to avoid the issue?

Broader liturgical context

To set the scene for the views expressed and the positions adopted by Maimonides, a few general remarks need to be made. The leading talmudic academies of Iraq had made a powerful impact on the rabbinic situation in the course of the previous four centuries. Their dynamic efforts had succeeded in laying down standard interpretations of the Talmud, in legislating for much of the Jewish world, and in centralizing Jewish religious practice. In the liturgical area, an attempt had been made to establish an authoritative version of the prayers through the development of an actual prayer-book. In this connection, such Ge'onim as R. Natronai and R. Amram had, in response to enquiries from the developing communities of Spain, offered them instructions about how precisely they should formulate their prayers. For their part, the Jews of the Holy Land remained determined to maintain their own liturgical traditions even in the face of scurrilous attacks by their Babylonian brethren as, for instance, on the part of Pirqoi ben Baboi. By the twelfth century, the general guidance issued by the rabbinic leaders in Iraq had had a profound effect on the synagogal customs of many communities but the next stage of development was again of the particular rather than the universal and saw the proud emergence of local liturgical interpretations in such centres as Spain, North Africa, Franco-Germany, Italy and Byzantium.[9] In Egypt itself, Jewish refugees arrived in numbers from other countries and ensured the existence there in the Fatimid period of a few competing traditions. The most famous example of such liturgical variation is that documented by the twelfth-century Jewish traveller, Benjamin of Tudela:[10]

---

8   See the reference below to *Mishneh Torah, Tefillah* 13.1 in the section entitled 'Specific comments in the *Mishneh Torah, Tefillah*'.
9   This whole development is described in detail in S. C. Reif, *Judaism and Hebrew Prayer: New Perspectives on Jewish Liturgical History* (Cambridge, 1993), pp. 122–206.
10 M. N. Adler, *The Itinerary of Benjamin of Tudela. Critical Text, Translation and Commentary* (London, 1907), Hebrew text, pp. 62–63.

There are two large synagogues in Cairo, one belonging to the Jews of the land of Israel and the other to those of Iraq...They follow different usages with regard to the pentateuchal lectionaries, the Iraqis having the custom of reading a portion each week, as is done in Spain (and is our own tradition) and concluding the Pentateuch on an annual basis, while the Palestinian Jews do not do so but divide each portion into three and finish after three years. The two communities do, however, have an established custom of uniting and praying together on the festival days of Simhat Torah and Shavuot.

If, in addition to those fleeing the Crusaders, we take into account the absorption into Fatimid Egypt of Spanish and North African Jews, as well as a strong community of Karaites, it will be clear that the matter of the form of the daily prayers was likely to have been a highly controversial one.

Principles

In so far as principles are concerned, the first point to be made is that there are undoubtedly contradictions between Maimonides's various works in connection with certain aspects of prayer. When he is composing a code or a responsum his attitude is not necessarily the same as when he is laying down principles of religious philosophy. In the last-mentioned area he can claim that it is naive to presuppose that we pray in order for our prayers to be answered, that it is impossible to describe God, that it is theologically objectionable to compose poetry that is heavily laden with rich and complex epithets and metaphors, and that the meditative worship of the intellectual is a higher ideal than the performance of sacrifices or the recitation of fixed prayers.[11] On the other hand, in his code he proceeds on the assumption that Jews are obligated to pray in a sincere fashion and to use the formal texts provided by rabbinic tradition. There are also more general tensions within his work that do not necessarily relate to the difference between the halakhic and philosophical approaches. For example, he tends towards the notions that worship in the heart ('avodah shebelev) requires personal submission to God and to see this as an elitist model while at the same time continuing the geonic tendency to compromise in this connection and to set standards that can be met by the ordinary individual. Similarly, he recognizes that at the popular level there is a major need for a religious establishment and centralized communal life and appears to look with a certain degree of envy at Islam's

---

11   See, for example, Guide I.59 and III.32, ed. Pines (see n. 2 above), pp. 140–42 and 529 and ed. Schwarz (see n. 2 above), pp 149–51 and 536.

achievements in connection with discipline and authority. Where congregational unity competes with the purity of the rite, he opts for the view that the former takes precedence. As far as midrash is concerned, pre-sinaitic activities (such as those of the biblical Patriarchs) have no normative standing and cannot function as precedents so that Maimonides cites the midrash about patriarchal prayer in his laws of *melakhim* but not among those of *tefillah*. A direct link can, and indeed must, be made between sacrifices and prayer, as has been done by the talmudic rabbis, so that the earlier historical form can be acknowledged but the latter, in its ideal existence, is indubitably superior.[12] Part of Maimonides's rationale here was surely to justify, by reference to such a talmudic notion, his approval of liturgical centralization, authority and standardization.

Of particular interest is Maimonides's introduction to the section on prayer in his *Mishneh Torah* code where he refers to the passage in Nehemiah 13:24 about the loss of Hebrew on the part of some of the Judeans and uses this as a justification for the formulation of the *'amidah* benedictions by Ezra and his court.[13] Blidstein is probably correct in explaining that Maimonides is here presupposing a move from the spiritual ideal of the Torah regarding prayer to the pragmatism of historical reality while he is at the same time adhering to the notion championed by his fellow scholars of Iraq and Spain that the loss of Hebrew was to be deplored. Blidstein is, however, perhaps stressing the halakhic and linguistic angles while underplaying the possibility of a more theologico-historical interpretation. Surely Maimonides is here seeking a historical – or, more accurately, quasi-historical – peg on which to hang his idea of liturgical authority and his approval of the move from spontaneity to standardization. I believe that Blidstein is too cautious in his explanation of what motivated Maimonides to lay such emphasis on the need for the liturgical rites to be fixed. In this connection he argues (in my translation from the Hebrew) that "there is no convincing reason to argue that Rambam created the myth of historical standardization in order to meet the narrow needs of his own day. On the other hand, it is reasonable to suppose that the motivation for his consistent stress on the work of Ezra, as he strictly interpreted it, lay in the message that such work could convey to his contemporaries who were taken with the idea of

---

12   I am particularly indebted here to Gerald (Ya'akov) Blidstein who has penned an excellent summary of Maimonides's halakhic approach to prayer, with some variations of interpretation and emphasis to which I shall draw attention as the theme is discussed; see his *Prayer in Maimonidean Halakha* (Hebrew; Jerusalem and Beersheba, 1994), especially pp. 9–52, 69–74, and 123–43.

13   Blidstein, *Prayer*, pp. 38–42.

granting themselves freedom to introduce innovations into liturgical texts."[14] Blidstein's first claim flies in the face of the fact that a major liturgical struggle was taking place in the Eastern Mediterranean Jewish communities of the twelfth century with regard to the degree of standardization that should be applied to the texts of the prayers and that those promoting such a process were very much in need of "historical" precedents. To my mind, his second claim lays too much stress on the freedom of individuals. It was not a matter of individuals seeking freedom but rather of locally dominant communal rites, such as that of the land of Israel, being inherited, practised and defended.[15]

Two more sources may be cited to add to the overall picture in this area and to exemplify the point that there is a radical as well as a conservative element in Maimonides's views and decisions regarding liturgical practice. One of his responsa rules that it is in order for individuals to recite chapters of Psalms and collections of supplicatory verses at home but not in synagogue where the standard should be that of the weakest, whose devotional concentration – a vital factor for Maimonides – would suffer from such lengthy additions. In another of his responsa, he courts controversy by his firm rejection of liturgical poetry but he patently avoids laying down the law on such issues in his code.[16]

Individuals relying on the prayer-leader

There are two additional responsa that are worthy of note in this context since they demonstrate how brave and innovative Maimonides could be when the need arose and how he sought to justify his rulings by drawing attention to their importance in removing the danger of public Jewish embarrassment. The first of these reads (in my translation from Blau's Hebrew rendering of the Judaeo-Arabic):

> If one of the congregation says the 'amidah quietly while the prayer-leader is offering his prayer, he has done his religious duty. Equally, if one does not recite the 'amidah personally, even if he is competent to do so, he can fulfil his duty by listening to the 'amidah recited by the prayer-leader ... One who hears is equivalent to one who answers in all instances and one who says 'amen' is equivalent to the one reciting the benediction ... I shall also

---

14   Blidstein, *Prayer*, pp. 124–25.
15   With reference to the document drawn up by Palestinian Jews in Cairo in 1211 in an attempt to protect their liturgical traditions, see the discussion and the citations of earlier research by M. A. Friedman, '"A controversy for the sake of heaven": studies in the liturgical polemics of Abraham Maimonides and his contemporaries', *Te'uda* 10, ed. M. A. Friedman (Tel Aviv, 1996), pp. 245–98.
16   Ed. Blau (see n. 4 above), vol. 2 (Jerusalem, 1960), no. 261, pp. 490–92, no. 180, pp. 328–29, and no. 207, pp. 363–66; see also Elbogen, 'Ritus' (see n. 1 above), p. 321.

describe to you a custom of ours, concerning the 'amidah of shaḥarit and musaf on shabbat and festivals, that I regard as necessary and appropriate because of the large numbers in the synagogue, a custom that is similar to what you do locally on Rosh Ha-Shanah. I also arrange for us to do this when minḥah is so delayed that I fear that the formal hour of dusk is approaching. I rule that the prayer-leader [immediately] recites the 'amidah out loud together with the qedushah and there is no disadvantage in this for anyone since a congregant who cannot recite his own prayer can do his duty by hearing the prayer-leader's prayer and one who is competent to do so may recite the 'amidah together with the prayer-leader, word for word...By doing this we arrange for everyone's obligation to be met in an obvious way, and avoid the kind of public act of desecration that occurs when congregants regard the repetition as an occasion for joking and mockery. On other daily occasions, when there are fewer learned congregants present, the 'amidah is recited twice, quietly and then out loud.[17]

The second of these reads (again in my translation from Blau's Hebrew rendering of the Judaeo-Arabic):

The custom you mention of reciting the 'amidah out loud twice is absolutely wrong according to all views and a terrible error for those who are competent to pray since they recite their prayers in everyone's hearing and this constitutes an act of gross ignorance ... If congregants do not recite the quiet 'amidah at all but follow the prayer-leader's recitation with the qedushah, reciting the text if they know it, or simply listening if they do not, and bowing with him as necessary, they all meet their obligation in an organized and orderly fashion and a lengthy service is avoided. A public embarrassment for the Jewish people is also avoided since otherwise non-Jews see Jews spitting, coughing and paying no attention during the prayer-leader's repetition. So this is my view about the correct procedure these days, for the reasons I have outlined.[18]

Specific comments in the Mishneh Torah, Tefillah

2.17: In those places where rain is needed in the summer, such as in the 'faraway sea-isles', it should be prayed for in the shome'ah tefillah benediction whenever necessary.

There is a talmudic report that the Jews of Nineveh sought a ruling from the Patriarch, R. Judah, about whether their need for rain in the summer should be addressed by way of a special prayer included in the ninth benediction of the 'amidah concerning agricultural prosperity or rather included in the sixteenth benediction where individual

---

17   Ed. Blau (see n. 4 above), no. 256, pp. 473–76, and no. 291, p. 548.
18   Ed. Blau (see n. 4 above), no. 258, pp. 483–84.

requirements are usually inserted.[19] On the basis of the response that favoured the latter option, Maimonides constructs a more general rule that applies to distant places. In his mishnaic commentary[20] he is more emphatic and stresses that the ninth benediction can refer to only to the land of Israel and that a prayer for a rainfall that would be disastrous for the area of one's own domicile would be a logical absurdity.[21]

> 3.7: Permission is granted to pray the evening service on Friday and Saturday nights before its time because that service is optional and the timing is therefore less critical.

Although the Talmud records the practice of Rav to recite the evening prayer before dark on Friday evening and of R. Josiah to act similarly on Saturday evening, there are detailed talmudic discussions about this and some attempts by the later halakhic authorities to limit what appears to be a considerable liturgical leniency.[22] Maimonides, on the other hand, provides clear support for such a leniency as long as the *shema'* is recited again at a later hour when it is dark.[23]

> 4.1: Even if the time for prayer has arrived, it cannot be undertaken unless the body is in a state of purity and clothed, the area is free of contamination, there is nothing pressing on the worshipper's mind and he can concentrate properly.

Maimonides summarizes the various talmudic rulings with regard to the preparations that are needed before one commences one's prayers.[24] His summary of the requirements essentially covers the three areas of personal hygiene and purity[25], suitable environment and correct frame of mind.[26]

---

19 BT, *Ta'anit* 14b. With regard to the 'faraway sea-isles', it is interesting that as late as the nineteenth century an Asian Muslim visitor to England was describing it as 'the end of the world where the sun appears, far to the south, as weak as the moon. It is a small island which seems on the globe like a mole on the body.' See E. B. Eastwick (ed.), *Autobiography of Lutfullah, a Mohamedan Gentleman and his Transactions with his Fellow-creatures* (London, 1857), p. 406.
20 *Commentary on the Mishnah, Ta'anit* 1.3, ed. J. Qafiḥ, *Seder Mo'ed* (Jerusalem, 1963), pp. 330–31.
21 Rubenstein, p. 42; Rabinovitch, pp. 170–72; and Kaplan, pp. 137–38 (see n. 3 above for full references).
22 BT, *Berakhot* 27b; *Ṭur, 'Oraḥ Ḥayyim*, no. 293.
23 Rubenstein, pp. 45–46; Rabinovitch, pp. 188–91; and Kaplan, pp. 148–50 (see n. 3 above for full references).
24 The sources are generally to be found in BT, *Berakhot* and are cited in the commentaries detailed in n. 40 below.
25 See his ruling in *Mishneh Torah, Berakhot* 6.2, as discussed below.
26 Rubenstein, p. 47; Rabinovitch, pp. 198; and Kaplan, p. 155 (see n. 3 above for full references).

4.6: It is the general custom in Babylonia and Spain that one who has suffered a seminal discharge cannot pray until he has bathed his whole body in water, in order to fulfil the biblical requirement 'Prepare to meet your God, Israel' (Amos 4:12).

Maimonides displays something of an ambivalence in the matter of pre-liturgical ablutions. He acknowledges that the emission of semen no longer requires a ritual bath[27] and that only in Iraq and Spain was it still customary for a person to bathe his body after intercourse and before prayer. In a letter to R. Pinḥas Ha-Dayyan, he responds strongly to those who are critical of his ruling.[28] He points out that the custom of performing such an ablution was practised in Spain and Iraq and not in Byzantium, Franco-Germany or Provence and evoked some amusement among non-Spanish Jews who saw in it the influence of Islam. At the same time, he stresses that he personally still follows the Spanish custom and that reports to the contrary about his behaviour are unfounded, untrue and mere figments of imagination. Behind his anger is a frustration with the need to follow local and not personal traditions and a tension about the degree to which special washing is an integral part of the ideal preparations needed for prayer.[29]

4.8: Prayer should not be recited in a place which is, or might be, ritually impure.

From this passage and a number of others elsewhere in the code, it is clear that Maimonides follows the PT and not the BT in explaining that the reason why prayer is not appropriate at a cemetery is because it is a place of ritual impurity, not because of consideration for the dead who are buried there.[30] He sees this latter consideration as belonging to magical beliefs and practices, and therefore forbidden. Special buildings should not be erected at the tombs of the righteous since their deeds are their memorials. Visits to cemeteries should not therefore be made in such religiously questionable contexts or in order to pray but as an encouragement to contrition and humility; otherwise the time would better be spent on Torah study.[31] What is reflected here is

---

27 See BT, *Berakhot* 22ab.
28 See his 'Letter to Pinḥas Ha-Dayyan' in *Letters and Essays of Moses Maimonides*, ed. I. Shilat (Hebrew; Maaleh Adumim, 1988), especially pp. 437–38.
29 Rubenstein, pp. 49–50; Rabinovitch, pp. 205–6; and Kaplan, pp. 162–63 (see n. 3 above for full references). Kaplan's translation 'there is no such custom' is somewhat misleading.
30 PT, *Berakhot* 2.3 (4c) and BT, *Berakhot* 18a. See also his comments in *Mishneh Torah, Shema'* 4.8, *Ta'anit* 4.18 and *Avelut* 4.4.
31 Y. S. Lichtenstein, 'The Rambam's approach regarding prayer, holy objects and visiting the cemetery', *HUCA* 72 (2001), Hebrew section, pp. 1–34; and on his attitude to superstition, see also Elbogen, 'Ritus' (see n. 1 above), p. 319.

Maimonides's opposition to the use of magical notions and superstition in a liturgical context that should strive for what he regards as more purely spiritual and theological achievements.[32]

> 4.19: For *'amidah* prayers recited at intervals, such as those of the festivals and the *musaf* for *Rosh Ḥodesh*, one should reduce the possibility of errors by preparing one's formulation and only then set about reciting it.

The general ruling of R. Eleazar b. Pedat is that one should always rehearse the precise wording of one's *'amidah* prayer before reciting it (apparently by heart) and the talmudic discussion concludes that this applies to any such prayer that has not been recited for thirty days.[33] While that discussion refers only to Rosh Ha-Shanah, Yom Kippur, *'peraqim'* and thirty days, Maimonides interprets the reference to thirty days as a specific allusion to Rosh Hodesh prayers and suggests the rationale that underlies the ruling.[34]

> 5.5: Correct clothing for prayer includes head-covering.

Although some talmudic sources associate head and face covering with distinction or special piety,[35] it was still widely regarded in the early Middle Ages as no more than a custom to cover one's head for prayer.[36] Here Maimonides includes it with other preparations relating to one's clothing that are recorded in the Talmud[37] and gives it a statutory status rather than regarding it as an optional custom.[38]

> 6.2: When praying with the community one should not prolong his *'amidah* prayer unduly but he may do so when praying alone.

There is a talmudic report by R. Judah b. Ilai that R. Akiva would in public worship be brief in the recitation of his *'amidah* prayer so as not to burden the congregation with waiting for him while in private he would considerably extend his liturgical activities.[39] Maimonides bases his ruling on this report but appears to soften its impact in two ways. Instead of referring to congregational inconvenience, he avoids giving

---

32 Rubenstein, p. 50; Rabinovitch, pp. 209–10; and Kaplan, pp. 164–65 (see n. 3 above for full references).

33 BT, *Rosh Ha-Shanah* 35a.

34 Rubenstein, pp. 54–55; Rabinovitch, p. 223; and Kaplan, pp. 178–79 (see n. 3 above for full references).

35 E.g. BT, *Shabbat* 156b.

36 See *Massekhet Soferim*, ed. M. Higger (New York, 1937), 14.12, pp. 265–66; E.T., ed. I. W. Slotki (London, 1965), pp. 280–81.

37 See BT, *Shabbat* 10a.

38 Rubenstein, p. 57; Rabinovitch, pp. 232–35; and Kaplan, pp. 186–88 (see n. 3 above for full references).

39 BT, *Berakhot* 31a.

any reason and redefines "lengthy prayer" as "over-lengthy prayer", at the same time avoiding altogether any reference to "abbreviating" such as occurs in the talmudic passage. He also indicates that lengthening one's prayers in the private context is not a requirement but merely permitted.[40]

> 7.9: The popular custom in most of our cities is to say the morning benedictions one after the other in the synagogue, whether there is an obligation or not, and this is wrong since benedictions should be recited only when there is an obligation.

In spite of the well-established custom of reciting the morning benedictions in the synagogue together with the statutory prayers, Maimonides strictly follows the talmudic understanding of these benedictions as relating to particular activities associated with rising in the morning and not to general praise of God.[41] He is adamant about the application of the principle that benedictions may be recited only when they are required and about the erroneous and inappropriate nature of the custom. He repeats this view in a responsum and it is defended powerfully and at length by his son, Abraham,[42] but his ruling did not achieve widespread acceptance since authorities before and after him found ways of justifying it.[43]

> 8.9: By responding amen to the reader's prayers one meets one's liturgical obligations but only if one is unable to pray personally.

In a talmudically recorded controversy between R. Gamliel and the Rabbis, the former argued that the one leading the congregation in prayer could meet the obligations of all the participants, including those who were competent to pray for themselves, while the latter restricted this to those who were unable to recite their own prayers.[44] In this ruling, Maimonides opts for the majority view, thus giving the prayer-leader less halakhic power and less central liturgical authority. In his responsa, however,[45] he appears to support the view of R. Gamliel, laying less stress on the individual function and more on that

---

40 Rubenstein, p. 63; Rabinovitch, p. 254; and Kaplan, pp. 204–5 (see n. 3 above for full references).
41 BT, *Berakhot* 60b; see also Elbogen, 'Ritus' (see n. 1 above), pp. 327–28.
42 Ed. Blau (see n. 4 above), vol. 2 (1960), no. 187, pp. 342–44; *Abraham Maimuni Responsa*, eds A. H. Freimann and S. D. Goitein (Jerusalem, 1937), no. 83, pp. 120–26.
43 Rubenstein, p. 73; Rabinovitch, pp. 279–82; and Touger, pp. 26–27.
44 BT, *Rosh Ha-Shanah* 34b.
45 See the responsum quoted above in the section entitled 'Individuals relying on the prayer-leader' and n. 17 thereon.

of the community although it has been argued that there he may have in mind different circumstances.[46]

> 9.13: On sabbaths and festivals, *musaf*, like *shaharit*, is recited quietly by the individual and then loudly by the prayer-leader.

In this case, Maimonides's codified ruling is more conventional and conservative than one of his responsa. While here he records the need for a repetition of the *'amidah* by the prayer-leader at both the *shaharit* and *musaf* services on sabbaths and festivals, in his responsa he reports that circumstances had forced him to adopt a more radical view.[47] Given the lack of attention and decorum that such repetitions encouraged on occasions when the synagogue was particularly full, and the way in which this was bringing Jewish worship into disrepute among the Muslims, he had suspended these particular repetitions in his synagogue.[48]

> 10.2: If the prayer-leader makes a mistake [other than] in [the first and last three benedictions of] the *'amidah*, my view is that he should not repeat it all because this would be a burden on the congregation.

Despite the apparently opposing view about this recorded in the BT and PT, Maimonides rules that the prayer-leader who errs in his public recitation of the *'amidah* should correct himself.[49] When, however, he is reciting the *'amidah* privately beforehand he need not do so since this would be troublesome for the congregation by holding up its proceedings. There is manuscript evidence that Maimonides applies this to all *'amidah* benedictions, not only to the first and last three.[50]

> 11.5: The custom in Spain, North Africa, Babylonia and Israel is to light lamps in the synagogues and to spread carpets on the floor on which to sit, while in Christian cities Jews sit on chairs.

Maimonides's reference to the synagogal practice of communities in Islamic countries and how it varies from that of those in Christian environments is not typical of his code. What he appears to be arguing is that sitting on a carpeted floor is a perfectly acceptable part of liturgical decorum for his congregations, perhaps polemicizing against those who argue that standing is preferable or that the use of chairs and benches is more dignified. Were there perhaps moves in such

---

46   Rubenstein, p. 81; Rabinovitch, pp. 313–20; and Touger, p. 57.
47   See the responsum quoted above in the section entitled 'Individuals Relying on the Prayer-leader' and n. 17 thereon.
48   Rubenstein, p. 89; Rabinovitch, p. 345; and Touger, p. 82.
49   PT, *Berakhot* 5.4 (9c) and BT, *Berakhot* 34a.
50   Rubenstein, p. 91; Rabinovitch, p. 350; and Touger, pp. 86–87; *Tur, 'Orah Hayyim*, no. 126.

directions in Spain in the twelfth century that inspired such a polemical stance on his part?[51]

> 13.1: Although some have the custom of completing the pentateuchal lectionary over a three-year period, the widespread custom among all Jewish communities is to take only one year, beginning just after *Sukkot* and ending at *Sukkot* time the next year.

While Maimonides here appears to remain neutral about the Palestinian lectionary, his son, Abraham, reports[52] that he was definitely opposed to the customs of the émigré community from the Holy Land that had settled in Cairo, but was forced to remain silent about this in order to avoid communal strife.[53]

Specific readings in his prayer-book

Some fairly randomly selected readings, as preserved in the Oxford manuscript of Maimonides's prayer-book earlier mentioned, will now be closely compared with their equivalents in some of the earliest Sefardi manuscript liturgies,[54] and with the prayer-books of such geonic and medieval authorities as Sa'adya Gaon, Amram Gaon, Judah ben Yaqar,[55] Solomon ben Nathan, Abudraham,[56] and of the most traditional Yemenite rite, which, as Elbogen appreciated, was particularly relevant to the study of the prayer-book of Maimonides.[57]

---

51 Rubenstein, p. 98; Rabinovitch, pp. 372–74; and Touger, pp. 110–11.
52 Rabbi Abraham ben Moshe ben Maimon, *Sefer Ha-Maspik Le'Ovdey Hashem, Part Two, Volume Two*, ed. Nissim Dana (Ramat-Gan, 1989), pp. 180–81.
53 Rubenstein, p. 117; Rabinovitch, p. 431; and Touger, pp. 162–63.
54 The manuscripts consulted were the earliest relevant liturgies in the collections of the British Library, London (= BL), Bodleian Library, Oxford (= Bod.), and Cambridge University Library (= CUL). See G. Margoliouth, *Catalogue of the Hebrew and Samaritan Manuscripts in the British Museum*, vol. 1 (London, 1905), nos 692–94, pp. 346–54; A. Neubauer, *Catalogue of the Hebrew Manuscripts in the Bodleian Library*, vol. 1 (Oxford, 1886), no. 1132–35, cols 328–30; S. C. Reif, *Hebrew Manuscripts at Cambridge University Library: A Description and Introduction* (Cambridge, 1997), nos 389 and 392, pp. 240–42.
55 *Siddur R. Saadya Gaon*, eds I. Davidson, S. Assaf and B. I. Joel, (Jerusalem, 1963²) (= RSG); *Seder Rav Amram*, ed. E. D. Goldschmidt (Jerusalem, 1971) (= SRA); Judah ben Yaqar, *Peyrush Ha-Tefillot Ve-Ha-Berakhot*, ed. S. Yerushalmi (2 vols; Jerusalem, 1968–69) (= JBY).
56 *Siddur Rabbenu Shelomo ben Nathan*, ed. S. Ḥagi (Jerusalem, 1995) (= SBN); *Sefer Abudraham* (Warsaw, 1877) and *Sefer Abudraham Ha-Shalem*, ed. S. A Wertheimer (Jerusalem, 1963) (= A).
57 *Tiklal* of Yaḥya ben Joseph ibn Ṣaliḥ (Jerusalem, 1894) (= T) and Z. Madmoni, 'Ha-Rambam ve-nusaḥ ha-tefillah shel Yehudey Teman' in *Yahadut Teman: Pirqey Meḥqar Ve-'Iyyun*, eds I. Yeshayahu and J. Tobi (Jerusalem, 1976), pp. 273–94; Elbogen, 'Ritus' (see n. 1 above), p. 320.

This may help clarify whether Maimonides followed a particular tradition or preferred an eclectic liturgical version and establish the degree to which his practice was followed in later prayer-books.

1. EDG 193, 11–12: ברוך שאמר in בשבחו ובזמרו.[58]

So RSG (var.), SBN, T, and Bod. Opp.Add.8vo.18, with plural suffix in SRA as variant (בשבחיו ובזמיריו); A cites R text as erroneous, feminine plural as SRA, and his own text as plural suffix, as also in BL Add. 27126 and Bod. Can.Or.108; JBY, BL Add. 18690, Bod. Laud.Or.27 and CUL Add. 541 have feminine plural; CUL Add. 1204 has feminine plural altered to plural suffix and Bod. Opp.Add.8vo.17 appears to have the singular for the first word and the plural for the second; see also SBN in *qaddish* where there are a number of noun forms with plurals apparently ending in *waw* e.g. לעילא לעילא מכל ברכתו שירותו תשבחותו נחמותו וטבאתו.

2. EDG 194, 11: **End of** ישתבח: מלך גדול התושבחות אל ההודאות אדון כל המעשים הבוחר בשירי זמרה חי עולמים. [consistently spelt so: התושבחות].[59]

So SBN (but not consistently), SRA, T, BL Add. 18690, BL Add.27126, all four Bodleian MSS consulted, and CUL Add. 541; but not RSG, JBY or A; CUL Add. 1204 has an alteration from תושבחות to תישבחות.

3. EDG 194, 12–13: **After** ישתבח: וקורא השירה עד סופה כמנהג המקום.[60]

So RSG, SBN, T; but [SRA?] JBY, A, BL Add. 18690, BL Add. 27126, BL Or. 5866, all four Bodleian MSS consulted, CUL Add. 541 and CUL Add. 1204 all have it before.

4. EDG 195, 14: המאיר לארץ ולדרין עליה.[61]

---

58 S. Baer, *Seder 'Avodat Yisra'el* (Rödelheim, 1868) (= Baer), p. 59; *Siddur Oṣar Ha-Tefillot*, ed. A. L. Gordon (corrected and expanded edition, Vilna, 1923, Hebrew pagination) (= OT), pp. 89–90; I. Elbogen, German edition = G, *Der jüdische Gottesdienst in seiner geschichtlichen Entwicklung* (Frankfurt am Main, 1931; reprint, Hildesheim, 1962), pp. 83–84; Hebrew edition = H, התפלה בישראל בהתפתחותה ההיסטורית (eds J. Heinemann, I. Adler, A. Negev, J. Petuchowski and H. Schirmann, Tel Aviv, 1972), pp. 65–66; English edition = E, *Jewish Liturgy: A Comprehensive History* (trans. and ed. Raymond P. Scheindlin, Philadelphia, Jerusalem and New York, 1993), pp. 73–74; B. S. Jacobson, *Netiv Binah* (Hebrew; 5 vols; Tel Aviv, 1968–83) (= Jacobson), 1.192–94; N. Wieder, 'Fourteen New Genizah-Fragments of Saadya's Siddur together with a Reproduction of a Missing Part' in *Saadya Studies in Commemoration of the One Thousandth Anniversary of the Death of R. Saadya Gaon*, ed. E. I. J. Rosenthal (Manchester, 1943), p. 268 and *The Formation of Jewish Liturgy in the East and the West: A Collection of Essays* (Hebrew; 2 vols; Jerusalem, 1998), 2.507–8.

59 Baer, pp. 59 and 75; OT, p. 123; Elbogen G, pp. 85–86, H, p. 67, E, pp. 75–76; Jacobson, 1.226–28; S. C. Reif, *Shabbethai Sofer and his Prayer-book* (Cambridge, 1979), pp. 156 and 267–68; C. E. Cohen, 'Ashkenazic mishnaic reading traditions in eighteenth-century grammatical treatises' (Hebrew), *Leshonenu* 62 (1999), pp. 274–79.

60 Baer, p. 73 ; OT, pp. 117–21; Elbogen G, p. 86, H, p. 67, E, pp. 75–76; Jacobson, 1.218–26; J. Mann, 'Genizah fragments of the Palestinian order of service', *HUCA* 2 (1925), pp. 281–85, reprinted in *Contributions to the Scientific Study of Jewish Liturgy* (ed. J. J. Petuchowski, New York, 1970); E. Fleischer, *Eretz-Israel Prayer and Prayer Rituals as Portrayed in the Geniza Documents* (Hebrew; Jerusalem, 1988), pp. 275–91; Elbogen, 'Ritus' (see n. 1 above), p. 328.

So RSG, SBN, T; but SRA, JBY, A, BL Add. 27126, BL Or. 5866, all four
Bodleian MSS consulted, CUL Add. 541 and CUL Add. 1204 all have ולדרים.

5. EDG 195, 31: כאמור לעושה אורים גדולים כי לעולם חסדו התקנת מאורות
לשמח עולם.[62]

So SBN (והתקנת...עולמך) and T; Bod. Opp.Add.8vo.17 and Bod.
Opp.Add.8vo.18, with third person for second person; but not RSG, SRA,
JBY, A, BL Add. 27126, BL Or. 5866, Bod. Laud.Or.27, Bod. Can.Or.108,
CUL Add. 1204 and Add. 541.

6. EDG 196, 13–15: In the אמת ויציב response, every <u>second</u> word
has conjunctive *waw*.[63]

So SBN (for at least the first twelve expressions); but in RSG all have *waw*
except יציב, and *waw* is attached to all the epithets in SRA, JBY, T, A, BL
Add. 18690, BL Add. 27126, BL Or. 5866, all four Bodleian MSS consulted,
CUL Add. 541 and CUL Add. 1204, sometimes with a note specifying
and/or explaining the use of *waw* in each case.

7. EDG 197–198, 11: The השכיבנו prayer "ends" <u>ברוך</u> שומר עמו ישראל
and then adds <u>ברוך</u>...ברוך יי לעולם אמן ואמן ימלוך יי לעולם אמן ואמן <u>ברוך</u>
<u>אתה יי</u> המולך בכבודו חי וקיים תמיד ימלוך לעולם ועד ונהגו מקצת העם להוסיף
פסוקין באמצע ברכה זו.[64]

So RSG, SBN and T; but there are two full benedictions in SRA, JBY, A, BL
Add. 18690, BL Add. 27126, BL Or. 5866, all four Bodleian MSS consulted;
CUL Add. 541 has the word אמן at the end of each.

8. EDG 199, 11: In benediction 7: ראה בעניינו וריבה ריבנו ומהר לגאלינו.[65]

So T, BL Add.27126, Bod. Opp.Add.8vo.18, Bod. Laud.Or.27, Bod.
Can.Or.108 and CUL Add. 541; but not in RSG, SRA, SBN, JBY, A or BL Or.
5866, Bod. Opp.Add.8vo.17 and CUL Add. 1204, all of which prefer וגאלנו
מהרה.

9. EDG 199, 14: In benediction 9: ברכנו יי אלהינו בכל מעשה ידינו.[66]

So T, BL Or. 5866, Bod. Opp.Add.8vo.18, Bod. Laud.Or.27, Bod.
Can.Or.108, CUL Add. 541 and CUL Add. 1204; but RSG, SRA, SBN, JBY,
A, BL Add. 18690, BL Add. 27126 and Bod. Opp.Add.8vo.17 prefer ברך עלינו.

---

61 Baer, p. 76 ; OT, p. 127; Elbogen G, p. 17, H, p. 13, E, p. 17; Jacobson, 1.230–31; Reif,
    Shabbethai (see n. 59 above), pp. 306–7.
62 Baer, p. 79 ; OT, pp. 132–33; Elbogen G, pp. 19–20, H, p. 15, E, p. 16; Jacobson, 1.235;
    Wieder, *Formation* (see n. 58 above), 1:155–57, reprinted from *Sinai* 76 (1975), pp. 116–
    18.
63 Baer, p. 84 ; OT, pp. 142–43; Elbogen G, p. 22, H, p. 17, E, p. 21; Jacobson, 1.254–60;
    Reif, *Shabbethai* (see n. 59 above), p. 211 and chapter 15 of the present volume.
64 Baer, pp. 168–69; OT, pp. 272–74; Elbogen G, p. 102–4, H, pp. 78–80, E, pp. 87–89;
    Jacobson, 1.410–14; Elbogen, 'Ritus' (see n. 1 above), pp. 323 and 329.
65 Baer, p. 91 ; OT, p. 164; Elbogen G, p. 48, H, p. 37, E, pp. 42–43; Jacobson, 1.279; Y.
    Luger, *The Weekday Amidah in the Cairo Genizah* (Hebrew; Jerusalem, 2001), pp. 92–96.
66 Baer, p. 92 ; OT, pp. 166–67; Elbogen G, pp. 49–50, H, pp. 38–39, E, p. 44; Jacobson,
    1.280–81; Luger, *Amidah* (see n. 65 above), pp. 103–13.

10. EDG 199, 27: **In benediction 14:** תשכון בתוך ירושלם עירך כאשר דברת
ובנה אותה בניין עולם במהרה בימינו.[67]

So JBY, T, A, BL Add. 18690, BL Add. 27126, BL Or. 5866, all four Bodleian
MSS consulted (in a later hand in Bod. Can.Or.108 and with an addition
about the throne of David in Bod. Opp.Add.8vo.17), CUL Add. 541 and
CUL Add. 1204; but RSG, SRA and SBN have רחם or על ירושלים.

11. EDG 200, 14–15: **In benediction 19:** וברכנו כולנו (כאחד) ממאור פניך כי
ממאור פניך נתתה לנו יי אלהינו תורה וחיים אהבה וחסד צדקה ושלום וטוב בעיניך
לברך את עמך ישראל [בכל עת] בשלום.[68]

So (apparently) SBN and T; RSG has במאור and then ממאור; JBY has באור and
then במאור ; but SRA, A, BL Or. 5866, Bod. Laud.Or.27, Bod. Can.Or.108 (in
a later hand), and CUL Add. 541 have באור twice. BL Add. 18690, BL Add.
27126, Bod. Opp.Add.8vo.17 and Bod. Opp.Add.8vo.18 have more
substantially different versions.

12. EDG 201, 17: **In 14th benediction for Tish'ah BeAv:** רחם יי אלהינו
עלינו ועל ישראל עמך...ברוך אתה יי בונה ירושלים.[69]

So RSG, SRA, SBN, JBY (both!), T and CUL Add. 1204; but A, BL Add.
18690, BL Or. 5866 and all four Bodleian MSS consulted have נחם.

13. EDG 202, 16–25: *Qedushah:* שליח צבור מברך לעולם ברכה שלישית בנוסח
זה. נקדישך ונעריצך ונשלש לך קדושה משולשת כדבר האמור על ידי נביאך וקרא זה
אל זה ואמר קדוש קדוש קדוש יי צבאות מלוא כל הארץ כבודו וגדלו מלא עולם
ומשרתיו שואלים איה מקום כבודו משבחים ואומרים ברוך כבוד יי ממקומו ממקומך
מלכינו תופיע ותמלוך עלינו כי מתי תמלוך בציון ובימינו תשכון
תתגדל ותתקדש בתוך ירושלם עירך לדור ודור ולנצח נצחים ועינינו תראינה במלכות
עוזך כדבר האמור בשירי קדשך על ידי דוד משיח צדקך ימלוך יי לעלם אלהיך ציון
לדור ודור [הללויה] לדור ודור נגיד גדול ולנצח נצחים קדושתך נקדיש ושבחך אלהינו
מפינו לא ימוש (לעולם ועד) כי אל מלך גדול וקדוש אתה ברוך א' יי האל הקדוש.[70]

So RSG (with אז ברעש גדול), T, SBN (minor variants) but others (including
many manuscripts) vary or are more complex. The battle for one simple
qedushah on all occasions was undoubtedly in the process of being lost by
this time.

67 Baer, p. 96 ; OT, p. 170; Elbogen G, pp. 52–54, H, pp. 41–42, E, pp. 47–48; Jacobson,
    1.285–86; Luger, *Amidah* (see n. 65 above), pp. 150–58.
68 Baer, p. 103 ; OT, pp. 181–82; Elbogen G, p. 59, H, p. 46, E, p. 53; Jacobson, 1.296–99;
    Luger, *Amidah* (see n. 65 above), pp. 196–208.
69 Baer, p. 96 ; OT, p. 171; Elbogen G, pp. 53, 129 and 181, H, pp. 42, 97 and 136, E, pp.
    48, 107–8 and 147; Jacobson, 1.327; see also J. Heinemann, *Prayer in the Period of the
    Tanna'im and Amora'im: Its Nature and Its Patterns* (Hebrew; Jerusalem², 1966), pp. 35–
    40 and 48–51; revised English edition, *Prayer in the Talmud: Forms and Patterns* (Berlin
    and New York, 1977), pp. 48–56, 70–76 and 288–91; and chapter 9 above.
70 Baer, pp. 89–90 and 218 ; OT, pp. 159–60 and 337–38; Elbogen G, pp. 61–67, H, pp.
    47–54, E, pp. 54–62; Jacobson, 1.307–10 and 2.205–6; Elbogen, 'Ritus' (see n. 1 above),
    p. 324.

14. EDG 205, 12–15: In the *musaf* prayer there is <u>no specific</u> <u>mention</u> of the detailed biblically ordained sacrifices, the shabbat *musaf* including: ‏כסדרן ומוספין‏ ‏ושם נעשה לפניך את קרבנות חובותינו תמידי'

‏כהלכתן [ו]את מוספי יום המנוח הזה נעשה ונקריב לפניך באהבה כמצות רצונך כמה‏
‏שכבת עלינו בתורתיך על־ידי משה עבדך <u>לא נתתו מלכינו לגויי הארצות</u> ולא הנחלתו‏
‏מלכינו לעובדי פסילים [גם] במנוחתו לא ישכנו ערלים לבית ישראל נתתו זרע ישורון‏
‏אשר בם בחרת חמדת ימים קראת אותו א"א רצה נא וכו'.‏[71]

So T and A; but RSG, SRA, SBN have the verses while there is discussion, or variation between *musafim*, in JBY, BL Add. 18690, BL Or. 5866, all four Bodleian MSS consulted, CUL Add. 541 and CUL Add. 1204.

15. EDG 214, 3–6: **Re specific mention of sacrificial details ordained in Torah:** ‏נהגו העם בכל תפלות המוספין כשהוא אומר כמו שכתבתה‏

‏עלינו בתורתך על ידי משה עבדך מזכיר קרבנות היום כמו שהן כתובין בתורה‏
‏וקורא אותן הפסוקים ואם לא הזכיר כיון שאמר כמו שכתבתה עלינו בתורתך שוב אינו‏
‏צריך.‏

16. EDG 208, 11–12: **In the *musaf* prayer for festivals:** ‏והשב ישראל‏

‏לנויהו כהנים לעבודתם ולויים לדוכנן וישראל למעמדן וארמון על משפטו ישב ושם‏
‏נעלה.‏[72]

So T and SBN (‏ולוים לשירה ולזמרה וארמון‏) with close similarities in RSG (+ the variants); but not SRA, A, the British Library and Bodleian MSS consulted, or CUL Add. 541.

17. EDG 203, 3–9: **Re *qaddish*:** ‏שליח צבור אומר קדיש לעולם קודם כל תפלה‏

‏ואחר כל תפלה ואחר שאמר סדר היום בכל עת שיאמר סדר היום יתחנן מעט ויאמר‏
‏קדיש וכישלים לקרות בתורה ובכל עת שיתחנן בדברי תחנונים כשיגמור תחנוניו יאמר‏
‏קדיש. נוסח הקדיש: יתגדל ויתקדש שמיה רבה בעלמא דיברא כרעותיה וימלך‏
‏מלכותיה ויצמח פורקניה ויקרב משיחיה ויפרוק עמיה בחייכון וביומיכון ובחייהון‏
‏(וביומיהון).‏ [‏סדר היום‏] is the ‏קדושא דסידרא‏.[73]

So (similarly) T, SBN and CUL Add. 541; but not RSG, SRA, JBY, A, the Bodleian MSS consulted (with the possible exception of Bod. Opp.Add.8vo.18 ?), the British Library MSS consulted, or CUL Add. 1204.

18. EDG 208, 17–19: ‏וכנוסח הזה [של פסח] הוא מתפלל בחג השבועות ובחג‏

‏הסכות <u>בלא חסרון בלא יתר</u> אלא שבחג השבועות הוא אומר את יום טוב מקרא ק' הזה‏
‏את יום חג השבועות הזה זמן מתן תורתינו באהבה זכר ליציא' מצ'... וכן בחג‏
‏הסוכות...וכן בשמיני עצרת.‏

---

71 Baer, pp. 239, 334, 352–53, 397 and 425; OT, pp. 363–64, 451, 462, 526 and 567; Elbogen G, pp. 117, 126, 136 and 145, H, pp. 89, 95, 102 and 110, E, pp. 98, 106, 114 and 122; Jacobson, 4:14–48; Elbogen, 'Ritus' (see n. 1 above), p. 325; see also the section entitled 'Early musaf prayer' in chapter ten above.

72 Baer, p. 355; OT, p. 464; Jacobson, 4.45; see also chapter nine above, section 7.

73 Baer, pp. 129–31; OT, pp. 82–83; Elbogen G, pp. 92–98, H, pp. 72–75, E, pp. 80–84; Jacobson, 1.365–73; Elbogen, 'Ritus' (see n. 1 above), p. 329. See also D. De Sola Pool, *The Kaddish* (Leipzig, 1909) and A. Lehnardt, *Qaddish: Untersuchungen zur Entstehung und Rezeption eines rabbinischen Gebetes* (Tübingen, 2002).

19. EDG 215, 27 – 216, 3: **In grace after meals:** וטובו הגדול לא חסר לנו
ואל יחסר לנו לעולם ועד כי הוא זן ומפרנס לכל כאמור פותח את ידיך ומשביע לכל חי
רצון ומכין מזון לכל בריותיו אשר ברא ב"א יי יי הזן את הכל. נודה לך יי אלהינו ונברך
מלכינו כי הנחלתת(נו והנחלת) את אבותינו ארץ חמדה טובה ורחבה ברית ותורה (חיים
ומזון) ועל שהוצאתנו מארץ מצרים ופדיתנו מבית עבדים על תורתך שלמדתנו על
חוקי רצונך שהורדעתנו ...[74]

20. EDG 26, 9–10: **grace:** הטוב והמטיב (אשר) [ש]בכל יום ויום (הוא מטיב עמנו)
הוא גומלנו חן וחסד ורחמים וכל טוב:

So T, with close similarities in JBY and A, and some in SBN, but not in RSG,
SRA or SBN or any of the Bodleian MSS consulted. BL Or. 5866 has some
readings that are similar to the latter part of the first benediction but not to
the section cited here from the fourth benediction.

Characteristics

1. Tensions: Theological tensions are regularly encountered in the
various aspects of Maimonides's liturgical work. Among the main
clashes that stand out are those between the spiritual ideal and the
reality of life, between the maximalist demand for elitism and the need
for popular guidance and support, and between the championing of
individual intensity and the trend towards communal standardization.
Other competitive trends include the practical halakhah vis-à-vis the
historical interpretation, the congregational setting versus the domestic
location, and the individual's inherited tradition as against the local
community's custom.

2. Innovation: The relevant sources reveal instances in the field of
liturgical decision-making in which Maimonides expresses brave,
radical and novel ideas that do not necessarily reflect the opinions of
the post-talmudic authorities or the established customs of these who
adhere to their rulings. He opts for the non-repetition of the 'amidah for
musaf, argues the need for brevity and the avoidance of congregational
boredom and loss of concentration, and sometimes demonstrates a
moderate tendency that avoids imposing strictness on the community.
He distinguishes what should be said in the synagogue from what
should more correctly be recited at home and displays an awareness
that different geographical circumstances may justifiably lead to variety
of practice. He is concerned to maintain an association between
physical and spiritual purity and to promote its relevance to the
liturgical sphere.

---

74 Baer, pp. 554–59; OT, pp. 239–43; Jacobson, 3.55–66; see also the study of a Genizah
    text of *birkat ha-mazon* in chapter eighteen below.

3. Traditionalism: Maimonides is strongly committed to the continued application of talmudic principles[75] and rulings and to a basic adherence to the formative Iraqi or Babylonian (but not necessarily Sa'adyanic) rite, rather than that of the land of Israel. There is in his work an anxiety to maintain the religiosity of prayer and a reluctance to abandon well-established phraseology. He respectfully takes note of customs, even when they are numerous and varied, but is careful to distinguish between what is halakhically required and what is an optional custom, sometimes adopting what appeals to him and at other times choosing not to codify what he regards as merely customary.

4. Form and Content: Maimonides appears to be content with the use of Rabbinic Hebrew (MH) and Aramaic in the prayers and is not among those who wish to "correct" the Hebrew style in accordance with the language and grammar of the masoretic Bible. It is important for the worshipper to adhere to a theme within each section and not to lose sight of that theme because of expansions and diversions. Successful prayer requires suitable and adequate preparations, physical as well as spiritual, congregational as well as individual. He has no problem with the inclusion of biblical verses but does not propose an extension of the practice, just as he is impatient with too much variety and essentially prefers to adhere to the skeletal liturgical format, rather than opting for a highly specific version. The issue of precision is applied by him to spiritual aims rather than to textual options. He expresses objection to superstition and magic and demonstrates a clear propensity towards the logical and the systematic and the concretization of abstract principles.

5. Place among Rites: His preferred liturgical text is akin to earlier rather than later Sefardi traditions (which came under the heavy influence of the Zohar and the kabbalists). It appears to belong to North African and Egyptian circles although the possibility should not be ruled out that the liturgical practices of such circles might have been identical with at least part of the earlier Sefardi tradition. It may well be that he adhered to a Sefardi minhag at home and that what he is formally and authoritatively offering to the Jewish public is an Egyptian rite. Whatever its provenance, his formal rite stands on the crossroads at which the highway of Babylonian centralization splits up into more minor roads leading to independent geographical units, all with their own adjustments, rationalizations and standardizations. He is a broad supporter of the liturgical preferences of the geonic authorities but an approach that incorporates a more strongly localized

---

75   See Elbogen, 'Ritus' (see n. 1 above), p. 325.

interpretation, manifestation and adjustment of those preferences is still clearly in the future.

6. Success: Unless we are to assume (without any evidence or rationale) that Maimonides adopted a pre-existent Yemenite rite in his halakhic work, it seems highly likely that he had the most influence on Yemen (*baladi* not *shami*), a conclusion that matches the other historical evidence about his impact on that community. His influence elsewhere was more limited because of controversies about his works, the lack of a widespread prayer-book version associated with his name (such as those of the geonic leaders Amram and Sa'adya), and the substantial inroads made by the mystics into the liturgical field. What also perhaps played a part was his son Abraham's reputation as a mystic rather than a continuator of his father's liturgical traditions, and it should not be forgotten that in the subsequent period the centres of Jewish religious leadership moved from Egypt, Eastern Mediterranean and Mesopotamia to Spain, Franco-Gemany and Italy.

Overall conclusion

Maimonides's liturgical work reveals a number of tensions about theological priorities and preferences. He was capable of innovation where the circumstances demanded it but was broadly committed to the continued application of talmudic principles, while remaining aware of the distinction between legal requirement and customary practice. What is uncovered in his comments is a contentment with basic Hebrew liturgy and a preference for intense preparation over unnecessary expansion, especially of the mystical variety. His preferred liturgy appears to be Egyptian/North African and to stand between the centralized Babylonian rite and the variegated traditions which flowed from it. It made a major impact only on the Yemenite rite and appears to have lost much of its influence in the increasingly powerful centres of Europe.[76]

---

76   An early draft of this paper was given at a conference organized by Professor Mark Geller at University College London and I am grateful to him for his invitation and to Professor Mordechai Friedman of Tel Aviv University for a number of helpful comments that I have incorporated into this fuller version.

13

Modern study of medieval liturgy

My first objectives in this chapter are to summarize how the first century of Genizah research impacted on the scientific study of the Jewish liturgy of the early medieval period and to note briefly how the views of the outstanding nineteenth-century savant Moritz Steinschneider in this field relate to more contemporary notions. I shall then offer an overview of some of the major developments in the study of rabbinic liturgical theory and practice that have taken place in the past fifteen years, particularly, but not exclusively, as they have been informed and inspired by fresh Genizah discoveries.

Pioneers

It is now well over over a century since Solomon Schechter, following the hints and hunches of earlier scholars and literary explorers, adopted a more dynamic and determined approach than such predecessors and succeeded in bringing to Cambridge from the Genizah of the Ben Ezra synagogue in Cairo over 140,000 fragments, representing some seventy percent of what had survived there from medieval Fustat into the modern period. As a result of this transfer of such a rich resource from a parochial provenance to an environment where it could be academically exploited, and the inspiration that Schechter provided for scholarly work to be undertaken on similar collections elsewhere, the whole topic of Jewish studies has undergone what is tantamount to revolutionary development. One of the many specific areas to derive substantial benefit from the novel Genizah documentation and its careful analysis has been the study of Jewish liturgical texts and their evolution, particularly the emergence of a formal and authoritative prayer-book from a loose collection of competing versions. It is therefore appropriate to summarize the Genizah's past contribution to this field of research and to indicate the nature of more recent work and its significance.[1]

That initiative of Schechter was due in no small part to his imaginative intellect and his scholarly industry, and it was these two characteristics of his that led him to a speedy appreciation of the

---

1   For the history of the Cambridge Genizah manuscripts and their overall contribution to scholarship, see S. C. Reif, *A Jewish Archive from Old Cairo: The History of Cambridge University's Genizah Collection* (Richmond, Surrey, 2000).

intense scholarly significance of the material he had brought back from Cairo. Once he set to work in Cambridge on sorting, classifying and identifying the precious fragments entrusted to him, it took him only a little time to set down for his contemporaries, and indeed for subsequent generations, general guidelines as to how the Genizah would affect scientific Jewish learning and specific comments on how it would contribute to the historical analysis of Hebrew liturgical texts.[2] In the well-known but still astonishingly perceptive report that he wrote within a few months of his Cairo expedition and that he later entitled 'A Hoard of Hebrew Manuscripts,' he described such texts in the following terms: 'As to liturgy, the Genizah offers the remains of the oldest forms of the worship of the synagogue and these throw much light on the history of the Jewish prayer-book ... they restore to us the older forms of the 'original prayers.'"[3] Although he regarded the reconstruction of such early versions as among scholarship's most urgent desiderata, and devoted some energy to setting such a process in motion, Schechter himself succeeded in publishing only a small number of the Genizah fragments relevant to this field. These contained rare and early versions of such central rabbinic prayers as the *'amidah*, the *qaddish*, and the blessings attached to the reading of the *shema'*.[4]

If the truth be told, however, Schechter was not the first scholar to utilize Genizah material for the critical study of the development of Jewish prayer and of synagogal custom and it was at Oxford and not at Cambridge that such items were initially acquired and studied. Before Schechter undertook his productive journey to Cairo, his elder contemporary at 'the other place,' Adolf Neubauer, had been working for some time on the description of the Bodleian Library's extensive collection of important Hebrew manuscripts. In that context he had given some attention to Genizah fragments that had been added to that collection from the early 1890s and his efforts in this connection, as in many others, had no doubt been partly motivated by the traditional

---

2   On the character and achievements of Schechter, see Norman Bentwich, *Solomon Schechter: A Biography* (Philadelphia, 1938), my essay in the *Oxford Dictionary of National Biography* (Oxford, 2004), 49.207–10, and the bibliography cited there. Schechter's descriptions of the Cambridge Genizah material originally appeared in *The Times* of 3 August 1897 and in *The Jewish Chronicle* of 15 October 1897 and of 1 April 1898, and were reprinted together under the title 'A hoard of Hebrew manuscripts' in his *Studies in Judaism*, (3 vols, Philadelphia, 1908), 2.1–30.

3   Schechter, 'A hoard' (see n. 2 above), pp. 10 and 18.

4   Schechter, 'Genizah specimens: liturgy', *JQR* 10 (1898), pp. 654–59 and his 'Nusḥa ba-qaddish', in *Gedenkbuch zur Errinerung an David Kaufmann* (Breslau, 1900), Hebrew section, pp. 52–54.

scholarly rivalry between England's two famous centres of scholarship that had its productive as well as its more contentious aspects.[5]

Appreciating that such fragments had a novel contribution to make to Jewish liturgical research, Neubauer invited his nephew, Adolf Büchler, then in Vienna, to subject them to his critical scholarly eye. Büchler spent two periods of study at the Bodleian between 1891 and 1893 and, when Neubauer's non-Jewish colleague and successor, Arthur Cowley, published the second volume of their *Catalogue of the Hebrew Manuscripts* in 1906, he acknowledged the assistance provided by Büchler in describing these items.[6] One particular manuscript attracted Büchler's closer attention, containing as it did details of the triennial cycle of pentateuchal and prophetic readings that was still current among the Palestinian Jews living in Cairo after the first Crusader invasion of the Holy Land. He published a lengthy and seminal article on this subject in the *Jewish Quarterly Review* of 1893 but, somewhat surprisingly, neither he nor his uncle gave the Hebrew liturgical fragments the fuller attention and publicity that they deserved.[7] The way was therefore left open to their competitor in Cambridge to steal the limelight in this connection.

Although it is customary in many Jewish scholarly circles to downplay the role of Anglo-Jewish academics in the development of *Wissenschaft des Judentums*, the fact is that in the matter of the study of the liturgical material in the Genizah collections, the contribution of those who were born in England, or who did a major part of their research there, was not insignificant. Following the lead given by Neubauer and Büchler, and encouraged by Schechter, Israel Abrahams, subsequently Schechter's successor in the readership in talmudic and rabbinic literature at Cambridge, also published fresh manuscript versions in this field. In 1897, he identified and transcribed important

---

5   The results of Neubauer's work appeared in his *Catalogue of Hebrew Manuscripts in the Bodleian Library*, eds A. Neubauer and A. Cowley (2 vols; Oxford, 1886–1906). A revised and augmented edition of the first volume, prepared by M. Beit-Arié and R. May, appeared just over a decade ago (Oxford, 1994). See also my two articles (which touch upon such rivalries): 'The discovery of the Ben Sira fragments' in *The Book of Ben Sira in Modern Research. Proceedings of the First International Ben Sira Conference 1996*, ed. P. C. Beentjes (Berlin, 1997), pp. 1–21, and 'The Damascus Document from the Cairo Genizah' in *The Damascus Document: A Centennial of Discovery*, eds J. M. Baumgarten, E. Chazon and A. Pinnick (Leiden, 2000), pp. 109–131.

6   See Cowley's remarks and those of Bodley's Librarian in *Catalogue of Hebrew Manuscripts* (see n. 5 above), pp. iii–v.

7   A. Büchler, 'The reading of the Law and Prophets in a triennial cycle', *JQR* 5 (1893), pp. 420–68, and 6 (1893), pp. 1–73; both are reprinted in J. J. Petuchowski, *Contributions to the Scientific Study of Jewish Liturgy* (New York, 1970), pp. 181–302. See also 'The Damascus Document' cited in n. 5 above.

and hitherto unknown texts of the various parts of the Passover
Haggadah and correctly ascribed them to the geonic period.[8] Part of the
academic career of Abrahams was spent at Jews' College and it was
there that an even more successful scholar, born in Galicia, received an
important part of his scholarly training and began to take a serious
interest in the Genizah.

Europe, USA and Mandatary Palestine

Jacob Mann studied there and at the University of London between
1908 and 1915 and was no doubt influenced by one who had already
been something of a Genizah pioneer, the then Principal of Jews'
College, Adolf Büchler.[9] Mann's primary interest in the Genizah turned
out to be in the history of Jewish communal life and culture in Palestine
and Egypt under the Fatimid caliphs but he also collected, deciphered
and annotated many liturgical texts.[10] He exploited these to reconstruct
many elements of the Palestinian rite as imported into Cairo by the
refugees from Christian persecution but he was cautious enough not to
make exaggerated claims about the degree to which his discoveries
represented a pristine version from the Holy Land. As he himself put it
in the fundamental study that appeared in the second volume of the
Hebrew Union College Annual, 'But it is a moot question, and one very
difficult to solve, whether in that house of God *Minhag Ereṣ Yisrael* was
adhered to in its purity without any admixture of a *local* Egyptian
custom (*Minhag Miṣrayim*) such as can be detected in Sa'adya's Siddur
... Egyptian Jewry seems early to have become divided in matters of
ritual into Babylonian and Palestinian sections.' Mann's research
covered a number of central liturgical topics, among them the morning
prayers for weekdays, sabbaths and festivals, and the grace after
meals.[11]

---

8   I. Abrahams, 'Some Egyptian fragments of the Passover Hagada', *JQR* 10 (1897), pp.
     41–51, where he acknowledges his debt to Schechter and also cites fragments from
     the Genizah collections of the Bodleian and of E. N. Adler. On the history of Genizah
     scholarship in Anglo-Jewry, see Reif, 'Fragments of Anglo-Jewry', *The Jewish Year
     Book 1998*, pp. lviii–lxvii.
9   See the brief biography by V. Reichert, 'Jacob Mann 1888–1940', *AJYB* 43, (1941), pp.
     407–14.
10   By 1916, Mann had already researched a long list of Cambridge Genizah fragments
     of historical interest, as is reported in the diary of the Cambridge University
     Librarian, Francis Jenkinson, for 8–9 June of that year, Cambridge University Library
     MS Add. 8754, p. 47. Such research resulted in his *The Jews in Egypt and Palestine
     under the Fatimid Caliphs* (2 vols; Oxford, 1920–22; reprinted edition with preface and
     reader's guide by S. D. Goitein; 2 volumes in 1; New York, 1970).
11   J. Mann, 'Genizah fragments of the Palestinian order of service,' *HUCA* 2 (1925), pp.
     269–338, reprinted in Petuchowski's *Contributions* (see n. 7 above), pp. 379–448.

There were also scholars in continental Europe and in the United States who successfully made use of the Genizah discoveries in the early part of the twentieth century for tracing the history of the prayer-book in the late geonic and early medieval periods. In France, Israel Lévi published newly found texts of the *shema'* benedictions, the *'amidah* and the *qaddish*,[12] while in Germany Ismar Elbogen, on the basis of photographs of Genizah fragments that he had ordered, was the author of instructive and insightful articles that dealt with problematic liturgical expressions, with festival prayers, and with textual developments in the *'amidah*.[13] Perhaps even more significantly, Elbogen compiled a comprehensive guide to Jewish liturgical history from the biblical age to the modern period.[14] Although he had done important research on the medieval Genizah fragments, and was aware of the textual variations between the rites of Babylon and Eretz Israel that they reflected, Elbogen regarded as pivotal and innovative the role of the talmudic rabbis in fixing the basic texts of the standard prayers. For him, the subsequent thousand years constituted a period of decadence as far as the central prayers were concerned, the creative element having been relegated and restricted to the realm of liturgical poetry.[15]

In the matter of the historical study of Jewish liturgical texts, the legacy of Schechter was taken up at the Jewish Theological Seminary of America in New York by Louis Finkelstein. He amassed a wealth of evidence from the Genizah, from other manuscripts, and from early printed sources which he exploited for his textual, literary and

12 I. Lévi, 'Fragments de rituels de prières provenant de la Gueniza du Caire', *REJ* 53 (1907), pp. 231–44.
13 I. Elbogen, 'Geschichte des Achtzehngebets', *MGWJ* 46 (1902), pp. 330–57 and 513–30, independently published in Breslau, 1903; *Studien zur Geschichte des jüdischen Gottesdienstes* (Berlin, 1907), published in English as 'Studies in Jewish liturgy', *JQR* 18 (1906), pp. 587–99, and 19 (1906–7), pp. 229–49 and 704–20; reprinted in Petuchowski's *Contributions* (see n. 7 above), pp. 1–51.
14 The original German version was entitled *Der jüdische Gottesdienst in seiner geschichtlichen Entwicklung* (Berlin, 1913, 1924, 1931) and was updated in a Hebrew version (Tel Aviv, 1972), edited by J. Heinemann, assisted by I. Adler, A. Negev, J. J. Petuchowski and J. Schirmann, and translated by J. Amir, under the title התפילה בישראל בהתפתחותה ההיסטורית. That Hebrew version formed the basis of the English translation *Jewish Liturgy: A Comprehensive History* by Raymond Scheindlin (Philadelphia and New York, 1993).
15 See Elbogen's remarks, in Scheindlin's translation, p. 213: 'But this [creative] power failed at the end of the talmudic period, and was followed by a slack time, when further development was hindered by severe persecution .... The later generations ... were content with collecting and securing the treasures that they had inherited from their predecessors .... But in the area of independent creativity, their powers were inadequate, and they could only content themselves with taking over ready-made thoughts and themes, developing them and filling them out .... The age of free additions, of independent work on the liturgy, was past, and the existing foundation was considered binding and immutable.'

historical studies of the earliest versions of the 'amidah and the grace after meals. In contrast to the reservations expressed by Mann about the recovery of pristine texts, Finkelstein concluded that original and authoritative versions had existed in Judea in the Second Temple period and that Rabban Gamliel had succeeded in establishing their authenticity and maintaining their purity. For him, the path to the rediscovery of these original versions lay by way of the signposts preserved in the Palestinian liturgical texts from the Genizah.[16] The problem is that Finkelstein did not distinguish carefully enough between what he defined as the Palestinian version, as he globally described it, and the various versions that were in use at a number of points in time in the different communities of the Holy Land. This liturgical interest in early medieval Palestine was also expressed in modern, mandatory Palestine during the 1930s when the Hebrew University scholar, Simcha Assaf, also published Genizah texts of its characteristic prayer rites.[17]

More recent studies

The first hundred years of Genizah research in the field of Jewish liturgy have been witness to two distinct scholarly trends. One has concentrated on building fundamental theories of development and historical reconstructions, while the other has preferred to limit itself to citing the manuscript evidence and the variant texts that belong to different times and places. During a period of over fifty years of productive and inspirational scholarship, my distinguished teacher, Naphtali Wieder, to whose work I shall shortly return, identified and described hundreds of liturgical Genizah fragments, explained how various texts emerged and developed, and traced the relationships between the various rites, particularly those of Palestine and Babylon.[18]

---

16 L. Finkelstein, 'The development of the amidah', *JQR*, NS 16 (1925), pp. 1–43 and 127–70, and 'The birkat ha-mazon', *JQR*, NS 19 (1928–29), pp. 211–62. For recent assessments of Finkelstein as scholar and educator, see M. B. Greenbaum, 'The Finkelstein era', H. E. Goldberg, 'Becoming history: perspectives on the Seminary faculty at mid-century' and B. R. Shargel, 'The texture of Seminary life during the Finkelstein era', in *Tradition Renewed: A History of the Jewish Theological Seminary* (2 vols, New York, 1997), 1.161–232, 353–437 and 515–64.

17 S. Assaf, 'Mi-seder ha-tefillah be-Eres Yisra'el' in *Sefer Dinaburg*, eds Y. Baer, J. Guttmann and M. Shova (Jerusalem, 1949), pp. 116–31 and 422. He also made use of Genizah fragments for his edition, with I. Davidson and B. I. Joel, of *Siddur R. Saadja Gaon* (Jerusalem, 1941; 1963²).

18 Four particularly important items were: 'Fourteen new Genizah-fragments of Saadya's *Siddur* together with a reproduction of a missing part' in *Saadya Studies*, ed. E. I. J. Rosenthal (Manchester, 1943), pp. 245–83; *Islamic Influences on the Jewish Worship* (Hebrew; Oxford, 1947), originally published in *Melila* 2 (Manchester, 1946);

In preparing his scientific editions of various liturgical works and prayers, Daniel Goldschmidt also made use of the Genizah source, especially in his historical study of the text of the Passover Haggadah.[19] For his part, Alexander Scheiber wrote on Genizah items that testified to Karaite views of rabbinic prayers and that provided rare formulations of the grace after meals.[20]

Some forty years ago, Joseph Heinemann seriously called into question what he dubbed the 'historical-philological approach' and attempted to effect a revolutionary change in the direction of Jewish liturgical research. His contention was that no single, original version had ever existed, and he pointed to the extensive textual variety to be found in the Genizah manuscripts as evidence of a total lack of liturgical consistency or unity among the Jewish communities of a thousand years ago. If, then, the talmudic rabbis and their immediate successors had not established definitive versions for the prayers, the role of the critical scholar, as he saw it, was not to set out in pursuit of non-existent pristine texts but to utilize the form-critical method to identify the various types of Jewish prayer and their provenances.[21]

After dominating the field for fifteen years, Heinemann's theories themselves came in for serious criticism at the hands of the world's leading scholar in Jewish liturgical poetry, Ezra Fleischer. According to him, it was Rabban Gamliel who introduced the revolutionary concept of fixed and written versions of the daily rabbinic prayers in the second Christian century. The variants to be found in the Genizah are not a reflection of earlier inconsistencies and variety but of the influence of those who composed and recited synagogal poetry. So innovative and creative were they that they encouraged the development of scant

'Genizah studies in the Babylonian liturgy', *Tarbiz*, 37 (1968), pp. 135–57 and 240–64; and 'An unknown benediction on reading the chapter *ba-meh madliqin*', *Sinai* 82 (1978), pp. 197–221. These are all reproduced in the collection of his articles referred to in n. 33 below.

19　A list of his publications, prepared by Naftali Ben-Menahem, appears in his collected essays *On Jewish Liturgy: Essays on Prayer and Religious Poetry* (Hebrew; Jerusalem, 1978). See also his edition *The Passover Haggadah: Its Sources and History* (Hebrew; Jerusalem, 1969).

20　A. (Sandor) Scheiber, 'The Rabbanite prayer-book quoted by Qirqisani', *HUCA* 22 (1949), pp. 307–20; '*Qiṭ'ey birkat ha-mazon*', *SRIHP* 7 (1958), pp. 147–53; 'Prières Rabbanites chez les auteurs Karaites', *REJ* 125 (1966), pp. 213–19. All three articles were included in his collected essays *Geniza Studies* (Hildesheim and New York, 1981), European language section, pp. 1–14 and 261–67, and Hebrew section, pp. 51–57.

21　The original Hebrew edition, with the English title *Prayer in the Period of the Tanna'im and Amora'im: Its Nature and Its Patterns* (Jerusalem, 1964) was updated by the author and translated into English by R. Sarason. It was published as *Prayer in the Talmud: Forms and Patterns* (Berlin, 1977). The introduction offers a summary and justification of his novel approach.

respect for the maintenance of traditional texts even in the standard and central prayers.[22] Fleischer made another major contribution to the field by way of an instructive Hebrew volume on Eretz Israel prayer and prayer rituals, in which he cites many important Genizah texts and subjects them to careful historical and literary analysis.[23]

In addition to these major contributions, brief mention may be made of the work of a number of younger scholars that appeared before 1990. Tsvi Groner traced the development of the confessional benediction ha-'el ha-solḥan, while Lawrence Hoffman analysed fifty-nine liturgical controversies in the geonic period.[24] Genizah fragments that testify to a Jewish prayer for the caliph and to the views of Jewish mystics were published by Paul Fenton while I authored articles on 'emet ve-'emunah, and on the liturgical titles given to sabbaths and festivals.[25]

What the Genizah has revealed

It should be clear from the overview just offered that the search for the original version of the standard daily prayers of rabbinic Judaism represents only one element of the scholarly study of Jewish liturgy in the geonic and early medieval periods as it has been conducted on the basis of the Genizah evidence over the period of a century. Other aspects of the subject have received close attention and the result of the

---

22 A list of his publications, prepared by T. Beeri and S. Ben-Ari, appears in his *Festschrift* entitled *Knesset Ezra: Literature and Life in the Synagogue: Studies Presented to Ezra Fleischer*, eds S. Elizur, M. D. Herr, G. Shaked and A. Shinan (Hebrew; Jerusalem, 1994). See, in particular, his articles: 'On the beginnings of obligatory Jewish prayer', *Tarbiz*, 59 (1990), pp. 397–441; 'Inquiries concerning the triennial reading of the Torah in ancient Eretz-Israel', *HUCA* 62 (1991), Hebrew section, pp. 43–61; 'Rejoinder to Dr Reif's remarks', *Tarbiz*, 60 (1991), pp. 683–88; 'Annual and triennial reading of the Bible in the Old Synagogue', *Tarbiz*, 61 (1992), pp. 25–43; 'The *Shemone Esre* – its character, internal order, contents and goals', *Tarbiz*, 62 (1993), pp. 179–223; and 'Le-sidrey ha-tefillah be-vet ha-kenesset', *Asufot* 7 (1993), pp. 217–60.

23 E. Fleischer, *Eretz-Israel Prayer and Prayer Rituals as Portrayed in the Geniza Documents* (Hebrew; Jerusalem, 1988).

24 T. Groner, 'The concluding blessing of the confessional prayer' (in Hebrew), *BIA* 13 (1976), pp. 158–68; L. A. Hoffman, *The Canonization of the Synagogue Service* (Notre Dame and London, 1979).

25 P. Fenton (= Yosef Yinnon), 'Tefillah be'ad ha-rashut u-reshut be'ad ha-tefillah', *Mimizraḥ Umi-Ma'arav*, 4 (1984), pp. 7–21; *The Treatise of the Pool* (London, 1981); S. C. Reif, 'Liturgical difficulties and Genizah manuscripts', in *Studies in Judaism and Islam Presented to Shelomo Dov Goitein*, eds S. Morag, I. Ben-Ami and N. A. Stillman (Jerusalem, 1981), pp. 99–122, reproduced in an updated form as chapter 15 of this volume, and 'Festive titles in liturgical terminology' (in Hebrew) in *Proceedings of the Ninth World Congress of Jewish Studies 1985* (Jerusalem: World Union of Jewish Studies, 1986), Division C, pp. 63–70.

relevant research has been the creation of a new and better understanding of historical developments. What the Genizah has revealed may be summarized in two paragraphs.

Firstly, there are novel or otherwise unknown benedictions that were subsequently forgotten or rejected for halakhic reasons, such as those used in connection with recitations of the *shema'*, collections of Psalms, the Yom Kippur confession, and the second chapter of the mishnaic tractate *Shabbat*; and with the kindling of lights at the onset of the sabbath, and the washing of the hands (three versions) during the *seder* of the first eve of Passover. Scholarly research has been enriched by previously unknown texts of the *qaddish*; the *'amidah* for weekdays, sabbaths and festivals; the morning benedictions and the grace after meals (including the sections beginning *ha-rahaman*); and the references to special days in the body of standard sabbath and festival prayers. There have also been indications of a more extensive usage of Psalms and other biblical verses; novel ceremonials associated with the use of the Torah scroll in the synagogue; a variety of pentateuchal and prophetic lectionaries; and the honorific mention of living personalities in the prayers.

Furthermore, the inclusion of the Ten Commandments and of the Song at the Sea as integral parts of the liturgy, and of mystical and messianic expansions to the *qedushah*, *shema'*, *qiddush*, *havdalah*, and Passover Haggadah, have been newly identified. It has, in addition, been possible to trace the influence of what were clearly the two major rites, that is, those of Eretz Israel and Babylon, on the formation of all later prayer texts, as well as the success that each had in leaving traces of its customs on the traditions and preferences of the other. The use of Hebrew, Aramaic and Judeo-Arabic has been noted not only in prayers and liturgical poems that had traditionally been expressed in one or other of these particular languages but also in other contexts where the expected language is somewhat surprisingly replaced by one of the others. The data uncovered has testified to the wide dissemination of liturgical poems, their success in winning an honoured place in the synagogal worship, and their remarkable degree of influence on the content and formulation of the standard prayers.[26]

26 Examples of all these liturgical phenomena may be found throughout the publications cited in the footnotes of this chapter. See also S. C. Reif, *Judaism and Hebrew Prayer: New Perspectives on Jewish Liturgical History* (Cambridge, 1993), pp. 143–45 and M. Margaliot, *Hilkhot Ereṣ Yisra'el Min Ha-Genizah*, ed. I. Ta-Shma (Jerusalem, 1973), pp. 127–52.

Steinschneider

Earlier in this chapter, note was taken of the pioneering efforts made in the late nineteenth and early twentieth centuries by such scholars as Neubauer, Büchler and Schechter in the realm of the critical and historical study of Jewish liturgy, especially on the basis of fresh manuscript evidence. Before moving on to detailed summaries of more recent research based on the Genizah discoveries, it will perhaps be instructive to take account of the views of one of the major figures who preceded these rabbinic specialists and whose scholarly assessments appear to have become more, and not less, relevant and accurate in the light of recent studies. It is well recognized that there are numerous areas of scientific Jewish studies (*Wissenschaft des Judentums*) in which Moritz Steinschneider excelled and to which he made seminal scholarly contributions. Although there is no denying that, in his view, Judaism had died and that such studies constituted a valid means of according it a decent burial, it is equally true that his pessimistic educational philosophy did not prevent him from completing many essential works of reference – perhaps it even inspired him to undertake them before it was (to his mind) too late![27] In his analysis of Jewish literary history he demonstrated an astonishing depth and breadth of knowledge of Jewish books and authors, as well as recording some outstanding insights into the nature and the development of particular areas of literature.[28] In the present context it will be interesting to cite three statements of his with regard to liturgical history (in the now quaint-sounding English translation of the Victorian period):

> 1. Since we have found in the literature of the Halacha and Haggada an expression of all the intellectual interests of life, we shall not expect prayer to have been an isolated development. And, in fact, the whole liturgical literature of the Jews stands in the closest connexion with the development of the Midrash, and particularly with the earlier period of its foundation, in which the Jewish prayers assumed their peculiar character. For the usual Jewish prayer-book consists of elements belonging to a period of 1000 years, and offers to criticism a field of greater difficulties than the

---

27 This view is cited in D. Biale, *Gershom Scholem: Kabbala and Counter-History* (Cambridge, Mass., 1979), pp. 1 and 227, since it was apparently Scholem who made Steinschneider's remark so well known.

28 The original German version of his study of Jewish literature appeared in J. S. Ersch and J. G. Gruber's *Allgemeine Encyclopädie der Wissenschaften und Künste* under the entry 'Jüdische Literatur' in volume 27 (Leipzig, 1850), pp. 382–84. The English version appeared under the title *Jewish Literature from the Eighth to the Eighteenth Century* (London, 1857) and a Hebrew translation entitled ספרות ישראל was produced by Tsvi (Henry) Malter and published in Warsaw in 1897.

Midrash, from the absence of all external criteria; while the accounts preserved in the Midrash, of prayers being composed by certain Rabbies [*sic*], must be received with caution, as the prayers now in use with the same beginnings have in many cases been enlarged. Moreover those Rabbies must not be considered as their authors, but merely as having handed them down.

2. At what time men began to pray at stated hours, and consequently to have a fixed ritual, when and how congregations first met for prayers and public worship elsewhere than at the Temple, and when the relation between *reciter of prayers* Cantor (חזן, שליח צבור) and congregation (קהל) was developed, are questions not yet satisfactorily determined; nor has it even been asked, whether the ancient prayers were propagated orally, or written down by their composers!

3. This, with the old variations, now extant, and also the argumentum e silentio, that in the Talmud nothing upon liturgical writings occurs, makes it more probable, that the older prayers were not circulated among the people in writing. By their spreading from the centre or authority, by the gradual interpolations of individual doctors and reciters, by the tendency to arrange and settle things constantly evinced by the Halacha (as the object of which certain prayers were now considered), by the continual increasing care in retaining that which was once produced, by the growing respect for learned writers and the need of a uniform public worship, and by a combination of all these causes, the dissemination of written prayers must have gradually advanced.[29]

In the view of Steinschneider, then, there were close connections between the evolution of rabbinic prayer and the overall development of wider rabbinic literature. He argued that much remained to be done in the critical study of the time and place of the earliest rabbinic prayers, and of the specific roles of the individual, the congregation and the scribe in the transmission of text versions. His understanding was that the commitment to writing increased in the context of the rabbinic leaders' interest in strengthening throughout the diaspora the authority of halakhah and its dispensers, in ensuring the preservation of their religious traditions, and in standardizing the nature of Jewish public worship. Over 155 years may have passed since Steinschneider expressed these views but it is remarkable to what degree they sound contemporary, insightful and relevant in the context of current research.

My liturgy book

Since it is indeed some specific items of research, published since 1990, that form the focal point of the second part of this chapter, it will

---

29   These citations are from pp. 54, 55–56 and 58 of the English edition.

perhaps be helpful to begin by summarizing what was covered in the volume that I published some twelve years ago and that was based on work done until the early 1990s. In that attempt to provide a fresh scientific overview of Jewish liturgical history, three chapters were devoted to what may with some degree of justification be called the Jewish medieval period in that it comes between the talmudic age and the past three centuries of modernity. In covering the millennium that ranged from the seventh to the seventeenth century, the volume dealt with a number of central topics. Firstly, it traced the process by which there emerged a formal, authoritative liturgy that was committed to writing and attempted to explain such a development by reference to the influences of political centralization, the challenges of other religious groups, and the standardization of Jewish religious law. It was argued that the emergence of the synagogue at the centre of Jewish religious life and the adoption of the codex for transmitting rabbinic traditions played central roles in the developments of the geonic age.[30] The next chapter moved on to what are often referred to as the 'high middle ages' and traced the manner in which the Babylonian rite had a major influence on the prayer-books of later communities while that of the Palestinian homeland left only remnants of its traditions. As the newer centres became stronger and more independent, they opted for their own liturgical expression and there emerged a host of textual variations between and within the oriental and occidental communities. Leading scholars and major works focused on the text, obligation and meaning of prayer and the bound prayer-book greatly extended its content from simple text to compendious, synagogal and communal coverage.[31]

In the remainder of the study it emerged that the major themes of the immediate pre-modern centuries were demographical change, the revolution of printing and the growth of mysticism. The self-assured and cultured Jews of Spain came to dominate the forms of worship in the synagogues of their new homelands and the wide availability of printed editions had a democratizing effect on the evolution of texts. The mystical trends of Egypt, Franco-Germany and Spain reached their peak in Safed and no longer had to enter the prayer-book by the back door. Introductory and concluding sets of prayers increased in number while internal and external censorship forced textual amendments. As more systematic thought was given to the ramifications of communal prayer, so the claims of theology, grammar, women, non-Jews and departed relatives competed for liturgical attention, thus laying the

30   Reif, *Hebrew Prayer* (see n. 26 above), pp. 122–52.
31   Reif, *Hebrew Prayer* (see n. 26 above), pp. 153–206.

foundations of more revolutionary developments in the subsequent period of political emancipation.[32]

Wieder as trail-blazer

In many ways, the most important publication of the past fifteen years in the field of Jewish liturgy was a collection of studies that were originally written in the course of the previous half-century. Naphtali Wieder's researches into the text of the prayer-book began during the Second World War when he was one of the remarkable band of scholarly refugees from central Europe who took up residence in Oxford and brought a refreshing input into academic Jewish studies in the United Kingdom. Wieder, a brilliant lecturer, an outstanding researcher and an inspired compiler of scholarly data, who taught at Jews' College and University College in London, and then at Bar-Ilan University in Israel, deciphered and closely analysed hundreds of Hebrew codices and Genizah fragments from many collections around the world and published numerous articles in periodicals and *Festschriften*, mostly in Hebrew.[33] An astonishing characteristic of his work is how often he was a trail-blazer in a field of Jewish studies whose insights and interpretations were neither widely noted nor adequately appreciated until many years later. He was the scholar who first drew detailed attention, in 1947, to the liturgical innovations proposed by Abraham Maimonides in thirteenth-century Cairo and pointed to the characteristics they had in common with the contemporaneous Sufi attitudes to worship. His *Judean Scrolls and Karaism*, which appeared in 1962, was the first balanced, historical and non-polemical attempt to trace the detailed parallels between these two Jewish sects, and for many years his liturgical studies quietly but convincingly set the tone for critical examination of Jewish prayer-texts from talmudic to modern times. He consistently overwhelmed the reader with extensive and intricate data, only moving slightly towards the presentation of a broader, historical overview in his later work. Either because of his reticence to address his scholarly publications to any more than a few leading specialists, or because what he was attempting to say was not yet fashionable (or was he perhaps simply

---

32   Reif, *Hebrew Prayer* (see n. 26 above), pp. 207–55.
33   Naphtali Wieder, *The Formation of Jewish Liturgy in the East and the West: A Collection of Essays* (Hebrew; 2 vols; Jerusalem, 1998).

not engaged in the correct institution?), it took many years for the remainder of the academic world to catch up with him.[34]

The appearance of two volumes of his collected articles rectified the situation and have undoubtedly made a major impact on the field. Although the texts of the previously published items were unfortunately reproduced photographically rather than reset, the author added new material and made fresh comments to many of these, as well as contributing five fresh studies. English articles were translated into Hebrew and important indexes were prepared by P. Zackbach but, sadly, there were no English summaries for the student less familiar with contemporary Hebrew. What immediately strikes the reader of the two volumes is the author's range of competence. Thoroughly convinced as he always was that proponents of *Wissenschaft des Judentums* should not be one-subject scholars but had to range widely across Hebrew and Jewish literature, he clearly demonstrated his own practical adherence to this philosophy by explaining talmudic, halakhic and mystical passages, annotating midrashic and poetic sources, commenting on Aramaic and Judeo-Arabic texts, and subjecting liturgical formulations to linguistic as well as historical analysis. It will be no surprise even for those less acquainted with his work to come across articles that reconstruct the history of prayers, readings and expressions such as *yismaḥ mosheh, kol nidrey,* the morning benedictions, *ba-meh madliqin, qeṣ, barukh hu u-varukh shemo,* and the widely forgotten blessings for virginity and wine.[35] What may attract greater attention, and perhaps a degree of astonishment, is the extent to which such a variety of factors led to adjustments in the wording of some daily prayers. Some Jews found that the numerical value of two uncomplimentary words in the *'alenu* prayer (להבל ולריק) was equivalent to that of the names of Jesus and Muhammad and this inevitably led many others to do their utmost to alter these, and also some other words in that prayer. An archaic formula used to draw the congregation's special attention to the next

---

34 See his volumes *Der Midrasch Echa Zuṭa: Übersetzung, Kommentierung und Vergleich mit Echa Rabbati* (Berlin, 1936); *Islamic Influences on the Jewish Worship* (Hebrew; Oxford, 1947; reproduced from what had originally appeared in *Melila* 2 (Manchester, 1946); and *The Judean Scrolls and Karaism* (London, 1962), recently reproduced from the first edition with the author's addenda, corrigenda and supplementary articles by the Ben-Zvi Institute (Jerusalem, 2005). Wieder's life, from his birth in Sziget, Hungary, in 1905 to his death in Jerusalem in 2001, is a remarkable scholarly tale which I tried to summarize in an English article 'A scholar's scholar: Naphtali Wieder, 1905–2001', *Le'ela* 51 (2001), pp. 67–78, and in a Hebrew version 'Professor Naphtali Wieder: rabbinic scholar, teacher and liturgical researcher', *Pe'amim* 96 (2003), pp. 163–75.

35 Wieder, *Formation of Jewish Liturgy* (see n. 33 above), pp. 295–322, 368–90, 199–218, 323–51, 492–501, 259–80, 619–21 and 234–41.

part of the service was the dramatic use of the word הקול in the sense of
'hearken!' but once the original meaning and context became unclear it
was amended to הכול and differently understood. The problematic and
unattested expression בני מרון in the Mishnah *Rosh Ha-Shanah* 1.2 and in
the *musaf 'amidah* repetition on New Year is simply a corruption of the
single Greek word *noumeron* (Latin *numerus*), in the sense of 'a column
of soldiers'. There are a number of early liturgical manuscripts that
testify to the old pronunciation preserved in the word that appears as
rabbouni in Mark 10:51 and John 20:16.[36] If the word חבר was widely
perceived to refer to a distinguished scholarly leader, the phrase חברים
כל ישראל became problematic since it was manifestly untrue, and
alternative phraseology had to be substituted. The European Jews were
familiar with so many languages in which an expression very similar to
the Hebrew *fi* was crude and offensive that they felt obliged to
eliminate it from the prayers, and indeed from masoretic texts, and
replace it with the forms *feh* and *piy*, even if the context made such
forms grammatically inappropriate. The enigmatic liturgical use of the
word הוא may still convey a meaning that it already had in the Qumran
scrolls, namely, that of a divine epithet.[37]

Also important for the development of Jewish liturgical study are
the general trends that Wieder convincingly identified throughout his
liturgical researches. Versions that are widely characterized as
Palestinian may sometimes appear in what are undoubtedly
Babylonian texts and historical developments should therefore not be
oversimplified. The logic, order and clarity of the prayers came to have
major significance and any item that did not meet what were regarded
as the required standards was subject to adjustment or replacement.
When a rabbinic reticence to use biblical verses was overcome and they
were used in the liturgy, the sense presupposed is not uncommonly to
be found in the interpretations given to them in the standard talmudic-
midrashic sources. While Sa'adya Gaon constructed his prayer-book on
the basis of contextual and philosophical considerations, the
amendments made to it by his successors were often motivated by a
desire to make it more user-friendly and liturgically convenient. The
rabbinic use of Psalms selections is at times parallel to Karaite and

---

36 Wieder, *Formation of Jewish Liturgy* (see n. 33 above), pp. 453–68, 181–84, 440–47 and
    502–6.
37 Wieder, *Formation of Jewish Liturgy* (see n. 33 above), pp. 141–54, 469–91 and 395–439.
    It is interesting to note that the well-documented reading *benoumeron* for *bney maron*
    appears to have become a theological issue in contemporary Jerusalem with a
    conservative rabbi, David Golinkin, arguing the emendation and an orthodox one,
    Dovid Kamenetsky, defending the standard printed version; see the former's article
    'Solving a mahzor mystery' in the *Jerusalem Post* of 7 October 2005 and the latter's
    letter of response in the issue of 16 October 2005.

Christian custom and changes attributed to the kabbalists of Safed may be identified in earlier literature, albeit with different rationalization.[38] Early texts such as those from the Genizah should not be lightly dismissed as erroneous but may provide the only remaining testimony to a long-forgotten liturgical practice. Wieder also contributed in the region of a hundred additional texts to the reconstruction of Sa'adya's *siddur* and its transmission and carefully pointed out those instances in which he called into question liturgical theories proposed by A. Mirski, A. M. Habermann, E. Fleischer, I. Ta-Shma and M. Bar-Ilan.[39] In sum, what Wieder convincingly demonstrated is that there is hardly a word, a phrase or a paragraph in the medieval Hebrew prayer-book for which the assiduous researcher cannot uncover a dynamic and controversial history.

In a conference held in Denver in 1998 and devoted to Jewish and Islamic liturgy, Shalom Goldman devoted his presentation to Wieder's Hebrew monograph on *Islamic Influences on the Jewish Worship*. He argued that the work displayed remarkable erudition, was rich in primary rabbinic sources, and contained copious and provocative notes. He regretted that Wieder's description and analysis of Abraham Maimonides's liturgical innovations and the relevant Judeo-Arabic texts had not received the attention they deserved.[40] In fact, Wieder's monograph has now re-appeared in the new volume of his collected essays and Mordechai Friedman has made considerable progress in preparing a study of the liturgical controversies between the son of Maimonides and his contemporaries. That study has to date taken the form of various scholarly articles which deserve summary and assessment in the present context.

Battle against Palestinian Jewry's prayer-book

Friedman has expanded the earlier Genizah researches of such scholars as Jacob Mann and Ezra Fleischer and impressively clarified the history of the liturgical controversies between the Palestinian and Babylonian

---

38 Wieder, *Formation of Jewish Liturgy* (see n. 33 above), pp. 561–621 and 352–57.

39 Wieder, *Formation of Jewish Liturgy* (see n. 33 above), pp. 561–658; 52 and 361; 393–94, 441 and 521; 179, 274, 287, 289 and 646–67; 613; and 764–66.

40 S. Goldman, 'An appraisal of Naphtali Wieder's *Islamic Influences on Jewish Worship* on the fiftieth anniversary of its publication', *Medieval Encounters* 5/1 (1999), pp. 11–16. That issue of *Medieval Encounters* consists of nine of the papers delivered at the conference devoted to '*Avoda* and '*Ibada*: Ritual and Liturgy in Islamic and Judaic Traditions' arranged by Seth Ward at the University of Denver, Colorado, in March, 1998. See also Y. T. Langermann, 'From private devotion to communal prayer: new light on Abraham Maimonides' synagogue reforms', *Ginzei Qedem: Genizah Research Annual* 1 (2005), pp. 31–49.

communities.[41] There were undoubtedly Palestinian liturgical practices, still in existence in the Middle Ages and relating for example to the synagogal lectionaries, that had had their origins in the age of the *tanna'im*. As the authority of the Babylonian Talmud grew during the amoraic and geonic periods and the associated application of its religious law and ritual took increasingly greater hold on the wider communities of the Near East and the Mediterranean area, attempts were made to force these practices followed in the homeland to come into line with the views of the diaspora majority. One of the most famous and powerful examples of attacks on the Palestinian rites was that of the Babylonian scholar Pirqoi ben Baboi of the eighth and ninth centuries. He not only objected to the alternative cycles of pentateuchal and prophetic lectionaries and the inclusion of benedictions, petitions, mystical texts and poetry but also noted how the Babylonians had had to convince the Palestinians to recite a daily *qedushah*, and expressed his opposition to their reading the Torah at the afternoon service of a festival, as well as of the regular sabbath. The synagogue of the Palestinian Jews in Fustat, which, according to Friedman, may well have been built as early as the beginning of the seventh century, before the rise of Islam, was one of the havens of the 'western' customs and it is possible that early in its existence it had developed a compromise custom whereby its congregants read from their texts according to the Babylonian cycle but listened to a communal reading from a scroll that adhered to their own ancient practice.

By the beginning of the thirteenth century, most of the Palestinian communities and their customs had disappeared and the emigrés in the Ben Ezra synagogue in Fustat were left alone to carry the banner of their traditions and to defend them against growing opposition. Conscious as they were of the responsibility, they drew up a kind of 'trust deed' in 1211 which summarized their liturgical formulations and synagogal customs, including the special roles of the Torah scroll and the reading of the Song of the Sea (Exodus 15) and the Ten Commandments (Exodus 20), as well as the more extensive use of liturgical poems and biblical verses, and confirmed their adherence to these. No sooner had they done so than one of their number addressed an enquiry to one of the leading halakhic authorities (*rosh ha-seder*) in

---

41   Mann touched on the subject in his volumes *The Jews in Egypt and in Palestine under the Fatimid Caliphs* (2 vols; Oxford, 1920–22; reprinted in one volume with preface and reader's guide by S. D. Goitein, New York, 1970) and *Texts and Studies in Jewish History and Literature* (2 vols; Cincinnati and Philadelphia, 1931–35; and the reprint of Philadelphia-New York, 1991, with Gershon Cohen's important essay on 'The reconstruction of gaonic history'), while Fleischer dealt with it in some detail in his *Eretz-Israel* (see n. 23 above); see Friedman (n. 45 below) for further details.

Egypt who had emigrated there from Iraq, R. Joseph ben Jacob. In his missive, he argued the importance of adhering to their traditional ways in the face of pressure to change, claiming earlier acceptance of these by non-Palestinian rabbinic luminaries, and questioning the standing of any other rabbinic court to dictate otherwise. There is little doubt that he hoped for a formal ratification of his community's intention of continuing what many had come to regard as its heterodoxical ways and equally little doubt that Joseph's responsum was designed to disappoint such an expectation and to demonstrate a total unwillingness to brook any departure from the established Babylonian, now virtually universal, practice. While Maimonides had defined the Palestinian customs as erroneous, he had recognized the strength of their communal adherence to these. He had unsuccessfully attempted to put a stop to the triennial cycle of lectionaries and had reluctantly declined to stir up further controversy by ruling further against the rites of the Jews from the Holy Land. Joseph ben Jacob was considerably less tolerant of deviations from what he regarded as the norm and, adopting or perhaps continuing the maximalist position of Pirqoi, he defined such deviation as nothing less than heresy. This approach was virtually identical to that of his contemporary, Abraham b. Moses, the only son of Maimonides himself.[42]

Sufi Rabbi

Friedman has also added to the research of Wieder, Goitein and Fenton in the matter of the role of Abraham b. Moses as leader of the Cairo community on the one hand and of the Jewish Sufi-like mystics on the other.[43] Abraham's ambition, like that of both R. Joseph ben Jacob and R. Yeḥiel ben Eliaqim was to eliminate the Palestinian liturgical customs from the Cairene community but part of his agenda was also to force the adoption of pietistic customs in the synagogue not as an option but as a religious requirement. He saw the standardization of prayer-texts, lectionaries and synagogal customs as well as the wider use of ritual ablution, of kneeling and of prostration as vital to the

---

42   M. A. Friedman, 'Opposition to Palestinian prayer and prayer rituals as portrayed in responsa found in the Geniza (from the responsa of R. Joseph Rosh Ha-Seder)' in *Knesset Ezra* (see n. 22 above), pp. 69–102.

43   N. Wieder, *Islamic Influences* (see n. 34 above); S. D. Goitein, 'Abraham Maimonides and his pietist circle' in *Jewish Medieval and Renaissance Studies*, ed. A. Altmann (Cambridge, Mass., 1967), pp. 145–64 and his earlier Hebrew version of the paper in *Tarbiz* 33 (1963), pp. 181–97; P. B. Fenton, 'A mystical treatise on prayer and the spiritual quest from the pietist circle', *Jerusalem Studies in Arabic and Islam* 16 (1993), pp. 137–75. See also the article of Langermann (see n. 40 above) which argues for some earlier individual use of prostration in the Spanish Jewish community.

improvement of the spiritual experience during prayer and as practices that should be adopted by all congregants because they had originally been part of standard Jewish observance, subsequently preserved only by the Muslims. He himself was convinced that he had won a major victory against the 'Jerusalemites' by unifying the customs of the Babylonian and Palestinian Jews in the early period of his authority and took pride in the fact that he had achieved more in this respect than his great father, who had been unable to overcome the powerful opposition of R. Sar-Shalom (Zuta) Ha-Levi ben Moses, the Palestinian leader.

Various Genizah documents do, however, reveal that the war of words between him and his opponents continued from the time of his father's demise in 1204 virtually until his own death in 1237. Initially, the practice of referring to the leader of the Jewish community in parts of the synagogal liturgy (reshut), as well as in official documents, as an expression of allegiance, had to be abandoned by the leadership because of objections to Abraham's authority and ideology and it took almost a decade before he was able to re-assert this right for himself. Only by taking such action could the leadership forestall the creation of additional synagogues that would regard themselves as independent of the communal leadership. His opponents saw Abraham's pietistic campaign not as a defence of tradition but as a radically novel religiosity bent on mimicking Sufi practice and his rejection of Palestinian practice as an attempt to destroy well-established and authentic rituals. So incensed and desperate were they that on more than one occasion they appealed to the Muslim authorities to rule that his modes of worship were unconscionably innovative. He, for his part, was so convinced of the rectitude of his arguments that he found support for them in tannaitic sources. According to his interpretation of a passage in the Tosefta,[44] there was already then an established custom uniformly to kneel in rows facing the ark where the scrolls were kept and to conduct all the prayers in the direction of Jerusalem.[45]

Recent Genizah research has demonstrated that a Hebrew responsum written by R. Yeḥiel ben Eliaqim, and previously discussed by Abrahams and by Mann, was penned in 1211 and related to the controversy between Abraham Maimonides and his opponents about the use of the reshut as an acknowledgement of the authority of .

---

44 Tosefta, *Megillah* 3(4).21 (ed. S. Lieberman, p. 360, ll. 77ff).
45 M. A. Friedman, '"A controversy for the sake of heaven": studies in the liturgical polemics of Abraham Maimonides and his contemporaries' in *Te'uda* 10, ed. M. A. Friedman (Tel Aviv, 1996), pp. 245–98.

Maimonides's son.[46] It turns out that R. Yeḥiel was not from Aleppo but from Byzantium or Christian Europe and that he was active in Fustat from 1211 until at least 1238. His responsum was composed in reply to a request for guidance from the supporters of Abraham M. who thought that the newly arrived scholar might be willing to speak out against the earlier removal of the *reshut*. The favourable and unequivocal response that they received was inspired by the developments of the previous six years and reflected the increased success and growing power of Abraham M.. It contributed to the re-introduction of the *reshut* and the consequent recognition of Abraham's authority in acts of communal worship, as well as in formal documentation.[47]

During the thirty-year period in which Abraham held the leadership of the Cairo community, those loyal to the Palestinian traditions in the Ben Ezra synagogue fought hard against his attempts to change communal worship by eliminating their customs and introducing pietistic rituals. It would appear that a Genizah letter addressed to the court physician, Samuel ben Solomon Ha-Levi, entreating him to intervene with the Sultan in defence of these traditions, was drafted in response to the pro-Abraham offensives of 1211, including the attack of R. Joseph ben Jacob on the extensive use of liturgical poetry by the Palestinians. The subject of the letter and the type of request make this identification a plausible one and it fits neatly with other developments known from the Genizah. While Maimonides had been prepared to tolerate liturgical poems for the sake of avoiding communal controversy, he recited his prayers in his own study-centre where they could be avoided. His son and his supporters took a firmer line and demonstrated in their rulings a determination to rid the synagogue of liturgy that they regarded as a departure from the halakhically authorized formulations and a distraction from the required concentration. Those anxious to enlist the support of the Muslim court against such an approach claimed that those promoting it lacked integrity and probity and were set on depriving them of a synagogal activity that was of major cultural and aesthetic importance and constituted one of the few spiritual pleasures left to them.[48]

---

46   I. Abrahams, 'A formula and a responsum' in *Jews' College Jubilee Volume*, ed. I. Harris (London, 1906), pp. 101–8; J. Mann, *The Jews* (see n. 41 above), 1.237–41 and 267, and 2.301–5.

47   M. A. Friedman, 'R. Yeḥiel b. Elyakim's responsum permitting the *reshut*' in *Mas'at Moshe: Studies in Jewish and Islamic Culture Presented to Moshe Gil*, eds E. Fleischer, M. A. Friedman and J. A. Kraemer (Hebrew; Jerusalem and Tel Aviv, 1998), pp. 328–67.

48   M. A. Friedman, 'A bitter protest about elimination of *piyyuṭim* from the service: a request to appeal to the Sultan', *Pe'amim* 78 (1999), pp. 128–47; see G. Khan, *Arabic*

It should also be noted that Gerald Blidstein's examination of the
halakhic work of Abraham M. has revealed the degree to which he was
conscious of the competing claims on him as an individual pietist on
the one hand and as a communal leader on the other. Attempting a
balance of the theological and the practical sides of his commitments,
and seeing this as a continuation of his father's similar efforts, he
argued for a reciprocal relationship between the individual and the
community. He claimed that his quarrel with those who were opposed
to his elitist spiritualism was not with the broader community but with
some of its specific leaders.[49]

Circumambulating the Temple site

Some comments on research developments in another area of ritual
devotion are now in order. While it had already been appreciated that
saints, tombs and holy places had played an important liturgical role in
Judaism, Christianity and Islam, particularly in the area of pilgrimage
and more popular religion, there was some suspicion that references to
the dead in acts of worship had their origins in Christian circles.[50] The
recent researches of Josef Meri have, however, demonstrated more
clearly the extent to which veneration of relics, of the dead and of holy
books was also a major element in Muslim and Jewish spirituality. The
object was to achieve blessing and intercession for the worshipper and
the ritual included the recitation of verses and prayers,
circumambulation of the site, and the use of water and earth from the
sacred source. Some activities at the Ka'ba were already characteristic
of pilgrimage to Mecca at least from, if not earlier than, the time of
Muhammad. Unsurprisingly, the theologians were not always
enamoured of this form of religiosity and there are known objections
on the Muslim side from Ibn Taymiya in the thirteenth century, on the
Karaite side from Sahl ben Maṣliaḥ in the tenth century, and on the
rabbinic side from the Ge'onim Nissim, Sherira and Hai.[51] It therefore
emerges that the concern with the dead in Ashkenazi liturgical practice
from about the eleventh century may have had earlier oriental
precedents, even if some of the more immediate inspiration was
derived from local Christian custom. As far as liturgical rituals at holy

---

Legal and Administrative Documents in the Cambridge Genizah Collections (Cambridge,
   1993), nos. 65-66, pp. 291–94.
49 G. (Y.) Blidstein, 'The congregation and public prayer in the writings of Rabbi
   Abraham, the son of Maimonides', Pe'amim 78 (1999), pp. 148–63.
50 Reif, Hebrew Prayer (see n. 26 above), pp. 218–20.
51 Josef W. Meri, 'Aspects of baraka (blessings) and ritual devotion among medieval
   Muslims and Jews', Medieval Encounters 5/1 (1999), pp. 46–69 (see n. 40 above).

sites are concerned, current studies of medieval Rabbanite and Karaite custom vis-à-vis pilgrimage to Jerusalem attest to an additional manifestation of the role of the holy place in popular worship.

Two of these studies, by Ezra Fleischer and Haggai Ben-Shammai, deserve closer attention. That the Genizah texts reveal the special prayers and biblical verses recited by pilgrims on their visits to Jerusalem was already noted by Jacob Mann and more recent research has been done on the subject by Mordecai Margaliot, Elhanan Reiner and Moshe Gil.[52] Ezra Fleischer has now closely examined some ten Genizah fragments, eight of them from Cambridge, and added substantial detail to our knowledge of the ceremony and the recitations that accompanied each part of the approach to the Holy City, the circumambulation of its walls, and the final arrival at the Temple Mount.[53] It is not yet clear where each of the gates mentioned in the Genizah texts was actually located but it can be postulated with some confidence that the custom of adding to the spiritual dimension of a visit to Jerusalem by such liturgical activities, formally entitled in Judeo-Arabic ṣlw't 'l'bw'b 'lqwds (='Prayers at the Gates of Jerusalem'), was already well established by the time of the Crusader invasion at the end of the eleventh century. Although there are some minor inconsistencies in the data provided in each of the fragments, an overall picture emerges and permits a number of important conclusions. The twenty names actually refer to the ten gates of the city (rather than the Temple Mount) and the Jewish quarter was at that time to the south of the Temple Mount, between the Temple wall and the southern city wall. The ritual may be traced in both Rabbanite and Karaite circles, and it would appear that it was the 'Mourners of Zion' who instituted the practice. The biblical verses recited at each gate were chosen to match its name and the special prayers and supplications were added to these verses only at the first and last 'stations'. Some of these were known from other liturgical contexts and took the form of benedictions and poetic items were also used, in one case borrowed from the mystical *hekhalot* texts.[54]

---

52 J. Mann, *Texts* (see n. 41 above), 1.459; M. Margaliot, *Hilkhot 'Ereṣ Yisra'el Min Ha-Genizah*, ed. I. Ta-Shma (Jerusalem, 1973), pp. 138–41; E. Reiner, 'Concerning the Priest Gate and its location', *Tarbiz* 56 (1987), pp. 279–90; and M. Gil, *Palestine during the First Muslim Period (634–1099)* (Hebrew; 3 vols, Tel Aviv, 1983), 1.519–33.

53 The Genizah fragments are T-S K27.2, NS 265.13, H10.278, H11.72, NS 315.276–77, NS 154.46, NS 195.23, NS 208.73 at Cambridge University Library; Adler 2893, f. 2b at the Jewish Theological Seminary of America in New York; and Heb.f.100.35–36 at the Bodleian Library in Oxford.

54 E. Fleischer, 'Pilgrims' prayer at the gates of Jerusalem' in *Mas'at Moshe* (see n. 47 above), pp. 298–327.

Ben-Shammai's study is concerned with a Karaite manifestation of such a ritual. He deals with a manuscript that has preserved a large fragment of the *Book of Concealment* (*Kitab al-tawriya*) by the Karaite author Yeshu'ah ben Judah (hitherto not attested in specific text) dealing with the interpretation of difficult pentateuchal expressions.[55] The colophon is dated 1046 and is followed by a lamentation on the destruction of Jerusalem and the Temple which is remarkable not only for its language and content but also for what it reveals more generally about the period and the ambience in which it was composed. Its few lines have much to tell us about the ceremonies of the 'Mourners of Zion' in Jerusalem during the eleventh century. Locals and pilgrims participated in ceremonies in the course of which they recited the book of Lamentations and other poems that bemoaned the loss of Jerusalem and the Temple and expressed sorrow about their current state. They walked around the walls of the city reciting biblical passages and prayers at particular sites and such leaders and scholars as Yeshu'ah ben Judah, who apparently composed this lamentation, were among the participants in this moving mourning ritual.[56]

Tensions between custom and halakhah

Although the close study of medieval halakhic and liturgical texts currently being done by scholars in North America does not generally match its equivalent in Israel, a recent volume is an exception to this rule and undoubtedly constitutes a helpful contribution to our understanding of the development of the Hebrew prayer-book in the Middle Ages. Although based on her doctoral dissertation, commenced with the late and lamented Jacob Petuchowski, Ruth Langer's study is of a higher standard than many such efforts produced for such a purpose.[57] In addition to defining how the talmudic authorities justified their replacement of the Temple worship with the adoption of regular prayers for daily, sabbath and festival use, and tracing some of the ramifications of Jewish liturgical controversy in the modern world, the body of her work is concerned with the tensions created in the geonic and medieval periods between those who wished to follow a narrow

---

55 The manuscript is Firkovich II Evr.-Ar. I 4816 in the Russian National Library in St Petersburg.
56 H. Ben-Shammai, 'A unique lamentation on Jerusalem by the Karaite author Yeshu'a ben Judah', in *Mas'at Moshe* (see n. 47 above), pp. 93–102.
57 R. Langer, *To Worship God Properly: Tensions between Liturgical Custom and Halakhah in Judaism* (Cincinnati, 1998). She has also written an important critique of the views of E. Fleischer in *Prooftexts* 19 (1999), pp. 179–204 but that is concerned with the earlier rabbinic liturgy rather than with its medieval development.

interpretation of talmudic principles in the area of prayer texts with
those who accorded at least equal authority to established custom and
practice. She exemplifies these tensions by dealing with the three major
issues of a) the halakhic status of non-talmudic benedictions such as
those for the tokens of virginity and for the priest to recite at the
redemption of the first born child; b) the acceptability of the insertion of
piyyuṭim (liturgical poems) into the body of the standard prayers as
well as around them; and c) the individual recitation of the *qedushah*, in
the three contexts of the pre-*shema'* benedictions, the *'amidah*, and the
qedushah desidra after the *'amidah*. A great wealth of texts, from Genizah
fragments, codices and printed editions, are cited, translated and
annotated and although the general treatment is thematic, there is also
an accompanying analysis that pays close attention to the historical
development.

In a different context I have made a few critical comments in
connection with some definitions, presuppositions, translations and
omissions in Langer's treatment.[58] For our purposes here, we may
summarize some of her important conclusions that appear to me to be
perfectly acceptable interpretations of the evidence. There is
throughout the medieval period a tension between the acceptance of
established custom and the desire to standardize halakhic theory and
practice. This is also manifest when rabbinic authorities who are used
to prayers as they are recited in one centre being confronted with
alternative and, to their mind, questionable formulations preferred in
another. Decisions are made that are undoubtedly seen as halakhic but
they are reached under the influence of historical, geographical and
cultural considerations as well as what might be described as more
clinically legal ones. In Langer's words: 'Liturgical halakhah thus was
shaped not only by the historical circumstances of its great codifiers,
but also by changes in the cultural status of minhagim. These changes
altered the balance between the authority of the particular minhag and
the authority of the relevant halakhah.'[59] Substitute 'textual variants'
for 'minhagim' and the broader point is made. Tendencies in one centre
did not match those of another and even within major rites one has to
be aware of internal divergences. Responses to such difficulties varied
from the total acceptance or rejection of a tradition to various degrees
of compromise being made with it, sometimes in the form of amended
or conflated texts, other times in the form of an ideological, historical
or exegetical re-assessment. While the mystics left their mark on the
prayers at a number of junctures in liturgical history, there was always

---

58   See my review in *JSS* 46 (2001), pp. 344–47.
59   Langer, *Worship* (see n. 57 above), p. 251.

some ambivalence about whether the prayer of the ordinary individual should be on a par with that of the ascetic and what the textual ramifications would be of either decision.

Internal dynamic assessed

While it was common some twenty-five years ago to bemoan the limited extent of scholarly work on the medieval history of the Hebrew prayers, it must today be acknowledged that the range of recent work in the field has been such that it is impossible to do it justice within the limitations of a chapter such as this. All that may be done in these concluding remarks is to note the existence of other important work and leave closer assessment of it to another context. Those interested in a full bibliographical survey may take advantage of the excellent guidance provided by Joseph Tabory of Bar-Ilan University.[60] Robert Brody has explained Sa'adya's approach to liturgical innovation and has identified new material in his published descriptions of Rabbinica among the Cambridge Genizah material.[61] Meir Bar-Ilan has produced a monograph on mystical prayer[62] while a study by Yehezkel Luger has recorded the numerous texts of the various 'amidah benedictions according to the Palestinian rite.[63] Editions of the work of Shabbethai Sofer and Solomon ben Nathan of Sijilmasa,[64] as well as an English translation of Elbogen's classic, have appeared.[65] Collections of useful

---

60 See J. Tabory, *Jewish Prayer and the Yearly Cycle: A List of Articles*, supplement to *Kiryat Sefer* 64 (Jerusalem, 1992–93), and a substantial collection of addenda to that publication that appeared together with his facsimile edition of the Hanau prayer-book of 1628, eds J. Tabory and M. Rapeld (Ramat Gan, 1994). See also his bibliography 'A list of articles about synagogues' in the Hebrew section of *Kenishta: Studies of the Synagogue World* (Ramat Gan, 2001), pp. 63–147. Tabory has also surveyed the latest developments in the whole liturgical field in a Hebrew article entitled '*Tefillah*' in supplementary volume 3 of the *Encyclopaedia Hebraica* (Jerusalem and Tel Aviv, 1995), cols 1061–68 and in an English essay in *Prooftexts* 17.2 (1997), 115–32.

61 R. Brody, 'Saadya Gaon on the limits of liturgical flexibility' in *Genizah Research after Ninety Years*, eds J. Blau and S. C. Reif (Cambridge, 1992), pp. 40–46; *Hand-list of Rabbinica in the Cambridge Genizah Collections: The New Series* (Cambridge, 1998).

62 M. Bar-Ilan, *The Mysteries of Jewish Prayer and Hekhalot* (Hebrew; Ramat Gan, 1987).

63 Originally a doctoral dissertation (Bar-Ilan University, 2 vols, 1992), it was later published as Y. Luger, *The Weekday Amidah in the Cairo Genizah* (Hebrew; Jerusalem, 2001).

64 סדור המדקדק הגדול בקי בכל חדרי התורה מה"ר שבתי סופר ב"ר יצחק מפרעמישלא תלמיד הלבוש, יוצא לאור יצחקי דוד והרב סך יצחק הרב ידי על בלונדון הדין בית כ"י ע"פ, eds I. Satz and D. Yitschaki (Hebrew; 5 vols; Baltimore, 1987–2002); *Siddur R. Shelomo b. R. Natan*, edited and transcribed by S. Ḥagi (Jerusalem, 1995).

65 *Jewish Liturgy: A Comprehensive History by Ismar Elbogen*, ed. Raymond Scheindlin (Philadelphia, Jerusalem and New York, 1993).

essays have been published by the late J. J. Petuchowski[66] and by Israel Ta-Shma,[67] and edited by Joseph Tabory.[68] A series of volumes have been edited by Paul Bradshaw and Lawrence Hoffman,[69] a linguistic study of the Yemenite rite has been completed by Isaac Gluska[70] and Uri Ehrlich has published an interesting analysis of gesturing in Jewish prayer.[71] My own contribution has been by way of a number of essays in Hebrew and English publications, most of which are being reproduced in this volume.[72]

What Wieder points out in the cases of *kol nidrey* and *'alenu* could justifiably be applied to many others in the medieval history of the Hebrew prayer-book. In the first instance, he writes: 'The Babylonian *ge'onim* rejected it completely; the Karaites criticized it strongly; the halakhists of every generation persistently drew attention to the halakhic and ethical problems bound up in its recitation.'[73] In connection with the latter prayer, his comments include the following: 'One generation of substitute expressions gave way to another or both came to be used in conflated versions. New textual formulations were created as a result of the struggle and against a background of constant deletions and erasures.'[74] This assessment of the internal dynamic of medieval Hebrew prayer-texts is one that has undoubtedly been fortified by the scholarly researches of the past decade and a half.

66 J. J. Petuchowski, *Studies in Modern Theology and Prayer*, eds E. R. and A. M. Petuchowski (Philadelphia and Jerusalem, 1998).
67 I. M. Ta-Shma, *Early Franco-German Ritual and Custom* (Hebrew; Jerusalem, 1992); *Ritual, Custom and Reality in Franco-Germany, 1000–1350* (Hebrew; Jerusalem, 1996); *The Early Ashkenazic Prayer: Literary and Historical Aspects* (Hebrew; Jerusalem, 2003).
68 J. Tabory, *From Qumran to Cairo: Studies in the History of Prayer* (Hebrew and English; Jerusalem, 1999); *Kenishta* (see n. 60 above) and *Kenishta* 2 (Ramat Gan, 2003); see also his *Pesaḥ Dorot: Peraqim Be-Toledot Lel Ha-Seder* (Tel Aviv, 1996).
69 P. F. Bradshaw and L. A. Hoffman have edited six volumes in the series 'Two Liturgical Traditions' published by the University of Notre Dame Press from 1991 until 1999.
70 Isaac Gluska, *The Yemenite Weekday Prayer: Text and Language* (Hebrew; Jerusalem, 1995).
71 Uri Ehrlich, כל עצמותי תאמרנה (Jerusalem, 1999), published in English as *The Nonverbal Language of Prayer: A New Approach to Jewish Liturgy* (Tübingen, 2004).
72 See the details of the original places of publication given at the end of the preface to this volume.
73 Wieder, *Formation of Jewish Liturgy* (see n. 33 above), p. 368.
74 Wieder, *Formation of Jewish Liturgy* (see` n. 33 above), p. 466.

14

Solomon Luria's Prayer-book

Introduction

It is not an uncommon phenomenon for the greatness of a famous personality and the general value of his work to be widely, if somewhat uncritically acknowledged by scholars prior to the thorough and critical examinations that might establish the validity of such estimates on the basis of sound evidence. Such uncritical acknowledgement, originating in the respect bequeathed by tradition and fortified by the need for constant reference to the personality's writings and also perhaps by simple scholarly intuition, is certainly not to be underestimated; at the same time an up-to-date scientific study remains a desideratum. My remarks are well exemplified by the case of the famous talmudist and halakhic authority, Rabbi Solomon b. Yeḥiel Luria (c.1510–1574). Reference is often made to the outstanding contributions of this sixteenth-century scholar but no comprehensive, critical biography has yet been attempted. It will perhaps be helpful to note some of the general work that has been done to date on this personality before an attempt is made to describe a special contribution he made to the development of Jewish liturgy.

Bibliography

At the turn of the century Samuel Abba Horodezky took the first steps towards the composition of a biography but his essay was limited to a selection of interesting quotations and references from certain of Luria's works and made no attempt to place him in any meaningful historical, religious, or intellectual context.[1] Simon Hurwitz's *The Responsa of Solomon Luria* was never intended to be more than a loose translation, paraphrase and digest of the original, for popular rather than scholarly consumption.[2] Simcha Assaf added to the sum total of knowledge of Luria's life and work and essayed a brief evaluation but, as he himself wrote:

---

1   *Le-Qorot Ha-Rabbanut* (Warsaw, 1911), pp. 123–44.
2   Originally published in New York, 1938, it was reprinted by the Bloch Publishing Company there in 1969.

במאמר זה לא באתי אלא ...על המהש"ל לא נכתב עדיין המחקר הממצא והמקיף שהוא ראוי לו
³להוסיף משהו לתולדותיו ולתולדות ספריו.

More recently Hayyim Reuben Rabbinowitz summarized his life's
achievements in an article commemorating the four hundredth
anniversary of his death. He stressed his fearless disagreement with
major figures, criticism of the corruptions of the day and enthusiasm
for a return to the talmudic sources. The article also made reference to
his liturgical customs, knowledge of Sefardi traditions, preference for
accurate Hebrew and competence as a textual critic but none of the
findings are in any way novel, nor is any mention made of the existence
of a prayer-book composed by him.[4]

Liturgy

Luria's rabbinical activities certainly included involvement in a variety
of liturgical matters and all the available evidence in this field requires
to be collected and analysed as a contribution to the reconstruction of
his total personality. His responsum no. 64, which deals exclusively
with the prayer-book,[5] his editions of specific sections of liturgy and
liturgical poetry,[6] as well as his various comments on talmudic
passages that touch upon the general theme of prayer,[7] constitute part
of that evidence and, as such, will require attention. A less well known
effort of his in this field needs, however, to be brought to the attention
of the scholarly world in more than general terms. Luria's apparently
extensive commentary on the prayer-book, known to us only from its
quotation in the manuscript commentary of Shabbethai Sofer of
Przemysl, is a rich source yet to be effectively quarried for liturgical
scholarship and it is to this subject that the remainder of this article is
devoted. The manuscript once belonged to the London Beth Din and
Beth Hamidrash, where it was deposited by Chief Rabbi Solomon
Hirschel (1762–1842), but on the sale of that collection at auction in
New York it has passed into private hands.

---

3   'Mashehu le-toledot Maharshal' in Louis Ginzberg Jubilee Volume, Hebrew Section (New
    York, 1946), pp. 45–63.
4   'Ha-Maharshal – ha-gibbor shebahavurah', Hadorom 44 (1977), pp. 254–65.
5   His collected responsa, containing a number of relevance to liturgical matters (e.g.
    29, 44, 48, 63 and 86, as well as 64) first appeared in Lublin, 1574, and an English
    translation of no. 64 was published by B. Berliner, 'Rabbi Solomon Luria on the pray-
    er-book' in Jews' College Jubilee Volume, ed. I. Harris (London, 1906), pp. 123–39.
6   E.g. Zemirot published in Lublin 1596 and with Nathan Spira's Birkat Ha-Mazon in
    Venice 1603, and a tehinah published in Zevah Todah edited by Eleazar Perls
    Altschuler in Prague, 1615.
7   E.g. his Yam Shel Shelomoh (New York, 1959) on Yevamot, chapter 12, section 29, 62b,
    Bava Qamma, chapter 7, section 37, 71, and Hullin, chapter 1, sections 48–52, 10–11.

Work on Luria's prayer-book

Naturally, it was not until the discovery of Shabbethai's manuscript commentary on the Ashkenazi prayer-book that anything was known about Luria's equivalent work which, it turned out, was one of its most commonly quoted sources. Over a century and a half ago, Adolph Neubauer published that part of Shabbethai's 'General Introduction' (הקדמה הכללית) to his *siddur* that detailed his sources and contained the following note on Luria's prayer-book (I quote from the original manuscript rather than from Neubauer's version which contained a few minor but misleading errors):

גם את זה עשה האלדים והמציא לידי את הסדור שכתב לעצמו הגאון מהרש"ל. וכבר היה אותו הסדור
בירושלים תוב"ב ביד הגאון מהר"ר וישל זצ"ל כי הוא היה חתנו של מהרש"ל ז"ל ועתה הובא אותו
הסדור לידי ומצאתי בו דקדוקים וחדושים מאשר מצא הגאון זצ"ל בסדורים ישנים שהביא בדבריו
כגון סדורו של רש"י. ורמ"ח. ורא"ק. ור"י ברונא. ור' אביגדור קרא. והרבה כאלה הגאונים שהביא
הגאון מה שמצא בסדורים שלהם. ולפעמים כתב סתם ספרים מדוייקים אכתוב את כל אחד בשמו
במקומו אי"ה.

'Thanks to Divine providence I have obtained the prayer-book written for himself by the great scholar, Rabbi Solomon Luria. This prayer-book was previously in the possession of his son-in-law, the late, distinguished Rabbi Fischel, in Jerusalem, but it has now been brought here to me. In it I have found grammatical comments and novel explanations cited by Rabbi Luria from such old prayer-books as those of Rashi and Rabbis Moshe Ḥazzan, Abraham Klausner, Israel Bruna and Avigdor Qra. Many other such liturgical authorities are similarly quoted by Rabbi Luria. Sometimes he simply refers to 'accurate texts' and I shall, God willing, note each of these instances as it occurs.'[8]

David Kaufmann republished this passage, together with Neubauer's few errors of transcription,[9] and Abraham Berliner took the subject further by correcting some of these errors and publishing Shabbethai's 'General Introduction', in which a number of direct quotations are made from Luria's prayer-book.[10] Unfortunately, knowledge about Luria's prayer-book made no further progress following Berliner's work, and both Simcha Assaf[11] and Yizhak Raphael,[12] in articles on

---

8   *Israelietische Letterboode* 11 (1855–56), pp. 1–5. An edition of the whole of Shabbetai
     Sofer's prayer-book has now been published סדור המדקדק הגדול בקי בכל חדרי התורה מה"ר
     שבתי סופר ב"ר יצחק מפרעמישלא תלמיד הלבוש, יוצא לאור ע"פ כ"י בית הדין בלונדון על ידי הרב יצחק סץ
     יצחקי והרב דוד, eds I. Satz and D. Yitschaki (Hebrew; 5 vols, Baltimore, 1987–2002); the
     reference to Luria in the 'Special Introduction' is to be found there in 1.92–93.
9   *Ha-Asif* 5 (1899), pp. 125–29.
10   *Abhandlung über den Siddur des Schabtai ha-Sofer aus Przemysl* (Frankfurt am Main,
     1909).
11   See n. 3 above.

Luria, based their comments directly on his publication and the earlier work of Neubauer and Kaufmann. Assaf's list of quotations from Luria's prayer-book published by Berliner is indeed neither wholly accurate nor complete. For his part, Raphael makes the statement:

סידורו של מהרש"ל אבד והוא ידוע לנו מתוך המובאות ממנו בהקדמתו לסידורו של ר' שבתי הסופר
מפרמישלא (הוצאת אברהם ברלינר...).

He was apparently unaware that the actual commentary itself in Shabbethai's prayer-book is a much richer source for the reconstruction of Luria's prayer-book. Incidentally, it should also here be noted that the article on Luria in the *Encyclopaedia Judaica* mentions Luria's edition of sabbath *zemirot* but wrongly attributes to him a commentary on the grace after meals and makes no reference at all to his prayer-book or to any other liturgical matters.[13]

It was in the context of my work on Shabbethai Sofer of Przemysl that I first dealt with the Maharshal's contribution to the development of the Ashkenazi prayer-book. Both in my doctoral dissertation of 1969 and in my Cambridge University Press volume[14] I gave some attention to Solomon Luria as one of Shabbethai's major sources and inspirations.[15]

My research produced three main results concerning Luria's prayer-book i.e.

1. Like Shabbethai after him and the Maharil before him, Luria was one of a long line of 'correctors' (as it were) of liturgical Hebrew who preceded and to a large extent inspired the work of Heidenheim and Baer. They believed that there could be only one form of correct Hebrew, the standard Ben Asher Tiberian system finally adopted for the Bible; all remnants of variant systems were to be eliminated e.g. – *akh* for –*kha*, *hef'el* for *haf'el*, preformative *mem* with *segol* for *ḥiriq*, interchange of *qameṣ* and *pataḥ*, indication of *qameṣ qaṭan* by use of *waw*, and non-biblical vocabulary. Luria's famous attack on Isserles for his failure to write grammatical Hebrew was partly inspired by this campaign to establish biblically correct Hebrew in all aspects of

---

12 'Hanhagat Maharshal' in the *Sefer Yovel* for S. Federbush (Jerusalem, 1960), ed. J. L. Maimon (Fishman), pp. 316–29.

13 Volume 11, cols 579–82. The confusion apparently arises out of the fact that Luria's text and commentary on the *Zemirot* were published together with Nathan Spira's commentary on the grace (see n. 6 above).

14 *Edition of Shabbathai Sofer's Ms. Commentary on the Sabbath Services according to the Ashkenazi rite, with Introduction and Notes*, University of London, under the supervision of Professors Naphtali Wieder and Siegfried Stein. The manuscript was at that time no. 37 in the collection of the London Beth Din and Beth Hamidrash (henceforth LBD MS); *Shabbethai Sofer and his Prayer-book* (Cambridge, 1979).

15 See the references indexed under the entry 'Luria, Solomon b. Yeḥiel (Maharshal)' on p. 363 of the book.

Hebrew literature.[16] Modern linguistic research has shown the fallacious nature of the correctors' theory, while at the same time acknowledging its debt to them for having preserved many old variants, subsequently standardized out of existence.

2. In arriving at his conclusion, Luria made use of and cited a large number of liturgical manuscripts and editions, as well as halakhic, grammatical and masoretic works and demonstrated the same critical and independent, scholarly approach. Among the sources cited by him, and preserved for us by Shabbethai Sofer, were Abraham Klausner, Jacob Naqdan, Joseph Ḥazzan of Troyes, Jacob b. Moses Mollin, Meir b. Barukh of Rothenburg, Israel Bruna, Avigdor Qra and some forty other luminaries, of whom the most frequently quoted are Rashi, Eleazar b. Judah of Worms, Solomon b. Abraham ibn Parḥon, Simeon b. Ṣemaḥ Duran and the Qimḥi family.

3. About a quarter of the 423 quotations from Luria's prayer-book cited in Shabbethai's commentary were made available to scholars and a number of these were analysed, explained and set in the relevant scholarly context, whether linguistic, liturgical, halakhic, theological or social. Examples of such comments are Luria's preference for ואמרו אמן over ונאמר אמן at the end of prayers[17] and רוב מעשיהם over כל מעשיהם after the morning benedictions;[18] his animosity towards the recitation of שיר היחוד and similar 'hymns';[19] his rejection of הן הן as an error for הן הם [20] of

---

16   In his responsum no. 6 (see n. 5 above). On aspects of the cultural and historical backgrounds to Luria's work, see N. E. Shulman, *Authority and Community: Polish Jewry in the Sixteenth Century* (New York, 1986) and J. Elbaum, *Openness and Insularity: Late Sixteeth Century Literature in Poland and Ashkenaz* (Hebrew; Jerusalem, 1990).

17   LBD MS, f. 53v:
ואמרו: ובסדור מהרש"ל כתוב וז"ל ואמרו אמן יש צרפתים שאומרים ונאמר אמן בסיום תפלתם וטעות הוא בידם כי למלאכים התמידים אצלו הוא אומר ואמרו אמן ע"כ עכ"ל.
See Reif, *Shabbethai Sofer* (see n. 14 above), pp. 288–89; eds I. Satz and D. Yitschaki, 2.237.

18   LBD MS, f. 7v:
כי רוב מעשיהם: כ"ה הנכון אבל אין לומר כל מעשיהם דהא יש בידינו תורה ומצות אלא גרסי' רוב וכן הגיה מהר"ם בסדור שלו ואין לומר כל. סדור מהרש"ל.
See Reif, *Shabbethai Sofer* (see n. 14 above), pp. 142–43 and 251; eds I. Satz and D. Yitschaki, 2.28.

19   LBD MS, Introductions, f. 29v:
והנה נוהגים ברוב קהלות אשכנז לומר שיר היחוד הזה בכל יום רק במדינת רוסיא בקהלות אשר נהג בהם רבנות הגאון מהר"ר שלמה לוריא ז"ל אין אומרים אותו כל עיקר. ושמעתי מפי רבים מזקני הדור שהגידו לי ששמעו את מהרש"ל שהיה דורש בק"ק לבוב ובק"ק לובלין בתחלת בואו לנהוג שם רבנות ואמר בדרשותיו שאין לומר שיר היחוד מפני שמצא שחיבר אותו מין ובעבור זה היה מוחה בכל קהלות מושבותיו מלאמרו.
See *Shabbethai Sofer* (see n. 14 above), p. 76, n. 56c; eds I. Satz and D. Yitschaki, 1.89–90.

20   LBD MS, f. 61v:
הן הם יודו: והאומרים הן הן או הם הם טועים כי הן הם גימטריא מאה ברכות שמודי' ומברכי' מאה ברכות לומר בכל יום סדור מהרש"ל.

the insertion of the word רבים between רעים and נאמנים in the *nishmat* prayer,[21] and of the addition of the phrase ואלהי אבותינו after אלהינו in various instances;[22] and his recording of the two alternative vocalizations מְשֻׁבַּח בָּאוֹמֶר for מְשֻׁבָּח וְאוֹמֵר[23] and הַגִּבּוֹר לָנֶצַח for הַגִּבּוֹר לָנֵצַח[24] in the sabbath morning service, and of Maharil's custom of spitting once in the *'alenu* prayer.[25]

Obviously the ultimate aim must be to publish all these quotations, accompanied by scientific annotations. This is, of course, precluded in the present context, limited as it is by considerations of space, but I hope it can be undertaken at a later date.[26] Meanwhile I shall content myself with making known a few more of the Maharshal's comments, this time with the emphasis on the generally liturgical rather than the purely linguistic elements.

Detailed examples

A. From *'Ahavah Rabbah*

כן תחננו: וכן כתב מהרש"ל בסדורו וז"ל ולדברי הצרפתים שמוסיפים ואומרים כן תחננו ותלמדנו גם בזה אין רוח חכמים נוחה בהם שהרי נעלם מעינם וטחו עיניהם מראות שכתב רבינו החסיד ז"ל

See Reif, *Shabbethai Sofer* (see n. 14 above), pp. 149–50; eds I. Satz and D. Yitschaki, 2.318.

21 LBD MS, f. 61r:
   ומהרש"ל כתב בסדורו וז"ל רעים ונאמנים כ"ה והאומרים רעים רבים ונאמנים עליהם נאמר ורבים מעמי הארץ כי לא נמצא אף בפסוק עכ"ל.
   See Reif, *Shabbethai Sofer* (see n. 14 above), p. 148; eds I. Satz and D. Yitschaki, 2.317.

22 LBD MS, ff. 61r and 33r:
   ואלדי אבותינו: ס"א לא כתיב אלו ב' תיבות ואלדי אבותינו סדור מהרש"ל.
   See Reif, *Shabbethai Sofer* (see n. 14 above), p. 146; eds I. Satz and D. Yitschaki, 2.315 and 2.129.

23 LBD MS, f. 64v:
   משבח ואומר: ס"א משובח באומר סדור מהרש"ל.
   See Reif, *Shabbethai Sofer* (see n. 14 above), p. 163; eds I. Satz and D. Yitschaki, 2.331–2.

24 LBD MS, f. 62r:
   הגבור לנצח: בסדור מהרש"ל כתוב ס"א לנצח הלמ"ד בשב"א והנו"ן בפת"ח והצד"י דגושה וצר"י בהולד נח בפת"ח לפני החי"ת מענין חזק ונצחון כמו לנצח על מלאכת בית ה' (עזרא ג').
   See Reif, *Shabbethai Sofer* (see n. 14 above), p. 152; eds I. Satz and D. Yitschaki, 2.320.

25 LBD MS, f. 52r:
   כי מהרש"ל כתב בסדורו מהרי"ל כשהגיע ללא יושיע היה מקיא פעם אחת.
   See Reif, *Shabbethai Sofer* (see n. 14 above), pp. 50 and 89, n. 22, and *Tarbiz* 44 (1975), pp. 202–3; eds I. Satz and D. Yitschaki, 2.224.

26 Following the publication of his Hebrew article 'Ashkenazic mishnaic reading traditions in eighteenth-century grammatical treatises', *Leshonenu* 62 (1999), pp. 257–83, I was in touch with Dr Chaim Cohen and shared with him my transcriptions of Luria's comments from the original manuscript. He was then planning to annotate and publish these, apparently in our joint names.

שבברכת אהבה רבה יש בה ארבעה מיני לימודים ואלו הן ותלמדם א' ללמוד ב' ללמוד ג' וללמד ג' תלמוד ד'
וכו' ומאריך שם בראיות ובטעמים.[27]

Although Luria here bases his exclusion of the word ותלמדנו on the view
of the German Hasidim that the root למד is used in four different ways
in the paragraph אהבה רבה and that the text of the benediction without
the word ותלמדנו already has four such instances,[28] he is clearly aware of
the deep-seated textual problem that has given rise to the discussion.
He rightly refers to the fact that the French, i.e. the old French or north
French, pre-Ashkenazi rite has the extra word תלמדנו,[29] and to his
observation may be added the note that it also occurs in the Italian rite[30]
but is absent in the Babylonian, Sefardi and Yemenite versions.[31] It is
not clear from the quotation from his prayer-book whether Luria is
objecting to only one word or the whole phrase but there is certainly
manuscript evidence for no small degree of doubt about all three words
כן תחננו ותלמדנו.[32] In addition, the relationship of the phrase to what
precedes and follows it is unclear, the use of the *waw* consecutive
(ותלמדם חקי חיים) in a liturgical Hebrew passage, though by no means
unique, was apparently regarded by some as suspect; and there is
controversy in the sources as to whether the suffix of that verb refers to
'us' or 'them', Hebrew נו-, ם- and מו-. This is not the place to attempt a
solution of the whole problem; suffice it to say that such a solution is
probably to be sought through a different division of the phrases, and
may also involve a realization that the verb חנן could here be a parallel
to למד and a possible vocalization וּתְלַמְּדֵנוּ\מוֹם for מוֹם. In any
event, Luria's instinct about the additional use of the word ותלמדנו after
תחננו proves to be correct.

---

27   LBD MS, f. 30v; eds I. Satz and D. Yitschaki, 2.119-20.
28   See *Siddur of R. Solomon ben Samson of Garmaise including the Siddur of the Ḥaside
     Ashkenaz*, ed. M. Hershler (Jerusalem, 1971), p. 89, and *Sefer Arugat Habosem*, ed. E. E.
     Urbach, (4 vols; Jerusalem, 1939–63), 4.93–94, citing British Library MS Harley 5529,
     f. 14r.
29   E.g. *The Etz Hayyim*, ed. I. Brodie (Jerusalem, 1962–67), pp. 1, 84 and *Maḥzor Vitry*, ed.
     S. Hurwitz (Nuremberg², 1923), 1.65. The relevant old French manuscripts also
     support this reading but, interestingly enough, so does a Genizah fragment at
     Cambridge University Library, T-S 8H10.21:
     ובעבור אבותינו הצדיקים אשר בטחו בך ותלמדמו חוקי חיים מלפניך כן תחננו ותלמדנו.
30   E.g. ed. S. D. Luzzatto (Livorno, 1856), ff. 1, 14a and *Maḥzor Roma* (Bologna, 1540),
     before the morning *shema'*.
31   The texts of Sa'adya (eds Davidson, Assaf, Joel, Jerusalem, 1963², p. 14), Amram (ed.
     N. Coronel, Warsaw, 1865, p. 5a; ed. A.L. Frumkin, Jerusalem, 1912, 1.195–96; ed. E.
     D. Goldschmidt, Jerusalem, 1971, p. 14; ed. D. Hedegård, Lund, 1951, Hebrew text,
     p. 20); Maimonides (ed. E. D. Goldschmidt in *Studies of the Research Institute for
     Hebrew Poetry* 7, Jerusalem, 1958, p. 192); Abudraham (ed. Warsaw, 1877, p. 45); and
     the *Tiklal* of Yaḥya b. Joseph Ṣaliḥ (Jerusalem, 1894), 1.34a.
32   See *Oṣar Ha-Tefillot*, ed. A. L. Gordon (corrected and expanded edition, Vilna, 1923
     Hebrew pagination), 1.133a–135b for examples of the variations.

B. Following the *Shema'* of R. Judah Ha-Nasi

אתה הוא עד שלא נברא. ובסדור מהרש"ל ז"ל בסדור הטוב כתב אתה הוא שבראת העולם ואתה הוא
משבראת וכן עיקר והאומר משנברא נמצא מחרף משמע כאלו אחר בראו כך מצאתי. וכן יש לומר וכן
נראה לומר בשביל מנין תיבות ועיין ותמצא עכ"ל.[33]

At first glance it would appear somewhat strange that the *Siddur Ha-Ṭov* is objecting to a text that is cited from the Palestinian Talmud by some of the medieval authorities. The fact is, however, that the passage is more likely to be one of those that emerged in the land of Israel in the geonic period and were subsequently incorporated into some versions of the 'Yerushalmi'.[34]

A knowledge that the present passage did not actually belong to the authentic talmudic text may indeed have been a factor in Luria's offering a different reason for justifying its retention. Unease about the formulation of the doxology may be traced back to the earlier manifestations of what we may call, for convenience rather than with scientific accuracy, the various non-Palestinian-orientated rites. While the Italian and Ashkenazi prayer-books[35] were generally content to follow the text as it occurs in some early (Palestinian?) Genizah texts,[36] many old French, Sefardi and Yemenite *siddurim* either effected a change or adopted a less ambiguous phraseology.[37] Apparently aware of the possible understanding of the preposition עד in a future, temporal sense and the prefix -מש as a subordinate clause of reason, they felt that there was a danger of the phrase being misunderstood to mean 'you are He until the world is no more and as a consequence of its being created', an obviously heretical thought. The most common way out of the difficulty was to substitute the two unambiguous prepositions קודם and אחר.

The theory that it was a possible misunderstanding of עד in the future sense that led to such a change is supported by the existence of

---

33   Formerly LBD MS, f. 8r; eds I. Satz and D. Yitschaki, 2.32.

34   See V. Aptowitzer, *'Unechte Jeruschalmizitate'* in *MGWJ* 55 (1911), pp. 419–25 and *Introdutio ad Sefer Rabiah* (Jerusalem, 1938), pp. 276–77; and S. S. Feiginsohn's השמטות מירושלמי on chapter 9 of *Berakhot* printed with the Yerushalmi edition of Jerusalem, 1960.

35   As followed by Luzzatto (see n. 29 above), 1.9a and S. Baer (*Seder 'Avodat Yisra'el*, Rödelheim, 1868), p. 46. See also the Warsaw 1865 edition of *Seder Rav Amram*, p. 2, and the text cited (but not adopted) by Abudraham (see n. 31 above), p. 36. The evidence of Ashkenazi and Italian manuscripts and early editions is overwhelmingly in favour of this text.

36   E.g. Cambridge University Library Genizah fragments T–S 6H2.10 and 8H10.1.

37   See *The Etz Hayyim* (see n. 29 above), p. 70 and *Maḥzor Vitry* (see n. 29 above), p. 60; Maimonides (see n. 31 above), p. 189; Judah b. Yaqar, *Peyrush Ha-Tefillot Ve-Ha-Berakhot*, ed. S. Yerushalmi (2 vols; Jerusalem, 1968-69), 1.60; and ed. Amsterdam, 1661, p. 24a; *Tiklal* (see n. 31 above), p. 14a.

two other Genizah texts[38] which exchange the position of the two phrases, reading: אתה משנברא העולם ואתה הוא עד שלא נברא העולם.

The author of that particular version clearly felt that references to the past (משנברא) should precede those alluding to the future (עד). While the *Siddur Ha-Ṭov* offers another alternative, Luria uses the argument about the number of words that was so common among the earlier German Hasidim to plead the case of the status quo.[39]

C. In the Festival '*Amidah*

את יום השבת הזה: וכתב מהרש"ל בסדורו וז"ל אין לומר את יום המנוח הזה כי מנוח עם הארץ היה
ודו"ק עכ"ל.[40]

The background to this comment constitutes a good example of the pressure that was being exerted on the established Ashkenazi rite of the sixteenth century to conform to its Sefardi counterpart. Contrary to what is generally supposed, the pressure was not exclusively the result of the spread of the work of the Sefardi kabbalists but at this stage owed as much, if not more, to dominant codes. In this case the Sefardi version could also claim not only to go back at least as far as the geonic period but also to tally with the old French and Yemenite rites. The tenacity with which יום השבת הזה held on to its place in the Ashkenazi and Italian rites may also indicate a good pedigree and an early alternative[41] but both expressions may at an even earlier stage have been newly introduced into a context which had previously included references only to the relevant festival and not the sabbath. The picture is not yet totally clear but it may well be that the biblical term is indeed the older and that the non-biblical form took its place in some communities in the geonic period as a reaction against Karaite tendencies towards exclusively biblical use or, perhaps, more simply, in order to provide an alternative word to accompany the name of a festival which could not be said to mean festival itself. At any rate it was fighting off the challenge of מנוח and the controversy can still

---

38 Cambridge University Library Genizah fragments T–S 8H9.1 and 8H9.7, the former also placing both phrases after and not before אתה הוא בעולם הזה ואתה הוא בעולם הבא. British Library MS Add. 26954 inserts אל after the first two words.

39 In his edition, LBD MS, f. 8r, Shabbetai Sofer adopted the text אתה הוא עד שלא בראת את העולם ואתה הוא לאחר שבראת את העולם and is apparently the target for the criticism made of such changes by David b. Samuel Ha-Levi in his commentary (*TaZ*) on *Shulḥan 'Arukh*, '*Oraḥ Ḥayyim* 46:9.

40 LBD MS, f. 96r; eds I. Satz and D. Yitschaki, 3.520.

41 See Baer (see n. 35 above), pp. 347–48; *Oṣar Ha-Tefillot* (see n. 32 above), 1.915–16; *Sefer Hamanhig* (ed. Y. Raphael, 2 vols; Jerusalem, 1978), 1.170; *Sefer Maharil* (Warsaw,1874), p. 26a; Luzzatto (see n. 30 above), 1.94a, 108b, 146b, 152b, etc.; *Tiklal* (see n. 31 above), 2.34b, 39b etc. See also my Hebrew article 'Festive titles in liturgical terminology' in *Proceedings of the Ninth World Congress of Jewish Studies 1985/1, Division C* (Jerusalem, 1986), pp. 63–70.

clearly be traced in the eighteenth and nineteenth centuries.[42] The arguments against the use of מנוח include the contention that in biblical Hebrew it refers only to a place on which to rest part or all of one's body, that it is not the authentic Ashkenazi *nusah* and that in the Babylonian Talmud Rav Naḥman refers to Manoah as an עם הארץ[43]. Jacob Ṣemaḥ b. Ḥayyim cites this view in the name of his teacher, the Lurianic kabbalist, Samuel b. Ḥayyim Vital and according to him it means simply that one who uses the phrase is an עם הארץ. Samuel's father was a contemporary of Luria but it is not clear who borrowed the phrase about Manoah from whom. Whatever the origin, Solomon Luria cites it here in somewhat stark form. Perhaps he is hinting that just as Manoah is referred to in this way for following his wife and acknowledging her superiority so those who follow the Sefardi rite and regard it as superior are deserving of a similar epithet.

D. From the *Qedushah* in the *Yoṣer*

חיים ומלך עולם: אין לומר ומלך בוי"ו לפי שנראה כשתי רשויות וכן דעת מהר"ם ומהרא"ק אבל פסוק הוא בירמי' י' הוא אלדים ומלך עולם סדור מהרש"ל.[44]

Once the basic format of the most common liturgical texts was fixed at the end of the geonic period, and therefore somewhat less prone to controversy, commentators gave more attention to the detailed linguistic structure, both consonantal and vocalic, and to the sense that it did, or could convey. As a result, numerous words and phrases were identified as theologically suspect or prone to internal or external misunderstanding because of their ambiguity. Battle was thus joined between those in favour of clarity through emendation and those who offered novel interpretations to justify the retention of traditional versions. Although our earliest known prayer-books appear to be unanimous in recording the text of this phrase in the form given above, Meir of Rothenburg was obviously uneasy about its connotation and suggested the omission of the conjunctive *waw*. Stalwart interpreter as he was of the Ashkenazi custom, he nevertheless had personal experience of the extent to which standard Hebrew texts could be employed as weapons in the arsenal of theological disputations and it may have been for this reason that he made this particular suggestion.[45]

---

42 See e.g. Jacob Ṣemaḥ b. Ḥayyim, *Nagid U-Meṣaweh* (Amsterdam, 1712), p. 62b and Jacob Reischer (Backofen), *Ḥoq Ya'aqov* on *Shulḥan 'Arukh*, *'Oraḥ Ḥayyim* 487.1.

43 BT, *Berakhot* 61a (cf. also Bemidbar Rabbah 10.5) on Judges 13:11.

44 LBD MS, f. 29v; eds I. Satz and D. Yitschaki, 2.115.

45 It does not appear to be recorded in I. Z. Kahane's edition of his *Responsa, Rulings and Customs* (3 vols; Jerusalem, 1957–62), nor alluded to in Irving Agus, *Rabbi Meir of Rothenburg – His life and his works as sources for the religious, legal and social history of the Jews of Germany in the thirteenth century* (New York², 1970).

Luria's admiration for the learning and achievements of his predecessor are clearly expressed in his talmudic commentaries and in the comment under discussion he faithfully sets down the master's objection to the presence of the *waw* and the support for its removal on the part of Abraham Klausner, another of Luria's own major sources. At the same time he is clearly not totally convinced of the validity of the objection since he also notes that a verse from Jeremiah is similarly expressed and could be enlisted in support of the text as it stands.[46] Indeed, both Judah b. Yakar and David Abudraham, commentators on the Sefardi liturgy of the thirteenth and fourteenth centuries respectively, cite the same verse in their comments on the liturgical phrase.[47] The two views expressed by Luria are not only to be found in earlier sources; they also occur in their later equivalents, demonstrating that the argument continued for at least three more centuries. Both Seligmann Baer[48] in the name of Menaḥem Mendel Auerbach and the commentary of Ḥanokh Zundel b. Joseph in *'Oṣar Ha-tefillot*[49] record the view of Meir of Rothenburg but while the latter refers to Leib Saraval's preference for the biblical precedent, Baer draws a distinction between the liturgical and biblical forms. In the Jeremiah verse, he claims, the pronoun הוא removes all ambiguity while in the prayer-book there is no such aid to clarity.

E. The Correct Title of *Shemini 'Aṣeret*

ובסדורו כתב וז"ל שמיני העצרת הזה. רי"ן לא כתב חג העצרת רק את יום העצרת הזה כי לא כתוב בו חג שמיני. ונ"ל דטעות הוא דהא מי שלא חגג בסוכות חוגג בשמיני ונקרא עצרת. פי' חג הראשון עצור עדיין ולא יגרע מחול המועד והוא רגל לענין פז"ר קש"ב. ואמרינן במסכת סופרים בכל הרגלים אומרים חג חרץ מבראש השנה והרי שמחה נמי לא כתיב בשמיני מ"מ אומרים בו זמן שמחתינו. ונ"ל דילפינן בגזרה שוה עצרת דשבעות של פסח מעצרת דשמיני עצרת ובפרק אין דורשין קורא ליה שמוני ימי החג. ועוד דכתיב חג האסיף ובסכות זמן אסיפה ובריש מסכת תענית תנן ר' יהושוע אומר מיום ראשון של חג עד יום אחרון של חג הלכך יש לומר חג גם רי"ן מחק הה"א וכתב שמיני עצרת בלא ה"א וחדוש הוא עכ"ל.[50]

It is not only festival nomenclature but the whole issue of the status and origin of a festival that underlies the problem here. In Maharshal's well known liturgical responsum[51] he complements what he has to say in his prayer-book by citing both the view of Isaac Tyrnau's *Minhagim*[52] that the word חג is not apt since it is not used in connection with this

---

46   Jeremiah 10:10.
47   Judah b. Yaqar (see n. 37 above), 1.25 and Abudraham (see n. 31above), p. 43.
48   *'Avodat Yisra'el* (see n. 35 above), pp. 77–78.
49   Edition cited in n. 32 above, 1.258–59.
50   LBD MS, Introductions, f. 29r; eds I. Satz and D. Yitschaki, 1.88–89.
51   See n. 5 above.
52   Ed. Cracow, 1597, p. 34b, a view followed in British Library Ms Add. 26954 and eds Prague 1549–50 and Cracow 1578.

festival in the Hebrew Bible, and the argument of the Maharil, widely
followed in Ashkenazi manuscripts and early editions, that the word חג
is applicable and should be inserted between שמיני and עצרת.[53] Tyrnau's
view there elicits the same response as Jacob Naqdan's here, i.e., חג is
relevant as the *nomen rectum* of the construct עצרת but should not
govern the whole phrase, and Maharil's insertion of חג is rejected on the
grounds that the two words always occur together in biblical texts. As a
result, Luria had no option but to place it thus: את יום שמיני העצרת-חג
הזה.i.e. 'the eighth day, this additional part of the festival'. The fact is
that although Maharil's view appears to be a common one among the
medieval sources[54] various attempts were made to understand and
thereby to order the different sections of the phrase[55] and all of them
had to take account of the conflicting nature of biblical, talmudic and
later evidence. While the day is called simply יום שמיני and described as
an עצרת in the Hebrew Bible,[56] the rabbis referred to it as שמיני שלחג or
אחרון שלחג[57] and in the early middle ages the name שמיני עצרת appears on
the scene linking together two words that occur side-by-side in the
Hebrew Bible but are always separated by the Masoretes. Add to this
the further complications that the Talmud argues for a festival status
for this day only in certain limited aspects,[58] that the word עצרת has no
unequivocal interpretation,[59] and that there was obviously a strong
desire on the part of the standardizers of the liturgy to equate the
phrase here with the parallel יום חג and יום חג השבועות הזה, יום חג המצות הזה,
הסכות הזה, and you have the ingredients for a liturgical mêlée. David
Levy, author of the טורי זהב commentary on the *Shulḥan 'Arukh*,
faithfully follows Luria[60] and is taken to task for his pains in a most
energetic fashion by Wolf Heidenheim in his commentary on the
festival prayers.[61] To ensure that the modern prayer-books are not free

53 Ed. Warsaw, 1874, p. 52b.
54 E.g. Amram (see n. 31 above), ed. Warsaw, p. 51b, ed. Frumkin, 2.384, ed.
    Goldschmidt, p. 177; Abudraham (see n. 31 above), p. 161a; and R. Nissim Gerondi
    in BT, *Megillah* 31a; so Luzzatto (see n. 30 above), 2.165a, and Jacob Emden, *'Amudey
    Shamayim* (Altona, 1745) 1.369a and 2.23a.
55 E.g. Maimonides (see n. 31 above), p. 205 and the Yemenite *Tiklal* (see n. 31 above)
    2.81b have את יום חג שמיני עצרת הזה while *Maḥzor Vitry* (see n. 29 above), p. 445 has את יום
    שמיני לחג עצרת הזה with the added preposition to indicate the possessive state.
56 Leviticus 23:36, Numbers 29:35, Nehemiah 8:18.
57 BT, *Rosh Ha-Shanah* 4b and *Megillah* 31a.
58 BT, *Sukkah* 47a–48a.
59 L. Koehler and W. Baumgartner, *Hebräisches und Aramäisches Lexikon zum Alten
    Testament* (Leiden³, 1967–90), p. 825.
60 On *'Oraḥ Ḥayyim* 668.
61 In his commentary on the evening *'amidah* for Shemini *'Aṣeret*, in ed. Rödelheim, 1803,
    p. 46b and Krotoschin, 1838, pp. 17–18.

of controversy it need only be added that the Habad custom, with its currently wide and powerful influence, favours את יום שמיני עצרת החג הזה.[62]

F. In *Birkhot Ha-Shahar*

וכוף את יצרנו: וכתב מהרש"ל בסדורו וז"ל י"א וכוף את יצרי אבל שמעתי שאין לאמרו כי ארז"ל הכל בידי שמים חוץ מיראת שמים מצ' עכ"ל.[63]

Luria here objects on theological grounds to the alternative text that employs the singular pronominal suffix, not the plural. Since humanity has free will with regard to religious inclination there is no point in appealing to God to subdue it.[64] It is more likely, however, that this text choice arises out of a different theological consideration viz. whether prayers that are basically personal in nature and in origin should remain in the first person singular or whether once they have been incorporated into the synagogal setting they should be adjusted to the plural. The various talmudic or Talmud-based exhortations to which this phrase belongs, like the morning benedictions with which they came to be included, originated in a personal, domestic context[65] but later joined the standard synagogal liturgy. During this transformation there was obviously controversy about the degree to which their language should be altered to reflect the change. The variant noted by Luria may be found in the old French and Italian rites[66] and was still a common feature of many prayer-books, manuscript and printed,[67] some of which were known to Maharshal. He clearly intended to support the full transformation of the phrase into the standard liturgical style.

Other examples

Having given a few examples in detail it remains only to complete this chapter by making brief reference to a number of other interesting comments by Luria. He is clearly aware of the tendency to amplify

---

62 E.g. *Siddur Tehillat Ha-Shem* (New York, 1951), p. 253.

63 LBD MS, f. 6r; eds I. Satz and D. Yitschaki, 2.23.

64 Baer (see n. 35 above) p. 42, raises the same question and offers the answer that it is not for the removal of the evil inclination that we pray but for the ideal conditions in which we can ourselves subdue it.

65 See BT, *Berakhot* 60b.

66 E.g. *Mahzor Vitry* (see n. 29 above) 1.57; *The Etz Hayyim* (see n. 29 above) 1.65; *Mahzor Roma* (see the commentary) and Luzzatto (see n. 30 above) 1.4a (latter three without את). The singular form ותכוף את יצרי is also to be found in the text of Amram, eds Frumkin (see n. 31 above) 1.68 and Goldschmidt (see n. 31 above), p. 3.

67 Among Ashkenazi and French manuscripts consulted, British Library Add. 27556 and Add. 27208 and Cambridge University Library Add. 667.1 have the plural. The plural also predominates among early Ashkenazi editions (e.g. Soncino 1495, Trino 1525, Thiengen 1560, Cracow 1579 and Basle 1599).

liturgical phrases whenever the opportunity arises and sometimes
declares himself against this when he feels that the authentic text is
thereby compromised. Following this line he argues against the
insertion of the word לנו in the phrase אין אלהים זולתך in the morning
ge'ulah benediction on the grounds that the verse in 1 Chronicles 17:20
does not have it and against the appearance of the word נא in the
phrase איה אלהיהם because it makes no sense in the context. In the latter
case he chooses the linguistic argument rather than the possible
reference to the verse in Joel 2:17.[68] On the other hand, he is content to
fall back on the counting of the words of a prayer so popular with the
earlier German Hasidim when anxious to justify the retention of a
particular word. This is precisely what he does when noting and
opposing the objection made by some to the presence of the word זכר in
the verse ואל תשחית זכר שאריתנו of the *taḥanun* on the grounds that it might
be taken to mean 'do not destroy the memory of our remnant'
i.e.'destroy the remnant itself'![69]

The achievement of what he regarded as more elegant Hebrew is
apparently his motivation in his comments on the words איזהו and כיצד
in the mishnaic passages from *Zevahim* recited after the morning
benedictions. He notes the alternatives אי זה הוא and כאיזה צד and also
expresses his approval in the first case.[70]

Linguistic considerations also play a part in his decision to record,
apparently with at least some degree of approval, the readings לְלְמוֹד לא
לְלְמוֹד for the more usual לְלַמֵד לא לְלַמֵד in the hermeneutical principles of
Rabbi Ishmael[71] and למות ולחיים for the more usual לחיים ולמות in the *musaf*
'amidah for the New Year.[72] In the first case he cites the argument of
Abraham Klausner, based on Rashi's comments on Deuteronomy 4:10
that the root למד in the *qal* has a reflexive sense and in the *pi'el* a
transitive sense and that it is the first that is here required. The case for
לחיים ולמות is not put by Luria himself but Shabbethai Sofer maintains

---

68   a) LBD MS, f. 33r; eds I. Satz and D. Yitschaki, 2.129:
אין אלדים זולתך: ואין לומר לנו כי כ"ה בתפלת דוד בד"ה א' י"ז ואין אלדי' זולתך סדור מהרש"ל.
      b) LBD MS, f. 45r; eds I. Satz and D. Yitschaki, 2.184:
איה אלדיהם: וכתב מהרש"ל בסדורו וז"ל והכן בלבבך שלא שייך נא בענין הזה עכ"ל.

69   LBD MS, f. 47v; eds I. Satz and D. Yitschaki, 2.193:
זכר: ובסדור מהרש"ל ז"ל יש מדלגין זכר לפי דמשמע הזכר יניח אבל העיקר ישחית ח"ו לכך טוב לומר אל תשחית
שאריתנו כלל ולפיכך לא יהיה מנין תיבות רמ"ט אם ידלג זכר ול"נ אם ידלג זכר אזי יאמר כלל ודוק עכ"ל.

70   a) LBD MS, f. 10r; eds I. Satz and D. Yitschaki, 2.40: סדור מהרש"ל.
איזהו: אי זה הוא עיקר.
      b) LBD MS, f. 10v; eds I. Satz and D. Yitschaki, 2.43:
כיצד: ובסדור מהרש"ל כיצד ס"א כאיזה צד רא"ק.

71   LBD MS, f. 12r; eds I. Satz and D. Yitschaki, 2.51:
ללמד לא ללמד: ובסדור מהרא"ק ללמוד לא ללמוד בפ' ואתחנן ילמדון פירש"י לעצמו [כ"ה בכת"י; אולי י"ל
לעצמן?] וסוף הפסוק ואת בניהם ילמדון סדור מהרש"ל.

72   LBD MS, f. 152r; eds I. Satz and D. Yitschaki, 3.669: לחיים ולמות: אבל בסדור מהרש"ל הפוך
למות ולחיים.

that it could be justified either as an attempt at harmonizing the text with similar, contrasting expressions used earlier in the prayer or as a conscious change to avoid ending with the word 'death'.

Luria is not always so precise and analytical but can, on occasion, employ a lighter touch. A somewhat fanciful justification is given by him for the recitation of the benediction פוקח עורים before מלביש ערומים; 'The verse in Genesis 3:7 states *the eyes of both of them were opened and they sewed fig leaves* – there you have it, the opening of the eye followed by the clothing of the body!'[73]

If I may take Maharshal's lead and close on a quasi-homiletical note, albeit by way of a mixed metaphor, I hope that this eye-opener will have succeeded in clothing some of the bare facts about Luria's place in the history of Jewish liturgy.

---

73 LBD MS, f. 5v; eds I. Satz and D. Yitschaki, 2.17:

כן הוא הנכון לומר ברכת פקח עורים קודם ברכת מלביש ערומים...וכ"ה באבודרהם ובסדור מהרש"ל נתן טעם לסדרן זה וכתב שנסדרה ברכת מלביש ערומים אחר פקח עורים לפי שכתב ותפקחנה עיני שניהם ויתפרו עלי [עלה] תאנה הרי פקיחה ולבישה.

15

'Truth and faith' in Genizah Manuscripts

Introduction

There can be little doubt that liturgical Hebrew offers a potentially rich source of linguistic information for Hebraists and Semitists alike and that this applies not only to the colourful and innovative idiom of the *piyyuṭim*[1] but at least in equal measure to the more staid and normative language of the common daily prayers. That a substantial exploitation of this latter part of the source remains to be undertaken is due to a number of factors. Scholars fully *au fait* with the intricacies of the Jewish liturgy have, since the pioneering efforts of Zunz to provide a scientific basis for its study, traditionally occupied themselves with the general emergence of the various rites and the place which each of the notable prayers has come to occupy within these rites.[2] They have in only a minority of cases dissected these prayers in sufficiently minute detail to reveal the linguistic significance of individual expressions and no systematic study of the field has therefore emerged.[3] Scholars less

---

1   Although important work has been done in this area by I. Davidson, M. Zulay, H. Schirmann, A. Mirsky and E. Fleischer (see the useful bibliography in Fleischer's *Hebrew Liturgical Poetry in the Middle Ages*, Hebrew; Jerusalem, 1975), the contribution of the *piyyuṭim* to the evolution of the Hebrew language has yet to be fully evaluated. See W. Chomsky, 'The growth of Hebrew during the middle ages' in *Seventy-fifth Anniversary Volume of the JQR*, eds A. A. Neuman and S. Zeitlin (Philadelphia, 1967), pp. 121–36, and A. S. Halkin, 'The medieval Jewish attitude toward Hebrew' in *Biblical and Other Studies*, ed. A. Altmann (Cambridge, Mass., 1963), pp. 233–48.
2   E.g. I. Elbogen's *Der jüdische Gottesdienst in seiner geschichtlichen Entwicklung* (Frankfurt am Main, 1931); reprinted Hildesheim, 1962; Hebrew edition, (eds. J. Heinemann, I. Adler, A. Negev, J. Petuchowski and H. Schirmann, Tel Aviv, 1972); English edition, *Jewish Liturgy: A Comprehensive History* (trans. and ed. Raymond P. Scheindlin, Philadelphia, Jerusalem and New York, 1993); which, though regarded as the classic presentation of the subject, rarely deals with detailed linguistic matters.
3   What I have in mind is the kind of treatment undertaken by S. Baer in his *Seder 'Avodat Yisra'el* (Rödelheim, 1868,), by A. L. Gordon in the commentaries published in the prayer-book *Oṣar Ha-Tefillot* (I have here used ed. Wilna, 1928) and by A. Berliner in his *Randbemerkungen zum täglichen Gebetbuche* (Berlin, 1909). Among more recent scholars, N. Wieder, in his important articles now collected together in *The Formation of Jewish Liturgy in the East and the West: A Collection of Essays* (2 vols.; Hebrew; Jerusalem, 1998), is the only one to have applied all the tools of modern critical scholarship to this task, but B. S. Jacobson's *Netiv Binah* (Hebrew; 5 vols; Tel Aviv, 1968–83) is a valuable compendium and E. D. Goldschmidt has done

familiar with the subject, even if aware of the possible contribution to be made by a close analysis of liturgical Hebrew, have balked at the daunting obstacles which face anyone approaching the Jewish prayers without an acquaintance with their traditional recitation in the synagogal context.[4] In addition, as with so many areas of rabbinic study, little progress can be made until reliable texts in their earliest recoverable form have been established. This task is made particularly difficult in the case of the common prayers by their exclusively oral form in the early centuries of their existence, the tendency in the traditional sources to cite only the first words and not the complete text of well-known pieces, the corruptions which have taken place in the course of transmission and publication, the textual adjustments made to harmonize conflicting views and the alterations dictated by censorship, external and self-imposed. An all too familiar acquaintance with the traditional formulation, and its repeated recitation often almost by rote, have also served to conceal the difficulties inherent in a particular text or to produce unconvincing explanations for those which are acknowledged, and have consequently obstructed efforts to arrive at an authentic version.[5]

Three examples

Three examples, well-known to specialists, will readily illustrate how the critical examination of familiar liturgical phrases, made possible by the relatively recent availability of so much manuscript and early printed material, has repaid those who have undertaken the necessary research by revealing what appear to be more reliable texts, thereby contributing to a better understanding of Hebrew usage and vocabulary in the liturgical context:

1. The expression מעין הברכות occurring in the מגן אבות prayer recited after the 'amidah' at the Friday evening service had long presented difficulties to the commentator and translator. The traditional explanation had come to be that the sense of מעין in this context was equivalent to that occurring in the phrase מעין חתימה and that the word therefore comprised a preposition followed by a noun in the construct state; hence Singer's translation 'fitting forms of blessings' and many similar

important groundwork with his Jerusalem editions of *The Passover Haggadah* (1969), *Maḥzor La-Yamim Ha-Nora'im* (1970) and *Seder Rav Amram* (1971).
4   See my review in *JSS* 23 (1978), pp. 119–22.
5   The complex history of the vocalization of liturgical Hebrew is an additional complicating factor; see my *Shabbethai Sofer and his Prayer-book* (Cambridge, 1979), especially pp. 29–38.

renderings.[6] The rediscovery, in the course of modern manuscript research, of the use of the phrase מעון הברכות as a divine epithet, coupled with the realization that the occurrence of this phrase in the Yemenite version of מגן אבות was a witness to the original text rather than simply a variant, produced a definitive article by the late Gedaliahu Alon establishing the authenticity of the spelling with *waw* and pointing out that the phrase was not the object of the previous verb ונודה but belonged to the later group of divine epithets such as אל ההודאות and אדון השלום.[7] Alas, this has yet to be reflected in contemporary English versions of the traditional prayer-book.

2. In the standard editions of the Mishnah *Rosh Ha-Shanah* 1.2 it is stated that all the world's inhabitants pass before God כבני מרון. The precise sense of this otherwise unknown expression was the subject of controversy from Amoraic times[8] and the difficulty was imported into the early medieval liturgy by its incorporation into the moving *piyyuṭ* ונתנה תוקף which came to occupy such a central role in the Ashkenazi services for New Year and the Day of Atonement. Although various ingenious renderings have been suggested by modern lexicographers no less than by their earlier counterparts,[9] the word מרון has been popularly understood to mean 'sheep' or 'a flock of sheep'. Over a hundred years ago, however, N. Brüll[10] suggested that the expression might have been read by the Amora Samuel as one word and, following this suggestion, the reading כבנומרון was ultimately preferred by a number of scholars and, on the basis of the Greek νούμερον (Latin *numerus*), translated 'like a troop of soldiers'. The argument for this reading remained inconclusive until N. Wieder found important support for it in a number of medieval liturgical manuscripts and was thus able to demolish an essential prop in the defences of the traditional text.[11] Once again, modern editions have been tardy in giving practical expression to a theory produced by manuscript research.

---

6   *The Authorised Daily Prayer Book* (ed. I. Brodie, London, 1962), p. 160, following Baer (see n. 3 above), p. 191; see also I. Abrahams, *A Companion to the Authorised Daily Prayer Book; Historical and Explanatory Notes* (London, 1922; reprinted New York, 1966), p. 132.

7   *Tarbiz* 14 (1942), pp. 70–74, reprinted in his *Studies in Jewish History* 2 (Tel Aviv, 1958), pp. 128–32. For an early suggestion to alter the text, see A. Mishcon, 'Disputed phrasings in the siddur', *JQR* NS 7 (1917), p. 529.

8   See BT, *Rosh Ha-Shanah* 18a, and PT, *Rosh Ha-Shanah* 1.3 (57b).

9   The references are given by Wieder (see n. 11 below), p. 1.

10 *Jahrbücher für jüdische Geschichte und Literatur* 1 (1874), p. 187.

11 *JJS* 18 (1967), pp. 1–7. But see *The Jerusalem Post* of 16 October 2005 for an orthodox rabbinic attempt at a defence of the reading with *yod* on the basis of early printed editions.

3. The third example concerns the poetic formulation of the fifth of
Maimonides's *Thirteen Principles* in the *yigdal* hymn emanating from
fourteenth-century Italy.[12] The principle states that one must pray only
to the Creator and yet the equivalent line in the standard prayer-book
text of *yigdal* reads: הנו אדון עולם לכל נוצר יורה גדולתו ומלכותו making God the
subject of the verb יורה and referring to instruction proceeding from
Him rather than prayer addressed to Him. The rediscovery of the
variants וכל and יודה in the middle of the nineteenth century by the
enlightened Hebraist and rabbi, David Oppenheim,[13] and by S. Baer,[14]
in an anti-Christian polemic by Don David Nasi[15] and in a number of
early editions, provided a text more consistent with the original
statement of Maimonides and therefore more convincing. Both A.
Berliner[16] and A. L. Frumkin[17] offered support for this latter text and it
was cited in the popular *Oṣar Ha-Tefillot*[18] but it is the problematic form
which is still to be found in most prayer-books.[19] The change from לכל
to וכל has been made in a few cases but יורה seems to reign supreme.
Indeed, P. Birnbaum has recently followed Oppenheim's antagonist in
the matter, Abraham Abele Ehrlich,[20] and has defended the reading
with the argument that it bears the sense of 'relate', 'tell' in Biblical
Hebrew and is employed as the equivalent of יתפלל in one talmudic
passage.[21]

Whether the findings of modern scholarship are acceptable in each
of the above cases or judgement is reserved, there are a sufficient
number of similar examples to demonstrate the value of such
methodology for liturgical research. Although the scholarly procedure
is an obvious and familiar one it will perhaps be useful in the present
context to provide an explicit definition. The researcher is required to
recognize the existence of a difficulty, to question the validity of the

---

12 I. Davidson, *Thesaurus of Mediaeval Hebrew Poetry* 2 (New York, 1929), pp. 266–67, no. 195.
13 *Hamaggid* 11, no. 21 (1867), pp. 165–66.
14 See his additional notes printed before the text and commentary proper (see n. 3 above), p. 28.
15 ספר הודאת בעל דין (Frankfurt am Main, 1866), p. 10.
16 *Randbemerkungen* (see n. 3 above), p. 13.
17 *Seder Rav Amram Ha-Shalem* (Jerusalem, 1912) 1.22ab; see also Yaḥya Ṣaliḥ's commentary on the Yemenite *Tiklal* (Jerusalem, 1894) 1.110b.
18 See A. L. Gordon's commentaries on p. 53ab of ed. Wilna, 1928.
19 But see *The Hirsch Siddur: The Order of Prayers for the Whole Year* (E.T.; Jerusalem and New York, 1969), p. 3, where both words have been changed.
20 *Hamaggid* 11, no. 1 (1867), p. 6.
21 See his *Daily Prayer Book* (New York, 1949), pp. 11–12, where he cites Job 12:7–8 and Psalms 145:6–12, and BT, *'Eruvin* 65a, in support. Jacobson (see n. 3 above), 1.150, helpfully refers to Birnbaum's note in volumes 8–9 of ספר השנה ליהודי אמריקה (New York, 1947), but the page reference should be corrected from 334 to 335.

solutions traditionally offered, to bring a wealth of internal and external evidence to bear on the problem and, finally, to suggest an improved reading or understanding of the text.

It was in the course of my early work on the liturgical commentary of Shabbethai Sofer of Przemysl that I first gave any serious attention to the difficulties inherent in the standard text of the first sentence of the אמת ואמונה prayer in the *ge'ulah* prayer of the daily evening service.[22] My treatment of the subject was, however, in that context necessarily brief, and it was not until I examined a large number of Genizah texts at Cambridge University Library that I became aware of its complexity and set myself the task of dealing with it in greater depth. As in so many other cases, some of them treated in other chapters of this volume, such Genizah texts demonstrate clearly how often the complete codices of the later medieval ages have failed to retain important alternative readings that are preserved in those tantalizing fragments from Cairo.[23] The study has been undertaken in five parts. The first part is intended to demonstrate the problem and how it has been tackled in medieval and modern sources, the second to set it in the wider linguistic and liturgical contexts, the third to examine the evidence of Genizah and other manuscripts, the fourth to cite modern critical opinion on the origins of the אמת prayers, and the fifth to trace the lines along which a possible solution may be sought.

1.1 The Problem

The major rites are in agreement about the first sentence in the *ge'ulah* prayer which is to follow the recitation of the third paragraph of the *shema'* (Numbers 15:37–41) at the weekday evening service. In the current editions of the liturgy it runs as follows: אֱמֶת וֶאֱמוּנָה כָּל-זֹאת וְקַיָּם עָלֵינוּ כִּי הוּא יי אֱלֹהֵינוּ וְאֵין זוּלָתוֹ וַאֲנַחְנוּ יִשְׂרָאֵל עַמּוֹ

If familiarity with the text blinds readers to its difficulties, a survey of a sample of modern English translations will soon make them aware that there is no unanimous view about the sense the prayer here intends to convey. In the rendering of this passage, Orthodox, Conservative and Reform translations seem equally at a loss, as is made clear by the following examples:

---

22 *Shabbethai Sofer* (see n. 5 above), pp. 123 and 214–15.
23 For the Cambridge Genizah collections' overall impact on early medieval scholarship, see Reif, *A Jewish Archive from Old Cairo* (Richmond, 2000).

1. This is true and firmly established with us, that he is the Lord our God...[24]

2. True and trustworthy is all this and it is established with us that he is the Lord our God...[25]

3. True and trustworthy is all this. We are certain that He is the Lord our God...[26]

4. True it is, and certain, that the Lord alone is our God...[27]

5. We affirm the truth that He is our God...[28]

6. Truth and faith is all this, yea, it is established upon us that he is God our Lord...[29]

7. All this is true and firmly held by us, that He is the Lord our God...[30]

It is clear from the above examples that would-be translators of the prayer are confronted by three basic questions:

1. To what does the expression כל זאת allude?

2. What precise sense is conveyed by the words אמת ואמונה and what grammatical relationship exists between them?

3. Does the phrase וקים עלינו refer back to כל זאת or does it belong to the second part of the sentence in which the clause כי הוא יי אלהינו is its subject?

In order to establish what answers have traditionally been given to these questions and whether such may be regarded as scientifically tenable, it will be necessary to examine a number of outstanding liturgical commentaries reflecting a reasonably wide geographical and chronological spectrum. Before this examination is made, it should be stressed that the views to be found there are not necessarily unique nor even original to these sources but are conveniently presented there and are characteristic of the manner in which generations of rabbis understood the passage under discussion. It should also be noted that the statement cited in the name of Rav in the Babylonian Talmud, *Berakhot* 12a, that the morning prayer אמת ויציב is concerned with God's

---

24 *The Book of Prayer and Order of Service according to the Custom of the Spanish and Portuguese Jews*, ed. M. Gaster (London, 1901–6), 1. 69.

25 *ADB* (see n. 6 above), p. 119.

26 *DPB* (see n. 21 above), p. 196.

27 *Service of the Heart* (Union of Liberal and Progressive Synagogues, London, 1967), p. 66.

28 *Maḥzor for Rosh Hashanah and Yom Kippur* (ed. J. Harlow, Rabbinical Assembly, New York, 1972), p. 24.

29 *The Standard Siddur-prayer book with an Orthodox English Translation*, ed. S. Schonfeld (London, 1973), p. 91.

30 *Forms of Prayer for Jewish Worship* (Reform Synagogues of Great Britain, London, 1977), p. 35.

love and the evening prayer with our trust in Him, as expressed in Psalms 92:3, was the starting point for every commentator.

1.2 Solutions proposed

In the commentary on the Franco-German rite attributed to the eleventh century rabbi, Solomon b. Samson of Worms, published for the first time by M. Hershler,[31] the use of the word כלומר to introduce the explanation being offered is an immediate indication that there are difficulties afoot. The commentary goes on to explain the prayer in the following terms: 'It is a matter of certainty [i.e. of God's love] and trust [i.e. in Him] for us to observe (לקיים) all the ritual requirements (כל זאת) laid down by the rabbis in connection with the recitation of the *shema'* and its benedictions'. A further indication of the difficulties being encountered by the commentators is in the fact that he goes on to offer another explanation: 'All this that I have recited [in the last verse of the third paragraph of the *shema'*, i.e.] "I am the Lord your God who brought you out etc." is also a matter of certainty and trust.' The word קים is then taken as part of the next clause which is explained as a statement of conviction that 'the Lord is our God'.[32]

It is clear that as far as the words אמת ואמונה are concerned the example set by Rav in offering what would today be called a homiletical rather than a literal rendering is not only being followed but even bettered. This is indicated in a second commentary on the Franco-German rite, *Maḥzor Vitry*,[33] written by a student of Rashi, Simḥah b. Samuel of Vitry, and in this instance reflects the view of the master as known from other sources.[34] In this commentary it is specifically asked what trust (אמונה) is involved here and the answer given that man entrusts his weary soul to God at night and, although the soul would wish it otherwise, He keeps His faith with man and restores it to him refreshed in the morning.[35]

---

31   סידור רבנו שלמה מיוחס לרבנו שלמה ב"ר שמשון מגרמייזא (Jerusalem, 1972), p. 133.

32   כלומר, אמת ואמונה עלינו לקיים כל זאת לקרוא קרית שמע וברכותיה כאשר תיקנו. וגם אמת ואמונה, כל זאת שאמרתי אני יי' אלהיכם אשר הוצא' אתכם. ודבר זה קיים עלינו כי הוא יי אלהינו. For a justification of my rendering see the comments of Rashi, *Tosafot* and *Maḥzor Vitry* cited below. I do not believe that דבר זה refers back to כל זאת or it could have been given in those same words. The phrase כי הוא is therefore in apposition to דבר זה and not a subordinate adverbial clause of reason as it would have to be in Abudraham's interpretation.

33   *Maḥzor Vitry*, ed. S. Hurwitz (Nuremberg[2], 1923), pp. 77–78.

34   See *Siddur Raschi*, ed. S. Buber (Berlin, 1911), p. 213 and *Ha-Pardes*, ed. H. Ehrenreich (Budapest, 1924), p. 303.

35   ואי זו אמונה יש כאן. לפי שאין לך אדם שאין נפשו כאיבה עליו בלילה מרוב עמל וטורח שטרח ביום. וכשעולה ברקיע בלילה אין הנשמה רוצה לשוב בקרבו עד שאומר לה המק' שוב למקומך בתוך האדם איני רוצה לוותר

The tendency to adopt a more imaginative approach to the meaning of the expression אמת ואמונה is taken further in the work of Zedekiah b. Abraham Anaw of thirteenth century Rome. In the *Shibboley Ha-Leqet* he includes the view just cited from *Mahzor Vitry* in the name of Rashi but not until he has offered a more fanciful interpretation 'in the name of the Ge'onim'.[36] He points out that the numerical value of אמונה is one hundred i.e. מאה, apparently pursuing an idea already adumbrated in the Talmudic-midrashic literature according to which מאה is interpreted as prayer[37] and pointing to a similar use of the word אמונה in Exodus 17:12 to refer to Moses's prayers. As with so many attempts at *gematriah*, however, the equation is not quite accurate since אמונה = 102 and he is therefore forced to find the missing two in the dual recitation of the *shema'* each day![38]

In his fourteenth century commentary on the Sefardi liturgy,[39] David Abudraham of Seville has his feet more firmly on the ground. The somewhat disturbing כלומר is, however, again present, on this occasion introducing the comment that אמת refers to the Torah according to Psalms 119:142 and Proverbs 23:23, and אמונה to the precepts, as demonstrable from Psalms 119:86. He is not convincing, not indeed convinced, as is indicated by his provision of an alternative explanation which sees the expressions אמת and אמונה as descriptive of God's reliability and faithfulness, and quotes a section of *Midrash Tehillim*[40] in support of the homily about the soul already cited above from *Mahzor Vitry*. As far as the remainder of the sentence is concerned, he understands כל זאת as a reference to אמת ואמונה, the whole qualified by the adjective קיים, with כי introducing the reason. The sense thus conveyed is that everything just mentioned is established for the reciters of the prayer *because* He is the Lord their God.[41]

Some four centuries later, Abudraham's views about the homily on the soul and the equation of אמת with Torah and אמונה with the precepts are repeated – not without the ubiquitous כלומר – by Yahya b. Joseph

---

אומנותי כנגדו. הוא האמין בי והפקידך אצלי. שנאמר בידך אפקיד רוחי. ועושה הק' אמונה ומחזירה לו ובבקר
עושה לו נס ומחדש את כוחו ואינו חלש מכל מה שטרח אתמול

36   *Shibboley Ha-Leqet Ha-Shalem*, ed. S. Buber (Wilna, 1886), p. 21a.
37   See BT, *Menahot* 43b and PT, *Berakhot* 9.8 (14d) and the introductions to the various medieval liturgical commentaries e.g. the edition cited in the previous note, p. 1a.
38   אמונה בגימטריא מאה וזו היא תפלתו של משה רבינו שנאמר ויהי ידיו אמונה וגו'. והשנים היתרים כנגד ב'
      פעמים שקורין קריאת שמע ביום
39   *Sefer Abudraham* (Warsaw, 1877), p. 38b.
40   25.105b.
41   אמת ואמונה כלומר התורה שהיא אמת שנאמר אמת ותורתך וכתיב אמת קנה ואל תמכור וגו'. והמצות שהם אמונה
      שנא' כל מצותיך אמונה. כל זאת קיים עלינו בעבור כי הוא ה' אלהינו ואין זולתו

Ṣaliḥ of San'a in his commentary on the Yemenite liturgy.[42] In addition, he cites the alternative view that these first two words of the prayer refer to the last verse of the preceding paragraph, beginning 'I am the Lord your God'. What is novel here is that he also offers two interpretations of the next phrase כל זאת קיים עלינו both of which follow the vocalization to be found in the Yemenite liturgy viz. קָיֵּםand not קָיָם. According to the first, God has imposed upon Israel (קיים עלינו) the obligation to recite כל זאת i.e. אמת ויציב in the morning service and אמת ואמונה at the evening service; according to the second the obligation is to recognize and believe that He is the Lord. Another significant comment, which will later be discussed, is that the evening version of the prayer speaks of the future redemption while that of the morning service refers to the Egyptian redemption.[43]

The nineteenth-century German commentator on the traditional rabbinic liturgy, Seligmann Baer, has even less to offer than his medieval counterparts, contenting himself with a definition of the kind of benediction here being introduced and a comment that it is 'all this that we have read in the three paragraphs of the *shema'* which is אמת ואמונה'.[44]

It will be apparent from this brief summary of their views that the answers offered by some of the outstanding liturgical commentaries to the questions posited above are no more unanimous or convincing than the translations offered by contemporary prayer-books. No sound linguistic point is made regarding the sense of the words אמת ואמונה and any distinction made between them is of a purely homiletical kind, a welter of suggestions is made as to what is conveyed by כל זאת, and no satisfactory syntactical analysis of the whole sentence emerges. It is my contention that this state of affairs testifies to an early loss (or abandonment?) of the original import of the introductory words of this *ge'ulah* prayer and the consequent introduction of inaccuracies and variant readings into its text. There are already a number of indications in the commentaries cited above that the earliest talmudic comments about אמת ויציב and אמת ואמונה and variants in the text and vocalization of the latter (e.g. in the case of קים(ו)) may provide important clues for the solution of the puzzle. An attempted reconstruction of a more authentic text and interpretation will therefore require not only a survey of how the notable words of this prayer are used in other liturgical contexts but

---

42 P. 90a (see n. 17 above).
43 לזה אנו אומרים כל זאת קיים עלינו כלומר חייב לנו לומר אמת ואמונה וכו' כמפורש בדברי חז"ל ואמר כל לכלול גם מצות אמירת אמת ויציב ולזה תמצא שבספרי תימן מנקדים הקו"ף בחיר"ק. א"נ אמת ואמונה קאי אאני ה' אלהיכם שהוא סיום ק"ש. עז"א אמת ואמונה. כל זאת קיים עלינו. חייב לנו לידע ולהאמין כי הוא ה' אלהינו... ותקנו לומר אמת ואמונה בערבית על הגאולה של עתיד שאנו מאמינם שיקיים לנו הבטחתו ויגאלנו בקרוב
44 P. 166 (see n. 3 above).

also an examination of the variant readings offered by early medieval manuscripts and a study of elements in the prayer's earliest history.

2.1 Linguistic background

Before proceeding with these tasks it will be helpful to clarify the linguistic background of the expressions אמת and אמונה by making brief reference to the results of modern investigations into the senses they bear in Biblical Hebrew and how, if at all, they are to be differentiated. In the context of a blistering attack on the 'etymologizing' approach of certain Christian theologians,[45] James Barr has demonstrated that there is little basis for their tendency to treat these two words as 'nearly synonymous' and theologically 'almost indistinguishable'. While not denying that there are some instances in which it is not easy to distinguish them, he stresses that in general אמת is used for 'truth' as opposed to falsity and אמונה for 'trust' and 'fidelity'.[46] A. Jepsen has followed Barr in emphasizing this semantic distinction, dwelling on the differences in usage. While it is common to describe words and things as אמת, אמונה is only rarely used in this way, more often occurring as a quality or a type of conduct.[47]

Since, then, the words are neither generally interchangeable nor parallel in Biblical Hebrew usage, the construction אמת ואמונה would probably look strange in such a context, especially if intended to constitute two epithets for the same subject. Rabbinic Hebrew need not, of course, comply so strictly with biblical usage but it does seem that with regard to such common words and concepts, particularly in the case of their liturgical use, the tendency was to make further progress along the same semantic lines rather than to effect a revolutionary change of direction. Although a sound modern dictionary of Rabbinic Hebrew is still awaited, the lexicographical work available to us would certainly seem to bear this out in the case of the words under discussion.[48] The only evidence to the contrary which I have encountered is in N. Wieder's reference to the employment of the term אמונה by tenth-century Karaite authors and their Rabbanite opponents

---

45 *The Semantics of Biblical Language* (Oxford, 1961), pp. 161–205.
46 Barr, *Semantics* (see n. 45 above), pp. 198–200.
47 *Theological Dictionary of the Old Testament*, eds G. J. Botterweck and H. Ringgren, ET, J. T. Willis, vol. 1 (Grand Rapids, 1973), entry *'aman* by Alfred Jepsen, pp. 292–323, especially p. 317.
48 The entries in J. Levy, *Neuhebräisches und chaldäisches Wörterbuch* 1 (Leipzig, 1876), pp. 98, 103; M. Jastrow, *A Dictionary* (New York, 1960), pp. 76, 79; and *A Complete Dictionary of Ancient and Modern Hebrew by Eliezer Ben Yehuda of Jerusalem* (Jerusalem and New York, 1908–1959), pp. 275, 301–2, record little change from the meanings known from Biblical Hebrew.

in the sense of 'truth'. Wieder himself, however, points out that 'the usage… is rather uncommon' and his description of it as belonging 'to the style of the period' and being 'in vogue with Karaite authors' makes it unlikely that it has any relevance for our study of what is a much earlier rabbinic liturgical source.[49]

2.2 Liturgical context

The richest source of information for a survey of the manner in which אמת is used as an introductory word is the morning equivalent to the *ge'ulah* prayer in which אמת ואמונה is included at the evening service. The following examples occur:

1. אמת יציב ונכון: It is quite clear that אמת does not belong to the list of epithets qualifying הדבר הזה since there are already fifteen of these and it is this number, not sixteen, which is of significance in the structure of various prayers.[50] An additional support for this view is found in the absence of *waw* from the word יציב in many texts.

2. אמת אלהי עולם מלכנו: If אמת is taken as an epithet for אלהי עולם (so Jacobson[51]), the whole structure of the sentence becomes unbalanced.

3. אמת שאתה הוא יי: The use of the -ש after אמת is inconsistent with all the other examples and seems strange. I suspect that it is not original but cannot yet provide the necessary evidence for this.[52]

4. אמת אשרי איש שישמע: The אמת has somehow been lost in the Ashkenazi rite. It may well be that the introduction of -ש was one way of overcoming the difficulty in explaining the word אמת; the omission of that word may have been another.

5. אמת אתה הוא אדון לעמך

6. אמת אתה הוא ראשון

---

49 *The Judean Scrolls and Karaism* (London, 1962), pp. 89–90, and the recently reprinted edition with the author's addenda, corrigenda and supplementary articles (Jerusalem, 2005), pp. 306–7. See also *Siddur R. Saadya Gaon*, eds I. Davidson, S. Assaf and B. I. Joel (Jerusalem, 1963²), pp. 64–65.

50 The subject is too large to be dealt with here but see *Abudraham* (see n. 39 above), pp. 20a, 25b; *Ha-Pardes* (see n. 35 above), p. 95; *Siddur Rabbenu Shelomo* (see n. 31 above), p. 97; and the various medieval liturgical commentaries on the ישתבח, אמת ויציב and קדיש prayers.

51 On pp. 254–57 of the first volume (see n. 3 above) he points to the recurrence of אמת as an introductory word in the context of his discussion of the theological significance of each statement in the morning *ge'ulah* benediction but does not reach the same conclusion about the sense of אמת as that being reached here.

52 Cf. the phrases אמת כי אתה הוא דין and אמת כי אתה הוא יוצרם and their variants in *Maḥzor La-Yamim Ha-Nora'im*, ed. E. D. Goldschmidt (Jerusalem, 1970), 1.169, 171. see also 'Two Mishna fragments from the Cairo Genizah' by R. Mirkin in *Henoch Yalon Memorial Volume*, eds E. Y. Kutscher, S. Lieberman and M. Z. Kaddari (Jerusalem, 1974), p. 374.

7. אמת ממצרים גאלתנו: The אמת is once again absent from the Ashkenazi rite.

The main conclusion to be drawn from the above examples is that the word אמת is being employed neither in its absolute substantival sense of 'truth' nor as an epithet but as the equivalent of באמת in the sense of 'truly...', 'in truth...' or the English colloquial 'true...', introducing an affirmative response. Before any attempt is made to apply this conclusion to an interpretation of the אמת ואמונה phrase, however, there are two other instances of that phrase's occurrence in the liturgy where אמת can hardly bear this sense and which must therefore be accounted for. The first of these is אמת ואמונה חק ולא יעבר in the same morning *ge'ulah* prayer and the other the phrase מנוחת אמת ואמונה in the *'amidah* for the sabbath afternoon service. As far as the first is concerned, the words אמת ואמונה do not occur at all in Sa'adya's text which reads דבר קיים לעולם ועד חק ולא יעבר.[53] They occur as באמת ובאמונה in the versions of Amram[54] and Abudraham[55] where they replace Sa'adya's לעולם ועד and in the Yemenite rite the first phrase has דבר טוב וקים באמת.[56] Even in the Italian version (including the Roman rite) which is almost as long as that of the Ashkenazim, the אמת ואמונה belongs to the end of the first phrase rather than the beginning of the second.[57] It is therefore clear that it is only because the Ashkenazi version has become so expanded that אמת ואמונה has spilled over into the second phrase which it now introduces. It is also important in the present context to note that the original text, or at least the original sense, was probably באמת ואמונה. The phrase מנוחת אמת ואמונה presents no challenge to what has been stated above about אמת since neither that word nor אמונה are introductory or even syntactically independent in the context but are used in an adjectival sense, i.e. 'true and trustworthy rest'.

The various instances in which the word קים occurs in the liturgy will next be listed to see what relevance they have for the expression (ו)קים עלינו of the prayer under discussion. The first five are once again to be found in the *ge'ulah* prayer of the morning service while the remaining three are from the ברוך שאמר and עזרת אבותינו prayers of that same service and for the *'amidah* for the New Year:

1.   אמת (ו)יציב ונכון וקים... הדבר הזה
2.   הוא קים ושמו קים
3.   ומלכותו (ואמונתו) (לעד) קימת
4.   ודבריו (חיים) (ו) (קימים)

53   *Siddur* (see n. 49 above), p. 16.
54   Ed. Frumkin (see n. 17 above) 1.111b; ed. Goldschmidt (see n. 3 above), p. 19.
55   P. 26a (see n. 39 above).
56   Ed. Jerusalem 1894 (see n. 17 above) 1, p. 39a.
57   See ed. S. D. Luzzatto (Livorno, 1856) 1, p. 15a; דבר טוב וקים אמת ואמונה חק נתן ולא יעבור.
     The Ashkenazi version is: דבר טוב וקים לעולם ועד. אמת ואמונה חק ולא יעבור.

5.   דבר (טוב ו)קים

6.   ברוך (אל) חי לעד וקים לנצח

7.   למלך (ל)אל (רם ונשא) חי וקים

8.   כי אתה אמת ודברך (מלכנו) אמת וקים לעד (absent from some versions).

It readily becomes apparent from the above examples, which are by no means exhaustive, that קים is used to describe God, His name and His word(s) with suitable inflections for the feminine, as in the cases of אמונה and מלכות, and the plural. Equally revealing is the fact that in none of these instances is the word followed by the prepositions עלינו or לנו.

Where these prepositions do occur with the root קום it is with a verbal rather than an adjectival form, viz. the *pi'el* imperative קַיֵם. The phrase קַיֵם לנו meaning 'fulfil for us' and referring to a divine promise recorded in a biblical verse, occurs in the paragraph אתה הוא יי אלהינו בשמים ובארץ following the ברכות השחר and towards the end of the זכרונות benediction in the *musaf 'amidah* for New Year. Similarly, Mann has used Genizah material to demonstrate that the imperative קיים introduced a prayer for the messianic redemption in the evening *ge'ulah* prayer of the old Palestinian rite,[58] and Wieder, exploiting manuscript fragments from the same Cairene source, has established the existence of a prayer with the introductory formula קיים עלינו and the same petition in the morning *ge'ulah* prayer of Sa'adya's prayer-book, apparently the result of Palestinian influence.[59] Other verbal forms important for the present study include the use of the participle with אמונה viz. ומקים אמונתו in the second benediction of the daily *'amidah*, and the verse יחד שמך וקים מלכותך in the third post-*shema'* benediction of the evening service according to the Ashkenazi rite. On the face of it, this קים too ought to be a clear imperative and yet in *Mahzor Roma* and other Italian rites it appears as קַיֵם,[60] a phenomenon to which further reference will later be made.

3. Manuscript readings

The first point to be made in connection with medieval manuscript versions of the first sentence of the אמת ואמונה prayer housed at

---

58   'Genizah fragments of the Palestinian order of service,' *HUCA* 2 (1925), p. 303, reprinted in *Contributions to the Scientific Study of Jewish Liturgy* (ed. J. J. Petuchowski, New York, 1970).

59   'Fourteen new Genizah fragments of Saadya's *Siddur*' in *Saadya Studies*, ed. E. I. J. Rosenthal (Manchester, 1943), pp. 250–53; see also his *Formation of Jewish Liturgy* (see n. 3 above), 2.649.

60   See ed. Luzzatto (see n. 57 above) 1, p. 28a, and *Yosef Omeṣ* (Frankfurt am Main, 1928; reprinted Jerusalem, 1965), section 29, p. 9.

Cambridge University Library is that the majority of those examined, of both Genizah and other provenance and covering all the major rites, do not have a *waw* prefixed to the word קים.[61] In a number of Genizah texts this is the only variant from the current version[62] although it should not be forgotten that there are some manuscripts which follow the old Palestinian custom of reciting אמת ויציב in the evening as well as in the morning.[63] There are, however, two fragments which are probably to be counted among the earliest liturgical manuscripts from the Genizah and dated to about the eleventh century and which contain the following interesting text: אמת אמונה כל זאת קיים עלינו יי אלהינו ואנחנו ישראל עמו. In the first of these this continues מלכנו אין זולתו[64] and in the second אמת מלכנו ואין זולתו.[65] The sense of the text makes it reasonably obvious how this version is to be vocalized but any doubt is removed by two later fragments which have the same formulation.[66] In these the word קים is not only without a *waw*, as expected, but is also vocalized as a *pi'el* perfect קִיֵּם, as preserved in the Yemenite rite. What that rite and others have failed to preserve from the old rite, however, is no less significant. There is no *waw* joining אמת and אמונה, the subject of קיים is יי אלהינו so that there is no need for כי הוא, and the phrase אין זולתו does not belong to this first part of the prayer but to a subsequent statement, again introduced by אמת. The fact that all these elements are also present in the critical edition of Sa'adya's prayer-book[67] reconstructed from similar such manuscript material suggests that the text found in the Genizah fragments cited above has a sound pedigree. If it was indeed the original text, the degree of its perspicuity was apparently called into question and it was gradually abandoned in favour of the longer but more easily intelligible version. In that case, those manuscripts, including that of Maimonides's prayer-book,[68] which include the words כי הוא but in no other way depart from this suggested original text,

---

61 E.g. Add.379.1, Add.1490 (*waw* added), Dd.13.7 (*waw* scored through), Add.375, Add.634, Add.2987, Add.437, Add.438, Add.1752, Add.1204 and Add.1754.

62 E.g. T-S 10H1.7, T-S NS 153.68 and T-S NS 197.3.

63 See Mann (see n. 58 above), p. 303.

64 Add.3160.2. See the plate of this manuscript fragment at the end of this volume.

65 T-S 8H10.15. The same unvocalized text is found in T-S Misc.24.137.4a and T-S Misc.24.137.12a.

66 T-S 8H9.5 and T-S NS 153.14.

67 P. 27 (see n. 49 above).

68 'The Oxford Ms. of Maimonides' book of prayer', ed. E. D. Goldschmidt, in *Studies of the Research Institute for Hebrew Poetry in Jerusalem* 7 (Jerusalem and Tel Aviv, 1958), p. 194, reprinted in his collection of articles *On Jewish Liturgy. Essays on Prayer and Religious Poetry* (Hebrew; Jerusalem, 1978), p. 197. See also T-S Misc.28.247.

represent an intermediate stage in the process of evolution.[69] One of them even has these two words as a gloss above the word עלינו.[70]

The discovery of a number of additional Cambridge Genizah fragments containing the קיים (עלינו) messianic prayer to which Mann and Wieder drew attention is not in itself significant.[71] What does call for comment is the alteration which has been made to the word קיים in two of these. In one the text is not very clear but it seems to read יקיים לנו (further altered to יקיים על(י)נו)[72] while in the other there is no doubt at all that the word has been revocalized as קָיָּם.[73] The use of the third person rather than the imperative may simply be for consistency with the remainder of the prayer; the revocalization reflects the same dissatisfaction with the inclusion of a prayer for future redemption in the context of a reference to the past Egyptian redemption as that already encountered in the Italian version of קים מלכותך. What is of particular importance in the present study is that there was an interchange of the forms קָיָּם, קַיָם and קֵיָם in various parts of the liturgy.[74]

For the sake of completeness a few remarks should be made at this juncture about the following variations on the theme of אמת ואמונה:

1. אמת אמונה אמרה איומה: Employed as an alternative in the Saturday evening service; see *Siddur R. Saadya Gaon*, p. 123; Davidson, *Thesaurus* 1.273, no. 5985. Also found in Genizah texts, e.g. CUL T-S 13H4.3 and T-S NS 271.6, NS 271.18 and NS 271.60.

2. אמת אמונתך בשביעי קיימת גזרת: Employed as an alternative in the Friday evening service ; see *Siddur R. Saadya Gaon*, p. 110; Davidson, *Thesaurus* 1.273, no. 5986, and the slightly modified texts of the Italian and Roman rites separately listed by Davidson, 1.274, no. 6010. Also found in Genizah texts, e.g. CUL T-S 10H8.7, 13H4.3 and T-S NS 271.35.

3. אמת (ו)אמונה כל זאת פעלה ימינך: Employed as an alternative in the Saturday evening service but disapproved of by the Gaon Amram; see his *Seder*, ed. Warsaw, p. 31a, ed. Frumkin, 2.54a, ed. Goldschmidt, p. 81 and ed. Kronholm, pp. כ and 137.

4. אמת אמונה בריתך קיימת ליל זומן למופש: Another version, apparently for Passover use, found in CUL T-S NS 235.146.

5. אמת אמונה ונכון וקיים: A compromise version, used at least on festivals, incorporating elements of the morning and evening versions recorded in the Talmud. Found particularly in Italian manuscripts, e.g. Montefiore

---

69 T-S 8H11.4.
70 T-S A29.41.
71 E.g. T-S 6H2.1, T-S 6H3.7, T-S 8H11.4, T-S 8H23.10 and T-S 10H1.4.
72 T-S 8H10.6.
73 T-S NS 271.64.
74 Ashkenazi prayer-book, ed. Mantua, 1558, even has וְקַיָם in the אמת ואמונה prayer.

215 (see H. Hirschfeld, *Catalogue*, pp. 66–68), but also in CUL T-S NS 271.151.[75]

It may be deduced from the above that there were at one time a considerable number of texts employed at the various evening services in addition to the one which was destined to become the most familiar. They all contained the words אמת and אמונה but usually without conjunctive *waw* and in some of them the word אמונה is governed by a *pi'el* form of the root קום.

4. Modern critical views

The structure of the liturgy is of course regulated by the halakhah and therefore, ultimately, by the talmudic sources. It will therefore be useful to summarize the essential requirements laid down in these sources with regard to אמת ויציב and אמת ואמונה and to refer to the findings of modern critical scholarship about the origin and early development of these prayers. The overriding impression one receives from the relevant talmudic passages[76] is of a determination to establish that the *shema'* must be followed immediately by the אמת and *ge'ulah* prayers and that these in their turn must merge with the *'amidah*. For those who obey this latter instruction, there is even the promise of trouble-free days and the enjoyment of eternal life, an obvious measure of the importance which the rabbis attached to having their advice in this matter heeded. There is also the clear indication that the Tannaim differed on which topics were to be included in the אמת ויציב prayer and that at least one of them solved the problem by declaring that all suggested topics should be included. On the basis of these and similar sources, A. Spanier has expressed the view that the basic text of אמת ויציב was in the Thou-style and that of the אמת ואמונה in the He-style.[77] L. Ginzberg has stressed the independent nature of the *shema'* and the *'amidah* in the earlier tannaitic period and that the only prayer to follow the *shema'* was a short affirmation of its religious truths, a kind of אמן,

75 For fuller bibiographical details of the works cited in these five numbers see notes 3, 12, 17 and 49 above. The Warsaw edition of *Seder Rav Amram* was published by N. Coronel in 1865 and the Kronholm edition in Lund, 1974. Hirschfeld's *Descriptive Catalogue of the Hebrew Mss. of the Montefiore Library* appeared in London, 1904, and in a reprint (ed. R. P. Lehmann) in Farnborough, Hants., 1969.

76 Mishnah, *Berakhot* 2.2; Tosefta, *Berakhot* 2.1, 3.6 (10) (ed. Zuckermandel, pp. 3, 6); BT, *Berakhot* 9b, 12a; and PT, *Berakhot* 1.9 (3d). it is clear that the original intention of joining אמת to the third paragraph of the *shema'* was to ensure continuation. The verse in Jeremiah 10:10 was later used to justify the custom. There are other examples in the liturgy of this tendency to understand talmudic instructions in somewhat literal a fashion.

77 'Zur Formengeschichte des altjüdischen Gebetes', *MGWJ* 78 (1934), pp. 446–47.

which ultimately developed into a full repetition of those truths.[78] According to I. Elbogen, Rav's introduction of אמת ואמונה into the standard evening liturgy, to match the אמת ויציב of the morning, is to be seen as part of a process of enrichment which was the work of the Babylonian Amoraim.[79] L. Liebreich has put forward the theory that the אמת ויציב has attracted so many accretions that the current text of אמת ואמונה is nearer to the original form of the prayer with which it once was parallel,[80] while J. Heinemann has sought the origins of both prayers in the synagogue rather than the academy and has credited them with a considerable antiquity.[81] What is common to all the theories is the conviction that separate liturgical entities have here been strung together and that the אמת prayers were originally brief, simple and parallel but underwent considerable expansion as part of the stringing process. It may be added that the corollary of such a view is that the text at present before us and its traditional interpretation may be, with the exception of a few words, a far cry from what was recited and understood in the environs of tannaitic Yavneh or Usha.

There is one further piece of evidence to be presented before an attempt is made to reach some tentative conclusions. As has already been noted, Rav's differentiation of the אמת prayers to be recited in the morning and evening is supported in the talmudic sources by reference to the verse in Psalms 92:3, חסדך being taken as a reference to אמת ויציב and אמונתך to אמת ואמונה. The comments of both Rashi and the *Tosafot* on this source are most intriguing.[82] Rashi, having explained by way of introduction that the חסד which is the subject of the morning version refers exclusively to the Egyptian redemption and the Red Sea crossing, goes on to say that the evening version also includes references to future redemptions. He finds these references in the words הגואלנו, הפודנו and other participles which occur before any mention is made of the Egyptian redemption and which he understands as bearing a continuous sense and therefore alluding to divine marvels which we enjoy every day. What is even more remarkable is that if the latter part of his comments is taken as an interpretation of the central part of the

---

78 *A Commentary on the Palestinian Talmud* (4 vols; New York, 1941 and 1961) 1.215–16, and 3.359. Cf also the idea of the *haftarot* benedictions as an acknowledgement of the truth of the prophetic reading.

79 Pp. 262–63 (see n. 2 above); p. 197 in the Hebrew edition; p. 207 in the English edition.

80 'The benediction immediately preceeding [sic] and the one following the recital of the shema", *REJ* 125 (1966), pp. 151–65.

81 *Prayer in the Period of the Tanna'im and the Amora'im: Its Nature and Its Patterns* (Hebrew; Jerusalem², 1966), pp. 172–73; revised English edition, *Prayer in the Talmud: Forms and Patterns* (Berlin and New York, 1977), pp. 269–70.

82 BT, *Berakhot* 12a.

אמת ואמונה prayer, his introductory remarks may legitimately be understood as a commentary on its first sentence. His exact words are: וברכת אמת ואמונה מדבר בה אף על העתידות שאנו מצפים שיקיים לנו הבטחתו ואמונתו לגאלנו מיד מלכים and it is tempting to suggest that Rashi is here paraphrasing the first sentence as an expression of trust in the future fulfilment of a divine promise. The current text does not fit well with such an interpretation but Rashi's text may have been different or he may have preserved an interpretation which has outlived the text for which it had once been proposed. The *Tosafot* spell it out even more clearly, stating that אמונתך refers to the future: שאנו מצפים שישמור הבטחתו ואמונתו ויגאלנו מיד מלכים ובסוף ברכה חוזר לגאולה דפרעה. There was, however, apparently some dissatisfaction with this since the alternative explanation according to which אמונה refers to the trust that God will restore a refreshed soul to man each morning is also offered.

5. Tentative conclusions

The presentation of the evidence, as far as I have been able to gather it, is now complete and some conclusions have to be drawn. The essence of my argument is that the traditionally accepted interpretations, already presented above, are for various reasons inconsistent with this evidence and that some novel solution is called for. An attempt must be made to find such a solution and to this end I shall indicate along which avenues further exploration should be undertaken.

The suggestion that אמת, אמונה and קים are all epithets qualifying כל זאת is unsatisfactory because it has been shown that these expressions are linguistically, liturgically and grammatically incompatible in such a context. The forms נאמנה and קימת or, if loosely employed, at least נאמן, would have been required and there seems no reason why, if employed in this way, all these epithets should not have occurred together without the intrusion of כל זאת. Furthermore, those supporting this interpretation would be hard-pressed to explain the variant manuscript readings which omit כי הוא.

The alternative view that (ו)קים introduces a second statement also offers no satisfactory reason for the manuscript readings just cited. It also suffers from the weakness that the words קים עלינו are not used together in this way in the liturgy. The words אמת ואמונה would also have to be explained as a monolithic expression simply meaning 'true' and the objection to such a usage in Biblical and Mishnaic Hebrew would have to be ignored. It has already been suggested that it was difficulties with the precise sense of these two words in this context which led the medieval commentators to so many fanciful explanations which can hardly be taken seriously by modern scholars.

Although Yahya Ṣaliḥ partly subscribes to these homiletical interpretations, he also records and explains the vocalization קִים. His view that the sense here is 'has imposed an obligation on us', if perhaps reading a trifle too much into the text, is nevertheless not impossible. It is true that few objections to this aspect of his comments may be brought from the manuscript and historical evidence cited above but it does leave the words אמת ואמונה somewhat limp and vague and sheds no light at all on the puzzling comments of Rashi and *Tosafot* which he himself cites in part, as already indicated.

Still taking the Yemenite vocalization as the starting point, there are various possibilities for improving on Yahya's interpretation. A more convincing sense for כל זאת קים עלינו could be 'has fulfilled all this for us', i.e. God has kept his promise just recited in the third paragraph of the *shema'*, to be our God, 'and we are Israel His people'. The first two words could also be made to yield a better sense if it is recalled that the first of them is often used in the liturgy in the sense of באמת and both are given this sense here. Additional support for such a meaning is available in the variant reading באמת ובאמונה instead of אמת ואמונה which occurs in another context and has already been cited. The translation would then be 'In truth and faith, God has fulfilled all this for us'. Alternatively, אמת is only the introductory 'Truly' and not part of the remainder of the sentence, and just as in the third part of the sentence a claim is made about the fulfilment of God's promise so in the second part is the trustworthiness of what has been recited acknowledged in the words אֱמוּנָה כל זאת. Such a sense and vocalization would admirably fit Ginzberg's theory about the origins of the prayer as an אמן to what has gone before. it would also be linguistically significant. The translation would then be 'Truly, all this is acknowledged'.[83]

This novel treatment of the passage does not, however, provide any reference to the future redemption, apparently presupposed by Rashi and the *Tosafot*. It may, of course, be the case that they are reading the idea into קים עלינו but, if not, the possibility that קים was here originally קַיָּם as it appears in so many other cases, or יְקַיַּם, should be considered. Perhaps mention should also again be made of the possibility that there is here a remnant of some form of קים אמונה, 'keeping a promise'. Changes in other such petitions for the future redemption are well-known and some note has already been taken of them but the last phrase ואנחנו ישראל עמו, unless a later addition, would not fit well as the concluding portion of such a petition.

---

83 The reading in T-S Misc.28.77, though unclear, would appear to be אמת ואמונה בכל זאת. If this is so, it points to yet another possible interpretation, namely 'God has indeed laid upon us the obligation of belief in all this'.

There is the remote possibility that there is here some long-forgotten allusion to a popular text or its interpretation, a text such as Nehemiah 10:1 in which the expression כל זאת occurs in the context of 'making a covenant'. The covenant, אמנה, is, according to Rashi, the acceptance of God's kingship, strangely enough the same commitment as that traditionally associated with the *shema'*, and it may be added that the words ברית and אמנה are governed by none other a verb than קום in the *pi'el* in one of the 'Zadokite Documents';[84] but all this is probably no more than coincidental and produces only conjecture.

There are undoubtedly weaknesses in each of the explanations offered but I am fairly sure that I have established the existence of a problem and moderately hopeful that I have provided some clues that will ultimately contribute to its definitive solution.

---

84   *The Zadokite Documents*, ed. C. Rabin (Oxford, 1958), p. 39.

16

'Al Ha-Nissim: Its Emergence and Textual Evolution

The Canard

It is something of a canard in the historical study of Jewish liturgy to claim that the rabbinic prayers are essentially talmudic in origin and that the developments of the post-talmudic and medieval periods amount to no more than a tinkering with detail. Indeed, the doyen of Jewish liturgical research in the early part of the twentieth century, Ismar Elbogen, categorically limited the importance of those periods to what was achieved in the realm of liturgical poetry and was fairly dismissive of their whole contribution to the evolution of the statutory prayers themselves. More recently, Alan Mintz has argued that '...the prayerbook remains to this day essentially a document of the early rabbis.'[1] While it is undoubtedly true that the overall plan, the essential framework and the main beams of rabbinic prayer's structure were successfully completed by the talmudic teachers – both early and late – it must also be acknowledged that the more intricate layout, the decorations and the finishing were (*pace* Elbogen) all achievements of the later periods.. What is more, there was considerable dissension about precisely how to complete the task and about the ultimate appearance of the liturgical end-product. The degree of halakhic control, the need for total consistency, and the question of innovation were among the major matters of principle that occupied the minds of the post-talmudic authorities and there is clear and practical evidence in the manuscript fragments from the Cairo Genizah of particular trends towards textual clarification, expansion and adjustment.[2]

---

1   I. Elbogen, German edition (=G), *Der jüdische Gottesdienst in seiner geschichtlichen Entwicklung* (Frankfurt am Main, 1931; reprint, Hildesheim, 1962), pp. 271–72; Hebrew edition (=H), התפילה בישראל בהתפתחותה ההיסטורית (eds. J. Heinemann, I. Adler, A. Negev, J. Petuchowski and H. Schirmann, Tel Aviv, 1972), pp. 203–4; English edition (=E), *Jewish Liturgy: A Comprehensive History* (trans. and ed. Raymond P. Scheindlin, Philadelphia, Jerusalem and New York, 1993), p. 213; A. Mintz, 'Prayer and the prayerbook' in *Back to the Sources: Reading the Classic Jewish Texts*, ed. B. W. Holtz (New York, 1984), p. 406.
2   S. C. Reif, *Judaism and Hebrew Prayer* (Cambridge, 1993), pp. 122–52; and see chapter 11 of this volume.

In addition, there appears to have been a greater interest in spelling out the precise character of each liturgical occasion by way of targeted biblical readings, detailed sabbath and festival references, and highly specific insertions. Such an interest had already been partly indulged during the talmudic period but in a less systematic fashion and rarely without at least some element of controversy. What is especially interesting for the historian to trace are the manner in which certain prayers and formulas attached themselves to the liturgical corpus after the redaction of the Babylonian Talmud and how the process of their incorporation reflects the original talmudic principles and arguments and is itself reflected in the views of halakhic works and authorities of the geonic and medieval ages. For the linguist and the exegete it is also interesting to consider the textual variants that occur in such liturgical compositions and to speculate on their underlying reasons. It is commonly argued, to quote Mintz again, that 'before the Enlightenment, the idea of tampering with actual received words of the Siddur was unthinkable. To add or reinterpret – yes, but not to alter.' Is this view wholly borne out by a detailed examination of textual variation in the post-talmudic period?[3]

Ḥanukkah in talmudic prayer

In such a context, the treatment of the minor festivals of Ḥanukkah and Purim in the *'amidah* is especially instructive. The late fourth-century traditions recorded in the Tosefta represent the earliest instructions concerning this liturgical matter and make a clear distinction between what is to be done on the festivals which have a biblical origin and those that derive their authority from rabbinic tradition.[4] In the case of the former, which have an additional *'amidah* (*musaf*) representing the extra sacrifice offered in the Temple, the morning and afternoon *'amidot* include a reference to the festive day within the first of the final three benedictions (*'avodah*) while in the *musaf* service itself there is a specific benediction devoted to the holiness of the day, sandwiched between the first and last three regular benedictions. There is no instruction about the evening *'amidah* presumably because of its less obligatory nature, the textual reference to it clearly constituting, as Lieberman

---

3   Mintz (see n. 1 above), p. 425. On the matter of scribal transmission, see M. Beit-Arié, *Unveiled Faces of Medieval Hebrew Books: The Evolution of Manuscript Production – Progression or Regression?* (Jerusalem, 2003).
4   Tosefta, *Berakhot* 3.10, ed. Zuckermandel, p. 7, collated with *The Tosefta* ed. S. Lieberman (New York, 1955), pp. 14–15 and *Tosefta Ki-fshuṭa, Zera'im*, part 1 (New York, 1955), p. 39.

convincingly argues, an addition that has later been made to the traditions in the light of later practice.

An alternative view, in the name of R. Eleazar, suggests that the correct place for the insertion of a reference to the minor festival at the morning and afternoon 'amidot is the penultimate (hoda'a) benediction. As far as Ḥanukkah and Purim are concerned, there is no additional benediction in any of the 'amidot but merely a reference to the 'essential nature of the event' (מעין המורע). Should the one leading the prayer accidentally omit such a reference, there is textual ambivalence about whether he is required to repeat the prayer in order to include it, such doubt apparently arising out of the opposing halakhic views obtaining at different times.[5]

The Babylonian Talmud addresses the issue of whether Ḥanukkah should be specified in the grace after meals as part of the requirement to 'publicize the miracle' or should be ignored because it is not a biblically ordained festival.[6] A number of traditions are recorded as relevant to the discussion. Depending on how it is interpreted, one appears to suggest either that it need not be mentioned but, if it is, the most suitable place is the second benediction dealing with the land of Israel, or that it should be mentioned only in the 'amidah.[7] A second tradition is that its mention in the grace should follow the practice in the 'amidah, namely, in the thanksgiving benediction, which is the one dealing with the land of Israel. In the third tradition, the question is raised whether Ḥanukkah, which does not itself have an additional (musaf) 'amidah, merits specific mention in the 'amidot of the sabbath and New Moon days that coincide with that festival and that do themselves have musaf prayers. Both positive and negative responses to the question are cited. Interestingly, these two passages, from the Tosefta and the Babylonian Talmud, when compared with some passages in the Palestinian Talmud, appear to presuppose different texts and halakhic interpretations.[8]

5 The readings מחזירין and אין מחזירין both occur, the negative giving way to the positive when the more stringent view came to dominate.
6 BT, Shabbat 24a.
7 The original Hebrew reads: אמר רבא אמר רב סחורה אמר רב הונא אינו מזכיר ואם בא להזכיר מזכיר בהודאה. Rashi presupposes that the reference here, as in the third tradition cited, is to the second benediction of the grace but this is by no means unambiguous and he may have had a variant text before him.
8 The relevant passages are PT, Berakhot 7.4 (11c) and Ta'anit 2.2 (65c). There is an interesting discussion of the degree of variation by A. Hilbitz in Ḥiqrey Zemanim (Jerusalem, 1976), pp. 271–86. His attempt to harmonize the various views is historically questionable but his discussion is nevertheless most useful, especially for the development of all the halakhic issues touched upon here.

A number of important conclusions may be reached on the basis of these passages. Firstly, the matter of the specific mention of Hanukkah in the 'amidah and in the grace after meals was controversial. Equally open to discussion was the choice of the most appropriate benediction in which to insert such a reference, assuming that it did indeed require to be inserted. There was no unanimity about drawing parallels in this connection between the 'amidah and the grace after meals. Perhaps most important of all, there is no instruction about precisely how one is to word this 'mention'. There are hints that the content should relate to the expression of gratitude to God for favours received regarding one's life, the land that produces one's food, and the Temple worship, but no wording is suggested. In some instances the Talmud offers no prayer-text but does at least refer to the title of the relevant prayer. Here, however, not even such a clue is offered. Rashi explains that the reference is to the 'al ha-nissim ('for the miracles') prayer recited in the thanksgiving (hodayya) benediction of the 'amidah but it is perfectly fair to suggest that this reflects the position in medieval Franco-Germany and not in fourth-century Babylonia.

Geonic evidence

The evidence from the geonic period testifies to a somewhat different state of affairs. The post-talmudic tractate Soferim, dated to about the seventh or eighth century and including important liturgical traditions from the land of Israel as well as from Babylonia, and perhaps even redacted in Italy, specifies that on Hanukkah the worshipper is to recite a special prayer at the conclusion of the hodaya benediction of the 'amidah. It amounts to a request that God's miraculous intervention in the days of the priestly Hasmonean family led by Mattathias should now be replicated for those currently offering their prayers so that they will be eternally grateful.[9] Another source from about the same time, also with some Palestinian but with primarily Babylonian input, is the She'iltot collection of R. Aha of Shabha which offers two rulings in connection with Hanukkah liturgy.[10] Dates on which miraculous events occurred for Israel, such as Hanukkah and Purim, should be marked by the recitation of the benediction 'who wrought miracles for our fathers at this time'. The prayer 'al ha-nissim should be included in the

---

9   *Massekhet Soferim*, ed. M. Higger (New York, 1937), 20.6, p. 346 (E.T., ed. I. W. Slotki, London, 1965, 20.8, p. 313); see M. B. Lerner, 'Massekhet Sofrim' in *The Literature of the Sages. First Part: Oral Tora, Halakha, Mishna, Tosefta, Talmud, External Tractates*, eds. S. Safrai and P. J. Tomson (Assen/Maastricht and Philadelphia, 1987), pp. 397–400.
10   See Robert Brody, *The Textual History of the She'iltot* (Hebrew; New York and Jerusalem, 1991).

thanksgiving benediction of the *'amidah* but not in the grace after meals since one has a religious obligation to pray but not to have a meal.[11]

The halakhic code of a century or so later, *Halakhot Gedolot*, which has Palestinian content but is mainly the product of the Babylonian geonic environment, appears to repeat the rulings of the *She'iltot* which is not an unusual characteristic of that work. What is more noteworthy is that an Oxford manuscript of *Halakhot Gedolot* has no specific mention of *'al ha-nissim* but appears to go no further than the Babylonian Talmud, including only a general reference to 'mentioning' Hanukkah.[12] The only fully comprehensive and authentic prayer-book from geonic Mesopotamia is of course that of Sa'adya ben Joseph of Sura but the paradox is that it remains unclear whether his text represents a purely Babylonian version or one influenced by his Egyptian origins and his period of study in the Holy Land. Whatever its origins, his text is the earliest complete version of the *'al ha-nissim* prayer known to us and has five constituent parts:[13]

---

11   *Sheiltot, Vayishlaḥ* 26: וכד מטי יומא דאיתרחיש להו ניסא לישראל כגון חנוכה או פורים מיחייב לברוכי ברוך אשר עשה ניסים לאבותינו בזמן הזה... ומחייבינן לאדכורי בצלותא על הניסים ואינו חייב להזכיר בברכת המזון מ"ט תפלה משום דחובה הוא לצלויי מחייב אבל בסעודה דרשות היא לא חייבנו רבנן.

12   *Sefer Halakhot Gedolot*, ed. E. Hildesheimer, 1.163, 167, 169 (Jerusalem, 1971).

13   *Siddur R. Saadya Gaon*, eds. I. Davidson, S. Assaf and B. I. Joel, (Jerusalem, 1941; 1963²), p. 255:

על הנסין והגבורות והתשועות והמלחמות והפדות והפרקן שעשיתה עמנו ועם אבותינו בימים ההם ובזמן הזה. בימי מתתיהו בן יוחנן כהן גדול חשמונאי ובניו כשעמדה מלכות יון על עמך לשכחם את תורתך ולהעבירם מחוקי רצונך. ואתה ברחמיך הרבים עמדתה להם בעת צרתם ורבתה את ריבם ודנתה את דינם ונקמת את נקמתם ומסרת גבורים ביד חלשים ורבים ביד מעטים וטמאים ביד טהורים ורשעים ביד צדיקים ומזידים בכף עושי תורה. ולך עשיתה שם גדול וקדוש ולעמך ישראל עשיתה תשועה גדולה ופרקן. ואחר כך נכנסו עמך לדביר ביתך ופנו את היכלך וטיהרו את מקדשך והדליקו נרות בחצרות קדשך ועל כולם תתברך ותתרומם ותתרומם מן זיד פיה [ויש מוסיפים בו] וקבעו שמונת ימים הלל והודאה לשמך כשם שעשית נסין לראשונים כך תעשה לאחרונים ותושיענו בימים האילו כבימים ההם ועל כולם

   '(We thank you) for the miracles, the mighty deeds, the acts of salvation, the battles, the redemption and the rescue that you performed for us and for our forefathers in those days and at this time. In the days of Mattathias son of Johanan the High Priest, the Hasmonean, and his sons, when the kingdom of Greece arose against your people with the aim of making them forget your Torah and transgress your express instructions, you stood up for them in your manifold mercies in their time of trouble, pleaded their cause, represented their case, took revenge for them, handing the mighty into the power of the weak, the many into the power of the few, the impure into the power of the pure, the wicked into the power of the righteous and the insolent into the power of those who engage in Torah. You enhanced your great and holy reputation and brought about great salvation and rescue for your people Israel. Afterwards your people entered the shrine of your temple, cleansed your palace, purified your sanctuary and kindled lights in your holy courtyards. For all these things may you be blessed and exalted.' Some then add here 'They instituted eight days of praise and gratitude to your name. Just as you performed miracles for earlier generations, so do likewise for the later ones and save us these days as in those days, for all these things ...'

a. Gratitude for the miracles, victories and rescues perpetrated by God for us and our fathers at this time in earlier days.

b. Historical note about how the Greeks tried to suppress Judaism in the time of the Hasmonean high priest, Mattathias, and his sons.

c. Poetic summary of how God acted for Israel in this crisis and brought victory to a small and weak group of pure, righteous and observant Jews over a powerful and numerous enemy, with its contaminated and evil practices.

d. How this brought rescue for Israel and publicized the greatness and holiness of God.

e. Another historical note about how the victorious Jews reconsecrated the Temple and kindled lights there.

Sa'adya then notes that some worshippers add at this juncture (ומן אלנס מן יזיד פיה) another historical note (here designated 'f.') describing how the victors then instituted eight days of praise and thanksgiving and an entreaty asking for divine action at this time on behalf of the contemporary generation similar to what was done in those days for their ancestors. He is not averse to such an addition but is not enthusiastic enough to incorporate it in his standard formulation. He also notes that despite the fact that Hanukkah has no *musaf* prayer, there is no reason to object to the inclusion of *'al ha-nissim* in the *musaf* prayers of Sabbath and New Moon. As is well known, one has always to exercise caution in citing the texts to be found in the various versions of the prayer-book circulated for many centuries in the name of R. Sa'adya's predecessor, R. Amram ben Sheshna Gaon, because its sheer popularity led to its use in different liturgical communities where it was sometimes adjusted to match local custom. In the case of *'al ha-nissim*, however, the text is virtually identical with the sa'adyanic version, with the exception that section f. is included without comment.[14] We may apparently then presuppose that the sa'adyanic version was one that was prevalent in the Babylonian communities.

How then may we summarize developments in the geonic period with regard to the liturgical topic in hand? It was agreed that, while thanks were being offered to God in the *'amidah*, reference should also be made to the miraculous Hasmonean victory. This was expanded in three different ways. In one, the historical circumstances were simply chronicled while in another they were lyrically summarized. It may be the case that in the sa'adyanic version we can detect a fusion of the historical and the poetic formulations, sections b. and e. representing the former and c. and d. the latter. A third style opted for a link with the present and the future and requested a repeat performance of

---

14   *Seder Rav Amram Gaon*, ed. E. D. Goldschmidt (Jerusalem, 1971), pp. 97–98.

divine intervention. This is no longer history but eschatology and was a particularly common characteristic of the liturgical rite of the land of Israel in the period under discussion. It is possible that as in many instances in the development of the prayer-book, the ultimate response to the competitive existence of numerous options was to remove the element of controversy by including all of them in the standard formulation. Interestingly, these liturgical references to the Ḥanukkah miracle include the kindling of lights in the Temple, and rejoicing for eight days, but make no specific mention of the oil that marvellously lasted for eight days.[15]

Controversial entreaty

Be that as it speculatively may, there is no doubt that the inclusion at the end of 'al ha-nissim of the entreaty for miraculous divine intervention on behalf of contemporary Jewry invited some authorities to move one step further than R. Sa'adya and to express their discomfort with the practice. Citing R. Hai Gaon in support, the eleventh-century scholar, Judah ben Barzilai of Barcelona, points to the passage in the Yerushalmi[16] that distinguishes gratitude for past mercies from requests for future needs and notes the existence of a specific place for each in the 'amidah.[17] Such discomfort is expressed as downright opposition in the responsa of R. Meir of Rothenburg (=Maharam) in thirteenth-century Ashkenaz. Three comments are recorded in his name on the subject of the Ḥanukkah liturgy. Basing himself on the talmudic lack of unanimity about the need for a liturgical mention of Ḥanukkah, he limits its uncontroversial inclusion to the hodaya benediction in the 'amidah and offers his views on the correct formulation of two phrases in the 'al ha-nissim (of which more anon). His remaining comment, of relevance to this part of our discussion, is that the entreaty in section f. is inappropriate to the hodayya benediction.[18]

---

15   As in BT, Shabbat 21b. This point is made by B. S. Jacobson in his Netiv Binah (5 vols, Tel Aviv, 1968–83), 1.338.

16   PT, Berakhot 4.3 (8a). See the background to this in Mishnah, Berakhot 9.4.

17   Sefer Ha-'Ittim, ed. J. Schor (Berlin, 1902–3), p. 252.

18   Teshuvot, Pesaqim U-Minhagim, ed. I. Z. Cahane, vol. 1 (Jerusalem, 1957), nos 611–13, pp. 320–21:

תריא. ולהזכיר מעין המאורע [בברכה א' מעין ג'] בחנוכה ופורים לא צריך, דאפי' בברכת המזון איכא למ"ד פרק
במה מדליקין [שבת כד ע"א] דאין מזכיר, ואם בא להזכיר מזכיר בהודאה. אבל במעין שלש לא יעלה על לב איש,
כיון דליכא הודאה בברכה (דבעין) [דמעין] ג' אין מזכיר, דלא להזכיר מאורע בחנוכה ופורים אלא היכא דאיכא
הודאה בתפילה. [תשובות]

תריב. ואינו אומר בעל הנסים (השם) [כשם שעשית להם נסים וגבורות], לפי שאין תפלה בהודאה, ואומר רק
להודות ולהלל לשמך הגדול. [תשב"ץ]

This same view had been expressed about half a century earlier by Abraham b. Nathan of Lunel and the liturgical practice of Lunel cited in support.[19] Apparently it was only in the German communities that the opposition took hold, probably because of the major reputation of the Maharam, and the influence of his pupil, Meir Ha-Kohen who repeated the view in his commentary on the *Mishneh Torah* code of Maimonides,[20] with the result that the offending part of section f. gradually came to be deleted in most Ashkenazi prayer-books.[21] All the other communities, including the French, Italian, Spanish, North African, Persian, Rumanian and Yemenite, retained it.[22] Perhaps the defence mounted by R. Asher ben Saul of Lunel and Narbonne in the early thirteenth century[23] and by Abudraham in the fourteenth century assisted this proces of retention. They argued that entreaties on behalf of an individual's needs might be inappropriate but not those on behalf of the community as a whole.[24]

Early rites

A close examination of the early liturgical rites and authorities reveals a number of other interesting trends and developments. According to the Persian rite, thanks are to be given to God in section a. not only for the miracles but also for his special love (חסד) and in section c. the poetic

---

תריג. ואין לומר [להשכיחם] מתורתך במ"ם תחילה אלא תורתך בלא מ"ם, וכן הוא בסדר רבינו סעדיה, וכן כתב ה"ר מאיר מרוטנבורק. [אבודרהם]

19 *Sefer Ha-Manhig*, ed. I. Raphael (Jerusalem, 1978), 1.247: 'When I was a young man in the holy Jewish community of the city of Lunel, the view was that one should prevent the prayer-leader from reciting this piece.'

20 *Haggahot Maymoniyyot* on *Mishneh Torah*, in his comments on the liturgical text that follows the laws of circumcision at the end of the second book, on the passage dealing with the *hodayah* (second last) benediction of the *'amidah*.

21 See, for instance, S. Baer, *Seder Avodat Yisra'el* (Rödelheim, 1868), pp. 101–2. In the early seventeenth century, Shabbethai Sofer of Przemysl, who was most interested in such variations and in standardizing the Ashkenazi liturgy, makes no mention whatsoever of this part of section f. See the recent edition of his prayer-book, סדור המדקדק הגדול בקי בכל חדרי התורה מה"ר שבתי סופר ב"ר יצחק מפרעמישלא תלמיד הלבוש, יוצא לאור ע"פ כ"י בית הדין בלונדון על ידי הרב יצחק סץ והרב דוד יצחקי (5 vols, Baltimore, 1987–2002), 2.159–62.

22 See *Maḥzor Vitry*, ed. S. Hurwitz (2 vols, Nuremberg², 1923), p. 68; *Maḥzor Roma* (Bologna, 1540), pp. 49–50; E. D. Goldschmidt, *On Jewish Liturgy: Essays on Prayer and Religious Poetry* (Hebrew; Jerusalem, 1978), p. 294; *Siddur Rabbenu Shelomo ben Nathan*, ed. S. Ḥagi (Jerusalem, 1995), p. 74; *The Persian Jewish Prayer Book*, ed. S. Tal (Jerusalem, 1980), pp. 191–92 (MS, f. 99a); *Seder Tefillot Ha-Shanah Le-Minhag Qehillot Romaniya* (Constantinople, 1574), p. 35; *Tiklal* of Yaḥya ben Joseph ibn Ṣaliḥ (Jerusalem, 1894), 1.161b–162a.

23 *Sifran Shel Rishonim*, ed. S. Assaf (Jerusalem, 1935), p. 153.

24 *Sefer Abudraham* (Warsaw, 1877), p. 108; *Sefer Abudraham Ha-Shalem*, ed. S. A Wertheimer (Jerusalem, 1963), pp. 201–2.

summary also distinguishes between the circumcised and the uncircumcised (ערלים ביד מולים). The entreaty contained in section f. lists among current Jewish requirements not only miracles, as heretofore, but also 'release, salavation, mighty acts and wonders' (ופורקן וישועות וגבורות ונפלאות).[25] The specific identification of the wicked enemy of the Jews with the 'uncircumcised' is perhaps politically motivated by a desire to clarify that Muslims are not included among the 'powerful and numerous enemy, with its contaminated and evil practices'. The listing of additional substantives and epithets is a common characteristic of the liturgy of the land of Israel and is not a surprising find in the Persian rite which so often follows the liturgical custom of the homeland.[26]

The Roman rite also expands section f. with a request for wonders and miracles (כן עשה עמנו פלא ונסים) but, more interestingly, the equivalent text in the Rumanian rite makes no mention of miracles among the requests but prays rather for salvation (כן תעשה עמנו...והושיענו), perhaps laying the emphasis on a practical rather than a theological rescue. Equally significant is the addition to be found in Maḥzor Vitry to section e. Instead of ending the historical summary simply with a reference to the dedication of eight days to praise and thanksgiving, that work states the reason for such activity, namely, the multitude of miracles and wonders, thereby appearing to increase the status of the miraculous, perhaps at the expense of the historical.[27] Also opting for less of the historical data is the version of Maimonides, duplicated in the Yemenite prayer-book, which omits the reference to the institution of the eight days of Ḥanukkah earlier listed as e. in the description of the sa'adyanic text.[28]

Genizah texts

As in all such critical analyses of the textual history of early medieval rabbinic liturgy, it is essential to examine the evidence preserved in the manuscript fragments from the Cairo Genizah. Of some forty-six items to date identified in the Taylor-Schechter Collection at Cambridge University Library as having some Ḥanukkah connections, thirty-three

---

25 *Persian Prayer Book*, ed. Tal (see n. 22 above).
26 Reif, *Hebrew Prayer* (see n. 2 above), pp. 161–62. The issue of the circumcised non-Jew was a common point of halakhic discussion from talmudic times; see Mishnah, *Nedarim* 3.11 and BT, *'Avodah Zarah* 27a.
27 *Maḥzor Vitry*, ed. S. Hurwitz (see n. 22 above).
28 Goldschmidt, 'The Oxford ms. of Maimonides' book of prayer' in his collected articles entitled *On Jewish Liturgy* (see n. 22 above), p. 202; *Tiklal* (see n. 22 above).

have partial or substantial texts of 'al ha-nissim[29] and fifteen of these have textual evidence that is particularly significant for our discussion. At this point, only the relationship of each of these significant fragments to the literary history of the 'al ha-nissim prayer will be discussed. The linguistic variations in the detailed text will be discussed when all such readings engage our attention later in this chapter.

The major overall impression received is that the group of Cambridge Genizah fragments consulted are, with some important exceptions that will immediately be discussed, substantially in agreement with the literary structure and fuller text recorded by R. Sa'adya Gaon.[30] Since these fragments probably date from the tenth to the thirteenth centuries, and have Palestinian as well as Babylonian backgrounds, this would appear to indicate that the structure of the text had already been fixed by the ninth century, a conclusion that tallies with the evidence earlier cited from the geonic sources. It will be recalled that R. Sa'adya, and some of his successors, had some doubts about the inclusion of the final entreaty listed as f. in the summary of the contents of 'al ha-nissim offered above. Two of the earliest Genizah fragments in our list, both written on vellum, do not include this entreaty at all.[31] Interestingly, another fragment, which is undoubtedly from the eleventh-century land of Israel or the twelfth-century émigré community in Syria – since it elsewhere mentions Palestinian rabbinic leaders who functioned in the two decades just before the Crusader invasion and in the decade immediately afterwards – has all the sections of the prayer, including the entreaty.[32]

In spite of known tendencies in the Holy Land to opt for more fanciful poetic versions than those of their Babylonian coreligionists,

---

29   The 46 items are here listed, with the thirteen without texts of 'al ha-nissim given at
     the end of the list: 6H6.6, 8H10.14, 8H22.1, H5.146, H10.273, H18.4, H18.32, NS 89.36,
     NS 115.143, NS 123.126, NS 148.6, NS 150.2, NS 150.6, NS 150.150, NS 152.82, NS
     158.93, NS 159.113, NS 160.5, NS 164.111, NS 172.18, NS 195.43, NS 196.81, NS 197.16,
     NS 229.46, NS 235.170, NS 271.4, NS 271.162, NS 272.54, NS 272.67, NS 274.174, AS
     103.83, AS 105.197, AS 110.47; NS 32.18, NS 38.96, NS 150.151, NS 157.178, NS 159.86,
     NS 196.73, NS 204.40, NS 271.94, NS 272.132, NS 288.152, AS 105.41, AS 105.42, AS
     110.72. I have been made aware of some of these texts through the joint Genizah
     liturgical project of Ben-Gurion University of the Negev and Cambridge University
     Library being run by Dr Uri Ehrlich and my Cambridge colleague, Dr Ben
     Outhwaite. See the plate of manuscript fragment T-S NS 229.46 at the end of this
     volume.
30   E.g. T-S NS 89.36.
31   T-S H5.146 and T-S NS 115.143.
32   T-S 6H6.6; on this fragment see N. Wieder, *The Formation of Jewish Liturgy in the East
     and the West: A Collection of Essays* (2 vols; Hebrew; Jerusalem, 1998), 1.264 and E.
     Fleischer, *Eretz-Israel Prayer and Prayer Rituals as Portrayed in the Geniza Documents*
     (Hebrew; Jerusalem, 1988), p. 244.

that fragment is not one of those that include a poetic alternative to the simple version recorded by R. Sa'adya. In the latter's liturgy, the text offered is simply כשם שעשית נסין לראשונים כך תעשה לאחרונים ותושיענו בימים האילו כבימים ההם 'just as you peformed miracles for earlier generations, do act similarly for their descendants and save us in these days as in those times'. A poetic version of this entreaty, formulated as וכנסי פלאיך וכתשועת כוהניך 'as your wondrous miracles and the salvation of your priests' (similar to the text of *Soferim*) occurs in a number of Genizah fragments, sometimes in additon to the more prosaic formulation and on other occasions in a conflated version of both styles.[33] It was perhaps once an independent alternative which was widely replaced by the more standard formula but did not entirely disappear from all texts. There is also a simpler version of the entreaty that, unlike the sa'adyanic version, makes no mention of the earlier or later generations but simply requests wondrous miracles for the benefit of current worshippers (כן עשה עמנו נסים וגבורות), the text then reverting to the benediction's central theme of thanksgiving.[34]

It will be recalled that section d. of the prayer generally consists of two parts, the first noting how the events just described brought rescue for Israel and the second mentioning how they publicized the greatness and holiness of God. The Yemenite rite includes only the first part referring to wondrous miracles (פלא ונסים) rather than to rescue, perhaps in order to match both the previous section which deals with the marvel of the historical event and the subsequent section which requests similar miraculous intervention for the contemporary worshippers.[35] On the other hand, one of the Genizah fragments consulted includes a reference only to the events having consolidated God's great and fearful reputation, leaving the previous and subsequent sections to deal with Israel.[36] This may indicate, once again, that the stitching together of a number of original formulations, each with its own hermeneutical angle, led to questions being raised about consistency and textual adjustments being made in response.

Two other variants are here worthy of note and occur in a Genizah fragment that is written in a square hand on vellum but has detailed

---

33 T-S H10.273, T-S NS 158.93, T-S NS 196.81, T-S NS 229.46, T-S NS 271.4 and T-S NS 271.162; see n. 9 above for *Soferim* reference. Interestingly, T-S NS 271.4 has the continuation of the regular benediction with the words ועל כולם before the two entreaties but these two word are marked as a deletion. The two entreaties are then followed by the words ועל כולם, giving the impression that the entreaties were perhaps an addendum.

34 T-S 8H10.14 (with an alternative Aramaic formulation: כאלין יומיא ובכל זמן ועידן), T-S H18.4 and T-S NS 148.6.

35 *Tiklal* (see n. 22 above), 1.162a.

36 T-S NS 160.5.

and standard vocalization and is therefore unlikely to be among the earliest representatives of its type.[37] It replaces 'wars' (מלחמות) in section a. with 'consolations' (נחמות), an alternative reading that is perhaps motivated by a desire to present a pacific image to those who might be seeking in the Jewish liturgy pretexts to persecute those who perform it. Such an explanation may be supported by the fact that the same alternative occurs in a fifteenth-century Spanish prayer-book, published from manuscript by E. D. Goldschmidt over sixty years ago.[38] The second reading occurs in section e. and, instead of very generally referring to the 'praise and gratitude' (הלל והודאה) expressed by the victorious Hasmoneans, specifies, in the case of the first of these expressions, 'complete hallel' (הלל גמור). What has occurred here is that the expression has been understood to refer to the halakhic requirement of reciting all six specified psalms (113–118) and the original simple form therefore replaced with the technical liturgical term. By using the term גמור the scribe makes it clear that the shorter version – which omits the first halves of Psalms 115 and 116 and which is used, for instance, for the New Moon liturgy – is not to be employed in the case of Ḥanukkah.[39]

Linguistic variants

It remains to comment on some of the more noteworthy linguistic variants to be found in the detailed texts of the 'al ha-nissim in the various sources that have been cited above in connection with its literary structure.

1. הנסין 'the miracles': So RSG[40], P, T-S H5.146 and T-S H18.32; elsewhere predominantly הנסים. The alternative plural suffix in nun rather than in mem is a common characteristic of Mishnaic Hebrew (MH), particularly in its early forms, which is gradually reversed as Biblical Hebrew (BH) acquires its standard form as a result of the work

---

37　T-S NS 272.54.
38　Goldschmidt (see n. 22 above), p. 294; originally published in Kiryat Sefer 20 (1943–44), pp. 171–76.
39　See Elbogen (see n. 1 above), G, p. 125, H, p. 95, E, p. 105.
40　The abbreviations used here are as follows: RSG = R. Sa'adya Gaon, as in n. 13 above; P = Persian rite, as in n. 22 above; SRA = Seder Rav Amram, as in n. 14 above; MV = Maḥzor Vitry, as in n. 22 above; SbN = Solomon ben Nathan, as in n. 22 above; RMBM = Maimonides, as in n. 28 above; Rom = Roman rite, as in n. 22 above; Rum = Rumanian rite, as in n. 22 above; JbY = Judah ben Yaqar, Perush Ha-Tefillot Ve-Ha-Berakhot (2 vols.; Jerusalem, 1968–69); T = Tiklal, as in n. 22 above.

of the Masoretes and this has an impact on the MH used in the liturgy.[41]

2. שעשיתה 'that you performed': So RSG, and predominantly (but not always with internal consistency) among the Genizah fragments consulted and earlier cited.[42] This fuller orthography, with the addition of the letter *he*, for the second person masculine singular perfect form, which also occurs in the other verbs used later in the prayer, is commonly found in early rabbinic manuscripts, 'especially in Palestinian texts', as already pointed out by Segal.[43] It is standard at Qumran and is attested in archaic BH.[44]

3. עמנו ועם אבותינו 'for us and for our forefathers': So RSG, P, T and Rum but SRA and MV have only לאבותינו and this shorter alternative is also found in the later Sefardi and Ashkenazi rites.[45] The Genizah texts testify to those two versions[46], as well as to an intriguing third version that makes a link with the next passage and reads: שעשית ה' אלהינו (לאבותינו) על ידי מתתיה 'that you performed, Lord our God, (for our forefathers) through Mattathias'[47] Both Genizah fragments that record this third version reflect the rite of the land of Israel, as does another Palestinian fragment that adds the word ולנו after לאבותינו.[48] A reasonable hypothesis would be that originally one formulation, apparently recited in the Holy Land, stressed the historical miracle while the other, perhaps championed by the Babylonian authorities, wished to link the miracle with the current worshipper, perhaps to forestall the criticism that we cannot thank God in the *'amidah* for something that does not in some way relate to us. The commentary of

---

41 M. H. Segal, *A Grammar of Mishnaic Hebrew* (Oxford, 1927), p. 126; H. Yalon, *Introduction to the Vocalization of the Mishna* (Hebrew; Jerusalem, 1964), pp. 25–26; S. C. Reif, *Shabbethai Sofer and his Prayer-book* (Cambridge, 1979), pp. 306–7; E. Y. Kutscher, *A History of the Hebrew Language*, ed. R. Kutscher (Jerusalem and Leiden, 1982), pp. 121–22 and 129; M. P. Fernández, *An Introductory Grammar of Rabbinic Hebrew*, E. T., J. Elwolde (Leiden, New York and Köln, 1997), p. 63; A. Sáenz Badillos, *A History of the Hebrew Language*, E. T., J. Elwolde (Cambridge, 1993), pp. 35–36 and 191; and A. Dodi, 'The vocalization of a 13th century siddur' (Hebrew), *Leshonenu* 53 (1988), p. 70.

42 E.g. T-S 6H6.6, 8H10.14, 8H22.1, H5.146, H10.273, NS 89.36, NS 115.143, NS 148.6, NS 158.93, NS 159.113, NS 229.46, with inconsistency in T-S NS 271.162.

43 Segal, *A Grammar* (see n. 41 above), pp. 70–71.

44 Fernández, *Introductory Grammar* (see n. 41 above), p. 105.

45 E.g. Baer (see n. 21) above; *The Book of Prayer and Order of Service according to the Custom of the Spanish and Portuguese Jews*, eds D. A. de Sola and M. Gaster (London, 1901), 1.35.

46 The longer version occurs in T-S H5.146, NS 89.36, NS 115.143, NS 123.126, AS 105.197, while the shorter version is to be found in T-S NS 148.6, NS 158.93, NS 229.46.

47 So T-S H18.4 and T-S NS 160.5.

48 T-S 6H6.6.

Yaḥya ibn Ṣaliḥ on the Yemenite prayer-book argues such a case in his
defence of the longer version: דנס שנעשה לאבותינו שייך גם לנו כי לולא שנשארה
להם פליטה לא היינו אנחנו נמצאים בעולם דאם אין שורש ענף מניין 'the miracle that
was performed for our forefathers is also relevant to us since our
existence in today's world would not have been possible if they had
had no surviving remnant, given that branches cannot grow without
roots.'[49]

4. בימים ההם ובזמן הזה 'in those days and at this time': This text is what
substantially appears in all the rites and authorities[50] but sometimes
without the conjunctive *waw*[51] and with alternatives of האילו and האלה for
ההם.[52] The latter variation is easily explained by reference to the issue of
whether to follow BH or MH in the prayer-book but the matter of the
waw is not immediately explicable. Given that the second benediction
for the kindling of the Ḥanukkah lights has a similar mention of
miracles performed for one's ancestors, it is appropriate to take note of
the early variants that appear in versions of that text. Both the *She'iltot*
and Sa'adya have only the phrase בזמן הזה[53] while *Soferim* includes no
more than שעשה נסים, apparently without any mention of the time factor,
unless we are dealing simply with an abbreviated text.[54] Some of the
Genizah texts consulted have only the phrase בזמן הזה after שעשה נסים
with no reference to 'those days'[55] while others have the alternative
בימים האילו.[56] It therefore seems reasonable to suppose, as far as the
benediction is concerned, that it was possible at some stage to refer to
the miracles done בימים האילו which would have been the more rabbinic
form. To take this supposition a little further, such a phrase could have
been understood either as 'at this time' or 'in those days' and an
alternative for the former could have been בזמן הזה. In the על הנסים
prayer, the two readings were conflated, as often happened in
medieval Jewish liturgy, and the choice before the worshipper and the
copyist was either to understand the whole phrase as meaning that
God performed miracles 'in those days, at this time of the year', thus
justifying both readings, or to interpret God's actions as applying to
both then and now ('for us and for our forefathers'). In that case, a *waw*
would be inserted between them to indicate a reference to 'both in
those days and in our own time', giving more sense to the act of current

---

49 T (see n. 22 above), p. 161b.
50 RSG, P, MV.
51 SRA (possibly), RMBM, T, Rom, Rum and Abudraham.
52 T-S 6H6.6 and T-S NS 229.46.
53 See notes 11 and 13 above.
54 *Soferim* (see n. 9 above), 20.4, p. 344; E. T. 20.6, pp. 312–13.
55 T-S H2.124 and T-S H2.152, which contain the benediction as it occurs in the
    Passover Haggadah.
56 T-S NS 89.36.

thanksgiving as explained in the previous discussion. There is support
for such a reconstruction from the textual variation to be found at the
end of the final section (cited above as 'f.') which constitutes an
entreaty about the need for contemporary miracles and which will
receive attention in the final textual discussion below (no. 12).

5. מלכות יון הרשעה 'the wicked Greek kingdom': This is the most
common text, found in many Genizah fragments as well as in the
versions of SRA, RMBM, MV, SbN, Rom and Rum. RSG has only מלכות
יון without the moral qualification[57] and it is possible that such a
qualification, which is regularly used in rabbinic literature to describe
the Roman authority, was imported here. Perhaps this is why Judah
ben Yaqar offers an explanation and distinction. He argues the
possibility that 'wicked' is a suitable epithet for Greece rather than
Rome since the latter is more appropriately described as 'guilty' (חייבת)
or 'insolent' (זדון) which he regards as worse than 'wicked'. The
vocalization of the word הרשעה is also controversial, being construed as
either הָרְשָׁעָה (more commonly) or as הָרְשָׁעָה, as in the Persian, Yemenite,
Roman and Rumanian rites.[58] It would appear that the latter is a non-
standard form, gradually eliminated from various rites when the
prayer-book text came under the influence of the standard Tiberian
vocalization of Ben Asher.[59] The commentary of Yaḥya ibn Ṣaliḥ on the
Yemenite rite cites the opposing views of Joseph Karo and Hezekiah
ben David Da Silva, expressing personal preference for the standard
form but noting the traditional Yemenite choice of the other form.
Other commentaries puristically concerned with the adoption of the
BH model for liturgical Hebrew, such as Shabbethai Sofer and
Seligmann Baer, refer to the work of David Qimḥi and Elijah Levita,
arguing that הָרְשָׁעָה is an adjectival form, as in Ezek. 3:18, while הרשעה
can only be a noun, as in Zech. 5:8.[60] Alternatively, the original text was
מלכות הרשעה, with the first word in the construct case and the second a
noun and not an adjective, and it was the introduction of the word יון
(to exclude other kingdoms that might be thought to be wicked) that
created the grammatical anomaly.

---

57   So too T-S NS 115.143. T-S NS 89.36 has יום for יון, perhaps mistakenly considering
     this as more akin to BH! See the comments on הנסין above.
58   See n. 22 above.
59   For this kind of development, see M. Beit-Arié, 'The vocalization of the Worms
     Mahzor', Leshonenu 29 (1964–65), pp. 27–46 and 80–102 and Dodi, 'Vocalization' (see
     n. 41 above).
60   Bet Yosef on Ṭur, Oraḥ Ḥayyim 682; Peri Ḥadash on Shulḥan 'Arukh, same section. See
     also D. Qimḥi's Shorashim, ed. J. H. R. Biesenthal and F. Lebrecht (Berlin, 1847), s.v.
     רשע, with Levita's additional note, pp. 361 and 440; the prayer-book of Shabbethai
     Sofer of Przemysl (see n. 21 above), 2.160; S. Baer, 'Avodat Yisra'el (see n. 21 above).

6. לשכחם את תורתך 'to make them forget your Torah': So RSG, SbN and some Genizah texts[61] but the את is not present and the second word is given a prefix (ומתורתך) in SRA, JbY, P, Rom, Rum and T-S 8H22.1. Among other alternatives to be found in the early sources are לבטלם מתורתך as in RMBM and T-S NS 152.82; לשכחם ולבטלם מתורתך as in T and T-S 8H10.14; להסירם מתורתך as in T-S NS 160.5; and להשכיחם מתורתך as in MV. One problem that faced the early liturgical formulators and transmitters appears to lie in the double accusative of the simplest (and probably original) form לשכחם תורתך, which may have left the phrase somewhat ambiguous, and another difficulty lay in the meaning of the root שכח in the *pi'el* conjugation. In MH it carries the sense of 'making someone forget' or 'making someone neglect',[62] as intended here, but in BH the *pi'el* extends the meaning from 'causing to forget' to 'removing from memory' and therefore 'removing from existence'.[63] The ambiguity of the double accusative and the superstitious objection to associating Israel in any way with destruction could be removed by a change to the *hiph'il* conjugation[64] and/or by the insertion of the prefixed *mem* to the word תורה.[65] Such a change of conjugation is not uncommon in the linguistic development of the Hebrew prayers, as with מקדש/מקדיש/מקדש and מטבל/מטביל and מנהג/מנהיג/מנהג[66]. Other alternatives were to make use of a verb such as להסיר or לבטל, or, inevitably, to use two such verbs (לשכחם ולבטלם) to ensure clarity or to avoid the elimination of an established expression.

7. ונקמת את נקמתם 'and took revenge for them': The various medieval rites and liturgical authorities appear to be united in using the *qal* conjugation here but some Genizah fragments record the *pi'el* form וניקמת.[67] Both conjugations occur in BH but MH undoubtedly prefers the *qal* form. The use of the *pi'el* in some prayer-books appears to have been influenced by the verse in Jer. 51:36 which has two of the expressions

---

61 T-S NS 158.93 and NS 197.16.
62 See e.g. Tosefta, *Soṭah* 3.12, and Mishnah, *Avot* 2.2.
63 As in Lam. 2:6: שכח ה' בציון מועד ושבת; see *A Complete Dictionary of Ancient and Modern Hebrew by Eliezer Ben Yehuda of Jerusalem* (Hebrew; Jerusalem and New York, 1908–1959), p. 7092.
64 As in Jer. 23:27: להשכיח את עמי שמי.
65 Objection to this prefix was expressed by Maharam (see n. 18 above) and Abudraham (see n. 24 above).
66 Reif, *Shabbethai Sofer* (see n. 41 above), pp. 244–45 and 251–52. Compare also the alternative vocalization of the word משכחת in *Avot* 2.2 as a *pi'el* or a *hiph'il*; see S. Sharvit, *Tractate Avoth Through the Ages: A Critical Edition, Prolegomena and Appendices* (Hebrew; Jerusalem, 2004), p. 82. See also A. Dodi, 'Post biblical morphological features of a Spanish *machzor* from the 15th or 16th century' (Hebrew) in *Studies in Ancient and Modern Hebrew in Honour of M. Z. Kaddari*, ed. S. Sharvit (Ramat Gan, 1999), p. 193.
67 T-S NS 89.36 and T-S NS 271.4.

being used in this prayer and has the root נקם in the *pi'el* form: הנני רב את ריבם ונקמתי את נקמתך. Further evidence of a tendency on the part of some text transmitters to follow the biblical precedent in this liturgical context may be found in the prayer-books of Maimonides and the Yemenite rite. Both are apparently unhappy about the phrase דנת את דינם being permitted to come between two other phrases that occur together in the Hebrew Bible. In their texts it therefore precedes them.

8. מעטים 'few': Once again there is unity among the various medieval rites and liturgical authorities in using the adjective מעטים to refer to the Jews and contrasting it with the adjective רבים 'many' to refer to their enemies. What is surprising is that a substantial number of Genizah fragments use the alternative adjective מעוטים as the opposite of the unchanged word רבים and this certainly calls for an explanation.[68] The word מעטים in BH widely bears the sense of 'little', 'diminished', 'few', at times in antithesis to רבים or הרבה.[69] The Hebrew of the Second Temple period, however, as represented by such sources as Ben Sira and the Manual of Discipline, records the alternative adjectival form מועט, apparently derived from the *pu'al* or *hoph'al* conjugation, with the meaning of 'small in number, capacity or extent' and an opposite form in the word מרובה. Such a form also appears in MH but is joined by what appears to be a *qal* passive form מעוט which is used to convey the sense of 'limited', 'weak' or 'sparse' of people and of things, sometimes with negative overtones. [70] Given that the earliest liturgical Hebrew in rabbinic circles was more akin to MH than to BH,[71] the version of the Genizah fragments may represent a remnant of that language which was subsequently 'biblicized'. It appears to have been used here with no more specialized meaning than its biblical counterpart but simply as a MH alternative to it. What is particularly noteworthy is that in this instance the slate was virtually swept clean of such early evidence and only the Genizah texts testify to such a version.

9. ומזידים בכף עושי תורה 'and the insolent into the power of those who engage in Torah': So RSG and (partly preserved) T-S AS 110.47, while SbN and T-S NS 172.18 have ומזידים בכף עושי תורתך; T-S NS 229.46 has

---

68 T-S 6H6.6, 8H10.14, NS 115.143, NS 148.6, NS160.5, NS 235.170 and NS 271.4.
69 F. Brown, S. R. Driver and C. A Briggs, *A Hebrew and English Lexicon of the Old Testament* (Oxford, 1907), pp. 589–90; H.-J. Zobel in *Theological Dictionary of the Old Testament*, eds G. J. Botterweck, H. Ringgren and H.-J. Fabry (E. T., Grand Rapids, 1997), 8.452–58.
70 *Ben Yehuda of Jerusalem* (see n. 63 above), pp. 2855, 3152–53 and 3158–62; A. Even-Shushan, *Ha-Millon He-Hadash* (Jerusalem, 1979), pp. 1264, 1430 and 1432–34. Compare גסי רוח ומעוטי תורה in PT, *Sanhedrin* 1.2 (18c), and BT *Berakhot* 61a which includes both the BH and MH forms in virtually the same statement of moral advice first based on rabbinic tradition and then supported from scripture.
71 See chapter three of this volume.

ומזידים בכף עוסקי תורתך; T-S 8H10.14, T-S H5.146, T-S NS 158.93 and T-S NS 159.113 have ומז(י)דים בכף עוסקי תורה; T-S NS 115.143 (and T-S NS 271.4, with a defective spelling of the first word) have ומזידים ביד עושי תורה; T-S NS 271.162 has ומזידים ביד עוסקי תורה; T-S 6H6.6 has וזידים בכף עוסקי תורה; T-S NS 150.6 has תורתיך [sic] וזדים בכף עוזקי; SRA, T-S NS 160.5 have וזידים ביד עוסקי תורה; T-S NS 148.6, MV, Abudraham, P, Rom and Rum have וזידים ופושעים ביד עוסקי; T has ופושעים ביד עושי תורתך; RMBM has ביד עוסקי תורתך תורתך. The problem is precisely how to understand the nature of the loyal Jewish activity here described and how it stands in opposition to the behaviour of those who were attacking the Jews in the time of Mattathias. Is it the observance of the Torah or its study that the text has in mind and how does the Hebrew root זיד relate adversely to either of these activities? Is the dominant theme of the phrase political, theological or intellectual? That there is precisely such a problem of interpretation is confirmed by the comments of, among others, Joseph Karo, Hezekiah ben David Da Silva, Yahya ibn Salih and Seligmann Baer.[72] If we examine the other occurrences of the word זדים in the early medieval prayer-book, which are to be found in the *ge'ulah* benediction before the morning *'amidah* and in the twelfth benediction of the *'amidah* itself, the meaning would appear to be the political and religious enemies of the Jewish people, exemplified by the Egyptians at the Reed Sea and the Romans or Jewish apostates in the Roman world of the early Christian period.[73] A comparison of this phrase with all those that immediately precede it in the prayer would also support the idea that the contrast should again be between the small groups of loyal Jews and the powerful bands of insolent non-Jews. The variations on the text may therefore be understood as the attempts of different generations and circles to clarify precisely how they saw the miraculous deliverance. Perhaps those who were unconvinced that the word עושי could be used to refer to Torah students and loyalists (thinking that it meant only those who observe the Torah) stressed the importance of Torah study by opting for the less ambiguous term עוסקי[74]. The use of the pronominal suffix to convey the sense of 'God's

---

72 *Bet Yosef* on *Tur, Orah Hayyim* 682; *Peri Hadash* on *Shulhan 'Arukh*, same section; T (see n. 22 above), commentary, p. 162a; S. Baer, *'Avodat Yisra'el* (see n. 21 above). See also N. M. Bronznick in *Or Ha-Mizrah* 26 (1977), pp. 262–68.

73 See Y. Luger, *The Weekday Amidah in the Cairo Genizah* (Hebrew; Jerusalem, 2001), pp. 141–43. It is interesting that the earliest forms of the *ge'ulah* benediction, such as that of Sa'adya Gaon, describe the Egyptian persecutors with various expressions but do not use זדים. Perhaps this is another indication that the word was later adopted as a more biblical (or lyrical?) expression.

74 For the root לעשות in the sense of 'study', see e.g. *Seder Eliyahu Rabbah*, ed. M. Friedmann (Vienna, 1904), 6(7).38; the short *Tur* commentary on Lev. 26:3; S. Safrai in *Tarbiz* 38 (1969), pp. 90–91; and Bronznick (see n. 72 above).

Torah' was an attempt to strengthen the notion of the divine revelation (of both the Oral and Written Torah?). The problem of interpretation is aggravated by the fact that the BH word זדים, though still occurring as late as Ben Sira 11:10 (9), was not used in early rabbinic literature and has clearly been re-introduced from BH into the liturgy as a more poetic version of רשע.[75] Those who were uneasy about this linguistic change preferred the word פושעים and saw this as a better way of drawing a contrast between good and evil. It is more difficult to explain what may lie behind the textual variation זדים/מזידים.[76] Given that the word מזיד in rabbinic literature refers to Jews who deliberately flout the prescriptions of the Torah, is its use here possibly an attempt to contrast two groups of Jews, the loyal and the disloyal? In that case, could it have been motivated by an awareness of the presence of Jewish apostates among the Hellenisers or did it relate to the period of the text transmitter rather than to that of the Hasmoneans and simply represent vocabulary that was more familiar from early MH? Or are both hypotheses possible? As far as the variant יד/כף is concerned, the most likely explanation here is that כף is the poetic equivalent of יד in MH, preferred by those who wish to lyricize the liturgy to a greater extent and rejected by those who see the word more prosaically as the palm of the hand.

10. שם גדול וקדוש בעולמך 'a great and holy reputation in your world': So SRA and MV. There would appear to be hardly anything controversial about claiming that God enhanced his standing by his support of the Maccabees but the textual history of the phraseology here indicates otherwise. There is no reference to 'the world' in RSG or in Rum, the Yemenite *Tiklal* of Yaḥya ibn Ṣaliḥ mentions only what happened to Israel and says nothing of God in this section, and the word בעולם is used instead of בעולמך in P, Rom and SbN. The evidence from the Genizah complicates matters even further. A number of fragments make no mention of the word בעולם but they expand on God's action by describing his name as holy or revered as well as great (שם גדול וקדוש or שם גדול ונורא) and/or by referring to the 'great salvation' (תשועה גדולה) that he brought about.[77] The most common rendering appears, however, to be שם גדול וקדוש בעולם 'a great and holy reputation in the world'.[78] Others use the word בעולמך instead of בעולם but have a simpler description of

---

75 I. Gluska, *The Yemenite Weekday Prayer: Text and Language* (Hebrew; Jerusalem, 1995), pp. 212–14.

76 Unless we speculatively suppose that the similar sound of the word to that describing the Muslim sect of the *Zaydiyyun* inspired the change in the grammatical form.

77 E.g. T-S NS 89.36, T-S NS 160.5 and T-S NS 229.46.

78 T-S H5.146, NS 115.143, NS 148.6, NS 158.93, NS 235.170, NS 271.4 and NS 271.162.

God's great name, that is, שם גדול בעולמך.[79] The problem for those who preferred בעולמך to בעולם appears to have been the assumption that God had, as it were, to use the Maccabean victory to establish his reputation, which was apparently seen by some as *lèse majesté*. By indicating that the whole world was God's, at least part of this difficulty was removed. For those who made no reference to God but only to Israel, there was of course no theological difficulty of this nature. Commentators such as Judah ben Yaqar and Abudraham justified the retention of the theological concept by citing as a parallel the verses in Ezekiel 36:22–23 in which God declares that he is acting not for Israel but for the sanctification of his name, which had been profaned, and to make the world understand that he is God. Most interestingly of all, a Genizah fragment of the Palestinian rite has an alternative for the word בעולם, offering the reading שם גדול וקדוש בארץ.[80] The transmitter of this text is perhaps more concerned with tying the events to the land of Israel, unless he is uncomfortable with the rabbinic use of the word עולם as world and prefers the biblical ארץ.

11. **נכנסו עמך לדביר ביתך** 'your people entered the shrine of your temple': This reading, which is favoured by Sa'adya, is not the one that came to dominate among most of the rites and authorities. First of all, it needs to be noted that Maimonides and the Yemenite rite make no reference at all to the actions of the Jews in the Temple itself but move directly into the comparison of past and future miracles. For Rom, Rum, SRA, JbY, MV, and the later Ashkenazi and Sefardi prayer-books באו בניך לדביר ביתך is the preferred reading while a number of Genizah fragments testify to a greater degree of variation with the replacement of לדביר ביתך[81] by לבית בחירתך and read לבית בחירתך(י)ך נכנסו עמ(י)ך. The situation is further complicated by the existence of what may be described as conflated readings such as נכנסו בניך לבית בחירתך and באו עמך לדביר ביתך.[82] Evidence that such issues troubled some of the copyists is to be found in an early Palestinian Genizah fragment in which the word עמך has been scored through and replaced with בניך.[83] What appears to be occurring here is, again, an argument about whether biblical or mishnaic Hebrew forms are preferable in the liturgy. In the cases of באו and נכנסו, as well as דביר ביתך and בית בחירתך, the former represent BH while the latter are

---

79   E.g. T-S NS 272.54.
80   T-S 6H6.6.
81   E.g. T-S H5.146, H10.273, NS 89.36, NS 158.93 and NS 271.162.
82   So P and SbN and Genizah fragments T-S NS 172.18 and T-S NS 229.46; see also T-S NS 272.54 which has a lacuna but, given the space, seems more likely to have read באו than נכנסו and T-S NS 272.67 which has נכנסו בניך לביתך.
83   T-S 6H6.6.

examples of MH.[84] The distinction between עמך and בניך is less clear. Perhaps the former is the more prosaic form and the latter the more poetic. The unusual phrase that occurs in one Genizah fragment, that is, ודיכאו את מזבחך, is without doubt more in the rabbinic style, choosing as it does a term that is commonly found in late Palestinian Jewish Aramaic to describe 'ritual cleansing'.[85]

12. בימים האילו כבימים ההם 'these days as in those days': Further to the discussion in no. 4 above, it is interesting to note that again there are, among those which include such comparative chronological reference towards the end of the section,[86] some texts that offer only one phrase. Furthermore, where there is only one such phrase and not the double formulation listed at the introduction to this paragraph, the nature of that phrase varies from source to source. It occurs as בימים האלה (האילו) 'in those days',[87] בעת הזאת 'at this time'[88] and בעת ובעונה הזאת 'at this very time'.[89] There is also an intriguing Aramaic version which reads כאלין יומיא ובכל זמן ועידן 'as at these days and at all other times' which makes a differently worded comparison between the past and the other times.[90] If once again one of the early versions was of the order of ותושיענו כימים האלו 'and save us as at these days' the latter two words remain ambiguous and could mean 'as also at this time' or 'as in those days'. All the formulations that use what I have called the comparative chronological reference – with whatever prepositions are employed with each noun, either *bet* or *kaf* – constitute attempts to avoid the ambiguity by incorporating both possible meanings and referring to the past and the present.[91] This would reflect the view of those who have no problem with the idea of making an entreaty specifically for the present while offering thanks for the past.

---

84 BDB *Lexicon* (see n. 69 above), pp. 97–99 and 184; *Ben Yehuda of Jerusalem* (see n. 63 above), pp. 503 and 2442–47. The expression בית בחירה appears in fact to be later rather than earlier MH.

85 M. Sokoloff, *A Dictionary of Jewish Palestinian Aramaic of the Byzantine Period* (Ramat Gan, 1990), p. 149.

86 *Soferim* (see n. 9 above) and T-S 6H6.6 have only a request for more miracles and no chronological addition.

87 SRA.

88 MV, Rom.

89 RMBM, P, T.

90 T-S 8H10.14.

91 See e.g. T-S H10.273, NS 148.6, NS 159.113, NS 195.43, NS 196.81, NS 229.46, NS 271.162 and AS 103.83.

Conclusions

On the basis of the evidence cited and the analysis of its content, a number of important conclusions are possible:

1. In the talmudic period, the special mention of Ḥanukkah in the liturgy was not definitively decided or worded. The geonic authorities, on the other hand, agreed that gratitude should be given liturgical expression in benedictions and in specially worded texts of a historical, poetic and supplicatory nature.

2. The Genizah texts testify to a fairly standard overall structure but also include some interesting textual variants that are worthy of discussion and explication.

3. Characteristics of Mishnaic Hebrew (MH), particularly in its early forms, are gradually replaced in the liturgy as Biblical Hebrew (BH) acquires its standard form as a result of the work of the Masoretes and this has an impact on rabbinic literature.

4. There is evidence of a tendency on the part of some text transmitters to follow the biblical precedent in the liturgical context, especially when a biblical verse may be used as a prototype.

5. The version of the Genizah fragments may at times represent a remnant of that language which was thought to have negative overtones and was subsequently 'biblicized'.

6. The fuller orthography, with the addition of the letter *he*, for the second person masculine singular perfect form תה–, is commonly found in early rabbinic manuscripts, 'especially in Palestinian texts' and still retained in a fair number of Genizah fragments.

7. A reasonable hypothesis would be that originally one formulation stressed the historical miracle while the other wished to link the miracle with the current worshipper, perhaps to forestall the criticism that we cannot thank God in the *'amidah* for something that does not in some way relate to us.

8. All the formulations constitute attempts to avoid the ambiguity by incorporating both possible meanings and referring to the past and the present. This would reflect the view of those who have no problem with the idea of making an entreaty specifically for the present while offering thanks for the past.

9. There was tension between those who saw liturgy as essentially current entreaties and those who saw it as strengthened by the historical experience.

10. Sometimes the historical circumstances were simply chronicled while at others they were lyrically summarized.

11. There is ambivalence about the place of eschatology and the supernatural.

12. It would appear that *ha-rish'ah* is a non-standard form, gradually eliminated from various rites when the prayer-book text came under the influence of the standard Tiberian vocalization of Ben Asher, or a later insertion has disturbed the grammatical construction of the phrase.

13. It is possible that such a qualification, which is regularly used in rabbinic literature to describe the Roman authority, was imported here.

14. The ambiguity of the double accusative and the superstitious objection to associating Israel in any way with destruction could be removed by a change to the *hiph'il* conjugation and/or by the insertion of the prefixed *mem* to the word תורה.

15. Is the dominant theme of the phrase זדים ביד עוסקי תורתך political, theological or intellectual?

16. The problem for those who preferred בעולמך to בעולם appears to have been the assumption that God had, as it were, to use the Maccabean victory to establish his reputation, which was apparently seen by some as *lèse majesté*.

17. The distinction between עמך and בניך is less clear. Perhaps the former is the more prosaic form and the latter the more poetic.

18. Elbogen helpfully cited the texts from *Soferim* and the *She'iltot* and accurately noted the opposition to the inclusion of the entreaty listed above as f. His claim, however, that 'Die Texte lauten seit Amr. bis auf die unvermeidlichen kleinen Abweichungen gleich' ('since Amram the texts have been identical except for minor and unavoidable variants') requires to be corrected in the light of the analysis offered above.[92]

In conclusion, while Alan Mintz may be correct in claiming that '...a religious or literary appreciation of the Siddur does not require more sharply refined historical knowledge' this analysis has surely demonstrated that the evolution of liturgical texts undoubtedly contributes in no small degree to the expansion of precisely such knowledge.[93]

---

92   Elbogen (see n. 1 above), G, pp. 58 and 130–31, H, pp. 45 and 98–99, and E, pp. 52 and 109.
93   Mintz (see n. 1 above), p. 406.

17

A Well-Known Hymn in Aramaic Guise

Mecca of Genizah scholarship

The world of scholarship's interest in the Genizah material in general and in the collections at Cambridge University Library has grown consistently in the course of the last few decades and in no way appears to be waning. Such interest is not limited to the identification, analysis and identification of the fragments, individually or in groups, but also extends into the history of the collections and how they came to be where they are today. This is especially true with regard to the Taylor-Schechter Collection at Cambridge because there are so many remarkable tales associated with its passage from an Egyptian synagogue to an English university.[1] While some of these tales have already been told, and told on numerous occasions, there are still aspects of them that remain to be described. What is well known and documented is the central role played by Shelomo Dov Goitein (1900–1985) in the rediscovery of some 40,000 fragment that had long been neglected, if not well nigh abandoned, at Cambridge University Library and in the process of their classification as the 'New Series' of the Taylor-Schechter Collection, followed by their further analysis ands description.[2] Somewhat less familiar are the contributions made by a number of other scholars who also made their way to what Goitein regarded as the Mecca of Genizah scholarship and worked devotedly in the fifties and sixties of the twentieth century in the Manuscripts Reading Room of Cambridge University Library, first when it was in the Anderson Room at the southern end of the first floor of the 1934 building, and more recently, over the last three decades, on the third

---

1   S. C. Reif, *A Jewish Archive from Old Cairo: The History of Cambridge University's Genizah Collection* (Richmond, Surrey, 2000), especially pp. 234–60; 'The Cambridge Genizah story: some unfamiliar aspects' (Hebrew) in *Te'uda* 15, ed. M. A. Friedman (Tel Aviv, 1999), pp. 413–28; and 'Giblews, Jews and Genizah views', *JJS* 55 (2004), pp. 332–46.
2   S. D. Goitein, *A Mediterranean Society: The Jewish Communities of the Arab World as Portrayed in the Documents of the Cairo Geniza*, 5 vols and index volume (Berkeley, Los Angeles and London, 1967–93), 1.1–28; 'Involvement in Geniza research' in *Religion in a Religious Age* (Cambridge, Mass., 1974), pp. 139–46.

floor of the newly extended West Bookstack.[3] They identified
hundreds, if not thousands of worn, faded and torn pieces, thus laying
the foundations for the extensive expansion of our knowledge in
various fields of medieval Jewish studies. Among such dedicated
visitors to Cambridge are to be counted Yefim Schirmann (1904–81),
Abraham Habermann (1901–80), Nehemiah Allony (1906–83), Shraga
Abramson (1915–96). Alexander Scheiber (1913–85), Moshe Zucker
(1904–87), Eliyahu Ashtor (1914–84) and Jacob Teicher (1904–81) and
the details of their efforts in this connection have not yet fully been
estimated and acknowledged.[4]

Liturgical fragment discovered

While the interests of such scholars ranged from poetry, belles-lettres
and book-lists to halakhah, history, exegesis and typography, the work
of my own late and revered teacher was in the field of liturgy. Naphtali
Wieder (1905–2001) was a pioneer in the close historical study of the
wording of the medieval rabbinic prayers and provided guidance and
set high standards for all those venturing into the dimly lit and
tortuous passageways of this intriguing area. Enthused as he was with
the novelty and importance of the Genizah material for the discovery
and understanding of the early medieval liturgical rites, Wieder took
every available opportunity to travel to Cambridge from London,
where he taught at Jews' College and later University College. There he
spent time sorting fragments, particularly of the Jewish prayers, from
large crates of unidentified material and transferring them to smaller
cardboard boxes, to which numbers were assigned in the New Series.
Thus it was that he was able to prepare manuscript material for this
own books and articles, as well as rescuing from virtual oblivion so
many items that would subsequently be of significance to later

---

3   See, for example, the Hebrew articles by N. Allony, 'Genizah and Hebrew
     manuscripts in Cambridge libraries', *Areshet* 3 (1961), pp. 395–425 and 'Genizah
     practices among the Jews', *Sinai* 79 (1976), pp. 193–201, and A. M. Habermann, *The
     Cairo Genizah and other Genizoth* (Hebrew; Jerusalem, 1971).
4   For some details of their work, see *Bibliography of the Writings of Professor Hayyim
     Schirmann*, ed. D. Pagis (Hebrew; Jerusalem, 1984); *Writings of Abraham Meir
     Habermann: A Bibliography*, ed. Y. David (Hebrew; Jerusalem, 1977); *Bibliography of the
     Writings of Professor Nehemya Allony*, ed. A. R. Tal (Hebrew; Jerusalem, 1984); *In
     Memory of Shraga Abramson* (Hebrew; Israel Academy; Jerusalem, 1997), ed. A.
     Choueka; A. (Sandor) Scheiber, *Geniza Studies* (Hildesheim and New York, 1981); *The
     Medieval Levant: Studies in Memory of Eliyahu Ashtor*, eds B. Z. Kedar and A. L.
     Udovitch (Haifa, 1988); and the brief appreciation of Teicher in N. Allony, *Studies in
     Medieval Philology and Literature: Collected Papers*, vol. 6, ed. Y. Tobi (Jerusalem, 1992),
     pp. 270–71. Teicher's daughter, Dr Anna Teicher, is now working in Cambridge on
     some biographical and bibliographical details relating to her father.

generations of specialists.[5] During one such visit, he set aside one such fragment and placed it in a box classified as T-S NS 160. What had attracted his attention was the fact that it contained a poetic Aramaic version of the liturgical hymn, *ve-'ilu finu*, 'If our mouths' and he intended to return to it at a later time and include it in a future study. Other commitments over the years prevented this and it has fallen to my lot to become the fortunate conveyer of the contents and significance of this fragment to those with special interests in medieval Jewish liturgy and poetry and thereby to continue in at least one small way the work of my distinguished teacher.[6]

The fragment in which this interesting hymn appears now bears the classmark T-S NS 160.11 at Cambridge University Library. It consists of one paper bifolium, with each of its four sides measuring 29 × 19 centimetres, and its physical state is more satisfactory than that of most Genizah fragments. The text is clearly written and easily legible and the written area covers 14 × 11 centimetres on the first folio and 15 × 11 centimetres on the second folio, while half of the verso of f.2 remains blank. The numbers of lines on each folio are as follows: f. 1r: 19; f. 1v: 20; f. 2r: 18; and f. 2v: 10. Although the style of the handwriting on f. 1 is not actually identical with that of f. 2 – with the text on the latter folio apparently added as a kind of gloss on f. 1 – there are no other grounds for supposing that the texts on each folio differ significantly in dating and location. In all likelihood we are dealing here with a square oriental hand of the eleventh century. The first folio contains a *yoṣer* formulation for the intermediate Sabbath of the Passover festival by Joseph al-Baradani. The central portion of the *yoṣer* is apparently the work of a liturgical poet with the name Eleazar and the *zulat* section was perhaps composed by Dosa or Judah b. Benjamin. The formulation is Babylonian, as indicated by the fact that the *zulat* is based on the prophetic reading about the dry bones from Ezekiel 37 which is the prophetic reading for the intermediate sabbath of the Passover festival

---

5   For the results of his manuscript research, see his collected articles, *The Formation of Jewish Liturgy in the East and the West: A Collection of Essays* (Hebrew; 2 vols; Jerusalem, 1998). On his life and work, see Reif, 'A scholar's scholar: Naphtali Wieder, 1905–2001', *Le'ela* 51 (2001), pp. 67–78 (in English) and 'Professor Naphtali Wieder: Rabbinic scholar, teacher and liturgical researcher', *Pe'amim* 96 (2003), pp. 163–75 (in Hebrew).

6   A few years before his death, during a visit I made to his home in Jerusalem, Professor Wieder handed me his transcription of this fragment and suggested that I work on it at some stage. In the preparation of this brief study, I have had the benefit of comment from Professors E. Fleischer, M. Beit-Arié, M. Gil and J. Sussmann. My late and much lamented friend and colleague, Professor Michael Klein, also had some helpful remarks to make in the area of targumic studies. I am grateful to the Syndics of Cambridge University Library for their permission to publish the text of the fragment and the plate that appears at the end of this volume.

according to the standard Babylonian rite. For the historian of liturgical texts, however, even more important here is the poetic Aramaic version of the hymn *ve-'ilu finu* which is to be found on the second folio of the manuscript and which requires to be analysed and explained.[7]

Hymn of praise

The earliest reference to a prayer beginning with the words *ve-'ilu finu* occurs in the Babylonian Talmud, *Berakhot* 59b, as the concluding section of the benediction for rain according to the view of R. Yohanan. As the talmudic text stands, all that is included are the opening words אילו פינו מלא שירה כים ('If our mouths were full of thanks and psalms'); the central phrase אין אנו מספיקין להודות לך ה' אלהינו ('we could not thank you sufficiently, Lord, our God'); and the concluding benediction בא"י רוב ההודאות('You are blessed, Lord, for favours in abundance').[8] By the time that the geonic authorities wielded power over the Babylonian communities (7th–11th centuries), the hymn beginning *ve-'ilu finu* had become an integral part of what is technically called the *birkat ha-shir* ('benediction of song') but had acquired the more popular name of *nishmat* (from it first word) and is described by Heinemann as 'the most exalted and elegant prayer in the hymnic style to be found in the statutory liturgy...noted for its use of numerous stylistic devices, such as the "rhetorical" *topos* "Were our mouths as filled with song as the sea"'.[9] By that time, the talmudic prayer had grown considerably, as is clearly documented in the early prayer-texts, both Babylonian and

---

7   On al-Baradani and his poetry, see T. Beeri, *Masdarim and Yozerot by Joseph Albaradani* (Hebrew; 2 vols; Jerusalem, 1990) and *The "Great Cantor" of Baghdad: the liturgical poems of Joseph ben Ḥayyim al-Baradani: annotated critical edition with introduction* (Hebrew; Jerusalem, 2002), especially the edition on p. 402. For the identification of these poems I am indebted to the Project for Research in Genizah Poetry, supported by the Israel Academy of Sciences and directed by Professor Ezra Fleischer. For the physical appearance of the fragment, see the plate at the end of this volume.

8   W. Jawitz, *Die Liturgie des Siddur und ihre Entwicklung nach der Urquellen untersucht und systematisch geordnet* (Hebrew; Berlin, 1910), pp. 66–69; I. Elbogen, German edition, *Der jüdische Gottesdienst in seiner geschichtlichen Entwicklung* (Frankfurt am Main, 1931; reprint, Hildesheim, 1962), pp. 113 and 211; Hebrew edition, התפילה בישראל בהתפתחותה ההיסטורית (eds J. Heinemann, I. Adler, A. Negev, J. Petuchowski and H. Schirmann, Tel Aviv, 1972), pp. 86–87 and 158; English edition, *Jewish Liturgy: A Comprehensive History* (trans. and ed. Raymond P. Scheindlin, Philadelphia, Jerusalem and New York, 1993), pp. 96 and 169; J. Heinemann, *Prayer in the Talmud: Forms and Patterns* (revised English edition, Berlin and New York, 1977), pp. 46 and 58–62; E. D. Goldschmidt, *The Passover Haggadah: Its Sources and History* (Hebrew; Jerusalem, 1969), pp. 64–68; B. S. Jacobson, *Netiv Binah* (Hebrew; 5 vols; Tel Aviv, 1968–83), 2.183–92.

9   Heinemann, *Prayer* (see n. 8 above), p. 241.

Palestinian, that are to be found in the various Genizah collections.[10] In connection with the ritual differences between these two communities, it should be pointed out that while in the land of Israel the custom was to recite the expanded *birkat ha-shir* on a daily basis, the practice in Babylonia was to say the *nishmat* prayer only on sabbaths and festivals.[11] What is more, the earliest sources indicate that the text of the *'ilu finu* hymn was at that time still rather simple and short, lacking those expansions that were destined to characterize it in later generations. Nevertheless, we can still be sure that already in the tenth century *'ilu finu* had a secure place among those parts of the fixed liturgy that brought the reading of the Psalms to a formal conclusion before the commencement of the benedictions preceding the recitation of the *shema'*.[12] Indeed, in the midrashic compilation *Tanna De-Be Eliyahu*, which is not later than the ninth century, the author echoes the *'ilu finu* hymn in some of the language that he uses to express the depth of his feelings: אם נעמוד אנו ובנינו ובנותינו ויהיה לנו פה כים ולשונינו כהמון גליו

ושפתותינו כמרחבי רקיע, אין אנו יכולים להודות ולומר לפניך ה' אלהינו... ('If we, and our sons and daughters were in such a state that our mouths were as the sea, our tongues like its powerful waves and our lips comparable to the expanse of the sky, we would still remain unable to thank you, Lord, our God, and to recite to you...'[13]

When the post-geonic history of the *'ilu finu* hymn is examined, it emerges that by that time its place, formulation and concepts have all undergone alterations and developments. One of the principal discoveries of Jewish liturgical research is that when a part of a particular prayer is relocated to a new context, other parts of that prayer ultimately follow the same path, at least in one of the familiar rites. No sooner had expansions been made in the *birkat ha-shir* of the morning prayer than they were also transmitted into the text of the *hallel* which it was customary to recite at the end of the Passover Haggadah. Thus it was, unsurprisingly, that *'ilu finu* found in the

---

10 See J. Mann, 'Genizah fragments of the Palestinian order of service,' *HUCA* 2 (1925), pp. 272–85, reprinted in *Contributions to the Scientific Study of Jewish Liturgy* (ed. J. J. Petuchowski, New York, 1970) and the texts of Genizah fragments at Cambridge University Library that are transcribed below in the appendix to this chapter.

11 *Seder Rav Amram Gaon*, ed. E. D. Goldschmidt (Jerusalem, 1971), pp. 69–70 and 119; Mann, 'Genizah fragments' (see n. 10 above), p. 275. Compare also the sources cited by E. Fleischer, *Eretz-Israel Prayer and Prayer Rituals as Portrayed in the Geniza Documents* (Hebrew; Jerusalem, 1998), pp. 197, 226, 230, 234, 239, 244, 264, 266, 268, 270, 288–89 and 306.

12 Fleischer, *Eretz-Israel* (see n. 11 above), pp. 92, 227, 230–31 and 239.

13 *Seder Eliyahu Rabba and Seder Eliyahu Zuṭa*, ed. M. Friedman (Ish-Shalom) (Vienna, 1904; Jerusalem, 1960), p. 163; see also *The Zohar*, ed. R. Margaliot (3 vols; Jerusalem, 1940–46), 2.138a; E. T., eds H. Sperling, M. Simon and P. P. Levertoff (5 vols; London, 1933), 3.396–97.

Jewish home a place that was hardly less honourable than its original location in the fixed communal prayers. As it became more popular with the Jewish worshipper, it was embellished with more lyrical words and expressions as when שבח was attached to שפתותינו, מאירות to עינינו, פרושות to ידינו, and קלות to רגלינו, and other such instances.[14] The hymn's ideas also had an impact on its poetic successors in later generations. The French and German communities of the periods of Rashi and the Tosafists saw the composition of such liturgical poems as *aqdamut millin* by the *ḥazzan* Meir b. Isaac Nehorai. That poem served as a poetic introduction to the Aramaic translation of the Torah reading on the festival of Pentecost. Similarly, there was another such poem, *ilu pumey ve-khol nimey*, that was included in the *Maḥzor Vitry* among the *reshut* compositions recited by the reciter of the Targum version of the verses of the prophetic reading. Both such poems, it should be noted, were composed in Aramaic.[15] The *Sitz im Leben* of these poems – that is to say, their use as introductory material to targumic versions of biblical texts – was obviously instrumental in the choice of Aramaic but it should also be noted that these poets of the high middle ages still had the interest and competence required to make such a use of the Aramaic language. Indeed, both Sefardi and Ashkenazi composers of liturgical poems did not stop at such developments but also abandoned the classic styles of content and formulation inherited from their predecessors. For their part, they created various innovative expansions of the *nishmat* prayer that departed significantly from the original source.[16]

---

14 See the responsum cited in the name of Hai Gaon in *Sha'arey Simḥah*, ed. S. B. Bamberger (Fiorda, 1861–62), pp. 100–101, and the following prayer-books: Maimonides in 'The Oxford Ms. of Maimonides' book of prayer', ed. E. D. Goldschmidt, and (reprinted from *Studies of the Research Institute for Hebrew Poetry in Jerusalem* 7 (1958), pp. 183–213) in his collected articles entitled *On Jewish Liturgy: Essays on Prayer and Religious Poetry* (Hebrew; Jerusalem, 1978), p. 194; Judah ben Yaqar, *Peyrush Ha-Tefillot Ve-Ha-Berakhot*, ed. S. Yerushalmi (2 vols; Jerusalem, 1968–69), 1.93; Abudraham (Warsaw, 1877), p. 89 and *Sefer Abudraham Ha-Shalem*, ed. S. A Wertheimer (Jerusalem, 1963), pp. 164–65; *Maḥzor Vitry*, ed. S. Hurwitz (2 vols; Nuremberg², 1923), 1.148 and 1.153; Jacob ben Judah Ḥazzan of London, *The Etz Hayyim*, ed. I. Brodie (3 vols, Jerusalem, 1962–67), 1.79. All of these liturgies testify to the fuller version while the Ashkenazi (but not the Old French) and the Italian prayer-books do not include all the expressions here noted until a later period. On this and on the *waw* prefixed to the first word of *'ilu finu*, see S. C. Reif, *Shabbethai Sofer and his Prayer-book* (Cambridge, 1979), pp. 145–46 and 254–55.

15 See Y. Lewinsky, *Sefer Ha-Mo'adim* (8 vols; Tel Aviv⁹, 1970), 3.137–61; *Maḥzor Vitry* (see n. 14 above), pp. 159–65.

16 See I. Davidson, *Thesaurus of Mediaeval Hebrew Poetry* (4 vols; New York, 1924–33), 3.226–34; E. Fleischer, *Hebrew Liturgical Poetry in the Middle Ages* (Hebrew; Jerusalem, 1975), pp. 395–402 and 461–63.

To return to the Genizah manuscript here being discussed, the Aramaic text will now be transcribed, accompanied by an English translation, and by textual and linguistic comments on the one hand, and notes on its content, sources and formulation on the other. In an appendix, a critical comparison will be made between the manuscript and the parallel formulations to be found in the regular prayers included in R. Sa'adya Gaon's prayer-book and in two other Genizah fragments from the land of Israel.

Aramaic Text

1. ואי פומנא מליא אודוון ותשבחן עתיקין / ולישן דילן כנחשולין רגשין לא שתיקין
2. ושפוותנא כפותיא דרקיעין / וארקין ועיננא כתרין נהורין ובעורין דלקין
3. וידנא כנשרין באוירא סל[קין]ן / ורגלנא כאילא וטביא בקלילות ערקין
4. ושמיא וארעא מגילין ופיתקין / וכל אעין צֻמֲחִין קלמוסין עזיקין
5. ועֵינַאוֵן דיותא נבעין לא פסקין / וכל דביה רוח ממללא זעטוטין ודעדקין
6. וכתבין קלוסין לא הוו מספקין / על נסן דעבד לעם מטנס פריקין
7. ענאמאי אוכח בְּכֵאיבִין ושלפוקין / מנא אמטר לעמוי וּבְשֶׁלָוָא מתפנקין
8. ואפקנא בריש גלי לעין כל מעיקין / בזע טינרין ומיין נפקין
9. אוריתיה יהב לנה למהוי בה עסיקין / [וּ?]כְתָב מפרש בלוחין כגלוף בעסקין
10. ואשמעיננא פיתגמוהי בקלין אברקין / דנהוי דחלין לשמיה ולה מתזקין
11. דַבְרָנָא לדירא דקדשא למחסן גוהרקין / ועד כען סעיד נא ומרחמוהי לא שביקין
12. עלנא לברוכי שמיה במיכנש סבין ודרדקין / למהוי גופנא לפקודוהי דרופתקין
13. קבֵּל צלותנא כבני תנא זעקין / יהי שמיה מברך לעלם ד[עני?] ע]שיקין
14. **ממ[צ]רים גאלתנו יי אלהינו**

English Translation

1. If our mouths were full of thanks and psalms
Our tongues as strong as ceaseless storms
2. Our lips as wide as skies and lands
Eyes twice as bright as burning lamps
3. Our hands could soar like eagles skywards
Our feet could race gazelles and hinds
4. If sky and land were scroll and board
And every tree grew hardy nibs
5. Our eyes wept ink in ceaseless flow
Our youngest speakers all took part
6. And never ceased from praising God
For rescue from Egypt, for wonders wrought
7. God smiting its folk with pain and plague
Then feeding his people with manna and quail
8. Our proud depart he showed the foe
A rock was smitten and water flowed
9. He gave us his Torah to muse and mind
Tablets inscribed, commands enshrined
10. His words came forth with flash and roar
We feared his name but were not harmed
11. Given holy shrine and noble thrones
His aid and love have never left us
12. Obliged to praise him, young and old

To keep his precepts with body and soul
13. Receive our prayers, as creatures wailing,
Who heeds the oppressed, God's name be blessed
14. **YOU REDEEMED US FROM EGYPT, LORD OUR GOD**

Textual and linguistic comments

1. Each line of the poem ends with the rhyme ‎-קין. I have transcribed
every two lines on one line of the text here, with a slash to separate
them. The layout of the lines in the manuscript is haphazard. Since it
does not match the structure of the poem and depends entirely on the
space available on the paper, I have taken no account of it in the
transcription.

2. I have not transcribed here the various punctuation marks to be
found in the manuscript since the scribe has attempted to mark the
ends of the poem's lines in accordance with the rhyme but there is a
clear lack of consistency in his work.

3. Line 4: Because insufficient space was available to the scribe to
transcribe the whole of the word ‎אעין in the previous line, he has filled
that line with half of the *alef* of that word, with a point above it, and
repeated the whole word in the next line.[17]

4. Line 4: The word ‎צמחין is pointed as a *pi'el* or, more accurately, an
Aramaic *pa'el* in the manuscript. The participle carries a transitive sense
and its object is the word ‎קלמוסין. All the pointing to be found in the
manuscript under discussion has been transcribed above.

5. Line 4: The spelling of the word ‎עזיקין appears to me to constitute an
example of the interchange of *'ayin* and *het* that is a common
characteristic of the linguistic tradition of Palestinian Jewry. It does
however remain moot whether such an interchange is to be exclusively
traced to that particular geographical and cultural background.

6. Lines 5–6: The use of a vocabulary that includes such terms as ‎זעטוטין,
‎דעדקין (and its alternative ‎דרדקין in line 12) and ‎קלוסין undoubtedly has a
distinguished pedigree in the early linguistic history of rabbinic

---

17   For examples of such scribal techniques in medieval Hebrew manuscripts, see M.
     Beit-Arié, *Hebrew Codicology: Tentative Typology of Technical Practices Employed in
     Hebrew Dated Medieval Manuscripts* (Jerusalem², 1981); B. Richler, *Hebrew Manuscripts:
     A Treasured Legacy* (Cleveland and Jerusalem, 1990); C. Sirat, *Hebrew Manuscripts of
     the Middle Ages* (E. T., Cambridge, 2002); the series of volumes entitled *Manuscrits
     Médiévaux en Caractères Hébraïques*, eds M. Beit-Arié and C. Sirat (Jerusalem and
     Paris, 1979–); and M. Beit-Arié, *Unveiled Faces of Medieval Hebrew Books: The Evolution
     of Manuscript Production – Progression or Regression?* (Jerusalem, 2003), pp. 32-48.

literature, not only in the land of Israel but also in the Babylonian communities.[18]

7. Line 6: Since there was insufficient space for the whole word מטנס in line 5, the scribe has filled that line with its first letter, *mem*, with a dot above, and written the whole word in the next line.

8. Line 7: The poet is here alluding to the Egyptians in accordance with Genesis 10:13 (and 1 Chronicles 1:11) which lists the Anamites as the progeny of Misrayim. The fuller spelling of the word is a common feature of those writing Judeo-Arabic texts during the classical Genizah period.

9. Line 7: With regard to the word ובשלוא, the space in the previous line is again filled with part of the next word – in this case with its first three letters and with a line above – and the whole word is written in the next line.

10. Lines 7–8: Although all the other pointing to be found in this manuscript is that of standard Tiberian Hebrew, it is noteworthy that in the cases of the words אמטר and ואפקנא there is a use of the hamza sign that characteristically occurs in Arabic vocalization. The scribe apparently wished to stress the value of the glottal stop in the initial 'alef of these two words.

11. Line 9: It seems likely that the meaning of the Aramaic word עסקין is here identical to that of the Hebrew word דיברות . The parallel use of the roots עסק and דבר is well-known in Jewish Aramaic texts and what we appear to have here is an expansion of such a use. In the view of editors of Aramaic poems, Yahalom and Sokoloff, the characteristic form in Palestinian Jewish Aramaic is עסיק.[19]

12. Lines 11–12: The verbal form סעידנא is written as two separate words in the manuscript although there is no doubt that it constitutes a perfect tense with a first-person plural pronominal suffix, similar in form to the word ואפקנא that occurs earlier in line 8. One should perhaps take into the account the possibility that we have here a remnant of a linguistic tradition to write the suffix separately from the verb.

18 See, for example, Tosefta *Sanhedrin* 2.5 (ed. M. S. Zuckermandel, p. 416); Sifrey Deuteronomy, §356, ed. L. Finkelstein, p. 423; PT, *Ta'anit* 4.2 (68a), *Sukkah* 5.4 (55b) and *Rosh Ha-Shanah* 4.7 (59c); BT, *Bava Meṣi'a* 66a and *Bava Batra* 21a; Targum Onqelos on Exodus 16:14 and Numbers 23:10.

19 M. Sokoloff and J. Yahalom, 'Aramaic piyyutim from the Byzantine period', *JQR* 75 (1985), pp. 309–21. See also their volume *Jewish Palestinian Aramaic Poetry from Late Antiquity* (Hebrew; Jerusalem, 1999), pp. 88–89 and 254–56.

13. Lines 11–12: The words גוהרקין and דרופתקין occur in the Babylonian Talmud but to the best of my knowledge are not a feature of the regular vocabulary of the Palestinian Jewish literature of the middle ages.[20]

14. Line 13: The letters that are here printed within square brackets have been lost in the manuscript so that the restored reading must remain conjectural. It is, however, clear that we are dealing with two separate words.[21]

15. Line 14: The scribe makes use of the ligature of *'alef* and *lamed* that was widely used by the writers of Judeo-Arabic texts to be found in the Genizah material. This whole line is preceded by a significant space indicating that it is not part of the liturgical poem but refers to the text of the common prayers. It provides us with important evidence as to the point in the *nishmat* prayer at which the poetic insertion was made.

Notes on content, sources and formulation

1. Lines 1–4: Unlike the basic text of the *'ilu finu* hymn in the geonic period, the version in this manuscript makes no reference to the sea in its first verse but adds epithets to each of the parts of the body in the other five verses and inserts other details, without departing from the basic metaphor employed in the hymn.

2. Line 1: אודוון ותשבחן עתיקין : The author is creating a link between the recitation of those chapters of Psalms that are included in the *hallel* (or the *pesuqey de-zimra*) and his own poem. The sense of the phrase is that, however numerous and ancient these psalms may be, they cannot fully describe the miracles performed by God for the people of Israel when they left the land of Egypt.[22]

3. Line 1: כנחשולין : Compare Targum Jonathan on Jonah 1:4, 11–13 and 15 which employs the word נחשול to translate the two Hebrew roots סער and זעף in connection with the powerful storm at sea.

4. Line 2: כתרין נהורין : Compare Targum Onqelos on Genesis 1:16.

5. Line 3: כאילא וטביא : The names of these two animals are usually found together in the Hebrew Bible, as in Deuteronomy 12:22 and 1 Kings 5:3; see also 1 Chronicles 12:8.

---

20 See BT, *Ta'anit* 20b, *Bava Meṣi'a* 73b and 85b, *Giṭṭin* 31b and *Sanhedrin* 99b.

21 In the expression בני תנא, the second word is an Aramaic translation of the Biblical Hebrew תנים while the form בני is simply a direct loan from Hebrew. On the 'wailing' of such animals, see Isaiah 13:22, Micah 1:8 and Job 30:29.

22 Compare the lines that occur in the *aqdamut* poem (as transcribed in the sources cited in n. 15 above): גבורן עלמין ליה ולא ספק פרישותא. דיו אלו ימי וכל מי גויל אלו רקיעי קני כל חורשתא. דירי ארעה ספרי ורשמי רשותא כנישותא

6. Lines 4–6: In similar fashion to that adopted by the author of the poem *'aqdamut millin*, our poet also inserts into the text of the *nishmat* prayer mentions of the writing implements of the scribe and the speaking ability of the community. He does this in order to give concrete expression to the notion that even if such facilities are grossly increased they will not prove adequate to praise the acts of God in the required fashion.

7. Line 4: מגילין ופיתקין : The author is here referring to two extensive writing materials; compare the use of these two expressions in Targum Esther 9:32 (אתכתבת מגלתא בפטקא).

8. Lines 5–6: This is perhaps an allusion to the work of the liturgical poets (כתבין קלוסין) and their attempt to praise God for the redemption of the Jewish people from Egypt. The mention of children and little ones (זעטוטין ודעדקין) in addition to scribes paints a picture of a complete and vibrant community.[23]

9. Lines 6–11: While the simpler, original hymn makes general reference to 'the good deeds that you have done for us and our fathers' (הטובות שעשית עמנו ועם אבותינו), this poetic version systematically enumerates each of the miracles in an order that differs from that of scripture and with additions to the classic aggadic sources.[24]

10. Line 7: At this point, the author begins to list the wonders performed for the Israelites in Egypt and in the wilderness, in the manner of many Hebrew poets in countless poems, from as early as Psalm 78; compare Psalms 105:14 and Numbers 11.

11. Line 7: Tanes is the Greek name of an Egyptian city, used by the Greek and Aramaic translators of the Bible, as well as by the liturgical poets, to describe Egypt as a whole or specific places in it such as Ṣo'an, 'On and Pithom. Here the poet is probably referring to Exodus 14:2 and to the name Pithom. According to the aggadic interpretation in Mekhilta, פי החירות refers to Pithom and is given the longer name because of a play on the word חירות i.e. 'that is where Israel were made free' (שם נעשו בני ישראל חורין).[25]

---

23 Compare also line 12 of the text and the notes thereon offered above in comment 13.

24 For the details of these miracles according to midrashic aggadah, see Ginzberg, *Legends*, as listed further in comment 12.

25 Compare the Aramaic Targumim on Genesis 41:45 and 50, on Exodus 1:11 and on Numbers 13:22 and see *Mekilta de-Rabbi Ishmael*, ed. J. Z. Lauterbach (3 vols; Philadelphia, 1933–35), 1.188 and eds H. S. Horovitz and I. A. Rabin (Frankfurt am Main, 1931), p. 83; *Mekhilta D'Rabbi Šim'on b. Jochai*, eds J. N. Epstein and E. Z. Melamed (Jerusalem, 1955), p. 48.

12. Line 8: For details of the miraculous events associated by the aggadists with the splitting of the Red Sea, see L. Ginzberg, *The Legends of the Jews* (7 vols; Philadelphia, 1909–38), 3.18–36.

13. Line 8: On the 'smiting of the rocks'(בזע טינרין) and surrounding events, see Psalms 78:15, 20 and 24, and the Targum on these verses.

14. Line 9: This line appears to allude to the famous aggadaic interpretation according to which the letters (עסקין) of the Ten Commandments were inscribed in such a miraculous fashion on the tablets that they could be read normally from both sides (משני עבריהם).[26]

15. Line 10: Compare Exodus 19:10–25, especially verse 16, and the midrashim on these verses as cited, for example, by M. M. Kasher, *Torah Shelemah* (New York, 1953), vol. 15.

16. Line 11: לדירא דקדשא : Compare the Targumim on Exodus 15:13.

17. Line 11: The word גוהרקין apparently refers to 'the glorious thrones' (like 'the glorious crowns') of Torah, kingship and priesthood.[27]

18. Line 11: ועד כען סעיד : What we have here is a reworking of the Hebrew verse (חסדיך) עד הנה עזרונו רחמיך ולא עזבונו ('until now your mercies have helped us and (your acts of love) have not left us' which occurs in the standard text of *ve-'ilu finu* after the phrase ממצרים גאלתנו ('You redeemed us from Egypt'), as in R. Sa'adya Gaon's prayer-book, p. 119.

19. Line 12: The author here re-stresses the communal context in which the benediction is recited.

20. Lines 12–13: The poet once again explains the obligation of the whole community to praise God and to observe his precepts and concludes the poem with an appeal to God to hear their prayers.

21. Line 14: A return at this point to the standard text of the *nishmat* prayer actually leads to a duplication of part of the content since the story of God's miracles and of the exodus from Egypt have already appeared in the poetic version. Perhaps the poem was originally intended to be recited in place of a more substantial part of the standard Hebrew text.

Literary and linguistic contexts

A closer examination of some other aspects of this Aramaic poem raises broader issues that are worthy of further discussion. Its style parallels

---

26 See BT, *Shabbat* 104a; the Aramaic Targumim on Exodus 32:16; and Ginzberg, *Legends* (see comment 12), 3.119 and 6.49–50.
27 Compare *Mekilta*, ed. Lauterbach (see n. 25 above), 2.70 and ed. Horovitz-Rabin, p. 146; and *Mekhilta*, ed. Epstein-Melamed (see n. 25 above), p. 96, on Exodus 15:13.

and echoes those of Targum Onqelos and the fixed prayers of the early medieval period. Its vocabulary, grammatical forms and modes of expression closely match the language of the halakhic authorities who held spiritual and cultural sway over much of the Mediterranean area at the end of the geonic period. At the same time, it has to be acknowledged that, although there are no clear indications of the kind of Galilean Aramaic that is characteristic of so many targumic versions to be found in the Genizah collections, there are some linguistic elements that appear to have originated among the communities of the land of Israel. It therefore seems justified to challenge the supposition that in the case of texts of this sort the language may always be identified as a pure and independent form of either Babylonian or Galilean Aramaic. Is it indeed wholly possible to distinguish forms of Aramaic in such a clear-cut fashion? Are all examples that earlier scholars have identified as Eastern Aramaic undoubtedly Babylonian in origin?[28] Given the incontrovertible existence of trilingualism on the part of the Jews in the post-geonic period, it hardly seems surprising to encounter texts in which there are switches between these three languages.[29] It is not unlikely that one of the aspects of this linguistic and literary process was the development whereby Aramaic dialects came to be used that did not represent particular geographical areas. The scholarly authors of the later period chose to write Aramaic in order to expand the range of their literature and made use of a variety of earlier styles and characteristics that were borrowed from a number of different sources.

The matter of the precise literary genre to which this Aramaic poem belongs is also an intriguing problem. Although it is clearly neither a prayer nor a targum in its own right, it is also not a liturgical poem of those standard and familiar types produced by the oriental communities in the Genizah period. On the other hand, the context is clearly that of the fixed liturgy and the intention is obviously to attach it to the *nishmat* prayer. The fragment calls to mind the relatively late central European custom – one that has not yet been found among the oriental communities – of inserting poetic compositions before the *'ilu finu* section of the *nishmat* prayer. If, however, one compares it with

---

28 For exemplary studies of the problems relating to the text and language of the Babylonian Talmud, see S. Friedman, *Le-Ilan ha-yuhasin shel nushey Bava Meṣ'ia* in *Meḥqarim Be-Sifrut Ha-Talmudit*, ed. S. Romm (Jerusalem, 1983), pp. 93–147, especially pp. 122–29, and *Talmud Arukh: BT Bava Mezi'a VI* (Hebrew; Jerusalem, 1990); see also the article by Kasher cited in n. 31 below.

29 There are numerous examples of such linguistic exchanges between Hebrew, Aramaic and Judeo-Arabic in various contexts, as discussed in S. C. Reif, 'Aspects of mediaeval Jewish literacy', in *The Uses of Literacy in Early Mediaeval Europe*, ed. R. McKitterick (Cambridge, 1990), pp. 148–49.

these later European addenda, both Sefardi and Ashkenazi, it stands
out as something quite other.[30] However poetic the format of our
Aramaic poem, its simple style and its closeness to the basic text of the
prayer into which it is inserted appear to indicate that, unlike his later
European counterparts, the author was not interested in adding fresh
prayer content but was most anxious to add detail that was in no way
at odds with the basic liturgical material before him.

The manner in which our author re-works the material before him
is basically similar to that employed by the Aramaic targumists when
they added to the scriptural source but remained thoroughly loyal to its
basic content. Recently published research work on such targumim
have demonstrated the existence of many types of translation and
supplement. In addition to the well-known Targum Onqelos, Pseudo-
Jonathan and Yerushalmi renderings, there were also targumic
collections that followed the sabbath and festival lectionaries or treated
particular chapters or verses of scripture, as well as more general types
of *tosefta* (additamenta) versions. In a number of respects, our Aramaic
poem, though connected to the fixed liturgy rather than to the biblical
text, is similar to such targumim and makes use of words and
expressions that are linguistically typical of targumic Aramaic.[31]

Given that we have established that the text before us is a liturgical
poem, we must now enquire whether there are literary and linguistic
predecessors, descendants and siblings. The largest corpus of Aramaic
liturgical poems from the post-talmudic period is that created by
Byzantine Jewry and this has been the subject of recent research by
Michael Sokoloff and Joseph Yahalom. Their conclusion is that such
poems were composed in honour of Jewish festivals, particular biblical
books and important events in the daily life of the community, and that
their language is Galilean Jewish Aramaic. Some of these poems
survived into later periods and were still being used, for example, in
the Ashkenazi communities of the Tosafists.[32] What we may therefore
have in T-S NS 160.11 is a composition that is similar in aim and usage
to those Aramaic poems of Byzantium and Franco-Germany but
certainly does not employ a language and style that is wholly
comparable with theirs. It seems reasonable to suppose that it is an

---

30 Compare the poem here being discussed with those cited and listed by Davidson
    and Fleischer (see n. 16 above).
31 See R. Kasher's discussion 'A new Targum to the Ten Commandments according to
    a Geniza manuscript', *HUCA* 60 (1989), Hebrew section, pp. 1–17, in which he notes
    the rich variety of targumim and traditions on this scriptural passage and explains
    how such a variety relates to dialect, translation and literary genre. Compare M. L.
    Klein, *Genizah Manuscripts of Palestinian Targum to the Pentateuch* (2 vols; Cincinnati,
    1986), vol. 1, introduction.
32 See Sokoloff and Yahalom, 'Aramaic piyyutim' (see n. 19 above), pp. 311–12.

example of a literary genre that belongs to the history of Hebrew poetry at the end of the geonic period and that is linked to the emergence of the new centres of Jewish life that replaced those of Babylon and the Palestinian Jewish homeland. As long, however, as no similar such poems have been found and identified, it will not be possible to be more precise about its historical and literary milieu.

By way of completion, a few sentences should now deal with the context in which the poem was recited. The first point to be made in this respect is that such a recitation was obviously attached to the *nishmat* prayer. Since the ritual practices of the communities of Babylon and Palestine are known to have differed as to when that prayer was recited, there are two possibilities that immediately come to mind. Our poem was recited either in the sabbath morning service or as part of the weekday prayers. But account should also be taken of a third historical option. Perhaps our author's intention was to include his composition among the special prayers recited on Passover. In that case, it could have been attached to the morning service of the festival, or of its intermediate sabbath, like the other poems that appear on the remaining folios of our fragment, or it might have been recited as part of the *hallel* section of the Passover Haggadah of the first evening. Since the Genizah has revealed fragments that contain novel Aramaic versions of parts of the Haggadah that are generally familiar to us in Hebrew, such a phenomenon need not be regarded as rare or exceptional.[33] The references in lines 5 and 12 to 'youngest speakers' and a gathering of 'young and old' (Aramaic originals: זעטוטין ודעדקין and במיכנש סבין ודרדקין) may certainly allude to the Jewish communal gathering in the synagogue but one cannot rule out the important possibility that the author has in mind the domestic Passover seder. If that is indeed the case, what emerges is that the community in which he operated apparently had the custom of extending the range of the *hallel* beyond what is to be found in R. Sa'adya Gaon's prayer-book and in many Genizah fragments. It is true that the remainder of our fragment's content deals with the morning service for Passover and not with the seder of Passover eve but it has also to be acknowledged that we cannot know for sure what precisely the scribe had in mind when he copied the Aramaic poem on to this bifolium. It is not outside the realms of possibility that he chose to copy a text for the Passover *seder* on to this piece of paper because it had some spare space and had no

---

33 See, for example, the early Genizah fragment, T-S H2.152. Close attention has already been paid to this fragment but without specific discussion of the Aramaic passage. See S. C. Reif, *Published Material from the Cambridge Genizah Collections: A Bibliography 1896–1980* (Cambridge, 1988), p. 74.

intention of linking our poem with the other Passover poems previously transcribed here.

Date and provenance

It remains to offer some brief and qualified conclusions about the date and provenance of this *'ilu finu* text before us. Given the limited information available to them and the considerable danger of making serious errors of judgement, Genizah scholars are generally cautious and circumspect about committing themselves in such matters. Nevertheless, some encouragement may be given to further discussion by offering, with due care and hesitation, a few tentative suggestions about the origins of our Aramaic poem.

The first point to be made in these concluding remarks is that it is difficult, perhaps even well-nigh impossible, to establish whether the poem here is in the handwriting of its author or in that of a copyist who may or may not have been close to the author in time or location. If the latter is the case, note has to be taken of the fact that the copyist may have admired the poem enough to copy it but not enough to mention the name of the original poet, although such anonymity is not uncommon in the Genizah texts. But if we are dealing with a copy, there is little that it can definitively convey about the date and provenance of the original. Furthermore, if that original goes back to the earlier geonic period, how are we to understand the fact that the linguistic and literary confidence appears to contradict such a dating? On the other hand, the poem may be an autograph and may represent, as already suggested, a kind of addendum to the other poems in the manuscript. In that case, it must be dated later than the composition of such items and that would mean that it cannot be earlier than the end of the tenth century and that the linguistic and literary evidence would tally with the proposed dating. It should also be stressed that the calligraphy of the poem makes it difficult to date it later than the end of the eleventh century. As far as provenance is concerned, the handwriting is oriental and, as has already been suggested, there are good literary and linguistic reasons for not seeking its origins in the land of Israel, among the Babylonian communities or in the Byzantine world. That having been said, we are left with the option of the Jewish centres in North Africa and Egypt. Since the discovery of such Genizah fragments as the one before us is primarily associated with the community of Fustat (old Cairo), and we have detailed and reliable information about the fusion of various liturgical rites in that city, we have to be satisfied with the least improbable suggestion, namely, that the provenance of the poem is in North Africa or Egypt during the time of R. Hai Gaon and to conclude that it was absorbed into the Cairo corpus of liturgical poems soon afterwards.[34]

There is some basis for one further suggestion about the precise background of 'ilu finu. One of the other liturgical poems in our manuscript came from the pen of the poet and ḥazzan, Joseph al-Baradani of Babylonia, whose compositions are found in many Genizah fragments.[35] His son, Nahum, followed in his footsteps as poet and ḥazzan and was either a representative of the Babylonian yeshivot in North Africa or simply settled there permanently. After many years of residence in Qayrawan, Nahum received a letter from R. Hai Gaon requesting his return to Baghdad to occupy his late father's post as senior ḥazzan of its communities. At that point, Nahum sent a collection of Hebrew books to Egypt and in the course of time he asked his representative there to sell them in the land of Israel. After Nahum's death, his heirs and the bookseller were engaged in a dispute before a rabbinical court in Sicily with regard to the profits made on that transaction.[36] What emerges is that members of the Baradani family were active in the south eastern Mediterranean at the end of the tenth and the beginning of the eleventh century and that some of Nahum's Hebrew books were available on the market in the area at that time.[37] Such data makes it possible to propose that texts that had once belonged to the poet Nahum al-Baradani were sold to others and ultimately found their way into the Cairo Genizah.

Perhaps, then, T-S NS 160.11 at Cambridge University Library is a survivor of that collection of books. In that case, the poems that appear on the first part of the bifolium were written in North Africa and 'ilu finu was either added there or at a later date in Fustat. About a quarter of a century ago, Goitein expressed the hope that scholars would one

---

34 See S. D. Goitein, 'The Cairo Genizah as a source for Mediterranean social history', *JAOS* 80 (1960), pp. 91–100; *A Mediterranean Society* (see n. 2 above), 2.155–70; Fleischer, *Eretz-Israel Prayer* (see n. 11 above), pp. 215–18; and J. L. Kraemer, 'Return to Messina – a letter from the Cairo Geniza', *Mediterranean Historical Review* 4 (1989), p. 364.

35 J. Mann, *Texts and Studies in Jewish History and Literature* (2 vols; Cincinnati and Philadelphia, 1931–35; and the reprint of Philadelphia-New York, 1991, with Gershon Cohen's important essay on 'The reconstruction of gaonic history'), 1.151–53; M. Gil, 'The Babylonian yeshivot and the Maghrib in the early middle ages', *PAAJR* 57 (1991), pp. 85–89. See also the work of T. Beeri cited in n. 7 above.

36 Mann, *Texts* (see n. 35 above), p. 122 and Goitein, *Mediterranean Society* (see n. 2 above), 3.300–301.

37 M. Ben-Sasson has prepared lectures and conducted seminars on the history of Jewish libraries at that time and informs me that he hopes to complete the study and submit it for publication at some future date. Meanwhile, see N. Allony, *Studies in Medieval Philology and Literature: Collected Papers*, vol. 5, *Bibliography and Book Art*, ed. Y. Tobi (Jerusalem, 1992) and Goitein, *Mediterranean Society* (see n. 2 above), 2.228–39.

day discover the fate of that collection of books.[38] Although some of the conclusions that I have drawn above with regard to our one Genizah fragment remain partly in the realm of the speculative, this analysis may have made at least a small contribution to the realization of Goitein's hope. Be that as it may, we now have a new poetic version, in Aramaic, of the *'ilu finu* hymn which indicates that scholarship has yet to become fully acquainted with the story of how such poems were added to the prayer stock during the late geonic period.

Appendix

In order to permit a comparison with the text of our fragment, I now cite the text of the *'ilu finu* poem that is attached to the *nishmat* prayer as it has been transmitted in three of the earliest sources:

Prayer-book of R. Saʿadya Gaon, p. 119:

ואלו פינו מלא שירה כים לשוננו רנה כהמון גליו ושפתותינו כרחבי הרקיע ועינינו כשמש וירח
וידינו כנשרי שמים ורגלינו כאילות אין אנו מספיקין להודות לך ייי אלהינו ולברך ולקדש את
שמך מלכנו על אחת מאלף אלפי אלפים ומרבוא רבבות פעמים הטובות נסין וגבורות שעשית
עמנו ועם אבותינו מלפנים ועד הנה ממצרים הוצאתנו ייי אלהינו מבית עבדים פדיתנו מלכנו
ברעב זנתנו ובשבע גדול כלכלתנו מחרב הצלתנו מדבר מלטתנו מחלאים רעים רבים רפיתנו
מלכנו ועד הנה עזרונו רחמיך ייי אלהינו ולא עזבונו עכשו

Cambridge University Library, Hebrew MS Add.3160.3:

אילו פינו מלא שירה כים ולשונינו רנה כהמון גליו ושפ ושפתותינו כמרח[בי הרקיע] ועינינו
כשמש ויריח וידינו כנשרי שמים ורגלינו כאילות אין אנו מספ מספיקין להודות לך יי אלהינו
ולברך את שמך מלכנו ולומר לפניך יי אלהינו ואלהי אבותינו אחת מאלף אלפים ומרבי רבבות
פעמים הטובות שעשית עמנו ועם אבותינו ממצרים גאלתנו יי אלהינו מבית עבדים פדיתנו ברעב
זנתנו ובשובע כלכלתנו ומחרב הצ הצלתנו ומדבר מלטתנו מחליים רעים רבים דליתנו אבל
אברים שפלגתה בנו [וכו]

Cambridge University Library, Hebrew MS Add.3160.5:

אילו פינו מלא שירה כים וַשפתותינו ולשונינו כהמון גליו וַשפתותינו כמרחבי רקיע אין אנו
מספיקים ולומר לפני יי אלהינו ואלהי אבותינו אחת מאלף אלפי אלפים ומרבי רבבות הטובות
והנחמות שעשיתה עמנו ועם אבותינו מלפנינו ממצרים גאלתנו מבית עבדים פדיתנו ברעב זנתנו
ובשובע גדול כלכלתנו ומחרב הצלתנו ומחלאי[...][39]

---

38 Goitein's precise words on p. 301 of the passage cited in n. 36 above were: 'Whether the rest of the books belonging to them had been sold, returned to them, or spoiled by rainwater (as happened occasionally in Jerusalem), we may learn some day'.

39 See also Cambridge University Library, Genizah texts T-S NS 150.23 and 159.1.

18

A Genizah Fragment of Grace After Meals

Tracing ideas

Any genuine attempt at reconstructing the form and content of medieval Hebrew prayer must ultimately be dependent on the sound decipherment and analysis of the manuscript evidence. If one is researching the situation in the Eastern Mediterranean of about a millennium ago, the primary source is undoubtedly the rich collection of material from the Cairo Genizah. Through its old, worn and fragmentary pieces, much has already been revealed about the development of post-talmudic Jewish liturgy but the picture still remains hazy and incomplete.[1] An overall sense of what occurred is gradually emerging and this is especially true in connection with the Babylonian and Palestinian rites and their input into the later evolution of the oriental and occidental rites. It must be admitted, however, that the details of the process are yet to be convincingly mapped. If this is true with regard to the philological and historical aspects, it applies even more to the tracing of theological ideas and their adjustment by way of the close examination of liturgical texts. Obviously, scholars cannot justifiably speculate on how such ideas were maintained or altered without basing themselves on the critical comparison of a fair number of accurately reconstructed texts. At the same time, it has to be acknowledged that no reliable theories about such developments will emerge unless there is an interest in building them. Here we are confronted with a virtual *tabula rasa* because of an exclusive preoccupation with the recording of textual variations on the part of some specialists and a conviction that different words merely reflect the same theology on the part of others.[2] The purpose of this study is to make a modest contribution, in a small area, to the history and theology of medieval Jewish liturgy by way of the critical examination of one Cambridge Genizah fragment of the rabbinic grace after meals. Some information will be provided about how the piece found its way to Cambridge and a description will be offered of its codicological and

---

1   M. Schmelzer, 'The contribution of the Genizah to the study of liturgy and poetry', *PAAJR* 63 [1997–2001] (2001), pp. 163–79; see also chapter 12 of this volume.

2   See the collected work of D. Rappel, *Piṯḥey Ha-She'arim: Gates to the Jewish Liturgy*, eds. Y. and N. Rappel (Tel Aviv, 2001).

palaeographical nature. Following a transcription of the Hebrew text, a
number of textual variants from each paragraph will be discussed and
the importance of these will be assessed for various aspects of Jewish
liturgical history. Finally, an attempt will be made to compare each
paragraph with other medieval versions and to draw some general
conclusions.

Description

According to Cambridge University Library's records, its Hebrew
manuscript Add. 3162 was purchased by the Oxford Egyptologist, the
Reverend Greville J. Chester, in Egypt and presented to the Library in
1891.[3] Given that geographical and chronological background, and the
fact that the other thirty-two items that Mr Chester presented to the
Library all have the standard characteristics of Genizah texts, it may
confidently be assumed that this manuscript also derives from that
same Cairo source.[4] Each of its four paper folios (in two bifolia, stitched
together at top and foot of folios) measures 15 × 10 centimetres, ff. 1v–
3r have Hebrew text on 13–14 lines, while there is scribbling on f. 1r
and f. 4v is blank. Although there is significant staining and damage,
the loss of text is minimal and the manuscript constitutes a complete
text of the set of blessings following a meal (*birkat ha-mazon*), including
an extensive list of הרחמן ('May the Merciful One...') verses. The text on
f. 1v is headed by the phrase בשמ' רחמ' ברכת מזון ('In the name of the
Merciful One, the grace after meals') and concludes on f. 4r with the
Judeo-Arabic note כמלת אלברכה בעון אללה ('The end of the grace, with the
help of God').[5] Two systems are used for filling lines in which there is
insufficient space for a whole word. According to one, the first half of
what resembles the letter *alef* is used (f. 1v, line 11) and in the other the
first letter of the word is transcribed (f. 2r, line 13) but the whole word
is then written again in the new line. The end of the text is indicated by
a dot with a circle around it (f. 4r, line 7). The letter *kaf* throughout the
text has an unusual shape that makes it appear almost like *mem*. The
vowel points are standard Tiberian with an occasional *rafeh* sign but
there is no *ḥaṭaf* under the *ḥet* of the word הרחמן, which is sometimes

---

3   This information is recorded in the Manuscripts Class Catalogue at Cambridge
    University Library. I am grateful to the Syndics of the Library for their permission to
    publish the text and the plate that appears at the end of this volume.

4   S. C. Reif, *Hebrew Manuscripts at Cambridge University Library: A Description and
    Introduction* (Cambridge, 1997), pp. 30 and 32.

5   In my brief description of this fragment in *Hebrew Manuscripts* (see n. 4 above), I
    misread the final letter of the third word of this Judeo-Arabic sentence. It is
    definitely a final *nun* and not a *zayin*.

abbreviated to הרח.[6] The word של is treated as a prefix and not an independent entity and there is some *plene* spelling, as in the case of the word ששמתה (f. 2r, line 7). The second person masculine pronominal suffix follows the Mishnaic Hebrew *-akh* and not the Biblical Hebrew *-kha*. At the end of the third benediction, the last word is followed by two dots indicating the conclusion. There is then a space before and after the word אמן. This is perhaps a reflection of the talmudic discussion concerning the use of 'amen' at the end of benedictions in general and this benediction in particular and the difference of opinion concerning whether it is to be declaimed or recited quietly.[7] In view of all the data just given, there is a *prima facie* case for establishing the original provenance of the manuscript in the Syro-Palestinian-Egyptian area in the classical Genizah period. Dr Edna Engel of the Hebrew Palaeography Project at the Jewish National and University Library in Jerusalem has tentatively suggested to me that it should be dated to the twelfth century.[8]

Text

1v

בשמ' רחמ'   ברכת מזון

ברוך אתה ייי אלהינו מלך העולם | הזן את העולם כולו בטוב בחסד | וברחמים נותן לחם לכל

בשר | כי לעולם חסדו עמנו וטובו | הגדול לא חסר לנו ואל יחסרינו | מלכינו מזון מעתה ועד

עולם | בעבור שמו הגדול כי הוא זן | ומפרנס לכל ושלחנו ערוך לכל | והתקין מזון לכל

בריות[יו אשר]‏[9] | ברא כרחמיו וכרוב חסדיו | כאמור פותח את ידיך ומשביע | לכל חי רצון

ברוך אתה ייי הזן

2r

את הכל.   נודה לך ייי אלהינו | כי הנחלתנו ארץ חמדה טובה | ורחבה ברית חיים ותורה חיים ומזון

| ועל שהוצאתנו מארץ מצרים | ופדיתנו מבית עבדים ועל | חוקי רצונך שהודעתנו ועל | בריתך

ששמתה בבשרינו ועל | תורתך שלמדתנו ועל חיים וחן | וחסד ופרנסה וכלכלה שאתה | חונן

ומלוה אתנו בכל עת ובכל | זמן ועל כולם ייי אלהינו אנו | מודים לך ומברכים את שמך | הגדול

והקדוש לעולם ועד | כאמור ואכלת ושבעת וברכת

---

6   Some of these various features are exemplified in the plate that appears at the end of this volume.

7   BT, *Berakhot* 45b; compare PT, *Berakhot* 5.5 (9c) which does not specifically refer to this example of the use of *amen*.

8   I am grateful to Dr Engel for this helpful suggestion which was made to me at the Library in Jerusalem early in 1997. On the matter of scribal transmission, see M. Beit-Arié, *Unveiled Faces of Medieval Hebrew Books: The Evolution of Manuscript Production – Progression or Regression?* (Jerusalem, 2003), with comments relating to the matter of line-fillers on pp. 32–48.

9   This is the only place in the manuscript where the paper has disintegrated and left a lacuna in the text.

2v

את ייי אלהיך על הארץ הטובה | אשר נתן לך וזכר לנו מהרה | את ברית אבותינו ובטובך |

הגדול תשבע נפשינו ונודה | לשמך הגדול סלה ברוך אתה | ייי על הארץ ועל המזון: | רחם

ייי אלהינו עלינו | ועל ישראל עמך ועל ירושלם | עירך ועל ציון משכן כבודך | ועל הבית הגדול

והקדוש אשר | נקרא שמך עליו ומלכות בית | דויד מהרה תחזירה למקומה | בימינו ובנה את

ירושלם בקרוב

3r

והעלינו לתוכה ושמחינו בבנינה | ברוך אתה ייי הבונה ברחמיו | את ירושלם: אמן | ברוך

אתה ייי אלהינו מלך העולם | אבינו מלכינו אדירינו קדושינו | קדוש יעקב המלך הרחמן | הטוב

והמטיב שבכל יום ויום | הוא מטיב עמנו הוא גמלנו | הוא יגמלנו לעד חן וחסד | ורחמים וכל

טוב הרחמן | ימלך לעולם ועד. הרחמן | ישתבח בשמים ובארץ. הרח' | יתהדר על כסא

כבודו. הרח'

3v

יוליכנו קוממיות. הרחמן | יצילנו מעניות. הרחמן | יגער בחושבי רעתינו. הרח' | יסיר

מחלה מקרבינו. הרח' | יברך מעשה ידינו. הרח'. הרח' | יצליחנו בכל דרכינו. הרח' | יטע תורתו

בלבינו. הרח' | יברך השלחן שאכלנו עליו | ישימו כשלחנו שלאברהם | יטע בו כל מעדנים יסדר

| עליו כל תענוגים. הרחמן | יפרוס עלינו סוכת שלום | הרחמן יהיה לנו עוזר

4r

וסומך. הרחמן יזכינו לביאת | המלך המשיח ולחיי העולם הבא. | מגדיל ישועות מלכו ועושה |

חסד למשיכו לדויד ולזרעו | עד עולם. עושה שלום | במרומיו הוא ברחמיו יעשה | שלום על

כל ישראל: |

כמלת אלברכה בעון אללה:

Variants

For the purposes of this brief paper, only a limited number of the numerous, interesting variants will be listed and discussed, and they will be cited according to folio and line as in the above text:

1. F. 1v, l. 5: The use of the word עמנו indicating that 'God's love is with us' is recorded in the twelfth-century Franco-German *Maḥzor Vitry*. It is, however, specifically opposed by the Spanish liturgist David Abudraham on the grounds that it does not appear in the original biblical phrase and is theologically suspect in that it limits the divine love to Israel.[10] It occurs in numerous Genizah texts and the reason for its inclusion may be an interest in stressing the Jewish relationship with God and a reluctance to use the purely biblical formula in favour of an adjusted rabbinic one.[11]

---

10 *Maḥzor Vitry*, ed. S. Hurwitz (2 vols; Nuremberg², 1923), 1.52, *Sefer Abudraham* (Warsaw, 1877), p. 174, and *Sefer Abudraham Ha-Shalem*, ed. S. A Wertheimer (Jerusalem, 1963), p. 322.

11 See Genizah texts CUL T-S NS 159.10 and 230.15, and T-S AS 104.76 and 107.181. Another Genizah fragment in which the word עמנו has been added to the biblical phrase is CUL T-S Ar.37.262 which contains an expanded version of the text to found in Sa'adya's prayer-book; see *Siddur R. Saadya Gaon*, eds I. Davidson, S. Assaf and B. I. Joel, (Jerusalem, 1941; second edition, Jerusalem, 1963), p. 102. See also L.

2. F. 1v, l. 5: The form טובו rather than ובטובו is a reflection of earlier texts in which reference is made to God's goodness, almost as an hypostasization, in both halves of the sentence, apparently in an original form that read **וטובו** הגדול לא חסר לנו ואל יחסר לנו כל **טוב** ('His divine goodness has never failed us nor will any of his goodness ever fail us'). An alternative such as לחם or מזון was later employed in order to avoid the duplication of the word טוב, or because its original sense was no longer clear, and to make a more specific reference to the provision of food. Such alternatives then became the subject of the whole sentence and the first use of טוב was adjusted to an adverbial use by the addition of a preposition, i.e. ובטובו or ומטובו, so that it was no longer God's goodness that had never failed or would never fail but rather the food that was provided by God's goodness.[12] The current phraseology appears to represent a transitional stage between the two formulas.

3. F. 1v, l. 6: The expansion of the second phrase mentioned in the previous note into ואל יְחַסְרֵנוּ מלכינו מזון ('and May our King never allow us to lack food') and the use of the *pi'el* conjugation appears to give God, as it were, a more active role in preventing a lack of food. Given that the subject of the entire first paragraph of the grace is the divine provider of food, and the possibility that in an early phraseology the sense of טוב was as an epithet of God, perhaps this expanded version has still preserved such a sense in its use of the *pi'el*.[13]

4. F. 1v, l. 10: In the various versions, one of two alternative verbs is employed to describe God's provision of food, both of them in the *hiph'il*, namely, מכין or (as here) התקין. The former is Biblical Hebrew while the latter is Mishnaic Hebrew and the option chosen in a

---

Finkelstein, 'The Birkat ha-mazon', *JQR*, NS 19 (1928–29), p. 243, and B. S. Jacobson, *Netiv Binah* (Hebrew; 5 vols; Tel Aviv, 1968–83), vol. 3 (1973), p. 55.

12 The phrase begins with וטובו (but also includes the words לחם and/or מזון) in Genizah fragments CUL T-S NS 159.10 and 230.15, and T-S AS 104.70 and 105.94 while T-S AS 107.181 has the word with the preposition, ובטובו. See also Finkelstein, 'Birkat ha-mazon' (see n. 11 above), p. 243, and Jacobson, *Netiv Binah* (see n. 11 above), pp. 55–56. On this and similar variants, see *Hazofeh* 10 (L. Blau *Festschrift*,1926), pp. 213–15.

13 Compare the ending of the first paragraph of the fourth benediction in the later Ashkenazi and Italian rites (לעולם אל יְחַסְרֵנוּ), as in S. D. Luzzatto (ed.), מחזור כל השנה כפי מנהג ק"ק איטאלייני (2 vols; Livorno, 1856), 1.101a, and S. Baer, *Seder 'Avodat Yisra'el* (Rödelheim, 1868), p. 559. On the use of הטוב for addressing God, compare the conclusion of the penultimate benediction of the 'amidah in numerous Genizah texts, many of them reflecting the Palestinian rite: הטוב לך להודות ('O Good One, who deserves thanks'); see Y. Luger, *The Weekday Amidah in the Cairo Genizah* (Hebrew; Jerusalem, 2001), p. 186. Genizah fragments CUL T-S NS 230.15 and AS 104.176 have another version that may represent an intermediate stage: וטובו הגדול לא חיסרנו ואל יחסר לנו מזון.

particular line of tradition consequently reflects that tradition's notion of what kind of language is preferable in the rabbinic liturgy.[14]

5. F. Iv, l. 12: Whether or not to conclude the body of a liturgical text, immediately before the benediction itself, with a biblical verse was a controversial matter and rites were not always consistent in their practices. Of the three verses commonly used with the first three paragraphs of the grace (respectively, Psalms 145:16, Deuteronomy 8:10 and Psalms 147:2), this version has the first two. Among the words used to introduce the verses are ככתוב, כאמור and לקיים. In this version, כאמור is used in the first benediction and ככתוב in the second (f. 2, l. 14).[15]

6. F. 2r, l. 2: The phrase הנחלתנו ארץ ('you have given us a land as an inheritance') presupposes that the worshipper is in the land of Israel, while the alternative הנחלת את אבותינו ('you have given our ancestors a land as an inheritance'), which occurs in many other versions, is undoubtedly more suited to those praying in the diaspora. The former version is, however, still retained by Sa'adya and perhaps also by Maimonides (about whose preference there is some textual doubt) before later giving way more widely to the latter. Earlier Genizah fragments often begin the benediction with the phrase על ארצינו ועל נחלת אבותינו, perhaps an alternative Palestinian version and position for the phrase being discussed.[16]

---

14 Some examples of liturgical objection to the Mishnaic Hebrew stem תקן are discussed in S. C. Reif, *Shabbethai Sofer and his Prayer-book* (Cambridge, 1979), pp. 127, 188, 195, 220, 298, and 303–4.

15 On the matter of the inclusion of a verse, see PT, *Berakhot* 1:8 (3d) and the interpretations offered by N. Wieder, *The Formation of Jewish Liturgy in the East and the West: A Collection of Essays* (Hebrew; 2 vols; Jerusalem, 1998), 1.285–91 (originally published in *Tarbiz* 43 (1974), pp. 46–52), I. Ta-Shma, '*Eyn omrim berakhah pasuq*' in *Sefer Raphael*, ed. J. E. Movshovitz (Hebrew; Jerusalem, 2000), pp. 643–51, and Jacob ben Judah Ḥazzan of London, *The Etz Hayyim*, ed. I. Brodie (3 vols; Jerusalem, 1962–67), 1.166. For the variation in the introductory word, see Finkelstein, 'Birkat ha-mazon' (see n. 11 above), pp. 243–57, and Jacobson, *Netiv Binah* (see n. 11 above), pp. 55–59. Among Genizah fragments, CUL T-S K8.7 (= J. Mann, 'Genizah fragments of the Palestinian order of service,' *HUCA* 2 (1925), no. 18, reprinted in *Contributions to the Scientific Study of Jewish Liturgy* (ed. J. J. Petuchowski, New York, 1970)) and Bodley, Heb. f. 47 (*Catalogue of the Hebrew Manuscripts in the Bodleian Library*, vol. 1, ed. A. Neubauer (Oxford, 1886); vol. 2, ed. A. Neubauer and A. E. Cowley (Oxford, 1906), no. 2734) have the verse while CUL T-S AS 102.22 and AS 107.181 do not.

16 *Saadya* (see n. 11 above), p. 102 and E. D. Goldschmidt, 'The Oxford Ms. of Maimonides' book of prayer' (reprinted from *Studies of the Research Institute for Hebrew Poetry in Jerusalem* 7 (1958), pp. 183–213) in his collected articles entitled *On Jewish Liturgy: Essays on Prayer and Religious Poetry* (Hebrew; Jerusalem, 1978), p. 215. See also Finkelstein, 'Birkat ha-mazon' (see n. 11 above), pp. 247–49 and Jacobson, *Netiv Binah* (see n. 11 above), pp. 57–59. Among Genizah fragments that have the introductory phrase and/or the word הנחלתנו are CUL T-S K8.7 (= Mann, 'Palestinian order' (see n. 15 above), no. 18), NS 154.95, 235.173 and 271.14, and AS 108.134.

7. F. 2r, l. 3: Among the subjects required by the talmudic teachers to be mentioned in the second paragraph of the grace are God's covenant with Israel and the Torah and these are linked up with the topic of daily sustenance.[17] Hence the phrase here that simply covers four topics: ברית ותורה חיים ומזון ('covenant, Torah, life and food'). The problem is that this version also includes later in the paragraph (lines 7–10) an expansion of each of these four topics. It may speculatively be proposed that what is probably being reflected here is a stage at which the expansion had found a place after various other appended phrases. It had not yet totally displaced the original but was co-existing with it, perhaps because their places in the paragraph were not contiguous.[18]

8. F. 2r, l. 12: In the most expansive versions there is here an expression of thanks to God's name and a wish for his name to be blessed forever, with a possible application of various epithets to His name.[19] Here in the statement אנו מודים לך ומברכים את שמך הגדול והקדוש ('we thank you and bless your great and holy name') the first half gives thanks directly to God and the second blesses his great and holy name. This version appears to represent a mid-point – though not necessarily a chronological one –between the shortest and longest texts.

9. F. 2v, lines 2–5: The passage immediately before the benediction in this instance is a plea for future sustenance: 'Speedily remember for us the covenant with our fathers and in your great goodness bring us satisfaction and we shall thank your great name forever'. There are at this point in some Genizah texts, in the Rumanian and, to a lesser extent, in the Italian rites pleas for future deliverance and restoration that undoubtedly have messianic overtones.[20] The text here appears to

17 BT, *Berakhot* 48b–49a and PT, *Berakhot* 1.9 (3d).
18 Only the four words, and no expansion of them, are to be found in *Saadya* (see n. 11 above), p. 102, *Siddur Rabbenu Shelomo ben Nathan*, ed. S. Ḥagi (Jerusalem, 1995), p. 118, and Genizah fragments CUL T-S NS 154.95, 159.120, 230.29, 235.173 and AS 102.22, and Bodley, Heb. f. 47 (Neubauer, *Catalogue* (see n. 15 above), no. 2734).
19 Contrast the version of *Saadya* (see n. 11 above), p. 102, and Genizah fragment CUL T-S NS 174.14, which read: אנו מודים לך ומברכים את שמך לעולם ועד ('we thank you and bless your name forever'), with that of *The Etz Hayyim* (see n. 15 above), 1.167, which has: אנחנו מודים לך ומברכין אותך יתברך שמך בפה כל חי תמיד לעולם ועד ('we thank you and bless you; may your name be blessed in the mouth of all living continually forever'). See also Finkelstein, 'Birkat ha-mazon' (see n. 11 above), pp. 247–51 and Jacobson, *Netiv Binah* (see n. 11 above), pp. 57–59. CUL T-S K8.7 (= Mann, 'Palestinian order' (see n. 15 above), no. 18) has יתברך שמך תמיד לעולם ועד while NS 197.14, though barely legible, appears to read ויתגדל שמך תמיד לעולם ועד.
20 *Seder Tefillot Ha-Shanah Le-Minhag Qehillot Romaniya* (Constantinople, 1574) = Rumanian rite, f. 80a; Luzzatto's מנהג איטאלייני (see n. 13 above), f. 100b; Finkelstein, 'Birkat ha-mazon' (see n. 11 above), p. 251, and Jacobson, *Netiv Binah* (see n. 11 above), p. 59; E. D. Goldschmidt, *On Jewish Liturgy* (see n. 16 above), p. 161; CUL T-S NS 271.128 and AS 107.181.

be more mundane, unless the phrase תשבע נפשינו (in which the verb is vocalized in the *pi'el* conjugation) carries a more figurative and spiritual sense.

10. F. 2v, l. 7: The prayer for Jerusalem occurs in the daily *'amidah*, the *haftarah* and wedding benedictions, and the grace. The factors common to all the versions and rites are the mentions of God's people Israel, the city of Jerusalem and the Temple, with amplifications of these and variations in their order.[21] The inclusion of the worshippers themselves among the potential recipients of the divine mercy, as flagged here by the inclusion of the word עלינו, is not universal and may reflect a concern to move from the people as a whole to the local congregation.[22]

11. Ff. 2v–3r: The simplest versions all make reference in the latter part of the third benediction to the return of the dynasty of David and some also include the rebuilding of Jerusalem and the restoration of the Temple service.[23] More complex formulations either expand on the messianic theme or prefer to stress the need for independence and security with regard to future sustenance, or sometimes do both.[24] The additional phraseology that is followed here is also used in some versions of the *musaf 'amidah* for festivals והעלינו לתוכה ושמחינו בבנינה ('bring us up into Jerusalem and grant us the joy of seeing it rebuilt') and lays the emphasis on the city's reconstruction.[25]

---

21 For sources and discussion of this Jerusalem benediction, see S. C. Reif, 'Some notions of restoration in early rabbinic prayer' in *Restoration: Old Testament, Jewish, and Christian Perspectives*, ed. J. M. Scott (Leiden, Boston, Köln, 2001), pp. 293–94, reproduced in an updated form as chapter 9 of this volume.

22 The word עלינו is not included (or, is excluded?) in *Seder Rav Amram Gaon*, ed. E. D. Goldschmidt (Jerusalem, 1971); collated with *Seder R. Amram*, part 1, ed. D. Hedegård (Lund, 1951), p. 45, and Goldschmidt, 'Maimonides' (see n. 16 above), p. 216, but otherwise occurs in numerous sources representing various rites and periods, including Genizah fragments such as CUL T-S NS 271.128 and Bodley, Heb. f. 47 (Neubauer, *Catalogue* (see n. 15 above), no. 2734). Similarly, *Mahzor Vitry* (see n. 10 above), 1.52, and Luzzatto's מנהג איטאלייני (see n. 13 above), f. 100a, add the word עלינו to the end of the phrase שנקרא שמך עליו.

23 As, for example, *Saadya* (see n. 11 above), Goldschmidt, 'Maimonides' (see n. 16 above), *Siddur Rabbenu Shelomo* (see n. 18 above) and the Persian rite (JTSA ENA 23), and Genizah fragments Bodley, Heb. f. 47 and f. 36 (Neubauer, *Catalogue* (see n. 15 above), nos 2734 and 2738), CUL T-S K8.7 (= Mann, 'Palestinian order' (see n. 15 above), no. 18) and AS 102.22. See also Finkelstein, 'Birkat ha-mazon' (see n. 11 above), pp. 253–54, and Jacobson, *Netiv Binah* (see n. 11 above), pp. 59–60.

24 *Amram* (see n. 22 above) in the form that we have it, p. 45, matches these formulations; see also *The Etz Hayyim* (see n. 15 above), 1.167, *Mahzor Vitry* (see n. 10 above), 1.52, Genizah fragments CUL T-S H18.8 and H11.74 (= Mann, 'Palestinian order' (see n. 15 above), nos 21 and 19), Luzzatto's מנהג איטאלייני (see n. 13 above), f. 100ab, the Rumanian rite, (see n. 20 above), f. 80a, and Finkelstein, 'Birkat ha-mazon' (see n. 11 above), pp. 255–57.

25 *Saadya* (see n. 11 above), pp. 151–52; I. Elbogen, German edition, *Der jüdische Gottesdienst in seiner geschichtlichen Entwicklung* (Frankfurt am Main, 1931; reprint,

12. F. 3r, l. 2: Although the use here of the definite article in the word הבונה occurs in some other Genizah texts and has survived in early versions of the Yemenite rite,[26] it is more commonly absent not only in the case of the shorter formula בונה ירושלים ('builder of Jerusalem') where the first word is construct and militates against such a form but even where the longer formula בונה את ירושלים is employed.[27] In the latter case, the use of the definite article is, strictly speaking, more grammatically sound and may even stress God's power but has been eliminated possibly by contamination with the alternative rendering.

13. F. 3r, lines 5–6: Although there is no consistency in the earliest Genizah fragments, the text after the opening benediction in the later versions and rites (but not here) generally included the word האל ('God') before any of God's other epithets.[28] Was the original ambivalence about opening the description with the word אבינו ('our Father') born out of a hesitation to over-emphasize God's fatherhood since this was so central a notion in Christian theology and such anathema to dominant Islamic conceptions of God? There is also variation with regard to the inclusion of a reference to God's holiness,

---

Hildesheim, 1962), pp. 132–40; Hebrew edition, התפילה בישראל בהתפתחותה ההיסטורית (eds J. Heinemann, I. Adler, A. Negev, J. Petuchowski and H. Schirmann, Tel Aviv, 1972), pp. 100–105; English edition, *Jewish Liturgy: A Comprehensive History* (trans. and ed. Raymond P. Scheindlin, Philadelphia, Jerusalem and New York, 1993), pp. 111–17; Mann, 'Palestinian order' (see n. 15 above), pp. 325–32; Jacobson, *Netiv Binah* (see n. 11 above), 4.14–27; and E. Fleischer, *Eretz-Israel Prayer and Prayer Rituals as Portrayed in the Geniza Documents* (Hebrew; Jerusalem, 1988), pp. 93–159.

26   As in Persian rite MS JTSA ENA 23, *Siddur Rabbenu Shelomo* (see n. 18 above), p. 120, and Genizah fragments CUL T-S K8.7 and H11.74 (= Mann, 'Palestinian order' (see n. 15 above), nos 18 and 21), and Bodley, Heb. f. 47 (Neubauer, *Catalogue* (see n. 15 above), no. 2734). The *Tiklal* of Yaḥya ben Joseph ibn Ṣaliḥ (three vols, Jerusalem, 1894), 1.168, omits the definite article and has a note objecting to its addition. See, however, earlier manuscripts of the *Tiklal* (e.g. CUL Add.1200, f.151r, Add.1727, f. 222v, Add.1729, f.87r, and Add.1754, f.103v) which have the definite article, and Finkelstein, 'Birkat ha-mazon' (see n. 11 above), pp. 253–58.

27   *Saadya* (see n. 11 above), p. 102, *Amram* (see n. 22 above), p. 45, Goldschmidt, 'Maimonides' (see n. 16 above), p. 216, Bodley, Heb. f. 36 (Neubauer, *Catalogue* (see n. 15 above), no. 2738) (אלהי דוד הוא בונה את ירושלים), *The Etz Hayyim* (see n. 15 above), 1, p. 167, and Luzzatto's מנהג איטאלייני (see n. 13 above), f. 101a.

28   *Saadya* (see n. 11 above), p. 102, Goldschmidt, 'Maimonides' (see n. 16 above), p. 216, *The Etz Hayyim* (see n. 15 above), 1.168, *Maḥzor Vitry* (see n. 10 above), 1.52, *Siddur Rabbenu Shelomo* (see n. 18 above), p. 120, Luzzatto's מנהג איטאלייני (see n. 13 above), f. 101a, Genizah fragments CUL T-S K8.7 and H18.8 (= Mann, 'Palestinian order' (see n. 15 above), nos 18 and 19), sometimes in the expanded form האל תתברך לעד or האל יתברך לעד. See also the Persian rite in MS JTSA ENA 23, Rumanian rite (see n. 20 above), f. 80a, Finkelstein, 'Birkat ha-mazon' (see n. 11 above), pp. 259–62, and Jacobson, *Netiv Binah* (see n. 11 above), pp. 34–35.

some of the early texts making no reference to it[29] while it appears here, and widely in the later rites, as קדושינו קדוש יעקב ('our Holy One, the Holy One of Jacob'), the words קדוש יעקב following the verse in Isaiah 29:23.[30]

14. F. 3r, lines 8–9: Although late medieval and early modern versions refer to both God's goodness to the worshippers (using the Hebrew root יטב) and His bestowal on them of a list of bounties (using the Hebrew root גמל) as activities of the past, present and future, this appears to be an attempt to impose a more balanced and rational structure on a looser, original sentence, with the support of statements made in the Tosafot and by R. Asher ben Yeḥiel of Toledo.[31] In the earliest texts there are sometimes as few as two expressions – one for each verb – and in other instances more than one tense is represented in the uses of the verb גמל.[32] In the case of our manuscript, the first verb occurs only as a participle, i.e. in the present tense. The second verb has the perfect and imperfect, which may carry the senses of the present (with or without a change of vowels) and the jussive: הוא מטיב עמנו הוא גמלנו | הוא יגמלנו לעד חן וחסד | ורחמים וכל טוב ('He is good to us; he provides (or, has provided) us, He will (or, may He) provide us forever with favour, love, mercy and all good').

15. The fourth benediction is followed by a group of short entreaties that address God as הרחמן ('the merciful one') and deal with a variety of special needs. The evidence of the earliest texts indicates that these were added in the post-talmudic period much in the same way as special pleas were appended to the end of the 'amidah. They provided an opportunity for the individual and/or the community to allude to the specific requirements of their time and place in their standard

---

29 *Saadya* (see n. 11 above) has no reference to holiness while Genizah text, Bodley, Heb. f. 36 (Neubauer, *Catalogue* (see n. 15 above), no. 2738), has מקדשנו קדוש יעקב.

30 Genizah texts CUL T-S K8.7 and H18.8 (= Mann, 'Palestinian order' (see n. 15 above), nos 18 and 19) and all the major rites and authorities.

31 Tosafot on *Berakhot* 46b and Rosh's section 22 on *Berakhot* 49a. *The Etz Hayyim* (see n. 15 above), 1.168, *Abudraham*, p. 176, and *Abudraham Ha-Shalem* (see n. 16 above), p. 326, order the tenses as present, past and future while the Italian and Ashkenazi rites in Luzzatto's מנהג איטאלייני (see n. 13 above), f. 101a, and Baer, *'Avodat Yisra'el* (see n. 13 above), p. 558–59, have past, present and future. See also *Sefer Ha-Manhig*, ed. I. Raphael (2 vols; Jerusalem, 1978), 1.223.

32 *Saadya* (see n. 11 above), p. 103, *Amram* (see n. 22 above), p. 46, Goldschmidt, 'Maimonides' (see n. 16 above), *Mahzor Vitry* (see n. 10 above), 1.52, *Siddur Rabbenu Shelomo* (see n. 18 above), p. 120, and Genizah texts CUL T-S H18.8 (= Mann, 'Palestinian order' (see n. 15 above), no. 19), T-S NS 230.29 and 230.74, T-S AS 102.22 and 104.45, and Bodley, Heb. f. 36 (Neubauer, *Catalogue* (see n. 15 above), no. 2738). See also the Yemenite, Persian and Rumanian rites as in *Tiklal* (see n. 26 above), f. 168b, MS JTSA ENA 23, Rumanian rite (see n. 20 above), f. 80a, Finkelstein, 'Birkat ha-mazon' (see n. 11 above), pp. 259–63 and Jacobson, *Netiv Binah* (see n. 11 above), pp. 64–66.

prayers.[33] As such, they came to be expanded but at the same time also acquired a degree of standardization that was to a large extent at odds with their original intent, not an uncommon feature of traditional rabbinic liturgy. Even in the fourteenth century commentary of David Abudraham, he was still able to offer the relaxed judgement that 'every worshipper may recite whichever of these he wishes and needs'.[34] For the liturgical historian they are especially interesting when they testify to special pleas that are not commonly known from other sources. In the case of the manuscript under discussion, the three texts that warrant particular attention are the fifth, sixth and seventh. They appeal to God to save the community from poverty (יצילנו מעניות),[35] to thwart the evil intentions of Israel's enemies (יגער בחושבי רעתנו),[36] and to remove sickness from among the worshippers (יסיר מחלה מקרבינו).[37] There is of course no way of knowing whether these pleas have been transmitted from earlier communities and situations as part of a traditional text but it is certainly possible that they reflect the problems of a community whose economic, political and medical conditions are not ideal.

Summary of data

The data provided above should now be interpreted thematically in terms of their relevance to the more general history of Jewish liturgy. Once again, the point must first be made that each of the textual preferences may not necessarily reflect the situation of the scribe committing it to writing since it may simply have been inherited and adopted from an earlier tradition. On the other hand, it will be possible by way of such a thematic assessment, and subsequently with the assistance of a synoptic analysis of the texts within each benediction and how they relate to other versions, to arrive at some tentative conclusions. These will attempt to locate the manuscript in the broader framework of the evolution of medieval Hebrew prayer.

---

33 Finkelstein, 'Birkat ha-mazon' (see n. 11 above), p. 234, exaggerates the antiquity of these addenda which are more accurately assessed by A. Z. Idelsohn, *Jewish Liturgy and Its Development* (New York, 1932), p. 124. See also Jacobson, *Netiv Binah* (see n. 11 above), pp. 66–75, and Genizah fragments CUL T-S H11.74 and H18.8 (= Mann, 'Palestinian order' (see n. 15 above), nos 21 and 19) for early examples of these addenda.

34 *Abudraham*, p. 176, and *Abudraham Ha-Shalem* (see n. 10 above), p. 326.

35 As in *Amram* (see n. 22 above), p. 46, Luzzatto's מנהג איטאלייני (see n. 13 above), f. 101a, Rumanian rite (see n. 20 above), f. 80b, and Genizah fragment CUL T-S AS 101.67.

36 *Saadya* (see n. 11 above), p. 103, and Genizah fragment CUL T-S NS 230.68.

37 *Saadya* (see n. 11 above), p. 103, Persian rite in JTSA ENA 23, and Genizah fragment CUL T-S NS 230.68.

It emerges from the texts discussed above in paragraphs 2, 6, 8, 12 and 13 and relating, respectively, to טובו, הנחלתנו, והקדוש, שמך הגדול, הבונה and האל, that there are here remnants of early formulations or tendencies that were amended or eliminated in most of the rites and versions as they evolved in the latter part of the Middle Ages. In addition, there are some phrases that have in them elements of the novel, rare or even unique. Paragraphs 3 and 9, with reference to יְחַסְּרֵנוּ and וזכר לנו note two such examples and also noteworthy in this connection are the inclusion of the two biblical phrases כרחמיו וכרוב חסדיו ('in accordance with his mercies and numerous kindnesses') and אתה חונן ומלוה אתנו ('you graciously lend us'). The first of these survived only in some Sefardi versions and in the Persian rite[38], and the latter, which was apparently an old Palestinian formulation, is to be found in the Persian and Rumanian rites[39]. Moves towards conflation or expansion, and tendencies towards literary and linguistic standardization are to be detected in the texts discussed above in paragraphs 7, 8 and 14, with regard to the phrases אנו מודים לך ומברכים את שמך הגדול, ברית ותורה חיים ומזון and the verbs גמל/יטב. The phrase לכל בריותיו אשר ברא, at the end of the first paragraph but not discussed above, may also represent a fusion of two alternatives, namely, לכל בריותיו and לכל אשר ברא.[40] On the other hand, there are also clear indications of the kind of inconsistency that perhaps predated or led to attempts at standardization, as in a) the case of והתקין; b) the use of verses towards the end of the benediction, noted in paragraphs 4 and 5 above; and c) with regard to the interchange of the words כי, אשר and the prefix -ש.[41]

In the matter of theology, some points that arose in the course of the textual discussion above should now be drawn together and summarized. The addition of the words עמנו and עלינו referred to in

---

38   Isaiah 63:7. See Finkelstein, 'Birkat ha-mazon' (see n. 11 above), p. 246, Jacobson, *Netiv Binah* (see n. 11 above), p. 56 and JTSA ENA 23.

39   Psalms 37:26. See Finkelstein, 'Birkat ha-mazon' (see n. 11 above), pp. 248, 250 and 252. The phrase is preserved in Genizah fragments CUL T-S NS 271.14 and 271.128, T-S AS 107.181 and 109.104 and partly in *Amram* (see n. 22 above), p. 45 (only מלוה), and the Persian rite in JTSA ENA 23 (שאתה חונן אותנו בכל רגע ובכל זמן).

40   Clear evidence for such a development may be identified in the variants to be found for this phrase, such as לכל, לכל הבריות, לכל מעשה ידיו, לכל אשר ברא, לכל בריותיו, and לכל בריותיו ולכל אשר ברא; ('for all', 'for all his creatures', 'for all that he has created', 'for all the creatures', 'for all the creatures and all the work of his hands', and 'for all his creatures and for all that he has created'). See Finkelstein, 'Birkat ha-mazon' (see n. 11 above), pp. 243–46, Jacobson, *Netiv Binah* (see n. 11 above), pp. 55–57. Genizah fragments CUL T-S AS 102.22 and AS 107.181, and Bodley, Heb. f. 47 (Neubauer, *Catalogue* (see n. 15 above), no. 2734) have לכל אשר ברא. *The Etz Hayyim* (see n. 15 above), 1.166, argues for לכל הבריות and objects to both אשר ברא and בריותיו.

41   See the Hebrew text above, 1v, lines 5 and 8, 2r, line 2; 1v, line 10, 2v, lines 2 and 10; 2r, lines 4 and 6–9, 3r, l. 7 and 3v, lines 8–9.

paragraphs 1 and 10 may indicate the presupposition of a closer relationship between God and the worshipping community. With regard to God's provision of food, the texts discussed in paragraphs 2 and 3 appear to vacillate between an ideology that accepts a direct, divine part in this process and one that prefers circumlocutions that would then leave God less open to blame for a conceived failure in this connection. Perhaps the worshipper's image of God also lies behind the use of the definite article with בונה and the lack of the word האל before the word אבינו noted in paragraphs 12 and 13. The former stresses a transcendental power not simply a process of reconstruction and the latter demonstrates no objection to beginning a benediction with an allusion to God's paternity. The pictures drawn of the future, messianic age, which are sometimes very colourful in Jewish liturgy, are somewhat more mundane in the phraseology noted in paragraphs 9 and 11. As far as the extended use of divine epithets is concerned, there are examples with regard to God's name and holiness cited in paragraphs 8 and 13 but no pronounced tendency in this manuscript to indulge in such language.

Synoptic comparison

If one lists each of the phrases recorded in the four benedictions of the grace as they occur in the manuscript under discussion and compares them with the earliest known witnesses of the rabbinic version of this prayer, the results are not all what one might expect. Far from fully matching the Babylonian or Palestinian rites or the subsequent oriental and European versions that succeeded them, the phrases appear to exchange their allegiances on a regular basis, not only from benediction to benediction but also within each benediction. In the case of the first of these (on the general provision of food), the first part of the text conforms to Genizah fragments that reflect various Palestinian versions of the tenth to the twelfth centuries and to the prayer-book of Solomon ben Nathan who flourished in Sijilmasa, south-west Morocco, in the twelfth century.[42] The remainder of the first benediction, on the other hand, has more in common with the Persian rite and some Sefardi versions, not all of them closely linked with the Babylonian tradition.[43]

The expansion of what was probably an original and talmudically sanctioned reference to ברית ותורה חיים ומזון ('covenant, Torah, life and food') into four descriptions of how these items relate to Israel is an

---

42   This applies to the phrases up to and including the word והתקין.
43   Compare the texts provided in Finkelstein, 'Birkat ha-mazon' (see n. 11 above), pp. 243–46, and Jacobson, *Netiv Binah* (see n. 11 above), pp. 55–57, and see JTSA ENA 23.

early post-talmudic phenomenon. Its occurrence here is most reminiscent of the formulations that are already found in some Genizah fragments of both the Palestinian and Babylonian variety and that are later widely followed, especially in the Franco-German, Rumanian and Persian rites. The remainder of the second benediction has most in common with the Rumanian rite.[44] The characteristics of the third benediction in our manuscript are parallel to those of the Persian rite and the prayer-book of Solomon ben Nathan of Sijilmasa, and, to a lesser extent, to those of the Rumanian rite.[45] Intriguingly, the situation with regard to the fourth paragraph changes again. Here, there is a close similarity with *Seder Rav Amram*, which presents itself as having originated with Amram ben Sheshna Gaon in ninth-century Babylonia, with the prayer text of Maimonides in twelfth-century Egypt, with the Rumanian rite and, to a lesser degree, with that of Persia.[46]

What then is the liturgical provenance of the manuscript being discussed? It appears to belong to those many Genizah texts that represent a mixture of what are commonly known as Babylonian and Palestinian elements. This should occasion no surprise since such texts do, in fact, generally outnumber those that may be characterized as more 'purely' Babylonian or Palestinian. It has more in common with *Seder Rav Amram* and Maimonides than it does with the prayer-book of Sa'adya ben Joseph Gaon of Sura. Given that it is now well recognized that the text of *Seder Rav Amram*, as it was transmitted for some three or four centuries after its author's time, was altered to match the notions of the scribes who were copying it and the rites of the communities in which it was being used, that work, as it has reached us, may itself also

---

44 The longer formulation, expanding on all or some of the four subjects approved by the Talmud, is to be found in Genizah fragments CUL T-S K8.7 (= Mann, 'Palestinian order' (see n. 15 above), no. 18), NS 271.14 and 271.128, AS 105.207 and 107.181 and in Goldschmidt, 'Maimonides' (see n. 16 above), p. 216, as well as in *The Etz Hayyim* (see n. 15 above), 1.167, *Maḥzor Vitry* (see n. 10 above), 1.52, the Rumanian rite (see n. 20 above), f. 80a, and Persian rite (JTSA ENA 23). Only the four words themselves occur in *Saadya* (see n. 11 above), p. 102, and *Siddur Rabbenu Shelomo* (see n. 18 above), p. 120, and in Genizah fragments, CUL T-S NS 154.95, 159.120 and 235.173, and Bodley, Heb. f. 47 (Neubauer, *Catalogue* (see n. 15 above), no. 2734). See also Finkelstein, 'Birkat ha-mazon' (see n. 11 above), pp. 247–52, and Jacobson, *Netiv Binah* (see n. 11 above), pp. 57–59.

45 Finkelstein, 'Birkat ha-mazon' (see n. 11 above), pp. 253–58, and Jacobson, *Netiv Binah* (see n. 11 above), pp. 59–64, *Siddur Rabbenu Shelomo* (see n. 18 above), p. 120, Rumanian rite (see n. 20 above), f. 80a, and MSS Bodley, Poc. 262 (Neubauer, *Catalogue* (see n. 15 above), no. 896) and JTSA ENA 23.

46 *Amram* (see n. 22 above), p. 46, Goldschmidt, 'Maimonides' (see n. 16 above), p. 216, Finkelstein, 'Birkat ha-mazon' (see n. 11 above), pp. 260–62, and Jacobson, *Netiv Binah* (see n. 11 above), pp. 90–93; Rumanian rite (see n. 20 above), f. 80a, and JTSA ENA 23.

be classed as a hybrid version.[47] Similarly, the text preferred by Maimonides is a reflection of his Andalusian origins as well as of his long residence in Egypt. Even the rites of Persia and Rumania, which are rightly said to incorporate Palestinian characteristics, undoubtedly fused those together with Babylonian and other elements before the split into the more standardized oriental and European rites that occurred in the twelfth and thirteenth centuries.[48] It may therefore be concluded that the manuscript here being analysed is just another example of the mixed, inconsistent and evolving versions that were typical in the age of Maimonides in the Eastern Mediterranean area. Such versions had opted for the overall structure and content of the Babylonian versions, together with some of the Palestinian traditions, but were still adjusting minor aspects of the texts to match their own preferences and propensities.

Conclusions

A number of more general conclusions, that are important for an accurate understanding of Jewish liturgical history, may also be derived from the data provided by this Genizah fragment of the grace after meals and from its relationship with other versions. The twelfth-century rabbinic liturgies clearly still displayed a considerable variety of textual detail that remained in flux even if the major factors had become more solidified. The crystallization of the definitively recognizable rites of Europe and the orient was only in its early stages. There were still tensions between traditional transmission and novelty, between inconsistency and standardization, and between the biblical and rabbinic varieties of Hebrew language. The image of God, the nature of his relationship with the worshipper, and the notion of the messianic era were all concepts that were, in their smaller detail if not in their major configuration, open to liturgical adjustment. Historians should be ready to find among the manuscript sources numerous examples of texts that are not purely Babylonian or Palestinian. They should be cautious about making facile claims about the *direct* dependence of later rites on one or other of these two alternatives, and should place *Seder Rav Amram*, as it has come down to us, among the *formae mixtae* of the post-geonic period and not within the purer

---

47   Wieder, *Formation* (see n. 15 above), 1.53 and 163, S. C. Reif, *Judaism and Hebrew Prayer: New Perspecives on Jewish Liturgical History* (Cambridge, 1993), pp. 185–87, and R. Brody, 'The enigma of *Seder Rav 'Amram*' (Hebrew) in *Knesset Ezra: Literature and Life in the Synagogue: Studies Presented to Ezra Fleischer*, eds S. Elizur, M. D. Herr, G. Shaked and A. Shinan (Jerusalem, 1994), pp. 21–34.
48   Reif, *Judaism and Hebrew Prayer* (see n. 47 above), pp. 161–64.

Babylonian versions of the ninth century. In plotting a graph of Jewish liturgical history in the high middle ages, and attempting to locate rites, texts and manuscripts within it, researchers should attempt to use all the factors at their disposal. These include linguistic, literary, historical and theological data as well as more technical palaeographical and codicological features. It should be recognized that there are considerable differences between the prayer-books of Solomon ben Nathan of Sijilmasa and the Sefardi rites and that this testifies to the fact that there were a variety of oriental rites that lay behind the North African and Spanish developments. It is consequently questionable to argue, as some recent researchers have done, that the North African rite is exclusively western and Sefardi rather than oriental and that this is borne out by its similarities to the versions of Sa'adya and pre-crusader Palestine. Our manuscript appears to belong to a genre that is in or close to North Africa and still retains mixed Babylonian and Palestinian elements as well as similarities to the modified version of *Seder Rav Amram* and the prayer-book of Maimonides. The prayer-book of Solomon ben Nathan is simply another example of the variety that still existed in North Africa in the twelfth century.[49]

---

49   My conclusions are therefore at odds with the theories proposed by S. Zucker and E. Wust, 'The oriental origin of "Siddur R. Shlomo b. R. Nathan" and its erroneous ascription to North Africa' (Hebrew), *Kiryat Sefer* 64 (1992–93), pp. 737–46.

Indexes

Index of sources

Manuscripts

Index of prayers and ritual

Index of names

Isserles, M., 258
Jackson, B., 72n
Jacob b. Judah, 196n, 320n, 338n
Jacob Koppel, 202
Jacob Naqdan, 259, 266
Jacob the Patriarch, 72, 120, 123–24, 167
Jacob Ṣemaḥ b. Ḥayyim, 264
Jacobson, B. S., 77n, 79n, 82n, 84n–85n,
    87n–92n, 109n, 131n–132n, 151n–
    156n, 158n–159n, 222n–226n, 271n,
    274n, 281, 297n, 318n, 337n–346n
Jaffee, M. S., 98n
Jakobovits, I., 166, 206n
Janzen, J. G., 114
Jastrow, M., 166n, 280n
Jawitz, W., 318n
Jenkinson, F., 232n
Jepsen, A., 280
Jeremias, J., 25n
Jerome, Church Father, 121n
Jick, L. A., 166n
Johnson, N. B., 53
Jolley, M. A., 54n
Jonquière, T. M., 73n, 116n
Joseph Ḥazzan, 259
Joseph b. Jacob, 246, 248
Joseph b. Moses Trani, 87n, 103n
Josephus Flavius, 28n, 73, 83n, 116
Joshua b. Qorḥa, 119n
Judah b. Barzilai, 86n, 297
Judah b. Benjamin, poet, 317
Judah (b. Ilai), 121, 218
Judah the Patriarch, 84, 215, 262
Judah b. Yaqar, 221–26, 262n, 265, 302n,
    305–6, 310, 320n
Kaddari, M. Z ., 281n
Kahn, E., 72n
Kamenetsky, D., 243
Kaplan, B., 208n, 216n–219n
Karo, Joseph, 179n, 305, 308
Kasher, M. M., 122n, 326, 327n
Kasher, R., 183n, 328n
Kaufmann, D., 257–58
Kedar, B. Z., 316n
Kessler, E., 99n
Khan, G., 189n, 191n, 248n
Kiley, M., 46n
Kimelman, R., 31n, 109n, 121n–123n
Kingsley, Charles, 22n
Kister, M., 58n–59n, 63n, 168n
Kitson Clark, G., 23
Klausner, Abraham, 259, 265, 268
Klein, M., 317n, 328n
Kodesh, S., 53n
Kohler, K., 37

Korah, 99
Kraemer, J., 163, 178n, 209n, 248n, 331n
Kraft, R. A., 44n, 73n
Kugler, R. A., 96n
Kutscher, E. Y., 281n, 303n
Kutscher, R., 303n
Lange, A., 52
Langer, R., 79n, 182n, 251–52
Langerman, Y. T., 244n, 246n
Lee, T. R., 66n
Lehmann, M. R., 40n
Lehmann, R. P., 286n
Lehnardt, A., 124n, 225n
Leib Saraval, 265
di Lella, A., 54, 61n, 65n
Leonhardt, J., 73n, 83n, 117n
Lerner, M. B., 170n, 294n
Levi, amora, 121
Lévi, I., 233
Levine, L. I., 4, 21n, 25n, 30n, 31n, 44n,
    100n, 146n, 181n
Levita, Elijah, 305
Levy, J., 280n
Lewinsky, Y., 320n
Lichtenstein, Y. S., 217n
Lieberman, S., 25n, 130n, 147n, 187n,
    281n, 292n
Liebes, Y., 155n
Liebreich, L. J., 136n, 158n
Limm, T., 39
Logan, J., 103n
Luger, Y., 133, 136n, 138n, 151n–156n,
    223n–224n, 253, 308n, 337n
Luria, Solomon, 12, 17, 80, 81n, 87n,
    103n, 255–69
Luzzatto, S. D., 261n–263n, 266n–267n,
    282n–283n, 337n, 339n, 340n–343n
Maccoby, H., 26n, 145n
Maharil (Jacob Mollin), 258–60, 266
Maier, J., 44n
Maimon, J. L., 258n
Maimonides, Abraham, 11, 17, 209, 219,
    221, 228, 241, 244, 246–49
Maimonides, Moses, 10–11, 16–17, 74n,
    78, 102–3, 179, 207–28, 246, 261n–
    262n, 266n, 274, 284, 298, 305, 308,
    302n, 304n, 306–8, 310, 311n, 320n,
    338, 340n–342n, 346–48
Malter, H. (Tsvi), 238n
Mann, J., 89n, 121n, 124n, 132n, 136n–
    138n, 151n, 156, 158–59, 177n,
    222n, 232, 234, 244, 245n, 247, 248n,
    250, 283, 284n, 285, 319n, 331n,
    338n–343n, 346n
Manoaḥ, Samson's father, 80, 81n, 263

Index of subjects and rites

Plates

המעריב ערבים אהבת עולם ישראל עמך
אהבת התורה ומצות חקים ומשפטים אותנו
למדתה עלכן בשכבנו ובקומנו ונשיח
בחקיך צורנו ונשמחה בדברי תורתך לעולם ועד
כי הם חיינו ואורך ימינו ובהם נהגה יומם ולילה
ברוך אתה יי אוהב עמו ישראל אבן סמיע
ישראל יי אלהינו יי אחד: כל אנו לו אוהב
כמא כתבנא אמת אמונה כל זאת קיים
עלינו יי אלהינו ואנחנו ישראל עמו מלכנו אין
וולתו הפודנו מיד מלכים

הגואלנו מכף כל עריצמ חזן הנפרע
לנו מצרינו המשיל גמול לכל איבי נפשנו העשה
נפשטו בחיים ולאנת לטות רגלינו . יפנו על
במות אויבידי רינו קבל ישראל ה עש

Plate 1: Cambridge University Library, Add.3160.2; see p. 284, n. 64

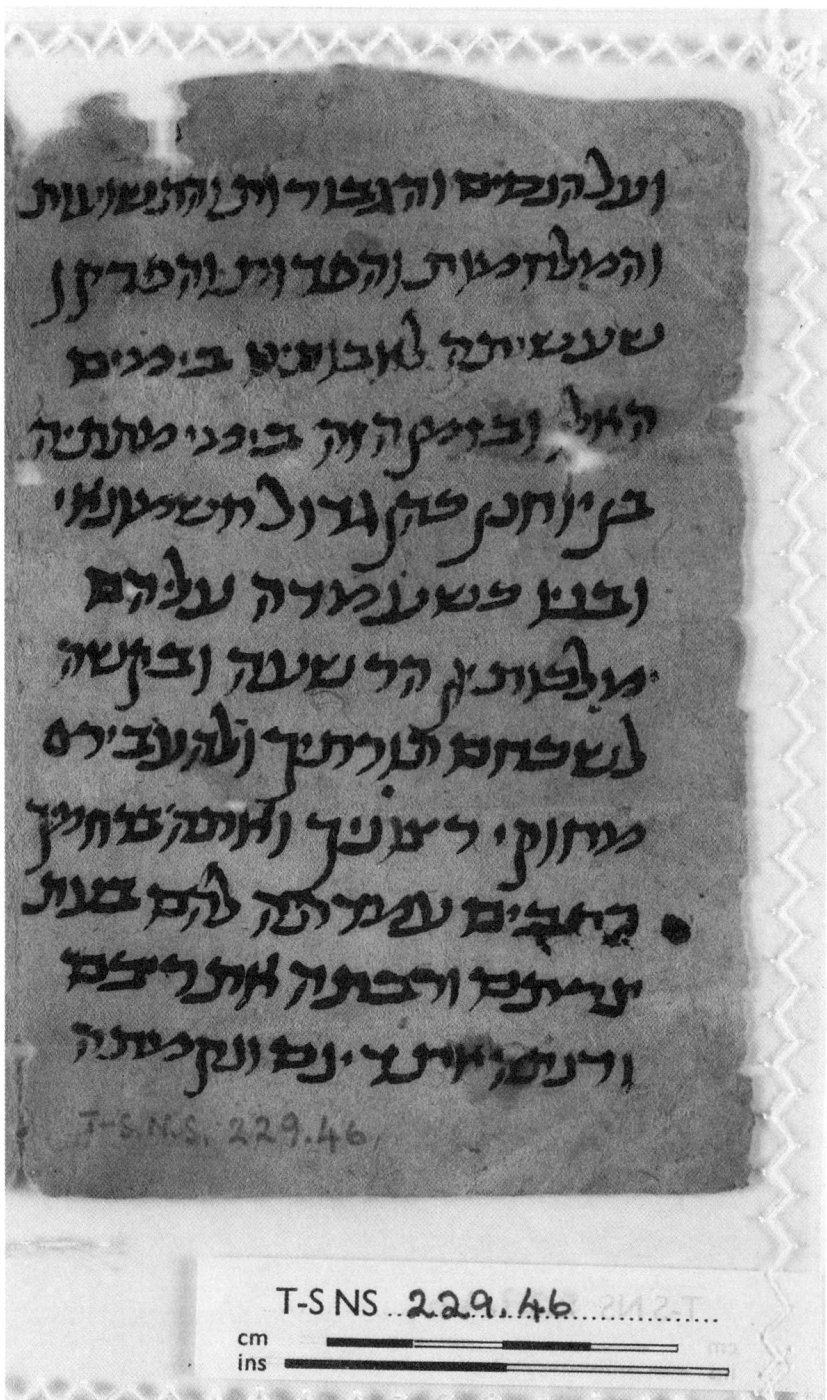

ועל הנסים והגבורות והתשועות

והמלחמות והפדיות והפרקן

שעשיתה לאבותינו בימים

ההם ובזמן הזה בימי מתתיה

בן יוחנן כהן גדול חשמנעי

ובניו כשעמדה עליהם

מלכות הרשעה ובקשה

לשכחם תורתך ולהעבירם

מחוקי רצונך ואתה ברחמיך

הרבים עמדתה להם בעת

צרתם ורבתה את ריבם

ודנת דינם ... ונקמתה

Plate 2: Cambridge University Library, T-S NS 229.46; see p. 300, n. 29

שני זונגורא כריבין ותהירך הדנר
מתעבר ארזין ומפגד עלפין הוא אאה
להין ומרי מלבין . ואילו פינו .
ואי פומנא מלוא אודוו ' ומשבחן
עתיקין ' ולישן דילך כפחשורלי הבצין '
לא שלטיקין ' ושפווהנא כפנודשא דקלעין
ואודקין ' ועינגא סמיך עמרין ובעמרין
דלקין ' וירוא כנשרין באורא סלו
ורגלנא כאילי ' וטביא בקלילות ברקין
ושמרא וארעא מגילין ופיתקין וכל צ
אען יממחין קלמוסין עליקין ' ולפנאוון
הותא וסבין ' לא פסדין ' וכל דביה דוח
כמללא זעטוטין ורסיקין ' וכתבין קלוסין
לא הוו מספסין על סין דעבור לעס לא
מטוס פריקין ענאמרי אוכח סבאיבין
וטולפויקין ' מנא אמור לעמיה וק
ובישלוא מתפנקין ואספא סריש גלי
לעין כל מפקין בזעפירדין ומיןנפקין '

בשם רחמ̇ ברכת מזון

בָּרוּךְ אַתָּה יְיָ אֱלֹהֵינוּ מֶלֶךְ הָעוֹלָם

הַזָּן אֶת הָעוֹלָם כֻּלּוֹ בְּטוּב בְּחֶסֶד

וּבְרַחֲמִים נוֹתֵן לֶחֶם לְכָל בָּשָׂר

כִּי לְעוֹלָם חַסְדּוֹ וּבְטוּבוֹ וְטוּב

הַגָּדוֹל לֹא חָסֵר לָנוּ וְאַל יֶחְסַר עֲב

מִלְבֵּינוּ מָזוֹן מִשְׁעָנָה וְעַד עוֹלָם

בַּעֲבוּר שְׁמוֹ הַגָּדוֹל כִּי הוּא זָן

וּמְפַרְנֵס לַכֹּל וְשֻׁלְחָנוֹ עָרוּךְ לַכֹּל

וְהִתְקִין מָזוֹן לְכָל בְּאֵ...

בְּרָא בְּרַחֲמִין וּכְרוֹב חֲסָדֶיךָ ׳

כָּאָמוּר פּוֹתֵחַ אֶת יָדֶיךָ וּמַשְׂבִּיעַ

לְכָל חַי רָצוֹן בָּרוּךְ אַתָּה יְיָ הַזָּן

Plate 4: Cambridge University Library, Add.3162; see p. 334